DO YOU BELIEVE IN MAGIC?

By: M. E. Nevill

Chapter 1

The street patrolman rousted the old man that street people knew as Old Walter from his makeshift bed of overflow garbage bags and discarded laundry stacked beside a dumpster behind The Wash Tub, where dryer vents provided warmth in winter and on cool late summer nights like tonight. The badged officer pointed the disheveled vagrant in the direction of the Broadway Street Shelter, but he soon became confused by the unfamiliar San Diego streets he found himself on. He stumbled upon a dark Lexus waiting at a street light—a green light. The motor was running, but the car was just sitting there idling. Walter steadied himself against the corner utility pole and pushed the crossing button. The light changed to red and the white LED walking man lit up, so he hurried across to beat the red hand. He had almost reached the curb when a Lincoln Navigator suddenly screeched to a halt behind the apparent stalled car. Six men wearing dark gray uniforms exited all four doors and surrounded the Lexus. Walter could hear them talking but could not make out their words because they had on helmets with dark shields. One produced a steel pipe from somewhere after examining the man inside and finding him slumped over the steering wheel. He then leaned back inside through the passenger door. Walter heard noises that sounded like body blows and then saw a wide spray of blood spatter against the inside of the windshield. He stepped backward, stumbling over the curb and staggered toward a shadowed side street, hoping none of the strange men had noticed him, like most people. But when the man holding the pipe withdrew from the car, he rotated around as if looking for him. He signaled two men who quickly overtook him as he tried to shuffle away. They grabbed him by the arms and dragged him back to the Lexus, where they hurriedly placed the victim's gold watch on his wrist, the pipe in his hands, and stuffed his pockets with blood-soaked money from the victim's wallet.

"No-no," Walter pleaded and discarded the pipe and pulled the money from his pockets, but blood was now smeared all over the front of his ragged coat. They pushed him to the ground, and all six took turns punching him in the stomach; then they jumped into the Navigator and sped away. Walter heard sirens in the distance, but he was in too much pain to get up and run. There was a great commotion when the units arrived, and he was quickly gathered up, handcuffed, and shoved into the back seat of a patrol car while being advised he was under arrest for the murder of Anderson Barksdale.

"That's him!" he heard a man's voice shout. "That's the man I saw back out of the Lexus with the pipe in his hands." Walter couldn't remember doing anything that the oriental witness was going on about to a policeman beside him taking notes. Anderson Barksdale was the county tourist commissioner, but he never got close enough to the car to recognize him. "I saw the whole thing from my window," the man continued, looking up at a pair of second-story windows over a Chinese restaurant. "I saw the Lexus pull up to the light; then he opened the passenger door. I saw him hit Mr. Barksdale over and over; and the blood…oh, all that blood; it was horrible."

"What about all those other guys?" Walter groaned as he struggled to sit upright in the caged back seat. "The ones in the uniforms and—and the helmets?"

"Shut up, deadbeat!"

Walter hadn't noticed the officer sitting in the front seat logging information about the incident onto a laptop. He could see an array of photos across the screen: a bloody pipe, Barksdale's wallet, bloodstained money, and three of himself…close-ups of his bloody hands and clothes.

"But I-I didn't do anything," Walter cried. "It was them—they did it."

Chapter 2

A two-inch digital announcement cast a blue hue across one corner of the bedroom, complimenting the chilly February night. Its aura hovered eerily over two sleeping figures lying in the bed next to the nightstand. Annette Rylan, the sleeping beauty under the abundant comforter, would resist stirring from its security where she was snuggled next to Phoebe, her near-constant canine companion, when the alarm sounded at 6:00 am. The moon was at its fullest in the clear southern California sky, but its glow could not seep through. Smoke-tinted windowpanes blanketed by vinyl shades and lined curtains saw to that. Total darkness was the number one rule. The second rule was total quiet; therefore, a pedestal fan set on high speed was in the opposite corner and served as a noise equalizer. Its gusts wiggled the clothes hanging in the closet and moved the floor-length curtains back and forth against the wall, and masked sounds of loud music, barking dogs, and cars with altered mufflers. Snoring or scratching would earn Phoebe a gentle nudge. Continued annoyance would be rewarded with a sweeping shove off the bed.

By definition, Phoebe was a female AKC-registered miniature chocolate poodle, always kept clean but never groomed in the pompous style of her breed. Annette Rylan didn't believe in frills; she was a down-to-earth southern girl, and her constant companion would always reflect the same style.

Annette was small in stature, worked at Molly's Day Care, and was often mistaken for one of the teens who hung out there after school and was a magnet to children of all ages. She was born and raised in the small college town of Natchitoches, Louisiana, and moved to San Diego two years after her father died of cancer. She would be thirty soon and couldn't take living in the depressed southern state any longer. Her mother and father were always content with their life on Cane River, but nothing made sense to her anymore with her father gone.

The silk-like strands of her light brown hair spread across the pillow and partially covered her face. Her nose was sprinkled with small freckles from summers spent outdoors growing up. She didn't like playing with dolls, so she was a fair opponent in softball, basketball, soccer, flag football, and tennis. She preferred the code that guys played by, which was by rules; she learned early on that girls liked to change rules to suit themselves. Her father taught her and her older brother, Keith, the laws by which Sonny Rylan lived. Her childhood arguments turned into debates when she got older and they inevitably became best friends. When he died, he took his rulebook with him and she didn't know what to do anymore.

Sonny Rylan graduated high school but never went to college. He was self-educated with books from the library, how-to manuals, YouTube, Tech TV, and the Discovery and History Channels. His style of debate was with a steady progression of reason and logic until he had you in total agreement with him. He would never buy what he could make himself and would pay no more than the lowest price he could negotiate. He bartered labor for labor when he built their two-story family home just outside of Natchitoches. His wife Stella, Annette, and Keith were the biggest part of his cheap labor.

Annette set out to travel the country with Phoebe who was still a young pup, to try and separate herself from the somberness that seemed to lurk everywhere. She took the I-10 West, bypassed congested Houston, and stopped in San Antonio. There was little solace at the Mall on the River or the Alamo, where the war with the Mexican army led by Santa Ana took the life of Jim Bowie and approximately 200 Texian soldiers.

With Phoebe always on her arm, she continued and toured Arizona's Mesa Verde National Park cliff dwellings. A young boy, perhaps ten years old, approached her while she was there. She thought that, like most kids, he wanted to pet Phoebe. But he handed her a small turquoise stone and said his grandfather, who was sitting behind him under a tree in front of a souvenir shop and dressed in full Indian dress, had sent him over to present the offering to the spirit that was traveling with her. The old man slowly stood up when she looked at him; then raised his arms and began to chant. Every person dressed in ancestral Puebloan gear turned to see who was the focus of his prayer. When the tourists began to whisper about what seemed to be a significant mantra, she pressed the stone back into the boy's hand and hurried to the parking lot.

The Pacific coast seemed to be calling her, so she followed the signs to Mission Beach when she arrived in San Diego by way of I-8. She placed Pheobe on top of the concrete wall that separated the sand from the boardwalk and let the sea breeze fill her mind with a liberating sense of peace.

Two years later, she lived fifteen minutes from the Pacific in the small Mesa Community in north San Diego County. Not comfortable with the Chargers yet, her sleepwear was New Orleans Saints football tee shirts and sweatpants. The discriminating young lady would never wear anything impractical as silk or satin. Her mother, Stella, who she resembled in appearance only, had given up on buying her daughter dresses by fourth grade, and she often told the story of when they went shopping at Sears for school clothes and the fight they had right there in the store over a tangerine dress imprinted with small white flowers. Annette screamed that it looked stupid, hid inside a clothes carousel, and wouldn't come out until her mother hung the hideous thing back on the rack. She learned to crawl and walk during the hippie era when wearing blue jeans became the norm and that's how she felt most comfortable.

Phoebe lay stretched out on her side in the crook of her mistress's knees. A fluffy tail was her only pretentious cut, and that was only because the vet took it upon himself to cut it in accordance with poodle etiquette two weeks after she was born. Annette's little brown dog would never win AKC's Best of Show at Westminster, have painted toenails, wear bows in her ears, or wear clothes, except when Molly took one of her notions.

Phoebe was born two days after Sonny passed from this earthbound world. She was the only puppy thrown by her mother, Coco, the family dog, who spent most of her time at Sonny's side. When Phoebe opened her eyes for the first time, it was Annette's face she saw through the tiny slits.

She was fed cereal and goat's milk from a fingertip or a doll bottle a week after birth. When Annette scolded Coco for abandoning her baby, Coco just looked at her as if to say in classic Sonny Rylan logic: *You want to be her mother, be my guest.*

A product of one man's influence slept peacefully in what appeared to be a tranquil predawn day, a holiday for some, Presidents Day. Annette was five-foot one, although she would argue anyone down that said she was less than five-two. She had thick and naturally tapered eyebrows and pale blue eyes, and her cheeks turned pink when she laughed. A dab of powder and lipstick would accentuate this natural petite-size beauty if she chose to wear it.

Annette was every child's favorite at Molly's. Although she had matured under the profound philosophy of her father, her mother taught her a few things about gentle persuasion, an old-fashioned Southern method of nurturing that resulted in people eating out of her hand. Annette emerged with the uncanny ability to demand cooperation from all in her charge and make them love it. *Nette,* the name kids gave her because it was easier to say, had a rapport with children that adults read about but couldn't pull off for themselves. Phoebe baited kids by performing tricks on demand, making it easy for Nette to reel them into her magical lair.

The comforter they lay on was splashed with various flowers and greenery like the hydrangeas and multicolored hybrid daylilies that nestle within the bank-side foliage common along the bayous that spread like small arteries throughout the Delta State. Phoebe abruptly twitched one ear. The humming fan could never desensitize her acute hearing or circulate the air enough to mislead her sensitive nose. She instinctively raised her head above the crest of a graceful fern and rose to her feet. She crept to the corner of the bed and stopped to look back when the tag on her collar jingled. Her mistress could be a real bear if a good night's sleep was interrupted. Phoebe had observed various bears on the Animal Planet television network and elephants, tigers, lions, dinosaurs and other animals that made threatening noises in nature's habitat. Annette's threats compared best to that of the black bear. She had never met one in real life, but for some reason, its growl had a characteristic that struck fear all through her little body.

Confident her movement hadn't disturbed her master, Phoebe slipped effortlessly from the bed to the carpeted floor. She looked back again to ensure the tag hadn't prodded her master's subconscious. She padded to the end of the dark hall and entered the brighter living room where the open drapes allowed the streetlight to fill the room. Two hops took her from the floor to the back of the sofa. She separated the slender white mini blinds with her black nose and peered onto Jewel Street. Two houses to the left and four on the right secured the three-bedroom abode on both sides. The typical residential neighborhood of tract homes was made of various shades of pastel stucco with attached garages and standard matching window shutters and tile rooftops. All garage doors within her view were closed and automobiles parked in their appropriate driveway and at its proper curb. Nothing seemed to be moving from one end of Phoebe's spectrum to the other.

But something had awakened her. She snorted an exhale and bolted from the sofa to the floor, then darted across the kitchen and pushed her nose and body through the doggy door. She came to a sudden stop at the end of the concrete porch and peered behind her to make sure the flapping sound of the plastic door against its magnet hadn't disturbed the *bear* in the bedroom. She looked at the bedroom window; everything seemed normal. Annette's ingenious precautions against noise made Phoebe's nighttime explorations easy. She resumed her endeavor and dashed down the steps. She crossed the yard and wiggled through a secret broken slat in the gray, weathered fence that privatized the backyard.

She was now in the alley that separated the backyards of Jewel and Antrim Way. Mesa was a community situated north of Miramar Naval Air Station. The alleyways were used for garbage pickup in past decades, but that was discontinued with the advent of automated trucks that limited service to the front curbs. The Mesa community sprang to life after Miramar built the elite training facility in what was then a total desert. The community grew from a modest size to an ever-increasing population of sixty-thousand. Mesa Retirement Village was at the North end of the street and around the corner. The *Village,* as it was affectionately called by its residents and neighbors, was a secure assisted-living retirement community that was state-of-the-art. The Village was where Phoebe was headed. Her instincts compelled her to run as fast as her short legs could carry her.

She leaped like a rabbit over ruts and tall weeds dotting the alleyway. Frankie and Johnnie, the two German shepherds next door, lethargically ambled closer to their chain link fence when they saw her dart past. They whined as if asking the little adventurer what she was up to tonight, but Phoebe couldn't waste time with through-the-fence gossip. She turned onto a path, a right of way, between two properties that took her to Antrim Way.

She paused momentarily between two driveways when she reached the sidewalk on Antrim. A low humming sound emitted from a three-foot tall green metal box. The box was bolted to a concrete slab and surrounded by a wall of box hedges, obviously, someone's endeavor to blend the hideous metal object into the manicured landscape. Its mantra was uncanny in the otherwise tranquil surroundings. Its combination of tones seemed to beckon her, like a call in the wild that hunters use to draw game closer into their crosshairs. She remembered seeing hunters on TV using instruments that made sounds like deer grunts and turkey calls that made these animals walk from the safety of thick woods right out into the open. She sensed the same danger coming from the ominous green box. Her instincts kicked in, reminding her there was no time to waste. Phoebe possessed an unusual sensory perception that set her apart from other canines.

She scooted across two front yards to the corner house where Scott Bolton lived with his mother. His bedroom was the only lighted window in the neighborhood. Scott was 10 years old and an advanced honors student at Mesa High School with an IQ of 160, although officially in the 10th grade. He was a computer science junkie that seemed to require little sleep, so it wasn't unusual for his alien lava lamp to be on at such an hour. The lime-green glow from the lamp illuminated his straight blonde hair and pale yellow pajamas as he sat at his desk near the window, reading a text in his notebook. He was about to reply to a chat buddy when something outside caught his attention. He rose quickly, removed his gold wire-rimmed glasses, wiped them with the tail of his pajama shirt and put them back on; then he leaned over the window sill and looked across the neighbor's four-foot hedge row. He rushed back to his notebook and switched to the video feed from the four surveillance cameras on the corners of the roof. His mother installed them and an alarm system because she was a single mom and worked long hours.

NC headed to The Village. Scott sent the message after reviewing the video; a reply appeared a few seconds later.

What's going on?

Phoebe didn't check for traffic when she crossed the corner because she felt there was precious little time. She had her private entrances to her favorite places in the neighborhood. She entered Mesa Village through the tall bushes and sufficiently spaced rungs of the iron fence behind them.

Impending danger had instinctively awakened the miniature poodle, and then a high-pitched tone straightened the hair inside her ears when she stepped out on her master's porch. Now, the trace of smoke she had smelled since the corner was getting funkier as she pumped along. The alert was getting harder to bear, but time was critical, and so far, she was the only one answering the alarm.

She ran alongside the house where an elderly resident named Lewis lived. He suffered from emphysema and once owned a terrier named Buddy, who had died. Phoebe often heard Lewis' neighbor Charlie say they were a perfect match because Buddy was as ugly as Lewis.

When Phoebe reached the backside of the house, she let herself inside through the special entrance Lewis had made for Buddy in the stucco. He had sealed it with mortar but didn't do a very good job, and the patchwork had crumbled. Phoebe had nudged her way through it with ease a long time ago. The smoke alarm was agonizing, but she would endure it to find Lewis. She put her head close to the floor and crawled between chairs and table legs until she found the living room. She ducked under a chair with a ruffled skirt that enabled her to momentarily escape the smoke that was getting thicker the further she went into the house. She broke from under the chair and crawled down the hall until she reached Lewis' bedroom. The room was hazy, but she could see him lying on the bed through her watering eyes. He had on blue pin-striped pajamas and his hands were folded across his stomach.

Phoebe saw the flicker of a small flame reflecting off the shiny wallboard in the bathroom across the hall. She jumped up on the bed and pounced on Lewis's stomach. She barked repeatedly and then moved closer and barked into his ear. He gave off a short moan that was followed by a cough.

"Phoebe…*cough*...Is that you? …*Gasp.*"

Phoebe tugged at his pajama shirt. Lewis tried to raise his head but was overcome by the lethal smoke. Afraid he was slipping away, she tugged at his shirt harder, tearing it and ripping off a small piece of material and a white pearl button. To the left side of the bed was a night table with a small intercom unit. It was more than three feet away, but Phoebe lunged and landed on top of it. She pressed a button with her paw, almost knocking the unit off the table. Phoebe heard static coming from the speaker and then a man's voice.

"Sup, Lou?"

"Gruff!"

"Phoebe?" the voice asked.

The smoke made Phoebe sneeze.

A second later, the voice returned, this time in a higher pitch. "Is that the smoke alarm?"

Phoebe answered with another, "Gruff."

"Why didn't it show up on the board? I'm calling 911; I'll be right there!"

The voice on the other end of the intercom was Gerry Ortega, who was Spanish/American and employed as a maintenance man at the village. Gerry supplemented his income by working the switchboard through the long and tedious nights. He manned the board dressed in the same khaki uniform from the afternoon's bout with an electric stove, water heater, and a gas grill. It had been a boring and uneventful night for the midnight voice of the Village. He was passing the time thinking about all the unfinished projects at home that needed his attention and how nice it would be to be in bed next to his wife, Cindy, instead of babysitting the switchboard to earn extra money.

A security guard pulled up outside the office about the same time as the intercom buzzed the switchboard. The guard rubbed his eyes as he opened the door of the white jeep that bore the official logo of Mesa Village. It was time for a cup of coffee and he knew that Gerry would have a fresh pot made about this time. He pushed his dark policeman-style cap away from his forehead and entered the front door. He frowned when he saw Gerry sitting at the switchboard flailing his arms. The security guard hurried over and heard Gerry yelling an address into the telephone receiver. The maintenance man planted the telephone receiver in the security guard's hand when he swung around and saw him standing there.

"Finish answering their silly questions, will you?" Gerry hollered and jumped up. "The security system didn't alert the switchboard and the smoke alarm is going off at Lewis's; keys in the jeep?" he asked and ran for the door.

"Well, yeah, sure," the guard said. The security guard had never seen the large man move so fast. He was out the front door and leaping over the side of the open-top jeep before he could finish the question and had started the engine before his six-foot frame was straight in the driver seat. He backed out of the parking space without looking behind him and shoved the gearshift into drive. The rear tires squealed and left a trail of black marks.

Scott realized something was happening at The Village when he stepped out on his front stoop. His chat buddy, who went by the name of Guardian, would be interested to know that Nightcrawler, the code name they used for Phoebe, was at the scene. Guardian had a particular interest in the neighborhood and Nightcrawler for some unexplained reason and always wanted to know when something curious happened. Scott saw headlights on Main Street through the tall hedges.

He eased the front door closed behind him after turning off the alarm, being careful not to wake his mother, whose bedroom was in the back of the house and who worked double shifts at the airport.

"What the…!" he gasped and staggered backward. He felt something run across the top of his feet; then he saw the small dark figure scampering past the hedges. He rushed to the edge of the hedgerow. "Nightcrawler," he called out in a whisper. Phoebe suddenly stopped, nearly tumbling after crossing the neighbor's driveway. She growled at the green transmission box between the two driveways and then darted onto the path. Scott heard sirens in the distance and saw more lights on Main Street in Mesa Village. He pulled out his iPhone.

Emergency at the Village, Scott quickly typed. *NC ran past me, headed home. I hear sirens, fire engines, maybe an ambulance.*

G: *Confirmation received on my end; Mesa FD rec 911.*

S: *I'll bet NC alerted them somehow.*

G: *Copy that.*

As Scott and G shared info, Phoebe sprang back onto the plush comforter and quietly settled into the caladiums and daylilies. The room was just as she left it. The clock was still making its blue statement. The fan rumbled, the clothes were quivering, and the drapes were slowly breathing in and out. She raised an ear and looked at the shaded window. The distant siren she heard on the way home was much louder now. Soon, the whole neighborhood would be awake.

Phoebe saw Annette's foot stir, and she quickly crouched into the folds of the comforter. Her master brushed the hair from her face, slowly rolled on her back, and threw one arm over her forehead. Phoebe crept closer and found her breathing getting increasingly profound. After a few seconds, she squeezed her eyelids together, fighting the oncoming wakefulness with a vengeance. A low moan turned into a high-pitched weeping sound in the form of a question. What had interrupted her best sleep in weeks? Phoebe fixed her eyes on her master's face. Was it possible she would drift back to sleep? Perhaps the fan would offset the noise.

"Ooh…um…ugh," Annette fretted. "What's that smell?" Phoebe had carried the scent of smoke home with her.

Annette's speech was slow and garbled and her southern accent almost discernible. She slowly rose, but only to her elbows, her eyes still closed. She hung her head in front of her and then rolled it back letting the ends of her hair brush the pillowcase. "Oh, God," she whispered as she lifted her head upright again. She arched both eyebrows which pulled her eyelids open as far as slits. She tried to focus on Phoebe in spite of the listlessness. "It's *you*!" She gnarled. "Ugh! Why do you smell like...?"

Phoebe dodged out of the way when her master sat up straight. Annette sniffed her tee shirt and then grabbed the comforter where Phoebe was lying and put it to her face. Then she heard the siren.

"That's a fire truck, oh my God," she blurted out, looking at Phoebe. "What…why…?" She turned to look at the tightly covered windows as if expecting to see lights flashing through them. "They're gettin louder, closer; it's in the neighborhood." She glared at Phoebe who was now standing at the end of the bed and staring back at her. "But I guess you know that don't you?" she scolded and then lunged for her. Phoebe scooted to the left barely missing her master's hands. "I smell you, Phoebe! You might as well come here." Annette was on her knees, spinning around on top of the bed, chasing after the sprightly little dog. She stopped when she noticed something hanging out of Phoebe's mouth. In the dark, it looked like a small piece of white paper. "Let me see what cha got? Have you been rootin candy from someplace?" Phoebe lowered her head and released a small piece of cloth from her mouth, dropping it on a maroon marigold print.

"What is this?" Annette asked picking up the blue and white striped material. She ran her thumb over the white pearl button. She stared at the small dog as if trying to ignore the revelation. She fought with the comforter that was now twisted and wrapped around her as she got out of bed.

Phoebe tried but failed to dodge the tide of covers that tumbled over her. She nudged her way to the surface and watched her master search in the dark for the sweatshirt and cap she had flung in different directions before getting into bed.

"What did you do?" Annette said as she dropped to her knees looking for the white Reeboks that had to be under the bed in the dark disorder. "Did anyone see you? God, I hope not!" she grumbled and rose as far as the edge of the bed with a shoe in each hand. She looked at Phoebe lying on top of the comforter. "What am I gonna do?" Annette threw her shoes down on the floor beside the bed and clutched what felt like the sweatshirt that was thrown over the headboard. She punched her arms through the sleeves and forced her head through the neckband all in one motion. She patted her hands along the top of the dresser until she found a hair tie and continued the blind search until she felt a red baseball cap. She secured the cap on her head, forced her toes into the Reeboks, and worked her feet further into them as she stepped into the hall. She fell into a kitchen chair just long enough to make a shoehorn out of two fingers and jam her heels into the shoes.

Phoebe hugged the wall and crept into the kitchen. She took refuge under the table in the corner of the dining nook. It was the same fortress she used to hide from the children Annette brought home until she could safely make a run behind the sofa or under a bed. She huddled quietly under the table until the gray sweats and the white Reeboks rushed out the back door. It closed with such force that the plastic flap swung back and forth past its magnet many more times than normal. Phoebe was mid-way through the chair legs when the door suddenly opened again.

"Don't you dare follow me," Nette shouted into the dark kitchen.

Phoebe lowered her head; fully aware this wasn't the last she'd hear of this.

Annette grabbed the handlebars of her bicycle and steered it across the porch while Phoebe crept through the doggy door and hid under a white wicker chair.

She guided the white Schwinn down the steps and across the backyard but turned her head before opening the gate. "Don't you follow me," she growled, knowing her confidant was somewhere within the sound of her voice. Annette took a running start and threw her right leg over the bicycle saddle. Sirens and horns were blaring down Gold Coast now, and Frankie and Johnnie, the German

Shepherds next door, were now competing for the angriest protest.

"Quiet, you two," Annette said with a stern bark of her own as she passed their chain link fence in the alley. Frankie and Johnnie obeyed her order for as long as it took her to clear the boundary of their domain, and then they started again.

Scott peeked around the hedge row beside his house just far enough to observe Annette turn onto the path. He had changed into a black windbreaker and sweatpants. His blond hair was cloaked under a black skull cap that was rolled down to his eyebrows. He scurried along the line of shrubs to the front yard.

Annette followed the same route between the houses as Phoebe. The city-owned the strip of land between the houses, and by right of way, its power lines ran through underground pipes from Antrim to Jewel, along with other service-related companies such as telephone and cable. This innovative practice resulted in fewer outages due to inclement weather and made neighborhoods more aesthetic. The house to her right had been vacant for several months so Annette wasn't thinking about the yellow moving truck that had been in the driveway for the past several days. She might not have cut as sharp a turn into the driveway, which resulted in the evasive action she was forced to take when she saw a man walking down the driveway incline. She was going too fast and he didn't see her because he was pulling a dark sweater over his head. She missed him, barely, and thought she brushed his white Nikes with her back tire. She whispered, "Sorry," when she passed him but wasn't sure he heard her because a fire truck was slowly turning into Mesa Village simultaneously. Annette looked back long enough to see the man plant his hands firmly on his hips. "Oops," she whispered to herself, but he looked unharmed and she kept peddling. Her neighbor across the alley, fifteen-year-old Robby Jones, had told her a family from Chicago had moved in and mentioned a *hot chick* with long dark hair and a father who was a real *ass.*

Scott watched Annette cross the street and glide around an ambulance that had slowed to turn through the open gates of Mesa Village from his crouched position behind the hedges that divided his property from his new neighbor, the one that Nette had almost run down. Other curious neighbors began to stagger outside, but the new resident headed back up his driveway.

Chapter 3

"Daddy, Daddy," the little girl cried while hiding in the shadows behind the screen door. "Come back inside, Daddy, pleeease!" Tears streamed down the face of the petite six-year-old who was desperate to see her father who had been outside too long in the torrent of flashing lights and uproar of hellish sounds. She wiped her tears with the sleeve of her pajamas, pasting strands of her wavy blonde hair to the sides of her feverish cheeks. The nightmare had started with blaring sirens that bolted her upright in bed. Red and white lights ran up and down the walls and across the ceiling, and for those first terrifying seconds, she had no memory of where she was or how she got there. She screamed while holding on to the mattress as the room spun along with the blue lights that were now flashing around the room at twice the speed. Her fourteen-year-old sister Nicky rushed in and switched on the light. By then her little sister was on the floor up against the wall in a corner underneath all her bed linens. Nicky cuddled Elizabeth close, as she had done countless times when she woke up screaming because of bad dreams or things she heard happening in the neighborhood that she was too young to understand. Nicky had been taking care of Elizabeth since she was born and was the only person who could calm the fear that often left her incapacitated.

"What arrogant show-offs!" Dr. Anthony Harding grumbled as he paced in the living room, fretting over whether to answer the emergency outside or stay with his daughters. "Is it really necessary to run sirens at this time of the night? How much traffic could there be at one o'clock in the morning?" Lightning-like strobes flashed against the white sheets that were serving as temporary drapes for the living room windows. When he heard Elizabeth's screams, he had just opened the door to look outside. He rushed to her bedroom, stumbling over a wooden rocking chair on the way. He whisked Elizabeth out of Nicky's arms and carried her to the living room, where he sat down in the rocking chair and cradled her close, hoping to soothe her fear. The front door was still open, so he could hear the sirens wind down as they reached their destination, perhaps a block away. Nicky slowly entered the living room with her arms folded in front of her. When she saw the open door, she knew it wouldn't be long before her father, the doctor, would be on the other side of it.

Elizabeth was relieved to hear her father's footsteps approaching after he walked outside but backed away from the door just in case something monstrous had switched places with him.

"Everything's okay, Lizzy," Tony said softly when he opened the screen door and saw the fearful look in her eyes. "It's just a couple of noisy fire trucks; you know, like the ones your Uncle Chris drives and like Grandpa used to."

"Is-is that Uncle Chris?" she sobbed.

"No honey, he and Grandpa are in Chicago." He knelt in front of her and gently placed both hands on her cheeks, wiped her wet face with his fingers, and then pulled her long hair back behind her ears. "There are apparently loud and noisy fire trucks in every town. I'll bet you didn't even know an ambulance drove by. Firemen are such drama kings," he scoffed. "They love to call attention to themselves. I should know I grew up in a family full of them."

"Back home in Chicago?" Nicky muttered scornfully. "We'll never see that place again."

"Sure, we will, Nicky," Tony Harding whispered. He kissed Elizabeth on the forehead.

"So, what's going on?" Nicky asked while picking up a hairbrush from an end table. Nicky had dark brown hair and eyes identical to her father's. Sooner or later, everyone got around to the painful reminder that there was no denying whom she belonged to; she hated hearing it. She might resemble the sorry excuse of a father, but she would never be like him. She would never make promises that would never be kept. Elizabeth inherited their mother's violet blue eyes and blonde hair; and her paranoia. Carol Harding had sought professional help, but it seemed the only solution the countless doctors had was in dozens of prescription bottles. Relatives went on and on at her wake about not being surprised by her tragic end. Nicky wasn't going to be surprised with the outcome of the move to San

Diego, because it was just her father's futile attempt to run away from his failures.

"Looks like a house fire in the first block of the retirement community across Gold Coast. I saw three engines and two buses. I thought I'd go see if they need any help."

"Ditching us again?" Nicky scowled and rolled her eyes up to the ceiling. "Come on Lizzy, I'll brush your hair until he gets back." She took Elizabeth by the hand and led her to the sofa, "whenever that might be."

"Nicky, stop it!" her father snapped. "You know I have a duty to use my training." Cardboard boxes full of medical books lined one side of the hallway, and many more were unopened inside the first bedroom to the right that Tony had designated his office.

"Everything always seems worse when it's dark, Lizzy, you know that," Nicky said while she gently brushed the tangles from the ends of her sister's hair.

"That's more like it," Tony sighed. "Okay, Nicky, you two stay inside," he ordered, pointing to the sofa. "I won't be long."

Nicky's mouth opened as if to argue the edict, but she changed her mind and buckled her arms instead.

"But Daddy, I don't want you to go back out there." Elizabeth ran to him and grabbed hold of his sweatpants. "Those dogs across the alley, they're scaring me." She looked over her shoulder toward the dark kitchen. She trembled and her eyes stretched wide open when she heard Frankie and Johnnie wailing beyond the kitchen door. She imagined the savage dogs tearing a hole through the screen and then breaking down the door. She foresaw their large teeth gnawing in all directions while spitting saliva. Her imagination often carried her off into dire circumstances. She let out a desperate gasp and grabbed her father's wrists. "No, you can't go," she could barely talk now and was shaking and hyperventilating. She covered her ears when she heard another siren. "Oh, no," she cried, squeezed her eyes shut and fell to her knees.

"Lizzy," Tony quickly picked her up from the floor. Her lips were swollen and drooling. "Look at me!" He knelt in front of her and rubbed her arms. "Just me," he whispered.

"Don't look anywhere else." He looked into her blue eyes that were gushing over with tears again. He ran his fingers repeatedly through her wavy blonde hair. It must have helped because her breathing slowed. "Nicky's going to get the timer from the kitchen and set it for thirty minutes," Tony told her confidently while looking up at his disgruntled oldest daughter. She was already responding to his instructions with a piercing glare. "I'll be back before the timer goes off. I promise…right, Nicky?"

Elizabeth looked up at Nicky awaiting the confirmation.

"Sure," Nicky said curtly.

Elizabeth jumped up from the floor and rushed to her sister and Nicky quickly enveloped her into her motherly arms. She watched with resentment as their father prepared his mindset for the probabilities that waited outside.

"Go on, Nicky, get the timer. I'll be back in thirty," he said in a tone sounding much like the one he used when talking to one of the first-year students at St. Joe's. His thoughts quickly turned to the possibilities that might have summoned at least three fire engines and two ambulances. It was a slightly elevated, mid-level response according to South Chicago Firehouse 11 protocol, so it was enough to assume a need for someone with his ER and Level 1 trauma experience. He pushed the door open and hurried down the front walk. He felt alert as always; ready to observe and assess as he had done hundreds of times at St. Joseph's State Hospital in South Chicago. The night air was cool; it helped neutralize the raging adrenalin flowing inside him. It had been two months since he had answered an emergency call and the stimulation was invigorating. He stuffed his hands inside the pockets of the hooded sweater and trotted across the street.

Elizabeth held the white timer out to her sister after guardedly turning on the kitchen light and retrieving it for herself. "Nicky, Nicky, turn it to thirty, hurry."

Nicky was at the screen door staring outside. She brandished a sneer before snatching the timer from her sister's hand. She set it and then turned the face around so Elizabeth could see it.

"He's supposed to be back before the arrow moves back to zero, see? But don't count on it." Nicky stuffed the timer in the pocket of her bathrobe and pushed open the screen door. "Come on, let's go have a look."

Elizabeth gasped. Their father gave them strict orders to stay inside, but she wasn't about to be left alone in the unfamiliar house with who knows what lurking inside. She grabbed the skirt of Nicky's bathrobe and followed her to the curb. Nicky craned her neck to see beyond the gates, but too many hedges surrounded the grounds. Elizabeth buried her face in Nicky's bathrobe but somehow found the courage to open her right eye and move the terrycloth just enough to see Scott and his mother standing at the curb in front of their house next door. She had dark blonde hair pulled back in a low ponytail, a phone to her ear, and an arm around Scott. They were both dressed in black. Elizabeth always hid behind the makeshift curtains when she saw Scott walking across the front yard. He was always carrying a tablet or laptop under his arm. He caught her outside once and tried to introduce himself. No one south of 31st Street smiled or waved and said hello as if they meant it. Scott suddenly waved to her, but his dark clothes made him appear threatening and she turned her face into the safety of Nicky's robe. She turned her head to the left, hoping nothing foreboding would come into view. Robby stood at the end of his driveway with his parents, Brad and Katie Jones, and his sister Marley. The family group seemed normal and unexceptional. Other curiosity seekers had made their way out into the street while others stood in their yards. Elizabeth buried her head into Nicky's bathrobe again as if doing so might reset the events to something less fearful. She heard the ticking sound of the timer in Nicky's pocket. It reminded her that Daddy would be back before the arrow reached zero. The neighbors in the street formed a huddle, and Charles Drake, who lived across the street, volunteered as a scout. He kissed his wife Donna on the cheek, patted their son Ray on top of the head, and jogged toward whatever had summoned the daunting trucks.

"See, he could have just left things to the neighbors," Nicky complained as she watched Charles Drake walking briskly past the gates of the retirement village. "They don't need his help," she sighed.

"Yo, hey there." Nicky heard a voice behind her, startling her from the resentful thoughts.

"Oh, God," she gasped. Lizzy hung onto the bathrobe as her sister turned around. "Oh, it's you, Robby." Nicky was suddenly very self-conscious of her appearance and pressed the top of her head. She had brushed the ends of her long hair in between Lizzy's consoling strokes but failed to give any attention to the frazzle that must be on top.

"I saw Doc take off just before Mr. D," Robby said. "Yo, little sis," he said to Elizabeth who was still hiding her face. She gathered more of the skirt and covered her ears.

Robby was much taller than Nicky and had brown hair so dark it looked black. The amber streetlights cast a halo image around the top of his head. His eyes were pale blue under the lights and luminous in the daytime. He acted confident and funny and was the first and only person she had met anywhere near her age. He tried to act all cool around her, but the crew from her old neighborhood had invented everything he was trying to lay down. But she appreciated how he sort of rescued her that first afternoon when they pulled up in the embarrassing ugly yellow rental truck. She had been at the mercy of her tyrant father until Robby rushed over and knocked him all out of kilter with his rank humor and insistence that he help unload the truck. He had made her smile, which was rare these days. Nicky looked toward the village and sighed. "Yeah, he always has his nose up in stuff like this." Robby was standing closer now, making her so nervous that she didn't even feel the cold. It was freezing in Chicago; she and Lizzy would be huddled under five blankets. The thought made her pull Lizzy closer. "Our mother always said he went to medical school to become a professional Good Samaritan," she finally said. She focused on the blue and red lights that twinkled through the tall shrubs surrounding the grounds across the street and wondered for the thousandth time why it was so important to move so far away. "He spends more time with them than with us."

"Well, I 'spoze that's cuz he took the oath, right; you know, the Hippocratic Oath?" Robby nudged her arm. "Yo, did I say that right? C*ratic,* or is it *critic*?"

"What?" Nicky looked up at Robby and shrugged her shoulders. She knew he was trying to make her smile, but the Hippocratic Oath had ruined their lives. It was his priority over everything, his oath to their mother, and his obligation as a parent. Life threw him a curve when their mother was killed in a car accident. It forced him to become their full-time father. Now he was on some sort of mission to reinvent their lives. Carol Harding managed just fine, even though it took prescriptions and alcohol to keep her going. Things might have been a little dysfunctional but they had it worked out.

"You ladies wanna come over and meet my folks and my boring sister?" Robby said, grinning.

"No," Nicky answered quickly. "We were told, or should I say, ordered, not to leave the house."

"And even so, here you are," Robby said in a melodic tune.

"So, what?" Nicky moaned.

"Come on, Nick," Robby coaxed.

Nicky gave him a *go-to-hell* look. "Leave us alone." Nicky tugged Lizzy's arm and moved away from him and fixed her gaze on the retirement village. She didn't know what to do with light-hearted preppy jargon. She wished he would say something unforgiving and give her a reason to shove her knuckles into his gut. Maybe punching someone would make her feel better. "Are all guys from California like you, Robby?" she asked.

"That sounds like something your old man would ask me," Robby replied. "Hey, what's that ticking noise? You got a bomb in your pocket?"

"What?" Nicky asked impatiently and remembered, "Oh, that, the timer." Nicky put her hand in her pocket. "Come on, Lizzy, let's go back to bed," Nicky huffed. "We've learned not to wait up for him." She guided Lizzy up the front walk.

"Comes with the oath, right?" Robby yelled to her.

"Bunk," Nicky grumbled.

"Yo, you better get back inside that house, young ladies," Robby growled, imitating their father's voice. "You too, little sis," Robby teased and rejoined his parents. Elizabeth looked back at Robby and smiled as she tagged behind Nicky.

The adrenalin pumping inside the steadfast Anthony Harding nullified the effects of the crisp night air piercing his face as he hurried toward the flashing lights in the block ahead. He trotted down the center of Main Street, hands in his pockets to ensure their warmth and the hood of the dark sweatshirt over his head. Just beyond a group of gathered elderly neighbors, he saw a cluster of vehicles parked at various angles of access to the front of a house with smoke trickling out the front door. He counted two paramedic buses, an indication of multiple victims, and at least four trained medics were on site, as well as two engines and a Fire Marshall truck. His heart would not be quelled until its ardent desire to help was satisfied. He had promised his daughters no more pagers, no more middle-of-the-night summons. The new position at the University of California at San Diego wouldn't require him to do so. A warm fog exploded from his mouth as if he had whispered the words: everything would *be different.* He was now close enough to see two paramedics carrying a stretcher to an adult victim lying on the ground. He exhaled another cloud of gray mist. One medic applied an oxygen mask while the other held a glucose bag beside them. Two firemen helped hoist the victim onto a gurney and pushed it to the rear of an ambulance. The firemen quickly reentered the house, passing another coming out, steering a wheelbarrow of smoking debris, which was quickly sprayed with retardant. *Everything will be different.* The words faded quickly when he reached the gurney. "Elderly male," he muttered as he stood over the victim. "Early seventies, breathing extremely labored, symptomatic of COPD now compromised by smoke inhalation." A paramedic hung a second bag from a silver mast attached to the gurney. "Meds for lung inflammation," Tony recited and addressed the medic. "How's his heart sound?"

Curious neighbors were corralled a safe distance away. Some anxiously held on to each other, some had their hands to their faces. A fire hose lay flat on the ground and was partially unrolled; fire extinguishers had put this one out. The smell of the chemicals and smoke filled the air. The summons was nothing near what he expected considering the number of respondents.

Charlie!" Annette's voice was inaudible over the rumbling generator inside the red truck parked at the curb. She laid her bicycle down near the elder's front porch. The Fire Marshall had backed the onlookers away from Lewis's property and onto Charlie's, roping it off with yellow caution tape. She spotted her friend in heavy insulated clothes and an earflap hat assisting a slow-moving neighbor lady to the waiting hands of a friend standing near the plastic barrier. Annette was relieved that Charlie's house was unscathed, yet troubled to see the activity next door at Lewis's. Charlie and Lewis were best friends and it would be tragic if something happened to him. "Charlie!" Annette gasped. She reached his side just as the paramedics rolled the gurney toward the ambulance. "Is that Lewis?" Her voice quivered.

"Everything's fine, everything's okay," Charlie said and patted her hands clamped around one of his arms so tight it had flattened the insulation in his puffy jacket. "Shush, shush! Gerry's got everything under control."

"What do you mean by that?" she asked and looked at the unmistakable figure standing near the head of the gurney. She let go of Charlie's arm and stepped toward the tape.

"Whoa!" Charlie yelped and pulled her back before she had a chance to raise it over her head. "You can't go over there."

"I have to make sure of somethin."

"I just told you; Gerry has everything under control," Charlie said slowly and with purpose.

Annette stared at Charlie for a few seconds, trying to decide whether to break away from him and dive under the tape. She chose to listen to the man she had learned to trust for the past two years. "Is Lewis really okay?" she asked with a calmer tone.

"He will be," he grumbled. "After he spends twenty-four hours in the hospital for observation and his body soaks up enough anti-inflammatory medicine to keep his lungs from flaring up…the old fool." Charlie shook his head. "He was smoking, of all things; can't stay away from those damn coffin nails. Said he just wanted one tiny drag before going to bed; humph! Missed the toilet and it landed in the plastic trash can next to it." Charlie rubbed his white mustache. "Honey, I just don't know what it's gonna take to make him stay away from those things."

"What about Phoebe?" Annette whispered. "She came home smellin like smoke, Charlie. Did Lewis say anything?"

"That's where Gerry comes in. You see, he's gonna ride along with Lewis to the hospital in case he starts rambling." Charlie and Lewis were among the original residents of the thirty-year-old retirement village. Annette's grandfathers died long before she was born, and he was the perfect image of what she thought one should be. Charlie took her into his heart just as easily because he could tell she had been brought up to respect her elders. His wife had been gone for ten years, and his children lived hundreds of miles away.

"What did Phoebe do?" she asked when she saw Charlie and the lofty maintenance man exchange nods.

"She buzzed Gerry on the intercom," he whispered. "She got him down here just in time. For some reason the smoke alarm didn't alert the switchboard like it was supposed to. Good thing it was Gerry working tonight; he just picked Lewis up out of the bed and carried him outside." Annette began to shake as if the night's chill had just hit her, so Charlie rubbed her arms through the sweatshirt with both his hands. "You should have more clothes on than this little girl."

"Does Lewis remember Phoebe bein there?" Annette opened her shaking hand and showed Charlie the piece of material with the white pearl button attached.

"Hey, look," he sighed. "As far as anyone knows, Lewis pressed the intercom himself, and Gerry heard the smoke alarm."

"So, you're sayin it was Phoebe?" She tried to suppress her trembling voice.

"Lewis was unconscious; Gerry heard her barking." Charlie took her by the arm and led her away from the crowd. They stopped in front of his porch next to her bicycle. "Is Phoebe okay?" he asked.

Annette could only nod because she was afraid of bursting into tears.

"Thank goodness, you scared me there for a second. Listen, everything's gonna be okay," he whispered intently. "Come on, Nette, honey, Phoebe saved Lewis's life. That's nothing to be upset over. Gerry will make sure Lewis doesn't give away our secret. Hell, he probably won't remember any of it anyway."

Annette nodded. "Okay, but I just smelled smoke on her, and then I heard the sirens; I didn't know what," She stopped in mid-sentence. "Her curiosity's gonna get her into somethin she can't get out of one of these days. She's just a little dog." Annette nervously rubbed her forehead and adjusted her cap. "Please don't let anyone find out she was here." She squeezed her friend's arm and handed him the torn piece of pajama shirt.

"Don't worry," Charlie assured her, closing his hand around the fabric and putting it in his pocket. "Go on back home now and get out of this night air."

Annette picked up her bicycle. "Call me tomorrow," she said.

"I will," he said. "Now get on home."

The victim before Dr. Anthony Harding was struggling to breathe. The story was that he inhaled a lot of smoke into his already diseased lungs. The mere two seconds it took him to draw in a single drag had set his lungs on fire rendering him helpless. He had made it as far as the bed and was lucky that the maintenance man had rescued him. The burden in the man's chest made Tony think about the first time he saw Arthur Gallows, the elderly man who presented in the emergency room at St. Joe's one night, which had initiated his journey to San Diego. Paramedics had brought him to the E.R. from O'Hare. His shirt was ripped off, and most of his clothes were removed. His flesh was gray, and he smelled of vomit like many of the malnourished street vagrants who came and went regularly. As it turned out, Arthur Gallows was a cardiologist stricken at the airport during a layover. The eighty-year-old was found in a men's room lying on the floor, clutching his chest. His wallet had been stolen, so it took the police a while to identify him. Tony diagnosed Mr. Gallows with a mild stroke and dangerously close to having a major heart attack. Like Lewis, he was lucky to have been found and brought to a Level 1 hospital. Mr. Gallows was also a long-time trusted friend of Dr. Rick Samuels, owner of the Samuels Family Practice where Tony was to start work on Monday. Arthur was impressed with the young doctor's meticulous care. And as they talked over the next few days, Tony confided his difficulties. Later, while waiting for transport after being discharged, Arthur took Tony's prescription pad from his scrub pocket, wrote Rick's address and phone number on the top sheet and signed it. "You remind me of Rick in his younger days," he said." He's building a new practice in San Diego. Use this if you're interested in starting a new life with your family; I believe there's something special about you." And then he put the pad back into Tony's pocket.

"Phoebe, Phoebe." Lewis's muffled mumbling brought Tony back from the flashback.

"Hey, Mr. Lewis, how are you feeling?" Tony whispered to the aged man on the gurney, who was frowning at him. Tony pushed the sweatshirt's hood back so the old man wouldn't think he was the Grim Reaper. "Is that better?" Tony asked, smiling. "I'm a doctor; you're gonna be fine. The paramedics are giving you medicine right now. Your house caught fire, and your friend here saved your life." Tony pointed to the tall man in the brown uniform standing at the head of the gurney. Lewis began to choke under the oxygen mask, so Tony lifted it and gently placed it under the old man's chin. He leaned forward because the old fellow was straining to say something.

"Phoebe?" The old man's voice rumbled as if his throat was full of flam. "Is Phoebe okay?" Then he groped at his chest with his fingers.

"Are you in pain, Mr. Lewis?" Tony asked quickly and grabbed a stethoscope from the pocket of a nearby paramedic and hooked it into his ears. Tony pressed the medallion to Lewis's chest. The front of his pajama shirt was ripped, and one of the white pearl buttons was missing.

Tony presumed Lewis must have ripped it off during his frantic battle to breathe.

"Did she get out okay?" Lewis garbled.

He moved the stethoscope over the old man's chest. "Are you feeling discomfort in your chest?"

Lewis slowly nodded and drifted off to sleep, whispering the name again, *Phoebe*.

Tony replaced the mask over the man's nose and mouth. The EMTs had gathered their gear and were ready to load their patient. The second ambulance had already driven away. "The patient is asking about someone," Tony reported when he returned the stethoscope.

"Yeah, I know," the paramedic replied as he packed the instrument away. "Those guys checked and re-checked," he said, pointing to the firemen rolling up the hose. "House is clear."

Tony approached the tall Latino in the smudged maintenance uniform. Gerry was born in Monterey, Mexico but had lived in the U.S. since he was three. His English was perfect, but he used his native tongue whenever he thought it was necessary. "Senor Doctor?" Gerry asked.

"Yes…uh…Si…Doctor Anthony Harding," Tony replied, pointing to himself.

"Esa senora is uh, companero of Senor Lewis," Gerry said. "Com…pan…ion...si? She's gone…fuera de poblacion. She's, ah, been notificar… uh, avisar ya." Then he said, as if laboring to explain in English, "Senor Lewis hablar...out of his head a little; confuso…comprendo?" he added as two firemen who were rolling up their hoses and who knew Gerry well shook their heads when they heard him speak in Spanish. "There ees no whon else," he seemingly struggled to say. Then he shook his head. "Let us no jump to conclusion, eh." he said, smiling.

"Si," Tony replied. "Let's not do that, but obviously, somebody must have thought the whole block was on fire," he sighed, intending his verbal afterthought to be his own.

"Si," Gerry replied softly.

Charlie made sure Annette was safely on her way home before turning his attention to Lewis again. He rushed back to the yellow caution tape when he saw the man in dark sweats attending Lewis. He was checking Lewis' pulse, listening to his chest through a stethoscope, and…talking to him. He watched him speak to the paramedics and then to Gerry, then suddenly look at his watch, animate a goodbye, and walk away briskly...toward Charlie. He greeted Charlie with a nod when he passed, then slipped the hood of his sweatshirt over his head. Charlie lost sight of him in the log jam of vehicles exiting the village. "Humph," Charlie grunted, "never seen him before."

Annette took the alley off of Gold Coast instead of Antrim Way. Too many neighbors lingered in the street, and she was never good at skirting the truth. Charles Drake was on his way home; he would relay the unofficial report to the neighbors.

Scott listened to all the Oh's and ah's when Mr. Drake told the crowd in the street about the small fire that started in Lewis' bathroom and that he surely would have died except for Gerry's quick action. But Scott had video of Phoebe aka *Nightcrawler* rushing to the scene long before Gerry.

Annette kicked off her shoes as she stumbled into the dark bedroom. One landed near the closet and the other next to the dresser. She dropped her sweatshirt on the floor at the end of the bed, yanked the red cap and hair band off, flung them both in the general direction of the dresser, and fell backward into the bed of hydrangeas and daylilies. Phoebe instantly appeared from out of the darkness and lay down beside her. The purring fan made all seem normal again. Annette rolled over and put an arm over Phoebe. "Everything seems okay, but it's a bath for you in the mornin little girl," she whispered. "I'm just too tired right now."

Phoebe let out a groan because she knew a Rylan lecture was due as well. She didn't know which she dreaded the most.

Tony reduced his run to a walk when he reached the driveway. A paperboy whizzed past him and dropped a newspaper at his feet, catching him off guard. "Man, you've gotta watch out for the bicycle traffic around here!"

he muttered and picked up the paper. There was a banner of red, white and blue flags across the top of the front page in recognition of President's Day. He paid little attention to the bold headlines except for the word, *Mistrial* that was visible on the top side of the folded paper. *By Sally Samuels* was printed under it. He might have opened the paper, but he looked up and saw his daughters sitting on the front stoop. They had retrieved their winter coats and a blanket and disobeyed his specific instruction to stay inside. *What kind of father am I if I can't make my children do something so simple?* he thought while noticing the neighbors disbanding and house lights along the street systematically going dark. "I thought I told you two to stay inside," he scolded, putting the paper under his arm.

"So, what happened?" Nicky asked.

"Yes, Daddy, what happened?" Elizabeth unwound her arms from around Nicky and scrambled to her feet.

"A fire started in the bathroom of one of the elderly residents," the father replied. He sat on the stoop, and Elizabeth immediately crawled into his lap. He had been a full-time father for over a year and still didn't know how to handle her panic attacks. He was grateful to see her acting normal despite everything that happened tonight, but she was capable of going into hysterics over the slightest thing at any given moment.

"Did anyone die?" Elizabeth asked eagerly, cupping her hands around the back of his neck.

Nicky didn't know whether to be resentful or grateful for Elizabeth's ability to capture her father's full attention with the slightest whimper.

"No, Lizzy, no one died," he said, trying not to upset her. "There was no fire, just a lot of smoke from a cigarette this old fellow threw in a trash can."

Nicky smiled as she listened to her little sister twist her father around with her questions. Soon she would suck all the anger right out of him. Before long they would go back to bed, all happy, and their disobedience forgotten.

Lizzy's imagination worried Tony. She could turn the most ordinary inconsequential event into something dramatic and scary. He had to be careful with details.

"What was his name, Daddy?" Elizabeth asked.

"Lewis, Lizzy, Lewis," he replied. "Hmm, you know, he did keep rambling about someone, but her name escapes me. They thought someone else might be in the house, but as it turned out, she wasn't. A Latino man explained it to me in Spanish."

"I didn't know you knew Spanish, Daddy?" Lizzy asked.

"I don't, Lizzy," Tony laughed. "But the house was clear."

"Did the man go to the hospital in an ambulance?" she quizzed.

"Yes, he did."

"Lewis!" she interrupted as if trying to be helpful and remind her father of the ailing man's name.

"Yes, Lizzy. Mr. Lewis has a lung disease, and he inhaled a lot of smoke. The paramedics are taking him to the hospital for observation. The doctors will watch his blood gases and determine when he can go home."

"Blood gases? Daddy, we have gas in our blood?" Lizzy screeched.

Nicky rolled her eyes and rested her head on her knees. She covered her head with her hands and wished Lizzy would just shut up.

"Not the kind you're thinking, Lizzy," her father replied. "Our blood is made up of many things. Please don't worry about this tonight, okay?" Tony said, yawning. "It's late. I'll be glad to explain it to you in the morning."

"Daddy, are there pictures of our gases in one of your books?" the little girl whispered as her father opened the screen door and led his daughters inside.

Tony helped them shed their coats and tossed them along with newspaper on the wooden rocking chair's seat. The timer in Nicky's pocket suddenly chimed.

"Ding!"

"See, I told you, Lizzy. Everything is different now," he sighed.

Scott's mother had been called in to work during all the commotion. Now Scott was reporting the details of the neighborhood emergency to his internet friend *Guardian.*

G: *NC called for help?*

S: *That's my deduction. Lewis is on his way to UCSD for observation.*

G: *Keep me posted on NC.*

S: *NC; what about Lewis?*

G: *Sending a new program; want your opinion.*

He got up to turn the alarm off when he saw Robby standing at the front door in the video feed from the security cameras.

"What ya doing, man?" Robby asked as he followed Scott to his bedroom.

"Your mom told Pop to let you stay at our crib tonight."

"Guardian sent me something to work on," Scott replied. "I don't think I'll be able to sleep now." They both looked down at the laptop. "Why don't you spend the night here? My mother doesn't want me to be alone; we can see your driveway from the window. It's practically like being at your house." They had a perfect view of the Harding front yard, the driveways, box hedges surrounding the terminal box, and Brad Jones' truck.

"I'll text Marley; she's up working on something," Robby conceded. "She can tell Mom and Pop I'm staying here." He crawled into Scott's bed and went to sleep while Scott decoded the material from his internet friend. The neighborhood was quiet now except for the purring terminal box between the driveways judiciously conveying encrypted information for its own.

Chapter 4

Any dyed-in-the-wool, ink-in-the-veins reporter who worked for the *San Diego Daily Post* could easily start their day as early as midnight. Lights in the press room were always on, and a crew was on standby to roll the presses. The Post printed thousands of pages every twenty-four hours, keeping the populous of San Diego and California abreast of all the southwest news. The early edition ran at 2:00 a.m. and was on the delivery trucks by 3:00. The underground presses seemed to run continually, and the third-floor newsroom was always alive with voices and telephone tones. A single, night editor was required on the press room floor at night to determine whether a breaking story had the legs to run in the early edition. Most reporters worked in a common area within the confines of their eight-by-ten cubbyholes. Six *Star Reporters* enjoyed the privilege of private offices with a TV, futon, mini fridge, and a raised gold star on their name tile.

Sally Samuels was a star reporter and presently reflecting on her contribution to today's early publication. She had composed, re-written, edited, and doted over a front-page headline story with a resolute strategy for two weeks. She'd been developing the deeply personal article for a year but couldn't make herself write it until now because, on Tuesday, an innocent man was likely to be found guilty of murder. Three hours earlier she was guarding the front page set up. Afterward, she watched the giant rolls of paper pass across the electronic printing plates from a catwalk. She followed the automated process through the cutting and folding process and observed the early edition as it was stacked, bundled, and conveyed to the loading dock. She stayed until the last loaded delivery truck pulled out. Some reporters have an anxiety that can't be quelled until they read their own words on printed paper and crave the rush that comes from hearing the reactions to their published work. Sally was no different, except for today.

She had been breathing freely for over an hour, including the twenty-minute drive to her home in La Jolla. She had no desire to hang around for the critique. Every word, sentence structure, and paragraph went around in her head as she walked her bedroom floor. Nerves took her downstairs once to refill her wine glass, but it was untouched on the dressing table. Foremost in her mind was that life as she knew it was over after today. Exhaustion finally silenced her conscious thoughts at three. In a matter of hours, her audience would include a faction that she genuinely feared disturbing. She hoped the wine would put her to sleep, but it only made her blood pump faster and her thoughts flow deeper. Her fan base was accustomed to her bleating outcry for the less fortunate but wouldn't fathom how far her pen had penetrated; that she had gone further than the expose' of a miscarriage of justice against a single homeless man who went by the street name of Old Walter. They admired the waves she stirred on behalf of the little guy; they trusted her. Some would cringe at the provocative stand she touted against her husband of five years, the highly regarded Randal Samuels, Head District Attorney of San Diego County. Others would shrug and say it was about time because they never understood why she married him in the first place. The story would grab the attention of The Group, her husband's largest contributor whose headquarters was in mountainous Escondido. Its influences were widespread and its enterprises self-serving. Its principals would react with knitted eyebrows and secret stares and assemble quickly to discuss the article and its effect on the political groundwork they were building.

Sally stood before a full-length mirror in her bedroom and tried to mimic a posture of strength. She needed to practice the effort it would take to hold her shoulders back and her chin up. First Amendment rights, professional duty, yes; that might pass for good reason, she told herself. Perhaps it was a move, although foolish, to advance her career; that might carry credence with the CEO's at the Daily Post. Would anyone consider inherent satisfaction? After all, her parents, Aggie and Park Stevens had been freelance writers who published mystery novels packed with adventurous exploits. She exhaled and her stance slumped. Sally was a popular figure in San Diego; a featured speaker at community functions. Her innate talent inspired and motivated readers at the grassroots level, always posing awkward questions and giving the average citizen a forum. She supplied their armor; her words became their words; they spoke the rationale of Sally Samuels to their neighbors and community leaders and ultimately to the touch screen behind a voting curtain. Today, the earliest risers would read all about the unethical practices of three prominent San Diego County legal system members on the front page of the San Diego Daily Post. They would find it hard to believe the accusation that her husband withheld evidence from the court in the current high-profile murder trial against Old Walter. She would report that Curtis Richards, Chief Criminal Investigator, and Assistant Medical examiner, Gordon Knight, had aided Randal in removing and concealing from the court, a crucial page from the M.E. autopsy report that described a different cause of death for Anderson Barksdale, San Diego's popular tourist commissioner. Sally would tell of how she had inadvertently discovered the page in her husband's safe. The discovery would seriously alter the State's murder case that her husband was presenting to a jury against the panhandler. This was an indisputable unorthodox way to disclose the missing evidence, but she felt it was necessary to ensure it was brought forth at all. A round table discussion with The Post's editors was pointless because politics would enter the debate while they were busy dissecting the article. The Post was a subsidiary of The Group and the story would never make it to press.

"Poor David," Sally muttered and walked away from the mirror. She couldn't face herself and think of David Dalton at the same time. He was her Executive Managing Editor. They had been friends since college where they had a short-lived romantic involvement. They had been inseparable friends for fifteen years until David met the woman of his dreams. How many projects had they worked on together? How many times had they confided to each other and had each other's backs? She hadn't breathed a word about this to him; she hadn't dropped one hint or clue. He was going to be furious. Tears welled up in her eyes and she allowed them to flow for a few seconds before she swiped them away. Did she have a prayer? Could she count on David's support? Her articles helped his circulation. The Post was among the top three papers in the State. Or would he be forced to cut her loose after being pressured to do so by the Board of Directors, which was largely made up of the seemingly mesmerized products of The Group? She had taken advantage of his trust tonight by telling him to go home to his family, that she'd put the early edition to bed. She had bypassed the night editor, and the press operators had no clue what she was up to. She knew how to disassemble and rearrange articles on the composing room computer. She knew how to set up a headline. He would be livid over the elaborate deception. *I'm not feeling so courageous right now, David,* she confessed to herself.

With her cell and their unlisted number turned off, the inevitable could be delayed somewhat, so Sally forced herself to slide between the satin sheets. With her head against the pillow, she thought of her early childhood and how the approaching spring always meant the end of another school year at St. Jude's boarding school. Her parents would call, and she would sit on the front steps of the Catholic School, anxiously awaiting their arrival in the latest model Mercedes. Their summers together were magical. They played games and traveled until the fall semester when they had to deliver her back to the Monsignor and the nuns for safekeeping while they went off to sell their books. Sally honed her journalistic skills while watching her parents develop and write their far-fetched mystery stories. They planned to retire when she graduated from high school. She used to sneak away from the nuns after lights out to a forgotten dilapidated chapel at the edge of Old Town. It was surrounded by an eight-foot stone wall with a strip of run-down classrooms behind a courtyard and a crumbling fountain in the middle, which was now reduced to a rain collector. The three crosses of Mount Calvary were carved into the church doors that creaked when she opened them. The plaster on the ceiling fell like sifting flour when she closed them. Spiders spun their webs lavishly from the weathered exposed beams. Occasionally, she saw a mouse scurry across the floor, so she curled her legs up underneath her when she sat in the pews to do homework and write short stories by flashlight; stories she knew the nuns would never approve of because they emulated her parent's style of mystery and scandal. A Spanish boy named Juan sometimes hid in the chapel as well to take refuge from his life. She helped him improve his English by allowing him to read her stories. One day, he sadly told her his family was moving to San Joaquin Valley to work in the fields. That's when he led her to a wall of empty bookcases in the sacristy behind the altar. He pulled one of the casings loose, and a panel of shelves swung out like a door. Behind it were stairs that led to a wine cellar that he said was a better hiding place if she ever needed one. He had heard tales of a secret tunnel beyond the wine cellar that the Aztec Indians and early Mexican immigrants used to travel between Mexico and California. Mexican soldiers used them for safe passage during their country's many wars. The beams and cross members in the underground structure had been made of a unique petrified wood, native only to South America. Conquistadors killed for the wood and used it to reinforce their ships against pirates and to make weapons and armor to battle hostile tribes. The tunnel was said to be two hundred miles long at one time, but most of it collapsed because scavengers had removed the rock-like beams. She hid her writings inside one of the old wine barrels in the cellar, along with her parents' books. She never told anyone about Juan, not David or even Randy. She intended to tell her parents, wanting to incorporate his character into a story, but she never had the chance because they died the following winter while traveling in France. A poorly maintained trestle gave way just when their train reached the mid-section. Her grief caused her to lose her memory of Juan for a time and question if he had ever existed. She never returned to the chapel, leaving the treasured magazines, books and writings to disintegrate along with the buildings.

Sally's bedside telephone suddenly rang, startling her. One arm struggled awkwardly from under the sheets. She raised her head and flung her dark auburn hair from her face. Randy always said he loved the way her hair always seemed to fall perfectly into place around her shoulders. She fumbled for the receiver, knocking it off its dock and onto the floor. She moaned, turned over, and swung her arm over the side of the bed. She groped the floor and nudged it with her hand making it slide two inches further under the bed.

"For God's sake," she sighed in support of the challenge it took her to sit up and find the cordless phone. "Hello," she mumbled into the voice pad. Her emerald green eyes opened wider after hearing a distorted voice in the earpiece. She had dozed off for a brief ten minutes and, for a second, thought everything was normal, and this was The Post calling with an assignment, a breaking story. She looked at Randy's undisturbed side of the bed, and then the nightmare she had created for herself returned. She had left messages for him everywhere earlier, his office, cell phone, but no one had seen him. Was he returning her calls? Her confusion vanished when the acoustical voice began to speak.

"Warn me?" she asked the altered orator. "How did you get… you listen…" Sally's anger quickly cleared the haze. She had no patience with crank callers, particularly when the validity of her stories was questioned. "My sources are...how dare you question…who's on the way? Ahh!" she shouted when the caller hung up before she could unload on him. She pressed star sixty-nine; there were three buzzes and then a click.

"This phone is disposable, Ms. Samuels," advised the gurgling voice. "And so are you."

Sally threw the phone on the bed. At the same moment, the bedroom door swung open. Sally turned her head and gasped, thinking for an instant that someone had broken in, someone connected to the phone call who meant to do her harm and dispose of her. She picked up the cordless from the bed and threw it at the open door. Randy's mighty silhouette was easy to recognize, even against the dim light from downstairs. Not many men could fill a doorway the way he could with his height and broad athletic frame. He was holding the early edition in one hand and switched on the crystalline overhead light without warning. Sally covered her eyes, trying to protect them from the sudden brightness reflecting off the prisms. She saw her husband's face through her cupped fingers.

"What have you done to me!" he roared, moving closer and throwing the newspaper down on the bed in front of her. Randy's commanding voice demanded everyone's attention in the courtroom, and it certainly had Sally's at this moment. Most of the inside sections of the Monday morning early edition scattered across the covers leaving Section A clearly in her view. Elusive Evidence Surfaces - Mistrial Imminent was printed in four-inch bold lettering across the top page.

Her intense green eyes dropped from the dominant headline she had agonized over earlier that evening to the article below that contained her byline. The art department had outdone itself with the red, white, and blue flags and swirling ribbons and faces of past presidents that decorated the border of the first page. Holiday sale inserts dripped to the floor off the satin bedspread. She slowly looked up at her husband, who was now standing at the edge of the bed, and judging by the glare from his steel gray eyes, she knew exactly what would happen between them. Nothing in her arsenal of seductive offerings could mend what she did. She had betrayed him on the grandest of scales.

"Why, Sally?" Randy asked as if he were grilling a witness. "Is this something you and your buddy Dalton thought you could get away with like you did in your old shock and awe tabloid reporting days? This is suicide, you know…for you…not me."

Sally pressed her lips together. Her plan was to remain silent and let him say what he felt. He had a right to be furious. "No, Randy," she said, shaking her head, "David had nothing to do with this. It…was…all me," she panted. "This is the way…I do things, Randy. You know me well enough," she whispered. "I tried to reach you, but…I'm sorry."

"Sorry? Sorry?" he roared. "That's not good enough."

"Those people have too much control over you," she blurted out. "Please, I've tried to talk to you about The Group and how they have completely taken over your life…and you."

"So that's why you did this?" Randy asked. "You're jealous of the time I spend with the company that will put me in the governor's mansion?"

"No, Randy, no," she replied. "Remember how suspicious you were of them in the beginning? Think, please!"

"I don't know what you talking about. Tell Dalton he's got until the next edition to print a retraction," he barked, raising his fist. "And you can start packing!"

Sally bit her bottom lip, trying to keep silent. She didn't have to explain herself to Randy. They had been married for five years. He told her many times that it was her gutsiness that he found so attractive. He had trumpeted it hundreds of times, both in public and private. He knew exactly who she was. Woefully, she wished she could say the same about him. "It's too late for a retraction, Randy. The evidence will soon be in the hands of the FBI."

Randy stared at her in silence. He opened his mouth, but Sally interrupted.

"Apparently, local law enforcement is on its way," she said, looking at the empty phone dock, "and, eventually, the FBI."

Randy grabbed the chair in front of the dressing table and threw it up against the small mirrored vanity, knocking over bottles of lotion and the glass of wine Sally had left there. The chair then ricocheted and rolled over twice before coming to rest beside the bed. He left the bedroom, slamming the door behind him which shook the wall, tilting two paintings. Sally jumped out of bed and grabbed her bathrobe. She wanted to scream at him but she was afraid the only thing that would come out would be incoherent blubbering through gushing tears. She could hear Randy's voice clearly over the thunder of his hefty footsteps storming down the stairs.

"You think I'm worried about the local law enforcement," he roared, and then he laughed, "ha, and the FBI?"

Chapter 5

The tiny solar garden lights along the walk would give way to dawn's first light in another hour. The sprinklers had just finished their ten-minute broad spray, and now the mini heads under the ground cover were spurting, feeding the cropped shrubs and trees surrounding the two-story brick, stone, and mortar home. A silver Cadillac moved slowly over the sculpted terracotta driveway and stopped beside the front steps. Randy Samuels stepped out and carefully closed the door as if trying not to disturb the chirping crickets and cicadas. He wore dark blue sweats and carried a leather duffle and canvas suit bag.

"Randy! What the hell?" Rick Samuels asked his younger brother after opening the solid oak door. "Lorraine's upstairs tidying up the guest room," he said, leading the way to the large family room. "That'll give us a few minutes to talk. What's in the early edition?" Rick Samuels was every bit as tall as his brother Randy but slimmer and had whiter hair. He had been practicing medicine in San Diego since graduating from the University of Southern California, where he completed his residency, concentrating on neurology. He clerked in neurology and worked under a fellowship program accredited by the prestigious ACGME and UCNS, where he engaged in both clinical and investigative work in new ways to approach the treatment of neurological diseases such as Alzheimer's, Parkinson's, Huntington's, stroke, epilepsy, and many others. Married forty years, Rick and Lorraine had two grown children: Myra, married with two children of her own, and Kevin, divorced and living with his parents temporarily, along with his son, Daniel. Rick and Lorraine were well off, thanks to Rick's importance in the medical community.

Randy handed his brother the early edition of The San Diego Daily Post. "Read this," he grumbled. "You'll understand why I got the hell out of there. I appreciate you and Lorraine allowing me to stay here until my people straighten this out. I told Sally to pack and get out, but who knows how long that will take."

"Let's go in my office," Rick said soberly after reading the headline. One whole wall of his office was reference books and awards. Paintings Lorraine bought in Europe, and a family portrait strategically balanced the décor on the opposite wall behind his desk, and a large window capped the room that looked out onto the deck and back yard. A set of wooden hand-carved lion heads bookends sat on a bookshelf directly across from his desk. Most of the children's craftwork was on display in the family room and kitchen, but he considered the pair of lion heads special because, during a better time in their relationship, Kevin made them for him in a high school woodworking class. Rick sat down at his desk, put on his reading glasses, and spread the newspaper in front of him.

"Oh my God, oh my God!" he repeated while he read the article. "Randy, is any of this true?" he finally said when he finished.

Randy was standing at the window looking out at the blooming garden patio. The deck lights were on, and he could see the lower level, the yard, and the swimming pool. His brother seemed to have a perfect life, wife, and family. Randy had remained single until five years ago. He and Sally lived a different life style than Rick and Lorraine. They were self-indulgent and never talked about having children; he thought they were happy. "No," Randy said emphatically and turned from the window. "We have a witness and forensic evidence. She found a discrepancy that's not my fault. And now she's blowing it up and making accusations; for what, for a story."

"You mean the missing evidence, the page she found in your safe that was omitted from the M.E. report?"

"I don't know where that came from or how that ended up in my safe," Randy roared angrily, "unless someone or *she* put it there."

"What about the M.E. testimony?" Rick asked.

"That's for Knight to explain," Randy bellowed. "I don't know how she convinced Dalton to go along with this. He'll suffer if I find out he's involved."

"Her old friend from college," Rick said, recalling the rumors of their college affair and infamous journalistic collaborations. "But why would she do this? Did the two of you have an argument?"

"No," Randy's voice growled. "This was purely out of the blue with no warning whatsoever. And she's not going to get away with it."

"God, Randy, I hate to say this," Rick reached for the silver humidor on his desk when he got up, then realized Sally gave it to him for Christmas and pulled his hand back. "But you knew her reputation when you married her. We talked about it, remember?"

"You were right, Rick," he said, returning to the window. "I wish I'd listened."

"Have you talked with the mayor or anyone at the State Capital?"

"I called the Lieutenant Governor," Randy replied. "He was already aware of the article and had informed the Governor. There will be meetings in a few hours, starting with the Judge and later with some people from The Group; I hope I haven't lost them over this. I didn't know where else to go, Rick. I'm sorry," he sighed.

"We're brothers." Rick went to his brother and stood beside him at the window and put a hand on his shoulder. "We stick together, no matter what. Our parents were fifty-five and sixty when we were born. They taught us to take care of each other because they knew they wouldn't live to see us grow. And that's what we've always done."

"And there was Uncle Arthur," Randy sighed.

"Yes, he was like a father to us after they were both gone," Rick sighed. "Hey, do you smell something?" Rick said, lifting his nose." Lorraine's in the kitchen cooking breakfast. Kevin and Daniel will be down when they smell that bacon." They both headed toward the door. "She doesn't do this very often, you know. I'm usually on my own at breakfast, which is my fault, of course, because I get up so early to go to the hospital. In fact," he looked at his watch. "I'll be headed there soon."

"When are you going to retire, for real, I mean?" Randy poked.

Rick reached for the two lion head bookends and turned them so the backs of their heads supported a small group of books. "When I fall dead in the halls of the hospital, I suppose."

"Are you talking about falling dead again?" Lorraine yelled when she heard their voices. "I wish you would tell him to stop telling people that, Randy. It sounds like a death wish. He hired another young protégé; someone Arthur met when he fell ill at O'Hare."

"Don't worry, he won't be able to cut it; no one has my brother's work ethic. Is it the young man you had me check on? Widower, two children, glowing record," he said, recalling the background check. "There was something about the way his wife died; oh yes, car accident, and there's a younger brother doing time. His diagnosis record, attention to detail, and success rate caught your attention."

"Coffee's ready," Lorraine said as she put plates on the dining table. "Juice is on the table."

"He's starting next week," Rick said.

"Are you talking about Boy Wonder again?" Kevin said, strolling into the dining room in his bathrobe. "Father doesn't usually like to talk about the hospital when he's home, but he just can't seem to stop himself when it comes to this new guy that Uncle Arthur bumped into on his way to New York."

"It was a little more than bumping into," Rick said. "And you're right, Kevin, I don't like talking about work at home."

"Honey, be nice," Lorraine whined and smoothed her son's hair to one side.

"How are you, Kevin?" Randy asked, sounding overly cordial.

"Advertising's kinda dried up right now, Uncle Randy," Kevin replied, swatting his mother's hand away.

"You'll find something, honey," Lorraine said. "A third of the country is unemployed. You and Daniel are doing fine right here with us, right Ricky?"

"Unfortunately, the guy that took Anderson's place brought his own team with him," Randy stated sarcastically before sitting beside his brother.

Kevin frowned at his uncle while pouring coffee into the cup Lorraine put in his hand. "Don't worry, Uncle Randy, you won't be seeing me around the courthouse."

"Kevin," Randy said, staring at his nephew while Lorraine poured coffee into his cup, "I don't need to remind you that the city council would have allowed you to keep your position if you and Andy hadn't hacked into the courthouse system."

"Which they would never have discovered if Andy hadn't been killed," Kevin said cynically, "triggering The Group to go snooping into his activities."

"Please, let's don't talk about that that horrible tragedy," Lorraine sighed. "Oh, look who is up?"

"Gramma, what are you doing up?" Kevin's five-year-old son, Daniel, was standing in the light of the dining room with a hand over one eye. He trotted to Lorraine and she pulled him onto her lap.

"Where are your tinted glasses, baby? You know what the doctor said about your eye sensitivity. Your Uncle Randy just arrived and we decided to have a big breakfast to celebrate. Are you hungry?"

He shook his head and slipped down from her lap. He ran to his grandpa, pulled on his shirt sleeve, and whispered in his ear.

"Of course," Rick chuckled. "Eat some of Gramma's bacon while I make our toast."

Lorraine looked at Randy and explained: "He likes to get up early and eat honey toast with his grandpa. Ricky puts him back to bed before he leaves for the hospital."

"How can you be sure he doesn't stay up and play on the computer after Father goes to work, Mother?" Kevin asked condescendingly.

"It's your job to ensure he doesn't, Kevin," she replied curtly.

Kevin grunted a laugh. "I was just harassing you, Mother."

"It seems that he's been playing on the computer too much," Lorraine graciously explained to Randy. "His pediatrician says he's suffering from eye strain, so he advised us to make him wear tinted glasses for a while."

"What's going on anyway?" Kevin asked while walking to the table with his coffee. "Why are you here at this time of the morning, Uncle Randy?"

"Pass him the newspaper," Randy bellowed. Kevin picked it up after Lorraine pushed it toward his end of the table.

"Whoa! Uncle Randy!" he gasped. His mouth hung ajar as he read the entire article. "I don't know what to say. What are you going to do?"

"First things first," he replied.

"I wouldn't know what was first if this was me."

Lorraine rolled her eyes, remembering how badly Kevin handled the breakup with his wife and how she and Rick were forced to hire an attorney to keep him from losing total custody of Daniel. Thankfully, the well-paid attorney could pass on a large sum of money and was vicious enough to convince Kevin's ex-wife to move away and never bother him again.

"I have a meeting with the Judge later today," Randy said. "But I really could use a couple hours of sleep."

"Come on, Randy," Lorraine said, pushing her chair back. "Bring your things upstairs. I'll show you which room is yours. And it's yours from now on if you like."

"You're an angel, Lorraine," Randy said, following her from the dining area. "Ricky sure is lucky to have you."

Kevin smirked when he heard his uncle's remark. "Yeah, well," he mumbled under his breath. He sipped his coffee and watched his father dote over Daniel. He thought how fortunate it was for him that grandchildren have such power over their grandparents. He would be hard-pressed for a place to live right now if it weren't for that bond.

"Come on, little man," Rick teased. "It's time for your nap. Grandpa has to go to work."

"Not even a kiss before naptime?" Kevin asked, even though his father was halfway across the family room with Daniel on his arm. Rick put Daniel down, and he quickly ran to Kevin, kissed him on the cheek, and immediately scurried back to his grandpa.

"Come on, Grandpa. Read me just one short story before you go to work."

They met Lorraine at the top of the stairs. She kissed her grandson and then went down to the dining room. Neither Kevin nor Lorraine spoke while she cleared the breakfast dishes, although they did throw sparring glances at one another. After loading the dishwasher, she walked to the table, took his empty coffee cup out of his hand and leaned in close. "How dare you be so disrespectful to your uncle!" she hissed. "You would be in federal prison now if it weren't for him. Please tell me that Daniel's eye problems aren't related to what you and Andy did. I overheard you talking on the phone to someone from The Group. You were talking about Daniel, and it sounded like you were in serious trouble. Don't worry, I didn't tell your father," she said when Kevin glared at her.

"Daniel will be fine," he said in a compromising tone.

"Thank goodness for your uncle's special relationship with The Group."

"Yes, they are exceptionally loyal to Uncle Randy, aren't they?" Kevin sighed and then picked up the paper again.

Chapter 6

Dawn was beginning to seep around the edges of Annette's bedroom curtains. She turned off the alarm to keep its irritating beeps from shattering the peacefulness. The early AM sirens had interrupted a dream about her father. Sonny Rylan had died at age fifty-eight of oat cell carcinoma. It took a mere eighteen months for the disease to wither his body, hollow his face, leave his hands and arms bruised from intravenous needles and then finally take his life. Annette and her mother witnessed every moment of the torture they should have put a stop to months before. But doctors had filled their heads with statistics and reasons for hope. She remembered her mother's uncombed strawberry-blonde hair and the way her blue eyes clashed brilliantly against the redness surrounding them. Her brother's flight from Denver had been delayed. Everyone always said that Keith could have been his father's twin.

Phoebe patted her shoulder as if trying to comfort her master. Annette rubbed the back of Phoebe's ear in return. "Why did your mama have just one special puppy?" Phoebe licked her master's nose. "What would she think if she could smell you right now? You stink to high heaven." Annette cupped her hand over Phoebe's nose and shook it. Then she hid her hand under the flowered comforter and moved it back and forth. Phoebe chased the fictitious animal tunneling beneath the fern, darting her head to the right and left, pouncing after the moving varmint. She dove into the greenery, popping her head out every few seconds looking for the finger creature. "We should have let him die at home, Phoeb," she whispered to her little confidant when the game was over. Annette and her mother were so tired those last few days that they could barely hold their heads up. Neither one of them wanted to leave the other alone. Coco watched them struggle to keep their eyes open from her customary spot between Sonny's side and his right arm. The two women sat alone in the dimly lit room and watched him fade in and out of a morphine stupor, moving his fingers occasionally, always feeling for Coco. She would acknowledge him by licking his hand. Neither of them could speak nor breathe when he finally took his last breath. They waited for him to inhale, for his chest to rise, or for his fingers to move. It was like being suspended in time when there was no sound or air. "Crap! I'm late!" Nette shouted when she looked at the clock. "Why didn't you tell me it was after six?" she said, jumping out of bed. "You know I have to be at Molly's by seven."

Phoebe sprang to her feet and watched as her master shuffled around the bedroom. She wondered if she had time to jump to the floor and scoot under the bed before Annette remembered the bath she had promised.

"That's not workin," Annette scolded as Phoebe whined and shook as she looked up from the shower floor, hoping the yearning expression would render sympathy. "You're the one that ran into the house full of smoke." She squatted down, squeezed the bottle of baby shampoo, and began to scrub the little dog. "What am I gonna do with you?" The scrubbing slowed to gentle messages as she thought of how Phoebe had saved her dear friend who probably didn't have many years left. She didn't want to think about losing someone else.

Phoebe wiggled out from Annette's punishment after a brief toweling. The poodle scampered into the living room, shaking her body, rolling on the carpet, and rubbing against the sofa, trying to use every means to remove the water.

"Phoebe!" Nette yelled from inside the shower. "Come back here and get this towel."

Phoebe sprang into the hall and stopped at the bathroom door. She stuck her nose in the door and then pushed her way inside. She quickly grabbed one corner of the towel lying on the floor in her mouth and ran out of the bathroom. She tugged it behind her down the hall and into the living room.

"Close the door! You're lettin in the cold air," her master yelled and reached from behind the shower door and slammed the bathroom door closed.

Phoebe held one end of the towel with her mouth; the rest lay on the floor behind her. She laid on it, rolled herself up inside and began to squirm.

Annette slipped into jeans and a black and gold Saints graphic long-sleeved sweater. She ran a brush through her wet hair in the kitchen while she doctored her coffee with sweetener and milk. Phoebe ate her breakfast from a bowl next to the refrigerator, where she watched her master through her own wet, stringy locks. Annette's white Reeboks paced back and forth across the kitchen floor in front of her; slowly at first, and then faster. Phoebe buried her nose in the bowl, hoping to avoid the brewing lecture.

"You know our lives will never be the same if people start makin somethin out of your *talent*, Phoeb," Annette finally blurted out. "People can't handle things they don't understand." Annette stopped pacing and dropped to her knees beside Phoebe. "People blow things all out of proportion, jump to conclusions, and make things up. Why?" she said when Phoebe cocked her head. "Because they're afraid of things they don't understand. Jesus, I don't understand how you do what you do, and it scares me. How did you know what had happened at Lewis' last night? Was it some kind of super dog-sensitive hearing or smell?" Annette sat down and leaned her back against the refrigerator door. "And last August, when you took off from me in the parkin lot at the Bowlin ally and led me to that car with the baby locked inside? How did you know it was in there? He wasn't cryin or anything. And a couple of weeks ago, when you distracted those people outside the movie theater just before a truck turned the corner and jumped the sidewalk." Annette let out a long moan. "We've found somethin here, Phoebe; somethin that feels right." Annette looked up at the window over the sink as if she could see out into the peaceful neighborhood from her position on the floor. "I don't want anything to change that. People around here have accepted us for who we are. Hum," she exhaled, "I don't know if that really says much because they pretty much accept everything. Back home, I always felt like the oddball cuz I never liked goin out and partyin and actin like a redneck fool." Annette sighed and leaned her head back against the refrigerator.

Phoebe cocked her head and raised one ear. Annette closed her eyes, wondering if her damp little confidant could really understand or if she was just talking to herself.

"Anyway, if you can understand what I'm sayin, please be careful. You're my…best friend, and I don't want to lose you." Annette leaned forward, grabbed her ankles, and pulled her legs close to her chest. "It's like you're the last thing Daddy left me. Somehow, when I talk to you, I feel like I'm talkin to him. You were there, inside Coco when he died." She reached down and stroked the top of Phoebe's head.

Phoebe lay down on the floor in front of her master with her head between her paws. Then she put both paws over her nose and whined.

"Oh, please!" Annette moaned. "I've seen this act before."

Phoebe quickly sat up, put her front paws on Nette's knees, then jumped over them and wiggled into the small space between her legs and chest. She began to lick her master's nose and eyes.

"Stop it, Phoebe. You know I don't like that. Ugh!" Annette reprimanded as she pried Phoebe away from her face. "I have to go. It's a holiday, and there's no tellin how many will be there today, so you have to stay here." Annette carried her coffee cup to the back porch and sat it on the porch railing. She felt a nudge against her leg and looked down. Phoebe was standing at her feet with her favorite pillow in her mouth. Annette muffled a chuckle, thinking it must have been quite a struggle to get that worn-out fringed throw pillow through the doggy door. "You're not goin," Annette said, shaking her head and pretending to ignore her. "Uh-uh; not after last night."

Phoebe wagged her tail and reinforced her clutch on the faded maroon print cushion.

"I don't think so," Annette sang melodically.

Phoebe cocked her head to one side and then flung the pillow in the air. It landed against Annette's stomach and dropped to the floor. They both looked at the pillow lying on the concrete and then at each other.

"Forget it!" Annette growled.

The pillow was faded and worn and looked ready for the trash but it had been part of Phoebe's layette inside the cardboard box where she opened her eyes for the first time.

Therefore, she liked having it nearby, and they spent many hours playing catch with it.

"Okay, if you can bring this to me before I get through the gate, you can come with me to Molly's," Annette challenged and quickly grabbed the pillow. She threw it in the air, landing on the top of a 10 ft. Juniper tree. "Ha! See ya this afternoon, pal," Nette said. She grabbed her bicycle by the handlebars and guided it to the gate.

Phoebe ran around the tree several times and finally dove inside. The shrub began to vibrate until the pillow fell through the inside branches. Within seconds, she ran out from under the juniper with the pillow in her jaws.

Annette was about to close the gate behind her when Phoebe raced through it with the treasured pillow. She stopped in front of the bicycle and wagged her tail with such vigor that the rear half of her body swayed back and forth. Annette's mouth opened, but she couldn't think of a point to argue. Phoebe cast the cushion into the air again. It looked like a rag doll with its tattered fringes and limp body turning over and over. It bounced off Annette's forehead and fell square into the wire basket attached to the handlebars.

"Okay, you win," she sighed and held her arms out.

Phoebe jumped into her arms, making panting noises like suppressed shouts of joy. She tried to thank her master with a lick to the face, but Nette bobbed her head back and forth, avoiding the gratuitous kisses. Annette fluffed the pillow, placed Phoebe on top of it and peddled down the alley toward Gold Coast. Frankie and Johnnie followed the bicycle with their eyes, not stirring from their horizontal positions. Annette peered over the fence across the alley from the two German Shepherds where her friends, Jim and Julia used to live. Then she remembered the near miss in the driveway the night before and sped up.

Molly Ward was the proud manager of the daycare that bore her name. Children six months and older played and learned their fundamentals under her wistful eye and the meticulous care of her staff. She owned the daycare at one time but fell into financial straits after an expensive expansion and trying to keep up with growing state licensing and code requirements. The State took over and allowed Molly to remain as its manager.

"Hi there, Mr. McKenzie," Annette said as she glided passed the elderly gentleman strolling up Molly's driveway. The tall pedestrian of slight build threw up a hand and waved. He squirmed occasionally as he walked as if trying to adjust the brown corduroy pants and matching dark brown polo sweater.

"I like your new duds," she said when they met in the garage.

"Kids sent me this for Christmas. Thought I'd best get a little wear out of it; not very comfortable though; not like my old flannel."

Annette's eyes sparkled, as they often did when she was around the elderly and children; it was as if she was set free while in the company of the two extreme generations. Mr. McKenzie scratched Phoebe on the head. She licked his hand in return.

"What's she doing here?"

"What—do you mean?" Nette stuttered.

"Well, you know," he began and then leaned closer. "After last night," he whispered. "I kinda figured she'd be in the dog house today, heh, heh."

"Very funny, Mr. Mac, but I don't know what you're talkin about," she said frowning.

"Oh, of course," the elder said and put a finger to his lips. "We're not supposed to talk about it."

"I knew bringin you here today was a bad idea!" she whispered to Phoebe after Mr. McKinsey went inside.

"You're here early, dear," Molly teased from her seat at the kitchen table. Molly was short and plump and wore a muumuu most of the time and preferred her short black hair in tight curls that sprang back into place whenever one of the children pulled on them. She wore bright red lipstick and rose-colored blush.

"I didn't sleep so good," Nette replied, noticing Molly's peculiar stare. Molly had always reminded Annette of her grandmother on her mother's side. She, too, was short and chubby and had an infectious laugh. Annette had inherited her height, or lack thereof, from her grandmother. "Did you hear the fire trucks last night?" Annette asked sheepishly. Clearly, something was on Molly's mind.

"Oh, Yes," Molly sighed and outstretched her arms, beckoning Phoebe. "Oh, Phoebe; you're wet?" Molly gasped when Phoebe jumped in her lap. Then Molly laughed so hard that her whole face turned red when Phoebe shook as if playing on sympathy.

"Yeah, she rolled in somethin really foul last night." Annette waved one hand in front of her nose as if to clear the air. "I couldn't stand her." *Who am I kiddin? She knows what happened, just like Mr. Mac.*

Molly whispered something into Phoebe's ear and then got up and retrieved a towel from a cabinet.

"Poor baby, we can't just let you dry willy-nilly." Molly searched further until she found a brush. "Come on, little darling, I'll make you all pretty." Molly plodded into the front room and eased down in a comfortable chair in front of a double window so the twosome could watch the parents coming up the front walk with their children. Annette followed them as far as the archway that divided the rooms and studied Molly doting over Phoebe.

"We might just have a magic show later to celebrate the holiday," Molly told Phoebe. "And you must look your best because you're the star." Molly rubbed Phoebe's nose against her own and then turned her head and winked at Annette standing in the archway.

Annette smiled, shook her head, and thought, even if Molly did act a little fickle, her heart was always in the right place. Perhaps years of looking after children had taken its toll. Molly gave Phoebe a treat and started talking to her in baby talk as if she was one of the toddlers.

"You remember what day it is, don't you dear?" Molly said as she messaged Phoebe with the towel. "Oh, I almost forgot, Jeffrey called; his grandmother is dropping him and Justin off later. He said something about his dad signing some papers today."

"Papers," Nette scowled.

"Something wrong?" Molly asked.

"Larry's been lookin at land in Escondido," Annette replied. "I didn't think he was serious. He's probably plannin on cookin somethin up there or relocating his fencin operation."

Two more staff members entered the kitchen.

"Whose voice is that?" the tall blonde asked.

"What are you doing here so early?" the second woman chimed in.

"Hey, I'm always on time," Annette shouted, and then whispered, "Mostly."

Molly tried to suppress her amusement, but her face turned red, and she burst out a single laugh.

Mona Spencer was married, in her mid-twenties, with dark hair and of Spanish descent, and was actually shorter than Annette. She gave her a friendly nudge when they met in the kitchen.

"Are you sick?" asked Lisa Wilson, who was twenty-four, married, and taller than all the staff members. She had long blonde hair and always pulled it back in a ponytail.

"What's the big deal, anyway?" Annette roared. After a pause, they all laughed at the same time.

"You are so messed up, Nette," Lisa taunted.

Molly hired Annette on the spot when she appeared at her door one day with Phoebe on one arm after she heard the children playing in the backyard. However, Annette avoided getting too tight with married couples like Lisa and Mona because she learned from heartbreaking experiences that a single woman in the mix often created jealousy between partners. Either the wives were spending too much time away from their husbands, or the husbands found her straightforwardness and tomboyish style a little too charming.

Mona had mastered English long ago but cherished her Spanish heritage and spoke her native tongue whenever possible. She was taking Internet college courses through the University of Southern Cal in L.A., where she had already received her teaching credits and was now working on a second art major. Mona's husband, Tim, was a great guy until he popped too many beer tops. When Mona complained, he only became obnoxious and proceeded to down a whole six-pack to spite her, sometimes more. Mona didn't drink, so it was a sore subject.

"Jeffrey and Justin will be here later," Annette said. "I picked them up from North Park Friday and took them to their grandmother's because they hadn't seen Larry in two days. He's lookin at land up in Escondido, and I'm worried about what will happen to them if they move up there."

"It may not happen," Mona said. "You know Larry; full of big ideas."

Annette took a large tub of butter and a carton of eggs from the fridge. Lisa and Mona looked at each other curiously.

"What are you doing?" Lisa finally asked, and Mona cupped a hand over her mouth to hide the grin on her face.

"I'm makin breakfast!" Annette said and cracked an egg into a bowl.

"You can't cook!" Lisa said, batting her eyes.

"Well, I can do this, and microwave, and, and," she stuttered and then gave in to their teasing.

"You pour cereal!" Lisa said, laughing.

Annette spent as little time in front of the stove as possible growing up. Stirring pots in the kitchen didn't interest her, but she was never more than two feet from her father's elbow. He had more interesting projects than chopping celery, carrots, and onions. As a result, she could fix her bicycle and tune up a lawn mower by the time she was seven and service her own car by the time she got her learner's permit.

"Fire trucks woke her up," Molly said when she abruptly appeared in the kitchen with Phoebe on one arm. "That's why she's here early."

"I was *on time,*" Annette said defensively while she scrambled the eggs and poured them into a skillet.

"Fire trucks?" Mona asked, looking at Molly and then Nette.

"We're going to the back for a blow dry and brush out and who knows what else." Molly's eyes were full of mischief. A snicker slipped out as she turned and waddled down the hallway.

"What happened, Nette?" Mona added.

She started to answer but they noticed smoke forming above the skillet full of eggs. Lisa grabbed the wooden handle and quickly removed it from the heat.

"You'd better let me do this," she said.

"Somethin's stuck on the burner, that's all," Annette argued.

Mona grabbed a paper plate and began fanning the smoke over the stove. "I hope the smoke alarm doesn't go off. The Group's security will call."

Annette was reminded of the security system that hadn't worked at Lewis' the night before and the only way Gerry knew the fire alarm was going off was because of Phoebe pressing the intercom.

"What was Molly talking about?" Lisa asked and moved the skillet to a cold burner.

Annette frowned at Lisa and took the skillet back. "Mona, would you quit fannin that stupid plate!"

All three women looked at the bright yellow scrambled eggs in the skillet.

"You see? Perfect!" Nette bragged.

Mona tapped Nette on the top of the head with the paper plate. "Well? What about the fire?"

"Well, uh," Annette began but the smoke alarm beeped once. "Oh God! Mona, go fan over there under the sensor." Annette told them about the fire and that Lewis was taken to the hospital.

"Poor Lewis," Mona gasped.

"I couldn't sleep so, that's why I'm here," her voice waned. Had she given the account too fast? Had it sounded phony? *Please don't ask about Phoebe.* She had told the truth, generally speaking, without mentioning Phoebe's participation or how freaked she was because the same smoke could have overcome Phoebe, and no one would have noticed her because she was so little or perhaps not given it a second thought. After all, she was only a dog. She felt the color draining from her face and turned away.

"Nette, are you sure that's all?" Lisa asked. "You don't look so good."

"You look like you saw a ghost," Mona added.

"That's all," she defended. She snatched up the pan and quickly emptied the eggs into a bowl.

Mona gently placed her hands on Nette's shoulders. "You had another dream about your father, didn't you?" she whispered. "I recognized that look. I know you don't like talking about it; it's okay." Mona gave Annette a hug, "Migraine; si?"

Annette nodded her head.

"I'll start the bacon, senorita."

According to Lisa's taste test, Annette's scrambled eggs turned out quite good, but the savory aroma of Mona's bacon lured everyone to the kitchen. She inevitably had to fry two more pounds to keep up with the demand.

Parents were greeting each other differently this morning as they arrived with their children. They had something on their minds other than the usual *hello and how-are-yous*. They each had their own copy of the early edition of the San Diego Daily Post and were talking about an article by Sally Samuels. Annette was relieved to hear the subject was about something other than the fire at Mesa Village. In fact, no one mentioned it at all. While she was rushing around to get ready for work, everyone else was picking up the early edition from their yards, coffee shops or convenience stores. Stories by Sally Samuels were often topics for discussion, which Annette assumed was her objective, but something about this article had induced more striking comments than usual. Voices seemed to ring louder every time someone new arrived. Another oddity was that they weren't just dropping off their kids and hurrying to work. They were lingering to talk. Annette stopped to listen after filling the last cup of orange juice. One mother offered Lisa a copy of the Post, which she took and immediately started reading. "It's about the Barksdale murder case," she told Annette. "A page of pathology notes surfaced that contained information about his cause of death. Sally Samuels says it was purposely removed from the original medical examiner's report. The notes were found in a manner that suggests evidence tampering. The report revealed that Anderson Barksdale died of an aneurysm."

"That's gonna turn that slam-dunk murder case of her husbands on its ear," another mother interrupted.

A third woman chimed in. "I'll bet he went berserk when he read this. I knew Sally was a crusader, but I never thought she'd screw her husband just to get a headline."

The first mother rebutted. “At least the old Sally is back. She’s been way too preoccupied glorifying that asshole's case instead of looking out for us.”

Annette’s curiosity drew her into the archway.

“Now look at her,” the second mother interrupted. “She’s saying that part of the M. E. report was purposely omitted, or stolen, by the D.A.’s office, her husband, and others involved; can this be true?”

The gathering hummed in agreement that it must be true if it was allowed to be printed in the newspaper. It was the third mother’s turn to read an excerpt. “Such misconduct could grant the defense a quest for a mistrial and allow the accused derelict, known only as Old Walter, to go free.”

The first mother folded her paper and held it up. Annette could read the large headline from across the room.

Mona eased into the archway and stood beside her. “Wow,” she whispered.

Annette remembered friends on the boardwalk at Mission Beach talking about Old Walter. Homeless for sure, but by all accounts, wouldn’t hurt a fly. Some vendors and locals from the area had sat in on part of the court proceedings and said the charges were bogus. The only good thing about it was that Old Walter now had a roof over his head and three square meals daily.

“Mona,” Nette whispered. “Let’s get these kids out of here.” Annette pushed the orange juice jug into Mona’s arms, collected the juice cups, and put them on a tray. “Take them out to the back porch. They don’t need to hear all this junk.”

“This way, mucho niño’s and niña’s,” Mona said, waving them toward the back door.

“Mona,” Annette whispered. “Get the tablecloth and some napkins and the chocolate milk…”

“Alto, senorita, I’m just one person here,” she snickered as she coaxed five youngsters that had just arrived with their carping mothers toward the back door.

“Sorry,” Annette said and grabbed a gallon jug of chocolate milk off the table and then pressed it into the arms of a passing seven-year-old. “There you go, handsome.” She wrapped his arms around the jug. “Carry this outside for Miss Mona. Delegate, Mona, delegate," Nette said, grinning.

Caught up in the enthusiasm, Mr. McKenzie picked up an open copy of the Posta mother had laid on the table beside him and began to read aloud.

"Anderson Barksdale, a prestigious member of San Diego County tourism commission, was believed to be the victim of a robbery and subsequently murdered by a local derelict. It was first reported that Mr. Barksdale was sitting alone in his car at a traffic light in the downtown area near Balboa Park when he was brutally attacked by the panhandler. An iron pipe containing Mr. Barksdale's blood and the derelict's fingerprints was found in a gutter near Mr. Barksdale's Lexus."

The first mother looked over his shoulder when Mr. McKenzie paused to reflect. "However," she continued, "information contained in the stolen medical examiner notes show that Mr. Barksdale died as a result of an aneurysm that burst deep within his brain before the presumed fatal blow; that he was already dead when Old Walter stumbled up."

The elder took over again. "Mr. Barksdale's brain was autopsied, and a comprehensive description of the hemorrhage was detailed in the M.E. notes. Mr. Barksdale was likely unaware anything was wrong, and death most likely occurred within seconds." Mr. McKenzie slowed down as if to absorb the words he was saying. "The jury has listened to false testimony, and therefore, a mistrial should be declared." The two orators looked at each other. They had read the details of this robbery/murder so many times in the Daily Post that they knew it by heart. They had seen the murder victim's face and filed footage of the crime scene on the morning and evening news for the past six months to the point they barely paid attention anymore. There was a new twist to the story now and Sally had presented it to them in her usual flamboyant style. "Isn't she great?" Mr. McKenzie concluded. He looked at Annette standing in the archway as if expecting a confirmation from her, but she remained expressionless.

"Why wasn't a press conference called?" one mother gripped. "Downtown always announces breaking news by press conference. Now everyone is quoting Sally."

"She's all they have to reference," Mr. McKenzie eagerly replied.

"So, Randal Samuels is guilty of conspiracy!" a woman's voice rang out.

"I'll bet he's doing a lot of rethinking about his lovely wife this morning," said a woman as she left through the front door.

Every adult in the room was expressing some sort of amusement over the miscarriage of justice, the people involved and the reporter that broke it to them; everyone except Annette who didn't care much for gossip or politics. Sally Samuels made a choice to write this article, and she would have to live with the consequences. That's what Sonny Rylan would say.

Peace didn't return to the daycare until the parents were gone. The burning questions would remain unanswered until the next clue was revealed, perhaps in Sally's next column, *if there was one,* which was another consensus of some during the way too lengthy discussion. She had them all by one big hook. There had been a witness, an oriental restaurant owner. Why didn't anyone mention the man who swore he saw the whole thing from a window above his store and identified Old Walter as the assailant? Did they forget about him? This was too complicated for the ordinary citizen or daycare worker.

"Kevin Samuels and Anderson Barksdale were best friends, right," Mona asked when she appeared beside Annette. "Did Kevin talk to you about this trial business?"

"Why would he talk to me about it?" Annette asked.

"Well," she said, "you told me he used to hang on the fence behind his son's dugout," Mona said, snickering, "and talk to you, I just thought…"

"Mona, please!" Nette groaned. "Don't even pretend I know Kevin well enough to talk to him about anything personal. He asked me out, but I ain't never goin anywhere with that sorry, egotistical...ugh!" Annette's shoulders quivered as if the nerves in her spine tingled. "He ain't nothin but a slitherin swamp snake. It was awful how Andy died, but there was always somethin creepy about those two."

"Si," Mona sighed. "And it was probably because they were so close that his Uncle Randy took a personal interest in the case."

"The Rylan's would have done the same for the family," Annette said in agreement. "I wonder, though, about the witness?"

"What witness? I don't remember a witness," Mona said, frowning. "Hey, are all the Rylan's like you?" she suddenly quipped.

"Why?" Annette huffed.

"I don't know if I want to be around to see more than one Rylan take up for the other," Mona laughed.

"Mona," Nette laughed, "you just might need a Rylan someday."

"I have my familia, extremo mucho gracias," Mona replied with added accentuation.

Nette shook her finger, "Quit pullin that Spanglish on me!"

"Vamos, vamos," Mona said and waved her hands. "I need a Rylan right now to help me pick up out here.

"Vamos, yourself," Nette replied and followed her friend outside.

While playing catch with a soccer ball, a little girl with blonde pigtails curled in ringlets and blue eyes tugged on Annette's jeans. She wore a shirt resembling a flag and the same patriotic-colored ribbons tied around the top of her pigtails.

"Hi there, sweetie pie," Nette said, squatting to her knees. "My goodness, you have the biggest blue eyes of any little girl I've ever seen. Nette patted her on the nose with one finger.

"Are you Nette?" the little girl asked.

"Yes, that's me," Nette replied.

"Do you have a dog named Fee-Bee? One of the ladies said you might let me play with her. Can I—please?"

"She's with Miss Molly right now," Nette replied. "What's your name? I don't believe we've met."

"Elizabeth Harding, I'm from Chicago. My daddy drove us all the way here in a big yellow truck full of our stuff.

We live two blocks from here. He had to run some errands, and my sister is at home…" Her voice drifted off, and Annette noticed her attention waning as she looked around the room.

"So, you have a sister?" Annette asked quickly.

"Yes, uh, Nicky; she didn't wanna come. She and Daddy had a big fight over it. Can I see Phoebe?" she begged, clasping her hands in prayer while bobbing up and down on her toes.

"I'll call you when Miss Molly brings her out. In the meantime," Annette took Elizabeth by the hand and guided her toward the swing set. Annette pointed to a little girl sitting alone on one of the swings. "See that little girl?" Elizabeth shaded her eyes with one hand and nodded. "Run over and introduce yourself. Her name is Claire. She's really shy and doesn't have many friends, so she could use someone to play with."

"You promise to call me when Phoebe comes out?" Elizabeth asked.

"I promise," Annette said and gave one of Elizabeth's pigtails a yank. Annette grimaced, remembering the yellow truck parked in Jim and Julia's old driveway. *That must have been Elizabeth's father I nearly ran over last night.*

Chapter 7

"Everybody, come on, come on, hurry!" Molly announced with a great commotion. "Now that the parents are gone, we can have our *secret* magic show."

Annette and Phoebe exchanged glances as Molly hurried past with the little dog in her arms. "Molly, what did you do?" Annette gasped.

Molly had brushed and blow-dried Phoebe's hair into a floozy fluff. Red, white, and blue bows were secured on each ear, and a bracelet of red glass stones was around her neck. She had fashioned a skirt from a flag, painted her toenails red, and put a scrunchy around her pompom tail.

"Let's set up girls, so we can get started," Molly shouted and gave a directional wave to Annette and Mona and then pointed to the back door.

Annette and Mona headed to the storage shed outside to fetch a mess table that would convert to a stage. Lisa went to a cabinet in Molly's office to get the long red tablecloth and the props for the magic show.

Molly swooshed her hand through the air again, motioning the children to sit in a semi-circle on the front room floor. "Oh, by the way," Molly said as Annette and Mona shuffled by with the folded mess table. "Charlie called; they're keeping Lewis another night."

Annette was on the leading end of the table and stopped immediately.

"I didn't hear the phone!" Mona complained after the abrupt change in pace.

"He called me on my cell," Molly stammered. "Or, uh, or maybe I called him; anyway, Lewis is fine." Molly gave Phoebe a hug and shuffled around in a circle as if they were waltzing. Phoebe's head swayed back and forth with the motion. "Lisa, do we still have that CD with the patriotic music?" Molly asked and dipped and swayed away toward the pantry.

"Come on, Nette, this thing is getting heavy," Mona complained to her friend on the other end of the table.

"She knew how worried I was about Lewis," Annette whispered. "How could she forget to tell me?"

"We're lucky she doesn't forget something really important," Mona said. "She's getting more absent-minded every day. She should see a doctor."

"You can't trust doctors," Annette quipped. "They talk down to you and tell you whatever, and those nurses and pink ladies just smile and tell you everything is gonna be fine; they all lie." Annette fostered contempt for hospitals and doctors. Two weeks of tests in a Houston Cancer Center earned her father a bottle of experimental chemotherapy in a black bag. Four hospitals took their turns directing radiation at the tumors that rose on his chest and his right side that were as large as baseballs until they burned his skin away and exposed their yellow tinge. Doctors implanted a port in a juggler vein after the last of the veins in his arms and hands collapsed. It seemed torture was his best chance of survival. The mysterious chemo left him with no appetite and unable to tolerate food, not even a morsel of a cracker. By the time the nausea subsided, he could no longer swallow. Annette picked up her father's chart from a window cove in his room one afternoon and read that the doctors had reduced the chemo. She asked a first-year resident to explain and he told her frankly that they needed to be saying their goodbyes. All the reassurances and statistics had been rhetoric of false expectations. She nearly collapsed when she realized that the words of hope she had been holding onto were nothing but bullshit. The intern was too green to know he was supposed to be patronizing. He told her to watch for stiffening in the neck; it would mean the disease had traveled up the spinal cord to the brain. There had never been any hope. Morphine was the only medication being administered the last three days of his life after the lordly doctors and kindly nurses suggested the family allow the IV to be removed to allow his kidneys to fail. They were finally done with him.

Annette collected Elizabeth and Claire from outside. Molly handed the decorated little dog to her and a black robe and scurried away. She had found four vampire robes left over from Halloween in the supply closet. Molly stopped in front of the center stage and clasped her hands together as Lisa and Mona finished pressing the folds of the red tablecloth draped over the mess table.

"Listen, everyone," Molly said, raising her voice as she turned to address the assembly of impressionable youngsters. "Before we start the Magic Show, I want to have a little chat with you."

"Couldn't you talk her out of this?" Nette whispered to Phoebe. Phoebe shook her head as if thwarting off a pesky fly. "Well, there ain't no way I'm wearin this stupid robe." Annette threw it over a nearby chair.

"Okay, okay, my darlings," Molly said as the children chose between the small chairs that Mona had arranged in rows and the floor.

Phoebe placed a paw in her master's hand. "Yes, I see the red nails," Annette winced. "Come on, admit it, showing off is what you do best, right?" Nette teased. Phoebe let out a whine as they eased toward the center of the table that was now officially the stage. "I tried to talk you out of coming here today, remember?" Annette whispered.

Annette placed her bejeweled dog on the stage. The audience of children giggled at Phoebe's appearance, and they all scooted closer to get a better look. Phoebe positioned herself in the middle of the stage while Molly continued her pre-performance orientation.

"Some of you have seen our Magic Show before," she began, "but I see a few new faces in the crowd; so not all of you are familiar with Phoebe's magic."

Phoebe slowly scanned the audience, and indeed, there were many faces she didn't recognize. Molly's typical carefree personality had transformed into a woman of focus and captivating delivery.

"For those who have not taken the oath before, we will do it now."

"Oath?" some in the crowd whispered.

Molly's resolute voice caused murmurs of concern and raised eyebrows among the young faces of the audience. "If you'd rather not take the oath or participate in the magic show, you may simply go outside and play. One of my girls will be happy to go with you." She raised an open hand that pointed to the direction of the backyard that was beyond the kitchen. All eyes followed her hand, but no one moved. Molly's prelude had them totally spellbound. "You must promise never to tell anyone what you see here today." She waved a warning index finger in front of her face. The black cape flowed with her arms as she moved around, waiting for a response, but no one spoke or moved. "Particularly, your parents," she continued. "They must pass a special test only given by me personally or by her master," she pointed to Annette, allowing the cape flow as she moved, "before they can be told about Phoebe's secret." There were giggles from within the audience. "Her secret is ours and ours alone."

"Phoebe's secret; what is Phoebe's secret?" faint whispers repeated throughout the crowd.

She looked into the eyes of each child sitting on the floor in the first row. "Do you *promise* not to tell?" she asked intently. Molly slowly scanned the remaining rows one by one, repeating: "Do you *promise* not to tell?" The children acknowledged her with hypnotic nods.

"Wow," Elizabeth whispered to Claire. "Wait till I tell Nicky about this." Claire didn't answer, which wasn't unusual for she rarely spoke to anyone. She was Elizabeth's age and lived with foster parents. Her mother was in rehab and as far as she knew, she didn't have a father.

"What did you say?" Molly whispered quickly. "Who said that?"

Elizabeth scooted behind Claire and out of Molly's sight.

"There is a responsibility that comes with this secret," Molly added, straightening her back. "A big responsibility," she continued, "a huge responsibility."

"Okay, Molly!" Nette interrupted, fearing she was scaring the kids. "It's time to get started with the show; everybody promises, right?"

"Right, yay!" the children answered while clapping their hands.

"What?" Molly blinked her eyes as if startled. "Yes, now we will go on with the show." Molly shuffled away from the center stage but stopped at the end of the first row and flung the cape around as she turned back to the audience. "Just remember that Phoebe won't be able to perform magic shows anymore if one of you breaks their promise."

"Molly!" Annette whispered firmly. "Let's do this, now!" Annette turned to the audience. "Okay, everybody, here we go," she announced, hoping to sound lighthearted enough to lessen any anxiety Molly's prologue might have created. Annette nodded, and Phoebe, seated at center stage waiting for her queue, rose up on her hind legs and showed off the red toenails and navy scrunchies. She cocked her ears and moved her head from side to side to display her red bows and the rest of the patriotic gear. Annette noticed Elizabeth sitting on her knees in the front row and covering her mouth with her hands. Somehow, she couldn't resist making the newest member of *Molly's Magic Club* part of the act. "Elizabeth, would you like to be Phoebe's assistant," Annette asked, extending an arm in the little girl's direction.

"Me?" Elizabeth gasped and scooted closer to Claire. Claire gave her a nudge and a nod of approval.

"Phoebe needs a dancing partner," Annette said, winking at her. Phoebe inched closer to the edge of the makeshift stage and whined.

"Well, okay, yes," she said timidly, placing her small hand in Annette's. "What do I do?" she asked, staring at Phoebe as she got up.

"Well, first, tell everyone your name," Annette said, trying to put the little girl at ease in front of the audience.

"Elizabeth Harding." She said slowly. She could see the two-to-five-year-olds that made up the first two rows on the floor. The older kids sat in chairs behind them. She was too nervous to notice the adult daycare workers lined up against the wall in the rear.

"Very good," Annette said in character, which required her to sound like the master of ceremonies in a circus. Elizabeth looked at Phoebe and straightened her posture to take on her part. Annette saw Molly standing beside a bookcase containing children's books and videos. Her hand was suspended over a jam box, and her index finger was poised and ready. When the master of ceremonies nodded, Molly pressed the play button, and jubilant sounds of flutes and stringed instruments filled the front room with a rhythmical ballet overture.

"Behold our ballerinas!" Annette's voice commanded an atmosphere to match the ceremonial sounds. Elizabeth looked at Phoebe. The little dog was standing up on her hind legs. So, Elizabeth stood on her tiptoes and raised her arms over her head. "Outstanding!" Annette, the announcer, exclaimed. Elizabeth imagined herself in an enormous theater with soft footlights glowing just beyond her feet and embellished balconies on either side of the stage. The audience was full of important people wearing tuxedos and sequenced dresses. They were clapping with gloved hands, and their faces were full of admiration.

Phoebe began to turn in a circle and Elizabeth immediately started to twirl. Phoebe danced all the way across the top of the stage to the end and Elizabeth followed in unison to the opposite side. Elizabeth's mother encouraged her daughter to use her imagination, and that's how she amused herself while her mother slept the day away. She would pretend to be an ice skater in the Olympics, a cast member of Disney on Ice, or the star of a dance video on MTV. Today, she was a ballerina dancing on the Chicago Theater stage with her new friend, Phoebe. They made four passes together and then Annette declared the next trick.

"Now…it's time for the magic hoop trick."

Molly's eyes twinkled with excitement and then she pressed the pause button and awaited the master of ceremonies next command. Phoebe leaned on her front elbows and pushed her rear and fluffy tail up as if to bow. The audience responded with giggles. Elizabeth followed quickly with her gracious curtsey of her own.

Nette handed the little girl a large embroidery hoop. "Okay, ladies and gentlemen; Elizabeth, Phoebe's assistant, will now hold the hoop in the air."

Elizabeth gripped the large hoop and marched behind the stage. Molly pressed the start button again, and a noble rhythm of trumpets erupted. Elizabeth held the hoop four inches above the red tablecloth. Phoebe paused to study her assistant's steadiness.

"Come on, Phoebe," Elizabeth beckoned. "We're an act." Phoebe snorted a short sneeze; drums began to roll, and she easily leaped through the hoop.

Annette wiggled her fingers, directing Elizabeth to raise the hoop higher.

Elizabeth felt herself becoming part of the music that seemed to grow louder and faster with every pass Phoebe made through the prop in her hand. It seemed that Phoebe's jumps were higher and came faster than the master of ceremonies was commanding. "Higher," she could hear her say; but her voice was out of sync because Phoebe was already in the air. Annette nodded, and Phoebe returned to the starting position in the middle of the stage and awaited the next intro. Elizabeth was awestruck as Annette took the large ring from her. "She's magnificent," she whispered without realizing she'd said a word. Had she seen a dog fly? It was like she jumped farther and lingered in the air much longer than a dog should be able to. She had never seen an animal trick, not even on TV, that compared to this. The flutes and xylophones tingled, and snare drums turned into clapping hands. Elizabeth was totally caught up. Phoebe was bowing again, so she did the same. The volume of the pompous music went down, and Annette handed Elizabeth a cheese cracker. She offered the reward to Phoebe in the palm of her hand, and she quickly crunched it up.

"Now tell Phoebe to sit up," Annette said and handed her another cracker. "Don't give it to her until she does it, okay?"

Elizabeth nodded. She held the cracker in the air and gave the command trying to copy Annette's authority. Phoebe rose on her hind legs, held her front legs and dangled her paws.

Awes filled the room as Elizabeth surrendered the treat. Phoebe dropped to the floor of the stage. Annette twirled her finger around, and Elizabeth mimicked the motion with her hand. Phoebe began to roll across the stage until she neared the edge. Elizabeth squealed with delight. The music from the player gave out a note of horns and cymbals. Molly pushed the stop button after allowing a long finale.

"Time to play catch," Annette announced. She produced an orange tennis ball and threw it to Phoebe which she caught in her mouth and then slung it back to the master of ceremonies. The ball made a snapping noise in her master's hand. She threw it up in the air, and it came down toward Phoebe, at which time she bounced it into the audience with her nose. A kid in the third row grabbed it and threw it back toward the stage. Phoebe watched the ball, moved from side to side to align herself, and then caught it easily in her jaws. The little dog immediately tossed the ball to her pint-sized assistant. Elizabeth had never been able to catch a ball in her life and huffed when the ball landed squarely in her cupped hands.

"Now, will someone call out two numbers that will add up to ten or less," Annette asked as she began to pace back and forth in front of the stage. She held her hands behind her back as if she were a college professor challenging a theater of students. One of the small boys in the second row raised his hand.

"Your name, young man?" the ringmaster said, raising one arm to present the young audience member.

"Jamie," he yelled.

"Jamie, what are the two numbers that add up to ten or less?"

"Two-plus-two," Jamie said, bouncing excitedly in his squatting position.

Annette effectively repeated his addition problem. "Two-plus-two, Phoebe!"

"Ruff-ruff-ruff-ruff," Phoebe replied.

"Someone else," Annette challenged as the floor full of children clapped. Only seconds passed before another set of numbers pierced the air.

"Three-plus-two," someone shouted. Phoebe barked out the five digits immediately. Elizabeth could hardly contain herself while standing behind the stage. She was anxious to be part of the act again so she shouted out the next addition problem, "one-plus-one!"

Phoebe turned to face her questioner, "Ruff-ruff," making Elizabeth gasp.

Annette paused briefly and looked up into the air as if trying to pull a new task out of the air. "Okay," she said and turned to face the audience. "Does anyone know multiplication…anyone," Annette slowly scanned the faces.

"Three times three," one of the older kids yelled out.

Phoebe looked at her master and snorted. She sounded off nine yelps slowly, luring everyone into counting along and wondering if she would stop when she reached the solution. Sets of numbers began to fill the room all at once and from all directions. Phoebe looked directly at each child when answering their individual problem.

"Now, the fabulous Phoebe will do her greatest trick," the announcer revelled.

Molly pressed the play button again. A drum roll sounded from the small speakers. There was a shuffling in the audience as the children squirmed and looked at the person on their left and right. Elizabeth took her place on the floor next to Claire. What could possibly be greater than what she'd already done? The children muttered and shrugged their shoulders. Annette held up a large black and gold New Orleans Saints World Championship bandana by her fingertips and made a cylinder around Phoebe. Elizabeth's eyes widened, and she tried not to blink. She held her breath and crawled closer to the stage. She didn't want to miss whatever was about to happen.

Molly waited for her queue to depress the stop button and silence the drum roll that would add a more dramatic effect when Annette removed the bandana. She leaned closer to Lisa and Mona while she waited. "I love this part." They each nodded in agreement.

Annette raised her palm and asked for quiet. This was Molly's queue, and she pressed the stop button.

"Abracadabra!" Nette chanted and closed her eyes for effect. Then the master of ceremonies pointed to the scarf, and with a swish, she jerked the black and gold scarf away. The fabulous Phoebe had disappeared.

The audience of impressionable preschoolers in the first two rows gasped. Their little jaws dropped, and their eyes grew large. The older children were quiet for three seconds; then, they asserted where the magic dog might actually be. They wanted Annette to raise the red tablecloth so they could see the hidden opening in the table.

Elizabeth scooted under the table without hesitation and without anyone seeing her. There were scary red shadows under the table, but there was no little dog, no hole in the table, and no false compartment. She raised the cloth to look behind the table; Phoebe was not there either.

The seconds that passed seemed like minutes. Finally, Annette raised the bandana and covered where Phoebe once stood. The littlest children sitting on the floor rocked up on their knees. The older ones leaned forward in their chairs to better see the illusion. She held the scarf tightly between her fingers and shaped it into a cylinder again.

Molly bowed her head, trying to contain her chuckling. This was the most exciting part of the performance; the grand finale and timing were crucial. There would be such surprise on her children's faces, and they would believe. They would believe in magic, even if only for a little while. Her attention wandered from her duty momentarily when something outside caught her attention. The door leading to the backyard yielded only a narrow view. But it was enough to see someone in the yard. She had seen him before, once on the front walk and twice in the corner of the garage beside the toolbox. She saw him sitting at the kitchen table once, but like always, in the blink of an eye, he was gone. She told Annette about the apparition but stopped short of telling her who she thought it might be, fearing it would upset her. But there he was again: the tall, slender man dressed in a brown leather jacket and wearing a floppy brown hat. He was standing inside the swing set between the glider and the rings, holding onto one of the poles and looking directly at her. He let go and stepped beyond the limits of the open door. Her attention returned to the ongoing entertainment, and she suddenly realized she had missed her cue. Annette was nodding at her and frowning as if the cue might have been given more than just a few times. Most of the audience was looking at her, so she quickly readied her hand over the play button.

Annette announced in true ringleader fashion: "Ladies and gentlemen, boys and girls may I present to you, Phoebe, The Magic Dog!"

Molly pressed the button, and a band played a triumphant theme through the small stereo speakers. Annette whipped the black and gold scarf away, and to the children's awe and amazement, Phoebe was sitting there, posed in a sitting-up posture and cocking her head from side to side. Annette moved away from the stage, allowing Phoebe to receive all the applause and glory. The group whooped and clapped.

Elizabeth did neither; she heard no hoopla around her except for a single voice. *Elizabeth, Elizabeth.* The kids around her were scrambling to their feet, following the direction of Annette and the other workers who had beckoned them into the kitchen for snacks. She couldn't take her eyes off Phoebe on the stage because she was staring at her too. "Yes, yes," Elizabeth whispered.

Carol Harding often took her daughter to the roof of their apartment building. She would bring toys for Lizzy to play with while she lay in the sun, and at night, they would watch the stars. Her mother repeatedly told her daughter that she was special, but Elizabeth never understood what she meant until this moment.

Chapter 8

Neither the early morning disturbance nor the holiday was going to alter Anthony Harding's itinerary. "Okay," the methodical father said at breakfast after clearing his throat. "Here's the plan." He shifted in his chair to face Nicky. "There are some things I need to do today and since there's no school, I want you and Lizzy to go to Molly's Day Care. The people are nice there, and you should get to know them since you'll be going there to check on your sister after school for a few weeks." He looked at Lizzy and smiled. "Or until she feels comfortable." Lizzy returned his smile but Nicky suddenly coughed as if a piece of cereal had suddenly lodged in her throat. Lizzy gasped, seeing the look on her sister's face. "So," he continued, "when you two finish breakfast, get dressed, and I'll drop you off on my way to the hardware store." Tony noticed Elizabeth's fearful expression. "This way, your sister," he said pointedly, turning to Nicky. "Look, don't fight me on this, Nicky!" he said after reading the opposition on her face.

Nicky's mouth was open, but instead of resisting, she bowed her head, pressed her lips together, and stared at the pieces of cereal floating in her milk. Elizabeth expelled a sigh of relief because the panting panther she had just imagined her sister to be had faded away. "She needs to make some friends at Molly's," she heard her father say. Lizzy forced the sides of her mouth apart. She tried to smile, but it looked more like she was in pain.

"It'll give both of you a chance to meet some new kids," he added. "Someone other than that idiot next door," he muttered in a low voice. "Lizzy will feel better if you're there. You know how she gets around strangers." Tony sealed the deal by nodding his head. He had learned from many years of supervising one of the busiest trauma units in Chicago that success comes from planning and organization. Incorporating these methods into his new life as a single father would help him greatly. Unfortunately, in this case, an ugly ten-minute argument ensued with Nicky that put serious cracks in his plans.

Nicky pushed every button she could think of. *What are you really up to? Don't make this sound like it's all about what's best for us. It's so you can push us off on somebody else so you can do whatever you want. You're always gonna be late or not show up. We always end up on our own. That's the real plan, isn't it? How convenient that Molly's is so close to where we live. How convenient our schools are only a few blocks away. Haven't you noticed that I might be too old for daycare? We did just fine without you before. How much are you paying them to take up your slack?* And the final button: *You're treating me just like you treated Mama. She never had a life either, thanks to you.*

Elizabeth sat silently when the outburst first erupted. She saw the veins in her father's neck rise and his face turn red. When he started reprimanding Nicky, his voice reminded her of thunder that started in the distance and became louder as it got closer. When he rose from his chair, it fell backward and hit the wall; Elizabeth closed her eyes. She envisioned a lion with its jaws opened wide, its teeth long and sharp with saliva dripping from the tips. Its eyes were yellow like fire, and its ears were slanted straight back. The animal's truss fell over its burly shoulders that protruded as if set to attack. Elizabeth squeezed her eyelids tighter trying to squash the vision of the angry king of beasts. But then she saw a bright flash, like lightning. She covered her ears with her hands to muffle the thunder that was bound to follow.

"Mama," Lizzy's voice quivered. She began to sob and blubber unrecognizable words. She fell off her chair and curled into a ball on the floor. This brought Tony to his knees beside her moaning apologies.

Nicky snatched up the breakfast dishes and deposited them firmly in the sink, then went to her room resolving that she would never speak to her father again. Tony carried Lizzy to the sofa and, after a few minutes, called Nicky to the living room. She could stay home, but the rest of the plan would remain in place. He would take Lizzy to Molly's on the way to the hardware store and she would check on her sister on school days for a few weeks but refused to explain how long that meant when he sensed another rebuttal. It would depend on her attitude.

He looked at Lizzy sitting next to him on the sofa. "Does that sound okay to you?"

She wrapped her arms around his neck, grateful the king of beasts was gone.

Tony reworked his agenda and decided Nicky would wait for the telephone and cable service while he was out. Her instructions were to call him as soon as he arrived. "Don't go next door," he stressed. "Call me if anything unexpected happens." He wouldn't have liked the sneer Nicky directed at him when he turned his back or the rolling eyes as he left with Lizzy in tow. He spent thirty minutes shopping for the items on his hand-written list in the hardware store. A white dry-erase board caught his eye. A bulletin board was just the thing to help him organize a daily routine. He looked at his watch. If he hurried, he might have time to make some minor repairs to the house and finish unpacking his office. As he moved forward in the checkout line, he heard two checkout ladies chatting across their adjacent registers. Tony compared the items in his basket against his list while he waited, trying not to eavesdrop. But the subject matter had a familiar ring.

"Gerry said if Phoebe hadn't called him on the intercom, Lewis might not have made it." A woman wearing a blue smock standing behind the register in Tony's line was leaning over the side of her booth talking to the cashier next to her. Her nametag identified her as *Cindy*. The cashier next to her, whose tag Tony couldn't see came back with an account of her own while moving a customer's items across the scanner in front of her.

"Thank God! Remember when Mrs. Wilkerson fell into the bathtub full of water and hit her head? Phoebe pulled the plug and…oh." The adjacent checkout girl stopped talking when Cindy gave her the hush sign with her finger after realizing Tony was listening.

Cindy cleared her throat. "Did you find everything you were looking for, sir?" She quickly moved into position in front of her register. Her manner changed dramatically into that of a no-nonsense checkout clerk.

Tony removed the items from his buggy and Cindy began scanning them.

"So, who is this Phoebe? Sorry, I overheard you just now," he apologized, but she scanned his items silently. "I live near the retirement village; I was there last night," he explained. "That's what you were just talking about, right?" He looked back and forth, waiting for one of them to answer but neither acknowledged. "Lewis, I heard you talking about Mr. Lewis."

No response.

"I was telling my daughters what happened when I got home, but I couldn't remember the lady's name Mr. Lewis whispered to me; it was Phoebe, the person you were just talking about. And I spoke to Gerry, a big fellow."

Again, there was no response as they moved their eyes back and forth at each other. Cindy sighed as if annoyed. He couldn't blame either of them because he had sort of barged in on their private conversation.

"I'm sorry, sir, I'm not sure what you're talking about," Cindy said as she quickly bagged his items except for the bulletin board, which she left loose in his shopping cart.

Tony handed her his credit card, which she had taken from him without further comment. He looked back as he pushed the cart through the automatic doors. The two women returned to their gossip as soon as he cleared the threshold. He put the checkout experience out of his mind as soon as he turned onto Antrim Way.

"Damn!" Tony cursed out loud at the sight of Nicky sharing one half of a boat trailer tongue with Robby. The boy's father owned the covered tri-hulled fishing rig that was in dry dock for the winter in half of the Jones driveway. "I can't trust her to do anything I tell her!" Robby had been knocking on the door several times a day, and Tony had either sent him away or just didn't answer after seeing him through the peephole. He was just a little too eager, an untrustworthy trait from where Tony Harding came.

Nicky imagined hearing her father growling her name as he pulled into the driveway. She stood up quickly and put sufficient distance between herself and Robby. The tall boy simultaneously bolted to attention and clasped his hands behind his neck as if demonstrating his innocence. He had on dark shades and a red do-rag. A black tee shirt with cut-out sleeves revealed a chain tattoo on his upper right arm. Low-riding cut-offs hung below the IZOD logo of his boxers.

"Good God!" Tony muttered. He ran a hand through his thick hair and tried to gather his composure before exiting the car. Nicky's hair was pulled back in a ponytail, and she had on lipstick and blush. She was projecting every bit of eighteen in her form-fitted, one-size-too-small pink sweater and skinny jeans. She slowly walked toward him on the balls of her feet. She was expressionless as she waved the cordless in front of her to display proof that she was doing as instructed and yet obviously doing what she wanted. Tony emerged slowly while removing his sunglasses.

"No phone calls Daddy," Nicky reported. "But this guy stopped and left a business card." She glanced at Robby who quickly produced a small blue card from his back pocket and began to flip it around his fingers. "He just left; that's why we're out here. I thought he was the cable guy, but..."

"Fo-real, Doc," Robby interrupted and handed the card to Tony between two fingers.

"How are you, Robby?" Tony slammed the car door. His disapproving voice rumbled as if full of gravel.

"Bitchin' Doc, and you?" Robby replied and put his right fist up, attempting a fist bump, which Tony ignored and walked past him. Nicky glared at her father for his rudeness.

"Well, I guess we'll see you later, Robby, goodbye." He made a quick motion with his head directing his daughter to move toward the door. "Nicky, I need your help inside; we still have unpacking to do." He grabbed Nicky by the arm and guided her up the front walk.

She didn't resist his tugging but stumbled just before they reached the front stoop. He was spouting a list of urgent things that *absolutely had to be taken care of today*. She could feel Robby staring at her even though seeing his eyes through the dark glasses was impossible. She blushed with embarrassment and put a hand to her face to see if it was as hot to the touch as it felt underneath her skin.

"Dude, you fo-sho?" Robby asked, interrupting him after he'd reached *unpack medical reference books* on his list. Robby took several large steps, putting him ahead of them, and grabbed the screen door handle. He pulled it open and smiled. "I've been dyin' to see your crib now that you've had time to, you know, settle in."

Nicky's father squelched his annoyance but couldn't hide the anger veins that were protruding from both sides of his neck. Nicky shook her head and tried to signal him to shut it down.

"Yo, Nicky said you went shopping," Robby continued nodding and pointing to Tony's green plastic bag. He inched forward and thumped the hardware store logo with two fingers. "You need, you know, some help?"

"What are you doing?" Nicky whispered.

Tony's jaws tightened. He glared at Robby and then he turned to Nicky. "No!" he answered sharply. He looked at her as if Robby's behavior was her fault. "We've got it!" He gave Nicky another push closer to the front door. Nicky looked back at Robby.

"Later," she managed to whisper as she stumbled into the house.

"Well, I'm right next door if you need me," Robby said after Tony closed the door in his face.

Tony put the shopping bag on the kitchen table. "Nicky!" he growled.

Nicky materialized in the doorway. "Your room finished?"

"Sort of," she replied.

He pointed down the hall as if directing her there. "You can help me unpack the books when your room is finished."

"Right," she replied and disappeared into the hall.

"I don't want you to have anything to do with that kid. I don't like posers."

"Say what?" Nicky asked, reappearing in the doorway. "What the h-; what do you know about posers?"

"Plenty," Tony replied. "Now go."

Nicky rolled her eyes upward and went to her room. She sat on the edge of the bed that Robby and her father had put together the day before. She remembered sneaking a peak at the tall boy on the opposite end of the labor every time he passed a room she was unpacking. Her father continuously spouted instructions to him without showing much appreciation for his help. She helped Lizzy settle into her room first. They never had rooms of their own before, and Lizzy was apprehensive about sleeping alone. Last night's commotion hadn't helped. But Nicky looked forward to having her own sanctuary. She picked up a rolled-up poster sticking out of an unpacked box and held it up like a saber. She slipped the rubber band off, allowing it to unroll across her bed. It was a collage of the Chicago Bulls team members in front of a city backdrop. She crammed it back into the box without rolling it back up, crushing it. She pulled a basketball from another box and wrapped both arms around it as if hugging an old friend. She had purposely left four boxes unpacked and lined up at the foot of her bed. They contained verification of the life she'd been forced to give up because she was the unfortunate daughter of Tony and Carol Harding. There were items packed in envelopes, flowered boxes, and zip-lock bags that eulogized everything that used to be important to her. There were basketball trophies and plaques and a snapshot of the Southside Boys and Girls Club Dream Team. There were blue ribbons and red ribbons; things that meant nothing anymore. Her father never came to her games and never saw her win anything. Her mother was there only because the gym was within walking distance of her favorite bar. There was no one to share this with anymore. It was as if everything represented in the boxes never happened so there was no point in unpacking any of it. She released the ball from her lap, and it rolled across the room and disappeared into the dark closet. She grabbed the MP3 her father had bought her for Christmas. It was a pretty good gift considering, but she would never tell him that because he thought too much of himself already. It was priceless during the cross-country trip because she could tune him out whenever she wanted. She searched the music file until she found an appropriate melancholy tune by Adele to inaugurate her haven. Then she took a gold-framed photo from one of the boxes. She sighed as she looked at the young woman's sparkling eyes and blonde hair that reflected off the photographer's spotlights. Nicky witnessed Carol Harding's addiction to prescription drugs and alcohol progress from the time she was eight years old and wasn't that surprised by the news that she'd been killed in the car accident. She knew it was her mother's fault even though the Chicago Tribune reported she had the green light when the mail truck t-boned her car. There was sufficient whispering throughout the Harding family afterward to confirm her theory.

"I guess you couldn't help it," Nicky reflected. "Now I'm in your prison; you left it to me. Some inheritance."

"What's wrong now?" Tony muttered and rapped the silent monitor with his fingers. The computer murmured in a low tone as it attempted to boot up again. The processor suddenly went silent. *Connection not compatible with hardware* stared back at him. He rushed out of his office thinking he had narrowed the problem to a connector. There was no light under Nicky's bedroom door, but he reached for the doorknob anyway. "Hey," he whispered. The slim light from the hallway guided him inside. The earlier frustration over his daughter's disobedience was replaced with a new problem requiring him to run another errand. For some reason, the music buzzing from Nicky's earbuds reminded him of how his two older sisters used him as their Guinea pig to work out their latest dance moves when he was young. Being the oldest brother somehow allowed him the honor. They would push back the living room furniture and roll up the rug when their father was at work. He learned to jitterbug, twist, jerk, mash potato, bump, and countless others he couldn't remember the names of. The toe of his Nike caught the corner of one of Nicky's boxes, and a couple of trophies made a ping noise when they knocked together. He quickly realigned the box and sat on the bed beside her. He removed one of the earbuds and gently shook her shoulder.

She opened her eyes and the tranquil expression on her face turned to a frown. She quickly rolled over, turning her back to him.

"I'm going to the computer store, I'll be right back," he said as he scrutinized her lethargic posture. "Nicky, are you okay?"

"Why are you in my room?" she moaned. "I'm fine, I was asleep."

He saw Carol's picture beside her on the bed and Nicky's fingers reaching for the edge of the fluted gold frame. "I won't be long." Tony left the room feeling like he'd been punched in the chest. He closed the door and leaned against it. He wanted to remind Nicky not to open the door to Robby while he was gone. But his mind went blank when he saw the portrait of Carol and the vibrant young woman she used to be. She had become a woman who lived to feed her habits, numb to any guilt of stealing her children's college money, something he didn't know about until after the funeral. He thought he'd successfully kept that from her, but somehow, she managed to sweet talk someone into letting her withdraw it. And yet, there was Nicky, lying next to her mother's photo, holding on to her by the tips of her fingers after all she put her through. Tony found the connector he needed at Computer World and headed home.

When he reached Antrim, he pushed the left-hand signal to turn. Everything seemed peaceful and quiet at his house so he steered right instead and drove through the open gates of Mesa Village Retirement Community.

The name *Mesa Village* was formed with decorative metalwork in each iron gate, something he hadn't noticed the night before because of the overabundant flashing lights that had eclipsed everything else. Now, he could see the perfectly trimmed shrubs, flowerbeds with plentiful varieties of annuals, and manicured lawns with tall trees and outstretched limbs that conveyed a certain serenity. The houses were almond-colored stucco with varied styles of freshly painted shutters. Midway down the block on the right he saw yellow tape staked around one of the yards. He pulled up to the curb and eased out of the Olds. Nothing stirred except the yellow tape swaying lazily and the birds chirping blissfully as they hopped between the tree branches. Tony carefully stepped over the tape. It wasn't until he reached the bottom step leading to Lewis's front door that he recognized the mucky rank of smoke residue from the days when his father took him to the firehouse. Periodically, Carl Harding would insist his eldest son go to the station with him and do ride-a-longs. The veteran fireman was determined to turn all three of his sons into the soldiers that he was and to *carry on the family tradition.* Tony wished he could erase the memory of Captain Harding's indoctrinations. There was more yellow tape dangling loosely around the front door. It had been crisscrossed but was now torn in two. He slid his sunglasses into his shirt pocket and peeked through the open door.

"It's okay if you want to take a look," a husky voice behind him said.

Tony quickly turned around to see who had caught him intruding. A short and somewhat stocky man with a white mustache and a straw hat plodded across the yard from next door. His shoes sank into the deep grass, laboring his stride. He swung his arms far out in front of him to keep his balance while he looked up at Tony standing on the stoop.

"There's no danger; the police put that tape up as a precaution." His voice strained initially but became more relaxed when he reached the steps. "Mostly smoke damage is all. Some of the other neighbors and I have been going in and out all morning. We're trying to prepare everything for Lewis when he comes home tomorrow. He's gonna stay next door with me until the cleaning service is finished, and that won't be until after the insurance adjuster makes his report. Charlie Warren," he said, offering Tony his right hand.

Tony bowed his head and smiled sheepishly as if embarrassed by being caught like a common curiosity seeker. "Anthony Harding." They shook hands. "Just moved in over on Antrim. I was here last night, and I wondered how everything turned out. It's an excellent sign if he's being released tomorrow."

The older man removed his hand-molded straw hat and wiped his forehead with a blue shop towel he pulled from a rear pocket. "I just hope he learned his lesson and doesn't try smoking again."

"He was a little incoherent last night…rambling, you know. I was afraid he might suffer complications."

The old man shook his head and put his hat back on. "You know, I think I remember seeing you here last night. I was standing over there in the crowd." Charlie pointed to his front yard. "You had on dark sweats. You were kneeling beside Lewis over by the ambulance." He pointed toward the curb. "I wondered who that was."

"I'm a doctor," Tony said. "I was head of a trauma unit at St. Joseph's Hospital in Chicago. Emergencies are my trade; I guess I can't resist them."

"Had me fooled; I thought you were just an ordinary working stiff like the rest of us in those sweats and Nike's and all." Charlie looked down at Tony's Nike's and then leaned forward to look at both sides of his head. "Hair's a little long; sure you're a doctor?"

"I sort of let my doctor's image go to the wayside for the past month or two. It took us nearly a month to pack and drive cross-country. Got here three days ago; we're still unpacking."

"Family?" Charlie asked.

"Single father, I'm afraid; two daughters, fourteen and six."

"That can't be easy," Charlie said, chuckling.

"Yeah, well, my life has been a little upside down this year." Tony looked at the front door again. "Going to practice at UCSD; that's something else I'm going to have to get used to after flying by the seat of my pants for the past fourteen years." Tony stepped closer to the door as he spoke. "Was there a lot of damage?"

"Nah, come on in," Charlie said. "Smells like crap though. I'm doing Lewis's laundry over at my place." Charlie led Tony through the living room.

"He's lucky the fire was so well contained," Tony said as they passed an open hutch in a small dining area with four shelves crammed with pictures and knick-knacks. He stopped to look at them. "I've heard people say it's their pictures they regret losing the most when their house burns. Lewis is lucky that these are only covered with smoke. He wiped the gray soot from the glass of one of the photos and smiled when he recognized a younger Charlie and Lewis.

"That's us with Leon Hart," Charlie whispered. Leon went missing twenty years ago after his wife, Ellie, died.

His family even hired a private detective to find him." Charlie shook his head. "I hope he found his peace; maybe he's with her by now." He led Tony through the hall and into the bedroom. "Lewis is over at UCSD in the north wing on the third floor."

Tony waited by the bed while Charlie shuffled through Lewis's closet. "That's where Gerry found Lewis," Charlie said. "It's a good thing he managed to call him on the intercom."

Tony imagined Lewis trying to reach for the small white box on the dusty table from the bed at least six feet away. "Hum," Tony said. "So, he stood over there when he called for help." Tony took three long steps from the bed to the table.

"Gerry said he heard Lewis choking," Charlie said from inside the closet, "and the smoke alarm."

"Look at all the paw prints on top of the table," Tony said, moving closer. "Does Lewis have a cat? No, actually, these are bigger, more like a dog." Tony bent down to get a better look. "Hum..."

"A cat must have got in through the front door," Charlie said, appearing quickly from the closet with several shirts draped over one arm. Tony was squatting on his knees, looking at the rug beside the bed. "There are quite a few cats around here," Charlie continued as he watched Tony examine the rug. "Everybody keeps feedin' 'em. If you leave your door open, they just come right in. Looking for something down there?"

Tony rose quickly and shook his head. "Oh no, I'm sorry, paw prints are on the floor too. Did you say Lewis was found in the bed? It would seem the covers would have been disturbed."

"Yeah, I straightened the bed," the elder replied gruffly, "after the Fire Marshall left."

"Lewis tore his shirt; I expected to see signs of struggling," Tony said. "Last night, he kept feeling for the missing button and calling out someone's name."

"Think the insurance adjuster might find that suspicious?" Charlie asked. "Maybe I should put the bed back like I found it." Charlie rolled the covers back and then bunched them up. "There, that's about right." Charlie escorted Tony out of the bedroom and pointed out the bathroom across the hall and the trashcan where the cigarette had ignited the plastic liner and paper. Charlie said the smell was making him nauseous, so they didn't linger. They met Gerry in the living room. He was holding a box fan in each hand.

"Oh, Gerry," Charlie called. "Did you get the electricity going?" Gerry nodded. "Okay, get those things cranked up. This place needs some fresh air really bad; might want to crack some more windows."

"Whew!" Gerry gasped when he reached the hallway. "Smells bad all right; heard from the adjuster yet?"

"Expecting him any time," Charlie replied. "Hey, Gerry, you remember this fellow from last night? Dr. Anthony Harding; he just moved in over on Antrim."

"Yes, sir, I do, very well," Gerry said. He put one of the fans down and shook Tony's hand.

"Good to meet you, Gerry," Tony said. "So, you carried Lewis out of here...great job. Thank God Lewis managed to get you on the intercom."

Gerry picked the fan up. "Yes, sir, thank God I heard the smoke alarm." Gerry looked at Charlie and frowned. "Well, I really have to hurry; I've gotta get over to the north side and fix a water heater as soon as I get through here. Nice to meet you, Dr. Harding; see you later, Charlie."

"Gerry's in charge of the village maintenance," Charlie reported after nodding goodbye to Gerry.

Before Tony knew it, Charlie had ushered him out the front door and all the way to the middle of the front yard.

"Yeah, I wish that adjuster would hurry," Charlie muttered as they walked. "He's got a lot of people stuck in a holding pattern. The sooner he finalizes his report, the sooner we can officially start cleaning up."

"Charlie?" Tony asked, interrupting Charlie's chatter.

"What is it, son?" Charlie asked, thinking this guy had asked too many questions already. Why couldn't he just talk about the wonderful California weather like everybody else does when they move here?

"It's Gerry," Tony began, "he spoke to me in Spanish last night, but just now, I didn't hear a trace of an accent."

"He spoke to you in Spanish last night?" Charlie repeated. "Oh, well," Charlie said, stalling, as he waited for a reasonable answer to materialize. "Oh, yes, Spanish," he finally said, chuckling. "Gerry does that with strangers sometimes. He had a rough upbringing in Mexico, and then he was taken advantage of a lot after he moved north of the border. Sometimes when he gets upset or anxious about something, like last night's situation, he reverts to his childhood language."

"But his English is so perfect," Tony said. "And there's something else. Lewis thought someone named Phoebe was in the house. He said her name several times."

Charlie held his breath and then rubbed his mustache. "I don't know why he was calling her name." He shook his head. "Lewis was alone, by himself, and called Gerry on the intercom. Gerry just said so."

"Yes, but who is…" Tony began.

"Phoebe wasn't anywhere around here last night. Lewis was rambling…lack of oxygen, you know."

"He kept touching the rip in his shirt and calling her name," Tony continued. "He thought she was still in the house." Tony realized the old man was looking at him funny. He was frowning, and his fists were planted firmly on his hips.

"You sure you're not that insurance adjuster?" Charlie asked with a gruff.

"Oh God, I'm sorry, Charlie," Tony said, apologizing. "It's a habit. I've been analyzing medical situations for so long that I just can't stop asking questions sometimes. Please forgive me."

"Hey, nothing wrong with an analytical mind," Charlie said. "Keeps people like me on their toes. Do you play poker? Me, Lewis, and Molly; she runs the daycare in the next block; we get a table going at the senior center once a week."

"Molly?" Tony asked. "My six-year-old is at her daycare right now. I just never pictured Miss Molly as a poker player."

"We only play for pennies," Charlie said. "Some people think Molly's getting a little senile, but let me warn you, she uses that to her advantage."

"You're not making me feel so great about leaving my six-year-old with her, Charlie," Tony quipped.

"Molly's got a damn good crew over there," Charlie replied. "They do all the work; Molly plays with the kids. All the parents are crazy about her."

Tony turned to Charlie when they reached the Olds. "Charlie, I'm really sorry this happened to your friend." Tony put his hand on the old man's right shoulder and squeezed it. "Lewis is very lucky that he could reach the intercom and that Gerry came so quickly. And he's very fortunate to have such caring friends waiting for him when he comes home."

Charlie acknowledged with marked silence and a simple nod because a lump had formed in his throat.

"You know, Charlie, Dr. Samuels told me I'd be doing part-time clinic work at a retirement home affiliated with UCSD."

"That's probably us," Charlie said with renewed gusto. "UCSD is part owner of this place and Molly's," he said, "along with a conglomerate called The Group. We get special treatment because of it. So, sounds like we might be playing poker pretty soon."

Tony wondered if special treatment meant that every firehouse for miles was required to respond to every simple trashcan fire. But he'd already tested Charlie's patience enough with his questions. "Well, I should get back home. I have a fourteen-year-old at home alone."

"Single father means double duty," Charlie chuckled. "Divorced?"

"Uh, no; my wife died in a car wreck a year ago," Tony replied and put his sunglasses back on.

"That's terrible!" Charlie huffed. "I'm so sorry. Look, you moved into a great little area here; neighbors look out for each other. And if you ever need anything, I mean anything, you just holler."

"Thank you, Charlie." Tony eased into the front seat of his car, grateful that his curiosity had led him through the gates of Mesa Village. A peaceful feeling came over him as he waved to Charlie after making a U-turn to head home. He was positive that moving here was the right thing. Thank goodness for that chance meeting with Arthur

Gallows. *"Thank you, Lord,"* he said to himself. He hadn't been to church since Carol's funeral and for a long time before that. He had noticed a church down the street on Gold Coast. Maybe he could make a new start in that direction too.

"Oh, man! You guys are gonna get me sent to boot camp." Nicky nervously paced back and forth within the small area in her father's office that was cleared of boxes. She stopped long enough to peek through a partially opened mini blind. Then she squatted to her knees to check Robby's progress with his friend Scott, examining the back of her father's modem.

"Hold on, babe," Robby said. "Let him do his thing."

"This is not cool," Nicky had told him when she opened the door after he ran over as soon as he saw her father leave and rang the bell. Robby enlisted Scott's help when Nicky said her father went to the computer store after experiencing a problem with his PC. "This is whack, Robby!" Nicky begged. "You said it wouldn't take long."

"Yo, it's cool, chillax," Robby replied. "My man's got this."

She went to the window again. "Hurry up! If he can't fix it, just put everything back exactly like it was and get out of here! Remember, it has to be exactly how it was, or he'll know." She sat down on a box of books and put her head in her hands. "Oh, man! This is so messed up." She quickly lifted her head when she heard a car pull up in the driveway, the motor idle and then stop.

"Oh, my God," Nicky stood up and looked through the mini blinds. The Oldsmobile was in the driveway. She grabbed a fist full of Robby's tee shirt neckband and pulled.

"You're choking me!" he gagged, struggling to his feet and rubbing his throat. Then they heard the car door slam. "Did that sound intentionally loud to you?"

"He hates it when people slam doors," Nicky gasped.

They both rushed to the door, trying to fit through at the same time and then burst into the hallway where Robby fell against the wall. Scott was oblivious to the commotion and continued his troubleshooting, using a flashlight he found on the floor behind the computer. Nicky and Robby froze in the living room when they heard the deadbolt rattle and saw the doorknob turn. Her father locked them both when he left and had just discovered the breach. The front door suddenly opened wide.

"I tried to warn you, punk," Nicky whispered. She sucked in a deep breath and then let out a long sigh as if it was her last.

"What's going on here?" Tony bellowed. He slammed the door; it shook the entire front wall of the living room.

Robby moaned something inaudible, but Nicky straightened her back and squared her jaw. She knew how to handle this; she could stand up to her father or anyone who got in her face. Her friends south of 31st Street taught her well. Maybe this was the fateful final straw, the fight that would send her back home to them.

"What are you doing here?" Tony growled at Robby. Tony's eyes looked like piercing daggers. The veins in his neck rose as he repeated the question louder, "What are you doing here?" he said, stepping closer, "In my house and alone with my daughter." Robby took a step backward.

"I let him in," Nicky said, stepping forward and between them.

Tony walked around her to confront Robby again. He reached up, pulled the due rag off his head, and threw it on the floor. Her father's fists were clenched. She knew what to do if he raised them to Robby; she would jump in the middle of his back and wrap her arms around his neck. She did it before when a friend's brother got crazy and started shoving everyone in his way to get to the dude he was after. He eventually threw her off, but not before someone with the right street cred stepped up. Friends watched one another's back in South C, but she was in Preppy Ville now, and Robby would run like a scared puppy. Nicky saw a spot of light race across the wall in the hallway behind Robby and remembered Scott was still in the office.

Robby's eyes were fixed on Tony's. "Yo, sir, uh," he stuttered. "We were just trying to…uh, well, I thought Scott…" He shuffled his feet toward the door while he tried to sputter an explanation. Tony followed every footstep to the point that it seemed they were waltzing. Their final step pinned Robby's back against the front door. "Don't blame Nicky, sir. I asked Scott over to uh…" His throat was dry, and he swallowed hard. "…look at your computer." Robby put a hand behind his back and found the doorknob. He slid along the face of the door until he reached the edge, then quickly pulled it open and squeezed through.

Nicky clenched her teeth. Robby had ditched her and Scott. Her father pushed the door closed and slapped his open hand against it. She heard the dull thump of the deadbolt slip into its slot. He stood facing the door with his back to her for what seemed like, a whole minute. *I'm ready, bring it on, old man. Go ahead; smack me.* She watched his back expand and contract before he finally turned around.; she raised her chin. *I can't wait to start packing.* But he rushed past her.

"What's that?" he huffed.

She turned in time to see him charge into his office. Now it was Scott's turn to take the heat. She didn't follow him; instead, she went to her room, her sanctuary. She lay down and listened for the turmoil.

Tony grabbed the door and shoved it all the way open. The thin panel of wood covering the door crackled under his grip, and the hinges squealed against the pressure. He turned and faced the desk with his arms out, ready to catch the intruder with the flashlight. The orb of light he saw in the hallway was now projected against the wall behind the desk just above the printer. It suddenly shifted upward making a half circle on the ceiling. There was rustling under the desk; he leaned closer and reached for the chair, but it began to roll backward. A pair of brown Sperry's and khaki pants protruded from under the desk.

"What were you doing down there?" Tony growled to the boy that barely came to his shoulders when he stood up. "I should have you arrested!"

Scott was unnerved. "Well, Dr. Harding," he said while brushing his pants and the front of his shirt. "You're up and running now." He straightened his glasses, which were knocked to one side.

"You fixed it?" The veins in Tony's neck were protruding again.

Scott seemed perplexed by the doctor's anger and extended his right hand. "Yes, sir; I'm Scott Bolton; I live next door. Surely you've seen me crossing your yard." Scott awkwardly lowered his hand when the doctor failed to reciprocate the proper greeting. "There were four bent prongs inside one of your ports. It probably happened during the move. Hope you don't mind that I straightened them out with a needle nose I found in your garage. What kind of system are you running?"

Tony slowly absorbed the context of what Scott was saying. "You were in my garage?"

"I returned them, sir, and you're plugged back in." The ten-year-old looked at the blank monitor. "I'll gladly upgrade your operating system if you like."

Tony opened a bottom drawer that contained a box of installation disks.

"Hum," Scott said as he looked through the box. "Wow."

"What's *wow*?" Tony asked and eased into the high-back chair.

"Well," Scott replied, putting a disk in the PC tray, "you just don't see Windows 98 anymore." The computer began its routine start-up. "It was a good system in its day, but hardly anything runs with it anymore."

The slow loading process gave Tony a chance to think. "How is it *you* and Robby friends?"

"I don't always get his humor," Scott replied, "but that's not unusual because I don't get a lot of people's humor. He's a pretty good musician; he plays several instruments. I engineer the digital sound for his group." Scott pointed to the screen. "Dr. Harding, click to continue. You'll want to subscribe to the Internet through the local cable, but don't waste your money on the SDCT enhancement service. It won't connect you any faster, and it's riddled with problems, viruses."

"Yeah, sure," Tony replied.

"Dr. Harding, I don't know how you plan to use your computer, but you must upgrade."

"That's what the kid at Computer World told me," Tony said.

"I have more RAM than anyone here because I work on complicated projects. I'm taking a first-year college engineering course over the Internet that requires faster speeds; my astronomy course allows me ten minutes a month with the Hubble Telescope. I also write and translate code."

Tony looked up at Scott and squinted. "You wouldn't be putting me on, would you? Because that sounds as wild as something your friend Robby would say."

"No, sir," Scott replied.

"Alright then," Tony said, waved a hand at Scott, and signaled him that it was time to leave.

"If you need any more help, Dr. Harding, just let me know," Scott said. "I've written an excellent virus protection; I'll be glad to install it for you," he continued as Tony walked him to the door. "I have a savvy chat buddy that keeps me abreast of new tech and viruses."

"Chat buddy, huh? How well do you know this chat buddy?"

"I met him online, but he's okay. I checked him out myself."

"If he ever asks you to meet him somewhere…well, tell your parents or me…I know how to take care of someone like that."

"There's just my mother; she knows about Guardian…that's his name."

"Look, kid, Scott, don't do this again," Tony said, waving his index finger in his face. "Next time, I'll tell your mother. Does she know you stay up all night on the computer?"

"Sure," Scott replied, unfazed by his threat. "She works long hours at the airport; we keep in touch by cell. I hang with Robby or Annette, another neighbor when she's not home. More than likely, I'll never know my father because my mother used a sperm donor."

"Oh, jeez," Tony gulped.

Nicky lay on her bed in the dark when her bedroom door flung open.

"Nicky!" Tony called as he flicked on the light switch. His tone was unbelievably upbeat, considering how mad he had been. "Please don't let Robby or anyone in the house again unless I'm here. Now go check on Lizzy. I'm going to…"

"Go check on her yourself!" Nicky retorted. "I know you don't want me to have any friends; you just want me to be your slave."

"Nicky, don't do this," Tony warned.

"What do you expect me to do? Stay in the house and do only what you say I can do?" Nicky ran out of the bedroom.

"Where the hell are you going?" Tony shouted.

"To the stupid babysitter's," she yelled.

Tony reached the kitchen just in time to see the back door slam. He walked to the door and opened it. "Dinner's in an hour," he yelled.

In South Chicago, checking an ally before entering was always best. But Nicky didn't care as she slammed the gate behind her. She just wanted to get away from *him*. She stopped short when she heard a hissing noise behind her.

"Yo, Nicky, Nicky," a voice called to her.

When she turned around, Robby was easing around the corner of the fence. "You can come out, Robby," she sneered. "Scott took the heat for you."

"I just talked to Scott; everything's cool," he said.

She shoved him in the chest when he got close to her. "My father doesn't want us to be friends."

"I'm sorry, Nicky," Robby whined. "Hey, at least he let you out of the house. Where you headed?"

"I'm going to check on my sister at Molly's," she grumbled.

"You need some company?" he asked.

"Are you serious? Didn't you hear what I just said? Just leave me alone!"

"Look Annette up when you get there. She's someone you can talk to…about anything."

Tony fell into the wooden rocking chair in the living room. He gently tapped one foot on the floor, started a slow rocking motion, and thought how glad he was that he hadn't sold it in the garage sale he organized before leaving Chicago. His mother rocked all five of her children and seven grandchildren in this chair. He rocked Nicky in it when he was in med school and working two jobs. Carol could never seem to hold on to one. The chair creaked loudly, complaining because his rocking had become so intense. He looked at his watch. “Better start dinner.”

Chapter 9

Lisa opened the kitchen door with concern because the nappers had only been down for ten minutes, and she could hear rowdy voices approaching.

"I win!" a blonde teen yelled when he suddenly burst through the back gate, anticipating victory over his brother. Jeffrey tried slamming it closed on him, but Justin was right behind him.

"No, you don't!" Justin shrieked and shoved the gate wide open again. Justin was slightly shorter than his older brother Jeffrey and only seconds behind him as they both howled in juvenile rivalry while racing across the yard. Lisa couldn't tell whose body hit the back wall of the house first because there was only one loud thud.

"Ha-ha, I won!" Jeffrey shouted as he rolled away from the striking point.

"In your dreams," Justin panted, sliding down the wall beside him.

Lisa ran out onto the patio as more tweens trotted through the gate.

Annette appeared next, holding a basketball under one arm. "Close the gate, will ya girls," she said, addressing the following few. "Oh God!" she gasped, wiping her forehead with her shirt sleeve. "I just can't keep up with you guys anymore."

Jeffrey and Justin were seventh- and eighth-year middle school students whose voices cracked between two octaves while they argued over who beat who. Annette aimed the basketball at them and threw it. Justin caught it after it bounced off the wall.

"Let's go again," Justin yelled, "and this time, we'll have an official judge, won't we, Nette?"

Jeffrey snatched the ball away from him. "Come on." Justin grabbed the ball back, and Jeffrey pushed Justin to the ground, and they began to wrestle for it in the grass.

"Both of you are in big trouble if you wake the babies!" Lisa scolded from the patio. "Nette, can't you do something?"

"Sorry, Miss Lisa," Jeffrey whined, pushing himself off Justin and sitting on the ground.

"Did you see who won, Miss Lisa?" Justin asked.

Lisa huffed and stormed back into the kitchen.

"It was a tie; now zip it," Annette yelled.

Lisa scolded each child in a whisper as he or she passed by her and gave Annette a more meaningful blameworthy stare. "Were we makin too much noise, Lisa?" Annette bit her lip and grinned at her friend for she knew she had been equally as loud.

"Do you think?" Lisa said with an enhanced whisper.

"Sorry, Miss Lisa," one of the kids answered in a deep voice. Giggles followed.

"No wonder these kids like you so much; you're just like them."

"Sorry, really; where's Phoebe?"

Lisa pointed to the hallway. "Taking a nap with Elizabeth; it seems they've bonded."

Annette turned to the group infesting the kitchen. "I'll be back in a minute. I don't wanna hear you from the bedroom." The crew recognized the edge in her voice to mean she was to be taken
seriously.

Phoebe was snuggled next to Elizabeth on a blue mat under one of the windows. Claire lay asleep on a mat next to her in the dark room. Phoebe's eyes expressed a yearning to be rescued as her master tiptoed toward them, but Annette put a finger across her lips, giving her the shush sign. She eased to the floor, and the little brown dog tried to inch closer, only to have Elizabeth secure her with a gentle hug.

Annette looked up at the luminous stars pressed to the ceiling and whispered to Phoebe. "This reminds me of our backyard." Elizabeth's eyebrows knitted together at the sound of the voice in the room. "Sometimes, at night in the summer, I lie on my back in the grass." Phoebe looked up at the ceiling while Annette scratched the top of her head. "When I was a kid, I used to think the sky was flat just like that ceilin until this one night when I and Daddy were checkin trotlines; sometimes we'd just sit and stare at the sky for no reason." She paused, visualizing the scene in her head. "Well, Daddy explained that we live in a galaxy called the Milky Way and he pointed out its spiral clusters and the big dipper and little dipper and as many of the visible constellations. It sure made me feel small."

"Is that where heaven is?" Elizabeth whispered. Her eyes were open now.

"Yes," Nette replied as the stars on the ceiling reflected in Phoebe's eyes.

"Is my mommy up there?" Elizabeth whispered so low that she could barely be heard.

Phoebe pointed her nose to the ceiling, and suddenly, the fluorescent stars began flicking.

"Ohhh!" Elizabeth gasped, "I wish Nicky could see this. Maybe she wouldn't want to go back to Chicago so bad and stop arguing with Daddy."

"She's homesick," Annette sighed. "Sometimes I kick back in my chair at night in the backyard and imagine that my family and friends are looking up at the stars at the same time as me. After all, everybody looks at the stars at night, right? It makes me feel like we're still connected."

"You miss your daddy?" Elizabeth whispered.

"Yes, he's up there with your mom. He passed away a couple of years ago."

"They're together," Elizabeth's voice drifted.

Annette leaned over to make sure Elizabeth was asleep. A teardrop fell from her eyes onto the little girl's forehead, and she sponged it away with a kiss. "Stay with her Phoeb," she whispered. Phoebe obediently rested her head on Elizabeth's chest but looked up in time to see her master wipe the remaining wetness from her eyes. Annette held many fond memories of the father who raised her to be independent and confident and missed him sorely.

By now, most adolescents were paired off in front of one game or another, PlayStation, Xbox, or Nintendo. Those waiting to rotate in were texting or watching TV. "You guys bout ready to go to the gym?" Annette whispered to Jeffrey, who was playing chess with Mr. McKenzie. His back was to Justin, who was playing a game on his phone. "No way this group is gonna be quiet till naps are over."

Jeffrey looked up from the chessboard when he saw a girl in a pink sweater with a long dark ponytail walking through the front door. His eyes widened and he immediately straightened his posture.

"What?" Annette asked, turning to look. The girl scanned each face in the room as if looking for someone.

Jeffrey elbowed Justin, but he continued to focus on his game. He elbowed his brother a second time but received a counter-jab. "Justin, look."

Justin grunted a complaint and then heard the sound of chess pieces falling. He turned when a white bishop rolled up against his knee. Mr. McKenzie held his breath as Jeffrey clumsily stepped over the carpet of kids.

"Hi," Jeffrey's adolescent voice crooned. "Can I help you?"

"Chill, Jeffrey," Annette said, straining to whisper while gingerly stepping through the obstacles. "I'm Annette," she said, gently placing her hand on the girl's shoulder. Instead of reciprocating the greeting, the girl withdrew her shoulder, leaving the caregiver's hand hanging in midair. "This is Jeffrey."

"Hey," he said, shifting his weight from one foot to the other, trying to mimic a cool side-to-side shuffle. Justin suddenly appeared beside Jeffrey and nudged his arm. "This is my brother, Justin." Justin smiled but was too shy to speak. His blushing said it all. She nodded to them without smiling.

"Are you lookin for someone?" Nette asked, crossing her arms.

"My sister, Elizabeth Harding."

"She's sleepin right now," Nette replied. "You must be Nicky."

"I need to make sure she's okay," Nicky huffed.

"Check it out… sista's got tude," Jeffrey wailed.

"Shush!" Annette scolded.

"Where's my sister?" Nicky demanded.

"Nette told you; yo sista's takin a nap," Jeffrey said and shuffled from side to side again.

Nicky clenched her fists.

Justin jabbed his brother in the ribs with his elbow. "Cool it, bro."

"She started it," he replied and shrugged his shoulders.

"Okay!" Nette exclaimed. "Let's give her some space. Get your posse and wait for me out back." Jeffrey high-stepped through the crowded floor again, tapping friends on the shoulder. "Elizabeth's in the first bedroom on the right," Nette said, pointing to the hallway. "You can come to the gym with us if you want…while she's sleepin. We're gonna shoot some hoops."

"Hoops?" Nicky glared at Annette. "Elizabeth freaks out sometimes when she wakes up alone and doesn't recognize..."

"Sure, I get that. We'll wait for you out back."

"Whatever," the girl mumbled.

"She's hot," Jeffrey blustered when Annette met them outside.

"Somebody ought to put her in her place," someone else commented. "Yeah, where does she get off…" another began.

"Okay, okay," Nette interrupted and sat atop a picnic table. "That's enough; she's just testin the waters. She ain't gettin away with nothin."

"So, let's go to the gym without her," Justin said, stealing the basketball from a friend's hands.

"No, we're gonna hang here like I said." Nette looked at Justin's friend. "You just gonna let him take that ball away from you?"

"Man, I'd never thought those two were sisters," Justin said as he dribbled the ball around the patio.

"You and Jeffrey are nothin alike either," Nette said. His friend stole the ball from under his hand, and Justin ran after him. The dribbling and keep-away contest evolved into football. They tussled on the ground for a few minutes and then realized the ball was gone.

"Looking for something?" Nicky was standing in the middle of the yard, balancing the basketball on the end of her index finger. She spun the ball with her hand and then passed it to her middle finger. "So, where's this gym?" She asked.

"Follow me." Nette jumped down from the picnic table. "Let's go, guys."

"Yeah," Jeffrey sneered. "Let's see if this girl's got game."

Phoebe licked Lizzy's hand and whined. "What did you say?" Lizzy whispered. "Yes, yes." She sat up and stretched her arms above her head, and yawned. She quickly pulled them down to her sides when she realized she was surrounded by yellow sand. Twinkling stars in a dark sky surrounded them from horizon to horizon. She felt completely safe despite the transformation because Phoebe was lying in her lap. "Is this the Milky Way?" she whispered, but the little dog shook her head. Fireworks exploded around them, and Elizabeth giggled. "It's a celebration." She could see the earth above the panoramic view. "Oh, I see, we're on the moon. Mama always wanted me to do this." Lizzy lay down in the sand, cuddling Phoebe, and fell into an even deeper sleep.

Chapter 10

Ground meat and onions sizzled in a skillet, contrasting the slow, lazy bubbling sauce in the soup pot sitting on the next burner. Tony moved the meat around as it browned, spooned it into the soup pot, and gently stirred the thick tomato mixture while it expelled a few beads of sauce at him. Fortunately, he had commenced the culinary venture with a bib apron, adorning himself in the traditional Harding style of double wrapping the sash around the waist and tying it in front. A colander of cooked spaghetti was in the sink with lukewarm water trickling over it. He gently blew over a spoonful of sauce and tasted it. He shook his head and thought that maybe his sister was right; their mother's secret ingredient must have been the cookware. Betty was sure the heart and soul of what no one could grasp was embedded in the fifty-year-old Magnalite. Betty and Catherine divided it after she died and were still trying to equal the tantalizing tastes it produced. Tony quickly reduced the sauce to simmer, covered it, and turned off the faucet when he heard a noise. He grabbed a dishrag and peered into the living room. There hadn't been much sun lately, but this afternoon, it was shining through the front screen door, revealing two distinct silhouettes standing on the stoop. A rumbling growl immediately formed deep within his throat. "Nicky's not here," he said through the screen, twisting the dishrag in his hands.

"Yo, Doc, uh, Doctor Harding," Robby began. "We're sorry about being up in your crib, I mean, your house, without your permission. And, uh, especially about messin with your gear."

Tony frowned and wrapped the ends of the rag around his hands.

"It was totally me," Robby continued, "I just sort of schmoozed my way in."

"Doctor Harding, may we come in?" Scott asked, attempting to manage the situation.

Tony raised a suspicious eyebrow. "Alright, let's hear what you have to say." He opened the screen door.

When he crossed the threshold, Robby looked down at the doctor's right hand. It was closed in a tight fist, and the colors of his knuckles were alternating between pink and white. A hammer was on a nearby end table, likely used to hang pictures, and well within reach of Doc's pulsating hand.

Tony saw Robby looking at the hammer, so he looked at it and then gave the boy his most intimating glare.

"Doctor Harding," Scott said, interrupting the coercion. "Robby knows that I'm sort of the person that people call when they have a problem with their computer, and of course, you didn't know that."

Tony reacted with an intentionally menacing look. Robby tried to swallow, but his throat had turned completely dry.

"We understand why you were upset," Scott continued. Robby gave Scott the thumbs-up, indicating he was doing a great job and then nodded for him to keep going.

"We had no ill intentions." Scott deepened his voice, trying to sound more mature. "We understand now that you have certain house rules. We are truly sorry we upset you, and it won't happen again." Scott nodded, satisfied he had expressed their regret properly.

"That's right, Doc." Robby chimed in. "We are sincerely sorry."

Scott prayed that Robby wouldn't ruin what good he might have accomplished.

"This was all my bad, fo-real, Doc. I talked my bro here into coming over. Sometimes I get a little on the carried away side when I'm tryin to do someone a solid. Do you feel what I'm sayin? It won't happen again, yo." Robby bobbed up and down on the balls of his feet as he spoke.

"Hum," Tony muttered; the two boys looked at each other because Tony was holding the rag with both hands and twisting it tighter and tighter. "You two better make damn sure you stay away from here when I'm not home; do you understand?" Tony said, raising his voice.

Both boys nodded in silence.

Robby was slightly taller than Tony. His ball and toe rhythm gave him a view of the hallway over the doctor's right shoulder. Tony suspected Robby was looking for Nicky and sidestepped to block his view.

"I told you, she's not here," he growled.

"Oh no, man, I was just thinking," Robby crooned. "My sister Marley wants to meet Nicky. She's a senior, and she's got some clothes and stuff she wants Nicky to look at. You think it would be okay if they hooked up later?" Robby saw the suspicion on Dr. Harding's face.

"You're sister, huh?" Tony asked suspiciously.

"Doc, dude." Robby placed a hand on the father's shoulder. "Chill, man; the streets up in Mesa are cool; we have each other's back."

"Ohhh," Scott sighed.

Dr. Harding's face turned pink, and the creases between his eyebrows burrowed deeper. He raised the twisted dish rag. Robby's eyes widened when it reached chest level.

"Oh, God," Scott moaned. Robby quickly removed his hand from Tony's shoulder. Scott grabbed a fist full of Robby's shirttail. "Well, thanks, Dr. Harding; I-I guess we'll be going," he said, pulling Robby's stubborn body toward the door.

"I'll tell Marley to give Nicky a shout later." Robby's voice quivered as Scott jostled him through the screen door.

Tony slammed the door behind them and popped the dishtowel like a whip on his way back to the kitchen. He chuckled over his success at putting a good scare into the boys and returned to stirring the sauce until he heard the doorbell.

"Christ!" he growled and turned off the burner. "What do I have to do?" he asked, jerking the door open. "Look, you two-Ohhh," he gasped. "I-I'm sorry. I thought you were someone else." Tony stammered because a woman was standing on the other side of the screen door, a drop-dead beautiful blonde with amazing hazel eyes. She wore a blue uniform with an insignia on the pocket that appeared to be a dish tower. Her hair was pulled back into a ponytail that cascaded down her back through the hole in the back of her cap with the same logo. Tony acted purely on instinct when he looked her up and down twice. She cradled a clipboard in one arm and held a pen in a ready-to-write position. There were stretch wrinkles around the top two snaps of her form-fitted and somewhat undersized uniform shirt.

"You must be talking about the two boys that just left here," she said, smiling.

"Y-Yes," Tony said, stuttering while gathering his composure. He opened the screen door to get a better look at her.

"You must have put the fear of God into them," she added, looking directly into his eyes. She had pink moist lips and perfectly polished teeth.

"Well, they, uh, were up to some mischief earlier, but I made my point." She had Tony's total attention, so he didn't notice Robby and Scott peering around the corner of the garage.

"Man, she's a fo-real life-sized Barbie Doll, all dressed up in her work clothes outfit of the day," Robby sighed.

Scott pushed his glasses up his nose to get a clearer view. "Yeah," he said with a long exhale. Her clothes looked as if they were molded to her body, leaving little room for the imagination.

When she asked if she could step inside, Dr. Harding didn't hesitate. He backed up against the doors and allowed her to pass.

"Ohhh, cold busted, Doc," Robby sneered.

She caressed the clipboard against her chest like a schoolgirl protecting her homework, and when she passed him, she gently brushed the bib of his apron with her shoulder. Then she paused and looked up at him and smiled.

Tony had no problem reading her classic bedroom eyes. She opened and closed them slowly as if expressing appreciation for the man she was looking at. All ill temperament was now completely flushed from his body.

"Uh, I've got a teenage daughter, and—uh, those two were…" His voice faded to a whisper.

"That's okay, Dr. Harding," she said, rescuing him from his self-consciousness. She looked at her clipboard again and then put it behind her back. "I understand; I have three brothers." She smiled sweetly, straightened her back, stretched her chest, and squared her shoulders. The wrinkles around the snaps tightened, and the gaps between the snaps widened, exposing a minimal amount of flesh. "I've been well schooled in what goes on in a man's mind.

And, I guess that's why," she paused to laugh, "I'm still very single."

They silently admired each other for another few seconds, which, fortunately, gave Tony enough time to come to his senses. He realized the young woman had called him by name and had even addressed him as *doctor*. "Uh, how do you know my name?" he asked curiously. He didn't know how things were in San Diego, but if someone came to your door and addressed you by your name in Chicago, you'd better look for the rest of the gang waiting outside. He'd never been a victim of such a crime, but he had seen the results of home invasions. Robby and Scott ducked behind the corner when Tony leaned out the door to check the front yard.

"Well, you see, Doctor Harding," she began, casting her eyes at the floor and then taking a deep breath to store up for a long speech. She looked up quickly and began her fully rehearsed pitch. The bashful ploy sunk another hook into him.

"The reason I'm ringing your doorbell today is that the company I work for, San Diego Cable Technology," She paused for a second and coyly made eye contact with him again, "a company that's been serving the county for twenty years wants to introduce every new cable subscriber to the latest technological apps available to enhance their service. Your cable company provides us with the names of their new customers so we can offer them, you, our enhancement program." She held several brochures out to him. He reached for them, and his heart picked up when she wrapped her fingers around his hand. He had been here before, and he knew what came next. The signals were old-style seduction, though she couldn't be more than twenty-five.

"I thought I had all their services," he replied politely. "I can't imagine what we're going to do with the hundred or so channels we already have."

She pouted, blushed, and smiled again and then gathered her enthusiasm.

"Well, Doctor Harding, it's simple, SDCT doesn't offer more channels. Your cable company wants you to have the very best service. Therefore, they want to ensure you're aware that SDCT can enhance what you presently have. For example," She moved closer, nudged her shoulder against his arm, and took one of the brochures from his hand. "They told you about bundling your television cable, telephone, and internet service."

"Yes, but I…" She reached across his arm and pointed to another brochure.

"With the enhancement package, your computer speed will be supercharged; your HDTV will receive the strongest signal, and your telephone service will include your cell phone with unlimited data. What do you think about that?"

Tony shifted his weight away from her. "My cable company doesn't provide that?"

"No," she replied enthusiastically. "San Diego Cable provides the hardware, the infrastructure, and basic services, but SDCT has more advanced technology," she insisted. "SDCT makes watching television and surfing the net much more enjoyable. We must solicit our customers, but San Diego Cable doesn't want to lose anyone to those dish people. SDCT provides top-quality and personalized service over and above any other. It's well worth the few extra pennies it costs."

Something about how she said personalized service stuck in his mind, and he felt his heart pound again. "Can I think about this and get back to you?" He asked. "I'm watching my pennies these days."

She was insensitive to Tony's reluctance. "Of course," she said, smiling. "Doctor Harding," she whispered, "what would you say if our company introduced you to this service free of charge for the first three months? We want you to experience it?" Her eyes were brilliant; who could refuse her? "I want you to experience it." She paused. "Believe me, Doctor Harding, this is where cell phone, television, and internet technology is headed, and you can be one of the first to receive it…free."

Why not take it? It's free. She made it sound so exciting and easy. He was sure that cable enhancement wasn't the only thing she talked about. But there was something odd about her presentation, and the way she said his name, *Doctor Harding*, was unnerving. She had perfect hair and a perfect body, and the sparkling eyes that were fascinating at first gave him an eerie feeling. He remembered how easy it was to give in to pretty nurses who flirted with him at St. Joe's, and there was always one around batting her eyes at him.

"Well, it seems you caught me at a bad time," he replied, inching backward and away from her. But she migrated forward along with him. "All this sounds very interesting, but I'd like to think about it."

"Sure, Doctor Harding," she pouted in disappointment. She held the clipboard in front of her again, jotting something down.

Tony tried to look over the board's top edge, but she raised it, restricting his view. When she flashed her eyes at him every few seconds, he noticed her pupils opening and closing strangely, causing her to blink as if trying to clear floaters away. "Are your eyes bothering you?" he asked when she finished writing.

"Why, no, Dr. Harding," she said, looking at him with great concern. "Why do you ask?"

Tony shook his head. "Did you have Lasix?"

"Why, yes, Dr. Harding. I did have Lasix about a month ago." She moved closer again. "Is there something wrong?" She opened her eyes wider.

"Oh, only a month, well, that explains it." Her pupils seemed to shrink and flare at will in the uniformly lit room. "There's not much I can really see with the naked eye; I'm sure everything's fine." Tony opened the screen door.

"Oh, okay," she blushed. "Listen, there's a hotline at the bottom of all the brochures. Any of our customer service reps will be glad to answer any of your questions 24/7. You can leave a message for me if you like." She opened her clipboard and pulled out a dark blue business card. "Ask for Rebecca, I'll come right over and take care of whatever you need."

Tony took the card and slipped it inside one of the brochures.

"I can give you my personalized service. And maybe I'll let you examine my eyes again with something more than your naked eyes."

"That was freaky," Tony said out loud when he closed the front door behind Rebecca. She waved goodbye wiggling her fingers in front of her face when she passed him on the way out. He expelled a sigh of relief now that there was a solid door between them. He threw the brochures in a tray on the desk in his office where the rest of the housewarming junk literature was stacking up. It would all be thrown out eventually, but her image would remain for a while. The old Tony would have locked the doors, closed the blinds, and given her everything she asked for. But he had emerged from Carol's death a different man. He was listening to his heartstrings now. He didn't know if it was fear or desperation that led him to San Diego, but this is where he was going to square off with himself over the past and build a future with his children.

Robby and Scott stood in the shadows inside the Jones double garage. They watched Rebecca bend over the hedge that surrounded the green terminal box. She unlocked the clamps and stood up to write notes on her clipboard.

"I think the chic needs some help with that cover," Robby whispered.

Scott grabbed for his arm but missed. "No! Where are you going?" Robby sauntered to the box while Scott took out his cell phone and began texting.

"Hello there," Rebecca said sweetly. She bent down to lift the cover off the small terminal station.

"May I assist?" Robby asked. Just as they squatted down to grab hold of each end of the tub-like cover, the top snap of her uniform shirt snapped apart. Robby had never been so close to so much cleavage.

"Thank you," Rebecca said after they placed the green case on its side in the driveway. "Do you live here?" she asked and pointed to Robby's garage, acting as if she didn't notice how much of her chest was exposed.

"Yeah," he replied. "My pop bought all your services from this dude, Bob." He tried to look directly at her face, but he couldn't help making quick glances at her open shirt when she looked at the clipboard or down at the terminal. "Bob was a former linebacker for San Diego State, and my pop loves football so...."

"Yes, I know Bob. He's sweet, like you."

Robby's mouth was dry again. He was finding it difficult to keep from looking down at her uniform shirt and hoped the second snap would go ahead and give way.

"How do your parents like their service?" she asked as she worked. She smiled at him flirtatiously and seemed to enjoy the exhibition.

"Are you kidding, they love it," he sighed as if in a daze. "I mean, they *really* love it."

"That's what I like to hear."

"My sister stays rooted in front of her puter. She's an honor student now; she was tanking before hooking up with you guys and most likely would a never brought home any kinda skin."

"Really," Rebecca asked. "How has it helped you?"

"Well, I don't surf like she does or watch much TV like Mom and Pop, sorry. I use a laptop, but it's to store music on."

"Listen," Rebecca purred. "If you can help me with something, I'll make it worth your while."

"Worth my while," his voice cracked.

"I think I used the wrong sales approach with your neighbor, Doctor Harding. Do you think you could convince him to use our service?"

"Worth my while," Robby repeated.

"Yeah, how about six months of free service? Your parents would like that, wouldn't they?"

"Six months free?" Robby wheezed. Her eyes had Robby awestruck. He had never seen eyes that sparkled like hers.

"Tell your mother and father. Oh, here," she reached down and picked up her clipboard. She took a business card from a compartment and handed it to him. "Give them my card. If Doctor Harding signs on, I'll see to it that SDCT rewards you with six months of free service. Just call me when you think he's ready."

It was a dark blue card identical to the one the man had left with Nicky earlier.

"Yo, I'm sorry, this dude was by this morning and left one of these," Robby said. "I gave it to Doc myself."

"Don't you let him call anyone else but me, okay? I'll give you the rest of my cards just in case you lose that one." She took several more cards from her clipboard and handed them to Robby, and continued the inspection and note-taking. “Ready to help me put the cover back on?”

Robby helped her replace the lid, followed her like a puppy to the van, and watched her drive away.

“Dude, why are you hiding in here?” Robby said to Scott when he returned to the garage. “Who are you texting?”

“I told *G* about her. Whatever you do, don’t let Doc sign with SDCT.”

“But she told me we’d get six months of free service. Look, she gave me some of her business cards.”

“I don’t care. *G* says it’s not safe. Their signals are not secure.”

“Aw, screw *G*,” Robby scowled. “What does he know? We’ve had it for over a year, and it’s cool. My Mom and Pop dig the hell out of it. They never used to do crap together, and now they can’t wait to sit down and watch TV together. Remember how they used to hate on my music and me? You need to take heed, little dude; this *G* guy is probably a pedophile. What do you know about the creep anyway?”

“He’s not a pedophile,” Scott argued. “He teaches me how to read data and write code.”

“Yeah, I’ll bet,” Robby jabbed.

“It’s not like that. He said SDCT is dangerous, and I believe him.”

Robby put the business cards up to his nose, inhaled, and then sighed. “They smell just like her.”

“Get real,” Scott scoffed.

Two hours had passed since Tony sent Nicky to check on Elizabeth. Dinner had been ready for an hour; they were late. He had tapped the face of his watch for the last time; he grabbed his keys to go look for them just as they walked in the back door. “It’s about time!” he growled. They both looked at him with surprise over his anger. He was also caught off guard when he looked at Nicky’s face. Her cheeks were flushed, and her hair was damp and frizzy; the blush and lip gloss that had made her look so mature earlier was gone. She resembled the little girl he knew long ago…before St. Joe’s demanded so much of his time, before Elizabeth, and before the divorce. “Look, girls,” he said, softening his tone because it must have alarmed

Elizabeth, judging by the look on her face. "Spaghetti and meatballs, fresh salad and garlic bread, your favorite Lizzy. And I must say, one of my best efforts. I'm gonna grill burgers tomorrow night. That's your favorite, right Nicky?"

Nicky answered with a smirk and then directed Lizzy to the bathroom to wash her hands. When they returned, Nicky was in her bathrobe, her hair wet and loose from a shower, and Lizzy hummed a tune.

"Something you heard at Molly's?" Tony asked, holding out his youngest daughter's chair.

"Something Phoebe taught me."

Tony quickly stepped behind Nicky's chair, but she grabbed it before he could touch it. He started to ask her why she looked so sweaty before, but Lizzy's humming got louder.

"Who did you say taught you that?" Tony asked.

"Phoebe," she replied, swaying her head back and forth.

"Phoebe," Tony muttered. "Hum. So, what did you do at Molly's, Nicky? You looked, uh…."

"Nothing!" she said curtly. "It's my turn to set the table." She got up and went to the cabinets. "I was playing basketball," she relented, pulling out three plates. "I used to play at home." She turned her head and looked at him.

"I know," he replied and got up from the table and walked to the stove. He grabbed a potholder and a spoon.

How would you know? Nicky sneered under her breath. Your precious career was more important than anything I did.

Tony returned Nicky's glare as he carried the sauce pot to the table. Nicky never let an opportunity go by to burn him for his lack of parenting. Didn't his passion for medicine account for anything? Didn't she realize that things were tough for him too? Things may have got out of hand and he lost his way, but he was on the right track now.

Nicky put the plates on the table, hoping with all her heart that she was making him uncomfortable. Nothing could make up for the years of responsibility he had strapped her with. When her mother got pregnant, everything went even further downhill. Her pregnancy caused a hormonal imbalance, and then there was post-pregnancy depression. Her OBGYN prescribed antidepressants and anxiety pills. She went to another doctor for insomnia, and after years of doctor shopping, she was addicted to painkillers. The pills and the drinking went on and on, and then there was pot and amphetamines. Nicky learned how to live without the support of a father and to depend on no one. She cut her eyes at him; he looked ridiculous in that stupid apron, and she hated the self-serving expression on his face every time he tasted something he cooked, like it was some sort of conquest.

"Nicky, speaking of basketball," Tony said when she sat down. "I've been meaning to ask about the basketball team at your school."

Nicky's fork slipped out of her hand, making a clanking sound when it landed on the table. She moaned somethin inaudible when she picked it up. Basketball was over, just like every part of her former life. Playing around with Jeffrey and Justin today was a fluke. "Please don't," she snapped back at him.

"I realize half the year is gone, but you never know, they might let you in." Tony ladled the sauce over Lizzy's spaghetti. "I'll go by the school office in the morning."

Nicky remained silent; she wished he would just stop talking. When he attempted to pour the sauce over her pasta, she took the large spoon from his hand and did it herself. She wasn't the little girl he turned his back on seven years ago. A bitter taste filled her mouth as she twirled her spaghetti. In a few weeks, the novelty of this place would wear off. He'd go back to what he loves most, and life would return to what it was before, except now they were two thousand miles away from home.

"Lizzy," Tony said, "tell me about Phoebe. What is she like?"

Elizabeth's eyes widened, and she hurried to swallow her food. "Oh, Daddy, Phoebe is wonderful. She can do magic tricks! And Miss Annette told me a story that Phoebe turned into an incredible adventure." Elizabeth leaned closer to the table. "The wind picked us up. It took us past the clouds, even beyond the Milky Way." She spread her arms as if flying, leaning from side to side. "This is called banking Daddy. The stars were different colors, and they felt warm when we passed near them."

Tony stared at his daughter and chuckled because of her enthusiasm as she told the story.

"The man-in-the-moon winked at us, and we stopped there and built sand castles out of the moon dust. We were so tired that we went to sleep right there. Nicky, I could see all your friends from there." Nicky stopped chewing and stared at her sister.

"Ahem," Tony said, clearing his throat.

"It was the funnest dream I ever had…ever!"

Tony sighed as if relieved. "So, you do know you were dreaming, right Lizzy?"

"Miss Molly made us promise that we'd never tell anyone about Phoebe's magic, 'specially our parents."

"Why is that?" Tony said.

"Parents have to take a test before they can see her magic," she boasted. She dug her fork into the plate of spaghetti.

"So, Phoebe works at Molly's and she was part of a magic show?" he asked and then looked at Nicky for confirmation. "I'll have to compliment her on how much she impressed you. Why do parents have to take a test?"

Elizabeth propped an elbow on the table and leaned her head against her hand. "I'm not sure; I think Miss Molly wants to make sure parents don't go around telling other grownups. She's afraid something might happen to Phoebe."

Tony tried to process Lizzy's chronicle and turned to Nicky.

"She was taking a nap when I got there," Nicky sneered.

"But you just told me, and I'm a parent," he asked Elizabeth.

Nicky squeezed her lips together and pressed her napkin against her mouth to hide the smile on her face. It was amazing how her little sister could lead her father around in circles.

"I didn't tell you what she did, just that she can do magic."

Tony realized that Lizzy had turned a simple piece of entertainment at Molly's into something exceptional.

Nicky shrugged her shoulders. "Nobody mentioned a magic show."

"Of course not; that's because it's a highly protected seeecret," Elizabeth accentuated. She looked at her father and smiled. "Daddy, Nicky doesn't have to look out for me anymore when I'm at Molly's because Phoebe said she'd take care of me. And Nicky, you can share your day with your friends every night when you look up at the stars."

"Where did you hear that bunk?" Nicky grumbled.

"Okay, Lizzy, that's enough chatter," Tony said impatiently. "Eat your dinner."

If Nicky's defiance wasn't enough to deal with, Elizabeth's grasp on reality made things even more slippery. Why couldn't Carol take better care of herself and her children?

"Oh, Nicky, by the way, the idiot from next door and his nerdy friend came over while you were at Molly's."

"Don't you mean the hormone factory?" Nicky asked sarcastically.

"What's a hormone factory?" Lizzy asked.

Tony wiped his mouth with his napkin. "It's a teenage boy who acts stupid around girls. Puberty causes hormones that make adolescent boys act like idiots."

"Ohhh," the little girl replied slowly while she pondered the explanation.

Nicky closed her eyes, took a deep breath, and tried to tune out her father. She thought about the 50 consecutive free throws she had made earlier at the Mesa Village gym. Jeffrey and Justin cheered her on initially but got bored after thirty goals. Nobody could beat her on the court; she had the plaques and trophies to prove it. Basketball taught her how to achieve and be a winner. And she was determined to have a life of her own someday without her father. She was tired of his orders and opinions. She looked at him as he ate his self-proclaimed perfectly prepared spaghetti and thought *If he would only stop talking*.

"Nicky, please don't let anyone in the house when you're here alone. And remember, always, always, check the peephole first. You just never know…"

"Not anyone; even if it's one of my friends?" The words just slipped out.

"Nicky, listen," Tony began, but Nicky cut him off.

"You don't want me to have any friends do you?" The bottoms of the chair legs scraped the floor when she stood up, making a screeching sound. "What the hell do you want me to do? Go to school, come home, and lock myself up in the house?"

Tony began to stutter. "Nicky, I-I didn't mean it that way. It's just that this afternoon there was a knock on the door and…"

It was too late; her voice was already at another level. "The neighborhood we came from was a hundred times worse than this one. I came and went as I pleased and managed to care for Elizabeth and our mother just fine. But you wouldn't know that."

Both girls jerked when Tony slammed his fist on the table. "Don't talk to me like that, Nicky," Tony snapped. "The point is I want you to be careful!"

"Why?" she asked. "Why now?" Nicky sat back down and put her hands to her face. All she had to do was eat dinner and go to bed; all she had to do was put up with him for four more years. *I'm smarter than this.* She looked at Lizzy, who was playing with two action dolls. They were beside her plate, and she pretended to feed them spaghetti. She was humming her new song as if nothing was wrong. *If only I could escape like that.* "You can pretend all you want, Lizzy," she said to her little sister, "but I'm never going to see my friends again." She looked at her father. "I'm never going to have any friends."

"I think you need to calm down, young lady," Tony said. "We'll discuss this later." He left the table.

Robby nervously bounced on the edge of his sister's bed, waving a cordless phone at arm's length, beckoning Marley to take it from him. She sat with her back to him in front of her white vanity covered with jars of various creams, makeup bottles, fingernail polish, perfumes, and jewelry trees. She inspected her eyes from different angles in the oval mirror trimmed with pictures of friends and high school mementos. She picked up a small bottle of eye drops, put her head back, and poured several drops in each eye. "Oh, that feels so much better," she sighed. Then she selected a lavender-scented lotion and rubbed it over her arms.

"Yo, come on, Marley," Robby coaxed. "I'll do the number; you do the talking. I told you he is a hard-ass; he'll never let me talk to her if he answers."

"Quit whining like a three-year-old," she scolded.

"Please, Marley." Robby moved closer and wiggled the phone over her shoulder so she could see it in the mirror's reflection.

"And what do I say if *daddy-hard-ass* answers?"

Robby quickly taped out the digits and handed her the phone. "Just ask for Nicky; use your charming voice. You know, the one you use when you're suckin' up to your teachers." Robby grinned. "Work him like you do Pop."

Marley huffed. "You're not supposed to know I do that." She started to throw the phone back at him, but she heard Nicky's voice answer. "Oh, Nicky," Marley said, surprised and yet relieved. "TG, it's you. Listen, girl, can you scoot yourself over here? I've got a ton of stuff that's way too small for this senior girl that I just know would look hot on you. It would be a shame for my Mom to Goodwill em." Marley looked at Robby and shrugged her shoulders. "Well, how about if I bring them over, like now?" Marley grimaced because she had a report to finish before going to bed.

Nicky quickly closed her bedroom door and leaned against it. "I went to Grand Mall with my dad a while ago, so I don't think so," she whispered. "My little sister's already gone to bed, and he's doing sentry duty, checking doors and turning out lights." She quickly switched off her bedroom light. "Maybe we can get together tomorrow or something. I'll have to figure it out." Nicky moved away from the bedroom door and eased down on the edge of her bed. "Your stuff's really cool Marley, but I can't imagine my old man letting me out of the house in the stuff I've seen you wearing."

Robby grabbed the phone away from Marley. "Nicky!" he said. "Look, I'm really sorry we got you in trouble."

Nicky sighed. "Thanks, Robby, but none of this is on you. It's all about my dad and me. We hate each other."

"I've been right where you are, Nicky," Robby said. "My pop used to hate my music. He thought I should watch football and sling wrenches like he does. I found someone to talk to."

"I was failing school," Marley whispered into the phone from over her brother's shoulder. "And there was so much tension."

"He'll wear down, Nicky," Robby said into the phone, "You'll see."

"I don't know what kind of world you live in, Robby, but people had to look out for themselves where I came from." Nicky thought she heard a door close in the hall. "I gotta go, he's coming." She quickly turned the phone off, shoved it under her pillow, crawled into bed, and pulled the covers over her head.

Robby stared at Marley, who had moved to a chair in front of the computer. "Man, her dad's got her so messed up."

Marley smiled, sympathetic for her little brother, while she filled the printer with fresh paper. "Another hard-luck girl with a despicable daddy?" she said, shaking her head. "Like Cass Burns, your girl from last summer? Some things are just unfixable, baby bro."

"Cass's dad is just mean. Doc's gonna chill once he gets used to things around here; I can tell."

"Like Mom and Pop got over whatever they had stuck crossways," Marley sighed.

"So, is that what changed you, Marley? Mom and Pop chillin' out?"

"Maybe, I'm not sure." As Robby left her bedroom, Marley turned the swivel chair to face the monitor. "I think it was because of this," she whispered as she laid both hands across the keyboard. After being introduced to and falling in love with the world through the internet, Marley had amazingly turned into an honor roll student. She was in the running for senior class valedictorian and had earned a full scholarship to the University of Southern California. The report she was working on was a bit lengthier than required, but that's how Marley did things these days. She was quite the improved student since her mom and pop bought the cable bundle that included the enhanced San

Diego Cable Technology service. She smiled as the papers fell one by one into the tray. She stacked the pages together and inserted them into a red report cover. Her moves were almost hypnotic, robotic. She reluctantly moved the mouse to the shutdown icon. She was compelled to remain online, but the internet told her it was time, so she took her hand off the mouse and reached for the eye drops again. She moved to the edge of the bed, where she sat and stared at the monitor until it went into sleep mode; only then did she lay down and close her eyes.

The neighborhood was quiet outside Marley's room, except for the transmission box between the driveways that purred its enhancing data communication through the SDCT cables, as did all the green boxes positioned throughout Mesa, San Diego, and the southwest. All the lights except the one glowing lava lamp in Scott's bedroom were out.

Scott's text to G: *Dr. Harding will be working for Samuels Family Practice; has 2 daughters, 14/6; EXTREMELY overprotective."*

G: *And Lewis?*

S: *To be released in am.*

G: *Nightcrawler?*

S: *Magic show at Molly's today.*

G: *Including the grand finale?*

S: *Affirmative.*

G: *Check your email; sending something to decode.*

"Cool," Scott said, smiling. He wiped his glasses and looked at Robby, who was already asleep beside him. He rushed to his laptop and waited with great anticipation for *G's* coding challenge.

Chapter 11

That evening, as dusk was giving way to darkness, while Anthony Harding was vigorously tapping the face of his watch, emphasizing to his daughters they were an hour later than expected, a black Lincoln Navigator with dark tinted windows was making its way up a five-mile alternate of Highway 15. A small blue sign at the main highway introduced the narrow stretch of road as a *Scenic Route.* The Navigator climbed the outer edge of the mountainside with great caution, slowing in the curves and then picking up speed in its short, straight stretches. It passed a spacious lookout point where more small signs encouraged tourists to stop and view the magnificent rock forms and identified evergreen trees and blooming shrubs and the unique plant life that secluded the mega-million-dollar homes that sparsely dotted the slope below and where sightseers could digitize spectacular California sunsets. Twilight succumbed to it all in what seemed like an instant, transforming the magnificence into foreboding. The monarch of shrubbery, trees, and boulders took on a new posture, seeming to dare anyone to pause for any reason. The Navigator rounded a sharp curve on the narrow two-lane road and was promptly consumed by the hillside. However, followers would never notice its departure from the horseshoe-shaped slice in the rock because their attention would solely be on the astonishing Spanish mission-style mansion before them that had been ingeniously built into the side of the hill. The driver would automatically slow to see the structure in all its glory before the road hooked back to the left. It was brilliant white in the daylight and decorated with varieties of vines that bloomed on the walls with dazzling pinks, yellows, and reds year-round. The ground cover was immaculate, and the shrubs were pristine. The surrounding evergreens were tall and protective of the three-story structure that surged upward to a bell tower with arched open windows. The roof was of molded red clay tiles shaped like troughs that fit inside each other. Each story had bays of balconies with canopies. There were abundant styles of windows: arched, oval, leaded, stained, and blocked. In the evening, the red roof tiles appeared to sizzle off the setting California sun. At night, hundreds of sparkling prisms dangled from the lighted chandeliers that hung in every room of every floor, accentuating murals and pastel-colored walls. Two spotlights jutted upward, annunciating the bell tower, and smaller floodlights revealed mosaic artworks that were sporadically engraved on a stone wall that enclosed the visible property. Small *"No Trespassing"* signs were posted beside the locked front gates and intermittently within the flowerbeds along the side of the road. There was no shoulder for parking along this strip of road and no turnouts for tourists. The fortress was meant to behold and not enter. Prevailing queries about its worth and who might reside there would continue until the route merged with the original demanding Highway fifteen. The SUV wheeled its way through the deep forestry after exiting the scenic route and traveled a narrow stone roadway that was closely surrounded by ill-kept brush and trees. Its wheels up-heaved the overgrowth causing leaves to gust in all directions as it rushed along. It forcefully blew through a veil of hanging growth that gingerly returned to its original posture while the Navigator approached a carport made of larger stones laden with vines and brush. The SUV stopped inside the passageway just long enough for four men in dark suits to exit from three doors. Then it sped away to another vanishing point as the figures disappeared into the rock wall through a door held open by an invisible doorman. The foursome crossed a poorly lit foyer and entered an elevator after each agent pressed his right hand firmly on a glass box on the wall next to the door. Once inside they removed their glasses and looked into a mirror above the door to complete their authentication by facial recognition. A failed screening process at this point would route the car nonstop to a fourth underground level, the basement, where the divergent would be dealt with. One of the agents tapped the screen on his tablet and then frowned.

"What are they doing, Shep?" he whispered to the large black man looking over his shoulder. The man grunted, replaced his dark glasses, and straightened his tie, revealing rings of gold and colossal diamonds on both hands. They were transported three levels below ground where they disembarked in unison. The agents separated in pairs, parading left and right toward their respective quadrants to the north and east, passing a silver logo on the wall that identified the complex as *The Group* headquarters. The sounds of muffled voices, printers, and pecking keyboards assured them that the Sub-level 3 technicians were diligently working in their cubicles. The multi-level complex included two levels of living quarters, meeting rooms and offices and a rooftop helicopter pad. Highly trained technicians worked in the three underground levels constructed within the mountain. Their assignment…to induce citizens of the southwest to better themselves, or not, by whatever means The Group dictated. The persuasion, delivered by an exceptional internet signal that entered a subject's brain through nerve bundles behind the optic nerve, spawned unique neuronal responses as impulses of multicolored lights were dispersed across the intellectual cortex, infusing it with information or specific instructions.

The rural setting in Escondido offered The Group headquarters few security situations. The rugged terrain and hillside forests were sufficient camouflage for the underground operation, and the acres of adjoining farms and ranches with meager herds of horses and cattle acquired by the corporation widened its safe perimeter and offset unwanted traffic. The architectural masterpiece supported a revolution quite different than the time period the stately Spanish mansion represented. Its demands were more cynical than the Mexicans and Indians who battled over territory with the Californios and Americans. Senior Agents Joseph Rodriguez and Willis Shepherd headed the Southwest operation and had been ordered by a cluster of high-ranking White House officials to rectify a problem that had developed overnight, which could impact their political hold in the high electoral delegate state of California.

Two senior-level engineer/tech specialists sat back-to-back at their stations at the end of their production table in the north quadrant. They were taking a break from the priority assignment that had everyone on alert since midnight. Their khaki coveralls were unzipped from neck to waist, exposing their geek-themed t-shirts, freeing their arms and elbows to better compete against each other in an urban war game set in the city streets of San Diego. Ty Hemil was twenty-six and slightly taller than the elder twenty-eight-year-old Colin Sadler. He leaned back in his worn and torn swivel chair, allowing his long legs to spread out comfortably under the table. Colin's elbows were propped on the armrests of his stately leather swivel chair while his pupils contracted as exploding grenades and carbine flashes and discharges from anti-tank/assault guns went off on the screen in front of him. Colin had two well-cultivated years with The Group over his opponent and took particular care to pass his valued experience onto his younger colleague. Ty admired the subtlety and finesse of Colin's game. He often noted Colin's perpetual poker face regardless of the circumstance. The direr the event, the more rigid his stance. Ty, however, preferred putting his flamboyance and superior eye-hand coordination on display.

"I'm annihilating you, Kemo! Nothin's gettin past my laser tank, dude." Ty's blue eyes sparkled as he crowed. "You better do something with your squad leader; I'm right behind him."

"Expendable," Colin replied casually.

"Your general's unprotected," Ty warned.

"It's time to change your contacts, bud because you're in for a big surprise."

Ty wrote the game program with a mask application so their fun would go undetected by their supervisors, and it was his duty to watch the entrance while they sneaked in the gameplay. Before the midnight alert, they were training techs in the west quad to do the toilsome task of manipulating minuscule portions of people's lives by using low-level electromagnetic light waves, a process the CIA developed with the help of a handful of scientists using optogenetics, a method that allowed the techs to influence its subjects' shopping habits at the mall or grocery store, decide what route to take to work or what television programs to watched. Techs in all four quadrants on Sub Level 3 had the power within their fingertips to seed and light up the necessary neural pathways to arrange promotions, terminations, marriages, divorces, traffic jams, or airline delays as required by The Group. As Senior Engineers, Ty, and Colin's assignments were a bit more tedious, such as inspiring sales presentations or motivating financial decisions by stimulating intellectual behavior. The top priority assignment was determining how Sally Samuels's article in the *Daily Post's* early edition got by their impeccable surveillance structure before it went to press. Significant keywords from the article, such as Randal Samuels, Anderson Barksdale, or Old Walter, should have been captured by a data surveillance system within The Post. The article should have been intercepted as the piece was being composed. Colin and Ty had spawned gossip, casual conversations, and heated debates in hopes of unearthing any tidbit of how Sally slipped the story past them and, most importantly, the why and where she got the information. Could there be another story in the works; because there was always more when Sally started a campaign? They successfully manipulated the CEOs at the Post to be appropriately outraged and motivated Sally's husband, Randy, central to the conspiracy accusation, to spend the night at his brother's, where he would receive sympathy and support. Their superiors would be pleased with their skilled management. Repercussions were near non-existent, so they were treating themselves to a little urban warfare.

The backs of their chairs bashed against each other, however when Ty abruptly tapped the kill symbol seconds before the elevator doors separated. They bolted to their feet, shoved their arms back inside their sleeves, and pulled their khaki coveralls over their shoulders. They backed away from their stations and stood nearly at attention as their battlefield screens converted to the standard company pattern. Colin feared Ty's manner of ending the game might have dropped the masking. One mouse move might reveal its frozen action frame if it was running behind the screensaver.

"Colin! Where are the hourly updates?" Joseph

Rodriguez bellowed as he approached his protégé's station. Colin and Ty were the two senior agents responsible. "I've seen nothing since we landed." Joseph Rodriguez was Latino and displayed a high-level green ID tag. The menacing-looking agent, with his wavy hair swept behind his ears and a minimum of gray at the temples, threw his tablet down across the table from Colin's station and docked it with the mainframe, giving neither tech as much as a glance even though they were standing conspicuously ridged. His transitional lenses adjusted quickly to the well-lighted room and revealed his dark brown, nearly black eyes. The two techs watched the agents take their seats and log into the highly secure system, resisting the temptation to look at one another, fearing that even their eye movements would give away the fact that something was out of the ordinary.

"Still nothing," Rodriguez groaned. "Not even footage of her pilfering around the M.E. office? She must have suckered someone into doing it for her." Joseph Rodriguez's finger skated across a glass pad while he trained his eyes on the wide flat screen above him. "She'll regret trying to hang Randal like this." The agent pounded his fist on the countertop and then looked at Colin. "Not one of our millions of enhanced subjects has given off a clue?" he growled.

"We coaxed everyone, sir," Colin replied dutifully with his arms at his sides; "hundreds of times." His jumpsuit was open in the front, displaying an image of *Halo's Master Chief.* "The north and east quadrants are re-sifting every sector. Field ops are on alert and are reporting everything they hear, no matter how minor. We're streaming stimulation to incline open conversation about any account of suspicious activity."

"But we all know Sally doesn't share her secrets," Ty offered. "And she charms people into or out of doing whatever she wants."

Joseph's eyes narrowed. "So, Colin, who's she using her charm on? I must know how much she knows?"

"Perhaps Randal talks in his sleep," Ty quipped before Colin could answer.

Joseph Rodriguez glared at Ty.

"Quit kidding around," Colin said quickly before Rodriguez had a chance to reprimand Ty for his frivolity.

Luckily, something else caught the mentor's eye on his tablet, and his eyes moved to the monitor above him. The San Diego Cable Technology website materialized on all surrounding wide screens in the sector. He moved to a grid that displayed a map of subscribers. Thanks to The Group's innovative subsidiary, all were actively enjoying various modes of communication and entertainment. "Our growth has been significant in recent years," the agent said, admiring the stats on the screen. "All subjects appear to be receiving the stream and functioning within normal parameters." He moved his finger and tapped the glass. "Output is steady at the tourist attractions," he observed. Then his voice became soft, almost reminiscent. "And my witness," he sighed, "his memory of that night?"

"Altered," Colin replied, "too indistinct to remember the facts you imprinted and now wiped from the memory of everyone involved."

"Is the Convention Center on schedule?"

"Yes, sir, I've reassigned a capable team to oversee the Tech Expo this weekend. No need to worry about the Chinese delegation."

"Good, good; we can't afford any hiccups. The Expo's enhancement must be flawless." Agent Rodriguez rubbed his forehead. "What did we miss? If it wasn't for the people under our control within the FBI, we could have lost Randal. A prospective White House candidate can't afford scandals."

"As you are aware, sir, Randy has been called to a special session with the judge," Colin said. "Rigorous neuronal impulses are being transmitted to the Judge through his laptop. He will conclude that Mr. Samuels is innocent of his wife's accusations."

"Sir, I-uh, we worked out a strategy," Ty interrupted. "Mostly my work," he mumbled in a low voice toward his mentor, Willis Shepherd. Colin flashed a subtle frown to his partner. "The vagrant's public defender is going to propose a deal," Ty said, trying to suppress a grin for Colin's sake. "The details were worked out within the past hour, and I-we took the liberty of sending word to Mr. Samuels to meet you here tonight for dinner to discuss a long-range strategy."

"Why didn't I see this in the report?" agent Rodriguez growled.

"Sir, we were issuing it as you arrived," Ty offered, trying to sound convincing.

"And the status of Randal's hacker nephew, Kevin Samuels?" Rodriguez growled. "We must watch all our bases."

"Still out of work since Barksdale died," Colin replied, "but there is an opening at a small advertising company where he can't do us any harm. And, you should know, The Post won't be printing a retraction."

Ty spoke up after seeing Agent Rodriguez tighten his jaw. "Actually, sir, I sent the CEOs a suggestion to curtail Sally's work until they can verify the news of Sally and Randy's pending divorce that is spreading over Social Media and making readers suspicious of her motive for the article."

Colin returned to his station, hoping Ty would do the same. He watched The Group logo on the screen disappear when he touched the glass pad in front of him. To his relief, the usual dark gray nondescript screen and icons appeared. His brain must have been drained when he allowed his friend to egg him into the game. Everybody knew that nothing went on inside or outside of the complex that wasn't observed, recorded, and examined thoroughly by one means or another. *I must be more careful.* Only first-level techs got away with acting on their own whims. After advancing to the Second Sub Level, the majority were incapable of such notions. Only the most intelligent and loyal to the cause, like themselves, were allowed to keep their reasoning power. Lying was unacceptable, and they would be put in the basement for reorientation. Joseph Rodriguez had counseled him that too many trips to the basement led to institutionalization. The basement layout wasn't on any schematic of the complex that Colin had seen, and only agents of the highest level were allowed to enter and leave on their own accord. If confronted, they would not lie and willingly accept whatever reprimand they were given.

Ty returned to his unfashionable chair, his back to Colin once again. He knew Colin was sweating over being caught with his coveralls down. His friend was highly gifted and took issue with breaking the rules. Colin should know he'd never leave him out on a limb.

Ty's mentor, senior agent Willis Shepherd sat across from him, scrolling through numbers of his interest. "Future stats look favorable, Joe," he commented. Agent Shepherd was a stern-looking black man with a baritone voice. His body was large, and his suits were tailor-made. He was solid enough to surrogate as a bodyguard when The Group required it. "*New York Times* has killed the story for something else," he read from the text. "Nothing online in the USA; negative for *Chicago Tribune* and the *Washington Post.* Looks like our boys covered everything, Joe."

"Sir," Ty said, looking up at his advisor across the workbench. "I used an upgraded complacency program to soften interest. All will be copasetic in 24 hours like it never happened unless another event takes place. I have a few diversions ready, just in case: a political scandal in Massachusetts and a major allegation about a well-known Hollywood celebrity." Ty walked around the bench where Shepherd sat and looked over his shoulder.

"Agent Shepherd," he whispered. "Twelve diamonds; I thought I saw two more." He pointed to the glittering stones atop the large gold setting on the agent's left ring finger. "Sir, I admire your bling."

Shepherd opened his stout right hand, admired the new ring setting, and looked up at Ty. "Glad you like it, Hemil," he said, nodding. "You're the only one that noticed; added them over the weekend."

"You trained me well, sir." Ty looked at Agent Rodriguez from across the workstation. "I have some thoughts, sir, if I may?"

"Let's hear it," Rodriguez grumbled, leaned back in his chair, and folded his arms judgmentally across his chest.

"With respect, sirs," Ty began, standing between the two production tables and senior agents. "I'd like to explain The Post's decision. Indications are she's no longer an immediate threat to our project."

Rodriguez looked up over his glasses at Ty. Shepherd leaned forward, removing his dark glasses to better scrutinize the young tech assigned to his tender. He took a handkerchief from his breast pocket, wiped the lens and then put them back on. "Appearances are important," Shepherd countered. "A message must be sent; not only to Sally, but to our superiors."

"Affirmative," Ty agreed. "And it stands to reason that if Kevin Samuels and Anderson Barksdale could stumble onto our program, then surely Randy's clever star-reporter wife could take even better advantage. But any access she once had is now severed; no one in the courthouse will let her near their offices, even if she does manage to sneak past the security guards posted at each entrance. Her credibility is tainted; we have more time to strategize."

"The complacency program is a quick fix," Shepherd interjected. "But she's not likely to drop this. She's historically persistent, we have no control over her, and we have no way of knowing how or when she'll do something like this again."

"Absolutely, sir," Ty said, sounding as if he admired Sally's shrewdness. "Although she is part of the populace that seems to be immune to our program, our resources, in conjunction with our agents within the CIA, are far more reaching. We proved it with only sixty percent control over the southwest population." Ty could hear the rumbling sound of impatience as Rodriguez unfolded his arms. "And that's acceptable because it allows our endeavors to stay under the radar enough to maintain a cover."

"Humph!" Rodriguez groaned. Colin tried to get Ty's attention and give him the wave-off sign, but Ty purposely avoided him.

"Randy was supposed to destroy the page after removing it from the M.E. report. She interfered somehow, so we are inserting knowledge of his finding out that his wife took the critical page to plant it in his safe in time for the front-page story that accused him of evidence tampering. Emotional stories have always been her bait and hook," Ty said with a slight smile. "Emotions are like glue to the memory; it's a scientific fact. We'll use it against her. The Barksdale story was already poignant enough to plant itself deep in the heart of the public. Andy was among San Diego's most eligible bachelors, popular in every social circle. His murder had already rocked the county, and the trial of his alleged killer had everyone watching their televisions, computers, and tablets, awaiting reports on the latest testimony. He was on the tourist commission and planned to run for city council and eventually mayor. It's like San Diego had its own Casey Anthony trial. Sally's empathy toward the homeless man made her keep digging until she uncovered something, a discrepancy between the report and the M.E.'s testimony. And she presented it in a way that touched the public's emotions on every level."

"We have to keep Randal under our control," Willis Shepherd said. "He's only second generation to the enhancement but a perfect candidate for our interests; not like his bother, the brain surgeon."

"We can't let her turn voters against him," Joseph added; "or worse, steer scrutiny in our direction. People are aware The Group is his biggest contributor. We're the largest holding company in the southwest, and you know how hard it is to remain sanitized these days with everyone's distrust of big business."

"Drama sells papers," Ty continued. "She discovered early on that emotional issues stick in people's minds. It adheres to the memory like syrup and is nearly impossible to completely swipe. It seeps into the crevices we are painstakingly creating for our purposes. Is she purposely targeting The Group? That's hard to know for sure."

"We are spending a lot of time and money grooming Randal for the Governorship," Shepherd said. "After completing a successful term there, where he will miraculously straighten out the state's financial and political woes, we intend to finance his Presidential bid. He's our golden boy."

Agent Rodriguez leaned forward. His face was rigid, and his voice stern. "The Group and its subsidiaries operate under a common goal: to secure the White House and all branches of government. Our southwest headquarters will go forward with its efforts despite the current problem. If our labor continues to suffer because of Ms. Samuels' drama, we will eliminate her."

Ty broke the eerie silence that followed. "We can provide people to collaborate with Randy's accusation that Sally planted the page in his safe. He could make a public statement, something to the effect that he and Sally were headed for divorce, and this was her way of attempting to nullify their prenup, enabling her to secure half his finances. The standard prenup clause nullifies an agreement if either party can be proven to have performed an illegal or immoral act that would entitle her to sizeable alimony and half the assets he acquired during their five-year marriage. We can conjure up witnesses to support his accusations just as you did with the Barksdale murder," he said, addressing Agent Rodriquez. "Randy will admit his only guilt was allowing her free reign of the courthouse. He could threaten to sue her, but he won't, of course, they'll settle."

"Emotional story; it could work," Willis injected. "He gave her too much access by allowing her to assist with investigations. Hell, he let her write his closings."

"Exactly," Ty said. "Managing the medical examiner's testimony will be easy. After all, the department handles thousands of cases, making it conceivable to get them confused. Then we can have him transferred out of the region. With our control over the TV stations and the Daily Post, it won't be long before people will be sick of hearing about the whole Randy/Sally affair."

"Alright," Joseph said as he stood up. "I'm sure you two understand the gravity of controlling this. The Chinese will be here this weekend to observe the Expo, and everything must go perfectly. "You two haven't been around here long enough to know how dangerous Sally can be; she never rests until she accomplishes her goal. And by the way, Hemil, we're at seventy-five percent, and by the time we take over the White House, we'll be at a hundred. The enhancement project was intended to be a subtle process from its inception. It's the greatest mass endeavor our government has ever undertaken. We will meet our objective to create a population of controlled citizens with varying degrees of intelligence who will willingly participate in turning this country into the most powerful in the world. The blue-collar population will be eager to cooperate with management; unions will no longer be necessary for lack of disgruntled workers. Humans are flawed," Rodriguez wailed as he moved closer to Ty, "they need strict supervision. Institutions are costly and ineffective. Gun control is impractical for people who lack the intelligence to know how to supervise it. People can't be counted on to live orderly lives without artificial help. Government management is cost-effective, and there's far less accountability. Humans allow themselves too many distractions," he said, squinting and standing face-to-face with Ty.

"Yes, sir," Ty sighed, wondering if he could possibly be referring to the game they were playing when they arrived.

"We've been indoctrinating people for thirty years using electromagnetic wave transmission, Hemil. Subsequent generations have inherited the gene, allowing us to turn on whatever group of neurons we wish, expand intelligence, and control behavior. The internet insurgence and its increasing applications allowed us to gain ground rapidly with more proficiently. By the time we get our candidate in D.C., the U.S. will be on the threshold of peace and world dominance. We will steer our country to greatness without challenge and be indebted to no one." Rodriguez then pointed to an array of widescreen monitors on a far wall. "In a few days, we will present the enhancement to the world at the Expo." The screens displayed real-time movements of exhibitors readying their various showcases inside the San Diego downtown convention center. "Ninety percent of participants will leave with a new perspective on how they should live. The Chinese delegation will be enlightened and open to our proposal and grant us permission to transmit from their country. Do you understand why The Group can't afford to have Ms. Samuels causing problems, Mr. Hemil?"

"Of course, sir," Ty replied dutifully. "We'll keep her under control. And I'm sure our engineers will manage the remainder of the population within The Group's timetable."

"In time, you're going to learn that trying to keep Sally Samuels under control wastes time!" Rodriguez growled. "I'd like nothing more than to dispose of her and that vagrant she's hell-bent on saving." He looked at his tablet.

"I see we've successfully persuaded the judge to declare a mistrial and release him. Have him picked up. Take him out over the ocean, no one will miss him."

"Surely, you're aware, sir," Ty challenged and looked to Colin for support, "how suspicious it will be if something happens to both of them."

"Excuse me, sir," Colin interrupted after clearing his throat. He held a pen up as if asking for permission to be heard. "The intentional murder of someone is totally against Group policy. Manipulating them into self-destruction, yes, but we can't just take someone out point-blank. Our superiors preach stringent rules about remaining low-key and not calling attention to ourselves. Wiping out Sally Samuels will create another investigation, more hype, and tie us up with more mass counter-manipulation. Too many people are emotionally invested in her."

"True enough," Willis Shepherd interjected. "But there are reasonable exceptions, such as when someone is interfering with a major objective."

"Shouldn't we give this more thought before breaking policy?" Colin asked. "Statistically speaking, we could set our project back by acting too hasty," he added while Willis and Joseph looked at each other, conceding that they should consider other options. "We've got our radar on her 24/7," Colin reported from his chair while looking at stats on the monitor in front of him that summarized the spying efforts. "We've got control over David Dalton, her longtime friend at the *Daily Post*. Her office is wired, and she adopted the weekly rag downtown. We've hacked into the computers in her office and at home. We put surveillance in the downtown condo. She's projected to move there now that she and Randy are estranged. Not to mention the feed we have courtesy of National Security from every surveillance and security camera in the country. We'll know the second she makes a false move. Sirs," Colin continued, "Ty's plan to discredit her makes sense. She'll have Randy's accusations to deal with, giving us at least a month of legal mêlée to brainstorm. I'm sure we can come up with an assortment of options. Murder gets complicated."

"Personally, I believe he has a partner," Ty added.

"But we've never picked up on anyone," Colin replied.

"We should put someone in the field that can get close enough to her to find out who it is," Ty said, "and possibly become her new confidant."

"Let me search the field ops..." Colin began.

"You know there's only one of us that can do it, Colin," Ty said and squeezed Colin's shoulders with both hands.

"What do you mean by us?" Colin said and stopped typing. "We don't do field work."

"Not us, Kemo. I'll have her eating out of my hand in a week," Ty boasted.

"That's ridiculous," Colin laughed and rocked back in his chair. "Anyway, you've got the hots for her, and that's why you should be the last person to go out on this one."

Rodriguez's eyes squinted behind his gray lenses.

"If that were true, then that's the very reason to put me on this. It'll give me a convincing degree of sincerity. I suppose you think she'd respond to your Mr. pan-faced-lack-of-enthusiasm? Sally and I share a common fearlessness; we both like taking chances."

Colin shook his head. "And what if your infatuation alters your loyalty?"

"I know how the *bonding factor* can erode an operation," Ty said. "But it can also be what closes the deal. Please don't doubt my loyalty." He looked at Willis. "I believe in The Group's purpose; this is where I belong, not inside this bunker. I'm a natural for field work." He turned to Joseph Rodriguez. "And practical experience is invaluable in becoming a good leader. You were originally in the field, weren't you, sir? I can do this."

Colin shook his head. "Ty..."

"Give me two weeks," Ty interrupted. "I'll bring you her secrets."

"Alright, Mr. Hemil," Rodriguez challenged. "I'll give you two weeks. Colin, I'm putting you in charge of this field ops idea. Make it workable, and I'll agree to it. Maybe it's time both of you expanded your horizons. But I insist you work up something to get rid of the derelict. I was forced to put him into play when Barksdale crapped out on us; I want his existence erased."

"Yes, sir," Colin replied.

Old Walter was Rodriguez's scapegoat when he was forced to create the homicide deception. The Group faced the risk of an autopsy exposing a link between his death and his abnormal brain structure that caused a weakened vessel to burst while he sat at a red light. Like any addict, Barksdale had overexposed himself to the effects of the electromagnetic waves associated with the enhancement and had bled to death within sixty seconds. A coroner's examination would have found a slightly swollen optic nerve, inflamed conjunctive nerves that carry information to the cortex, and unusually large, out-of-proportion gray matter that had developed to facilitate profuse neuronal activity. The Group had been surveilling Anderson Barksdale and Kevin Samuels for months because they had managed to hack into the enhancement program. Neither knew the exact reason for their increased aptitude, nor did they care as they voraciously continued their exposure. A covertly hidden dash cam depicted Barksdale slumped over the Lexus steering wheel. He was too well known to avoid a public investigation, so an undisputable cause of death was imperative. Old Walter stumbled upon the Lexus as ops arrived. The senior agent made the call; the inebriated old man was to be handed a steel pipe, *the murder weapon*, after an operative used it to crush Barksdale's skull, obliterating evidence of the enhancement effects. Other evidence was to be planted, but to further convince law enforcement and other emergency personnel whose progress he managed with controlled street lights and traffic congestion, Rodriguez conjured up a witness. He woke a third-generation restaurant owner who lived above his Chinese eatery on the same corner by remotely turning on his computer and having it announced that he had mail until he got up to investigate. The restaurant owner stared at the monitor, received Rodriguez's instructions, and was compelled to go to the window that overlooked the street. He visualized the vagrant backing out of the car with a pipe clutched in both hands, disregarding the team of operatives working the scene. He was Randy Samuels' star witness for the prosecution.

"Colin, keep my restaurant owner happy. See that his fourth-generation son continues to receive the enhancement in proper increments. We can't afford another incident."

"He should be fine; he was born with the altered DNA within his neurons. His generation is the easiest to control."

"Yes," Rodriguez agreed.

"May I reiterate that we merely abandon Old Walter?" Ty suggested one last time. "*Probabilities* has predicted Sally will get him out of town within twenty-four hours of his release."

"Sorry, Hemil," Joseph Rodriguez growled. "He's a loose end."

"Sir, Randy's ten minutes out," Colin advised.

Joseph Rodriguez glared at Ty. "Hemil, your idea is risky…for you. I'll pull the plug when you're straying off target."

"Yes, sir," Ty agreed enthusiastically.

Colin looked up from his keyboard and stared at his friend.

"Ty, are you sure…" he appealed.

"Thank you, sir, for allowing me this practical experience," Ty said, ignoring his friend.

"We'll be watching, so don't screw up," Rodriguez growled.

"Yes, sir," Ty replied.

"Your infatuation with Sally is amusing," Rodriguez grumbled, "but you have no idea." He nodded to Shepherd to follow him.

The two senior agents retreated to the elevator, where they ascended to the mansion above where they would meet with Randy Samuels, enjoy a fine dinner, celebrate their accomplishments, and indoctrinate him with the provocative domestic spin that would become his belief. They would rest that night and then prepare for their distinguished guests' arrival from China.

Later, Colin Sadler and Ty Hemil sat at an engineering table and plotted a strategy to put Ty in the field. They decided it would happen at *The Campus Voice,* a weekly paper kept alive by volunteer college journalism students trying to get experience in putting a paper together. The articles mostly concerned college matters and personal opinions on school, local, or state issues. Students rotated in and out every semester. Sally had taken The Voice under her wing and occasionally took time to tutor a revolving student if he or she displayed talent. Joseph Rodriguez had it under twenty-four-hour surveillance.

"Let's not shoot for running the operation, Ty," Colin jabbed while he uncurled a blueprint of the old downtown building. "Although I know it'll be hard given your ADHD personality."

They studied schematics of the building where *The Campus Voice* occupied the second floor over a vacant store space. A handful of students had converted it with Jared Dawson, a post-grad student, at the helm. The paper was free and survived on donations. Jared had to scrounge and keep equipment in repair, but he somehow put papers in the racks every Saturday.

"Be serious, Kemosabe. Running the paper would take too much time away from our objective. I can pass for a grad student, but I'd like to be more hands-on than that. Create a past for me, college and grade points, and a work history. Do that right away because you know she'll do a background check. And people will have to remember me. You'll handle that personally, won't you?"

"Been doing that stuff since second sub-level, bro," Colin sighed.

"She and Dawson are pretty tight," Ty deliberated. "I'll have to get her attention, or she'll think I'm just another pass-through."

"Dawson's not going to trust you with her," Colin said. "He's full of conviction, which, as you know, is The Group's archenemy."

"I've got an idea that will get his attention," Ty said. He rolled his chair closer to Colin. "I installed a new Phantom program in your admin to communicate privately."

"How do you think we'll get away with that?" Colin whispered.

"I've been testing it for a while."

"I don't think so," Colin argued. "They're letting you get away with it. That's wack, bro."

"It's invisible. Remember the game I wrote where Phantom hid our avatar from our opponents?"

"Don't talk about that in here," Colin interrupted. "We

only talk about that at the bar."

"I won't have time to explain the application, but you'll figure it out."

"We've never used Phantom in the field," Colin whispered, trying to keep his composure so he wouldn't attract the attention of the eyes on the other side of the dozens of cameras that observed all movement, inflections, and sound.

"It's simple, Kemo." Ty placed his hand on the drawing in front of them, pointed to the open office on the second floor, and pretended to discuss the placement of bugging devices. "It will appear like an encrypted stereogram. The 3D material will jump out at you from the text I send." Colin put a hand over his face and sighed as if regretting being a part of the field assignment. "Colin, Kemo," Ty said reassuringly, moving his hand to the second-floor area of the schematic. "We can do this; we have a tolerance for the enhancement that safeguards our chromosomes."

"Obviously, we experienced the same structured upbringing," Colin whispered. "Surely Rodriguez is aware. He'll be watching us closely."

"Perhaps he's testing us."

Colin frowned and shook his head, "All the more reason to be careful. He won't think twice about taking us to the basement if we screw up. Who knows what goes on down there?" Ty looked at another particular point on the table after Colin unfolded a map of the city of San Diego and placed it over the schematic of the newspaper office.

"I heard there's a secret room down there full of mad scientists."

"Ty!" Colin hissed. "Be careful of what you say around here! Don't take this so lightly. I will put you out there, but please remember they see everything. If at any time they catch you steering off mission, it will be the end of your chromosomes and mine."

"Trust me, Kemo." Ty looked toward the upper levels. "They're wasting their time trying to play God; history has repeatedly proven that it never works." Ty leaned in closer and laid his hand on the map of San Diego. "I don't trust Rodriguez, Kemo. He knows The Group's policy regarding murder, yet he has no problem taking out the vagrant. I think he has an agenda of his own. And why does he keep saying we don't know Sally like he does? He could have stopped Randy from marrying her, but he didn't." Ty tapped the drawing board with his fingers. "Truthfully, Kemo, I never expected him to go along with this, except that it allows him to keep closer tabs on Sally. I think he's the one with the infatuation."

Colin picked up a pencil and pretended to use it as a pointer over the city map. "So, you're jealous," he quipped and grinned at Ty.

"Just make sure everything appears to be by the book in here, and I'll take care of myself out there. I don't know about you, Kemosabe, but I'm definitely up for this challenge. I'm going to get my gear," he said and rubbed his eyes, "and replace these contacts. They're driving me nuts."

"Is that why you didn't see the elevator doors open sooner than you did?" Colin scoffed.

"Awe, man, I knew they were coming; did I make you jump?" Ty stood up and spoke loud enough for the eavesdroppers surrounding them to hear as he backed away from the slanted table. He gave his friend a fist bump on the shoulder. "Set me up with an entrance at The Voice," his voice dictated. "Have a crew clear my apartment and manage my landlord."

"Good luck to both of us," Colin replied. They shook hands and looked at each other like it might be the last time.

"We'll have a beer when this is over," Ty said.

"Hi-yo-silver," Colin whispered as he watched Ty's image fade away in the dimly lit corridor.

Brain enhancement was the CIA-digitized version of brainwashing. After the assassinations of John F. Kennedy, Robert Kennedy, and Martin Luther King, the agency solicited a group of scientists who were using electromagnetic light waves with mice and chimps to improve their skill levels. Their consideration was that everyone possesses higher intelligence, but it lay dormant until the genes for those neurons were seeded and exposed to the right illuminated magnetic fields. Volunteers were exposed to magnetic fields of light that created heightened neuronal activity in humans, and optogenetics provided the behavioral data associated with every part of the brain. The experimental project began to prove successful in small, controlled groups, so the government expanded the project to an area in the southwest that operated as The Group. In the early years, subjects received only electrified light signals through cable television. Progression in the sixties and seventies was slow but successful. The enhancement was delivered faster and more proficiently when digital signals transitioned into every home, office, and mobile device after the electronics explosion of the eighties and nineties. Low-level cable television enhancement continued, but The Group turned its focus to internet devices as its primary vehicle, not only because of its express popularity but because the technology also enabled The Group to synthesize the electromagnetic light waves to produce the behavior required of specific individuals. Investors poured their resources into improving the technology and consumers couldn't get enough of the products it spawned.

The only recorded fatality deemed a direct result of the enhancement, other than the recent Anderson Barksdale, was that of Eleanor Hart, a woman in her late fifties who lived in the Mesa Village Retirement Community. She died when a weakened artery wall in her brain burst. As a result, The Group abbreviated its signals to the elderly. Her husband Leon, however, couldn't let go of his wife's untimely death and approached any and all types of media to help him find out why his wife suddenly died, Sally Samuels being one of them. The Group tried to compensate by creating a windfall life insurance benefit, which he took and disappeared.

The Group bought Mesa Village, a minimally rated state-run nursing home. In five years, it was six blocks of one hundred homes, and it became one of the most progressive retirement communities in the country. Even the curtailed version of the enhancement turned the feeble residents into sharp-minded active people. Sally was impressed with the facility transformation and reported extensively about it in *The San Diego Daily Post.* It subsequently turned into a

San Diego landmark. But the enhancements needed to continue without Sally's interference. The Group's endeavor toward peace and global dominance depended on controlling her.

Chapter 12

The Campus Voice, a weekly circular operated solely by college students, was located on the second floor of an abandoned clothing store downtown near City College. Sally Samuels discovered the paper one afternoon after taking refuge from a rain storm inside its doorway and then sneaked upstairs after hearing voices. She was amazed that anything got published from the office of scruffy wooden desks with lopsided drawers and dented file cabinets with broken locks. The front door of the second-story project was riddled with pry marks between the door facing and the deadbolt lock. There were no private offices with plaques on the doors, just four distressed desks in the center of one common room. Two laptops sat open on each end of an old kitchen table. Hard but colorful fiberglass bucket chairs awaited the part-time associates. The Campus Voice contributors were mostly idealistic students who liked to display their opinions about campus issues, report on-campus social and scholastic events, and take the occasional stab at local or state concerns. The Voice allowed students to sit before a keyboard, vent their frustrations, and press enter. The periodical was hand-distributed to campus hangouts, convenience stores, and restaurants. Profits from the campus periodical were zero, but it reminded Sally of her meager start as a college reporter.

It had been two years since Jared Dawson graduated from San Diego State. Student apprentices wondered how long the post-grad would hang on at The Voice as they earned their diplomas, dropped out, or took jobs. Jared was the constant figure and, therefore, the intrinsic editor-in-chief.

"Sally?" Jared said when he looked up from his story about rising tuition fees. The young man of small stature sat perfectly in front of a PC in one of the hard-molded fiberglass chairs. He wore faded blue Dockers and a yellow Wild Animal Park tee shirt. His brown loafers were planted firmly on the floor as if ready to jump the second his cell phone chimed or to grab something off the fax machine when it rang. "I suppose Randy left…" he began but stopped after reading Sally's face.

Sally emitted a short nervous sigh when she sat down in the steel chair with tweed-covered cushions. It was the best chair on the floor, and Jared retrieved it for her whenever she came to see him, even if it meant removing someone from it. She pulled the chair closer to Jared's desk as if her visit was of a confidential nature. Privacy would be hard to come by from now on, even under the pale green painted-over sheetrock walls and the water-stained ceilings.

"Yes, he spent the night with Rick and Lorraine," she whispered. "Jared, I need to tell you something."

"You don't have to explain the article," he said, "I loved it!"

"Yes, well, David has restricted me to Section C stories until the board decides what to do with me. I'll be reporting on traffic accidents and convenience store robberies."

"You know you can write anything you like here," Jared said while his fingers continued to tap the keyboard. "No one pays that much attention to what college journalism students write about."

Sally kicked her black heels off and inhaled the clean, cool air that suddenly rushed in from the front windows that were cracked open.

"What?" Jared asked and clicked the mouse to save his copy. He smoothed his short sandy hair with one hand as if to spruce up for his hero and leaned forward. "I'm listening," he whispered.

"So, what's trending?" she asked, looking notably out of place in the neglected office.

Jared was disappointed she was stalling, but he obediently addressed her Twitter page. The message board was alive with conversation. He turned the monitor around so she could read it. It was moving quickly with all sorts of opinions and predictions. "They're waiting for you to post something."

Incompetent D.A. office; poor investigating; M.E. should be fired. Like Jared, many hoped she was finally out of the doomed marriage. *Sally never does anything status quo.*

The marriage will go down in flames. It will be nothing less than shock and awe.

"They're on your side for the most part," Jared said, but Sally just hung her head. "This would be the perfect time to get serious about that book you've been talking about…you know, *The Nightcrawler*."

"I'm not ready to tell that story," she said quietly as she looked behind her and around the room. "I'm still doing research."

"Come on," Jared coaxed. "We have fun playing around with it."

"Not now," she said and then shrugged her shoulders. "Besides, I haven't decided on how to open it."

"I know, you're savoring it; like all your great stories," Jared poked.

"And there's no ending," she replied. "How can I start unless I know how it ends?" Her voice became barely audible. "Or maybe I'm waiting for it." They stared at each other silently, and then she looked at the windows again.

"Do you want me to close them; are you cold?" he asked.

"No, the air feels good," she whispered.

"What's the matter then?" Jared had never seen so much dread on Sally's face. "Sally, please," he blurted out in a whisper that sounded like a hiss.

She shook her head and looked at the monitor again. "I'm not returning here after today; this place is probably already compromised." She turned the monitor away.

Jared knitted his eyebrows. "What are you talking about? These are your fans; they love you, and they admire you for your balls, I mean, your courage."

"Don't coddle me, Jared. They're emotionally challenged people who need someone to tell them what to think. Their opinions follow wherever the next big wave takes them. They have no courage, and I think I've just about run out."

"Don't sell your fans so short, Sally," Jared said. "They trust you more than you're willing to trust them, yourself, or me."

"Don't be mad, Jared," Sally whispered. "Of course, I trust you." She leaned forward. "I just don't want you to get…I don't want anything to happen to you…or this place that you care so much about."

Jared took the monitor over. “Tell me what to say; I’ll speak for you.”

“All the more reason to stay away. David’s already crumbling under the pressure of the Board,” she said. “He has a wife, a future to consider, and his children’s college. Some people will try and pressure you for information, or harm you because of our friendship.”

“What people; Randy’s people?” he asked, but she only stared back at him silently.

“So, what if this place goes bust? It probably should have been a hundred times already. I'll survive.”

Sally closed her eyes. “I’d never forgive myself if something happened to you, Jared.”

“What the hell is Randy really into?” Jared asked, barely able to hold his voice down to the level that Sally was trying to maintain.

“I always felt at home here, like I did when I was a little girl, and I...” she began. “My being here will cause you grief; the Board at The Post has connections that can make your life miserable. I came here to tell you, in person, why I can’t hang out here anymore.”

Jared’s jaw dropped two inches. “Uh-uh, no way; screw the board. Screw Randy. Sally Samuels doesn’t cower, and neither do I.”

Sally took a deep breath of the misty air from the front windows. “Everything seemed simple when I was your age, too.”

“Sally,” Jared pleaded in a whisper.

“David and I developed a writing style together in college in a place much like this one. We went on to be the hottest team in town,” she chuckled out loud.

“Go out on your own,” Jared said. “Freelance; write what you want. David changed his commitment and chose family life and that was a good choice for him. Make one for yourself now. I’ve been knocking around an idea of my own, an internet blog. There’s a guy coming by tomorrow that knows how it’s done. Who knows, I might meet the lady of my life tomorrow and start thinking about the conventional life. Circumstances change, Sally; people change, but it’s all good.”

“If you stay in the newspaper game long enough, Jared,”

Sally whispered, "a story will come along that is so personal that you just have to publish it, no matter how dangerous it might be."

The thin metal legs of Jared's chair creaked as he leaned back in the plastic chair, breaking the long silence that followed. "So, it was the bottom of the final inning..." he began.

Sally frowned as Jared leaned his chair back, rocking on the back legs, and strummed the tips of his fingers together.

"The bases were loaded," he recited. "Score...fifteen to twelve...visitor's favor." Jared's eyes animated with excitement. "Parents and grandparents, aunts and uncles held their breaths and clasped their hands as their favorite player walked to the plate." He hoped the narration of the book she'd fantasized about would prompt her to chime in. His voice became satirical. "Daniel Samuels slowly walked to the tee, swinging his bat unevenly as if it weighed fifteen pounds." Jared's voice raised a decimal. "Daniel stared at the outfield. His sights were set well beyond the reach of the players covering the large grassy field between the shortstop and the back fence. They were 5/0 for the season, which was pretty good for five-year-olds. The left fielder threw his cap in the air and the right fielder was turning in circles on the balls of his cleats while sifting dirt through the fingers of his mitt. They were oblivious to the loaded bases and the home run that would put Samuels Family Practice ahead by one and unaware of the team's secret weapon."

Sally shook her head and covered her eyes with one hand. "What are you doing?" she moaned.

"I'm trying to tell you...." The front of the chair hit the floor, and Sally's eyes widened. "What's this, the fans whispered?" he continued, pressing his fingers to his temples. "Is that a dog trotting out to the tee?" Jared stretched his arms as if presenting the scene in the aisle beside them. "A distraction, some suspected; or is it dutifully relaying a secret strategy from the coach." Jared leaned back in the hard plastic chair again.

"That was the worst opening I've ever heard," Sally laughed.

"The first time you saw Nightcrawler was at your

nephew's T-ball game, wasn't it?" he asked, but again, she only stared at him in silence.

"It would have to be more exciting and believable," she whispered. "My parent's openings were always enticing. But then they always knew their endings beforehand."

"The name Nightcrawler came from a kid in the stands, right? But her real name is…"

"Jared," Sally interrupted, "it doesn't matter. Please, delete The Nightcrawler outline from your computer. Go on, I want to see you do it," she said when he groaned and shook his head.

Joseph Rodriguez looked out over the sloping green hillside and sporadic ranches below from a large balcony on the second floor of the Escondido headquarters. It was one of the few places in the compound where he could speak without worry of being monitored. "Were you able to get some rest at your brother's last night?" he asked Randy Samuels, standing beside him.

"Enough," Randy replied. "You wanted to see me before I met with the judge?"

"This mansion has inspired me so much that I decided to build a similar compound on an island off the coast of Manzanillo. It's near the home of my great-great-grandparents. I have relatives that still live there. You should visit me there after you've completed your two terms as President of the New United States of America."

"That's an ambitious statement considering the present setback," Randy replied after a deep sigh. They turned and walked into a lavishly decorated office with two couches, a large hearth, and high-back chairs. A desk with a large flat screen monitor above it was at the opposite end next to a conference table. A three-tier crystal chandelier lighted the meeting room named the Cabrillo room after the painting hanging over the fireplace of Juan Rodriguez Cabrillo, Joseph Rodriguez's namesake, who discovered San Diego in 1542 for Spain, naming it San Miguel.

"No worries, my friend, the public emotions are already quelled," Rodriguez said, leading him toward the desk. "It's our influence over the Electorates that really matters."

"You might have the money to bribe the Electoral, but you can't suppress my wife, my ex-wife."

"Bribery is not necessary," Rodriguez chuckled. "And you let me worry about your ex. My team has already worked up a strategy." Joseph pointed to a laptop on the desk. "Your attorneys are dotting the i's on your divorce papers now and will email them shortly. Your wife isn't going to like your proposal."

"I'm sure she won't," Randy sighed.

"Your prenuptial has been tweaked and is already a public record." Rodriguez raised an arm, pointing the way to a hallway. "Brunch is being served in the dining room; I'll fill you in there. You should prepare yourself for what might happen if your wife refuses your generous settlement," he said as they walked.

"I'm more than prepared after what she did," Randy replied.

"That's what I wanted to hear," Rodriquez chortled.

"I'm sorry, Mr., I mean Dr. Harding," the school secretary stammered. She was standing behind a counter that shielded the busy assistant principal's office from the barrage of early morning business. "I just can't find Mrs. Sparks right now." She shook her head, apparently distracted by the beeping tones of a telephone somewhere behind her. She grinned at Tony and excused herself for the third time. Tony patiently watched the secretary flit from desk to office to desk, trying to keep up with the flow of students and teachers. His experience with demanding conditions had taught him that organization was the only way to maintain a semblance of control. There was certainly none here; the number of employees was out of balance with the work in the chaotic office. Seven students loitered at the counter, six were standing outside the door, and three more were wandering around on the wrong side of the counter. Six students sat in a row of chairs lining the back wall just outside the assistant principal office. He knew he would need the secretary's full attention if she was to grasp anything of what he wanted. Perhaps things would settle down after the first bell. "Okay," the secretary said, suddenly appearing with Nicky's schedule. "Mrs. Sparks is Nicole's third-hour Phys-Ed teacher.

"Is she the basketball coach?" Tony asked.

"Oh, no," the secretary said, shaking her head. "But she

can recommend students that show promise to Coach Burns," she said, looking up at him and blushing. "Dr. Harding," she sighed. "Somehow, you just don't look like a doctor."

"Do I look like a father that wants to speak to Mrs. Sparks?" Tony asked curtly. "Before she gets tied up in class?"

Student voices could be heard coming from all directions in the corridor. Some rushed by, while others lagged as if they had all day. The secretary's attention was suddenly drawn to something out in the hallway. "Ohhh! Do you hear that?" she gasped.

"What?" Tony replied, turning to look at the empty doorway. A teacher burst in, pushing a student ahead of him. He had the young boy by one arm and his black leather jacket collar. The secretary pointed to a specific blue plastic chair and the teacher forced him to sit in it. She hurried into the assistant principal's office while the teacher stood guard over the boy whose hair was so black it looked blue. He had a silver stud pierced through one nostril and another over his left eyebrow. The secretary signaled the teacher to bring the student behind the counter. He used the same diligent force to pull the uncooperative student out of the chair and then led him around the counter. Then, all three disappeared into the assistant principal's office. Tony surrendered in one of the plastic chairs until another boy, possibly seventeen, wearing a black leather jacket that hung to his ankles and more piercings than the previous kid, abruptly stormed into the office. He glared arrogantly at Tony as he passed.

"Looking for your friend?" Tony asked. He stood as the boy ignored him and kept walking. Students waiting at the counter quickly ran into the hall, and the ones in the chairs against the back wall stood up and shuffled toward a corner. Everyone else in the office seemed to freeze in place.

"You're not allowed back here, Jimmy," one man shouted when the boy boosted himself onto the counter. The man was crouching as if getting ready to duck under his desk.

Tony grabbed the boy's arm before he could complete the hurdle. "The man said you're not allowed back there, Jimmy," Tony growled. The boy tried to break loose, but Tony gripped his arm tighter and pulled him off the counter.

"I'm here for my brother," the boy demanded while trying to free his arm from Tony's clinched hand. "Heard he was in some kinda trouble; suspended or sumpin."

"See what's going on with that kid," Tony said to the man holding onto his desk with both hands. "But you're stayin' right here, Jimmy." Tony saw a security camera hanging from the ceiling. "You better cool it, kid; you're on video." Tony loosened his grip, and the boy jerked his arm free. Tony heard an exchange of muffled voices, and then the assistant principal came out pushing the young student ahead of him with the secretary following at a safe distance. The assistant principal placed the sign-out clipboard on the counter for Jimmy, but he shoved it off it and told him to sign it himself. He slapped his brother on the shoulder and signaled him to follow. The pair sounded like soldiers as their heavy boots pounded the tile floor in the hall. No office member moved until they heard the front doors slam closed. "Who are those punks?" Tony asked the assistant principal.

"Trouble," he bellowed. "I just suspended the younger one for fighting," he said as if directing the order to a nearby clerk. "He'll never make it to Mesa High, just like his brother." He signaled one of the students hovering in the corner to follow him, and he returned to his office.

"I'm sorry, Dr. Harding," the secretary said. "What were we talking about? Oh yes, Mrs. Sparks and your daughter and basketball."

It was impossible to have an uninterrupted conversation until after the second bell, and all the chairs were empty. The assistant principal appeared from his office and shook Tony's hand, thanking him for keeping the *delinquent* from jumping the counter. Tony asked him if there were more of these types that he should be concerned about since his daughter was now attending the school.

"There's a few that break dress code, smoke pot, and get into fights," he replied. "I keep suspending them. I pray they wait until high school before getting more serious ideas."

When he stepped outside the office, Tony looked at the empty halls for a minute. He heard the teacher's distant voices and smelled chalk and floor sweep. Something about the mint green walls and the specked floor tile made him think of St. Joe's, and for a moment, the school's pastel walls morphed into two-toned gray. In that instant he could see the doorways and exam rooms imprinted in his memory. X-ray equipment and instruments were laid out in perfect order, and ghostly shapes of nurses in white uniforms and aids in pale green smocks moved quickly as snippets of voices in heightened tones of urgency entered his head. The vision evaporated as quickly as it appeared. Every department of the state-run hospital was overwhelmed, just like the school office. But Anthony Harding led his trauma teams with commitment and composed perfection. Work was his life; it was the staple that held him together when he felt he had nothing else. It propped him up when his personal life had crumbled. He thrived on the adrenaline that came with urgency. For a brief second, he wondered why he left it. Then he remembered. His daughters were being stared at, whispered about, and pitied. He looked around again before pushing the door handle. No one had seen his awkward moment except for whoever was behind the security cameras scanning the entrance.

Nicky was standing outside classroom B36 holding the pink memo note that directed her to homeroom when a tall blonde with two inches of dark roots shoved her from behind, pushing her over the threshold.

"New kid's here," the girl with heavy black eyeliner sneered, strutting past her and then turning into the third row of desks and disappearing somewhere in the back.

"Not another poser," Nicky said under her breath.

The teacher addressed the class of twenty students. Everyone smiled when she introduced *Nicole from Chicago*. She began to read from her tablet, "Nicole has a six-year-old sister named Elizabeth. Her father is Dr. Anthony Harding of UCSD, and she enjoys playing basketball."

"It's Nicky," Nicky scoffed. "And I hate basketball.

"Okay," the teacher said when her students' expressions turned into frowns. "Sorry, Nicky. Your transcripts included a note that said you were quite good."

"It's wrong," Nicky quickly contested.

"Please accept my apology." She turned to the class. "Class, this is our new student, Nicky. Please say hello and make her feel welcome. Here is your schedule."

"Oh my God," Nicky thought as everyone greeted her in various pitches and no particular order. Embarrassed, she snatched the schedule from the teacher's hand, stormed to the back of the room, and picked the first vacant seat.

"Hey, *Plain Jane*," someone whispered. Nicky had picked a desk right next to the badly made-up blonde. She was referring to Nicky's plain blue tee shirt. "What's the matter? Didn't you feel like statin' on your first day?"

"Shut it!" Nicky snapped. "You statin' you're a bitch?"

"Chillax," she said as heads turned to look at them. "I like the tude, but I didn't put you here." The blonde snatched her schedule off the desk when Nicky turned to put her backpack down. "Let me scope this out," she said, looking at the card. "There's your locker number and combo at the top." She slid the paper back onto Nicky's desk.

"Keep your hands off my shit!" Nicky hissed.

"I'm Cass. You don't have to like me," she said when Nicky didn't respond, "but I can help you with the logistics."

"Don't you have your classes to go to?"

"Humph! I cut most of the time."

"Well, maybe that's what I'll do," Nicky replied.

"Cool, we can hang out with my friends and get high. But…"

"What?" Nicky hissed.

"You ain't the type to skip class," Cass said, shaking her head.

"Why don't you just mind your own business?" Nicky snarled.

Tony dozed off leaning back in his chair with the keyboard across his lap. He had been trying to catch his sister, Betty, up on the move's progress. They were eighteen months apart and his closest family tie. His older sisters taught him many things about girls, their plots and performances included. He woke up when the last spring of his swivel chair gave way to its gradual tilt. It was only a three-minute nap, but he felt recharged and hung the erasable writing board on the kitchen wall next to the back door. He directed Nicky and Elizabeth to sit in two kitchen chairs and spent thirty minutes demonstrating how the central communication board would simplify their lives. "We can each have a column," he said and printed their names in bold black letters across the top of the white board. Then he drew lines from top to bottom between their names, making three columns. "Lizzy," he had said to his youngest while holding a handful of colored dry-erase pens out in front of her. "You pick out a color to represent an urgent message."

Lizzy looked at the pens and spoke slowly as if afraid to respond. "I guess red."

"Great! That would be my choice too, red, urgent, you got it. Isn't that great, Nicky?" he said, but she silently frowned at him. He wrote out the word *urgent* with the red pen. "Anything we need from the store, we can make green. You know, like green veggies." He looked at Nicky and Lizzy as he printed the word *store* in green. "Blue can be for miscellaneous. We'll go shopping every Saturday." He turned to his daughters and nodded in approval of his well-thought-out plan to organize the Harding household.

The girls squirmed in their straight-back chairs as their father continued with example after example of messages that might need to be written on the board. He wrote them down in the appropriate colors under the family member column it applied to. Nicky and Elizabeth patiently sat through the presentation in silence, yawning periodically, hoping it would be the last each time he erased an example. In a weary voice, Elizabeth interrupted what she thought was his conclusion. "Daddy, can I just use the blue marker?" Nicky covered her mouth to hide the grin on her face. Elizabeth had rendered him speechless, and the expression on his face was priceless. *Old man, you are so lame.*

"Sure, honey," Tony relented with a sigh. "You understand what I'm trying to do here, don't you, Nicky? But she just stared back at him without answering. "I'll just leave these examples up here; you'll catch on Lizzy, you'll see." Later he cleaned the board, removing Lizzy's drawing of a flower and Nicky's note, *I want to go home.*

Tony decided to clear his head with yard work, but he noticed a small animal scampering under the camellias along the fence while raking. He knelt down to see whether it was a rabbit or a squirrel. "Must have gone down a hole," he muttered when he lost sight of it. Then he heard a scratching noise in the shrubs on the other side of the yard, so he jumped and crept across the yard. "Huh, nothing!" he grumbled after searching along the fence. A few seconds later, a rattling noise on the back porch drew his attention to the grill, whose cover was swaying. Tony eased to the back porch where the grill stood and quickly grabbed it by the handles and pulled it away from the wall, but there was nothing. Then the back gate leading to the alley made a clunking noise as if it had just closed. "What the hell?" He ran to the gate and opened it, but the alley was empty. When he closed the gate, he had an uncanny feeling that someone was watching him, and even though he saw a silhouette of a man in his peripheral vision standing beside the pile of leaves, he just raked. He turned to face the intruder, but there was nothing there. He armed himself with the rake and held it out in front of him in a defensive stance as he scanned the yard. Then he saw the top of someone's hat; someone was walking down the alley. Tony rushed to the gate again, but the alley was empty. He continued cleaning the yard, incessantly looking over his shoulder as he worked.

Brad Jones yelled from his driveway when he saw Tony putting bags of refuse next to the curb. "Hi there, neighbor!" The tall, robust man held a bright orange leaf blower in his right hand. He wore a snug red tee shirt over black bicycle shorts that accentuated his stomach. He swaggered like a linebacker as he careened toward him, tossing the leaf blower back and forth from one hand to the other like a toy. They met between their driveways next to the green cable box.

"Brad Jones," he said and extended his hand.

"Anthony Harding."

Brad had dyed-brown hair, a broad smile, and an enthusiastic handshake. "Katie and I have been meaning to come over and welcome you and your girls to the neighborhood," he said. "My son told us a little about you, Doctor Harding. Great day for yard duty, isn't it? I just bought this little beauty yesterday." Brad tipped the end of the blower across his chest. "Stihl's biggest and baddest."

"Yes, yes, great day," Tony replied.

"You know, you're lucky," Brad said with a resolute nod. "You got moved in before the rain started up again."

"Rain?" Tony replied. "I thought this was *sunny* California."

The green terminal box beside them made a short humming noise as if adding its comment, distracting Brad. He leaned over to examine the fiberglass cover surrounded by box hedges. "The only people who say that are the ones who don't live here," he finally replied. "It starts in December, but don't worry, from May till next fall, that wonderful sunshine will dry everything up, and then the brush fires start and…," Brad's attention waned to the box again.

"Is something the matter?" Tony asked. "Your weather can't be so bad," Tony said, trying to continue the conversation. "We were shoveling six inches of snow when we left Chicago."

Brad patted his shirt and pants pockets. "Oh, my cell is inside. We have the complete sports and movie package, plus their enhanced service. We can't afford to miss our programs, and Marley is working on something important for school."

"I have a business card inside if you want me to go get it," Tony offered.

"Naw, they're on my contacts list. So, how do you like Dr. Samuels? I heard you were going to work for him."

Tony smiled. "Robby?"

"Please don't get upset with my boy; his head might be in the clouds, but he's a good kid. Just run him off if he gets in the way."

"I have…I mean, I will."

"You can run Scott off, too, if you like. He's the little Brainiac that lives on the corner next to you. His mother works weird hours, so he stays with the lady across the alley or with us.

"I'll try and remember that."

Brad suddenly squatted to his knees and peered through the box hedges surrounding the green terminal box. He rubbed his broad hand across the vents on one side. "Maybe I should trim some of these branches and allow more ventilation," he said, struggling to his feet again. "Jim, the guy that used to live in your house, planted the hedges because Katie couldn't stand this ugly box. As you can see, everything Jim put in the ground grew bigger and better than anything in the neighborhood. You should have seen the vegetable garden that was in your backyard."

"The realtor must have sodded over it," Tony remarked.

"Jim was a chemical engineer," Brad continued. "We always accused him of spiking his fertilizer. He was blind, you know."

"But how did he…?" Tony began, but Brad interrupted.

"Irreparable retina damage," Brad continued. "He sank into severe depression after the accident. It happened right there in his, uh, your garage." Brad turned to look at Tony's open garage. "His wife, Julia, was sure he'd never put another seed in the ground. But then that little gal from Louisiana moved in behind us, and before long, there were rows of stakes strung together all over Jim's backyard. She made him use his cane to walk up and down the rows. And then there was Phoebe." Brad cleared his throat. "Well, Phoebe just worked her magic on him."

"Why did they move?" Tony asked, still pondering the name *Phoebe.*

"He won so many awards that every horticultural engineer in the state wanted him to come to work for them. He had an operation that restored the rest of his vision, and he accepted a position with the State Horticultural Service in Sacramento."

"That's amazing," Tony said.

"Did you have a yard in *Chicagoland?*" Brad asked. "Ha, while you were dodging all those bullets." Brad's eyes gleamed, pleased that he could produce a preconception about Chicago to match Tony's notions about California.

"No, not really," Tony sighed. "But I like having one now."

"Robby told me how the excitement over at the retirement village upset your little girl," Brad said. "My mother's been over there for ten years. She was diagnosed with Alzheimer's, and when she couldn't recognize us anymore, we moved her in. The funny thing, though, is that after a few months, she started getting better. You'd never know anything was ever wrong with her now. She's got a little arthritis, but her mind is back."

The two shook hands again, bid goodbye, and went about their respective yard duties. He thought it best not to dispute Brad's take on his mother's illness and remarkable recovery. Why did he feel ill-informed when he was so pleased with the outcome? Alzheimer's is a progressive disease that no one recovers from. It can be misdiagnosed because it falls under the umbrella of dementia and other similar diseases.

A loud noise suddenly erupted inside Brad's house as he hung the hedge trimmer on the garage wall. Everything on the wall vibrated on its hooks, and every can, box, and tool rattled. Tony rushed outside.

"Hello, Doctor Harding." Scott was standing in the driveway holding a silver laptop under one arm. "That was just Robby."

"That noise?" Tony gasped. "It sounded like a-a-"

"It's his amp. He sometimes forgets to turn the volume down when he switches over from his headphones. I hope he didn't break any of Ms. Katie's figurines again."

"Amplifier," Tony gasped.

"Yes, sir," Scott replied. "That was his electric guitar. I'm helping him mix sound variations." He gave the silver laptop under his arm a gentle pat with his free hand. "I wrote a mixing program."

Tony didn't acknowledge it because he repeated the words *guitar* and *amplifier* to himself.

"He plays the drums and electric keyboard as well. I guess I'll see you later."

Tony opened his mouth, but nothing came out. He saw Scott pick up a can of paint from the floor of Brad's garage that must have fallen off a shelf. Another loud shriek was discharged when Scott entered the house. *So much for the peaceful neighborhood, the realtor promised.* When Tony turned to go back inside the garage, he noticed a small brown shaggy dog sitting just inside the garage door, looking up at him and wagging its tail. "Where did you come from?" Tony asked.

The little dog cocked its head to one side.

"Who do you belong to?" He asked, noticing it had a collar and tag.

The little dog cocked its head to the other side.

"Get out of here! Shoo! Go home!" Tony growled.

Phoebe quickly stood up and darted around the corner and onto the path between the houses.

Marley sat at her desk in total command of the HP components in front of her. Her fingers skillfully danced over the keyboard and jetted across the mouse pad. Her movements were fluid, fast, and mechanical as if spellbound by the enhanced service that challenged her to keep up with its information. In minutes her thesis was complete and ready for print. She clicked the icon and triumphantly pushed herself away from the desk. Marley Jones was consumed with achieving utmost success and relished the scholastic edge she seemed to have over everyone these days. With an IQ of 130, the new Marley would be off to college this summer after earning her choice of scholarships. The SDCT salesman had predicted her success. Robby startled her when he opened the bedroom door. She hadn't been paying attention to the muffled vibration of tunes coming from his insulated room next door and hadn't noticed they'd stopped.

"Yo, Marley," Robby said as he entered. "What ya doing in here, looking at porn or something?"

"Funny boy," she sneered. "Can't you see I'm busy?"

"That report thing?" he asked. "Yeah, well, if you don't watch out, big sister, you're gonna burn out at eighteen."

"I'm sorry, Robby," she sighed. "You know how I get when I'm working; you scared the crap out of me."

"You didn't hear me knocking? I knocked like a b-zillion times."

"The printer must have…well anyway, what's that stuff in your hand?"

"Check it out, sheet music. I need you to make four copies for the band?"

"Seriously?" she asked. "You're going to copy-write, aren't you? Although, I don't know who'd want to steal this chicken scratch." Marley looked at her brother's sober face, grinned, and giggled.

Robby scooted closer. "This *scratch* is a symbol that Scott and I made up for some of the techno sounds we created; edgy, huh? I'm gonna show it to my music instructor and see what she thinks."

"Oh! I see, trying to impress teacher," Marley taunted, leaned closer, and squinted her eyes menacingly.

"Hey, cut it out, Marley; every serious music writer does this."

"So, do you intend to make this a career or something? I saw you looking at a music writing program last week at Computer World. Why didn't you just ask Mom and Pop to buy it for you? They would have you know; they're much more agreeable these days. I know you put it back on the shelf because you thought it was too expensive."

"Scott wrote a better one. He says those programs pick up Intruders that infiltrate systems and steal information. He hooked me up with a firewall and encoded everything; it's insane. It writes the music as I play it and has a sound bank for effects; awesome, right?"

"He's such a little Neutron," Marley quipped. "He keeps putting this anti-virus protection on my computer. I have to delete it because it interferes with SDCT upgrades."

"You shouldn't do that; he knows his stuff." Robby sighed, "Anyway, Mom and Pop spend too much money. They act like there's an endless supply."

"Well, lucky for you and your keyboard and electronic drums," Marley retorted. "And for my computer and the swimming pool they're going to put in this spring; and Mom's new car and Pop's truck and fishing rig…"

"Exactly," Robby interrupted. "It's ridiculous."

"I don't know," Marley said and swung her chair back around to face the monitor. "Two years ago, I'd have never thought I'd be in a computer club and be hanging with freaky geeks. And that everybody would think I was cool instead of a loser." She laid her hand across the mouse pad. "I'll always be grateful to them for buying this for me. I can't believe the difference it made in my life. Sometimes I even find it hard to recognize me."

Robby lay on his back across his sister's blue satin bedspread. He tapped his heels and toes on the carpeted floor in time with the printer, expelling the nervous energy that flushed through him as he thought of how things used to be. "Yo, remember bad-ass Bob, the salesman," he said. "It was like Pop met his long-lost soul brother. Bob was *The Man.* Pop was pretty much ignoring me anyway, but when he came along it was like I totally disappeared. It was Bob who insisted you get the computer." Robby frowned as he thought of his relationship with his father. *"Be a man!"* he mocked, imitating his father's hefty voice. "That's all he cared to say to me."

"You have to agree that everything is better now for everybody, even you," Marley said, lying beside her brother. "It's like everybody got re-invented."

"Mom and Pop got richer and happier," Robby agreed. "You got computerettes. Gramma even kicked it up a few. Things are just weird now." The last sheet settled into the paper tray.

"Are you sure it wasn't Cass that changed everything for you?" Marley sighed, "Your first love."

"Yeah, she pretty much dumped me after I stood her up at the station. I was sure ready to blow this place. We were gonna take the Amtrak and get as far away from our fathers as possible."

"But then you stopped to tell Annette goodbye," Marley said and sat up to gather the papers. "And that little dog of hers ran over here barking her head off, waking up Pop; and we had that intervention thing."

"Yeah," Robby sighed.

"I was pretty freaked," Marley moaned. "Pop was yelling, Mom was crying; everybody was shouting at each other, and you never shout."

"I couldn't take Pop's crap anymore," Robby sighed.

"I remember Pop's temper," Marley said soberly, "and being grateful he was yelling at you and not me. I was kind of afraid of him back then. Why do you think I used to stay out with my friends and then lock myself in my room?" Marley stroked the keyboard with the tips of her fingers. "Robby, this whole growing up thing is scary. I never thought I'd be going to college."

"Yo, I was never coming back," Robby said. "I just couldn't leave without telling Annette and Phoebe goodbye."

"Yeah, and she sold your ass out," Marley said and took the sheet music from him.

"If she hadn't sold my ass out, I'd be on some street corner right now freezing my butt off and playing for quarters instead of composing music on my own keyboard and writing programs with Scott. Trouble is, when I bailed on Cass, everything went sideways for her."

"I guess that's why she hangs with those scumbags now?"

"All hell broke loose between her and her father when he found out she was running away," Robby sighed. "She doesn't talk to me anymore."

"Humph!" Marley grunted. "Her ignorant father could use an intervention."

"My life got better, and hers still sucks. I don't blame her for hating me."

"Don't waste your time feeling sorry for her. Your copies are dropping."

"You're sure fast on that thing, Marley," Robby said as he watched her hand skate over the mouse pad.

"You know something that really scares me sometimes, Robby?" Marley looked at her brother while the printer produced the sheet music. "Sometimes I get the feeling that everything will suddenly turn back to how it was. You know, before all the money, before this." She looked at her computer and then at her little brother, who she somehow felt closer to since his run-away attempt. "Sometimes at night, before I fall to sleep, I wonder if all this will be gone when I wake up. It's like Mom and Pop went through this 'Back to the Future' time warp thing. And Gramma, her memory was supposed to fade away. Robby, please don't change or go anywhere. You're the only one I can talk to about this stuff. I need you to help me remember."

"Remember?" Robby asked, thinking Marley's voice sounded weird. It was like she was talking in her sleep. She was facing him, yet her eyes weren't really focused on him.

"Marley," Robby said and nudged her arm with his hand. "Yo, Marley," he repeated, grabbing and shaking her arm. Her focus returned, and she rubbed one side of her face.

"I must be tired; my face feels numb. I've been working on this thesis for five hours. Some kids in my computer club complain of the same thing when they work long hours; at least I don't get the headaches they do."

"Look, Sis," Robby whispered, "we've all been through some big changes, and it all happened really fast; we haven't had time to digest it. Look at you; I can show you pics from when you were a Miss Party girl two years ago. School is a challenge for you now instead of the drag it used to be. Yeah, you're actually an interesting chick now."

Marley stared at her brother. "How can someone so full of bullshit sometimes actually make sense?"

"Just imitating my mentor," Robby replied. "Annette keeps me grounded. She's my witness, proof of who I was, and who I am now." He picked up the printed pages, rolled them into a tube, and tapped it like a drumstick on both Marley's knees. "What you need to do, Sis is slow down a little; yo, take a break after graduation. Take the summer off and have some fun like you used to. Well, maybe not exactly like you used to."

"Robby, will you be my memory if I should ever need it? Will you remind me of who I used to be and how I got to wherever I ended up?"

"Sure, Sis," he said.

Four towers anchored in the mountainside near the Escondido mansion silently emitted potent electromagnetic waves into the atmosphere. They were received by six dedicated satellites that, in turn, relayed their commands to hundreds of booster transmission turrets capable of transmitting the specialized communication. Further disbursement went to the hundreds of thousands of exceptionally fortified terminals and junction boxes along the streets of the southwest, like the one between the Jones and Harding driveways. The specially designed magnetic field could compel responses to circumstances for select individuals from their various electronic devices. Households like the Joneses were unaware that many of their important decisions were planned and orchestrated by technicians sitting in front of a panel of keyboards deep within the mountains of Escondido.

Chapter 13

When Annette allowed the gym doors to slam closed, the rebounding sound from inside brought back haunting memories from The Boys and Girls Club of South Chicago for Nicky. “How big is this place?” Nicky finally asked when they had passed two tennis courts while returning to Molly’s.

“Bigger than any retirement community I’ve ever seen,” Nette replied. “The walkway just ahead leads to the Senior Center where residents meet and play cards and bingo and stuff. There’s a clinic and an indoor pool. The village is a happenin place for the folks that live here.”

“Sounds good for them,” Nicky sighed.

“Yeah,” Annette replied. “Somebody had a great idea when they dreamed this place up. So how was school?”

Nicky shrugged her shoulders and looked away. She didn’t want to think about the most humiliating day of her life when she had to recite the same introduction before every class that included her name, where she was from, her family stats, one younger sister, and a father who’s a doctor and a mother who died in a car accident.

“How ‘bout P.E.,” Nette asked, but Nicky sighed as if the whole day, including P.E., had been boring. “Who’d you get for P.E.?”

“Some stupid woman,” Nicky replied.

“Sparks?” Annette smirked.

“So, you know her?” Nicky asked.

Jeffrey was listening as he walked ahead and suddenly turned around and walked backward. “Mrs. Sparks teaches Home-Ec.,” he said. “You know, sewing and cooking and stuff like that.”

“And don’t forget, Biology,” Annette laughed.

“My Dad was supposed to talk to her, but she didn’t really have much to say to me. I was just happy I didn’t have to tell my life story again.”

“Why was your dad…?” Nette began.

“No reason,” she interrupted. “I left him at the school office this morning, but he gets distracted. He’s a doctor, sometimes things just happen, and he forgets about us.”

Although, he did write "see PE Teacher" on his stupid bulletin board.

"Huh," Nette whispered, looking at the smirk on Nicky's face.

"Well, I hope it was about changing PE teachers," Jeffrey ragged.

"I don't care," Nicky said.

"Hey, Nette, you should talk to Coach Burns," he said, tripping over his heels. "I bet he'd put her on JV."

"Yeah, if Burns wasn't such a butt-I mean," Annette blurted out and then bit her bottom lip.

"Ha, Ha, Nette, you said *butt*," Jeffrey snickered and waved a finger at her.

"Jeffrey, you know my talkin to Coach Burns is a bad idea. It never turns out well." She looked at Nicky. "And then he might take it out on you."

"You don't have to talk to anybody about me," Nicky sneered. "I can talk for myself. Besides, who said I wanted to be on JV?"

Annette looked at Nicky curiously. "Okay then," she said as they continued walking. Nicky was probably still grieving over the loss of her mother and her family and the friends she had to leave behind. "Burns likes to work your butt off and then chew on it. I think he forgets he's coachin middle school girls. I can't tell you how many times I've lost it because of his bullyin."

"Yeah, Nette goes insane; she got right up in his face once," Jeffrey said, laughing. "He treats his daughter Cass the worst."

"I met Cass today," Nicky grunted.

"I think Burns cares more about winnin than he does his daughter," Nette said. "He forgets that a sport is supposed to be a positive experience, instead..."

"Oh, please!" Nicky laughed. "Where do you come from, La-La-Land or something? Do you think the bitches on my block cut me any slack?"

Jeffrey and Annette exchanged raised eyebrows.

"Kids have enough to deal with these days without havin a teacher like him, that's all," Nette contended. "He has his warped idea of what winnin means. He gets some kind of insane satisfaction out of belittlin people in front of everybody."

"Whoa, Nette," Jeffrey warned and opened the gate for them.

"It's all about makin himself look good," Nette groaned. "One little insignificant mishap and he will be all down your throat."

"He acts like he's on steroids," Jeffrey added as he ran to walk in front of them again.

"I don't care," Nicky sneered.

"Cass shouldn't be subjected to his browbeatin," Annette added.

"Boohoo!" Nicky scoffed. She took the ball from under Annette's arm and bounced it off the ground at an angle from one hand to the other. "Just tell me one thing; does Cass play worth a shit?"

Annette nodded. "She's the best."

"She could easily play Varsity," Jeffrey said, "but she likes to screw up and piss off her dad."

Nicky learned how to cope with her screwed-up life by playing basketball. Her mother couldn't even open her eyes in the morning without a drink, and her little sister was stricken with anxiety because of their mother's unpredictability. She was used to life in South Chicago. She was thrown an unexpected curve with the move to San Diego. She used to hear people say life is a game; she had clung to basketball like it was a life preserver in South C. "Well," Nicky sighed. "I guess we all have our battles."

Molly's backyard was empty. "Man, we must be late," Jeffrey's two-tone voice screeched as he trotted to the door.

"Not by much," Annette said, looking at her watch.

"There you are," Mona said, waving her hands. "Do we have to put a GPS on you? Did you forget your cell?"

"Sorry, I put it on manner mode," Nette said. "Is anyone in trouble?"

Mona shook her head. "No, but we have a little girl with a very sad face in the front room who is worried about her big sister."

"Is—Is Lizzy all right?" Nicky stammered. The tough girl's face suddenly turned pale.

"Yes, she's fine," Mona attempted to explain before Nicky darted past. "I didn't mean to upset her," Mona whispered to Annette. "I think Lizzy is more upset because Phoebe isn't here." They followed Nicky as far as the archway. "Why didn't you bring her anyway? This one got attached to her very quickly."

"I don't know," Nette replied, watching Nicky help Lizzy gather her backpack and sweater. "I was hopin Claire would come back. Phoebe might have interfered with them playin together. Have you met their father? Nicky is really pissed at him because of the move."

"No," Mona whispered. "But Lisa says he's really hot."

"What?" Annette asked, and they both laughed.

"You know Lisa," Mona giggled. "She also said he was really nervous about leaving Elizabeth here."

Nette watched Nicky maneuver Elizabeth to the front door. The girls turned at the same time and waved goodbye.

"Let me show you something." Mona led Nette to a corner table and a pile of drawings.

"That looks like Phoebe and Elizabeth," Nette chuckled. Lizzy had effectively created the night sky by using fluorescent marking pens on a sheet of black construction paper.

"You know I'm majoring in art at San Diego State," Mona said.

"Si, seniorita," Nette replied.

"Si, excelente for a six-year-old," said Mona. "Kids have fantastico imaginacions; I love working with them. Sometimes their work is abstract, but they can tell me its story. This is an adventure that Elizabeth says she and Phoebe went on." The little girl in the drawing had bright yellow hair and sat in the crescent of a half-moon. A small brown dog with a green halo sat in her lap.

"This is amazing," Nette whispered and thought about the misty lime aura she sometimes saw around Phoebe's body when she drifted off to sleep.

"Si, she said these clusters are the ribbons in the Milky Way. Cool, huh?"

"What did she say about this?" Nette asked, pointing to the illuminated dog.

"Well, amigo mio, Lizzy said that sometimes Phoebe shines like one of the stars in the sky. This is special, si?"

"Si," Nette whispered.

Annette found Phoebe curled up in her favorite wicker chair on the back porch when she parked her bicycle beside the railing. "Hello, my little girl," she sighed when Phoebe raised her head. She hopped down, raced into the kitchen, and danced around her feet until Annette held out her arms. She sprang into them and immediately received generous hugs and scratches on the head. The little dog reciprocated with licks to the face.

"Phoebe! No! No! Stop! You know I can't stand that," Nette cried, darting her head from side to side to avoid the doggy kisses. "Somebody really missed you today," Annette crooned to her confidant as she carried her down the hall to the bedroom, moving her head back and forth to avoid Phoebe's constant attempts to lick her face. She raised a window and fell backward onto the bed of printed bayou foliage. "Shh, listen," she whispered. Phoebe snuggled close, and they listened to Robby picking out a tune on the guitar. "So, what's up with you and Elizabeth?" she whispered to Phoebe.

Phoebe grunted and rolled onto her back. Annette took the bait and scratched her belly.

"Stop tryin to change the subject," Nette said, propping herself up on one arm. "You know what I'm talkin about. She's impressionable, and you shouldn't encourage her."

Phoebe sneezed, rolled back on her belly, and snuggled close again.

"Quit bein all sweet; she needs to make friends with little girls her age, like Claire."

Phoebe sat up and whined and then barked at her master.

"Okay, I started it with the magic show," Nette conceded. "That's on me. We've talked about this, we have to be careful, especially around people we don't know, or they will mistake your talent for somethin else."

Phoebe whined as if in agreement, and they both lay down to listen to Robby.

"This reminds me of the bands that tune up before the festivals. You see, Phoeb, you don't know this, but people in Louisiana celebrate everything edible, and there's always music. There's the corn festival, pecan festival, pancake festival, rice, crawfish, sugar, soybeans, frogs, and couch on-de-lait, which is a roast pig."

Phoebe wagged her tail in response to her master's reminiscing.

Annette rolled on her side again and put an arm around her little dog. "I've been thinkin."

Phoebe shook her head.

"But Nicky's good at basketball," she argued as if Phoebe had read her thoughts. "I shouldn't talk to Coach Burns…should I?"

Phoebe groaned.

"I know, but she's good enough for JV. I'd like to see her make some friends. She's so angry." She pulled a pillow under her head. "I know that one," she said when Robby's work became a real song. "We haven't heard it in a while. He wrote it for Cass last summer." Nette cuddled closer to her confidant. "What am I thinking now?" she asked. "That Brad blames me for those two tryin' to run away?" Annette rolled to her back again and pressed her hands against her forehead as she replayed Brad's cutting words in her mind. *Interfering nosey woman,* and *why don't you mind your own business?* "This always happens to me. I might become Mr. Harding's enemy before I even meet him. Should I..." she began but was interrupted by Phoebe's tag when she shook her head. "Oh, what do you know about it?" Nette grumbled. "I wonder if Burns might be at the rec center tonight?" she sighed and drifted off.

Phoebe's tag made a soft ping noise when she crept to the edge of the bed. She looked up at a print on the wall of snow-capped mountains that overlooked a meadow of wild daisies. Annette bought it in Colorado when she visited her brother and his family. The yellow flowers in the picture began to sway in the wind, and she could hear the sound of trotting hooves. She could also hear Annette laughing and challenging her brother on horseback. Another wall had a scenic picture of the Gulf coastline that depicted breaking waves and pelicans lifting in the air after feasting on small fish jumping out of the surf. There were fishing trawlers in the distance, and somehow, Phoebe was aware of the oil rigs beyond the horizon. The scene transformed itself to include two small children, a brother and a sister. It, too, took on motion as the two began to run along the shoreline, flinging breadcrumbs in the air for the seagulls that caught the treats in flight. The tide curled in and out, and then, everything was still again. Phoebe turned around to gaze at a five-by-seven photo on the nightstand, taken at a Rylan family reunion. She seemed to remember it even though it had been taken fifteen years before she was born. Two shelves above the nightstand held Annette's treasured memorabilia. A family photo album was on the first shelf, along with a decorative box containing items that belonged to her father. A bottle of English Leather cologne with a stained label was on the shelf above. Annette said her father only wore it on special occasions and had it since high school. It had a wood top and an aged fragrance of its own. Annette took it down occasionally and held the top close to her nose.

Instinct was Phoebe's constant nemesis and a challenge for a creature her size. Once, a feeling of dread came over her at the Mesa Mall. She looked around and couldn't take her eyes off a young woman carrying a small child on her hip. She heard the woman say she was tired and needed to sit down for a minute. Instinct told Phoebe to run out in front of the woman before she reached the benches nearby. The woman stopped to admire the cute little dog whining and wagging her tail. She put her child down, and they spent a whole minute petting and laughing at Phoebe as she went through a series of tricks that included standing on her hind legs, dancing, and rolling over. Annette had just caught up to her when she heard a noise, and shards of glass began to fall from a huge skylight above them. The glass crashed onto a cluster of tables twenty feet from where they were standing, followed by pieces of steel. The woman screamed and clutched her child close to her as pieces of the skylight bounced toward them and came to rest inches from their feet. The woman looked for the little brown dog when she realized the distraction had saved them, but she was nowhere to be found. Mall Security discounted her story, and a reporter from Channel Four News interviewed shoppers and storeowners. No one had seen the mysterious creature. Annette had scooped Phoebe up, tucked her under her sweatshirt, and ran out of the mall. Phoebe was unscathed but suffered through one of Annette's lectures on the way home. Phoebe was feeling another instinct as she stared at the bottle on the top shelf. She knew instinct was something all animals were born with, but she also knew she wasn't like other animals.

Three young men in royal blue polo shirts with *Sun Recreation Center* logo stood behind the counter just inside the double doors. "How's it goin guys?" Annette said and greeted each with a fist bump. The center was open twenty-four hours and offered an abundance of activities. Darren, the shortest of the trio, was tanned with sun-bleached hair and hadn't taken his eyes off her since she entered through the automatic doors. Darren grabbed a towel from the laundry cart and hurried around the counter.

"Hey, Nette," he said, with his broad smile and perfect teeth. "Doris was looking for you; everything okay?"

Annette looked into his anxious blue eyes. "Sure; why wouldn't it be? Is she doin the seven o'clock?"

Darren didn't answer because he was caught up in her southern accent and sweet-smelling hair. She marched to a wall where the schedules were posted, with Darren following behind her. "Doris is in room three; here's a towel," Darren said and held a neatly folded white towel out to her.

"Thanks, Darren," Annette said politely and took the towel. "I'd better hurry before the equipment gets picked over."

Doris was a lean, well-toned black woman. She was extremely shy but had a commanding voice in the aerobics room. "Heard you were lookin for me," Nette said as she and Doris gathered equipment together.

"Yeah," Doris replied. "I was afraid you weren't coming. Ha! I think I had Darren worried too."

"He's such a dork," Nette sighed.

"He's a nice guy, Nette," Doris teased. "Why don't you give him a break and go out with him sometime? You'd make a cute couple."

"I'd be robbin the cradle."

"That doesn't seem to matter these days."

"Not gonna happen, Doris. Jocks like him are all brawn and no brains. I don't want to discuss it." Annette had her own philosophy about men. They were all slackers, heavy into competition, and lacking in responsibility. They were predictable and disappointing, so why bother? She had enough of the dating scene. Friendships worked out better and lasted longer than second-rate relationships that generally led to unpleasant words, hard feelings, and a permanent parting of ways.

"Listen, Nette, I really hate to ask you since you kept the kids for two days last week, but James has this thing at work tomorrow afternoon. I wondered if you'd do my four o'clock at the village if it's not too much trouble." Doris was a fierce instructor. She could pull every ounce of energy out of the wimpiest person yet embarrassed to think she might be an imposition on someone. Annette rarely let her get away with the shyness.

"Doris, quit makin it sound like you're puttin me out or somethin," Annette scolded. "Of course, I'll do it. Besides, the seniors will be grateful."

Doris grinned. "I don't work the seniors like I do this class. Why do you think I asked you to do it?"

"Well, I don't know how to take that, Doris, but I'll do it."

"Thanks, Nette, I owe you one, or one more, I should say. I'll give you an instruction sheet after class."

Annette took her position in the front row and waited for Doris to start the warm-up. "Doris, have you seen Coach Burns tonight?

"I saw him headed to the basketball courts about twenty minutes ago." Doris put her hands on her hips. "Why?"

"What?" Nette asked when she saw Doris glaring at her. "I just want to ask him somethin."

The dynamic instructor shifted her weight to one side. "Say that again. Do you hear yourself? Do you just want to ask him something? We both know how that's gonna turn out. So, you know what? I'm going to tell security to have one of those cameras follow you around."

"Please, not Big Brother!" Annette jibbed. "Besides, it won't be like that. I…think…I can talk to him, outside of a game, that is." Annette made short repetitive nods as she spoke, as she tried to convince her friend.

Doris put her headset on but hesitated before calling the class to attention. "Please wait until I leave before you talk to him." Doris had a nephew who played varsity basketball and two kids of her own in little league that had been officiated or umpired by Tom Burns. The two women often sat together in the bleachers, where Doris listened to Annette complain about his belligerence. The grumbling sometimes turned into verbal protesting and then into a face-to-face confrontation.

Annette left Doris's class wiping sweat from her face with Darren's towel and perspiration soaking her tee shirt and gym shorts. Tom Burns had ejected Annette from three Little League ball games and two basketball games as an officiating umpire. She had managed to shame him from swearing so much, but the league directors felt his discipline produced trophies. She slipped through the swinging doors to the gym, where two full basketball courts were bursting with action. The clatter from shouting players and echoes of bouncing balls collided from every direction. No one noticed the petite young lady with the ponytail and two-toned gray sweats, except the man standing behind her at the water fountain downing a handful of aspirins.

"What are you doing in here, Rylan," he bellowed.

Annette stopped and took a breath before she turned around.

"The women's showers are down on the other end." His voice got louder each time he spoke. "Are you lost?"

Annette gritted her teeth. Tom Burns appeared four times her size as he swayed toward her with water dripping from his chin. He popped the towel he was holding, threw it across his face, and wiped away the sweat and dribble. *What a repulsive sight.* She squeezed her lips together, trying to keep her thoughts to herself. He had large sweat beads on top of his balding head, and his hairy arms and shoulders were sweat-streaked. Annette gulped hard and pasted on her best smile. "Well, hello, Tom," she said politely. She could feel her blood pressure rising. At least she had Doris's super workout as an excuse for her red face. His chest swelled as he looked down at her; full of himself, as usual, and started bragging about how many games he won tonight and the scores. She took deep breaths as she pretended to care about the boasting. He suddenly got silent and looked at her funny, a little freaky.

"What the hell are you doing here anyway?" he asked.

"Well, Tom, I was looking for you," she said, smiling through her teeth.

"What's up?" He wiped his face again because more beads had broken out.

"Look-uh, this new girl moved into my neighborhood."

"Oh yeah?" Tom asked with a sneer.

What am I doin? She straightened her back and forged on. "She goes to Mesa Middle School, eighth grade; I've seen her play basketball. She's pretty good; I mean really good. She's wastin her time in Sparks' class. I think you could teach her somethin." The seconds it took him to respond seemed like forever. She had to be prepared for whatever he said and remain calm. She thought of her conversation with Doris. *It won't be necessary to call security.*

Burns wiped his arms with the towel and then his forehead again.

"So, you think she's that good?" he suddenly growled.

"Yes, I thought maybe you could drop in on her class and see what you think. You've got that eye, you know. She could be as good as Cass."

The coach frowned and then groaned. "Wouldn't that be nice?"

"Her name is Nicky Harding," Annette said nervously.

"Humph, well, since you asked, kid," he said smugly. "I'll look her up."

Annette was anxious to leave the gym, but there was one more thing she needed to say. "She's a little shy, Tom. I mean, if you decide to...just please, give her a break. You know what I mean." Annette took a couple of deep breaths to slow down her pounding heart.

Tom chuckled and then said, "Sure thing, kid." His taunting voice gave her a sick feeling as she left the gym. "Hey, you sissies, ready for a rematch?" he heard him howl.

She was almost to the front doors when someone called her name. Her height was always a disadvantage in crowds. She was sure she had slipped past Darren, who was working with a client in the weight room. Surely Doris was joking about having Security watch her.

"Nette!" the voice was getting closer. "Yo, wait up." Robby was wading his way through a group of people outside the racquetball courts. "Hey, how 'bout some ping pong?" he asked when he caught up to her. He had two orange paddles and a small white ball in his hands.

"Not tonight, Doris pooped me out. Where have you been lately?"

"I've been busy being a supportive friend to the new chick next door."

"You mean Nicky; I met her at Molly's."

"Hum, it's been a while since I've been to Molly's," he grinned.

"Molly's ain't no hook-up place," she laughed. "What are you bein so supportive about?"

"Her old man is a real control freak," he said as they walked through the exit.

"And how do you know that?" Nette asked suspiciously.

"Gimmie a break, Nette; all she wants to do is go back to Chicago. Her father's a doctor, and apparently..."

"Oh great! You know how I feel about doctors," Nette interrupted.

"He's gonna work for Dr. Samuels," Robby added while they crossed the parking lot.

"I'm sorry, I'm just not a fan of doctors," Annette whispered.

"So, why were you on the court just now?" he asked.

"I was talkin to Tom Burns about Nicky. She can really play basketball, and I should warn you, she met Cass."

"Well, that was gonna happen, I guess," he said as they reached Annette's Toyota. "Awe, man, I still can't get over those flags; they are so sick. Jose did a bitchin paint job. I love that American flag montage and how the stars explode from the stripes. My friend Todd wants you to put in a word; he'd like some flames across the hood of his Camaro."

"Yeah, well, he'll have to work for it like I did. I shuttled Jose's kids back and forth to the ballpark all last summer." She unlocked the back of the SUV, and a skateboard rolled out and fell to the ground.

"Seriously, Nette, we need to clean out the back of your 4-Runner," he said, picking up the skateboard.

"It's fine like it is; I never know when we might need somethin."

Phoebe lay on the bed, waiting for the blue digits on the clock to read *7:00,* the time she heard Annette say Doris's aerobics class started, before making her move. She crossed the alley and nudged between two slats to get into the Harding's yard. The door was open, and she heard a man's voice coming from the kitchen. She leaped onto the porch and crept closer to the screen door, slipping under the fitted gas grill cover when the pitch in the man's voice suddenly rose. She lifted the cover with her nose and looked into the kitchen. Nicky's father was apparently lecturing her on rinsing dishes before loading the dishwasher; she was standing beside its open door, staring impatiently at the ceiling. Phoebe heard Lizzy's voice behind her. The light from the kitchen window shone like a spotlight as she sat in a lounge chair in the middle of the yard in her nightgown. She held an action figure doll in each hand while carrying on an animated three-way conversation with them. Phoebe cocked her head and listened as the little girl changed her voice to three different pitches simulating each character. A small pink suitcase containing the action friend's accessories sat on an iron table with a glass top next to her. More of her friends were situated in her lap with their legs pointed straight out in sitting positions.

"I just wanted to make sure you knew exactly how…" Phoebe heard the man's voice again.

"I know how to do this," she heard Nicky argue. "Just leave me alone; why don't you call the hospital and check on that old man or something."

"I did, earlier," he said. "What about homework?" he asked, but there was no reply. Phoebe eased closer. "Well?" he repeated.

"I did it at school," Nicky finally said. "Please, I've been doing dishes since I was seven."

"Wait," he said. "Don't put the leftovers down the disposal; I have storage containers."

"Of course, you do," Nicky moaned.

Phoebe heard Elizabeth giggling and thought she might have been caught, but the little girl was still occupied with her dolls. She was sitting on her legs now and making her little friends dance in front of her on the chair. When she looked back, she saw a pair of white Nikes standing very near the door.

"Not the bulletin board," she heard Nicky groan.

"You'll have made a lot of friends by April," her father said.

"Erase that, I don't want a lame birthday party!" Nicky argued.

Phoebe crept closer to the door but heard Elizabeth's voice again. She would surely cause a scene if she saw her. She was standing in the lounge chair, and her dolls were on the glass tabletop. Their arms and heads were pointed upward as if watching her. She placed one foot on the armrest and then the other. Her pale blue nightgown hung below her ankles. The chair started to rock from side to side, and Phoebe's ears straightened.

"I think I can touch one of them," Elizabeth said to her tiny friends observing from their positions on the table. The chair began to tilt.

There was an ivy plant on a pedestal flower stand near the edge of the porch. Phoebe quickly pounced against it. The stand teetered, and the ceramic flowerpot wobbled around on its round base. She pushed it again, harder, and the pedestal stand fell over. The flowerpot crashed onto the concrete floor. Dirt and pieces of the pot flew everywhere; Phoebe scampered into the shadows.

Tony was trying to get Nicky to listen to his idea for a birthday present. When they heard the pot shatter, she had just opened her mouth in protest over putting a goalpost in the backyard. They looked out the open door at the same time, but Tony was the first to react when he saw Lizzy's right foot tangled in the hem of her gown and lose her footing on the arms of the lounge chair. "Oh, my God!"

Tony's voice sounded like a gush of wind. He grabbed the door, and his body exploded through the screen door. He was across the porch, and the yard before Nicky had time to take her first step toward the door. He arrived at Lizzy's side with his arms spread open just as the chair toppled out from under her before her head could hit the glass tabletop.

Nicky didn't have time to let out a sound. She stood at the door holding onto the door frame, not believing how fast her father had moved and that he had actually caught Elizabeth in time. The screen hinges had sprung past their limits, and the door swung freely and was lopsided next to the outside wall. Thoughts of how Lizzy could have broken her neck or fractured her skull came later.

"Lizzy!" Tony gasped. "What were you thinking?" he cried as he sat in the damp grass, cradling her in his arms.

"Daddy, I was trying to touch that star." Her eyes sparkled with delight as she looked up, and then she reached for her tiny friends who had fallen over on their sides. "I almost did it," she said to them. Their heads and arms were still extended outward, and it looked like they were now reaching out to her.

Tony looked up, hoping to see something magnificent that would explain why his daughter had attempted such a dangerous stunt. But there was nothing unusual in the sky, not a falling star or a comet, not even an airplane. He stood up and held Lizzy close like a baby. He carried her to her room, passing Nicky in the kitchen. Their eyes met briefly when he passed. "Take care of the kitchen, will you, Nicky?" he whispered.

Nicky tried to pull the screen door closed, but the hinges were sprung and bent, and the door was no longer square with the casing. She turned on the porch light. Dirt and ivy were scattered across the floor, along with pieces of the flower pot. "Lucky that happened," she whispered while turning off the porch light and closing the door.

Phoebe emerged from her hiding place and sniffed the dirt, the ivy leaves, and a piece of the broken ceramic pot. She pawed at the door; it opened just enough to allow her to scoot inside; the gurgling dishwasher diffusing her entry. She fondly looked for Jim and Julia sitting at the kitchen table drinking coffee, then trotted down the hall where she knew the bedrooms were. She followed the sound of the man's voice in the master bedroom at the end of the hall. She found him sitting on the side of the bed in the dark, whispering to himself; his hands folded together and pressed against his forehead.

"What am I going to do?" she heard him say. "Maybe I should have stayed with Betty. How can I possibly keep an eye on Lizzy 24/7? And Nicky is always going to hate me. I don't know if I can do this…God, please help me." He wiped his face with his hands and lay down. A clock on the night table read 8:00; her master would be home soon. When she turned to leave, she heard Elizabeth whisper her name loudly from the adjacent room, so she darted inside and jumped into her bed.

"I thought that was you. I missed you today," she whispered gleefully. Phoebe licked her on the cheek. "You missed me too?" Phoebe licked her cheek again while Elizabeth tried to muffle her giggling. Phoebe stayed with Elizabeth until she fell asleep.

Chapter 14

Tony looked up at the cloudy sky from the porch, recalling Brad's winter forecast. "When did he say I would see the sun?" he muttered to himself. "I should go for a run like I used; maybe it'll clear my head after last night." He had been up since 5:00 thinking about Lizzy. He turned to see what had crashed on the cement the night before. It had forced his attention to the backyard. But there was nothing; no evidence of the broken flowerpot he saw in his peripheral vision as he rushed by. The decorative ceramic pot containing the ivy was sitting on the pedestal stand, intact and without a chip mark. "There's an explanation for this," he whispered as he went to the dryer to retrieve his sweats. While running and mulling over last night's events, he met another runner wearing black sweats embossed with an emblem of three crosses. They nodded and continued in opposite directions. There was heavy traffic on Canyon Road so he turned left and ran until he reached Gold Coast, then trekked back toward Antrim. He trod past a church and saw the man in the black sweats jog into the rectory. The marquee outside displayed Mass times for The Mount Calvary Catholic Church and bore the emblem of three crosses. A half minute later, as he approached Jewel St., he recognized the white bicycle that had nearly run over him in his driveway. It was exiting the alley behind his house. He watched as the rider turned into Florence, the street that led to Molly's Day Care.

Nicky frowned at her father when they met in the hall as she and Elizabeth exited the bathroom.

"Nicky, did you pick up the ivy plant or whatever I heard fall last night?" he panted.

"Why is Daddy all sweaty?" Elizabeth asked.

"Who cares," Nicky moaned, nudged her into her bedroom, and closed the door.

"My hair is wavy like Mommy's; yours is straight like Daddy's," Lizzy said as she looked in the mirror while Nicky brushed her hair.

"I'm nothing like him," Nicky replied and slammed the brush on the dresser.

"I meant our hair." Lizzy looked at the glamour shot of their mother on Nicky's dresser, desperately trying to keep Phoebe's late-night visit a secret.

"Look at what I found in one of my boxes." Nicky handed her a case that contained a *Mary Poppins* video.

"I thought it was lost," Lizzy gasped. "It's my favorite; Mommy and I used to watch it."

"I know; I thought it might help you feel at home."

Elizabeth clutched the video case to her chest and looked at her mother's picture. "Just like home."

Nicky sat at the breakfast table with her head propped up on one arm, playing with her cereal. Lizzy held the Mary Poppins video tightly in one arm as she ate, keeping her lips pressed together in between bites to make sure she didn't accidentally blurt out anything.

"Lizzy," her father suddenly said. Lizzy's eyes widened; she sat up straight, fearing she might have said something without knowing it. "About last night," he continued. "I want you to know that I'm not mad at you, okay, but please don't try and climb on something so unstable again."

"Okay, Daddy," she sighed with much relief. Suddenly her nose began to sting. "Daddy, what's that smell?" she asked, rubbing her nose.

"I know; I found a bottle of cologne on my dresser this morning. Did one of you put it there?"

"No, Daddy," Elizabeth answered.

Nicky shook her head with disgust because of the odor.

"I picked it up by the wooden top, but it slipped off and spilled. I got a little on my pants and maybe on the floor." He turned to Nicky. "Nicky, did you see what fell last night?"

"The ivy plant," Nicky snipped. "It's all over the place out there."

"No, it's not; go look for yourself."

"Ask her," Nicky sneered, frowning at her sister. "Look at her; she's had a guilty face all morning."

"I didn't do anything," Lizzy whined when her father turned to her. "I was in bed all night, I promise."

Tony looked at Nicky again, and then it came to him; she was messing with him. It had to be her.

"Oh, okay," he laughed. "I get it. Well, anyway, I left a message for Mrs. Sparks yesterday, but she didn't call me back. How was P.E.?"

"Just great," Nicky replied.

"I'll try again today," Tony said.

"Don't bother. If I want to play on their lousy team, I'll take care of it myself." Nicky got up and put her bowl in the sink. She looked at the ivy plant sitting on its pedestal through the window. *What the...that's weird, it was in a hundred pieces last night.*

"It was her and the idiot from next door that cleaned up the mess outside, wasn't it?" Tony asked Lizzy when Nicky left the kitchen. She looked up at him and squeezed the Mary Poppins case tighter.

"What's that in your hand?" Tony asked.

"Mommy and I used to watch it together."

"Put it by the TV, and we'll watch it tonight," he said. "I'll call my boss today and tell him we're here."

"You'll be home tonight?"

"Yes, of course," he replied. "We'll watch it after dinner."

"Okay," Lizzy said, smiling. "But you probably should change clothes."

Tony changed his pants and wore a sports jacket, but the smell seemed embedded in his sinuses. He called the Samuels Family Practice from his cell after dropping the girls off at school. He watched raindrops as they accumulated on his windshield while the perky receptionist told him Dr. Rick was somewhere in the hospital and hadn't made it to the office yet, but she was sure it was okay to stop by. The University Hospital was a sprawling twenty acres, yet for some reason, Tony couldn't resist turning into the emergency entrance when he saw the large white-on-red directional arrow. He parked the Olds near the doors and ran through the now steadily falling rain. He could hear sirens in the distance and deduced two ambulances were thirty seconds out. Tony walked through the sliding doors and brushed the rain from his jacket. An ambulance wheeled in behind him, and as he would expect, there was a commotion. He heard the words *traffic accident* and *internal bleeding,* and the adrenaline began to flow.

The second ambulance arrived, *aneurism, stroke*. Doctors and nurses appeared from all directions. It had been a long time since he felt the rush the E.R. sparked inside him. Giving in to the impulse, he ran alongside the second gurney spouting his assessment. He asked for vitals, but no one answered. In ten seconds, the group had disappeared behind two swinging doors, and the corridor was suddenly quiet again. Tony stood frozen with his mouth ajar. He was sweating; his chest was heaving, and he scarcely heard the woman standing next to him.

"Are you all right, sir?" she said.

Tony swung around. Was someone asking for his help? No, it was a nurse in a pink uniform gingerly reaching for his elbow as if he were in need of assistance. He looked for a nametag.

"Are you a family member?" she asked.

"No…*Barbara*. I'm fine, I'm a doctor," he puffed. He saw that she wasn't convinced. She took him by the arm with both hands and gave him a gentle tug.

"Would you like to sit down for a minute?" she asked, trying to extend her most effectual care.

Tony shook his head and smiled at her. "I appreciate your concern," he replied. "I used to work in the ER, and I thought I could, well, I thought I might…well, yes, I'm fine."

She handed him a white hand towel which he took and wiped the sweat from his forehead.

"Actually, I'm looking for Dr. Samuels' office…Dr. Richard Samuels."

He noticed the nurse following his every motion with precaution; her arms extended in case he might weave.

"Doctor Samuels is on the fifth floor," she answered, looking at him warily.

"Yes, yes, the fifth floor, right."

"Go straight through these doors." She moved one hand just enough to point to a second set of swinging doors. "Just bear to the left, and you'll see a service elevator; I'll gladly escort you."

"I think I can find it," Tony whispered. "Thank you." Tony put the hand towel in one of her open hands.

"Are you sure?" she said, following him to the swinging doors.

"I've been here before, just not through this entrance," he replied.

"You'll be getting out at the rear entrance; you'll want to use the set of buttons at the rear of the elevator when you reach the fifth floor," she called after him.

Tony didn't recognize anything when he stepped into the empty fifth-floor hallway, and there were no directional signs showing the way to the Samuels Family Practice. So, he followed the sound of a woman's voice to the end of the hallway. It led to an open door that was a small room behind the reception desk of The Samuels Family Practice waiting room. A woman with stringy blonde hair sat behind the counter. She slowly pushed her swivel chair in a circle with one toe as she talked on her cell. She dropped the phone when she saw him.

"Dr. Harding!" she squealed. "You're here! That was you down in the ER? She leaped from her chair and took hold of his hand. "I'm Tonya! You remember me, don't you?"

"Um…." The receptionist sitting behind the counter two months ago had puffy red hair with green highlights.

"I was here when you came for your formal interview. We have been anxiously awaiting your return. Let me tell everybody, oh, I mean, let me go find Dr. Rick for you. Wait right here." She wore a yellow net skirt that fluttered like wings as she trotted around the counter and down a hallway.

Tony walked to the counter's edge and looked across the waiting area that would soon be part of his daily life. There were two rows of cushioned armchairs lined back-to-back in the middle of the room and more lining the walls. Light filled the room through partially opened woven vertical blinds. Three patients were sitting on a long sofa in front of the windows, staring at him from around a large broad-leaf potted plant that bordered the reception area. He smiled and nodded his head at the two women and one man as if to say hello, trying to project some semblance of professionalism after the scene Tonya made. He turned and looked behind him when their focus suddenly shifted to something over his shoulder. Tonya was hissing and waving wildly for him to join her in the hallway.

"Please make yourself at home in Dr. Rick's office; he will be right with you," Tonya chirped. "Can I get you anything, Dr. Harding…coffee…tea?"

He shook his head and smiled, indicating that he was fine, and she left him alone in the large office. Neurology reference books filled one-half of the doctor's west wall. It had been Rick Samuels' specialty for the majority of his career. He performed surgery less often now, content with the general practice he was building, although he did consult on special cases. The other half of the wall held a variety of reference books. The north wall was decorated with photos of Dr. Samuels and various medical field dignitaries including three general surgeons and four governors. There were certificates and degrees and awards and a gold plaque from The Group, a partner of the state-run hospital which also owned Mesa Village Retirement Community according to Charlie Warren. A bust sculpture of Hypocrites stood on a pedestal in the center of the library wall with a pair of high-back Victorian chairs on either side. The father of medicine's eyes seemed to follow Tony as he walked across the room toward the tall windows behind Dr. Samuels' desk. The double doors to his right were closed for his first visit but were now open. He saw a long conference table inside with several rolled-up blueprints on top and more reference bookshelves. The windows overlooked a small private courtyard with a fountain and a red brick circle walkway. He noticed a couple sitting on one of the iron benches facing the fountain. They seemed very involved with each other as they sat talking. "*It must be nice to have someone to share your life with.*" But Carol never got his passion for mending broken bodies. *Should I have given it all up and fixed her instead?* He thought about his best friend Harry, who interned with him at St. Joe's. Harry's father was a partner in a law firm that had offices in Willis Tower. He didn't have to struggle to pay his way through medical school as Tony did. He was Elizabeth's godfather, and they celebrated together when he got the acceptance call from Dr. Rick Samuels. He would never forget the night

Harry came to him with a heavy heart. Tony was putting his name on the shift board when he walked up from behind and touched him on the shoulder. He motioned him into a storage room and closed the door. He stammered around at first, not knowing how to begin. With considerable persistence on Tony's part, he finally told him that he had been checking on a homebound patient out by Cellular Field when he decided to grab a bite to eat before catching the red line south. He popped into a small pub to grab a quick sandwich. Harry's words were as hard to hear as they were for his friend to say. He was eating at the bar when he looked up in the mirror and thought he saw Carol sitting in a corner booth at the back of the pub. He slid off the barstool and walked over to say hello until he realized she wasn't alone. Harry was reluctant to go on with the account but told him she was with a man. They were nestled close together. The man had on a high-dollar gray suit with a matching silk shirt and red power tie. They were touching each other intimately. He returned to the bar stool and pretended to eat his sandwich but the sight had made him so sick he couldn't. He watched Carol slide off her jacket in the mirror; then there was a long kiss, and she allowed the man's hands to touch her everywhere.

"You know," Harry said, trying to console him as Tony braced himself against the storage room wall. "My father's firm can help you get custody of the girls. They have their own investigators. They can catch her in the act like I did, and then you can sue for sole custody."

Tony hung his head, unable to respond.

"There must be a security camera in the pub," he continued. "If we act fast, we might be able to get a court order."

Tony slid down the wall, sat on a cardboard box, and cradled his head in his arms. Harry had only told him what he already knew. The devastating day of reckoning had arrived. "Harry, we're divorced; she can see whoever she wants," Tony moaned. "And I don't want to bring Elizabeth into this; everyone thinks she's mine. I want to keep it that way. And I don't even have a home; I live here at the hospital."

"We'll get her on the alcohol and the drugs," Harry insisted. "My father will convince Social Services to make a surprise visit. You can count on Betty and Catherine to help you with the girls."

"She always manages to clean up her act when the court hearing comes around." Tony pounded his forehead against his forearms. "No judge will give me full custody."

Harry patted his friend on the shoulder. "It would help your case if you'd let my father use the Elizabeth issue."

"I won't do that." He took a deep breath and then relented and gave him permission to call his father. Tony called home after regaining his composure. A babysitter answered. Not realizing who he was, she told him Carol was meeting her husband at work, and they were going out for a late dinner. Four hours later, paramedics rushed through the emergency room doors with three accident victims. A mail truck had gone through a yellow caution light and T-boned a woman driver. She was wearing a seat belt, but alcohol could have been involved, and they lost her vitals on the way. The truck driver was pronounced dead at the scene, and his body was sent straight to the morgue.

Tony's team was busy in trauma room three, working on a serious gunshot wound, when Harry slipped through the swinging doors. Tony was bent over the table, and his team was dutifully watching their monitors as they hung IVs and slapped instruments into his hands as he called for them. Time seemed in short supply for the team working so hard to stop the bleeding. Tony knew someone had entered the room by the rise and fall of the noise level from outside the corridor. It wasn't the usual thump and swish sound of someone rushing in. Someone was wary of entering, cautious, hesitant, so Tony looked up expecting to see a lost relative. But instead, it was Harry, and he immediately knew something was terribly wrong. He made a gesture, pointing over his shoulder, to the other side of the doors. His mouth was moving, but nothing was coming out.

Carol's funeral was three days later. The darkest days of Tony's life followed. He overheard things like Carol had finally found her peace, but it felt like her demons were still hanging around and trying to find someone else to possess;

perhaps they were trying to seize control of him. Nicky treated him like a stranger, and Elizabeth asked endless questions he didn't want to answer. Betty and her husband John took them in. Carl Harding, Sr. pulled strings at police headquarters downtown. The retired fireman's years of heroism had gained him the utmost respect from all city departments. It had been agreed that the responding officer's report would read that the third fatality, the well-dressed man in the gray suit and red tie, had been standing at the corner hailing a cab and was an innocent victim of circumstance. This account wouldn't be questioned because, fortunately, he had not been wearing a seatbelt and had been thrown from the car, coming to rest in a proximity that would make the story work. Tony's mother passed away six months later, which brought him further down the slope of despair. He always thought of his mother as a saint for putting up with his father. Carl Sr. was rude and crude, and Tony hated the way he treated the family. By the time Arthur Gallows came along, he was more than ready to make a change. He was tired of his children overhearing people whisper about their mother. They all needed a fresh start somewhere far away from Chicago. The rain was coming down hard again, as if the sky was shedding tears for him. The couple below jumped up and ran inside the building. "*I did love Carol like that once. I would have married her even if she hadn't been pregnant.*"

"Well, Dr. Harding," said the amiable voice behind him. "You have created quite a stir throughout my office this morning."

Tony turned from the window and the grim memories. The tall and tanned white-haired Rick Samuels approached, and Tony shook his hand.

"It's great to finally be here."

"You looked a million miles away standing there; or perhaps just a couple a thousand…Chicago?"

Tony didn't want to admit how right he was. "I was looking at the amazing campus; I'm not used to so much space."

Dr. Samuels gave Tony's hand one last squeeze. "Please, sit down," he said and pointed to a leather chair in front of his desk. "How long have you been in town?"

"Almost a week now," Tony answered and gingerly held on to the armrests of the rich brown leather chair as he sunk into it.

"Have you taken the kids to the zoo yet…Sea World? Two girls, right?" Dr. Samuels sat down behind his desk and leaned forward. "You've got to show them the zoo. My grandson loves it. He's only five, but he knows all the endangered species that live there." He turned around and picked up a photo from a credenza behind him.

"Well, not yet," Tony said, shifting in the chair and trying to get comfortable. "My daughters are in school. We'll get around to it soon, I'm sure." Tony leaned forward to look at the photo. "Your grandson?"

Dr. Samuel's raised his eyebrows with pride. "Ah, yes, that little slugger right there." It was a photo of a softball team; he pointed to a boy kneeling on his right knee with a catcher's mitt cupped over his left and leaning on a baseball bat. A small dog sat beside him. The team wore red caps and shirts with *Samuels Family Practice* printed in script across the front.

"Great looking team," Tony said, nodding. "They're all laughing; that says a lot."

"Absolutely," Dr. Samuels agreed.

"Is that the team mascot sitting next to your grandson?" Tony asked.

"I guess you could call her that; some call her the assistant coach." The doctor rubbed his right thumb on the glass just over the face of the woman standing at the far-right end of the back row. "This is their coach," he whispered and nodded his head. "She took them to the finals last season. You'll get to see them in action this spring, I hope. I haven't convinced this little gal to re-up yet, but I'm working on it. The kids will do anything to please her."

Tony could see the radiance on the proud grandfather's face. "And that must be the rest of your family," he said, acknowledging several more pictures on the credenza.

Dr. Samuels put the team photo back and introduced him to the rest of the family, who were smiling from within the decorative frames. "This is my wife, Lorraine; we were on a trip in the Bahamas here. This is my daughter Myra, her husband Greg, and my two oldest grandchildren, Zack and Hope. And my son Kevin, a single father like you, and Daniel."

"You have a great-looking family, Dr. Samuels." Tony pulled his wallet out of his jacket and opened it. "This is Nicky and Elizabeth."

"Different as night and day, I see," he laughed. "Like my two. Your oldest looks like you, and the little one must take after her mother."

An awkward sensation rushed over Tony at the mention of his wife. "I have a picture of Carol," he said as he flipped the small plastic pages. "Ah, here we are. This was our engagement picture."

"Yes, just like her mother. You have two beautiful daughters."

"Thank you. I'm very proud of them."

Dr. Samuels stood up. "I have an idea," he said and walked around the desk. "I always get here early to beat the traffic, and I just finished up with my last patient. I'll give you another tour of the place and then take you to lunch."

Tony pulled himself out of the chair. "I was hoping I could look around again and sort of get my bearings before Monday."

"You can come in any time you want," Dr. Samuels said as they walked toward the door. "Tonya has your key card; it opens all office doors and the clinic at the Mesa Village Retirement Community. We open it once or twice a week depending on the demand as a convenience for the residents; some can't drive anymore. Oh, and by the way, please call me Rick."

"I practically live across the street from Mesa Village," Tony said.

"Yes, I know," Rick nodded.

Tony was more than ready to sink his teeth into the familiar. He had been a fish out of water for too long. It was an uphill battle getting to this point, and he was eager to get his future underway. He looked forward to seeing patients, touching medical instruments, and exercising his knowledge. Family practice would never be as electrifying as the ER or trauma, but it would give him a chance to balance his craft with fatherhood.

"Your office is right across the hall. Feel free to start moving your personal things in today if you like." Rick led him to a walnut door across the hall from his office. Tony looked at the tile on the door with his name on it before opening it, but they were all suddenly distracted by a commotion in the reception area, where there was a woman demanding to see Rick. Tonya was trying to get a word in and explain that he was busy, but she was insisting that he would see her if she would just tell him she was there.

"Someone you know?" Tony asked.

"I'm afraid so," Rick sighed. "You'd better hide in your office."

"Hide?" Tony asked.

"I'll come and get you when she's gone."

Tony caught sight of the auburn-haired woman in the dark blue suit and red heels as he opened the door. She was walking with great purpose toward Rick.

"I'm sorry, Dr. Rick," Tonya fretted as she trotted behind the woman. "I tried to stop her, but…"

"That's all right, Tonya. We know how rude my sister-in-law can be." Rick looked at Tony, who had only made it as far as the threshold. "Tony Harding, this is Sally Samuels. Doctor Harding is joining my staff next week. This is his office." Then he looked at Tony. "Sally is a reporter, Dr. Harding, so be careful what you say in front of her. She doesn't forget anything."

"Nice to meet you, Mrs. Samuels," Tony said politely. Sally's amazing green eyes widened when she looked at Tony. "It's so nice to meet you, Dr. Harding." Then she turned the emerald jewels to Rick. "Where have you been hiding Dr. Harding, Rick? How long has he been here?"

"Okay," Rick said with a start. "Dr. Harding, I'll be with you shortly." He nudged Tony inside his office and closed the door. "Tonya, make sure Dr. Harding gets his key card," he said. "Sally, in my office," he ordered.

Tony's office was half the size of Dr. Samuels's yet larger than any at St. Joe's. There was a cherry wood desk with a high-back leather chair, two armchairs that faced the desk, a file cabinet, and bookshelves on opposite walls. There was a single window with a view of an adjoining building and a parking lot. *Carol would have loved this. Well, maybe not the view; she would have complained about the view.*

"Well, I see you have your working clothes on, Sally," Rick growled, referring to the fitted blue suit and red stilettos. "I thought your editor would have fired you by now. I have no quotes for you if that's what you're here for; at least, nothing you can print." Rick peered out the window over the courtyard while Sally took the liberty of sitting in the brown leather chair in front of his desk.

"David is quite furious with me," Sally said softly, "the worst I've seen, in fact, but the board will decide my fate. Rick, you have to understand that Randy left me no choice." She scanned the ceiling but didn't see any obvious security cameras. "Walter is clearly innocent, and your brother is in too deep to drop the charges, even though the autopsy page I found cleared him. What would you have done?"

"Well, for one thing, I would have presented my evidence to the judge before printing it in the newspaper," Rick roared.

"Yes, well, I'm afraid Judge Yeager's reputation has always been to do favors from the bench," she returned. "He would have found some sort of legal grounds to disallow it, and the trial would have continued, leaving Walter to spend the rest of his life in prison."

"What is it with you and the homeless? Why was it necessary to save this one and screw your husband? Most of them are indigent alcoholics and drug users that would be better off confined."

"Walter shouldn't go to prison just because he's homeless. He was dragged into this to serve a purpose. I can't believe you'd minimize his situation this way. San Diego has wonderful shelters for people like him; I've showcased them many times, just like I did Mesa Village. Do you remember what I did for your retirement community in Mesa? Your project is a landmark thanks to the special sections I dedicated to it."

"It was an idea that would have succeeded with or without your support," Rick growled. "I don't have time or the desire to debate with you. Why are you here?" he asked sharply, knowing full well that the unscrupulous reporter wouldn't be in his office unless she had a reason. Any minute she would start pumping him for information. The cell phone in Rick's coat pocket vibrated as Sally bowed her head to gather her thoughts.

"I want to tell you in person how sorry I am for upsetting you and your family, and Randy. He's staying at your house, isn't he? How is he?"

"How do you think?" Rick said after reading the screen. "His case is spiraling into the depths of a mistrial as we speak; you may have ruined his career. You have some nerve coming up here pouting and saying you're sorry." Rick started toward the door. "It's my brother you screwed, remember."

"Rick, I love Randy," she said, turning in the chair and following his movement across the room. "I didn't do it for the story; I did it to jolt some sense into him."

"Blood is thicker than water, Sally," Rick said and opened the office door. "Randy will be staying with Lorraine and me until you move out. Now, I have an emergency downstairs."

Sally stood and walked slowly toward the door. She glanced at the statue of Hypocrites and then into the conference room where the rolled-up blueprints were neatly stacked on top of the table. "I see you finished the addition." She glared at him with her bright green eyes.

"Yes," he said, staring back at her.

"Will Dr. Harding be helping you with whatever you're doing in there?"

"It's where I go to concentrate," Rick growled.

"Problems concentrating, Rick?" she said, frowning as if actually concerned, but he only glared at her in silence. "I'm sorry about the direction this took, Rick," she said. "But Randy's principal donor has too much control over him, and others. We were a good team once."

"Teammates don't stab each other in the back!" Rick said sharply.

"Surely, you've seen it for yourself; how Randy has changed," Sally hissed. "Don't you care what happens to your brother? After what almost happened to Kevin?" she whispered as if someone were listening. Rick stepped aside as if inviting her into the hall. "Please tell Randy I'll be out by tonight." She looked back at the statue of Hypocrites. "I know you cherish everything Lorraine gives you, but honestly, that is a dreadful piece of artwork."

Rick watched Sally as she walked toward the reception area, then took the cell phone from his coat pocket and pressed a number.

"Your wife just left my office; we need to talk," he said and walked across the hall. Tony was standing next to Tonya, holding his key card, when he knocked and walked in.

"What did *she* want?" Tonya sneered when she saw Rick standing in the doorway holding his cell phone.

"She's probing as usual," Rick replied.

"I can't believe she showed up here demanding to see you after what she did to your brother, Randy," Tonya scorned.

"Wait!" Tony interrupted. "She's the one that wrote the story in the paper; the one that's all over the news…about your brother?"

Rick took a deep breath and shook his head with what appeared to be great impatience. "Yes, that's her, and my brother may lose his career."

"Oh man, I'm sorry. I've been so busy moving and enrolling the kids in school that I didn't put it together. No wonder you're so upset."

"She just walked past me, Dr. Rick," Tonya said.

"I know, Tonya," Rick assured her. "Next time she shows up, call security. Tony, son, I'm going to have to rain-check the lunch. I've got a call in to Randy and I'm needed downstairs in radiology."

"Of course, of course," Tony replied. "I can't imagine what your family must be going through. I would like to look around the office and the hospital, too, if you don't mind."

"Sure, help yourself," Rick replied. "I will call Lorraine and see what her plans are for this week. I want you and your girls over for dinner."

"You don't have to…" Tony began.

"Oh yes, I do. I will see if Arthur is in town, too, and call Myra and her bunch. I think Myra's oldest son is the same age as your Nicky, and my grandson Daniela year younger than Elizabeth."

"That would be nice, thank you," Tony conceded.

Rick looked down at his phone and frowned, "Radiology again."

Tonya moved closer to Tony and gave him a playful smile after Rick closed the door. "What areas of the hospital are you interested in, Dr. Harding? I'll be glad to give you the tour."

"Shouldn't you stay here and take care of the reception desk?"

"Well, I suppose I should," she grinned. "Darn!"

"I'd like to see ICU and the emergency area; perhaps cardiac and trauma."

"Well, you're going to want to wear this." She opened a closet door. "You have four lab coats; we handle the laundering." She took one of the white coats off a hanger and handed it to him. "Your ID card is in your top right desk drawer. Be sure and wear it when you're in any of the UCSD buildings."

Tony handed Tonya his sports jacket while he tried on the white coat. "Fits perfect," he said, pressing his hands against the front of it.

"Yes, it does," Tonya sighed admiringly, "perfectly."

The ID tag had his name, picture, and ID number, along with the *Association of The Group,* printed in small letters under the UCSD logo.

"You know," Tonya sighed, "you're the last Dr. Rick hired. I think he was waiting for the right person to put in this office." She smiled and turned the flirting on again. "Well, have fun, Dr. Harding. I'll alert the floors that you're touring. Sure, wish I could be the one to show you off." She turned and left his office with an obvious twist in her hips.

Tony went to the ER first and properly introduced himself to Barbara and the rest of the staff on duty. He learned the auto accident victim from earlier was in surgery, and the other patient had burst an artery in his brain and had bled out. He was glad to learn that Lewis had been discharged. He met a woman on the elevator and her daughter, clutching a dark brown stuffed dog.

Tony greeted them and pressed the second-floor button to ICU.

"I'm sorry for using this elevator," the woman apologized. "It's so much easier to find a parking place around back.

"I'm sure it's fine," Tony replied. "What's your name?" Tony asked the little girl.

"Crystal," she said shyly.

"Who's your friend?" he asked, patting the stuffed toy on the head.

"Phoebe," she replied.

"Phoebe?" Tony repeated; "unusual, and yet, somehow a popular name."

"When I told Molly at our daycare that we were moving up to Del Mar last summer, she made Crystal this stuffed toy as a going away present."

"Molly's Day Care?" Tony repeated.

"Yes, I think leaving Molly's was the worst part of moving," the mother said.

"My daughter is going there after school. There was a magic show on the first day, and she came home singing. I think my fourteen-year-old daughter likes it there too, although she won't admit it."

"Did you take the oath?" Crystal interrupted.

"Oh, I think that has something to do with one of Molly's games," the mother explained.

"Well, Lizzy did mention…" Tony said, rubbing his chin. "Something about an oath."

"I don't really know; that was just one of their games."

"Daddy broke his arm, and Phoebe's gonna use her magic to help him get well," Crystal declared and then caressed her stuffed poodle.

"That's great," Tony replied. "Us doctors need all the help we can get." The elevator door opened, and Tony stepped out onto the ICU floor. He introduced himself to nurses and technicians and visited patients randomly throughout the hospital. He ran into Crystal and her mother again when he was on the fourth floor. Her mother smiled and nodded, but Crystal, minus the stuffed dog, put a finger to her lips as if telling him to be quiet. She mouthed something to him that he thought was, *"Remember…it's a secret."* Tony smiled and winked at her, then pulled her father's chart. Mr. Magnoli was on his third round of antibiotics for an infection that had developed after surgery on his broken arm. He was alert and watching television when Tony entered his room. The humeral medial epicedial area had been crushed, and his surgery had been tedious. Two surgeons used screws and a special cement to put it back together. There was good reason to expect a long, slow recovery and months of therapy, provided the infection cleared up, and his arm didn't need amputation. Tony gingerly touched his fingers and introduced himself. Crystal had placed the brown stuffed dog between the injured elbow and his rib cage.

"Yeah, my little girl told me to leave Phoebe right here," Mr. Magnoli told Dr. Harding when he asked if he was comfortable with the stuffed toy so close to the point of pain. "And you know my arm's feeling better already."

Tony stepped into the elevator and pressed the button for the fifth floor, but it went all the way down first. He was shocked when the doors opened on the first floor, and Rebecca from San Diego Cable Technology stepped inside. She had on a red miniskirt and a white blouse. She stood against the wall and smiled bashfully.

"Dr. Harding, right?" she cooed. Tony nodded uncomfortably. "Second floor, please," she said. Tony pressed the number two button. "Your office is on five?" she asked, noticing it was the only lighted number.

"Samuels Family Practice," he divulged reluctantly. The car beeped, and the doors opened again. She stepped out and turned to look at him over her shoulder.

"I've been meaning to find an internist," she whispered. Tony was grateful that the doors closed quickly.

Chapter 15

Tony snatched the pink courtesy notice from under his windshield wiper. There was a one-hour time limit in the emergency parking area. A red Mercedes pulled up behind the Olds as he was wading up the paper. Sally Samuels was behind the wheel.

"Uh-oh," he muttered to himself.

The passenger side window lowered. Sally leaned over the seat and looked up at him. "Dr. Harding!"

"Yes, ma'am," Tony replied and walked to the window.

"I thought I missed you," she said. "You're in the wrong parking area."

"I know," Tony replied, showing her the crumpled notice. "Nice car, Mrs. Samuels, red and everything."

"I was hoping to take you to lunch if you don't have plans."

Tony was starving, but he didn't want to go anywhere with Sally Samuels.

"No, ma'am," Tony replied. "I don't have plans, and I don't mean to be rude, but my boss would be pretty upset to know I even talked to you."

"Well, that's honest," she replied. She leaned further down over the seat so she could see him better. "He wouldn't have to know about it."

Tony chuckled and shook his head. "Appreciate the invitation, but no thanks, ma'am." The Mercedes window slowly rose, and Sally drove away. Tony knew Rick Samuels was a highly educated neurosurgeon, a consultant to the top neurologist in the country, politically active within the American Medical Association, and practiced medicine for over forty-five years, yet this woman had totally unnerved him. Tony pulled into the University Mall parking lot and chose an Italian restaurant from the dozens of outer establishments. He was seated quickly as the regular lunch hour was over. Tony called Tonya after the waiter took his order. "You'll never believe who cornered me in the parking lot."

"I wish I would have been there," Tonya exclaimed after Tony told her that Sally Samuels had offered to buy him lunch. "I would have told the nosey bitch where to go. Dr. Rick is not going to like this." His plate arrived and he anxiously dug into the chicken fettuccini he ordered.

"How is your fettuccini, Dr. Harding?" a woman asked.

Tony expected to look up and see a waitress standing beside him holding a pitcher of tea, but regrettably, it was Sally Samuels. "You followed me?" he asked as he stood up.

"Well, I guess there's no point in trying to make something up, *Mr. Honesty*," she replied. "Yes, I did."

"Why? What do you want from me?"

"Please, Dr. Harding," she said. "Please allow me to sit down. I've already ordered and told the waiter to bring my plate to your table."

"Rick wasn't kidding about you," Tony grumbled. "I suppose it can't hurt." Tony walked around the table and put a hand on the back of her chair. "Just don't ask me any questions." She sat down, and a waiter quickly brought her plate and flatware.

"Would you like to see the wine list, masseur and madam?" he said, holding the menu out to them.

"No," she replied. "Not today, just water, please." The waiter cordially backed away. "Unless, of course, you'd like some Dr. Harding."

"Tea's fine for me," Tony said, pointing to his glass.

The waiter brought a glass of water, which Sally made him take back because it smelled funny, and requested a bottle of Evian. Her amazing green eyes were luminescent against her fair skin and auburn hair. He had to force himself to keep from staring. She picked at her salad and controlled the conversation with small talk until her Filet Minot arrived. Tony participated as little as possible. The waiter brought the bottled water and a glass. When she opened the bottle, Sally smelled the water and told the waiter it was much better, and he took leave once more. "You picked an excellent restaurant, Dr. Harding," she whispered as she poured the water into the glass.

"Too pricey," Tony said. "The chicken's dry; they went overboard with the pasta, and there's not enough sauce. Mine is better."

"You cook?" she asked as if surprised.

"My mother and two older sisters taught me," he replied. "Oh, I shouldn't have answered that," he said, shaking his head.

"Why don't you let me put our meals on my expense account? But that means I'll have to ask you a few more questions," she laughed.

"No thanks," Tony said, smiling back at her.

"So, what did Rick tell you about me?" she asked. "That I'm a back-stabbing bitch?"

"Not those words exactly," Tony replied, "but pretty close."

"Well, honestly, I know a little about you," she said. Sally took a sip of water and frowned as if it still wasn't to her liking.

"What do you mean?" Tony replied.

She leaned forward. "You're a widower," she whispered. Her expression was resolute, making her eyes even more alluring. "Your wife died in a car accident. She was on a date with a man named William Ferguson, a married investment broker. Your father had the police write their report to say he wasn't in your wife's car."

Tony put down his fork. He had never paid much attention to the name; he was just the man with the red tie; another one of her bad habits. He frowned, wondering how she knew all this.

"Your wife was an alcoholic and a prescription drug abuser," she continued. "Now you're raising your two daughters alone, which is a real challenge for you since you didn't spend much time with them before the accident. You lived with your sister and brother-in-law until moving here. Let's see, you have two sisters and two brothers. All are married except for your youngest brother, who is serving time in the Illinois State Prison for armed robbery."

Tony wiped his mouth with his napkin. "That's enough!" Tony signaled the waiter.

"Dr. Harding, wait," she said. "Rick hired you because you're talented and dedicated, because you stand up for your patients, and because of the impression you made on Arthur Gallows. You're not affected—uh, by politics," she said as Tony glared at her in silence. "Don't be angry with Rick," she said, putting her hand over his that was pressed hard against the top of the table. He tried to withdraw, but she pressed down harder, and after a seeming struggle of wills, she let go. "Rick uses Randy's resources in the D.A.'s office to check the backgrounds of his applicants," she replied. "He's been looking for the right person. He was especially impressed with your work ethic."

"Resources?" Tony groaned and shook his head. "Some of what you just said was wink and nod stuff, not public record." Tony hailed the waiter and paid him cash when he presented the bill. "I know what you're doing; trying to purposely upset me so I'll open up to you about whatever. I'll work this out with Rick myself," he said, getting up.

Sally grabbed his arm. "Rick needs your help with something more important than his practice, Dr. Harding. His son Kevin was a close friend of Anderson Barksdale, so he must tread carefully." She sighed as if fatigued.

"The man who was killed?" Tony asked.

"Yes." She said and leaned forward. "There have been others. Randy, the man I once knew and loved, has turned into someone I hardly recognize anymore," she paused for a second to look around as if someone might be eavesdropping. "I think he's past being able to see it for himself. He's allowed his largest contributor, The Group, too much control over his life."

"The company that's affiliated with USCSD?" Tony asked, but they were interrupted by the waiter.

"Is something wrong?" the waiter asked.

"Everything's fine, thank you," Sally replied, sat back in her chair, and took another sip of water. Tony left without saying anything further.

Sally's Mercedes passed Tony in the parking lot just as he reached his Olds. He took out his cell phone and called Tonya again.

"Tonya, is Rick still at the hospital?"

"Yes," she replied, "but he's consulting in the OR. Can I help you with something?"

"What time will he be in tomorrow?"

"Around five, I think; he's always here before I get here at seven. I leave his appointments for the next day on his desk every evening. Why?"

"Nothing, I'll see him tomorrow," he replied. Tony put his keys in the ignition and noticed the accumulation of raindrops across the windshield, and then Sally's Mercedes at the stop sign ahead at the end of the row. *She's probably waiting for me.* He waited twenty seconds, thirty seconds, a minute, but the Mercedes didn't move. He squinted, trying to see inside the car, but the windows were covered with a sheet of droplets. *She must be on her phone or texting.* The Mercedes began to roll forward slowly, but it didn't turn into the traffic lane. Tony stepped out of the Olds. The mist collected on his face as he watched the car creep along and stop when the front tires bumped the curb. Sally didn't emerge, so he walked toward the car. When he was five feet from the driver's door, he saw Sally slumped over the steering wheel. He pulled on the door handle, but the door was locked.

"Mrs. Samuels!" he yelled, after wiping the glass with his hand. She rolled her head to face the window. Her face was pale, and her eyes were glazed over. Saliva oozed over her bottom lip; she was holding her stomach with one arm. She floundered for the automatic door lock with her hand. Tony quickly opened the door after she finally found the button. "What's wrong?" Tony asked.

"My stomach," she moaned. "It must have been the water, it tasted salty."

Tony ran around to the passenger side of the Mercedes and opened the door. He crawled across the seat and slid Sally over to the passenger side. He strapped her in and ran back to the driver's side.

"What are you doing?" she mumbled.

"I'm taking you to the ER."

"No! Not the ER!" she gasped.

"Well, you're going to have to trust me," he replied.

Sally grabbed the door handle and unhooked her seatbelt.

"Don't do that," Tony yelled.

"I can't go there," she muttered. "They'll kill me." Sally rolled out of the car and fell to the asphalt. Tony jumped out and helped her to a standing position.

"Okay, just sit down then." Sally pushed away from him and stumbled around the open car door. She hugged her stomach with both hands and stepped over the curb onto the wet grass, almost slipping as she wobbled down the sloping hill. She stopped when she reached a large tree and leaned against it. Tony was right behind her. "You have to go to the ER now." Tony pulled his cell phone out of his pocket. "I'm calling 911."

"No!" Sally shrieked and knocked the phone from his hand. "Can't you do something? You're a doctor!"

"All right then," Tony conceded. "This isn't advisable, but you'll have to make yourself throw up."

"What?" she gasped.

"Bend over and stick your finger down your throat," he ordered. "If you don't, I will, so get started. Find the reflex area at the back of your throat," he instructed after her first attempt failed. Finally, she began to gag. "Keep it up until something comes up," he ordered. "Come on." After several attempts, Sally's lunch came up and splattered onto the ground beneath the tree. "Again," Tony demanded. Sally heaved, and more of her stomach contents poured out. "You need to flush with some water," he said.

"Back seat…or maybe the trunk," Sally gasped, and looked up the hill where her car was still lamely parked.

"Hold on to the tree and keep going for that reflex; I want all of it out!" Tony found a six-pack of Evian on the back floorboard and a towel in the trunk, then he parked her car next to the curb. He poured one of the bottles onto the towel on his way down the hill. "Put this on your face and neck," he said, handing her the cool, wet towel. He looked at the regurgitation on the ground and nodded approvingly. "Drink all of this." He opened another bottle from the package.

"I can't," Sally sighed as she leaned against the tree and pressed the towel to her face. "I feel better, I don't want to…"

"Drink as much as you can," Tony ordered.

"No, I can't," she whimpered. Tony grabbed the towel from her and put the bottle in her hand. She looked at him and shook her head. "All right, dammit!" she groaned and turned the bottle up.

"Keep drinking," he ordered.

"I'm going to be sick again."

"That's good," Tony assured her. "But listen carefully; it's important that you not let anything get in your windpipe. Because you don't want to go to the hospital, remember," Tony added when she frowned at him. "If you aspirate, I'll be forced to take you. When you're done with that bottle, drink another."

"Oh, God," Sally moaned.

Twenty minutes of drinking and throwing up passed before Sally's vomit was clear, and her stomach settled. They sat in the grass away from the tree and the stomach contents, their hair and clothes soaked from the rain. "Is there someone, a family member, I can call to come get you?" Tony asked as he lifted her eyelids to examine her pupils.

"No family," Sally replied. "My parents died when I was a teenager. I have no siblings. There was just Randy."

"Your eyes are clear," he said. "A blood sample would tell us if this is a virus or e-coli. In any case, you shouldn't drive. How about a coworker? And you have to promise me you'll go to the ER if this reoccurs."

Sally nodded. She pulled a cell phone from her coat pocket. "I must look awful, and this is a new suite. And I think my hair has puke in it. I may never drink water again." She pressed the keys on her cell phone. "I'll call a friend; he can take a cab."

"Come on then," Tony said. "Let's wait in the car and run the a/c in your face." Tony helped Sally to her feet and up the hill.

"Thank you for not taking me to the hospital," Sally said to him when they were sitting in the Mercedes.

"It was against my better judgment. But I did collect a sample to have tested." Tony started the car and turned the air vent toward Sally.

"Don't tell anyone it's mine; I'm insisting on doctor/patient confidentiality," she said when his facial expression expressed disagreement. She gave him a business card from her console, then leaned back on the headrest and closed her eyes. "You can leave a message for me."

"Well, that depends," he whispered and looked outside and saw a yellow cab turning in the parking lot.

"On what?" she sighed.

"On whether you keep your nose out of my business from now on," he replied. Tony looked at his watch. It was three thirty; school was out by now.

"Dr. Harding," Sally whispered without lifting her head, "be careful. I have reason to suspect The Group is more than just a holding company; it's responsible for some awful things, including what happened to Anderson Barksdale. Andy had a future in politics, but something went wrong. Now they've got their hooks in Randy." The cab pulled up, and a young man in khaki Dockers and a blue shirt jumped out of the back seat.

"Dr. Anthony Harding," Tony said when he got out and shook Jared's hand.

"Jared Dawson, editor of the *Campus Voice*. Sally said she was sick?"

"Mrs. Samuels may have eaten something not fully cooked and ingested a bacterium, but I believe she got it all up. She's a little shaky, and I don't think she should drive or be alone for a while. Can you keep an eye on her for a few hours?"

"Yes, of course," Jared replied.

"Do you have something like Pepto-Bismol or Dramamine to calm the stomach spasms?" Tony added. "It's possible she'll experience some diarrhea. If she starts vomiting again, please convince her to go to the ER."

"Sure; got plenty of the pink stuff at the office," Jared replied. "I'll make her comfortable, thanks." Jared slid behind the wheel of Sally's Mercedes and stared at her.

"I wrote my number on one of her cards," Tony added. "Sally, please go to the ER if…"

"Stop hovering, Dr. Harding," Sally whined. "I'll be fine."

Jared nodded a *thank you* to Tony, closed the door, and turned to Sally. "There's a cot downstairs and a bathroom with a shower. I've got a pair of clean sweats..."

"Just drive, Jared," Sally groaned. "You can drive, can't you? I've never actually seen you drive before; and why are you so dressed up?"

"Yes, I can drive," Jared said as he searched for the windshield wiper control. "There's someone I want you to meet if you feel up to it. He's a programming genius and says he can line me up with some cheap upgrade equipment. I left him holding down the fort."

Sally put the wet towel over her face and whispered, "You left someone in charge of your paper?"

Annette tried ice, heat, and ice again to ease her migraine. She drank warm milk, then herbal tea. It eased just in time to ride her bike to Molly's. "Molly, I'm worthless today," she whimpered when she walked in.

"Where's my baby," Molly said and held her arms out for Phoebe.

"Molly, not so loud, please; I'm battling a migraine."

"Why didn't you stay home, honey?" Molly scolded.

"I promised Doris I'd do her class at the Senior Center this afternoon."

"So, what if Charlie, Lewis, and the rest of them spend an extra hour sitting around?" Molly scowled.

"I can't let Doris down. She needs the money. Where's the ice bag?"

"Go sit in the living room, I'll get it." Molly waddled down the hall carrying Phoebe in her arms.

"Hey, seniorita, what's wrong?" Mona asked when she saw Annette with her arms wrapped around her face and forehead. "Ah, migraine."

"It must be the weather."

"I see, and did you have another dream about your father?" Mona asked, pulling up one of the tiny chairs.

"I can't remember; my head hurts."

"You and your father spent some good times together, si? So, did me and my papa." Annette lifted her sunglasses and looked at Mona because her voice sounded funny. Her hands were folded as if she were praying, and her eyes were puffy and red. They stared at each other in silence for a few seconds.

"You've been cryin," Annette finally said.

"I left Tim," Mona said in a low voice. Annette's mouth opened, but Mona interrupted. "It's his drinking; I can't take it anymore. Nette, I want my children to have a father like yours and mine. Tim doesn't understand what I'm saying; he denies the problem."

"Oh, Mona," Annette whispered, "I'm so sorry."

Molly passed them on the way to the kitchen to fill the ice bag. "I left Phoebe on the bed; she's waiting for you. What are you two whispering about?" Mona explained to Molly why she and her kids moved in with her mother.

Annette resigned to the bedroom. "I'm going to lie down now; my head can't even take my own thoughts." She woke later that afternoon to a voice whispering in her ear.

"Miss Nette, Miss Nette; Is Phoebe in here with you?"

Annette moaned even though the headache was gone. "Must I open my eyes?" she argued to herself, slowly raising her eyelids. "Elizabeth," she whispered when she saw her kneeling beside the bed staring at her. Phoebe raised her head from under the patch quilt Molly laid over them.

"There you are!" Elizabeth called out. "She's a good nap partner, isn't she, Miss Nette?"

"Elizabeth, what time is it?" Nette asked.

"I don't know; I just got here."

Annette sat up. "I need to get ready." She found her gym bag on the bed and started pulling things out.

Elizabeth climbed up on the bed and pulled Phoebe close to her. "You were talking in your sleep; were you dreaming?"

Nette wore her gym shorts and wrestled the tee shirt over her head and shoulders. "Yeah, I was dreaming about this big oak tree we used to have in our backyard. Its limbs were as big around as your body." Lizzy's eyes widened, and she cuddled Phoebe closer. "I loved climbing that tree." Annette found a ponytail tie and a hairbrush in the gym bag. "One afternoon, when I was about your age, I climbed higher than I ever had before and scooted out on a limb too far. When I finally looked down and saw how high I was, I got scared and started to cry." Annette brushed her hair back into a ponytail.

"Ooh!"

Annette sat down on the bed next to Elizabeth. "I looked down again and saw my daddy lookin up at me with his fists on his hips and his elbows stickin out. We had a dog back then called Sneaker; he was sittin next to my Daddy and lookin up at me too. Daddy asked Sneaker if he'd ever seen anything so funny and Sneaker bowed his head and said *yeowess.* Daddy and Sneaker used to talk to each other all the time."

Elizabeth giggled. "What happened? What?"

"Well, my daddy told me to either climb down the same way I went up or to jump."

"What did you do?" Elizabeth squealed.

"I tried to scoot backward, but the limb I was on started snappin and crackin, and then it broke and dumped me right off. I fell right into my Daddy's arms. My Daddy said I looked like I was flyin."

Elizabeth laughed and hugged Phoebe. "That was a great dream, wasn't it, Phoebe?" Phoebe replied by licking her on the cheek.

"Every pet we had loved my daddy."

"Could he talk to all of them?" Elizabeth asked.

Annette smiled. "Yes, he could; before he died."

"My Mama died too; before we moved here," Elizabeth sighed.

"I bet you miss her, just like I do my daddy." Annette kissed Elizabeth on the forehead and crammed her jeans and shirt into the gym bag. "I'm teaching an aerobics class next door at the Senior Center."

"Can Phoebe stay here with me?"

"You'll be gone by the time the class is over." Nette put the gym bag strap over one shoulder and wiggled her fingers, motioning Elizabeth to come along. "Let's find Miss Mona. She's feelin a little sad today and your drawin always cheers her up."

"Okay, but please bring Phoebe tomorrow," Elizabeth begged as she followed Annette into the front room.

"Lizzy, my favorite part estudiante," Mona said. "I bought some new coloring pens just for you." Mona pulled Annette aside after Lizzy sat down. "Larry can't pick up Jeffrey and Justin. He's held up somewhere, and their grandmother is busy, so he asked if you'd bring them home later."

"Did he say what's goin on?"

"No," Mona replied. "He was really evasive, but at least the caller ID wasn't the county jail."

"He's up to no good, I can feel it," Nette said, looking out the window. "I hate driving into North Park so late, especially when it's raining."

Tony looked at his watch. "If I hurry, I can catch the kids at Molly's," he said as he drove down Gold Coast. He turned the Olds into Molly's driveway and saw the white bicycle parked in the garage.

"Daddy, you just missed Phoebe," Elizabeth said when she looked up from the table and saw him.

"Phoebe, huh?" he said, picking up one of her drawings. "Lizzy, this looks like our old apartment building. How did you remember so many details of that place? The style of brick, the trim around the windows, the curved header over the entrance, and the decorative stones around the ledges; you even put people inside the windows and on the rooftop. You were only two years old."

"Hello, you're Lizzy's dad," Mona said.

"Olla, olla," Lizzy said.

"She's a great little artist," she said. "Such great detail for her age."

"And a great memory," Tony said.

Mona motioned him to follow her. Nicky and Justin were in the front room, sitting next to each other on small stools and watching Jeffrey and Mr. Mackenzie play chess. "Mr. Mackenzie is teaching the kids to play chess," Mona whispered.

"I gotta go, guys," Nicky said when she saw her father standing in the archway.

"If you're not in a hurry," Mr. Mackenzie said, "I'd like your daughter to see this next move."

"Oh man," Jeffrey sighed. "What move?" Nicky and Justin looked at each other and chuckled.

"Check and Mate," Mr. Mackenzie said and put Jeffrey's king in check.

"Ah, man!" Jeffrey moaned and fell backward off the ottoman he was sitting on.

Nicky laughed, and Justin slapped open hands with Mr. Mackenzie.

"That was cool Mr. Mac; I'll see you guys tomorrow," Nicky said and grabbed their two backpacks. She walked straight to Lizzy without speaking or looking at her father. "Let's go, Lizzy," she said.

"Crap! It's still raining," Jeffrey said when he looked outside. He pulled out a cell phone and punched some numbers. "She's not answering. She's just over at the Senior Center, Justin; let's run for it."

"Mesa Village Senior Center?" Tony asked. "It's on our way," Tony said when Justin nodded. "My car's in the garage."

"Cool, Doc," Jeffrey replied.

"Daddy, Daddy," Lizzy squealed. "Can we go too? You can meet Phoebe."

"We'll see Lizzy."

"We know what that means," Nicky muttered, leading her to the door.

Tony parked near the front door of the Senior Center. Jeffrey and Justin were in the back seat, and Nicky was in the front with Lizzy on her lap.

"I see Phoebe," Lizzy shrieked. "I see her! She's at the door." Lizzy grabbed the door handle.

"Wait, Lizzy," Tony said. "It's raining, don't open the door." He turned to the boys in the back seat. "There's an umbrella under my seat."

"Daddy, look!" Lizzy squealed again. "Phoebe…I see…look…Phoebe."

"Lizzy, please calm down," Tony said, fearing his daughter was on the verge of an anxiety attack. Her eyes looked wild, and she started hyperventilating as she spoke in broken sentences. She pulled the door handle and pushed on the door. Tony grabbed her arm, and Nicky wrapped her arms around her waist.

"Lizzy, please stop," Nicky begged.

Lizzy put her hands against the glass. "Phoebe," she sighed.

Phoebe was standing inside the door and suddenly looked up at the dark clouds while her master danced the two-step with one of the older men to Zydeco music along with three other couples.

Lizzy stopped pushing on the door when the rain suddenly stopped. “Phoebe moved the clouds!”

“That’s not…,” Tony said, but looked up and saw small patches of blue sky through the windshield. He turned to his daughters, but Lizzy was already running up the walk, and Nicky was getting out of the car. Jeffrey was gone, and Justin was sliding across the back seat.

“Wait,” Tony said, “Uh-wait-I, great!” All four were through the front doors before he could make a coherent objection.

Lizzy immediately scooped Phoebe up in her arms. Nicky, Jeffrey, and Justin went to the stereo cabinet. Everyone stopped dancing when Jeffrey pushed the eject button.

“Jeffrey!” Annette yelled. “What are you doin’, boy?”

“Nothing, just putting on some decent music,” he replied.

“I’d better not be rap!” she returned.

Piano music suddenly broke out from the upright in the corner. Robby was sitting in front of it, pounding a Stevie Wonder tune. “Yo, is this old-fashioned enough for you, Nette?” Robby hollered. Scott was standing next to him, tapping his fingers, almost in time with the music. Charlie strutted up to Nette and asked to cut in. Robby’s face erupted into a huge smile when Nicky sat beside him on the piano bench.

“What are you doing here?” she whispered to Robby.

“Visiting my grandma; she’s the one out there on the dance floor in the blue sweats. She uses a cane, except when she’s dancing.”

“That’s so cute,” Nicky giggled. Lizzy joined the group around the piano when she saw her father enter through the front door. She sat on the floor in front of Scott and laid Phoebe in her lap. The couples on the floor bounced up and down and around to the beat of Robby’s tune until he transitioned into a slower Ray Charles piece.

“How ‘bout this one?” he yelled

“It’s too old, too slow,” Annette yelled back.

“What do you mean too old?” Charlie said, “Reminds me of high school.”

“Sorry, Charlie,” Nette said, laughing.

"I must say, this is much better than aerobics," he added as he raised his shoulders and moved his feet.

"This is aerobics, Charlie," Nette replied while turning under Charlie's arm.

"We never dance like this in Doris's class," Charlie said, swinging her around again.

"Well, I can't help it if Doris' instructions got wet," Nette laughed.

"Look, there's Doc Harding." Charlie left her in the middle of the floor and trotted toward the door.

Justin brushed her hand. "Check this out, Nette." He began to waive his arms in the air while bending his knees and swinging his hips. The music changed again, this time to Van Halen.

"Now that's *my back-in-the-day*," Annette said, laughing, and began to step side to side to the beat.

"Doc," Charlie greeted, holding his hand out. "Welcome; we're doing a little cardio."

"Is that right?" Tony said and shook his hand. "How are you, Charlie?"

"Come on in and join the party."

"I was supposed to be dropping the boys off, but my girls have scattered; avoiding me actually."

"Kids, right? Have you met Annette and Phoebe?"

"Phoebe?" Tony asked. "Yes, I would definitely like to meet Phoebe."

"Robby, how 'bout that song you were workin on yesterday?" Annette asked as she joined him at the piano.

"Yo, I knew you were listening," Robby laughed. "Did it sound like a Louisiana song?"

Justin asked Nicky to dance, but she declined. "I'll dance with you, Justin," Lizzy said, handing Phoebe to Nette. Nicky saw her father approaching and quickly got up from the piano bench, rushed across the room to the stereo cabinet, and stood next to Jeffrey.

"You, see?" Tony said sheepishly to Charlie.

"You should stay a while, then," Charlie laughed.

"Hey, kid," Tony said, patting Robby on the shoulder, "this sounds a little better than some of the noise I hear coming from your house."

"Burn, Doc!" Robby replied. "So, I see you found our little hideaway."

"Yeah, well, I think I have an office somewhere in this place."

"Doc, this is Annette and Phoebe," Charlie said.

"It's nice to meet you," Tony addressed Annette. "Are you Annette or Phoebe?" Phoebe looked up at him from her master's lap.

"Annette," she replied. "This is Phoebe." Phoebe suddenly rose on her hind legs to greet him. "Phoebe, be still!" She put a paw out and touched Tony's hand. Tony instinctively put his hands out, and she crawled into his arms. "I'm sorry," Nette stuttered. "She doesn't usually do that with strangers." Phoebe sniffed Tony's neck and the side of his face and licked his cheek with the tip of her tongue.

"So, you're Phoebe," Tony whispered to the little brown poodle. "I believe she was in my garage the other day," he said, "and probably what I was chasing around my backyard." He looked at Charlie. "Charlie; is this who Lewis was calling for?"

Annette and Charlie looked at each other.

"Well, Doc—um—Lewis was delirious that night, lack of oxygen, remember?"

"Nice meeting you," Nette gasped and then snatched Phoebe from his arms and rushed away.

"What just happened?" Tony asked Charlie.

"Yo Doc, you just got dissed," Robby snickered, "big time."

"Don't be ridiculous," Tony mumbled and watched Annette join the kids at the stereo.

"Doc," Charlie interrupted. "If you have a minute, I'll show you the clinic."

"I'd like that, Charlie; Dr. Samuels gave me the keycard today."

Robby's tune morphed into *Blue Bayou*. She turned her head when she heard it. Robby was already grinning at her, and she returned the smile until she saw Charlie and Dr. Harding walking toward the clinic together. "Why were you so nice to him?" she whispered to Phoebe. Phoebe put her nose to Annette's cheek. "Jeffrey, get Justin; we're leavin."

Jeffrey waved to his brother. "Nicky, you wanna come? Nette lives right across the alley from you on Jewel."

"Yo, it's cool," Robby said when he saw Nicky frown. "I'll have my grandma tell your dad." He paid no attention to Scott, who was shaking his head. It took Lucy Jones about ten minutes to shuffle to the clinic door with the help of a footed aluminum cane.

"Dr. Harding," her voice quivered. "My grandson asked me to tell you they were going to Nette's. I'm sorry it took me so long to walk over here; it's this arthritis."

"Thank you, Lucy," Charlie replied, "I'm sure it's okay." But he noticed Tony was shaking his head. "Your job here is gonna be easy, Doc," Charlie remarked as they watched Lucy amble away. "We're a pretty healthy bunch here. I saw the look on your face just now. You don't have to worry about your girls when they're with Nette. Kids always hang out at her house; she attracts them like a magnet."

"She didn't seem so friendly to me," Tony mumbled.

"There's a reason for that," Charlie sighed. "I wasn't completely honest with you about Phoebe before. Phoebe was at Lewis's the other night but Annette wanted me to keep it on the down low."

"At least I know who Phoebe is now," Tony said. "I guess that explains Lizzy's fascination with her."

"Phoebe always finds the ones that need her the most," Charlie said. "You should hang out with us for a bit longer, Doc. We're not just a bunch of old fogies, you know."

Elizabeth stood in Annette's doorway next to Phoebe with a wary look on her face. "Nette, someone's knocking on your gate." Nette left Robby and Nicky at the table to reflect on the pieces of her chess game to peer through the back door. Jeffrey and Justin were in the living room playing the Xbox. Phoebe cocked her head as they watched the back gate open. "It's Daddy," Lizzy whispered to Phoebe. "I hope we're not in trouble." Nicky dropped the bishop she was holding.

"It's okay," Robby whispered and placed the piece upright on the board. "Nette's got this."

Tony stopped at the bottom of the steps. "Hello again," he said to Annette, who was standing on the porch by now. Phoebe darted around Lizzy, hiding inside the door, and ran down the steps. Tony looked down at Phoebe, who was jumping around his feet.

"Phoebe!" Annette scolded. "I'm sorry, she usually has better manners." Tony squatted to his knees and put his hands out. Phoebe jumped into his lap, wagging her tail and yipping a greeting. "Phoebe!" Annette reprimanded. She reached down to try and take her from him, but he stood up with her in his arms.

"She's a little wound up, isn't she?" Tony grimaced when Phoebe licked him on the side of the face.

"I'm really sorry," Nette apologized. "She's actin a little weird."

"Lizzy, is that you?" Tony asked when he saw his daughter kneeling just inside the kitchen door. She scrambled to her feet and ran to his side.

"Daddy, you have to see Phoebe do her tricks."

"It's time to go home, honey," he replied, "some other time."

"Please, Daddy. It won't take long, please!" Lizzy begged.

"Well, I-I…"

"Why don't you go get Phoebe's bowl?" Nette interrupted. Lizzy dashed into the kitchen and was back in a flash with the bowl. Lizzy kneeled in the grass, and Tony put Phoebe down beside her. "I now present the fabulous Phoebe," she said and outstretched her arms. Phoebe performed her tricks flawlessly at Lizzy's command. Annette brought out a large embroidery hoop. Lizzy raised it, and Phoebe jumped through.

"Well, I am impressed," Tony remarked when Phoebe cleared the hoop each time Lizzy raised it higher.

"Daddy, you haven't seen everything," Lizzy squealed. "You have to see her play ball and..."

"Lizzy, um, he doesn't have time to see *everything*," Annette interrupted.

"We really have to go," he said, looking at his watch. "There's dinner and baths and…"

"And you promised we'd watch Mary Poppins," Lizzy gushed.

"That's right," he said. "Go get your sister."

"She gets wound up," Tony said after Lizzy ran back into the house.

"She'll settle down once she gets to know everybody," Annette said. "Everything's bound to be a little strange to her right now…new home...new school…new friends. Shoot, I felt the same way when I first moved here." Nicky had a sour look on her face when she walked past Annette and her father.

"Wait a minute, young lady," Tony said. "Aren't you going to thank Miss Annette for inviting you to her house?"

Phoebe watched Nicky reluctantly stop at the gate and turn her head.

"Thanks, Nette; and thanks for explaining the chess pieces. And tell Jeffrey and Justin goodbye for me." Lizzy followed her but stopped to throw her arms around Annette's legs.

"Thanks, Miss Nette; I love you and Phoebe."

"You're welcome, I love you too," Nette said and waved goodbye. "You have two great kids, Doc. And welcome to the neighborhood."

"Yeah," Tony replied and started toward the gate. "What part of the South are you from?"

"Oh," Annette said, blushing. "Louisiana; I forget how I sound sometimes."

"I'm sorry," Tony sighed and blushed. "Crawfish and alligators?"

"Yeah," Annette laughed, "and armadillos and mosquitoes so big they pack you off." They both laughed. "Your house is kind of special to me and Phoebe," she said as she walked him to the gate. "I keep picturin my friend Jim in his garden and Julia, his wife, watchin him from the porch. I'm glad someone finally moved in; maybe I'll finally move on."

"You were good friends, I take it?" Tony said and remembered Brad telling him about Jim being blind and regaining his sight.

"Yes, very good friends," she answered. Annette bowed sheepishly and suddenly looked up when she felt raindrops on her shoulders.

"Uh-oh," Tony said, putting his hand out.

"The girls are welcome here any time," Nette said, wrinkling her nose and giggling as the tiny sprinkles hit her face. "Just thought I should say it, to make it official," she said and ran for the shelter of the back porch.

"Okay, sure, thanks." Tony ducked and weaved as if trying to dodge the raindrops as he closed the gate behind him.

"So, what did you think?" Robby asked while tapping the black king against the chessboard with one hand and the matching queen in the other.

"Think about what?" Nette asked.

"Doc, you know, Nicky's dad."

"I don't know," she replied. "He seems like a typical father I just met for the first time; how would I know?"

"He didn't like that Nicky and Lizzy were here," he said as he rhythmically tapped the pieces, "until you distracted him. And he really doesn't like me; that's why I hung back." Robby straightened in his chair and cupped his hands together. "Nette, seriously, you gotta help me figure out how to get on his good side cuz Nicky needs a friend, yo."

Annette laughed. "It shouldn't be that hard." She grabbed a handful of his hair and messed it up. "What's not to love?"

"Fo-real, Nette; he put on his good face for you," Robby said. "You have that effect on people. Maybe it's that southern thing, but I wish I knew how to make him like me."

"Okay." Annette sat down across the table from him. "My father was suspicious of every dude that came around; very few gained his respect. Offer to help him out with a little project or somethin. That used to work…sometimes."

"You wouldn't believe how totally *I don't need any help* he is," Robby accentuated.

"Oh, yes, I would," she replied. "I was raised by one."

Chapter 16

Annette carefully steered the 4-Runner through the streets of North Park with Phoebe sitting in her lap. Jeffrey was riding shotgun to help her navigate because the majority of the streetlights were knocked out, and it was pouring rain; Justin had the back seat to himself. “This is bad as drivin through Louisiana fog.”

“What did you think about Nicky’s dad?” Justin asked, leaning forward to help find their street.

“Well, he’s a doctor,” she replied. “So—”

“A doctor fixed my broken arm,” Jeffrey said, raising his left arm as evidence.

“That’s about all they’re good for; they just guess at the serious stuff.” She turned onto another dark street. “What did your dad say about the property up in Escondido?”

“There’s a lot of land, and we’ll be taking care of some horses,” Jeffrey replied.

“What does he know about horses?” Nette asked, squinting to see through the wipers that were set on high.

“Nothing,” Justin answered, “I think there are cows too.”

She slowed the Toyota; all the frame houses looked alike. At least the weather had pushed the loiterers off the streets and sidewalks onto carports and porches. As usual, they stared at the Toyota as it passed. No one ever bothered her when she drove through North Park. Larry said it was because of Jose’s American flag montage down each side of her truck. He was somewhat of a folklore artist; his painted tags were all over town. A man wearing a hooded coat suddenly broke from one of the groups and walked with intent toward the SUV. Phoebe stood up in her master’s lap when she heard Annette gasp. Another man rushed up behind him. Jeffrey and Justin watched them push and shove each other in the middle of the street from the rear window.

“Look at those fools,” Jeffrey laughed.

Phoebe made a groaning sound and lay back down in her master’s lap.

“Whose bitch is that?” yelled the man in the hooded jacket.

"No one's; none of us mess with the chick in the Toyota, dog," the other man yelled and waved his fists. "She takes care of the niño's up in here; you got it? She takes 'em where they need to be when there ain't nobody else, and sees to it they get back, see what em sayin?" The man sneered. "She lets 'em hang at her crib when it ain't safe up in here." He leaned closer to the hooded man. "You see Jose's tag? That means hands-off. Besides," he whispered, "the chick's got a bodyguard."

"Bodyguard?" the hooded man scoffed. "You're shittin me." He walked around in a circle until he faced the man again. "I didn't see nobody cep a couple kids. Man, I can get big bucks for that marked-up ride where I come from."

"Whatever, dog," the man said. "But there ain't none of us gonna help you. You need to listen, bro."

"We'll see about that!" said the hooded man and he pushed the other man away. The group on the porch moaned and snickered.

"We're here," Annette said and turned into the driveway of broken concrete. Annette and the boys jumped out but Phoebe stayed in the car. They scrambled up the steps and huddled under the overhang while Jeffrey opened the door. "Are you sure your dad's here? It's dark inside." Jeffrey led the way through the kitchen and into the living room. Larry was sprawled on the couch balancing a beer on his stomach and watching TV. He sat up when he saw them.

"Thanks for bringing the boys home," Larry said while clearing the phlegm from his throat.

Annette looked around the sparsely furnished living room. "Where's all your, you know, stuff?" she asked. The walls were normally lined with boxes containing DVD players, flat-screen TVs, cell phones, and other electronic gear that he had acquired by one illegal means or another.

"Got rid of it," he said. He pointed the remote at the TV, turning it off. "I'm out of the business."

"Really, for good?" she asked taking another long look around the room.

"Yeah," Larry replied. "Practically gave it away to a few other entrepreneurs. Once I put the word out, three trucks showed up, and fifteen minutes later, my inventory was loaded and gone." Larry stood up and directed Jeffrey and

Justin to the kitchen by waving his beer can in the air. "Got some pizza on the counter in the kitchen." Jeffrey and Justin raced each other to the kitchen, grabbed one of the large flat boxes on the counter, and went to their room. "There are some breadsticks, too," Larry added. "Go on and get all you want. There's plenty," he bragged. "You love bread sticks, don't you Nette?"

"I'm not really hungry, Larry; we ate sandwiches at the house, although it doesn't look it by the way they just attacked that pizza." She walked around the house again. "Wow Larry, I can't believe it's all gone."

"That's right," he said. "This deal up in Escondido is gonna pay me a hell of a lot more than what I've been making fencing electronics, plus it's legit. It'll be great for the boys to be up there in the country. I spent some time in the country when I was a kid before I moved down here and met Catrina." Annette began to pace back and forth across the living room which meant she was worried. "What?" he finally asked.

"What about the drugs, Larry?" she asked in a whisper so the boys wouldn't hear. "Are you out of that market too? Catrina is where she is because she got caught."

"Yes," he answered emphatically. "That was part of the deal," he whispered.

Nette sat down on the edge of the couch. "What deal?"

"I'm gonna live on a five-acre ranch next to The Group headquarters in Escondido. It will be mine if I prove that I can be responsible enough to maintain the grounds for five years. And you won't believe what they're paying me to do this. I should be rich in five years and able to send my boys to college."

"You realize this sounds too good to be true, Larry? And there could be real work involved?"

"Nette, I'm ready to shuck this," Larry said, gazing around the room. "I'm not smart enough or educated enough to make a real living, or ever have anything better. I've wanted to get out here in this neighborhood for a long time. If I don't, something bad is gonna happen to my boys. I don't want them to end up like me or in prison like their mother. This is my big chance to do something right;

to do something that's gonna be good for us. It's like a gift from heaven or something; I just can't pass it up."

"How did this guy find you, Larry?" Nette asked pointedly.

"I got busted by an undercover about a month ago, and one of the legal aides hooked me up with this representative dude looking to help someone willing to straighten out his life. It was an opportunity I just couldn't refuse. I'm doing it for Jeffrey and Justin."

Annette stared Larry straight in the eyes. "Are you sure it's on the level?"

"Yes," he replied. "It was all done legal, with a real estate agent and an attorney. I get the five acres plus a hundred thousand a month to keep the property cleared, the fences repaired, the livestock fed and the barns clean."

"A hundred thousand!" she gasped. "Larry…"

"I know how it sounds," said Larry, "but this is for real."

"Okay, but I'm gonna tell Jeffrey and Justin to call me if they think somethin's wrong."

"I get why you're skeptical," Larry nodded and looked at his beer can. "I appreciate how you feel about my boys. And believe me; they feel the same about you. We'll be moving up there in a couple of weeks; I want you to come up and see the place. There's plenty of room; you can stay for a weekend or as long you want." Larry looked at his beer can again. "Hell, I feel so good about all of this that I might even quit drinking. I think I just might; how about that?"

"Well," Nette whispered. "That would be somethin Larry. But let's not count your chickens yet." Nette frowned. "Will you have chickens?"

Larry laughed. "I didn't see any."

"Good, cuz I hate those nasty things."

Phoebe lay in the front passenger seat waiting for her master. Something, perhaps instincts, made her raise up and look out the rain-streaked window. She saw someone crossing the street and headed toward the Toyota. It was the man in the hooded raincoat they had passed before. He crouched down as he got closer; he had a crowbar in one hand; Phoebe growled. The rain suddenly came down harder, covering the mural with thick sheets of water, fading Jose's stars and stripes montage. The man intended to jack the vehicle, take it across the border, and perhaps get ten thousand dollars for it. He paused for a second after seeing a faint green hue emitting from inside the truck. He continued, deducing it was a refraction of the dashboard lights, but stopped again when a figure of a man appeared standing alongside the rear fender. The falling rain outlined a floppy hat that disbursed droplets to the top of his shoulders that became thicker sheets down his leather jacket. Unaffected by the downpour, the mysterious man moved forward, making a rumbling noise as he breathed, making the hair on the intruder's neck stand on end. A pair of green eyes appeared just below the brim of the hat when the figure raised his head. He had a baseball bat in one hand that made a smacking sound when he slapped it against his palm. The hooded man dropped the crowbar and pulled an AK rifle out from under his raincoat. The man in the leather jacket pointed the bat at him. Electricity shot out from the end and there was a loud bang as if lightning had struck it. A silver and blue bolt expelled in a straight line striking the handholding the high-powered gun. The gun exploded into pieces and flew in every direction. The man bent over, clutching his burning hand close to his chest, and cried out a few expletives.

"What are you, man?" he gasped, spitting rain from his mouth as he hunkered in pain while the man slowly lowered the bat. "What are you?" he yelled out again and lurched forward. There was another loud clap of thunder, and suddenly, the bat was an inch from his face. The hooded man turned his crippled body around and ran from the yard and out into the street splashing water under his feet as he pounded the inundated ground and uneven pavement. He ran stumbling, trying to put distance between himself and the apparition. He looked back and saw the figure fade as if the rain washed him away. The pain shot up his arm again as if reminding him to keep going. The group on the porch was hooting and scoffing about drunken nonsense and only laughed when he walked up ranting about the man with a bat that projected lightning. His story gave the stupefied group even more reason to wail. They hushed momentarily when he uncovered his burned hand and forearm.

"Would you look at that," one said after taking a drag off his self-rolled cigarette. "I told your ass to leave that Toyota alone. Call 911; that looks pretty bad."

Annette flinched when she heard the second clap of thunder. "I better check on Phoebe, that storm's gettin pretty wicked."

"Stay here until it blows over," Larry said. He grabbed an umbrella, but the rain stopped just when he opened the door.

"Looks like I caught a break," Nette said. They both looked up at the fast-moving clouds.

"It never thunders like that around here," Larry remarked.

"Sounds like home to me," Nette sighed. "You can have your earthquakes; I'll take a good ol' thunderstorm any day."

"Did I wake you?" Nette said when Phoebe jumped in her lap as she backed out of the driveway. Two police units were parked in the driveway of the house they passed before; an ambulance was idling at the curb. "Must a been a fight or somethin". Annette sped up when heads began to turn and look at her.

At first, Sally thought the thunder she heard was a car crashing in front of the building that housed the college newspaper. The door to the downstairs room where Jared left her to rest was partially open allowing a thin banner of light to shine on the wall. It also allowed her to hear Jared's muffled voice as he talked to someone upstairs, perhaps the guy he had left holding down the fort when he came to her rescue. Sally looked at her phone; she had slept three hours and had a message from David. She took a shower in the downstairs bathroom and changed into the black sweat suit Jared had left for her in a recycle tote bag, along with a pair of flip-flops. She shoved her soiled belongings into the eco-bag and set it down at the foot of the stairs leading to the campus newspaper office while trying to eavesdrop on the conversation. Jared's voice was high-pitched and enthusiastic, which made her all the more curious. She slowly climbed the stairs to the guardrail where Jared kept his bicycle. She peered around the door and saw him leaning over the shoulder of a man sitting in front of his computer. The man must have sensed her presence because he suddenly stopped typing and turned to look at her. He smiled broadly as if looking at a long-lost friend.

"Sally!" Jared gasped and rushed to her. "You look so much better; your color is back. Come over here; I need your opinion."

Sally slowly stepped into the office but stopped midway. "Who is this?"

"Let me introduce you," he replied waving at her to come closer. "Nate has created an outrageous new site for The Voice."

"You should never let just anyone use your computer," she grumbled and moved a few steps closer, stopping abruptly when Nate stood up. "Who are you?" she challenged the tall stranger.

"Sally! If you'll give me a second," Jared was bewildered by her discourtesy. "This is Nate Roberts. He's an IT consultant from USC in LA."

Sally turned to Jared and put both hands on his shoulders. "Jared?" she said staring into his eyes.

"I'm glad you're feeling better, Ms. Samuels," Nate interrupted. "Jared said you were really sick. I've been admiring your work for a long time. I can't believe I'm actually…"

"I don't care who he says he is," she groaned, staring into Jared's eyes and refusing to address the man claiming to be an IT tech.

"But Sally," Jared pleaded.

"He could be working for Randy." The corners of her mouth turned down. "I shouldn't have called you," she sighed and turned to Nate. "Don't waste your time Mr. Roberts; I was never stupid enough to write anything about Randy on any of Jared's computers." She left the room, rounded the guardrail, and descended the stairs.

Nate turned up his palms and shrugged his shoulders. "What'd I do, man?"

"She's having problems with her husband, and, and she was sick," Jared answered apologetically. "It's not you; I'll go talk to her."

"No, listen dude; it's obvious that my being here isn't a good thing right now. I'll come back tomorrow."

"I'll be here all night if you change your mind," Jared replied. "I've got dozens of ideas swimming around in my brain to use with this new program."

Sally heard footsteps coming down the stairs behind her. She was already regretting how she had treated Jared.

"It was nice meeting you, Ms. Samuels," Nate said, startling her as he stepped around her in the doorway. Jared appeared next and they watched Nate slip his arms into a dark all-weather jacket. He was tall and young like Jared, but to Sally, his face suggested a maturity that might have been gained by something weightier than IT work. He pulled the hood over his head and trotted across the street.

"You can spend the night if you like," Jared whispered.

"No," she whispered.

"Sally, please come upstairs; I want to show you how I'm going to expand The Voice to an online periodical. Nate installed a program that allows students, or anyone, to submit articles for approval from their own device. A link to *The Campus Voice* will appear on Facebook and every choice page. I never had the resources to make The Voice this sophisticated before. I'll have to invest a little money and hire some people. Actually, hire people, instead of begging for volunteers; isn't that insane? Nate says I'll make it back in no time with advertisers."

There was no question that Jared was excited about the project. The site could very well take off like wildfire. They sat on the stoop in the doorway and watched the rain bounce off the street. "Are you sure this guy's not scamming you for the investment money? And how many times have you told me you'd never sell advertising space?"

"Nate said I'd be able to pick and choose the ads."

Sally laid her hand on Jared's arm. "Let me check him out before this goes too far."

"Would you?" He placed his hand over hers. "I won't commit until you give me the go-ahead."

She put her hand over his trying to rein in this enthusiasm. "It'll take me a couple of days. In the meantime,"

"I'll be waiting," he replied; his face beaming.

"I'm sorry I was so rude before, Jared," Sally sighed.

"We discussed building a forum for you," Jared added.

"No forum," Sally said and pushed herself up from the stoop, ignoring Jared's effort to help her. She pulled the sweatshirt hood over her head and picked up the eco-bag at the foot of the stairs. "I should look like a street person in this, don't you think," she said. "My condo is only five blocks from here; I'd like to walk."

"That's crazy," Jared contested. "Look at the weather. Your car is around back; I'll get my raincoat."

"I've been walking these streets since I was a kid, even in the rain," Sally said after he returned with a dark green poncho. She told him many times about how she used to steal away from the convent as a young girl.

"You know," he laughed, "I'm sure nuns at St. Jude who tried to tame that little juvenile delinquent would be proud of you now, Sally."

"I'm sure the divine order was convinced I'd grow up to be a felon." Sally stepped out into the drizzle and headed in the opposite direction from Nate. Ominous clouds were blowing inland, and after a few blocks, she thought she heard footsteps behind her. Was it a mugger or someone Randy hired to follow her; Nate Roberts, perhaps, who could be one and the same? A store was ahead with a narrow entryway with a glass window showcase. She darted into it, pressed against a brick wall, and slipped behind a large planter. She began to re-think the decision to duck into the tunnel-like entrance when her follower stopped in the middle of the entryway. Water dripped from the hood of Jared's poncho and began to make a tapping noise on her shoulder. She peered between the plant stems and saw it was Nate Roberts. He moved on, and Sally exhaled in relief; then she nervously wiped the rain tacked to her face and hugged the brick that formed half of the shelter until she reached the edge of the glass showcase. She peeked around the corner and saw him walking slowly and looking from side to side in the next block. She slipped from her hiding place, quickly turned the corner, and backtracked a block. She gripped the cloth recycle bag that was now wet to the point that it no longer protected its contents. She crossed a street and walked toward the harbor, where vagrants were curled in sleeping bags under benches along the wide sidewalk at the harbor wall. More were wrapped in layers of clothing and salvaged plastic under the large bushes in the lawn between the sidewalk and the street. Sally took everything of value from the bag and shoved it into the pockets of Jared's sweatpants, then discarded the drenched bag into a garbage barrel. She passed several benches before choosing one. She loved to sit by the smelly harbor and listen to the water lap against the docks and the seagulls squeal and caw as they flew overhead or land on the dock posts to say hello and then take off again. Tourists and other passersby generally avoided eye contact with the homeless panhandlers that hung around West Harbor Drive. They didn't want to be seen enabling an alcoholic indigent by putting money in their outstretched palms. She closed her eyes and took in the aroma of mildew that permeated the harbor. She bowed and put her hand to her head when she heard the rustle of the plastic underneath her bench.

"Lee," she whispered. "Is that you?"

The bundle under the bench moved, and five gloved fingers appeared out from under it. "Yes, Miss Sally."

"The shelter will pick up Old Walter when he's released tomorrow," she whispered. "There are clothes for all of you at the warehouse; I'll leave the door unlocked. That should give me time to get him out of town before someone else grabs him."

The black lumpy figure beneath the bench spoke again. "Roger that, Miss Sally. Look on the ground by your right foot." The fingertips disappeared under the plastic clump, leaving a small, clear zip lock bag behind that contained a cell phone. Sally quickly picked up the bag and put it in the sweatpants pocket. "Drop your old one in the bay," the crusty voice said. "Your article has stirred up as much chatter from Escondido as when Barksdale died."

"I wish it would have made them lose interest in Randy," Sally whispered.

"They're only digging in deeper. You should assume your condo is bugged in light of what happened to you today. The star key will scramble all electronic devices within a quarter-mile; press it again to restore it. It's encoded so no one can hack or clone it."

"There's a new player, Nate Roberts; I think Randy sent him to The Voice to spy on me."

"I'm aware," he grunted.

"You should be at the shelter."

"I have a Metro card and a place."

Sally stood and walked to the safety rail that separated a row of boat docks from the public walkway. The water rippled around the rocking boats, lifting their slacked moorings up and down. She leaned on the rail and let her cell phone go. It didn't make a sound when it slipped into the water next to a piling. Frustrated and tired and almost looking like one of the homeless, she crossed several streets along the outskirts of the lamp district. She stopped at the Convention Center. Its upper decks represented the rolling surf and had been billed as an architectural wonder. It could handle twenty conventions simultaneously and was tagged for the next Democratic Presidential Nominating Convention. The city had its rough periods, and so had Sally, but she always thought of San Diego as the most beautiful city in the country, even in the rain. She wondered if she would survive trying to save it. Sally shuffled along the edge of the huge walkway in front of the Convention Center. She passed an outdoor restaurant on First Ave. The tables were empty, and the umbrellas were removed, but somewhere within the dark perimeter of the tables, she heard someone call her name.

"Ms. Samuels, is that you?" It was a man's voice.

She turned slowly, expecting to see a street dweller leaning against the building or crumpled under one of the tables. She quickly continued, hastening her steps when she saw the dark all-weather jacket glistening with raindrops.

"Mrs. Samuels?" Nate Roberts shouted after stepping into the light of a street lamp.

The flip-flops slapped the bottoms of her heels, throwing water up the back of her sweatpants. "Go away, or I'll call 911," she said loudly and walked faster.

"Please," he shouted and rushed to catch up with her.

She stopped abruptly and shouted, “Leave me alone.” They were facing each other now. Nate’s soft blue eyes looked down into her fiery green pools.
Sally shook her head, turned around, and continued to walk.

“We have to talk,” Nate said as he walked beside her.

“You don’t need my blessing to help Jared with his paper.” Her building was two blocks ahead on Island Avenue, so she made an evasive right turn.

“Yes, but I think Jared does,” he said. “I’m concerned he won’t commit without your approval. Did he tell you about the forum we created for you?”

“I told him not to do it.”

“You can participate from home.”

Sally stopped walking and looked up at him. “Listen to me very carefully. Jared can do whatever he wants, but there will be no forum, and I’m not going to contribute; I’m never going back there.” His pleading blue eyes were almost convincingly innocent. He raised his hands and pulled the hood off her head, then touched her damp hair and brushed her glistening cheek. He slid his hands down her arms until he reached her hands. “Mr. Roberts,” she whispered, resting her hands in his. “I know how powerful Randy’s backers are. It took everything I had to print that article accusing him of obstructing justice in the Barksdale case. I’ve been expecting retaliation.” She pulled her hands away and stepped back. “If you’re part of that, please leave Jared out. I promise you; he had nothing to do with it.” She pulled the hood back over her head and started to walk again.

Nate followed. “I’m not what you think I am.” Sally stared ahead as she walked, trying to ignore him. “Jared has talent, it would be a shame if he held himself back just because you didn’t approve. I’ll be out of the picture when *The Campus Voice* takes off. I don’t work for anyone; I’m in business for myself.”

“Nate,” she sighed. “I think I hear a semblance of sincerity in your voice, so please understand that I want Jared and his paper free of the suspicions surrounding me.”

“I do understand,” Nate replied. They both momentarily stopped walking. “And I’ll try my best not to bother you again, despite the huge fan I am of yours." He turned to walk away but stopped. He took something from his jacket pocket and put it in her hand. It was a small throwaway cell phone with the logo *IT Specialists* printed on it in red letters. "It's my business card. Press the green button and message me if you change your mind about the forum. *The Campus Voice* is going to lure a broader spectrum of readers. It will be really cool; you might want to be a part of it."

Nate Roberts was handsome and seemed passionate like David was a lifetime ago. Being part of such a project would be exciting and, perhaps, put her on a new career path. She snapped herself out of the delusion as she watched Nate jog away. He crossed at the corner and headed back toward the restaurant. Sally walked behind her condo building, crossed the street, and ducked into a narrow walkway beside a gift shop. She squeezed through one small space between the buildings after another until she reached a warehouse service door. She unlocked it with a key on her keychain and stepped inside. Rain slapped the sidewalk on the other side of a corrugated metal dock door. Security lights shined through the gaps around the door, enabling her to see the silhouette of a pallet load of sixty cardboard boxes labeled *Inmate Clothing*. She lifted a flap on one of the boxes to verify the contents. She grabbed the handle of a steel rod hanging over a beam beside the roll-up door. It had a hook on one end, and she used it to knock the locks out from under both sides of the door and then hung it back in its place. She exited by a utility cellar under the building, checking behind her every few seconds to make sure she wasn't being followed. She traveled through a maze of passageways that ended at a single door. She reached over the facing and worked her fingers along the edge until she found a key that unlocked it, replaced it, and entered the adjacent building. She followed another maze of hallways until she came to a door with a stenciled sign that read *laundry*. It opened into the housekeeping area of her condo building. She took the service elevator to the fourth floor and then the stairs to the sixth-floor penthouse. Sally had kept the penthouse after marrying Randy because she needed a place to be alone and think and write. She went to the bedroom and emptied the sweatpants pockets onto the bed. She picked up the cell phone Nate gave her and held it in her hand. The screen displayed a blinking icon, indicating he had a text message. Sally carefully changed behind a dressing screen into a more leisurely outfit, keeping in mind Lee's warning that her condo was most likely bugged. She carried Nate's cell with her to the living room and pulled back the drapes that covered one length of the room. She reveled in the spectacular view of downtown San Diego, the bay, and the Coronado Bridge. She poured herself a glass of wine and took it to the balcony. She leaned against the ledge, listened to the sounds of the city below, and watched the lights stream back and forth from Coronado Island as she sipped the wine. The alert from the tiny cell phone in her hand seemed to pulse in time with her heartbeat. *Nate Roberts, you must think I'm a fool.* She was too far up to hear it hit the pavement but leaned over the ledge anyway in time to see a service truck pass below.

Tony walked quietly through the house in his tee shirt and boxers, checking doors and turning off lights. He tried to close the kitchen screen door but the hinges had been bowed and twisted. He didn't even remember opening it after seeing Lizzy stumble on the armrests of the lawn chair. He went to the living room and turned the deadbolt. The evening had gone well; the family sat down and watched the entire Mary Poppins video together. Lizzy knew the songs by heart and entertained them by dancing along with Julie Andrews and Dick Van Dyke. He thought he heard Lizzy's voice when he approached her bedroom. He opened the door, but everything was quiet and still. He went into his room next to hers but stopped when he heard her giggle and make a shushing sound. He quickly stepped back into her room and switched on the light. Lizzy was sitting up in bed with a blanket over her head.

"Hurry!" she whispered rather loudly.

"Elizabeth!" Tony growled after pulling back the blanket. "What's that dog doing in your bed?"

"Why didn't you disappear?" Lizzy whined to Phoebe.

"What's that dog doing in your bed, Lizzy?" he demanded again. Phoebe jumped to the floor and scampered into the hall; Tony followed.

"Daddy, don't be mad," she cried, trotting behind him. Phoebe was sitting beside the kitchen door when Tony turned on the light. Lizzy was wide-eyed and breathing hard when she caught up to him. Tony opened the door, but Phoebe pranced to the middle of the kitchen instead.

"Outside!" he ordered.

"Ruff, ruff," Phoebe replied and then turned around in a circle and sat down.

"She doesn't want to go home, Daddy." Lizzy dropped to her knees on the floor beside her.

"Go on, get out of here," Tony growled.

"Ruff, ruff," Phoebe barked again, sitting in the middle of the kitchen floor.

"That's *no,*" Lizzy said, looking up at her father. "Once is for *yes,* and twice is for *no*."

"Lizzy, please." He said sternly.

"Maybe if you ask her nicely, Daddy; I think you hurt her feelings." Lizzy gently petted the top of Phoebe's head. "I think you scared her, and now she doesn't trust you." Phoebe licked Lizzy on the nose. "Yes, see, that's it," Lizzy said. "You hurt her feelings."

Nicky staggered into the kitchen, squinting one eye. "What's all that barking?"

"Phoebe's scared of Daddy," Lizzy whispered to her sister.

"That's enough, Lizzy," Tony growled. He looked at Phoebe and pointed to the door.

"Maybe she wants a treat," Lizzy cooed.

"Ruff," Phoebe barked, stood up, and wagged her tail.

"You see?" Lizzy squealed, looking up at her father. "That's *yes*. She wants a treat." Lizzy scrambled to her feet and darted to the refrigerator. She opened the door but was interrupted by her father.

"Lizzy," he growled, "close that door!" He reached down and scooped Phoebe up with one hand. Elizabeth's eyes grew wide when he put her out the front door. "She'll find her way home," he said, trying to reason with her.

"But it's raining," Lizzy sobbed.

Tony knelt on one knee beside her. "She'll be fine."

"Oh, God, not again!" Nicky sneered and returned to her room after her father frowned at her. Nicky's attitude wasn't worth dealing with because Lizzy was on the verge of something that might take a while to get under control. "Lizzy, she's just a dog. Dogs don't have feelings; they just live in the moment. She won't remember this fifteen minutes from now. I chased her out of the garage the other day. I told her to go home, and she did." Lizzy cried even harder, so Tony led her to her room, choosing not to ask how the dog got in her room in the first place. He pressed a wet washrag to her face and forehead until she calmed down. "Feel better?" he whispered.

She rubbed her eyes and nodded. "I know you don't understand, Daddy," she whispered, "because Phoebe's not like other dogs. She's a magic dog."

"Honey," Tony replied. "I know she's special to you, and she's been trained really well, but she has a home, and that's where she belongs. What if Miss Annette had been out in the rain all this time looking for her? You wouldn't want her to get mad at us because Phoebe was here, would you?"

"Miss Nette would know she was somewhere doing her magic," Lizzy said and turned on her side. Tony gave up trying to reason with his six-year-old and went to bed, but tossed and turned with worry for two hours before finally falling asleep.

Chapter 17

Ty Hemil, aka Nate Roberts, climbed the steps to his second-floor efficiency on 3rd Ave., hung his rain-soaked coat on the hook behind the door, and then went straight to the refrigerator and grabbed a bottle of *Life Water*. He turned the bottle up, finishing it all at once, and then threw it across the small kitchenette, where it landed squarely in the trashcan. He retrieved a laptop from the armoire in the bedroom section of the room and carried it to the bed. A message from Colin was waiting for him.

"Phantom working?" Ty replied to his friend's salutation, a single sentence telling him to check in.

C: *I see your message clearly over the bogus one about being settled in.*

T: *Made contact with Sally, but she didn't quite appreciate my charm.*

C: *Guess not, the device you gave her lost signal when it hit the pavement*

below her balcony. Surveillance verifies a truck ran over it.

"Seriously?" Ty responded while laughing out loud.

T: *I successfully injected the tracking device.*

C: *Transmitting loud and clear.*

T: *Was that us at the restaurant? Who was the lunch date?*

C: *Affirmative. Persuaded bartender. Lunch date is a new associate*

of Rick Samuels. Lives in Mesa near the retirement village.

T: *Did we follow the vagrant?*

C: *Lost him; limited facial rec from street cam.*

T: *He gave Sally something. Going back to the campus newspaper tomorrow;*

will scan their computers.

C: *Remember, eyes are on you.*

T: *Adios, Kemosabe.*

C: *Hi-yo!*

Ty plugged his earbuds into the laptop and listened to the recordings of Sally in the upstairs office of The Voice and

Jared at the foot of the stairs. While Jared was parking the Mercedes, the transmitter he injected under her skin between her shoulder blades was working perfectly. Everyone on Sub Level 3 was now tracking, listening, and waiting to see if Sally knew about The Group's mission to control the thoughts and actions of those living under the influence of the enhancement. He observed the exchange between Sally and the vagrant from a camera posted twenty feet away but the rain had played havoc with the video and their low voices. He leaned back against a pillow and listened to her 25-minute walk home after their exchange that should have only taken 10. He listened to her breathing, opening doors, shuffling, and moving things. The tracking device put her across the street and west of her condo. "What are you doing?" he sighed.

Tony huffed rhythmically as he ran through the neighborhood streets the next morning. He was compelled to jog further and cross Canyon Rd. he needed more time to sort out Elizabeth's relationship with Phoebe and pick apart his lunchtime conversation with Sally the day before. He met the man in black sweats again; they nodded good morning to each other as before. He saw Annette step out from the alley when he neared Jewel. Phoebe was prancing around her feet as Annette talked to her.

"Hey!" Tony hollered.

"Oh! Dr. Harding," she said, raising her head and looking at him through sunglasses.

"What's with the dark glasses and the cap pulled down so far?" he asked.

"I have a migraine comin on; I'm tryin to avoid the light."

"Do you have them often?" he asked with concern.

"Once a week, or so," she sighed. "Dr. Rick prescribed somethin, but it doesn't always work, and it wipes me out."

"You should try taking two low-grade aspirins," Tony offered. "It's the same as baby aspirin, but you have to take it every day. It opens the capillaries in the frontal area." He pointed to her forehead under her cap. "*Samuels Family Practice*," he said, reading the logo across the front.

"I coached for Dr. Rick last summer."

"That's you in the team picture I saw in his office, and Phoebe." Tony looked down at Phoebe standing at Annette's feet. "So, are you going to coach this year? Dr. Samuels really wants you to, you know." Phoebe yipped once, but Annette corrected her.

"I don't think so." She lowered the cap over her eyes. "I should go; talkin isn't good for me either."

"You'll know in about two weeks if the aspirin is helping." Tony looked down at Phoebe again. "Uh-actually, I was hoping to talk to you about something."

"What?" She replied impatiently.

"Last night, Phoebe was at our house, uh, in our house. It was kind of late, and I shooed her home. I thought you should know; in case you were looking for her. Unless that is, you normally let her run loose at night."

"No, she's not supposed to be out at night." She rubbed her forehead and looked down at Phoebe. "Were you at the Harding's last night?"

Phoebe bowed her head and rolled her eyes upward and replied in a low voice, "Ruff."

Annette pursed her lips together and put her hands on her hips. "We'll talk about this later," she said, addressing Phoebe. "It won't happen again."

"What?" Tony asked.

"What?" she returned.

"We'll talk about it later?"

"Oh," she said. "Uh, yeah; I'll make sure she's—I'm really not up to this."

"Uh, wait, one more thing," Tony said hesitantly. "Surely you've noticed that Elizabeth is..."

"Impressionable?" Annette interrupted, forcing a smile, "and smart, and has an imagination that's out of this world, and her drawings are awesome."

"But it's because she's so impressionable that I'm a little nervous about what's happening with Phoebe."

"So, what are you sayin?" Annette challenged.

"Is there something you can do to, uh, maybe, divert her attention away from Phoebe when she's at Molly's? Or, even better…" He gestured to the alley. "Leave her at home?"

Annette didn't answer right away. She put her hand on the bill of her cap while she fought the flush in her neck that was slowly moving up her face.

"I hope I haven't upset you," Tony said, confused by her silence.

"Well then." Annette reached down and picked Phoebe up, and handed her to Tony. "Would you please take her home and put her in the backyard for me? She has a doggy door."

"Well, I—I guess." Phoebe made herself comfortable in Tony's arms and watched him grope for what to say next. "I've upset you, haven't I?"

"Phoebe," Annette said, pointing a finger at her. Phoebe ducked her head down and nestled her nose into the bend of Tony's arm. "Dr. Harding is going to take you home, and I better not hear anything else about you roamin all over the neighborhood. Do you hear me?"

Phoebe whined and snuggled closer against Tony's chest.

"Yeah, right," Annette said, responding to the cuddling.

"Uh," Tony hesitated. "You, uh, don't really think she understood you?" he stuttered. "Just put her inside the gate?" he relented, reading the scowl on her face.

"Yes, please," Annette answered. "She won't give you any trouble, she likes you. And I'm late." She marched away without looking back.

Tony stood in the street holding Phoebe. He looked down at the furry bundle in his arms, and she looked up at him. "She's upset, isn't she?" he said. "Maybe it's just the migraine. Oh, wait; I'm not talking to you-I'm talking to myself; there's a difference." When Tony walked by, the two German Shepherds were lying next to their chain link fence. They both made an attempt at a single bark, but it came out more like a groan, far from Monday's early morning wailing that had terrified Elizabeth. Phoebe returned their greeting, to which one of them responded by wagging its tail. Tony opened Annette's gate and gently placed Phoebe on one of the small stepping stones that led to the porch. "Go on in the house like she said," Tony said to Phoebe, who was staring up at him. He waved his arm in the air and pointed to the porch. Phoebe scampered across the stone path and pranced up the steps. She turned around and looked at him, wagging her tail. Tony closed the gate and hurried home after he saw her jump through the doggie door. The girls were surely up by now, and he had errands.

Nicky and Lizzy were already sitting at the table when Tony finished showering. "What happened to the cologne on the dresser from yesterday?" he asked when he sat down. "Did one of you throw it out?"

"The stinky stuff?" Elizabeth asked.

"It's fine if you did because I was going to."

"No sir," Elizabeth said. "I don't know where it is."

"Be glad," Nicky said.

"It just appeared from nowhere and now it mysteriously disappeared?"

"Yes, mysteriously," Lizzy repeated.

"You don't have to take me to school today," Nicky said. "I have a ride."

Tony poured the milk over his cereal. "No, I'm taking both of you just like yesterday."

"But it's embarrassing," she sneered. "Robby's friend Todd has a yellow Camaro and picks him up every day; they can drop me off."

"Camaro; nope, not gonna happen," Tony said, and took a bite of cereal.

"Why?" she snarled back at him.

"Nicky, I'm not arguing with you about this. I don't know Todd. I'll talk to Brad, and then we'll see."

Nicky quickly rose from the table, stomped into the living room, and returned with the cordless phone. She put it down on the table in front of him. "Call Mr. Brad," she said. "Call him now, so I can go with them this morning."

Tony picked up the phone and put it back down. "I don't know the number."

Nicky picked up the phone, pressed the digits, and returned it. Tony heard the ringtone as she held the cordless out to him. He took the phone from her and went to the living room.

"Can I ride with you, Nicky?" Lizzy whispered from across the table.

"No," Nicky hissed.

"But why," Lizzy asked.

"Just shut up!"

"Are you coming to Molly's after school?" Elizabeth whimpered.

"I don't know," Nicky whispered adamantly.

"Don't ever put me in that position again, Nicky," Tony grumbled when he returned to the kitchen. "When I say no, that's what I mean. I'm going to allow it, just this once, and only because Brad vouched for this boy Todd, and you will take Lizzy."

"Robby talk's funny," Lizzy beamed, but Nicky gave her a dirty look.

"Yeah," Tony said and picked up his spoon again. "Be sure and tell me how funny he talks today on the way to school, Lizzy." He looked at Nicky as she glared back at him in silence. "You know, I saw some kids riding bicycles to school yesterday," he said.

"You're kidding," she gasped.

"I've been thinking about getting one of those parental cell phones, so you can call me in case of emergencies."

"Don't get one of those bunk bargain phones. I need a real one."

"Then get a job and help me pay for it," he rebutted. "Do you know how much those things cost? My father always said…" He stopped himself short and took a breath. He couldn't believe what came out of his mouth. Was he brain-dead? He never wanted to be anything like his father.

"Like father, like son," Nicky mumbled. She got up from the table and left the room in a huff.

"Daddy, can I be excused?" Lizzy asked. "I don't want Nicky to leave me."

"Lizzy, just a minute; I'd like to say something about last night," he said gingerly, trying to avoid an upset. "I don't want you to think I'm mad because Phoebe was in your room. Everything is fine; I spoke to Annette about it this morning, and she will make sure Phoebe stays home."

"But Daddy," Elizabeth said and then pressed her lips together as if trying to make sure she didn't say too much.

"If she comes to the door," he said, trying to reason with her, "don't let her in, she'll go home."

"Yes, sir," Elizabeth said and bowed her head. "But that's not what happened," she muttered as she stared into her cereal bowl.

"What did you say?" he asked.

"Can I be excused now, Daddy?"

Tony nodded, and Lizzy picked up her bowl and took it to the sink. She looked at her daddy sitting at the table, thinking *Mommy would have understood.*

Tony followed the Camaro to make sure his daughters were delivered to school safely, and then he headed to USCSD.

Tonya tried to suppress her enthusiasm when she saw him, but a couple of squeaks managed to slip out when she addressed him. "Why are you here so early?" She looked back at the empty waiting area, flinging her mop-style hairdo. "You know what? I bet it has something to do with this lab report with your name on it. It was brought up sometime during the night." She reached into a filing basket, retrieved a large white envelope, and handed it to him.

"Actually, I'm here to talk to Rick."

"Is something wrong?" she said with concern. "I don't like the look on your face, Dr. Harding. Something is wrong, isn't it?"

"It's personal. I'd appreciate it if you'd find him for me."

"It must be bad," she whispered and hurried to her desk in the reception area. She looked back at him while she picked up the phone.

Tony looked at the sealed white envelope in his hand. It had the hospital logo printed in the upper left corner and the word *Lab* stamped on it in bold black letters. His name and Samuels Family Practice, 5th Floor, were written underneath. He ran his finger under the edge of the flap and opened it. Inside was the report for patient *M. Smith.* It was printed on a single five-by-seven sheet of paper. It listed the properties contained in the sample presented by Dr. Anthony Harding on the previous date. The food described was as expected but with no presence of bacteria. Viral infection was reported as unknown because, *"blood sample n/a.*" The line for poisons had a notation, *"Os2O2 arsenic trioxide/poison"*.

"What?" Tony whispered. This would be so much simpler if there had been bacteria. Now he was obligated to report the findings to Sally and the authorities.
Tonya returned, announcing that Dr. Rick was in his office. She grabbed the corner of a filing cabinet as if trying to prepare herself for bad news when Tony told her not to bother escorting him. Tony folded the envelope and put it in the breast pocket of his jacket before knocking. He heard Rick's boisterous voice on the other side of the door inviting him in.

Rick was nearly at the door when he entered. The elder extended both arms, grabbed Tony's right hand, and clutched his arm affectionately. Dr. Rick Samuels had never shown any signs of misgivings toward him. Rick invited Tony to join him in the leather chairs on either side of the statue of Hippocrates. "Have a seat," he said, "and tell me what you thought of the hospital yesterday."

Tony eased into the cushy chair. "I didn't visit all the floors, of course, but everything looked clean; the staff was friendly, efficient, knowledgeable, and helpful."

"That's the kind of first impression I like to hear," he said. "What else? What about the lab report that came up with your name on it? What patient sparked your curiosity?"

"Lab report," Tony repeated. Of course, Rick would have seen the white envelope in Tonya's file basket. "Oh, that was a personal request. A patron fell ill yesterday in the restaurant I went to, and *he* refused to let me take him to the hospital. I felt compelled to—oh, did I break hospital policy?"

"No, not at all," Rick assured him. "I would expect that from someone like you. What were the results?"

"Inconclusive; actually, he's fine now."

"You know, that's what impressed Arthur about you, son; the extra effort you took with him. You took it upon yourself to call his family, spend time with him, brought him books from the hospital library. That's pretty old school by today's standards, but that extra attention has been proven to actually hasten patient recovery." The Hippocratic Oath was written in 400 B.C. and is taken by all doctors upon graduation from medical school. It's supposed to be their moral guide throughout their career. Tony's personal life might have been a mess but he never conceded where his work was concerned.

"Look, Rick," Tony began with a sigh.

"Is something wrong?" Rick asked. "You're not thinking of returning to Chicago, are you?"

"No sir," Tony replied. "Nothing could make me do that. I ran into your sister-in-law in the parking lot when I left here yesterday." Rick's face transformed immediately, just as Tony expected it would. The elder doctor closed his eyes while the corners of his mouth turned downward as if he'd tasted something sour.

"What did she do?" He moaned. "You wouldn't be here unless she upset you. He got up from the chair and walked to the window. "That woman is nothing but trouble. I wish to God Randy had never married her."

Tony stood up. "She told me things about my wife, the way she died, and my personal life that she has no business knowing; things that no one should know, especially my employer. I'd like to know why it was necessary to dig so deep into my personal life."

Rick turned from the window and returned to the center of the room. They stood facing one another with the impressive statue of the Greek physician standing between them like a referee. "Dr. Harding," Rick finally whispered. "I'm so embarrassed." He turned away from him and covered his eyes with one hand. "I never would have—I never intended—I don't know what to say." Rick Samuels was one of the most revered members of the medical community. He wrote papers published in top medical magazines and stood in front of hundreds to give lectures and presentations. But he was stammering for words as he went to his desk and slowly sat down while holding on to both armrests.

"And she made it sound as if Randy, you, and perhaps everyone is in some sort of danger," Tony said. "And it has something to do with The Group."

Rick bowed his head. "I used Randy's resources to check your employment history and references. Unfortunately, everything shows up when it's a request from someone with his credentials in the D.A.'s office. There were a couple of footnotes regarding your wife's cause of death and the accident. She obviously read the report before Randy gave it to me. I assure you..."

"Footnotes?" Tony cut in before Rick could squeeze in another excuse.

"The drugs and alcohol," Rick explained. "But you knew that, didn't you?"

Tony sat down in the chair across from Rick. The leather rumbled as if expressing his humiliation. "I didn't know how bad the pills were until after she died. I found prescription bottles from seven different doctors in her medicine cabinet. But the police said it was the impact of the mail truck that killed her."

Rick folded his hands together and leaned forward. He spoke in a more professional manner now, as he might with the family of a patient. "She only had a slim chance of survival, considering the amounts of amphetamines and alcohol in her system. And you don't have to worry about me telling anyone any of this."

"Some of what she told me can't possibly be on the NCIS sight," Tony growled. "Just how far is your brother's reach?"

"There are things about his work he doesn't share with me, son."

"Is something happening around here that I should know about?" Tony asked. "Sally mentioned Andrew Barksdale's death and your son, Kevin. And she said The Group has some sort of control over Randy."

"What Sally did yesterday is typical of what she's famous for," Rick said. "She wanted to unnerve you; throw you off balance. She wants something from you, Dr. Harding. Maybe information about Randy or my research, there's no telling. She's angry because The Group is grooming Randy for a future in politics. Stay away from her. I assure you that nothing we just talked about is in your personnel file. It contains only the glowing reports and recommendations from your employers and peers, and of course, Arthur's personal letter."

Colin Sadler studied the images from Dr. Samuels' office from his monitor in Sub Level 3. The view was from the statue of Hippocrates placed there by Lorraine Samuels and retrofitted with a camera and microphone by Group operatives. *This conversation could be damaging to Sally.*

"What are you looking for, my dear?" Molly asked Annette when she saw Annette riffling through the medicine closet.

"Molly, this is a childcare facility; why can't I find any baby aspirins?"

"Which one of the babies has a fever?" Molly said, waddling up beside her.

"It's for me," Annette replied.

"You have another migraine? Because if you do, I insist that you go see Dr. Rick again."

"Not yet." Annette followed Molly down the hall to the office, where she retrieved her purse and pulled out a small bottle of low-grade aspirin. "Lizzy's father suggested I take two baby aspirin a day."

"Oh? When did he do that?" Molly asked curiously.

"On my way here, just now," Annette replied.

"Hum," Molly hummed.

"Don't get any ideas, Molly. You know how I feel about doctors."

"I didn't say anything. I take one of these every day to thin my blood."

"Why, is somethin wrong?"

"No, no," Molly chuckled. "I'm being pro-active. Everybody at Mesa Village takes these." Molly handed the bottle to Annette. "Keep it, I have more. So, tell me what you think about Lizzy's father?"

"Nothin, but Phoebe's sure up to somethin. He told me she was at his house last night."

"Where is my little darling?"

"At home; Dr. Harding asked me to keep her there because Lizzy is too attached; he could be right." They walked to the kitchen, where Molly sat at the table, and Annette took the baby aspirin with a glass of orange juice.

"Phoebe has a way of picking out people that need her," Molly whispered, even though they were the only two people in the house. "Like Jim."

"Yeah," Annette sighed. "I remember how Phoebe used to trot alongside him in the garden and when he walked the neighborhood with his cane."

"Maybe Phoebe senses she's needed," Molly proposed.

Nette sighed to clear the memory of the remarkable neighbor who amazingly improved his capabilities to the point of becoming an award-winning horticulturist. "I guess kids and dogs are just naturally attracted to each other."

"Not all children get what they need from their parents," Molly said in a low voice, "and Phoebe's got a special gift."

"I know, Molly, but I really don't want to get that involved." Nette opened a cabinet, pulled out a stack of plastic bowls and cups, carried them to the table, and handed them to Molly.

"It's just you and me here, dear," Molly whispered. She held onto her hands cupped around the bowls. "Don't tell me you haven't seen him."

"Seen who?" Annette forced the bowls down onto the table and sat down next to Molly.

"The man in the brown jacket and the Indiana Jones hat, of course."

"Molly?" Nette took Molly's plump hands in hers. "What are you talking about?"

"Don't patronize me!" Molly fussed and jerked her hands away.

"Molly," Annette said tenderly. "When did you see this man?"

"During the magic show," she replied. "And every time Phoebe…you know," she whispered. "Is that Mona pulling up?" Molly quickly got up from the table and went into her office.

Annette had an aunt who claimed she saw spiders crawling on the wall and cats sitting in her windows; she also heard voices. This went on for years before she suddenly died from a massive stroke. She met Mona coming in from the garage. "Oh, Mona!" she gasped.

"Nette," Mona asked. "What's wrong?"

Annette sighed, remembering Mona's announcement from the day before. "I'm so sorry we didn't get to talk yesterday."

"Don't be upset, Nette; I'll be okay."

Annette put a hand up over her forehead. "And Molly," she whispered. "She's got me worried; she's actin funny."

"Again, she always acts funny," Mona said while hanging her jacket behind the kitchen door.

"She had a strange look in her eyes just now. She told me she's been seein this imaginary man."

"Lisa and I will keep an eye on her."

"What about you and Tim?" Nette asked. "Have you…?"

"No!" Mona cast her eyes down and walked past her. "He called me wanting to talk." Mona sounded both disappointed and angry. "But he didn't really offer anything different. He just wanted me to come home. I told him he couldn't be married to me and alcohol at the same time. I've made up my mind, and I'm not changing it."

Annette allowed Mona a minute to regain her composure. Being raised amongst the poor middle class in financially depressed Louisiana, Annette had seen more than her share of functional alcoholics with lost motivation. Tim's promises carried the same ring as the good ol' boys and gals from home who had a fresh beer in their hands at all times but no job and no home of their own. "Mona," Nette finally said. "I'm so sorry." She placed a hand on Mona's shoulder. "If you need to talk, you know I'm a good listener."

"Gracias, my good friend," Mona said, "perhaps later, during nap time."

Mona looked at the assortment of cereal boxes and plastic bowls and cups on the table. "What? No eggs?" They both laughed.

Sally walked to The Voice in the early morning mist to retrieve her Mercedes and then drove to The San Diego Daily Post. She parked in her designated spot in the parking complex and entered the automatic doors. She adjusted her shoulder bag and nodded proudly to the pretty young receptionist whose blonde curls flowed past her shoulders. The freshman secretary was dressed in trendy clothes and flaunted a huge smile when Sally approached her. The smile waned after the well-known reporter walked past her but was quickly re-set when Sally reached the first-floor elevator bank and looked back. Sally held her head high when she disembarked on the busy third floor into a wide hallway that led to the common newsroom area with six rows of desks that were enclosed with half-partitions. The regular nine o'clock staff meeting was over, and the energized reporters were already out on the street hoping to seize the day's headline. Three junior reporters were at their computers tapping out their copy to submit for a possible spot in the evening run. She took an extra second before entering her office to gaze at the tile with the embossed star she earned by being at her desk as early or as late as it took to perfect a story. A curious manila folder was on her desk. Assignments have been crappy since the early Monday edition. She passed everything beneath her talent on to Marcus Chew, a junior reporter who always seemed more than eager to bring her coffee, a muffin, or anything he thought she might desire. She opened the file and then slapped it closed. "The opening of a toy store; really, David?"

Tony bought a new screen door, leaned it against the wall on the porch, and spread newspaper across the concrete before opening the can of touch-up paint. As he dipped his brush into the can, he heard a jingling noise. "Awe, I don't believe it," he groaned when he turned and saw Phoebe standing behind him. "How did you get out?"

Phoebe shook her head, making the tag jingle again.

"Go home," Tony commanded. "Shoo!"

Phoebe shuffled backward a couple of steps and sat down, "Ruff-ruff."

"Humph!" Tony grunted and laid the brush down over the top of the can. He walked across the yard and opened the gate. "Come on," he ordered. Phoebe got up and trotted past him into the alley. "Go home!" he demanded. Phoebe ran to her master's gate, and Tony closed it hard to make sure it latched and went back to his chore, but when he finished painting the door casing, he looked around and saw Phoebe lying on the porch behind him. She wagged her tail when he looked at her. "I told you to go home!" He growled and then stomped his foot at her, making her jump to her feet. He hurried to the back gate and opened it, but she didn't obey his commands like before. He made a lunge forward, attempting to grab her, but she darted to the right. He chased her around the yard until she jumped up on the porch. She took shelter behind the screen door, leaning against the wall, causing it to slide forward. "No!" Tony shouted, and ran toward the door, grabbing it before it fell. The door frightened Phoebe and she ran into the open paint can, knocking it over. "Dammit!" Tony blurted out. Phoebe ran off the porch, leaving behind a pattern of zigzag black paw prints. "No!" Tony cried. She stopped in the yard as if waiting for Tony to restart the chase. "Look at what you did," he growled and grabbed a broom and pointed it at her. Phoebe jumped to her feet and scampered out the open gate. Tony slammed the gate and began the arduous chore of cleaning the paw prints and spilling paint off the concrete with mineral spirits. Just as he finished, he heard the jingling again. "No," Tony growled. "How did you…?" he began when he saw Phoebe laying the grass staring up at him. He rushed to the garage and found a self-closing hook that was attached to a nylon rope. He scooped her up, closed the hook around the metal ring on her collar, and then carried her to Annette's and put her down on the porch. He tied the rope around a post nearest the door. The rope was long enough to reach inside the house through the doggy door. "Now," he said, nodding. Phoebe cocked her head to one side. "I know you can't understand me." He pulled at the rope tied to the post to make sure it was secure. "I'm telling myself that this should hold you." He shook his head after Phoebe seemed to respond by cocking her head the other way. After realizing he had no idea how far away the little dog's water supply might be inside, he left but returned with a plastic bowl full of water. Phoebe licked his hand when he put the water bowl down which produced a rumbling sound from Tony's throat.

Tony sat down at the kitchen table to eat a sandwich after finishing the door. Reporters on the noonday TV news were prattling about things that meant nothing to him until he heard the name Randy Samuels.

Randy Samuels of the San Diego District Attorney's Office announced today that District Judge John T.

Yeager had declared a mistrial in the case against the man known as Old Walter in light of evidence brought forward early this week regarding the actual cause of death of Anderson Barksdale, a prominent member of San Diego's tourist commission. District Attorney Samuels advised that Anderson Barksdale actually died from a stroke caused by an aneurysm and not from the blow to the head he received. He confirmed there had been a mix-up in Medical Examiner reports, as alluded to in an earlier report this week in the Daily Post. The inaccuracies resulted in a First-Degree Murder charge by a grand jury. An internal investigation is being conducted regarding the chain of events that led to the confusion within the M.E. department. He emphasized that the papers found in his home safe were not related to the Barksdale case as previously reported. This has been verified by FBI investigators. It has also been determined that the elderly vagrant is mentally incapable of participating in his own defense, should future charges be brought forward.

Several file photos of Randal Samuels flashed across the screen, as well as of Anderson Barksdale and the homeless man, while the reporter read the script.

"Hello, Randal Samuels," Tony addressed the screen, "finally, a face to put with the infamous name." The brothers' resemblance was remarkable with the exception of Rick's hair being whiter and Randy's hair thicker. The report reminded Tony that he should have already told Sally about the traces of arsenic in the sample he collected. The Channel 4 reporter filled the rest of the slot with general file information about Randal Samuels being the future mayoral candidate and his aspiration to run for governor. He left the table in search of Sally's card.

"Sally, who is Dr. Anthony Harding," David asked after knocking and abruptly rushing into her office.

Sally looked up from her computer. "Come right in, David," she said sarcastically. "He works for Rick."

He was waving a small slip of ruled paper torn from a legal pad. "He just called for you and left this number." He dropped the small piece of paper on her desk.

"What, are you screening my calls now?" she asked. "No message?"

"It rang in my office for some reason. I tried to take a message." David had one hand on his hip. The sleeves of his white blue pin stripped shirt were rolled up to his elbows, which meant he was having a busy morning. His black-rimmed glasses were pushed up on top of his full head of black hair, and his forehead was sprinkled with perspiration. "Is this about a story, because he said it was important and could only discuss it with you?"

"No, I met him at Rick's office yesterday, and we had lunch," she replied. "Take that reporter look off your face; you're making my heart flutter."

David put his hands on Sally's desk and leaned closer. Their eyes locked momentarily. There was a time when all he wanted to do was look into those mesmerizing emerald-green eyes. But the zeal that stirred between them during their college years and their early days at the *Post*, when they were both young reporters contending for hot stories, was gone and never to be recaptured. Particularly when David realized how destructive continuing their style of reporting could be for his career. Sally had never forgiven him for turning "Establishment" on her. "Ahem!" David said nervously, clearing his throat. "I'm just concerned about you, Sally. You know that."

"Sure, you are." Sally's eyes narrowed as if they were about to eject daggers. "Until the board starts breathing down your neck; then all you're concerned about is your own ass."

"That's not fair." David tapped his knuckles on the desktop, and he pushed himself away from it.

"I'm sorry, David," she relented. "I know you're just doing your job, and I'm just blowing off steam. Who else would let me do that?" She smiled at him reminiscently. She wished she could see the old David sometimes, the passionate David to whom she could entrust her creativity, no matter how outrageous. She thought she had found that in Randy, but as it turned out, his life was more complicated than she could have imagined. "David, everything is fine," she said, smiling. "Look, I was just sending you an email." She picked up the manila folder. "I'm giving this one to Marcus. I'm busy this afternoon."

"Big surprise," David quipped and followed her to the door. "You've been passing stuff off to him all week. Listen, the Board wants…"

Sally stopped short at the door and turned around. "The Board wants what?" she asked, trying to suppress her impatience. "Listen, David." She poked him in the stomach with the rigid file folder. "Tell the Board I'm moving back into my old condo, and I have things to take care of."

"Sally," David said softly. "Everything's cool. Randy released a statement this morning and he didn't even mention you. The Board says it looks like we are—you are in the clear. You'll be getting lead stories again soon. Take as much time as you need to move."

"What statement?" She asked. "Do you have a copy?" She followed David to his office, where he presented her with the statement that had been released to all media outlets. "Barksdale's report was in his safe," she whispered after reading it.

"Be grateful that the D.A. office is letting this go as *misreporting* and departmental mix-up by someone on their end."

"There was no misreporting! The FBI was there; they saw the M.E. report. Someone should be charged with malfeasance. Fingerprints should have been taken and lie detector tests given." She shoved the news release back into David's hand and slapped the manila folder onto his desk. "Has everyone in this Godforsaken place been brainwashed?" She returned to her office and flopped into her chair. She looked around the room and then focused on the piece of paper David dropped on her desk. "One bright moment in this crappy day," she whispered. She slid the note into her shoulder bag and walked to the door. She reached for the light panel and paused briefly before pressing the button. "Lights out," she whispered, as if speaking to someone who might be hiding in the room.

"Ty, answer me…Ty," Colin called into the microphone of his headset. "Rodriguez and Shepherd were down earlier complaining about the lack of significant progress."

"Can't they see I'm lying groundwork?" Ty's voice returned in a whisper.

Colin looked at the array of screens in front of him and made a couple of keystrokes on the pad in front of him. Four screens projected views from within the office of *The Campus Voice*. "I see how busy you are," he said looking at a monitor above him showing Ty sitting in front of a computer. "Joseph repeated his threat to get rid of Sally in lieu of recent conversations."

"He allowed us two weeks," Ty whispered into the pea-sized unit deep in his ear.

"The lunch date, the doctor, left a message for Sally at the Post," Colin reported.

To maintain his cover Ty reached in his pocket for his cell phone and held it to his ear and then got up from his fiberglass chair and stood at the windows.

"He told Dalton it was important," Colin said. "It's about the lab report. There's a video from The Post where Sally used the word *brainwashed* when talking to Dalton. That kind of language will give Joseph the justification he's looking for."

"I'll get back to you," Ty replied when he saw Jared approaching.

"I just looked at the layout," Jared said as Nate put his phone away, "it's awesome."

"And ready to launch," Nate replied.

"I'm announcing the conversion in Saturday's edition and am putting up extra newspaper stands around the Tech Expo, where there should be plenty of advertisers for computer-related projects. I can't thank you enough for this, man."

Nate patted Jared on the shoulder. "Glad I could help."

The Group had been working for a year in preparation for the arrival of the Chinese after they agreed to attend the Tech Expo as their guest. Every piece of electronics on display was tied to The Group's control room. Expo attendees would move from exhibit to display and marvel over whatever their technicians inclined them to.

"*Sally Samuels Community* looks good," Jared added. "But you know she hasn't agreed to it yet." He went to his laptop and pulled it up. "Where did you get the college photos, like this one of Sally with her arms around David Dalton? They're apparently celebrating a story in the paper he's holding up; and this one of Sally and her parents. There's a lot of personal info here."

"IT consultants have their resources," Nate replied.

"Good to know," Jared said, raising his eyebrows. "Sally's fans should like it, but unfortunately, you'll never get her approval unless you can explain where you got all this."

"Yes, she has a suspicious nature, doesn't she," Nate jibed. "It's kind of sexy." He wrote a phone number down on the desk pad next to Jared's laptop. "Call me after you talk to her. I really wish I could be here to see her reaction, but I just got a panic call from a client over at UCSD." He headed for the stairs.

"Thanks, man," Jared said, projecting his voice enough to reach Nate, who was already loping down the stairs. "If you're scared, just say you're scared.

Chapter 18

Sally took the elevator down to the second floor and boarded a service elevator to the underground press room. Advertisement pages ran rapidly over and around large barrel-like rollers as she pranced through a maze of machines. She ducked into a janitorial supply room and squatted behind a large floor buffer. The sorters whined outside the door as she pressed the keys on the cell phone Lee gave her: *Walter, 3 pm today.* Thanks to Lee's application, the message disappeared and was automatically deleted when she pressed the send key. Then she took the torn piece of paper with Dr. Harding's number from her purse.

Tony fell asleep on the sofa with the phone lying across his chest after leaving the message for Sally while thinking about Robby and how he had stumbled out of the yellow Camaro that morning. He followed them to school and had been puzzled by the uncharacteristic look on the teen's face when he looked toward a group of kids gathered around a sporty blue Pontiac in the parking lot. He didn't think anything could remove the constant frivolous grin on the boy's face. Todd revved the motor, and everyone around the Pontiac turned to look, including the driver, whom Tony recognized as the disrupting older brother from the school office. Tony jerked and nearly ejected the phone off his chest when it suddenly rang.

"Hello," he answered. "Hello?" he repeated because all he heard was the sound of machinery, and he almost ended the call.

"Dr. Harding," a woman's voice whispered.

"Yes, this is Dr. Harding," he replied.

"I'm returning your call."

"Ms. Samuels?" he asked. "Are you okay?" Tony thought it strange that she was whispering when there was so much background noise.

"Yes, I'm in the press room; David said you called."

"It's about the lab results; there's something you should know."

"I told you not to do that."

“Your stomach contents contained a poison. You should take a copy of the report to the police.”

“Poison,” She gasped.

“Ms. Samuels?” Tony finally said after ten seconds of hearing nothing but the rolling presses.

“Please, just hang on to it for me.”

“Sure, I’ll make a patient file, and you can come in….”

“No,” she interrupted. “And don’t tell Rick, please. Keep the report somewhere else…in your car. I’ll send someone to get it.”

“Okay, I’ll put it in the glove box, but you really should get the police involved.”

“My husband knows too many people on the force,” she said.

“Do you think your husband had something to do with it?

“No,” she replied immediately.

“I’ll be guilty of negligence if I fail to follow procedure and file a report with county health regarding the restaurant. Other customers could be at risk.”

“Please don’t do that, Dr. Harding,” she begged. “No one else at the restaurant is at risk; it was meant for me. Just give the report to whoever I send.”

“Then you should be careful.”

“Yes, Dr. Harding, I know,” she said, and the presses went silent.

The organized lunch chaos at Molly’s was over. It was quiet time, and in a few hours, the school vans would arrive.

“What’s up with Molly?” Lisa whispered to Mona as they stood outside Molly’s door. “She’s been in her office all morning.” The two workers huddled together, considering which one of them should knock. “You think she’s playing Candy Crush? You remember how hooked she was on *Mario* last summer?”

“Nette said she was acting weird this morning before we got here. Maybe she just doesn’t feel like being with the kids today.”

“Maybe she’s making one of those stuffed Phoebe dogs,” Lisa said.

"No, no, que no puede ser, that can't be," Mona insisted. "She only makes those when one of the kids leaves us."

"I'm going to check on her," Lisa said. She stepped toward the door, but it suddenly opened, and Molly came prancing out.

"You'll never guess who just called," she announced and clapped her hands together. Lisa and Mona looked at each other because neither had heard the phone ring.

"What's goin on?" Annette asked as she walked into the kitchen. Molly's cheeks were red, and the two worker's jaws were open.

"Mrs. Carter called," Molly said giddily, then shuffled past Mona and Lisa and grabbed Annette's hands. "You know, the lady with the foster children." The three workers remained silent. "Claire will be on the van today," she said excitedly. "Isn't that wonderful?" She looked confused, seeing the look of concern on their faces.

"Molly," Lisa said, "would you like some water?"

"No, you remember, Claire is the…"

"The shy one that rarely talks to anyone," Annette said, finishing her sentence. "And when she does, it's barely above a whisper; that's great."

Molly nodded in agreement. "She's been begging to come back since the magic show. She wants to play with Elizabeth." Molly clapped her hands together again. "We'll have to do something special."

"Whoa, whoa, Molly," Nette said when she headed toward the hallway. "Let's not make a big fuss; we might put a scare into both of them. I think we should just let things play out between them naturally." Nette put both arms around Molly and hugged her. "This is wonderful, Molly; I've got a good feelin about this."

"You're right, dear," Molly whined. "I'm just so happy." Later, Annette and Mona carried their sodas to the back porch and sat with their feet propped up on the porch railing.

"I told you what it was like when I was a little girl, mi amigo," Mona said solemnly. "Where I grew up, everything under our feet was dirt; the floors, the streets. Our food wasn't fresh; our water wasn't clean. There were so many of us in one little house, sometimes there just wasn't enough food. Many succumbed to it and became los ladrones, robbers, and los asesinos, killers. Nearly all became alcoholics and drug addicts. There was no law to stop them. I was lucky; my mother moved to San Diego to live with her sister. She could only take in three, so my mother took me and my little brother. She chose us because the older one's paths were already forged. It was cramped living conditions, but we had good food and clean clothes, and we went to school. Tim has no reason to drink; he just does it because he likes to. He grew up with everything that we had to work hard to get. He doesn't understand what it's like to have nothing. He doesn't see that what he's doing will destroy him. I don't want our children to see it." Tears poured from Mona's eyes. "I will have my degree soon, and then I can teach full-time. I want to help the underprivileged immigrant children; the ones who are like me and my brother were. They need someone who's been through it to show them the way."

"Oh, Mona," Nette sighed. "I've only been as far as Tijuana, but I've seen the poverty beyond the tourist areas and the children on the street corners beggin for money, selling junk for whatever someone is willin to give them."

"They need to learn how to make an honest living," Mona said, "or they too will succumb to the lazy way, to the drugs that are so free-flowing there."

"Mona, there are poor folks where I'm from, too, lots of them. You'd think in this land of opportunity that people would get themselves out of the circumstances they grew up in. They just don't get how important it is to keep a job and to send their kids to school. They'd rather live on welfare than work, and drink or get high. It's like you said, they get lazy and quit tryin. My father and mother never had a problem finding work, and neither one of them went to college."

"I think that's why we are friends," Mona said softly. "We both appreciate what it takes to get what we want."

"I don't know, Mona. Your mother left Mexico to give her children a better life, yet I left Louisiana looking for something…what? I don't know."

"So, what have you found so far?" Mona asked.

"That people are the same everywhere."

"My children have to see their parents working towards something," Mona said, "like I saw my mother and my aunt and like you saw your mother and father. I don't want my children to think that it's okay to be a lazy drunk."

"I get it, Mona, I do."

"You know what, Nette," Mona said, "you should consider taking some college courses. The way you are with kids, a diploma would earn you more money." Something in the backyard suddenly distracted them. "Look there!" Mona pulled her feet down off the rail and sat up straight. "Nette, isn't that Phoebe?

Tony felt bad about losing his temper and tying Phoebe to the post on Annette's porch, so he crossed the ally and opened Annette's gate. He walked across the stone path, but when he reached the porch, he saw that Phoebe was gone, and so was the rope. He called her name and knocked on the door, but she didn't come out. *"How am I going to explain this?"*

Annette was carrying Phoebe and snapping the rope like a whip when she met Tony in the middle of Gold Coast. She wasted no time ripping into him. "Did you tie up my dog?" she growled.

"Yes, but let me ex…" Tony tried to say.

"Is that how you treat animals?" She reared back her arm again.

"No-I," Tony began and then grabbed her arm and took the rope from her.

"Phoebe has never been tied up in her life," she ranted. "Does she look dangerous to you? What's the matter with you?" She said, waving her free hand at him.

"I'm sorry," Tony said, ducking. "But I couldn't keep her out of my backyard. I was trying to paint and she kept appearing out of nowhere. Then she knocked over my paint can and tracked paint everywhere. It took me an hour to clean it up." She was gritting her teeth, so Tony kept his distance in case she decided to swing at him again. "I'm sorry; just do whatever to keep her out of my yard and my house."

Annette huffed and then turned around to go back to Molly's.

Tony looked at his watch and walked behind her at a safe distance. "It's time for the school van," he said. "I'll just get Lizzy up and..."

"No!" Annette gasped and turned around. She shoved her hand against his chest to stop him.

"What?" He said, trying to move forward.

"Elizabeth made a friend, Claire," she said, pressing harder. "Please, let her stay; let her stay as long as she wants today."

"But Phoebe..."

"I'll have Molly take her to the back; they can play cards. Please, it's important. Claire's a foster child and rarely interacts with anyone, but she did with Elizabeth," she explained. "It'll be good for both of them, don't you think?" She searched his chestnut eyes for a glint of understanding, but he looked angry. "I'll see that she gets home," she added; "I usually have a few kids with me anyway. Please!" She looked up at him again, noticing the laugh lines in the corners of his eyes and the creases on either side of his mouth. She smiled, wondering what kind of doctor allowed his hair to grow so far down on his neck.

"You're a strange woman," he sighed, shaking his head.

"I know," she replied. "And Elizabeth and Claire are two special little girls that need each other."

"Okay." Tony looked away for a second. "But you need to help me out with this Phoebe situation. By the way, how's the migraine?" he asked, remembering the early morning encounter that had put Phoebe in his charge.

"Better, actually," she sighed. "I guess Phoebe's lookin for Jim; that's why she keeps comin over. They were special friends." Annette lowered her eyes as if out of reverence.

"She must know by now that I'm not Jim."

Annette cut her eyes at Phoebe. "Yeah, you would think."

Tony stared at her as she returned to Molly's with Phoebe on one arm. *Did she say Molly and Phoebe would play cards? More strangeness.*

Sally was on the I-5 headed home when her cell phone rang. The caller ID read *Jared.*

"Hey," she answered. "Not today, I'm unpacking," she said when Jared asked her to stop by to look at the forum Nate built. "Send it to me, and remember, don't do anything until I look at it," she said and ended the call.

Ty sat on his bed and pulled up Sally's community forum on his tablet and, with a few swipes, launched Sally's forum to the World Wide Web and then sent an email to Colin. *"Kemo, maybe I can get her to talk to me now."* The forum had over a hundred hits within fifteen minutes.

Tony looked at his watch after closing the dishwasher. It was almost six, and dinner was ready. Neither of his daughters was home and he was having second thoughts about entrusting Lizzy to Annette. Elizabeth walked in just as he looked for Molly's number on the bulletin board.

"Where have you been, and where's Nicky?" he asked her. "Did you walk home by yourself?"

"Miss Nette walked me to the gate," she replied.

"And your sister?"

"We waited, but she never showed up. Can I watch TV?"

"Dinner's in twenty minutes whether your sister's here or not." An hour after dinner, he went to Nicky's room, hoping some sort of clue would jump out at him as to where she might be. A red leather photo album with gold trim he hadn't seen in years was lying on her dresser. He stared at it, thinking it might be best to leave the past alone. The chronicle started with wedding pictures of an almost unrecognizable young couple. He was barely out of high school, and Carol was seventeen and pregnant. It recorded the progression of her pregnancy, then her sitting in a hospital bed with Nicky in her arms, and then the young family standing in front of a baptismal. There were five more pages of the happy threesome. He looked up and saw his reflection in the mirror. *Why didn't someone warn me that being a med-student would be so hard on a marriage?* Someone had, but he never listened to anything his father had to say. He turned the page to a group shot of twelve students with smiling faces, wearing white coats. He grinned back at his classmates.

"Put that down!" He heard Nicky's voice demand. Tony turned around with the album lying open across his arms and saw his daughter standing in the doorway dressed in a red and white uniform. Her hair was wet, and her face was bitterly distorted with anger. She suddenly lunged forward, grabbed the album from him, and slammed it closed. "What are you doing in my room?" she growled and clutched the album close to her chest.

Tony's jaw dropped. "Young lady, this is my house, and I'll go in any room I want, any time I want." The voice he heard was the same resounding roar that he heard coming from his father too many times and it usually sent everyone scattering. "Where have you been?" There was that voice again. When did he start sounding like the person he despised? Nicky squeezed the red leather album tighter and, without saying a word, turned and ran down the hall. By the time Tony reached the kitchen, she was already out the back door. Elizabeth was on the floor in front of the television, mocking a song and dance from the Mary Poppins video. He realized that he had just sent Nicky scrambling in true Harding fashion.

Annette was sitting in the white wicker chair with Phoebe in her lap when she heard someone run through the alley. Phoebe jumped down and stood rigidly at the edge of the porch. "Hey!" Annette called out, but no one answered. "Looks like a kid," she whispered to Phoebe. Nicky was past the corner when Annette opened the gate and stepped into the alley. "Nicky, is that you?" she yelled and ran after her.

Nicky turned around and glared at her when Annette touched her arm. "Oh, it's you," she gasped.

"What on earth?" Annette whispered. "Did somethin happen?" Nicky had on a Mesa Middle School basketball uniform. "What did Tom Burns do to you?"

"Nothing," Nicky replied and looked over Annette's shoulder.

"Is someone chasing you?" Annette turned around to look.

"No," she shot back.

"Okay, well, what's goin on, what's this?" Annette pointed to the book Nicky had pressed against her chest.

Nicky loosened her grip. "It's my photo album."

"Can I see it?" Nette asked.

"I guess." Nicky seemed embarrassed by her behavior. Annette put an arm around her shoulder and led her through the gate and across the stone walkway to the porch, leaving the gate open so she would know she was free to leave if she wanted. They sat down on the top step. When she opened the album, Phoebe jumped in Annette's lap and sniffed Nicky's arm and the book and the cardboard pages.

"My mother gave it to me after Daddy left," she confided. "She didn't want to be reminded of him."

Annette put her hand on Nicky's shoulder. "Did you add some pictures?" Nicky nodded as Nette turned the pages. "This is your mom and dad?" A young woman with blonde shoulder-length hair dressed in jeans and a heavy red coat was sitting sidesaddle on a wooden golden palomino on a carousel. A young man with long shaggy hair wearing jeans and a dark coat had an arm around her as he leaned against the colorful steed. "They look so happy."

"Hmmm," Nicky grimaced.

"You know, I have pictures like this, too," Annette said. "Of my parents, I mean. They were really young when they got married. I hate lookin at my old pictures; they remind me of how old I'm gettin."

Nicky laughed. "But you're not old Nette."

"I'll be thirty in April, girl."

"No way!"

"Fraid so," Nette countered.

"That's weird; my birthday's in April, too." Nicky smiled.

"Look out; we got two independent Aries on the block. You do sort of remind me of myself. I have a great-aunt who used to chart horoscopes until she lost her sight. She always tacks on *that independent Aries* behind my name. But I really don't believe in that stuff."

"I'd like to be independent someday," Nicky sighed. "Like you and have my own house and car and a job."

"You will," Annette replied.

"How do you know that?" Nicky asked.

"Because you're already thinking ahead, but remember, you can't have the house and the car without the J-O-B."

"I've always liked this picture for some reason." Nicky's voice softened. "Sometimes I think I can remember this trip to the zoo." It was a picture of Nicky and her mother and father posed in front of a water fountain. "I remember the wind sprayed water on us. There were geese and cages with monkeys and foxes; it was the first time I ever ate cotton candy." She turned the page. "Daddy could ski but not Mama," she said, reminiscing over the two open pages with pictures of dark figures against bright white snowy hills.

The glamour shot of Carol Harding was in the middle of the next page. "Oh wow, she's beautiful," Annette gasped. "I'm so sorry you lost her. My father died not long ago, and not a day goes by that I don't think about him." Annette could feel her eyes sting. "When I dream about him, we touch hands, and it's as if all those months I watched him suffer with cancer never happened. It's so incredibly real." Annette squeezed her eyelids closed and took a deep breath to regain her composure.

"Yeah, well," Nicky began. "Sounds like you had a great dad. I'm glad for you. My dad and I don't have that kind of relationship. And my mother, she was a wreck." She turned over another page.

"I know you miss her, Nicky," Annette sighed.

"I suppose," Nicky said soberly. "But I've learned to deal with it. Thinking about it just drags me down." She turned another page and pretended to scan the photos. "I understand why she died. She's at peace now, in that better place people talk about. There's no point in getting upset over stuff out of my control. Growing up in South C taught me how to handle that sort of stuff." Nicky turned another page.

"What about Elizabeth?" Nette asked.

"She'll be okay. Haven't you noticed how Daddy dotes over her? It's sickening. I hope she forgets Chicago." Nicky turned to another page where there was a picture of her mother sitting on the third step of a wooden staircase. She had one-year-old Elizabeth in her lap and was dressed in a yellow tank top with spaghetti straps and faded Daisy

Dukes. Her eyes were heavily lined in black and shadowed in bright lavender. Her blonde hair was a teased mess. "This is who Mama was. Nothing she did surprised me, and she did a real number on Lizzy."

"I'm afraid to ask what you mean," Nette whispered.

"Mama took a lot of pills and drank and filled Lizzy's head with all kinds of crazy shit…sorry." Nicky reached over and petted Phoebe; Phoebe licked her hand. "I don't know how to explain Mama to Lizzy, and she doesn't understand that Daddy was M-I-A for five years. We would have been fine living with our aunt and uncle after Mama died, but here we are. So, I've decided that when I'm eighteen, I'm going back home to go to college."

"Nicky," Nette said. "I think that's a responsible plan, but in the meantime, you can get to know Mesa. And if you need a place to hang out or someone to talk to, Phoebe and I are right here."

"Thanks, Nette," Nicky replied. "But I've been making decisions for myself for a long time. You were right about Coach Burns; practice today was pretty grueling. I'm glad you gave me the heads-up about him, or I might have punched him." She grinned as if she was pleased with the whole experience. "He gives his daughter Cass most of the grief, but she kinda asks for it." Nicky smiled as if amused.

"Yes, I know," Nette whispered.

"Coach Burns asked me to practice with JV," Nicky said, trying to suppress her obvious pleasure over the invitation. "He might use me as an alternate; seems some of his looser players suffer from allergies and anxiety."

"Yes!" Nette exclaimed. They gave each other a high-five slap. Then something caught Annette's attention at the end of the stone pathway. It was Dr. Harding standing inside the gate. Nicky saw him an instant later and her face transformed immediately. He looked equally annoyed.

"Oh, hi there, Doc," Annette stammered. "Please come on in," she beckoned and managed a nervous smile. *"Dear God, please don't let a fight happen right here in my backyard."* She waved her arm in the air. "Come and join us." Phoebe jumped from her lap and ran to him.

Tony's face was rigid and his arms swung by his side like a soldier as he walked up the pathway. Phoebe circled his white Nike's forcing him to stop to keep from tripping over her. Without warning, she jumped towards him, amazingly high, compelling him to throw his arms out to catch her. His frown turned to a grin that produced the creases on either side of his face.

Annette gave Phoebe a suspicious squint when she saw her settled in his arms. In an act of desperation, she grabbed the album from Nicky's lap and turned to a random page. "Uh, tell me, is this really you?" She pointed to a photo of a dark-haired cyclist whose front wheels were off the ground, attempting some sort of acrobatics. For some reason, when he looked into her inquisitive blue eyes, his temper calmed. And when he noticed the freckles across her nose, his scant grin became a full-on smile.

"Well," he began reluctantly.

"You were doing a *wheelie!*" she laughed.

"A what?" Nicky gasped.

"I was a lot younger," he replied. Phoebe sneezed and nodded her head.

Annette returned the album to Nicky's lap. "And pretty skinny, too," Nicky grunted a laugh that ended with a smile. Tony sat beside his daughter, and Phoebe nestled her body into his lap. Her ears perked up in anticipation of the forthcoming conversation. Annette sat down on the other side of Nicky.

"I saw some pictures in here of y'all snow skiing.

"Nicky could ski some pretty nice hills when she was just Lizzy's age." Phoebe looked up at him as he spoke and then at her master, awaiting a response.

"I think you're gonna really like workin for Dr. Rick. He's one of the nicest people I know, for a doctor."

"He certainly has an excellent reputation," Tony said, withholding his recent discontent. "Do you have something against doctors?" Phoebe looked up at him and then her master.

"Sort of," she said. "It's personal." She put her hand on Nicky's shoulder. "Guess who practiced with the *Jr. Wildcats* today."

"Really? You should have called and told me where you were; I was worried."

"Yeah, well, there wasn't a phone handy, and my coach is kind of strict about leaving before practice is over.

"You don't have a cell?" Nette asked. "Every kid on earth has a cell phone."

"Ahem!" Tony cleared his throat. "We had this discussion already. A cell phone comes with responsibility."

"Exactly," Annette agreed. "There would be some rules, of course."

"Yes," he repeated. Tony frowned when he realized it sounded like he had just agreed to let Nicky have a cell phone. Nicky looked at her father and then Annette, and then looked at her father again.

"Does this mean you're gonna let me have one?"

"I, I don't know yet," Tony stammered. "Let me talk to my service provider."

"I get it; you're just making it sound like you're getting me one in front of Nette."

"There are all kinds of plans," Nette interrupted. "Some things will have to be agreed upon, right?" She leaned forward to look at Tony.

"Right," he said reluctantly. Nette leaned back and winked at Nicky.

"Daddy, I should take a shower and do some homework."

"Sure," Tony replied. "But we need to talk about this morning."

"What about it?" she asked.

"I have to know who you're riding with beforehand, okay?"

"Sure," Nicky replied. She stood, and the album slipped from her hands, and Tony grabbed it. Phoebe jumped clear of the sudden movement and landed in Annette's lap.

"Here, honey, this is yours."

"Yeah," she replied. She took the album and caressed it and then smiled at Nette before turning to leave.

"Yeah, Phoeb, I think she's gonna be okay," Nette whispered in response to Phoebe's yawning.

"Do you always talk to her like that?" Tony asked.

"Yeah, well, that's because she seems to understand every word I say." Phoebe lifted her snout to her master's face and gently sniffed it. Annette rubbed her face against Phoebe's soft hair and then kissed the top of her head.

"Lizzy thinks she's some sort of magic dog," Tony said and shrugged his shoulders.

"What did she say?" Nette frowned suspiciously.

"I'm sure it's because of the magic show you guys put on."

"That was just a little performance. Molly likes to do something special on days when attendance is more than usual; you know, to keep them entertained."

"That's what I told her. But she's certain it was something more than that." Tony looked at Phoebe, and she cocked her head to one side and then the other. "I can't seem to convince her that it was just parlor tricks. You already know she has an overactive imagination; I'm trying to keep her focused. I wasn't being mean when I asked you to keep them apart." Tony was caught up in her eyes again as he looked down at her sitting on the steps.

"I didn't think you were being mean," she said softly as she stood up. They were face to face now. "Thanks for lettin Lizzy stay. You know," she said after taking a deep breath, "Nicky's grievin, not only for her mother but for her friends and family and for everything familiar that she had to leave behind."

"I wasn't thinking about that when I decided to leave," Tony said. "I was desperate to get away from there."

"It might help if you tell her that and that you understand what she's goin' through. You know, show her some compassion."

"It felt good calling her *honey* just then. And she actually didn't go ballistic on me."

"You need to say those things to her as often as possible. I promise it will take the edge off her. Don't give up, no matter how hard she fights you. Basketball is going to help her make new friends and new memories."

"Thanks for being here for Nicky tonight," he said, trying to break the spell she seemed to have on him, "and for listening." He chuckled as he turned to leave. "And thanks for the cell phone thing. I'm going to look like a real ass if I don't get her one now."

"You're welcome." Annette put a hand up to her face to hide her smile. "That was one of those in-the-moment things. I'm sure y'all can agree on some rules."

Lizzy hadn't moved from in front of the television screen when Tony walked through the living room. "Are you okay, Lizzy?" he asked, but she was engrossed with the Mary Poppins video and didn't answer. He knocked on Nicky's door. "Listen, honey," he said after he heard her say come in. "About the album, it's been years, and I'd really like to look at it again if you don't mind." She didn't say anything. She glared at him for a second and retrieved it from the closet. "Thanks," he said, and after an awkward pause, added, "*Sweetheart.*" Nicky frowned at him suspiciously. *Why is this so hard?* When Elizabeth saw the album under his arm, she immediately jumped up from the floor to sit next to him on the sofa. She asked a multitude of questions about every photo. Nicky heard Lizzy's squeals and joined them. Later, Tony lay in bed in the dark, smiling. Then he heard the jingling sound coming from Lizzy's room again. He eased out of bed and tip-toed into her room. She was asleep, so he carefully pulled back the covers. To his relief, there was no little brown dog hiding under the covers. But when he turned around to leave the room, he saw a shadow in the hall. It was the likeness of a man. He ran out of Lizzy's room and down the hall, turned the corner, and leaped into the living room, but no one was there. He turned on every light in the house, including Nicky and Lizzy's bedrooms, waking them in the process. He and Nicky searched every room and closet until he was satisfied there was no intruder. Lizzy held onto his pajama pants, whimpering while he moved through the house. After witnessing his irrational behavior, he put her to bed with Nicky because now, she was afraid to be alone. Tony slept on the sofa for the rest of the night.

Sally watched the sun descend behind the city skyline from her downtown balcony. *I love San Diego sunsets.* She remembered whispering those words to Randy from the deck of their home in La Jolla. The Pacific sky was often ablaze with streaks of red, yellow, and blue, and then, in what would seem like an instant, the brilliant presentation would be replaced by a diamond-capped display in the dark blue water. *Are you looking at our sunset from our balcony? Will we ever have those sunsets together again? Someone may be listening to my words and watching what I do, but they can't read my thoughts; and my thoughts, my dearest Randy, are of you. God, please keep him safe.* She retreated to the living room and turned on the Channel 4 newscast. Footage of homeless Walter as he walked through the gates of the downtown city jail was airing while a standard script describing his incarceration and release played. A representative was escorting him from the Broadway Street Shelter. "Good job," Sally whispered when she recognized the large black woman with Walter. He was dressed in standard khaki prison-issue clothing. A conspicuous black Navigator was parked across the street. He would be safe for now because the man that would emerge from the van at the shelter would not be Walter, but a substitute wearing identical inmate clothing. Imposter Walter and the woman would amble into the shelter together, where hundreds of khaki uniforms had been distributed to every transitory resident that morning. Walter, still in the van, would then be rushed to a safe house where he would be groomed and relocated.

Chapter 19

The phone Lee gave Sally had been alerting at ten-minute intervals since 5:00 am. It was one of hundreds he had been stealing off semi-trailers on flatbed railcars that sat unattended at the downtown switchyard. A trusted out-of-work and homeless colleague encoded them, and Lee dispersed them to the members of his select network. It was an hour before Sally woke to the reminder. She reached for the familiar, the deeply carved edging around the night table next to the bed in her upstairs La Jolla bedroom, but instead, her fingers glided along a slick surface. Her arm fell against the pillow after opening her eyes and seeing the thousands of tiny Styrofoam beads in the white paste above her; a disheartening reminder that she might never wake up to the elaborately engraved panels that bejeweled the ceilings of her former home again. Sally and Randy's ideology and love for the best of everything drew them together but their passions had somehow cast them in different directions. Hers was a bleeding activist heart, and he showed little mercy to anyone in or out of the courtroom. They were the talk of the town, and the scuttle mongers had predicted their demise. Maybe that was the real reason she held on to the condo, in case they were right. She cuddled what should have been Randy's pillow and longed to feel his arms around her, to hear his voice, to speak to him, to swear at him, to pound his chest with her fists. Had he spent the night in their bedroom, looking at the sunset from their balcony? Did he miss her; did he regret her? Had The Group completely poisoned his mind against her? Did they send Nate Roberts?

The cell phone alerted again. According to the menu, there were two missed calls and three text messages from Jared. The message screen read, *Call me; Urgent;* and *911.* Her first thought was that the college periodical was now in worse shape than ever, thanks to Mr. Roberts. Sensing the eyes around her, she reached for a bathrobe while feeling a tingle in the middle of her back, so she rolled her shoulders, trying to rub the itch against the plush white cotton. Jared's voicemail told her Nate had launched her forum without permission, and he was fervently apologizing. Of course, the man caught Jared off guard by dangling conceivable success in his face. She texted Jared: *I had a bad feeling about him.* He replied just as the coffee finished brewing: *What should I do?*

The local morning newscasters were babbling nonsense when she turned on the TV, so she pressed the mute button and settled onto the sofa with a cup of coffee and her laptop. She logged onto the forum and viewed the site in its entirety. The posts were sympathetic, even encouraging. Most were glad to hear of the breakup and looked forward to her undivided attention again.

S: *Has* The Voice *gone viral?*

J: *No, just the forum. Tried to take it down, but it's passcode-protected.*

Posting flyers and announcing 2day.

S: *Good luck. Don't worry; I know this forum thing wasn't your fault.*

The *Bio* contained pictures of her parents that Nate could have retrieved from the archives of any periodical. There was an aerial view of a collapsed train trestle and a crumpled stack of cars amidst tall trees and rocks. The debris pile was at the bottom of a steep gorge where a small stream flowed around each side of the smoking wreckage. The same photo had been publicized in several national newspapers, along with her parents' passport photos that identified them as American passengers and victims of the horrible crash. She left copies of these same reports in the wine cellar under the chapel near Old Town twenty years ago. She clicked on a picture of her sitting on the steps with her parents at the Presidio Park Museum. It was the last one taken of them together. She often wondered what her life would've been like if they hadn't died. They taught her to be curious and to question everything. It was their influence that earned her the awards and the star on her name tile. It was also the reason she was alone, sitting in her condo playing games with Randy and his benefactors.

The TV station replayed the file footage of Old Walter and the large black woman walking out of the iron gates of the downtown jail. She closed the laptop and slipped Lee's cell phone inside a pocket of her robe on the way to the bathroom. When the hot water created enough steam to put beads on any camera lens that might be recording her, she disrobed and cleared the moisture from the mirror over the sink. She saw a small red pimple between her shoulder blades when she turned her back to the mirror. She plugged the drain, took a pair of scissors, and thrust the pointed end at the small red bump until the skin peeled back and dislodged a tiny object the size of a piece of rice. She quickly put it in the bathrobe pocket after it bounced into the sink. The small puncture wound felt like a bee sting when she stepped into the hot shower. Later, she sat in front of the dressing table, staring into the mirror, mechanically combing her hair. She had on a green sweatshirt, and the secure cell phone was now in the pocket of her jeans along with the small pellet. She put the brush down and stood up, then slipped her fingers into the jeans pocket and pressed the star symbol key on the cell phone. That was the last recorded image inside the condo by the techs in the Escondido facility for the next fifteen minutes. Disabled signals throughout the high-rise sent condo security and maintenance personnel and the underground team in Sub Level 3 scrambling to figure out what caused the significant shutdown. Sally went to the doorman first and told him she would be on assignment for a day or two and to have security keep an eye on her condo while she was gone; her husband had hired someone to watch her, so they might actually catch someone snooping around. She gave the doorman a one-hundred-dollar bill in payment for his loyalty. Then she proceeded to the basement and followed the utility route leading across the street to the vacant warehouse and exited by the rear door. She pressed the star symbol again after slipping into the back seat of a stalled taxi that had been abandoned by a patron after the vehicle went dead and the foreign taxi driver had given up trying to start it. He was mystified when the unit started after Sally got inside.

Nate Roberts was at the doorstep of the condo building within fifteen minutes after seeing steam billow and cover the camera lens hidden inside the a/c vent before the display turned into multicolored pixels and then blackness. When he arrived at the doorstep of Sally's building, the dutiful security guard wasn't allowing anyone inside until the alarm system was restored and the fire and police departments arrived to clear the building.

In Escondido, Colin Sadler propelled himself out of his chair and hurried to the north quadrant situation room, where a team was charged with monitoring every aspect of Sally's life. The team was in scramble mode. "What the hell was that?" Colin shouted when he looked at the array of blank screens. Twelve communication technician specialists were frantically typing and clicking to reconnect to the condo. "What else is down?" he shouted over the pattering.

"The whole building," one tech replied as he worked, "everything electronic."

"And a quarter mile perimeter surrounding Island Avenue," another reported.

"Sir, we're getting the building back now and traffic cams."

"How long were we down?" He looked at his watch.

"Fifteen minutes," a voice shouted from somewhere in the room.

"Get eyes on her ASAP."

"Got her," a tech shouted. "Tracking her moving north on I-5." Techs immediately took up pursuit with the aid of city surveillance cameras.

"Ty, are you there?" Colin shouted while he trotted back to his station.

T: *I'm at the condo. Security has it locked down. What did you guys do?*

C: *It wasn't us, Bud; it must have been her. We lost signal for fifteen minutes.*

She's tracking north on 5 in a Yellow Cab.

Ty went back to his apartment to review the condo surveillance. He watched footage of her reading the forum. Her nostrils flared when she looked up at the replay of Walter's release. "There it is," he whispered. He hurried downstairs and hailed a cab. The driver hadn't seen Sally today but told him her fares paid well when she was working a story; she often asked drivers to wait with the meter running. She tipped well, so cabbies now included Island Avenue on their route since her return to the downtown condo. Ty had the cabbie drop him at the

Broadway Street Shelter. He recognized the large black woman making beds from the news feed. She was in charge of four dormitories, and the busy woman shook her head in response to his inquiry about the man in her charge the day before. He had slipped out during the night, and she supposed he was on the street again. The occupancy of the shelter was sparse in the daytime, particularly when the weather was decent, so she gave him permission to look around. He counted six boarders wearing khaki shirts, pants and jackets and found an open cardboard box on the floor in one of the dorms stamped *Inmate Clothing.* He helped himself to one of the shirts.

"Who provides the clothes?" Ty asked the woman on his way out.

"Everything's donated," she replied almost defensively.

"Who donated the khakis?"

"Don't know, sir," she replied.

"Must have been the Department of Corrections," Ty remarked. "Walter had the same type of shirt and jacket on when he left the jail yesterday."

"We need more blankets and heavy coats," the woman moaned. "I just hope Walter found a blanket and a dry place to bed down. We were at capacity last night."

Ty nodded and left the shelter. The cabbie pulled up beside him as if he had been waiting. It seemed the twenty-dollar tip had earned him information. The driver had checked with his associates and someone had picked up a woman dressed in a green sweatshirt and jeans that could have been Mrs. Samuels. The fare ended at the Claremont Mall with a fifty-dollar tip. Ty alerted Colin when he exited the taxi.

T: *Kemo, a taxi took her to Claremont Mall. She's wearing a green sweatshirt.*

Monitor cabbie chatter; she tips big.

C: *Negative, we've got her on I-8 headed east.*

T: *She found the tracking device, Kemo.*

C: *We'll look in Claremont.*

Sally stepped off the city bus within a crowd of passengers at the Newton Shopping Center on Mesa Blvd. After releasing the cabbie at the Claremont Mall, she changed clothes in the dressing room of a small boutique and then boarded a bus to Mesa. She stuffed her auburn hair under a light blue riding cap that matched the pants and shirt she purchased for cash. She used a pay phone in a narrow hallway off a food court and sat amongst a small crowd of morning shoppers in the Market Place. She looked at the time display on her cell phone several times as she sipped coffee and pretended to read a *Nickel Saver* that was left on the table. She quickly dumped the coffee in a trash can when a man in a black suit and hat appeared outside the entrance.

Tony started his run late, and he didn't see the man wearing the church logo or Annette on her way to Molly's. His priority had been to sit down with his daughters at breakfast and explain, with some kind of rationality, what had happened the night before. They were due an explanation for his rousting them out of bed in search of a nonexistent intruder.

"I anticipated finding Phoebe under your blanket, Lizzy," he said. "I expected to see her, so my mind tricked me into seeing something in the hall. That's how the imagination works, get it?"

The silence around the table was deafening until Lizzy bounced from her chair, wrapped both arms around his neck, and said she got it. Yes, a logical explanation, but he still wasn't convinced he hadn't seen the shadowy figure in the hall that turned the corner and then leaped into the kitchen, because when he turned on the kitchen light, the rod hanging from the mini blind on the back door was swinging. But the doorknob was locked when he tried to open it, as was the deadbolt. He stepped outside, and all he heard was the swooshing of traffic a mile away on Canyon Road. There were no running footsteps or barking German Shepherds. He approached Canyon Road and slowed before crossing. A yellow sports car sped by, and for a split second, I thought it was Todd. It wasn't, of course, and he crossed after a black van passed.

"What do you see, Father; is it still bleeding?" Sally said and pulled the back of the blue shirt up over her shoulders and then turned to look at her reflection in the dresser mirror. “My shirt had blood on it.” The dresser had a small stack of prayer books on one end and a bible in the middle. The curtains were drawn closed, and the candle on a stand before a kneeling rail didn’t offer much light. She slapped the light switch next to the door and the apostolic faces within the frames on the walls seemed alarmed at the sight of a woman’s bare back. Sally believed in God; how could she not after being raised by His disciples with black habits, but she rarely depended on Him? Bible study classes at St. Jude’s always left her with more questions than answers regarding the chronicles of the life of Jesus of Nazareth. “Father, how does it look?”

“You can’t do that,” the man in the black turtleneck scolded. “Put your shirt down,” he said and reluctantly moved closer to observe the small wound. “There’s a puncture, maybe half an inch, and scratches. A band-aide with some antibacterial ointment should do.” He straightened and turned away. “I shouldn’t have sent the housekeeper home.” He kept his back to her as he spoke. “I’ll be right back. I thought you wanted to see Walter; I didn’t think you’d be removing your clothes.” He hurried out of the room, and Sally pulled the shirt completely off over her head.

“Father Clayton,” she whispered and followed him out the door. “Hurry, I want to make sure he’s okay.”

“Here,” the priest said, meeting her face-to-face in the hall. “Oh, please, Sally.” He held a band-aid out to her while shielding his eyes with the other hand.

“Surely, Father, at some time in your professional life, you’ve seen a woman in a bra before.” Sally took the band-aid and removed the paper wrapping.

“My profession doesn’t take me to places where women or men remove their clothes.”

“Really, Father, you’re kidding me; just do it.” She passed the band-aid back to him by the tip of her finger.

“Please, keep your back to me,” he ordered and gently pushed her shoulder to keep her back square. He nervously squeezed some ointment onto the gauze and pressed the band-aid firmly against her skin. He quickly busied himself with screwing the cap back on the tube. “Now, would you please return to the prayer room and put your shirt back on?"

"I should change clothes again," she said, facing him. The priest turned his head away. "I don't have any woman's clothes."

"Something of yours will do."

He pointed to the prayer room. "Look in the closet." He followed her as far as the door. "Sally, don't you think we're capable of taking care of Walter? You said we shouldn't communicate."

"Does Walter understand that he's going to Canada?"

"Yes; you're sure no one followed you?" The priest asked anxiously.

"I'm sure," she said and opened the door. "Do I look like a priest?" she said, grinning. She had on one of Father Clayton's black suits, white collar included. "I just need something to cover my hair."

"Your face is too feminine to pass for a priest. If anyone asks, you're a seminarian." He led her to a coat rack in the front office. "Take your pick, but the black derby is mine."

"I'll take the skull cap," Sally said. "Do seminarians wear skull caps?"

"Unfortunately, these days, they do," Father Clayton replied with a sigh. "The church van is out front; let's get this over with."

Sally settled into the passenger seat and turned around to grab the seatbelt. "Who's that?" she gasped.

"Who-where," Father Clayton said, twisting his body around one way and then the other, looking out the windows. "Oh, that guy running there? He's new in the neighborhood. We've been passing each other in the mornings."

"I think I know him," Sally said, remembering how close Dr. Harding lived to Mesa Village.

Scott was standing on the front walk when Tony returned from his run. "Did you miss your ride with Todd?" Tony huffed.

"No sir," Scott replied. "I'm home-schooling today as part of an enrichment option that allows me to work from my computer when I'm ahead of my class."

"How far ahead are you?" Tony asked as he walked to the front door.

"About nine months," Scott replied.

"That's a whole school year," Tony commented.

"Yes, sir. Actually, I'm three years ahead. I've been trying to slow my pace with extra work, but I keep edging forward."

"So, what's up?"

"I want to give you something, Dr. Harding." Scott reached into his Dockers. "I took these from Robby's room; he'll just think he misplaced them. The lady that came by your house the other day from SDCT gave these cards to Robby to pass out to his friends. He's under the misguided impression that he'll see her again if he sends her referrals. Robby acts a little adolescent, but he's a good guy and a pretty decent musician. You're not thinking about calling SDCT, are you? Because my reliable sources tell me it's not secure like they claim and is susceptible to viruses. I'd like to make sure your computer is fully protected, if you don't mind."

"Well, *my* reliable source, experience," Tony said, pointing to his forehead, "says stay away from anything that chick has to offer." He pointed to the business cards. "She ain't no cable technician."

"Good!" Scott nodded and smiled as if relieved.

"You know Scott, I've been meaning to ask you why it is, I never see your mother?" Tony said.

"She works double shifts at the airport," he replied. "She leaves early and comes home late and then sleeps. She leaves me notes, and we text."

"It's not right for a kid to stay home alone all the time," Tony said.

"We have it worked out," Scott replied. "When I finish school assignments, I hang with Robby or Annette."

"Well, tell her I'd like to meet her," Tony said. "If you're serious about my computer, come over after you finish your homeschooling. I'll call the office and have Tonya explain how to access the system. I wouldn't mind working from home too. Can you help me figure that out?"

"Sure, Dr. Harding; how about we start now?"

"Oh, no; schoolwork first," Tony said and opened the door.

"I can do it tonight," Scott argued.

"And that's another thing; it's not good for kids to stay up all hours of the night. I've seen your light on past midnight. A smart kid like you should know that people learn more when they have proper rest, so go home, do your schoolwork, and come back when you're finished."

"Yes sir," Scott replied, disappointed.

Tony turned to close the door but noticed Scott looking at him curiously. "What?" he asked the ten-year-old.

"In my defense Dr. Harding, I don't play games at night," he said and pushed his wire-rimmed glasses further up his nose. "I write programs and create virus protections and firewalls and decode encryptions. It's important work."

"Of course, you do, but it's also important that you be in bed by ten." Tony tapped a finger on his watch to make his point. "When did they start teaching encryption decoding in school?"

"It's internet courses, for extra credit."

"Hum, I'll see you later," Tony replied. "One more thing; you can hang out here too if you'd like. Elizabeth likes you for some reason. It's probably because you answer questions to her satisfaction better than I do."

Scott noticed a car turn into Antrim Way as he headed home. He watched it pass slowly in front of the Harding house and then quickly turn into the driveway of a vacant house in the middle of the block. He snapped a picture with his cell phone and rushed inside to share it with his internet friend, Guardian.

Rick grabbed the phone away from Tonya when Tony called asking about connecting to the office system. "Hey, son, we're having an informal barbeque at the house tomorrow evening. I'd like you and your girls to come. Better bring a date, or Lorraine will fix you up with one of our single neighbors. Tonya will forward you directions when she sends you the information you asked for. See you tomorrow evening."

Chapter 20

"We passed the gates," Sally said inquisitively when Father Clayton drove past the entrance to Mesa Village Retirement Community.

"They still live in the old section," he replied. "How long has it been since you've been up here?" He turned right after three more blocks.

"Too long, Father," she whispered.

"Most of the old units are already vacated for renovation, but Ms. Bonnie is still stalling," he said.

The church van pulled into a driveway in the middle of the block, and they both got out quickly. Father Clayton knocked on the door, and an elderly black woman with snow-white hair answered.

"Come in, Father, come in." Bonnie was thin and steadied herself with a wooden cane. She led them to the kitchen, pointed to the table, and instructed them to sit. She served them each a small plate of yellow cake. "Walter got up a little bit ago and is eating breakfast in his room. Curtis helped him shower and get dressed." She poured coffee into two cups at the counter, and Father Clayton quickly rose and carried them to the table. "I don't think he should go anywhere just yet, though," she said as she shuffled to the table and sat down. "He's got a cold and should stay with Curtis and me for a few more days. It's a long way to where he's going and a lot colder."

"I agree," Sally said, trying to disguise her voice from under the skull cap. "Is he running a fever?"

"A hundred," the old lady replied, and then leaned forward to get a better look at who she was talking to. She examined Sally's face from top to bottom and then looked at Father Clayton. "Who is this?" Then she addressed Sally. "Are you one of those gay priests?"

"I'm sorry, Ms. Bonnie," Sally apologized and removed the knit cap. Her auburn hair fell freely to her shoulders. "I'm incognito."

"That's a funny name," she replied and then looked at Father Clayton.

"No, I mean, I'm in disguise; I orchestrated, uh, planned Walter's move up here to Mesa; but no one can know I'm involved. People are watching me; I'd like to see Walter."

"I know who you are," Bonnie slowly moaned. "You're that Sally; the one that stirred up the stink in the D.A.'s office."

"I'm afraid so." Sally bowed her head sheepishly and looked down at her black coffee.

"Well; good for you for standing up for Walter. I lived on the streets before; back when I was in my forties. I lost everything because of my two sons. They sold drugs and robbed me of everything I had. They both went to prison; one is out and working down in San Ysidro, and the other was killed in a prison fight."

"I'm sorry," Sally whispered. "How are you?"

"I'm doing fine. Curtis and I have been together for fifteen years; I met him when I moved here. The folks up here are the finest in this God-forsaken world. Father Clayton is our liaison. He tells us when somebody in the community is in need. Like Lewis, after his house caught fire the other night; we all chipped in so he would be comfortable next door at Charlie's."

"If only the world could learn from your example," Sally said and gently touched Bonnie's hand.

Bonnie lowered her head and closed her eyes. "Thank you, Jesus, for sending Phoebe to help Lewis."

"The little brown dog," Sally began and looked at Father Clayton; he shook his head. "I've heard about her."

"Charlie told us not to talk about it."

"Of course; may I see Walter now?"

"Sure, follow me." The slight woman led them to a bedroom door where she knocked and then opened it at the same time. "Curtis, this is Miss Sally, the lady that sent Walter to us."

Sally and Curtis nodded to each other as she rushed to Walter, who was sitting on the edge of the bed. "Walter," she whispered. "It's so good to see you. Your haircut and clean shave make you look twenty years younger." She looked up at Curtis and winked. "Where did you get this beautiful brown corduroy suit?"

"His clothes were donated by the folks from the Village," Curtis answered.

"Some, under the pretext they were for Lewis," Father Clayton added.

"His outfit is from Mr. Mackenzie, and the coat from Charlie," Curtis said. "Some of the ladies went shopping for undershirts and socks. He has a whole new wardrobe for his trip to Canada."

"Walter, you feel warm," Sally whispered after hugging him.

"I don't feel so good," he groveled and coughed.

"I found this under the skin between his shoulder blades when I helped him shower," Curtis said and opened his palm.

"Father," Sally said, looking up at Father Clayton who was staring at the pellet in Curtis' hand. "The man we saw jogging is a doctor; he works for Rick and lives on Antrim."

"Sally, this is the same…" he began.

"I believe we can trust him," she said sternly. "Why don't you go get him? She grabbed the pellet from Curtis' hand and put it in her cassock pocket.

"But I haven't properly introduced myself yet," the priest said.

Sally looked at him with her serious green eyes. "Then this is a perfect time to meet your new parishioner."

"I suppose," he muttered. "Will you come with me, since you know him?" "It's best that I stay here, out of site. You've made cold calls before, Father; now go get him. She took Walter's hand. "You'll like Dr. Harding," she told him softly. "He's very nice and is an excellent doctor. He saved my life once," she said, patting his hand.

"Too bad he wasn't around for poor Anderson Barksdale," Walter said in a scratchy voice. "I'll never forget all that blood; it was even coming out of his ears and his nose; and his eyes, they were so red."

Sally smiled at Walter and gave him a hug. "I know, you're gonna be fine now." She looked up at Father Clayton again. "You're still here? Tell Dr. Harding to follow you in his car." The cell phone in Father Clayton's pocket vibrated; he looked at it as he left the room.

Tony had just clicked on the file from Tonya when the doorbell rang. He rolled his chair to the office window and looked through the mini blinds. A black van bearing the emblem with the three crosses was parked at the curb.

"Hello, Father," Tony said and held the screen door open for the man wearing the black suite and white collar.

"I'm sorry to barge in on you like this without calling first," the priest said, clasping his hands together as if praying as he stepped inside. "My name is Father Don Clayton. My church, Mount Calvary, is on the corner of Gold Coast and Canyon Road. I've seen you running in the mornings, and well, I didn't know your name or number…"

"Yeah, Father," Tony interrupted. "I've seen you too. It's good to finally meet you. I'm Anthony Harding, Doctor Anthony Harding." Tony put his right hand out, and they shook hands. "We moved in a week ago, my two daughters and me. I'm glad you stopped by; I was raised Catholic, and every time I pass your church, I think that I should start going to Mass again."

"Well, normally, that would make my visit easy," said the priest.

"I don't understand,"

"Well," he hesitated, "there's an older gentleman a few blocks from here that's sick, and someone told me you're a doctor, and I was hoping you would take a look at him; if you're not busy and it's not too much trouble, that is."

"Someone from the retirement village?" Tony asked.

"Well, yes," Father Clayton replied. "This older gentleman is staying with friends; he caught a cold, and we're a little concerned. Would you mind and perhaps prescribe something if necessary? He's running a slight fever."

"Let me grab my bag."

"Oh, could you follow me in your car?" the priest asked sheepishly. "I, uh, have another call to make and…"

"Not a problem, Father." Tony would never turn down anyone asking for help even if the solicitor did look suspiciously nervous. "I'll back the car out, and you can lead the way."

Tony evaluated Curtis as he led them to the bedroom. He was in pretty good health despite being seventy-four and more agile than Bonnie, who answered the door. Curtis was quick to brag, however, that Bonnie had graduated from a wheelchair to a walker and then to the cane in six months' time after a fall that broke her right hip. The elderly patient in the bedroom did not look as well. His apprehensive eyes moved nervously from Curtis to Father Clayton, who appeared to be just as tense as they exchanged frequent glances of silent communication. Tony sensed more might be going on than the priest had shared, but whatever it was, it could never compare to some of the tales that accompanied the patients brought to the emergency room at St. Joe's. Tony picked up the old man's wrist and felt his pulse. He took an instrument from his bag and tried to check his eyes, but Walter's eyes continued to move from Curtis to Father Clayton and now to Bonnie, who had entered the room. "What's your name," he asked the old man, trying to get his attention. Father Clayton suddenly moved around the bed and stood next to Tony.

"John, his name is John," the priest said. The old man frowned deeply and looked up at the priest.

"Okay, John," Tony said. "My name is Dr. Harding, and I live just around the corner. I will be working at the clinic here in the retirement village. Is it okay if I listen to your chest and take your temperature?"

Walter nodded. "She told me you're a good doctor," he whispered. "That you saved her life."

Tony looked at Bonnie, but she shook her head. He took his time, hoping it would help calm the old man down. "You know what I think, Miss Bonnie?" Tony finally said.

"What's that, Doc?" she asked, leaning forward against her cane.

"I think some good old-fashioned chicken soup would do wonders for John."

"I'll get right on that," she said and shuffled out of the room.

"But John, you'll have to stay in bed for another whole day; take two aspirins every four hours and drink lots of fluids. Your lungs sound good," he added after depressing a stethoscope to several places up and down his back. "But that could change in an instant with someone your age. You're going to have to stay warm and dry." He took a slip of paper from his bag and wrote something on it. "Curtis, take this to your pharmacist and tell him to mix this up for John. It's a vitamin recipe I made up. It'll help build up his immunity." He handed the small slip of paper to Curtis. "If you have any problems at the pharmacy, just call me; my cell number is there too. Your color tells me you're malnourished," he told the old man. "Do you live alone?" Tony received a delayed response preceded by more strange stares.

"John didn't eat much where he was staying," Father Clayton said nervously.

"You're going to be fine, John," Tony said and helped the old man lay down after Curtis left with the slip of paper. "Now that he's gone, maybe I can get a look at your eyes." But Walter's eyes were fixed on Father Clayton. "John, I need you to look straight ahead so I can..."

"Stop calling me John," he growled. "My name is Walter!"

"What?" Tony asked.

"I'm hidin' out, that's what," Walter replied.

"Hiding?" Tony looked across the bed at Father Clayton.

"No, no," the priest said and then looked at Walter. "You're staying here until you feel better." He turned to Tony again. "Then he's going to stay with relatives in, in, uh, uh, up north."

"Father," Tony said, shaking his head. "Face it; you're not a good liar. Listen, Walter, it doesn't matter what your name is or why you're here. I just want you to stay in bed, eat Bonnie's chicken soup, take vitamins and aspirin, and drink plenty of fluids."

"Not many doctors make house calls anymore," Walter sighed. "You seem like a good doctor, but you could use a haircut."

Tony smiled. "I like you too, Walter." He patted Walter on the shoulder and left the room. Father Clayton followed him.

"Dr. Harding," the priest whispered. "I'm sorry about the deception. It's for Walter's protection. So, if you don't mind, please don't tell anyone he's here or that he was ever here."

"Whatever you say, Father." Tony stopped just inside the kitchen. Bonnie was looking in the refrigerator and holding a package of chicken in each hand. "Let me help you with that, Miss Bonnie," Tony said, trying to ignore Father Clayton's assumption that he would spread gossip to anyone about a patient. Bonnie didn't have a chance to argue because Tony took the cartons from her and started scanning the refrigerator's contents for himself. "You just stand back, Miss Bonnie; I'll do this." Tony pulled out a bowl of peas, carrots, and green beans and put them on the counter beside the sink. "Do you have some potatoes and pasta?" he asked. The old woman pointed to the pantry. "Now, show me your seasonings." He looked at Father Clayton, who was standing at the kitchen door. "Didn't you tell me you had another call to make?"

Father Clayton began to stammer and stutter again. "Well, uh, yes, but I think I can spare another minute if you need some help."

"Find a pot suitable for boiling spaghetti," Tony instructed. "Fill it with water and put it on the stove. Take half of this…" He handed the box of spaghetti to him. "Break it up into four-inch pieces in a bowl. Miss Bonnie, why don't you give Walter a couple of aspirins with some water and make sure he drinks the full glass; then you just sit back and relax. I'll have this going in a jiffy."

"Well, I'll do just that," she said, smiling.

Tony shuffled around the kitchen, seasoning and mixing things together to his satisfaction. Father Clayton stood at his post, as directed, and stirred the spaghetti as it rolled in the boiling seasoned water. "Father, I understand your duty to secrecy," Tony whispered to the priest as they stood side by side at the sink, rinsing the spaghetti. "Just make sure Walter is completely well before he leaves. So, what time is Mass on Sunday? Haven't been to Mass in a few years or confession." Tony shook his head. "And forgive me, Father, for I have sinned."

The priest raised his right hand and made the sign of the cross. "Your sins are forgiven, my son; say three *Our Father's,* and I'll expect you on Sunday."

Tony left Father Clayton to finish the soup when the pharmacist from Walgreens called requesting verification for the script Curtis presented, but the passenger door of the Olds was ajar when he walked outside. Someone wearing a black suit, sunglasses, and a black skull cap was sitting in the seat, rummaging through the glove compartment. He thought about the punks dressed in black from Nicky's school. Could this be one of them hitting parked cars, looking for anything of value to pawn or trade for drugs? After all, he did the same thing when he was a kid. Most of the crew he ran with, however, moved on to major crimes and prison; like his brother. Tony dropped his bag on the sidewalk and made a quick surveillance of the street. The backup could be waiting in a parked car nearby. He pulled the door all the way open, grabbed the thief's arm, and yanked him out onto the sidewalk. The kid resisted and tried to break free of his grip. He swung at Tony with his free hand and kicked at his legs. "Be still; you're not going anywhere, punk!" Tony growled. "Besides, you fight like a girl."

"Oh my God," Father Clayton said, rushing up behind him, holding the bag Tony had dropped. "Dr. Harding, stop!"

"Wait a minute," Tony gasped when he saw the white band around the perpetrator's neck. "You've got on a collar!" He looked at Father Clayton with dismay. "Father, do you know this dirtbag?" He swiped the skullcap off the kid's head, and Sally's hair tumbled out. "What the hell?" He quickly released her arm and stepped back. "You!" he gasped.

"I can explain, Dr. Harding," Sally said. "I asked Father Clayton to bring you here. I was just getting the lab report from your glove box. You were busy in the kitchen, so I..."

"So, Walter was an excuse to get me over here so you could get the lab report," Tony said, growling at both of them.

"Yes," Sally answered.

"No," Father Clayton answered at the same time.

"Get out of my way," Tony said and slammed the passenger door. He snatched the bag from Father Clayton and rushed around the front of the Olds.

"Dr. Harding," Sally pleaded, running after him until he stopped beside the driver's door. "I can explain; don't be angry with Father Clayton."

"Oh, I'm almost sure you manipulated him into this," he chuckled. Father Clayton frowned and grimaced. "I don't want to hear anything you have to say, Ms. Samuels. Did you get what you wanted?" he asked as he opened the car door and slid behind the wheel.

"Yes, but," She said, standing beside the door. "Don't tell anyone you saw Walter or me here today. Please, it's important, not even Rick."

Tony glared at her and closed the door without saying a word. He started the car and drove away, screeching the rear wheels when he took off.

"He won't tell," Sally whispered and looked at Father Clayton as if assuring him.

Father Clayton took a deep breath. "Sally, don't get anyone else involved in this Walter thing; he has children." They watched the doctor turn around in the driveway next door and hurry past them.

"He works for Randy's brother; he'll be involved soon enough."

"What's the lab report about?"

"Nothing," she sighed and rushed back into the house.

The priest looked at his cell phone again. "The neighborhood watch took this picture of a suspicious Honda CRW."

"You have a neighborhood watch?" She looked at the picture and tucked her hair under the knit cap. "We better show this to Bonnie."

"What did Curtis find under Walter's skin?" the priest asked her later as he backed out of the driveway. "He had a wound like yours. I saw it when Dr. Harding examined him."

"A tracking device, I'm afraid," Sally sighed from the back seat. "Randy, or quite possibly his handlers, are having us followed. I took it from Curtis and stashed it in one of the vacant houses in the next block, but that won't throw them off for long."

"There's the Honda," Father Clayton gasped. "God help us," he sighed and recited the Lord's Prayer when Sally quickly lay down across the back seat.

"I wish I could be as convinced about God as you are, Father," she sighed and began to unbutton the black cassock.

"There are twenty-four undisputed miracles recorded in the Bible that were performed by Jesus during His teaching years," Father Clayton replied, checking his mirrors as he drove.

"And verified?" Sally replied while she wriggled out of the vestment. "You know a writer must have at least two sources of confirmation. I heard all the Bible stories when I lived with the nuns. But I also lived with two incredible writers that made their living embellishing stories."

"Four disciples went off to teach in different parts of the country yet penned identical accounts of Jesus' works. And yes, there were witnesses. Sally the truth is, you can put your trust in Jesus; all you have to do is ask Him."

"Do you know why I sought you out, Father?" Sally whispered while staring at a piece of church letterhead stationery on the front seat.

"Because of my proximity to the retirement village; or perhaps because of my acquaintance with the Monsignor at Calvary in Old Town."

"My parents reminded me sedulously that those three crosses meant either one of two things: a safe haven or a dire warning."

"You will always be safe in Our Lord's church, Sally," he said when he pulled up to the stop sign at Canyon Road. "Where to from here?"

"Drop me off at University Mall." She placed the cassock, including the skull cap, on the front seat. "Then go back and get Walter; have him wear this disguise. Move him somewhere else, somewhere they won't think to look."

It took Tony fifteen minutes to convince the pharmacist of his credentials and another twenty to oversee the mixing of the powdered vitamin. Scott was sitting on his doorstep when he got home. "School work all done?" Tony asked because Scott had his cell phone cupped in his hands.

"Who are you texting this time of day? All your friends are in school."

"My mom," he replied and tucked the cell phone away in his pocket. "There was a suspicious vehicle in the neighborhood, so I sent her the license number. She's gonna have TSA check the plates."

"What exactly does your mother do at the airport?"

"She's a coordinator, sort of," he replied, following Tony through the door.

"Hum, well, ok, let's see what Tonya sent me; and what's this virus protection you were talking about?"

"It's a prototype, but the strongest there is. My friend…I mean, one of my instructors sent it to me. I installed it on everyone's computer."

"You might as well put it on mine too."

"It was a stupid idea to plant something on her," Ty typed.

C: *We finally found her on the traffic cams.*

T: *No doubt she's aware someone is following her now. Is Walter in the house?*

C: *Yes, we were able to identify everyone in the house.*

Chapter 21

"Mona, your eyes are so red," Nette told her friend as they prepared for the day in Molly's kitchen. "You've been cryin haven't you?"

"No," Mona replied sharply. "I was up late preparing for my online final."

"Have you heard from Tim?"

"No." Mona sighed and then shook her head. "I mean, yes; but I didn't talk to him. I just let him talk to the kids; I was too busy." She left the kitchen and began to nervously pick up books and toys in the living room that were lying on tabletops and in chairs. "Everything is better now that I'm staying with my mother," she blurted out when she saw Annette standing in the archway watching her anxious behavior. "She keeps an eye on the kids so I can concentrate on studying. Tim was always interrupting me."

"God, Mona, that sounds a little obsessive."

"I'm not!" Mona growled. "Have you been talking to Tim?"

"No, it's just that I know a little somethin about being obsessive. Sometimes, you just have to let things happen on their own."

"This is my life's dream, Nette. It's what my mother wanted for me; it's what I want for me. Tim should be using this time to straighten himself out."

"Mona, you don't sound like yourself; is somethin else goin on?"

"What do you mean?" Mona said defensively.

"Is there somethin you're not tellin me, like maybe Tim's cheatin or somethin?"

"No, I told you; it's his drinking. He has to convince me that he's stopped, or I really don't have anything to say to him."

"Okay, okay," Nette nodded. "I get that, but it just seems like there's somethin more. You know how my gut tells me stuff."

Mona laid a stack of books she collected on a bookshelf. "I suppose this whole separation thing does have me a little weirded out."

"Listen, Claire's comin today." Mona immediately went to the table she set up for Elizabeth and Claire. She repeatedly straightened the coloring books and crayons. Then she turned as if looking for something else to do. She reached for the chess game that Mr. Mackenzie and Jeffrey were playing. "Mona, wait!" Nette yelled before she disturbed the pieces on the board. "They haven't finished." Mona looked up at Annette.

"How do you know Jeffrey's coming back?" she huffed. The whites of Mona's eyes looked like a roadmap of red lines.

"Mona," Nette said carefully. "You should talk to someone, a counselor, maybe."

Nicky found practice challenging because Tom Burns made her play strictly defense. She could dig, pivot, strip the ball, and charge the lane better than anyone on the JV team. Sooner or later, Burns would recognize her skills and allow her to score at will instead of making her pass the ball to someone taller. She was grateful for the grueling two-hour drill; it took her mind off the Chicago life that haunted her daily. The drills were familiar, but Burns insisted she guard. The foolish coach would learn soon enough that he was wasting her talent. He yelled at her every time she stole the ball and sprang for the goal. Her punishment was to memorize the numbered plays and practice each one with the team until she could execute them perfectly. Cass soon tired of his howling and retreated to the bleachers. Nicky faked a restroom request, sneaked to the second row, and sat beside her.

"Think your dad would care if we hung around after and played one-on-one?" Nicky whispered.

"I'm meeting friends," she sneered.

"My old team never held me back like this," Nicky sighed. "Your dad just doesn't get it."

"My dad hates street ball," Cass scoffed.

"Ever heard of the *Maravich figure 8*?"

"I can do that in my sleep," she sighed and shook her head. "He also despises hot-doggin." She turned her back to Nicky.

"What about the *Spider Dribble*?" Nicky asked, but Cass didn't answer. "So that's a no? What could he do to us after we sneak them into a game and win by a zillion points?"

"Get real, princess; that man will bench you so fast, you won't know what happened."

"The fans in the bleachers might have something to say about it."

"Our wimpy JV crowds?"

"So, let's give 'em a reason to show up."

"I hope no one minds, I parked in the garage," Tony said when he met Annette in Molly's kitchen. She waved him over to the archway between the kitchen and living room so he could see Lizzy and Claire exchanging Bratz accessories.

"Thanks," Tony whispered with evident relief on his face; "for talking me out of taking her home yesterday."

"They're good for each other," she said. "They both had a different start in life."

"Yeah," he replied with a guilty nod.

Annette looked up at him and, for some reason, couldn't take her eyes away from his. "I wanted to tell you, uh, I haven't had a migraine since I started takin' the baby aspirins."

"That's impossible, it never works this fast," he replied, not being able to look away either.

"It's true," she sighed.

"Thank you for calming Nicky down last night. As you can see, we don't get along so well. Word is you're good with kids."

"Word?" she laughed. "I like kids, and you have two great ones. Don't worry so much."

"Nicky's older and she remembers, well, the bad stuff between me and her mother." Tony bowed his head again.

"I just hope I don't live to regret telling Coach Burns about her," Nette said. "He's a real hard case."

"And I thought it was because I left all those messages for Mrs. Sparks."

"Maybe it's because we hit this from both directions."

"Maybe so," he said, smiling, trying to suppress his blushing.

"You know, I didn't know that doctors were allowed to let their hair grow so long. You're not one of those new-age doctors? You strike me as bein much more down to earth than that."

Tony laughed and shook his head. "No, I'm just a GP and a single father that's trying to be more responsible. And I'm going to get around to the haircut this weekend."

"I was just teasin; I actually like it. It kinda reminds me of home."

"You mean the guys in Louisiana?" he whispered, and Annette smiled.

"Why did you say just a GP?" she asked.

"Being head of a trauma department and working the ER was much more intense."

"Ah, an adrenaline junkie," she teased.

"I thought I heard a man's voice," Molly chirped, suddenly appearing from her office with Phoebe on one arm. "Dr. Harding, how are you? We were just playing a game of Battle."

"The card game?" Tony quizzed. "Oh look, something's in your hair."

"Oh my," Molly chuckled and pulled a piece of white filler from her tight curls and then sauntered back to her office. "What do you think, Dr. Harding?" Molly asked after quickly retrieving her creation. She held a stuffed animal in one arm and Phoebe in the other as if comparing them.

"I see who has the top rating around here," Tony said. "Let's see, which one is the magic dog?" Tony pointed to one and then the other. Molly blushed while trying to hold back a laugh.

"This one right here," Molly said and affectionately rubbed her forehead against Phoebe's nose.

"Molly, quit bein so silly," Annette scolded.

"Dr. Harding, you should give Nette and Phoebe a ride home," Molly said and handed Phoebe to Annette.

"Molly, stop it," Nette whispered, but the jovial woman paid no attention. "Besides, I rode my bike," she added. "I'm sorry, Dr. Harding," she said after Molly retreated to her office to put away the stuffed animal. "She's been acting weird all day. I wish you'd take a look at her sometime; oh, but you should really look at Mona first; her eyes are awfully red, and she's acting even stranger."

Molly suddenly burst from her office once again. "Mrs. Carter's going to be late," she announced excitedly. "Claire should probably go to your house, Nette." Molly waved at the girls to come along. "Dr. Harding will give you a ride to Nette's house. Maybe Lizzy could stay at Nette's until Mrs. Carter arrives." Molly raised her eyebrows at Tony. Phoebe looked at him and then at Nette.

"But, my bicycle," Nette whimpered as Molly nudged Annette and Dr. Harding forward with her hands.

"Come on, don't argue with the lady," Tony laughed as Lizzy and Claire ran to the car. "I'll come back for it later." Molly's face lit up, and she clasped her hands over her mouth when Annette finally gave in.

"I like your car," Annette said when they reached the Olds. "It reminds me of somethin my daddy would drive," she said while Tony ushered the two girls into the back seat.

"Well, it's paid for." He bent over to help Lizzy fasten her seat belt.

Annette dumped Phoebe in the front seat and then opened the back door and pulled Claire's seat belt across her lap. "I thought doctors," she said, pushing the belt into its fastener, "well, you know, drove big fancy cars." They both clicked the girl's seat belt fasteners at the same time and when Annette looked up, their faces were inches apart. Tony sighed something unintelligible, or maybe she felt so awkward that she couldn't hear what he said. She quickly backed out of the door and closed it. "What?"

"Not this doctor," Tony said from across the roof of the Olds.

"Claire, this is the smartest dog in the universe," Elizabeth proclaimed to her friend after Phoebe jumped into the back seat with them. "Wait till I show you all the tricks she can do? I wish everyone could be part of the Magic Club."

Annette looked at Tony. "That's just a…."

"Yeah, I know," Tony nodded, "just a game, right?"

"Right," Annette said. "Lizzy's a real chatterbox around Claire."

"Want to come in and inspect the place?" Annette asked when they pulled up in the driveway. Lizzy ran inside and grabbed some dog food from Phoebe's bowl. Claire mimicked Lizzy's actions and followed her to the backyard.

"Our floor plans are pretty much alike," Tony remarked as he looked around.

"Except I have three bedrooms," Nette replied. "I've been in your house many times."

"I turned the fourth bedroom into an office." She nodded, remembering that Jim had done the same. Tony noticed two recessed bookshelves on either side of the front windows. "What do you read?"

"Some of those are mine, and some belonged to my family," she said.

"You read Stephen King?" He sounded surprised and pulled down a thick yellow book.

"My dad read that to us when I was nine," she laughed. "It scared me to death."

"I bet; I could never allow Lizzy to read something like this. She'd have nightmares for a year."

"Jeffrey and Justin love all that spooky stuff," she remarked.

"Oh, something fell out, a photo." Tony bent down and picked it up.

"That's my dad and my brother, Keith." The photo was of two men dressed in camouflage jumpsuits. They were standing on either side of a freshly killed deer that was hanging from a chain attached to a rusty swing frame. "I took this just before they skinned and gutted it. I've always liked this picture. Daddy was so proud of my brother that day." She took the picture from him and looked at it. "Keith never let Daddy live this ten-point down," she said, sighed, and returned the book to the shelf.

"You're into astrology?" he asked and reached for a thin green hardback.

"That belonged to my aunt and those others too." She pointed to a small set of witchcraft and numerology hardbacks. "I kind of get Astrology, but not the other stuff. She used to read cards but she had to quit because people wouldn't leave her alone. I don't know why I keep them. I guess for sentimental reasons."

"You know, what a person displays on their bookshelf says a lot about them; what their interests are, what they think about. Some people might get the wrong impression."

"I don't care what impression people get of me," Nette said defensively. "Those books belonged to my family, and I'm a product of my family. What do you have on your bookshelves?"

"Medical books, mostly."

"I guess that's what you're all about then," Annette jabbed.

"I read everything I can to keep up with research and techniques."

Annette bowed her head. "Humph! Research," she whispered.

"What?"

"Nothing," Annette huffed. "We took my daddy to the best cancer research hospital in the South, and they couldn't do anything!"

"What kind of cancer?" Tony asked.

"Oat cell, carcinoma," she replied.

"That's a tough one," he sighed while shaking his head. "There's no cure for oat cell, not yet anyway; I'm not sure there will be for a long time."

"Yes, I know," Annette said and turned away from him. "But the doctors kept quotin us statistics and tellin' us there were experimental drugs that showed promise." She began to pace. "They sent us home from Houston four times with chemo covered with a black bag. They kept our hopes up when there really never was any." Annette's eyes burned, but she blinked the tears away. "A first-year intern told us the truth; we needed to…" Annette stopped pacing and took a breath. She released the words in an exhale. "Start thinkin about makin final arrangements."

"I'm sorry, that had to be tough. How long did your father live after he was diagnosed?"

"A year, but it seemed like he died months before that; the chemo destroyed his body."

"You know, sometimes doctors in research hospitals get caught up in their own trials and forget that families are hanging onto their every word. And then sometimes, families hear what they want to."

"Are you sayin that my mom and I heard what we wanted?" Annette glared at Tony and then stiffened her back and raised her chin.

"Oh no, I'm not saying that; I believe you. What I'm saying is that doctors have to be careful of what they tell families because…"

"Don't-don't; just don't say anything else," she said and then threw up her hands. "You doctors all stick together."

Tony grinned because of the way she was walking around in circles and ranting. Her face turned pink, which made the freckles across her nose glow. "I see you have some of the old Disney classic videos," he said, trying to change the subject, "and Bible stories." He chuckled to himself as he watched her pace.

"What's so funny?" she hissed.

"Nothing," Tony replied. "But your library does seem to swing from one extreme to the other."

"My kids have a lot of interests, so I keep a little of everything."

"I think you should take the books with the sentimental value and put them someplace where only you can admire them. Young curious minds aren't mature enough to understand these theories and have no business being exposed to such extreme ideas."

"Is that what you think?" Nette huffed.

"Yes," Tony replied.

"I don't teach children numerology or astrology," Annette insisted.

"Sure, you do. How many times have they asked you what's in these books? And how many times have you told them?"

"I-I don't tell them what, what…" Nette stuttered.

"You're their teacher." Tony raised his arms as if hanging a banner, "Witchcraft, approved by Annette."

Annette was speechless. "Huh!" she finally grunted. There was an awkward silence until they heard a car pull into the driveway. "That's Mrs. Carter," she said. "I'll get

Claire." She whirled around and disappeared into the kitchen, and then he heard the kitchen screen door close with a loud bang. He started to follow her, but Mrs. Carter opened the front door and called out.

"Yoo-hoo? Sorry, I'm late," she sang out. "Traffic is terrible downtown because of the Expo."

"Mrs. Carter." Tony reached out and shook her hand. "The girls are in the back; Nette's getting Claire. I'm Dr. Tony Harding, Lizzy's dad." After a few seconds of polite chitchat, Mrs. Carter scurried away with Claire. Annette had obviously been offended by his criticism because she didn't say a word to him except forbidding him goodbye while holding the door open.

"What an idiot!" Annette huffed, after closing the door. "What are you doin?" she growled because, for some reason, Phoebe was pulling on the hem of her jeans and backpedaling against the carpet. "What the heck?" Annette scowled and tried to gently shake her loose. Phoebe let go but ran to the kitchen door. "Just go through your door, dummy." But Phoebe barked twice. "Stop arguing!" Annette peered through the mini-blinds after Phoebe jumped through the doggie door; she seemed to be waiting for her in the middle of the backyard. "What?" she asked after opening the door. Phoebe immediately ran to the back gate and began barking. "Alright!" Annette opened the gate, and the little dog darted across the alley and pounced against the Jones gate.

When Tony turned onto Antrim, he saw Robby trotting across the driveways with a troubled look on his face. The tall, lanky boy laid his palms across the hood of the Olds when it pulled into the driveway as if trying to help it roll to a stop, then pressed his hands along the side of the car until he reached the door.

"Nicky's at practice," Tony snarled when Robby pulled on the door handle.

"Doc," Robby pleaded and pulled the door all the way open. Lizzy jumped out of the car when the automatic garage door began to open. "Doc!" Robby puffed. "It's-it's," he took a breath. "It's my sister, Marley; there's something wrong with her. Please come quickly. Her eyes are all bloodshot, and her head is hurting really bad."

"Where's your parents?" Tony asked while jumping out of the car.

"I've been trying to reach them." Robby's eyebrows were knitted so close together they almost met in the middle and both corners of his mouth were turned down.

Tony grabbed his black leather bag from the back seat and followed Robby across the driveways and past the terminal box that was humming, as usual. Todd's yellow Camaro was parked in the Jones driveway, which made him consider what he might find inside. Teens home alone have been known to raid their parent's liquor or medicine cabinets. He followed Robby through the front door where he saw Marley sitting on the sofa in the living room with her hands pressed together between her knees as if trying to keep them warm, or maybe trying to keep them still because she was trembling all over. Todd was sitting next to her, helplessly watching as she rocked back and forth. Scott was standing behind the sofa with his eyes trained on his cell phone, zealously moving his thumbs across the screen. Marley stopped moving when she saw her brother and Dr. Harding standing in front of her, and then she started again, rocking faster as if to make up for the lost seconds.

"Doc, we don't know what's wrong," Todd said anxiously.

Annette and Phoebe suddenly rushed in through the patio doors. "What's goin on?" she asked. "Phoebe..." Then she saw Tony standing next to Robby.

"Robby!" Marley cried out and then grabbed her brother by the arm.

"What happened?" Nette looked at Robby, but he shook his head and sat beside his sister.

"What's happening to me?" Marley's voice quivered.

"How long has she been like this?" Tony asked, kneeling down in front of her.

"She started acting funny on the way home," Todd reported. "She was complaining about her stomach at first and said she had to throw up. After that, she started acting like this, and now, look at her eyes."

Annette moved closer. The whites of Marley's eyes were red, like Mona's.

"Marley," Tony said, trying to get her attention. "I want you to think really hard." He touched her shoulder. "Come on, look at me." She slowly turned her body but held on to Robby's arm. "Look, I'm not accusing you of anything, okay, but I have to know if you're under the influence of anything or if you've taken any medication." Annette put a hand over her mouth and sat down on the arm of the sofa. Phoebe jumped up beside her.

"No," she said in between short breaths. Tony looked at Todd and Robby and then Scott. All three shook their heads. "Did you take anything after you started feeling bad?" he asked. She shook her head. Tony peered at each of the boys again, and they confirmed her answer.

"Dr. Harding, please, my head is hurting," she sobbed.

Tony opened his black bag and retrieved a stethoscope, a blood pressure kit, and a small flashlight. Todd surrendered his seat so Tony could better listen to Marley's heart, check her pulse and blood pressure, and look into her ears and eyes. "Robby, how long do you think it will be before your parents are home?"

"Pop's cell keeps going to voice mail, but he should be already on his way home from work. Mom is in a meeting somewhere; they're looking for her."

"I'm still trying," Scott interjected while working the cell phone keypad.

"What's wrong with me?" Marley whimpered.

"I think we should take you to the hospital and run some tests. Your optic nerve is swollen, and that should be addressed right away."

Robby's eyes immediately found Annette's. "Okay," she blurted out and jumped to her feet. "I'll be around the front in a second." She started toward the patio doors.

"No," Tony said decisively. Annette turned around, wondering if he thought she was incapable of driving someone to the hospital, just because she had a book or two on her shelf that he didn't approve of.

"Why-why," Robby stuttered. Tony paid no attention to Robby's stammering; he was busy packing his instruments. Scott sensed the tension and looked up from his phone.

"Annette," Tony said, not wasting time trying to analyze the frown on her face or wonder if she was upset with him.

"I'll do the transporting. I need you to watch Lizzy for me until Nicky gets home." She nodded without hesitation. "Robby and I will take Marley to UCSD in my car. Scott, you keep trying to reach Brad and Katie. You and Todd wait here until you either reach them or they come home. I'll call the ER on the way."

"Man, Mom and Pop are gonna freak," Robby screeched as he helped Marley to her feet.

Tony put a hand on Robby's shoulder and whispered to him. "If you want to help your sister, then you should let her hear only comforting and reassuring things from you. She's scared; you need to be her strength right now."

Robby nodded and put an arm around his sister's shaking body. "You're gonna be okay, Marley," he said. "It's cool; Doc just told me he's got a handle on this, and you're gonna be fine." Marley wrapped her arms around him as they moved toward the door. Dr. Harding walked ahead with his cell phone to his ear demanding a team meet them at the ER doors and that Marley should be rushed to Radiology for an immediate CT scan. Annette and Phoebe watched from the driveway, along with Scott and Todd, as the Olds made its hasty departure, hazard lights flashing.

Chapter 22

"I'm guessing brain tumor," said the X-ray technician as he and Tony walked through the radiology doors. "Or maybe an aneurism," he said, putting his glasses into his scrub pocket. "We've had a lot of those lately. Either way, Dr. Samuels is on his way; his interpretation will be more precise. One thing is for sure: he'll want to downsize whatever is putting pressure on the optic nerve ASAP. It's unfortunate to see a kid this age with something this serious." He pressed his lips together, shook his head, punched the large silver button on the wall, and disappeared behind the automatic doors.

I know it will be hard," Tony said after telling Brad, Katie, Robby, and Father Clayton, who had joined the family in Marley's room by now, that something unusual was on the CAT scan, "but please try to remain calm and convey the confidence you have in Dr. Samuels to Marley when she gets back from radiology. There will be a procedure, and it might sound scary, but remember that these techniques are performed daily in every hospital and that he is one of the most experienced neurosurgeons in the world."

Elizabeth cradled Phoebe in her arms as she led Annette through the house. "This is Daddy's office," she said, opening the first door in the hall.

"Medical books," Nette remarked as her eyes scaled the ceiling-to-floor wall of shelves that were filled to capacity.

"There are some plaques and certificates in that box on the floor that he's gonna hang on the wall in his office so patients will know he's a for-real doctor." They passed the garage entrance and stopped at Nicky's door. "This is Nicky's," she whispered as if she was inside.

"Better stay out of there, huh?" Nette replied with a whisper. Phoebe agreed with a snort.

"Let's go to my room, it's next to Daddy's." Lizzy pulled Annette by the hand into the next bedroom. "I didn't have a room of my own in Chicago." She scrambled onto the bed and let Phoebe loose. "A lot of bad things happen in our neighborhood, so I didn't mind sleeping with Nicky." She squeezed Phoebe closer. "She took care of me because sometimes Mama just couldn't."

"I'm sorry," Nette whispered.

"Sometimes she couldn't get out of bed; sometimes she was too sick to come home and would stay with a friend." Lizzy looked at a gold-framed photo on her dresser, a copy of the portrait in the photo album. "Everybody says I look like her."

"Lizzy, you don't have to worry about those things anymore; you're safe here."

"Things weren't so bad when we lived with our aunt and uncle. But we never knew when Daddy was coming home, like now. He promised everything would be different now, but I'm not sure. Nicky doesn't believe him." She gave Phoebe another gentle squeeze. "Can Phoebe stay and play with me, I mean, if Daddy doesn't come home tonight?"

"Honey, we'll stay with you until your daddy gets home," Nette replied. "How 'bout that?"

"Great!" Lizzy got up and went to the dresser and stood in front of her mother's photo. "Sometimes, when Mamma couldn't sleep, she would take me to the roof. We'd pretend we were somewhere else. She told me that someday when she was brave enough, she was going to just fly away. We would stand on the ledge and pretend…"

"What kind of ledge?" Annette gasped.

Lizzy moved to within an inch of her mother's face. "You wanted me to go with you," she whispered to the photo. "But I was too scared."

Phoebe looked at her master, who quickly asked, "Lizzy, it was a car accident, right?"

"A truck ran a red light and smashed into her car. It was the truck driver's fault, but," she sighed, "I heard a lot of whispering. People would stop talking when they saw me, and it made me feel like somehow it might have been Mama's."

"Lizzy," Nette whispered, "please don't let what other people say upset you. Enjoy your new friends and your new house, your very own room, and know that you are safe."

"I feel safest when I'm with Phoebe," Lizzy said and picked her up again.

Annette felt a twinge in her nose. "Lizzy, what's that smell?"

Lizzy giggled. "Daddy spilled some cologne he found in his room. It's terrible, isn't it?"

"It smells like," Nette stopped short when Phoebe suddenly jumped out of Lizzy's arms. "Where are you goin?" she said as Phoebe ran out of the room and down the hall.

"The cologne disappeared just like Phoebe in the magic show," Lizzy replied. "You want to watch TV?"

"Sure," Annette said. "How bout I order Pizza?"

"Yay!" Lizzy cried.

Annette lagged back and stopped at Doc's bedroom door. She was amazed at how much the fragrance resembled the aged bottle of English Leather that belonged to her father. Later, she woke up in her cushioned wicker chair on the back porch after hearing the gate hinges creak. She raised her head above the blanket and saw a man of slender build, wearing a floppy hat, slowly walking up the stone path. She strained to see his face, but the shadow of the brim made it impossible. He stepped up on the porch and bent down. She felt his hand gently touch her shoulder. She couldn't speak or move; she was paralyzed, frozen in a dream-like state. She finally forced herself upright, but a bright light suddenly blinded her. She rubbed her eyes and moaned a complaint and heard a voice, Doc's voice. He was squatted down in front of her and apologizing for waking her, saying he should have let her sleep. She slowly shook her head and mumbled that it was okay. Then she heard another voice, Charlie's.

"Glad you're back, Doc," she heard the old man say. She remembered curling up on the sofa with the blanket after putting the girls, along with Phoebe, in Nicky's bed. Scott had bedded down in Lizzy's room.

"I didn't mean to startle you," Tony whispered, seeing her initial confusion.

"No, no," Annette replied sleepily. "We were waiting for you." She looked at Charlie sitting in the rocking chair. She drew her legs up under her to make room for him to sit beside her. She looked at her cell phone on the end table. "We haven't heard from Robby for hours."

"How'd the surgery go, Doc?" asked Charlie. "Is Marley okay?"

"It went well," Tony said and sat down beside Annette.

"You're holdin somethin back; I can tell," Annette said.

"Rick performed a serious procedure," he said. "It makes the things I've done seem trivial by comparison."

"So that's good?" Annette asked impatiently.

"She's going to be fine," he replied frankly. "She'll be under close observation for a while, of course, but," he sighed. "Rick saved Marley's sight and most likely her life. I have never seen a case like this or laser surgery used this way with such proficiency. She was actually talking and sipping water when I left. It's no wonder Rick is so widely respected."

"I'm glad everything went well, Doc," Charlie said. "Now, I have to go tell Lewis."

Tony sat down next to Annette again after walking Charlie to the door. He noticed she seemed to hang on every word as he marveled over Dr. Samuels' skills, and he couldn't seem to stop himself from explaining the whole procedure to her. "He drilled a small hole in her skull and then went in with a microscopic camera and special instruments. He rearranged the excess tissue that was pressed against the optic nerve and a vessel."

"Why was there excessive tissue?" Annette asked.

"For some reason, Marley developed extra gray matter. It caused blurred vision and disorientation."

"Why, what caused this to happen?"

"It's an extraordinary case," he said, looking very somber. "Rick suggested her brain receptors have been unusually active; that her brain created new cells and tissue to accommodate the activity. A blood clot formed in a vessel in the enlarged area that he successfully suctioned. I'm definitely going to review her case with Rick," he said, reflecting on the multiple procedures he witnessed.

"Oh God," Annette moaned.

"I'm sorry; I didn't mean to scare you." Tony put a reassuring hand on her knee and quickly pulled it away as if embarrassed. "She should recover completely. It's just new to me; nothing like this ever came through my E.R. or trauma unit. Rick said he's actually familiar with the abnormality and the unusual receptor activity, so I'm anxious to discuss it with him."

"Poor Brad and Katie and Robby," Annette whimpered.

Tony started to touch her on the knee again but picked up her hand instead. Annette's eyes were locked on his, and he found himself somewhat captivated by her heartfelt emotions. He looked at his watch and then rubbed a hand over his face. "When I left, they were huddled in a corner in ICU Waiting. Some friends from Mesa Village brought Ms. Lucy over for a while. There were a lot of visitors, school friends, neighbors." A few seconds of silence passed as their eyes met and then Tony cleared his throat.

"You look tired," she said and put her hand on his shoulder as she got up from the sofa; Tony stood up along with her. "Thank you, for explaining everything. I told Nicky I'd have you wake her when you got home. She was really worried."

"I should let her sleep," Tony replied.

"Please, I promised," she insisted. "Tell her everything you told me; I think she can handle it. The girls are in Nicky's bed; Phoebe too. Scott's in Lizzy's room. I'll wake him and get Phoebe."

"They can all stay, under the circumstances," Tony relented with a smile. "Even Phoebe; I'll walk you home."

"That's not necessary."

"I'm not about to let you walk into that dark alley at this hour by yourself."

"That's very gentlemanly of you, but it's not the first time I've walked across the alley at night by myself."

"Don't argue." Tony opened the kitchen door.

Annette passed in front of him, desperately trying to suppress a grin. "Jesus, you sound like my father."

"I'll take that as a compliment." Tony escorted Annette safely to her back door. "Nicky and Elizabeth have spent far too much time alone; before we moved here. I promised them…" He inhaled and then let out a sigh as if alleviating a burden. "That stuff like tonight wouldn't happen again, so thank you for staying with them." He was afraid to linger for fear she might want him to explain what he meant, yet he didn't want to leave because he was feeling very compelled to move closer. His state of exhaustion was weakening his conviction to keep his life uncomplicated. Luckily, she didn't respond, and a few seconds of awkward silence followed.

"Would you do something for me?" she whispered. Tony wanted to tell her he'd do anything she wanted. "I suppose it's silly," she sighed, "but would you look at Mona's eyes tomorrow? They were red today, like Marley's. It could be because of her breakup with Tim, but…"

"Sure," Tony sighed and leaned a little closer.

"Thanks," she said, and quickly turned and left him standing alone in the dark.

He was hoping to talk to Nicky without waking Elizabeth, but when he reached out to touch Nicky's arm, Lizzy's head rose from her pillow, and then Phoebe wriggled out from under the covers. Nicky sat up, and Lizzy grabbed Phoebe as if bracing herself for terrible news. They listened while Tony explained Marley's condition, the surgery, and her good prognosis. Lizzy asked if she was in pain, if she was awake, and a dozen more questions. Nicky didn't say anything; she only looked down and picked at the lent on the bed linen.

"So," Nicky finally said, "you were gone all this time, and it was Dr. Samuels who actually did all the surgery."

"I wanted to stay, Nicky," Tony replied earnestly, trying to ignore her indignant attitude. He certainly expected something more heartfelt, but it was too late, and he was too tired to deal with her. *I should've gone with my first instinct and let them sleep*. It was those eyes, the cute southern accent, and the mussed-up hair that had persuaded him otherwise. "I was concerned about Marley," he continued. "And I know you are too."

"Well, Annette took care of us," she sneered and lay down, turning her back to him.

"When can we visit her, Daddy?" Lizzy asked anxiously. Phoebe's little round brown eyes peered at him as if awaiting his reply.

"I'll take you to see her tomorrow. And we can use my special entrance." Lizzy giggled at the idea of having a special way into the hospital. She couldn't go back to sleep, another thing Tony should have foreseen, so he and Lizzy went to the kitchen where he dished up some ice cream. They bounced a small rubber ball across the kitchen floor for Phoebe to fetch until she got tired and jumped into Tony's lap and started licking one side of his face. Lizzy gave her some water in a plastic bowl and she lapped it until she was satisfied and then looked up at Tony and burped. Tony and Lizzy laughed and agreed that, *on that note,* it was time to go to bed. It was 4:00 am when Tony finally crawled into bed. He fell asleep recounting the meticulous movements of Rick's hands as he guided the tiny lighted scope and laser scalpel throughout the inside of Marley's brain.

Scott eavesdropped in the hallway when Doc explained Marley's surgery to Annette and relayed the account to his internet friend.

S: *Marley Jones was suffering from a brain malformation and blood clot. There are no references to such in any medical site. Apparently, an increase in brain activity created excessive gray matter that pinched a vessel.*

G: *Interesting.*

A slit of sunlight shined through the bedroom curtains provoking Tony's eyelids. He turned his head slowly and peered at the clock on the night table. 10:00 stared back at him. Lizzy lay next to him with one arm over Phoebe. He eased out of bed and staggered through the hallway to Nicky's room. He looked in the bathroom when he discovered Nicky's empty bed. She wasn't in the living room or the kitchen or the backyard. But he found Scott standing at the end of the front walk holding his phone out in front of him.

"Good morning, Dr. Harding," he said and quickly put the phone in his back pocket.

"What's going on?" Tony asked. Two SDCT servicemen were working on the green box between the driveways. The cover was removed, and ribbons of cable were laid out in the driveway. Several of Katie's box hedges were bent over and broken.

"Cable's out," Scott replied. "Internet and local phone service too."

"Great," Tony said.

"They're retrofitting," Scott said sourly. "Now everyone's virus protection will have to be upgraded."

"Do you have any idea where Nicky is?" Tony asked, ignoring his concern.

"Yes, sir," Scott replied dutifully. "She went to the hospital with Annette. They were going to pick up donuts on the way. They've been gone for about three hours."

"What?" Tony gasped. "My daughter's been gone for three hours, and no one told me? Call her," he demanded, "use your phone; call Annette right now." Scott complied immediately. Tony looked down when he heard a growling noise and saw Phoebe at his feet, standing at attention and pointing her nose at the workmen. "What's going on with her?"

"She doesn't like those boxes for some reason," Scott replied while holding the phone to his ear. "It must emit a sound that disturbs her. Sorry, Dr. Harding, it went to voice mail. I'll text her."

Tony was leaning against the kitchen counter in front of the gurgling coffee pot when the telephone rang.

"Hey," Annette's voice said when he took the receiver off the wall and put it to his ear. "You didn't see our note?"

"What note!" Tony growled.

"The one on the whiteboard in the kitchen, the one Nicky said you guys leave each other notes on, which is a great idea, by the way."

Tony turned around and looked at the board. *700AM-Took Nicky to Hosp to visit Marley-Back B4 noon,* was printed in green across the middle of the board and signed: *Nette.*

"Nicky and Robby are in with Marley now. We'll be back in a little bit, I promise."

Tony stared at the note. "I-I'm sorry, I should have known you wouldn't just kidnap my daughter without telling me."

"Dr. Rick says she's doin really well."

"Okay, I have to go," he said, cutting the conversation short when he noticed Elizabeth standing in the kitchen doorway with Phoebe standing next to her. "Lizzy?" he said carefully.

"Are you leaving, Daddy?" she whimpered with her chest heaving. Her whole appearance expressed panic.

"No, Lizzy," he said and rushed to her. He knelt down in front of her and held her face gently between his hands. "I'm not going anywhere, honey. I was talking to Annette on the phone; she and Nicky are visiting Marley; she's doing much better. She wrapped her arms around his neck, and he picked her up and carried her to the wooden rocking chair. Phoebe jumped onto the sofa, rested her head on the armrest, and followed their rocking motion with her eyes. The television remote was just out of Tony's grasp on the end table next to Phoebe. She crawled over the arm of the sofa and nudged the remote with her nose, moving it closer to the edge where Tony could reach it. He pushed the power button, but instead of the Saturday morning cartoons that Lizzy was fond of, a blue screen appeared. Lizzy whimpered, and he rocked more earnestly, squirming in the chair until he found a comfortable position against the hardwood rungs and eventually dozed off to sleep. The next thing he heard was a Channel 4 news reporter's voice. He was alone in the chair, and the cable programming had returned in the middle of a live report from the biggest Electronics Expo ever held at the beautiful downtown *San Diego Convention Center!* Lizzy was at the kitchen table eating macaroni and cheese. The white bulletin board was wiped clean and water was filling the washing machine. Nicky was home.

A noise at the door woke Ty after he dozed off in front of his tablet. The green light on the electronic lock was flashing, which meant someone was using a key card to unlock the door. He put down the tablet and hid against the wall behind the door. When it opened, he grabbed the man entering the room from behind and slammed the door closed with his foot. He threw the intruder to the floor, where they rolled back and forth across the floor while the man tried to free himself from Ty's grip.

"Hey! Bro, it's me," the familiar voice strained.

"Kemo!" Ty immediately let his friend go, and they sat on the floor frowning at each other and catching their breath. "Sorry, man, but when I saw the keypad flashing, my mind just..."

"You weren't answering your COM or your cell, and you didn't answer the door. I've been out there knocking for three minutes."

"I was asleep; I was up late filing my report." He stood up and held his hand out for his friend.

"Yeah, I read it, but I got worried when the tactical assigned to you reported you hadn't left the apartment today." He looked out the only window in the apartment and signaled to the op sitting in a pickup truck across the street that everything was okay.

"I'm formulating my next play," Ty said, rubbing his eyes. "I really need to change these contacts again."

"Yeah, well, you don't mind if I look around while you do that?" Colin looked inside the kitchen cabinets over the sink and the stove and then the refrigerator and the microwave. "You couldn't find someplace bigger?" he remarked when Ty stepped out of the bathroom.

"I don't have time for frills," Ty sighed. "I've been thinking about Sally's trip to Mesa Village yesterday. The assignment is to find out if she knows about the enhancement and who she might be working with, right?"

"And?" Colin asked.

"Those people she went to see up in Mesa, the priest, the doctor, Old Walter, are just unsuspecting pawns. We need to find the vagrant from the other night, the one under the bench."

"North quad techs have been bringing in homeless men in khaki shirts and interrogating them in the basement."

"That's a waste of time; Sally created that deception by providing prison shirts to the Broadway shelter. I traced her steps and found boxes of them in a warehouse a block from her condo. That's the only thing I learned from the tracking device before she found it. She doesn't even snore."

"The reason I've been trying to reach you is because Joseph wants us at the Expo. One of our subjects was rushed into surgery last night. All enhancements have been dialed back or suspended until SDCT finishes troubleshooting the lines in the Mesa trunk."

"Mesa; that's part of the old original grid," Ty sighed, "where the first fatality occurred."

"I'm well aware," Colin said. "Four of the Chinese Heads of State Council Members arrived this morning. Joseph wants to make sure they are impressed."

"Yeah, sure, Kemo," Ty replied. "Man, two in the past six months. Barksdale and…who was it?"

"Marley Jones," Colin replied. "She lives next door to the doctor; yes, that doctor."

"Who handles Marley Jones?"

"Someone whose chair is empty by now," Colin replied. "We have ops stationed in a rental house on Antrim and the Expo is our priority for the moment." Colin walked to the door. "So, get dressed and meet me at the Convention Center."

Ty and Colin were paired together by Rodriguez and Shepherd because of their faultless programming skills. They quickly became experts at producing the necessary electromagnetic flashes required to stimulate both active and dormant regions of the brain. The proficient duo was picked to supervise the Sub Level 3 technicians in yielding the energy necessary to be received by the retina via the hundreds of millions of fibers in the optic nerve that, in turn, fired neurons connecting dozens more that lay latent. Fluid traveling through newly created canals, rearranged tufts and crevasses and created new cells that reshaped tissue. The Group was at the threshold of expanding its reach to the Far East and Europe with the cooperation of the Chinese. A flawless demonstration of the enhancement effects by the pair at the Tech Expo was imperative.

Chapter 23

Charlie dealt the cards around the table, then looked at his hand and shook his head. Annette was to his left, switching her five cards from top to bottom while Lewis, sitting next to her, played with the edges of his. Molly showed her hand to Phoebe sitting in her lap.

"What do you think, Phoeb?" Molly whispered and pointed to her cards. "This one, or this one?" Phoebe leaned forward and sniffed one of the cards. Brad's mother, Lucy, sat quietly next to Molly, pretending to study her hand.

Many of the residents from the village who were unable to go to the hospital, had gathered at the senior center to extend their best wishes to Lucy while she waited for an update on her granddaughter's condition.

"Okay, Nette," Charlie said, "you ready? Lewis, Molly, you and Phoebe are ready? Lucy?"

"Oh, I don't know, Charlie," Lucy whined.

"Take all the time you need."

Everybody anteed up a penny and then raised it once. Lewis and Annette threw their cards away, leaving Molly, Lucy, and Charlie.

"Quit cheating over there, Molly," Charlie bellowed when he saw her whispering to Phoebe again. Phoebe moaned when she noticed her master frowning at her suspiciously. "Let's see it, Molly," Charlie said.

"Well, okay, Phoebe and I have three kings and an ace."

Lucy spoke up as she lay her hand down. "I think this might beat you."

"My God, Lucy," Charlie said. "I can't remember when I last saw a royal flush." Charlie threw his cards down and shoved the pile of pennies toward her.

"Oh, my goodness," she gasped. Annette smiled, thinking how deserving it was that Lucy should win.

"You're such a good girl, Phoebe," Molly whispered and winked at Nette.

The number of visitors to the senior center picked up significantly at lunchtime. Several ladies from the retirement village made casseroles and desserts in honor of the Jones family, thanks to Scott's advertising the idea over social media. Lisa and her family, Mona, her children, and her mother, Jeffrey, and Justin and their grandmother, as well as the Drake's and most of Brad and Katie's neighbors, trickled in, as well as Doc and the girls, Gerry, the maintenance man and his wife, Cindy. Phoebe performed tricks and Robby accompanied music from the stereo on the piano. The spontaneous event was much appreciated by Brad and Katie, who excused themselves early to get some rest. Annette didn't want to leave Robby alone when the crowd dwindled, so she gave Tony the keys to the gym when Jeffrey asked if he and some friends could play basketball.

"She told me something was wrong," Robby said when she sat beside him on the piano bench, "but I just blew her off."

"How could you know, honey?" she said, squeezing his arm. "You were there when she needed you, that's what matters."

Tony returned from the gym later, bragging about the *wupin* he and Nicky put on Charles and Jeffrey. Annette couldn't help but notice that Nicky was trying to communicate something to her father with her eyes.

"What?" Annette finally asked.

"Well, we haven't actually seen the Pacific yet, so we were wondering if you'd tell us which beach is the best."

"Mission Beach is my favorite," Annette replied. "How bout we all go tomorrow after church."

"And, there's one more thing," Tony whispered and motioned for her to step away from the crowd at the piano. "My boss invited me to a barbeque at his house this evening. Apparently, if I don't bring someone, his wife will pair me up with a neighbor. Would you please come with us?"

"You and the girls?" she asked.

"Yeah-yeah," he stuttered. "All of us."

"I'll go, but on one condition," she said.

"Sure, anything," he said.

"Lorraine overdoes everything, no matter what the occasion, even barbeques. I'm gonna wear jeans, so do you still want me to go with you?"

"We'll all wear jeans," he said, grinning.

"And, keep Kevin Samuels away from me, he's a jerk."

"You keep Rick's wife from hooking me up, and I'll keep an eye on Rick's son."

"Deal," she said, and they shook hands.

Over one hundred thousand people paid to enter the San Diego Convention Center Saturday morning to play with and observe demonstrations of the future in electronics. On Friday, ten thousand had previewed the display of prospective PCs, laptops, notebooks, iPods, Smart Phones, large and small dimensional home appliances, water refinement systems, audio and video techniques, 3-D and Smart TVs, video recorders, cameras, video games, headphones, musical tuners and receivers, CD players, amplifiers, plasma monitors, security systems and intelligent home management systems. People ogled and were awed from the time the exhibition commenced at 8:00 am as Ty and Colin worked behind the scenes to make sure the SDCT signal was rendered properly to each and every consumer.

"It would appear the Curve OLED Smart TV has everyone buzzing," Colin said to Ty through the COM unit in his ear.

"Yep, and according to schedule," he replied as if bored from his observation point on the second-floor mezzanine. "Intelligent home management is next on the itinerary," Ty said, looking at his smartphone. "All good here, Kemo, how about you?"

"All is well," Colin replied from the control booth one floor above as he sustained the enhancement levels to each exhibit while the technicians below the Escondido mansion enabled the concentrated signals to the convention center. It was the responsibility of the elite pair to orchestrate each display as the Chinese State Council Members observed the sophisticated management from the adjacent VIP room. Convention attendees had no clue they were actually the ones on exhibition as they were induced from one venue to the next with a keystroke of Colin's trained hand. Investors and future consumers were amazed by certain products and then manipulated to shift their interest to another from the booth three floors above. Colin and Ty alternated their time on the board and the floor in two-hour shifts. Ty's floor shift had been uneventful until he spotted Sally in a red blouse and hair ribbon.

"You didn't call me," he said after working his way through the multitude to reach her. "You didn't find my calling card just a little fascinating?"

"I'm afraid not," she replied coolly and picked up a next-generation smartphone from a display.

"So, you didn't listen to the message I left for you?"

"I'm sorry, I misplaced it."

"Most people think it's a pretty inventive business card and press the button and listen; and can't resist making that call."

"I suppose it's a cute idea, but why would I want to call you Mr. Roberts?"

"So, we can discuss *The Campus Voice* and your forum." He bowed his head. "Listen, I'm sorry I launched the site without your permission. But you wouldn't talk to me; blame it on my ADD. I thought perhaps you might at least get mad enough to call me, if for no other reason than to tell me off. It was stupid, and I'm sorry."

"It was a stupid juvenile thing to do, but it's done."

"People should be reminded of what you went through to get to where you are. I've been a fan of yours all my life."

"Your life?" she laughed sarcastically.

"You're a hard person to make friends with."

"That's because you already proved yourself untrustworthy." She moved to another display.

"I know, I'm impatient."

"I don't like excuses, I don't like the way you took over Jared's paper, and I don't like being followed," she said sharply, seeming annoyed.

"I'm here because the convention center hired me to boost its security. I met Jared right here on the floor yesterday at the preopening. He explained his project to me, and I knew right away that I could help him. I'm staying a few blocks from here, and when I saw you walking home in the rain, I just couldn't help myself; I had to say something to you. My family has read everything you've written. That's how I know so much about you. Please forgive me for being an idiot."

"Your family," Sally said as if questioning his candor.

"My mother and father," Nate replied. Sally frowned suspiciously and moved to another exhibit. "Why are you here?" Nate asked as he followed her.

"I'm working," she replied, "observing, for the Post."

"I see." Nate smiled. "What are you doing later?"

"Really?" she sneered.

"Sorry; my ADD again. Would you like to see the convention floor from our vantage point?" Sally followed his eyes to the control booth.

"Our vantage point?" she asked curiously.

"My associate, Colin; we take turns watching the floor from there. I'd like you to see the unique way we control congestion…uh, with sound. We capture attention with music to keep people moving from venue to venue. You could write a great observational story from there," he bragged.

"Tell me, Mr. Roberts, do you have excess to the VIP area?" She shifted her eyes to the dark windows next to the booth.

"I might be able to sneak us in. Want to give it a try?"

"I'm going to move on now," she said with a laugh. "There's lots of ground to cover."

"Here, take another one of my business cards."

"I really don't want..."

"You never know when you might need my services," he interrupted. "I'm the best IT man in the southwest." Sally took the phone but dropped it in a trash bin after enveloping herself in a crowd that was quickly forming around the 3DHD TV exhibit.

"She dumped your phone again, bud," Colin teased when Ty entered the booth.

"It's like she's wearing a red flag," Ty sighed and looked at the wall that separated them from the VIP area next door, where Joseph Rodriguez and Willis Shepherd were busy certifying the enhancement's value to the Chinese Council Members.

"The way she asked about the VIP area could make some people think she knows what's going on there," Colin said. He pressed a key, and one of the monitors displayed a group of Chinese conventioneers suddenly looking to their left when a home management venue caught their interest for no apparent reason.

Rick and Lorraine Samuels lived in an affluent community in a northeast county called Rancho Bernardino, where homes were valued in the seven figures. Tonya's directions and Annette's having been there before made the home easy to find. Tony knew to expect a grand place after turning into the curved burnt-red terracotta driveway that led them to a circular parking area with a working fountain in the middle where a Black Lincoln Navigator and a Cadillac CST were parked. They took their time approaching the steps to admire the splendid grounds and the two-story stone and stucco house.

"I forgot how amazin this place is," Nette sighed.

"You've been here before?" Lizzy asked.

"I coached Dr. Rick's T-Ball team. His grandson, Daniel, was on the team."

"The doors look solid oak," Tony said, "and the fascia looks hand carved."

"Dr. Rick's wife, Lorraine, is responsible for most of the detailed work. She travels the world and either buys or incorporates a facsimile of what she can't buy into their home."

"I feel really out of place here," Nicky complained. "Why did we have to come?"

"Because we were invited," Tony replied and pressed the doorbell.

"Nicky," Annette said. "There's a basketball court around the back. If Dr. Rick's grandson Luke is here, y'all might be able to sneak away from the highbrows and enjoy yourselves."

"What's a highbrow?" Elizabeth asked.

"That's what my daddy uses to call people that have so much money they don't know what to do with it," Nette whispered to Lizzy. "They have a swimmin pool and a tennis court and an arcade."

"Cool," Nicky whispered.

"How old is this nephew?" Tony remarked just as one of the doors opened.

"You must be Dr. Harding," the man at the door said; "Annette, what a pleasant surprise." It was Kevin Samuels wearing a red Polo shirt and stone-washed blue jeans.

"How are you, Kevin?" Nette replied politely. "This is Dr. Tony Harding and his daughters, Nicky and Elizabeth." Tony shook Kevin's hand while Annette stood behind Nicky and Elizabeth, keeping her distance.

"Nice to meet you, Kevin," Tony said. "Annette and I are neighbors."

"And my son's favorite coach," Kevin said. "Please come in. Everybody's out on the deck. Just walk straight through to the French doors. You remember the way, don't you, Nette?"

Lizzy grabbed Nicky's hand as they stepped into the unfamiliar foyer. She looked up at the seven-foot hall tree next to the door that had eight antique brass double hooks and a large mirror. She grabbed Annette's hand as well when she looked up at the cathedral ceiling with large exposed beams when they entered the family room. There was a large fireplace on one side of the room with a hearth made of the same stone that surrounded the front door. Nicky remarked that it looked big enough to cook on, and Kevin affirmed her observation. Elizabeth let go of Nicky's hand at that point and clutched Annette's arm because the fireplace was twenty times bigger than any fireplace she'd ever seen. There was a big screen TV in one corner and large furniture everywhere. Every unique table, chair, window, and curio captivated her imagination.

"Is Daniel here?" Annette asked when they neared the French doors that led to the deck. "I thought Lizzy might enjoy playing the game I bought him for his birthday."

"Yes, the PlayStation game," Kevin said, sounding over-appreciative. "Unfortunately, we've had to restrict his gaming; he's been suffering from eye strain. His doctor advised the limitation and prescribed some eye drops and tinted glasses. It's hard to get him to wear them; you know how kids his age hate wearing glasses." He pointed to the stairs behind them next to the foyer. "They can play in his room later. He has plenty of other toys up there. Believe me, Mother always provides." Kevin opened the etched glass French doors. “The whole family is here; even Uncle Randy.”

“Rick’s brother?” Tony asked.

“Yes, and my sister and her family and a few neighbors.” There seemed to be 30 people standing around the deck in small huddles holding some sort of snack or drink, and more guests mingling around the pool area. Nette winked at Nicky.

“That’s Luke standin over by the divin board,” she whispered. “He plays center for Holy Christian; it’s a private school.”

Nicky smirked, pretending not to care. “Can you believe the stone-washed jeans that Kevin dude is wearing?” Nicky whispered to Nette, and they both snickered. “He’d get a beat down for wearing that in my old neighborhood.”

Tony coaxed his youngest daughter to release her grip on Annette’s arm and knelt down in front of her. “Lizzy, honey, we’re going to be meeting a lot of new people. We talked about this, remember? I’m going to introduce you to my boss, Dr. Rick, first. He’s right over there; the man with the white hair. Then we’ll meet his wife and family. You’ve already met his son, Kevin. Ready?” Lizzy nodded. “That’s my girl!” he said and gave her a hug.

“Could we please just get this over with?” Nicky groaned in a low voice.

Lizzy took the introductions well, and Nicky put on a polite smile for the *highbrows*. Rick greeted Annette enthusiastically. Lorraine was merely cordial, clearly disappointed that Tony brought Daniel’s T-ball coach, making it impossible to pair him up with a neighbor’s divorced daughter. She remarked that she almost didn’t recognize Annette without her little dog on one arm. Rick gave Tony a brief update on Marley’s stats after producing a Blackberry from his pocket. He made sure Tony felt welcome by personally introducing him to everyone, including his brother Randy, and reacquainted him with Arthur Gallows, the man who initiated his migration to San Diego. He took him on a tour of the grounds and stopped briefly at a small putting green behind the arcade building.

“Do you play?” Rick asked and picked up a putter leaning against the building.

"Oh, no," Tony replied, "never had the time or the money."

"It's a game of self-discipline." He held the club between his hands and swung it slowly above the grass. "I could see someone like you being very good at it. I've given Randy pointers to improve his game, but he does things his own way. And Kevin, well, unfortunately, most of the time, we don't get along well enough to even have a polite conversation."

"I'm sorry to hear that," Tony sympathized, thinking about his own fragile relationship with his daughter. He felt the weight of the club in his hands and made a practice swing.

"Ha!" Rick chuckled. "You're griping the club like a baseball bat. Loosen your wrists and straighten your right arm." Tony laughed, then tried it again and received an approving nod. "I guess you heard a few of my guests asking when I'm planning to retire and the remarks about the family practice being my way of phasing out of my career; some went so far as to wonder if you're the one I'm grooming to take my place."

"Yeah, I heard them," Tony replied.

"Truth is, I've diversified my interest. I must say, however, out of everyone I've hired, you would be my choice if that was my intention." Rick's expression suddenly turned more serious. "You met my son, Kevin. Lorraine and I raised both our children in a loving home, educated them well, and gave them every advantage, but we have two different children. Maya is happy, smart, and well-adjusted, but Kevin," he paused, "I believe he's damaged somehow. He's the reason I turned my attention to neuronal communication and curtailed my hectic practice. And then his friend Andy died so suddenly and tragically," he sighed. "There's research that proves neurons sometimes go awry when a certain protein electrifies untapped areas in the brain. This process can arouse the intellect, but it can also stimulate emotions, therefore driving some to do outrageous things. It changes the brain's architecture, enlarging it. Marley Jones' parents told me their daughter had turned her life around in recent years for the better, fortunately, but something happened to cause that change. The evidence is on her MRI."

"You think her brain was over-stimulated," Tony replied, "affecting her increased interest in learning and causing it to restructure within the architecture to accommodate the activity, thus constricting a vessel in the process, resulting in the aneurism."

"Authur and I have been collecting data for years on patients all over the southwest that have come into ER complaining of headaches and with swollen optic nerves and bulging gray matter and restricted blood flow. They have been described by loved ones and friends as having altered personalities. The case files are in the new addition."

"And you suspect Kevin is a victim of whatever this is because of his odd behavior?"

"I had hoped he would get better after Lorraine convinced him to go to counseling after his divorce, and he was put on antidepressants. But when he and Andy became partners, he seemed to go further off the deep end. After Andy died; he was so broken. He refused treatment of any kind."

"I appreciate you're sharing this with me," Tony said. "I'll be glad to help in any way I can. I suppose Marley's abnormality will be part of your research? You and Arthur could make history if you figure this out."

"Yes," he sighed. "I don't talk about any of this around the hospital. There are too many eyes and ears watching what I do. Brain function is far more complicated than most people understand. Our theory for now is the stimulation enters through the optic nerve, but I could use a new set of eyes to help give me some new perspective as to exactly how it's directed there. Our senses are largely what make us human; they are paramount to our decision-making, our consciousness, and our behavior. So, it could be one or all of them that are affected. I want so much to fix my son," he sighed. After a long silence, he took what seemed to be a deep cleansing breath. "Did the feel of that club grab your interest?"

Tony chuckled at the prospect of taking up golf and handed the club to Rick. "I think you already know enough about me to know the answer to that, but I am interested in you and Arthur's research."

"Listen, son; let me apologize again for Randy's thoroughness. None of what he found would have ever seen the light of day if it weren't for Sally."

"Well, the thing is, Sally believes The Group is somehow responsible for a change in your brother's behavior. Could there be any truth to her thinking, in light of the things you just told me?"

"She's the last person I want to know about my findings. She'll misconstrue everything I'm taking great pains to substantiate to the AMA. She'll only make it sound absurd; she thrives on the provocative. Please don't discuss any of this with her." The phone in his pocket suddenly buzzed. "It's Lorraine. I've been out of her sight too long."

Rick had billed the gathering as informal, but as Annette predicted, Lorraine had put out matching everything. There were red plates, utensils, napkins and red checkered tablecloths that resulted in many secret grins between Nette and Nicky over the ridiculousness. A full spread of barbecue from chicken, brisket, hamburgers, and brats to shrimp and lobster laid waiting with all the standard trimmings. A bartender stood ready to pour guests wine, beer, or mixed drinks into the appropriate etched glassware. Nicky kept her distance from Luke at first, but eventually, they struck up a conversation, and he invited her to sit down at a table with his friends. Elizabeth and Daniel sat across from Annette and Tony. When Daniel pushed the tinted glasses further up his nose, he smeared sauce on them, and Annette took them off his face to clean them. Lorraine appeared from out of nowhere, snatched them from her hands, and cleaned them herself with one of the red napkins. Annette grabbed Tony by the arm when she noticed Daniel's eyes.

"He must wear them at all times," Lorraine instructed after placing them on his face again.

"Doc," Nette whispered from behind her napkin as soon as Lorraine left. "What does eye strain look like?"

"Well, the vessels in the whites of the eyes become pink," he replied in a similar low voice.

"Please check Daniel's eyes; they look red to me."

He leaned forward. "I can't see anything through the glasses. Believe me; Rick would know if his grandson was suffering from anything like Marley."

"I'll slip them off his face; get ready." She raised her hands to reach for them but saw Lorraine looking their way.

"I'll take a look later," he said when he saw Annette take evasive action and wipe Daniel's cheeks. "If I see anything odd, I'll talk to Rick, okay?"

"Thank you," she replied.

There was dessert and coffee after dinner, but the bar and the pool area became the focal point for the adults. Tony and Kevin started a conversation while Nicky, Luke, and his friends escaped the boredom and stole away to the arcade building. Annette and Elizabeth followed Daniel up to his room. Elizabeth was in awe of the size of Daniel's room and the abundance of toys he had. Annette found some cards, and they sat on the floor to play Go Fish.

"Do your eyes feel okay, Daniel?" Annette asked when he raised the tinted glasses and looked at his cards. "What did your grandpa say about them?"

"To rest his eyes whenever possible," Lorraine answered from the doorway behind them. "I just came up here to remind you, Daniel honey," she said as she stepped into the room, "that you're allowed a limited amount of time to play video games and that you're not to use the computer at all." Then she turned to Annette. "I remembered how you always encouraged your young friends to go to your house and play them, so I thought I'd remind my grandson and you, of course, of the doctor's orders."

"Of course, Lorraine," Nette answered. "I would never let Daniel do somethin I knew would hurt him." Lorraine nodded and turned to leave, but something caught her eye when she passed Daniel's window. There was a car parked behind Dr. Harding's Olds in the circle driveway below; a red Mercedes. The distraught expression on Lorraine's face before she exited bewildered Annette, so she scooted across the floor to the window. She peered over the window sill in time to see Sally Samuels run toward the house across the circle drive below.

"Nette, I said do you have any dolphins?" Lizzy asked impatiently.

Nette turned away from the window and looked at the cards in her hand, then slid back to their game circle. "Did you see my hand when I was over there by the window?" she teased. "Yes, I have two dolphins."

"My wife always wanted a house like this," Tony said when Kevin's tour of the ground floor ended up in his father's office. He offered Tony a cigar which he declined, even after Kevin took one from the impressive silver humidor on his father's desk and tried to hand it to him.

"Mother doesn't allow us to smoke these anywhere except in here or outside, so I sneak in here to light one up every once in a while, and pour myself some of Father's special Scotch that he keeps hidden in the wet bar." Kevin offered Tony a glass which he also declined. "As you know, Dr. Harding," Kevin continued, "my father is a heralded neurologist and has received more awards than could ever be displayed here." Kevin took a drink from the gold-leafed glass while he scanned the plaques and scribed crests on his father's trophy wall. "Yes, neurology is the only thing my father has ever cared about." He looked down at his drink. "I suppose he's shown you the new addition?"

"No, not yet," Tony replied carefully.

"I'm surprised," Kevin remarked and moved to a wall of books. He placed a hand on the wooden lion head bookends and adjusted them to face his father's desk.

"I never cared to specialize," Tony said after they moved to the family room. "The ER and trauma were very fulfilling. My wife thought that because I was a doctor, we would automatically become filthy rich. My checks were always way too small to satisfy her."

"My wife," Kevin said, chuckling, "thought that because I came from money, I would provide her with this lifestyle. She was disappointed when my father wouldn't provide for us during our hard times. She left and got the money she wanted, but not Daniel. My mother saw to that."

"I guess we're both blessed with the single father label," Tony said.

"So, Dr. Harding, are you and Annette dating?"

"No, we're neighbors," Tony replied. "And you can call me Tony. I didn't particularly want to be fixed up with someone I didn't know, and she agreed to, well, you know."

"She's hard to get a commitment out of, but she is a good sport." Kevin showed him a grouping of pictures on the wall, all of which included Daniel.

"Rick has this photo in his office," Tony said, pointing out the team picture.

"She's different, isn't she?" Kevin said as he stared at Annette in the photo.

"Yeah, definitely," Tony agreed. They both looked up at the stairs when they heard footsteps bounding down them. It was Lorraine.

"Mother?" Kevin asked when she ran past him without stopping. She shoved the French doors open and rushed out onto the deck. "I'd better check on Daniel," he said. "Please excuse me."

"Would you like me to come with you?" Tony asked. "In case something happened, an accident?"

"No, thanks," he replied quickly. "I'll come get you if I need you." Kevin quickly finished his drink and rushed up the stairs.

Lorraine hurried through the French doors again, this time with Rick in tow. "I saw her pull up in the driveway," she huffed.

"But Randy left already, he had cases to prepare for," Rick explained as they crossed the room. "She has no other reason to be here." They passed Tony and headed to the front door; he couldn't resist following.

"Look!" Lorraine opened the door but stopped short of going through it. They stood in the doorway for a second, and then Rick turned to her.

"I'll take care of this, go back to our guests." Lorraine nodded and hurried past Tony, who had made it as far as the foyer next to Rick's office. "I'm sorry, son," Rick said to Tony from the doorway. "It seems Sally is on the premises somewhere."

"Is there something I can do?" Tony asked, but Rick shook his head, stepped outside, and closed the door.

Annette lay on the floor between Elizabeth and Daniel. They were taking turns shooting a small foam basketball through a hoop attached to Daniel's closet door when Kevin walked in. "Everything okay in here?" he asked and squatted down beside them. Annette stood up immediately and walked to the window. She realized her reaction had startled Lizzy because she followed her to the window and grabbed her hand.

"What made you think anything was wrong?" she asked Kevin.

"Because Mother just came running down the stairs acting crazy," he said.

"We were just fixin to go back down." She led Elizabeth to the door.

"Nette, please don't go yet!" Daniel whined.

"Yes," Kevin said, smirking. "Don't go yet."

"I'm sorry, honey, but Lizzy's daddy is probably wonderin where she is," she said and pulled Lizzy out of the room.

Tony heard a noise coming from inside Rick's office behind him. He put his ear to the door and heard shuffling and snapping noises, so he cracked open the door. Someone was crouched on the floor behind Rick's desk, picking up DVD cases. "Hello?" he said. "Who's there?" He walked inside.

"Close the door," a woman's voice ordered, which compelled Tony to comply. "I'm so glad it's you," Sally sighed when she stood up.

"What are you doing?" He was stunned to find Sally rifling through one of Rick's cabinets. "Rick and Lorraine know you're here. Rick is looking for you, and Lorraine is beside herself."

"I'll slip back out through the private entrance," she said, pointing behind her. "I have what I need."

"Yeah, what's that?" Tony asked, looking at the plastic cases in her hands.

"Nothing," she replied.

"That doesn't look like nothing; I'm going to get Rick…"

"Please, Dr. Harding, don't tell Rick or anyone." She put the DVD cases in a bag and pulled the strap over her shoulder.

"I'm afraid that's impossible," he said.

She moved closer and put both her hands on his chest. "I don't have time to explain, but..." Tony started to argue with her, but the door suddenly swung open. It was Annette and Lizzy.

"Oh," Annette gasped. "Doc, I heard your voice; I didn't mean to interrupt; come on, Lizzy." She took Lizzy's hand to lead her out of the room.

"No, no!" Tony replied.

"This is a surprise," Sally said and pulled her hands away from Tony.

"You two know each other?" Tony asked.

"Yes, from the ballpark," Sally quickly replied. "Where's your little dog?"

"Phoebe?" Lizzy whispered from behind Annette's arm.

"One of your daughters?" Sally asked Tony.

"Elizabeth," he said. He held his hand out to present her, but Lizzy hid behind Annette rather than expose herself to what she sensed was a threatening situation.

Sally looked at Tony and then at Annette and smiled. "Yes," she whispered fancifully and nodded her head.

"What?" Tony growled.

"The two of you," she replied and pointed back and forth between them.

"What are you talkin about?" Nette asked. "I'm just keepin up my part of a bargain, which is more than I can say for you," she said, glaring at Tony. "Where were you when Kevin had me cornered upstairs?"

"I was just about to come up when I heard…" Tony said and turned to Sally. "Where is she?"

"She went into that little hall over there by the window," Lizzy reported.

"Have we been politically correct long enough?" Annette asked.

"Sure," Tony said and placed a reassuring hand on her shoulder.

Kevin entered the office carrying Daniel on one arm. "What's going on in here?"

"I'll go find Nicky," Annette said, shrugging Tony's hand off her shoulder.

"Me too," Lizzy said, not willing to let go of Nette's hand. Tony and Kevin, holding Daniel, followed them only as far as the foyer, where Tony stopped and looked at his watch.

"You know, it's getting late, and we've got church in the morning. I'll just go say goodbye to Rick and Lorraine." He saw Annette standing outside through the glass doors. She turned her head and looked at him as if she had sensed him looking at her. "Well, Daniel," Tony said, "I hope your eyes continue to get better." He reached for the little boy's glasses. "Do you mind if I take a look?" Kevin pulled Daniel away. "I'm just curious." Tony lifted the tinted glasses and nodded. "Hum, what did his doctor prescribe?"

"I don't remember off the top of my head, sorry," Kevin replied somewhat grudgingly. "Mother takes him to the doctor; he had pink eye or something, and it apparently was complicated by eye strain."

"That was just weird," Annette sighed when they drove away from the Samuels' house.

"Rick is right; Sally is nothing but trouble," Tony groaned.

"I'm not just talkin about Sally," she rebutted. "There's somethin really evil about Kevin."

Probabilities analysis: 90% probability Sally Samuels was in the office, although her name was never spoken, and the video doesn't clearly show her face. It was definitely her Mercedes parked in the driveway.

Joseph Rodriguez clinched his teeth as he read the report and viewed the video from Dr. Samuels' home office.

Chapter 24

Nicky moved the hangers in Elizabeth's closet to one side until she came to a blue corduroy jumper. "I remember going when I was your age," she said. "We stopped after Daddy left, except for a couple of weddings and grandma's funeral."

Elizabeth was sitting in the middle of her bed, waiting for her sister to pick out an appropriate dress for her to wear to church. "Why didn't Daddy let me go to Mama's funeral?"

"Mama's funeral was a graveside service which means it wasn't in a church," Nicky explained. "Don't worry," she said when she saw the apprehensive look on her face. "Church is boring."

Tony skipped his morning run and gathered his daughters in the living room to explain the ritual of taking one day out of the week to honor Jesus, who was born both the Son of God and man and who died on the cross to wipe away the sins of all mankind. "And we believe this," he said when Lizzy looked more confused than ever and Nicky rolled her eyes, "because of the miracles Jesus performed as he preached to the people; and because He rose from the dead three days after being buried as he predicted He would to His followers the Apostles in order to prove He was the Son of God."

"Are we gonna be on TV?" Elizabeth interrupted, "I remember seeing church on TV."

"No, honey," Tony whispered, realizing she was too young and had missed the point.

"Will God be there?" Her voice quivered as if she were afraid to hear the answer.

"God is present everywhere, Lizzy," he replied. "We go to church because His son Jesus, told us to honor Him this way. We'll talk some more after you've had a chance to observe the service."

Elizabeth squeezed her father's hand when they approached the bottom of the church steps. She gripped the handrail reluctantly and looked up. The two bronze doors were twice as tall as her daddy and heavy because his knuckles turned white when he pulled on the handle. They passed through the foyer, where her father explained the wooden stairway to their left led to the choir loft, and the granite pedestal on the right was a baptismal pool. But she balked when they reached the entrance to the church proper. Six huge round marble columns held up two enormous domes that were painted with images of angels surrounded by clouds and pale blue skies. A long center aisle that ended at a raised area where the altar stood adorned in white and gold. Lighted candles on tall stands were on both sides, and a wooden cross was on the wall behind it. She started to bury her face in her father's coat but the colorful stained-glass windows above the cross caught her attention. The multicolored panes illustrated two angels holding raised trumpets. More stained windows of such scenes lined the walls. Her father nudged her forward but stopped briefly at a small marble fount where he dipped his fingers and then touched his forehead and his shoulders. He led her down the center aisle and ushered her into a row on the left near the back. The benches that her father referred to as pews gradually began to fill and it wasn't long before she could no longer see the altar. Soft organ music began to play from the choir loft, which made Lizzy's skin tingle. She imagined the sounds to be string-like waves that filled the domes above her. She rose up on her knees to watch the strings transform into wisps of air that moved over the heads of the people until they reached the front of the church, making the candle flames flicker and the white and gold garments covering the altar stir. She sat down between her father and Nicky and realized that being in church was nothing like watching it on TV and not at all boring. Elizabeth pulled on her daddy's sleeve and pointed to Annette when she spotted her sitting across the aisle. "Are we still going to the beach?" she whispered. He nodded and put a finger to his lips indicating that she should be quiet.

The service began with singing and then prayers spoken out loud. They stood and knelt along with everyone else and then sat down when Father Clayton climbed the steps of the pulpit. He read from the *Sacred Scripture* and then announced that thanks to the congregation's many prayers, God had guided the surgeon's hands perfectly, affecting the best possible outcome and prognosis for Marley Jones, and that God had given them yet again, another opportunity to witness His great mercy.

Charlie Warren was sitting on Annette's right and Jeffrey and Justin to her left. Robby was in the pew ahead with his parents. "Daddy," Lizzy whispered, "There's Nette." But he was already looking at her. After a while, the boredom set in, and she leaned against her father's arm. Father Clayton was talking about Adam and Eve and temptation, and her eyes drifted to the stained-glass windows above the cross, and they suddenly took on a life of their own.

Tony bowed his head as the priest spoke, reflecting on all the temptations he had given into over the years. Elizabeth's experience was quite different. Small bits of sunrays began to break around the edges of the mosaic of glass angels. As the sunlight intensified, the gleams began to jut out, extending like spears above the heads of everyone. Lighted beams climbed up the angel's arms like steps until the illuminations included the gold trumpets in their lofted hands. The array from one of the trumpets put a spotlight on Annette and an apparition of a transparent man wearing a jacket appeared behind her. Elizabeth was afraid to move or blink, thinking that any movement might cause the vision to evaporate. She barely heard her father whispering to her, asking if she was okay. She had been squeezing his arm and apparently holding her breath because she started hyperventilating when she came to her senses again and looked up at him.

"Honey?" he said. Lizzy looked across the aisle again, but the sun rays were now repositioned, and the vision was gone.

"I-I don't feel so good, Daddy," she sighed.

"Mass will be over soon; you want to lie down?"

"No," she whispered and looked at Annette again. "I saw—I saw *Him*," she whispered. "I saw God."

"What did you say, sweetheart?" Tony whispered.

"Daddy, I saw God," she said louder. She looked up at him as if waiting for him to explain.

"Come on," he said quietly when heads began to turn. He motioned to Nicky to stay and chastised himself on the way to the water fountain in the foyer for bringing Lizzy to church. He should have known better than to expose her to the majestic images that garnish the typical Catholic Church.

After the service, Father Clayton positioned himself on the top step outside where he shook hands with his parishioners as they exited, being particularly gracious with Brad and Katie when they appeared through the large doors. He hurried over when he noticed Tony and Lizzy. "Dr. Harding, welcome," he said, greeting them warmly. "And this is your youngest daughter."

"Elizabeth, Father," Tony said. "We're waiting on her sister Nicky."

"She must be in the group of kids inside gathered around Annette and Phoebe."

"She brought Phoebe to church?" Tony asked surprised.

"They're always together, so what's the harm? She's quieter than most of the babies. I noticed the two of you get up during my sermon."

"Lizzy wasn't feeling well. I think she was a little overwhelmed; it's her first time."

"Understandable," he said. "The Catholic Church is very ornamental; we have many beautiful statues. And priest vestments are a little different than other denominations," he added while running his hands across his colorful garments. Then he smiled at Lizzy. "You would probably enjoy our children's bible study that's held at the same time as the morning service. It concludes with prayer and snacks. We call it *Children's Church.* It's an excellent introduction to the Bible and it helps them understand the Mass."

"That is a great idea; don't you think so, honey?" Tony asked his daughter to which she replied with a nod. "You can learn about all the stories in the Bible just like I did when I was your age."

"Father Clayton," Lizzy asked timidly, "have you ever seen God?"

"No," the priest replied. "But I talk to him every day and all day long in my thoughts and prayers."

Elizabeth looked at her father and then at Father Clayton. "I saw Him, in there." She pointed to the large opened doors. Annette and Phoebe, along with Nicky, Robby, Jeffrey, and Justin, walked through them just as he turned.

"Well, Elizabeth," Father Clayton said and squatted down in front of her. "This is God's house and He loves it when we come visit Him. It fills His heart with joy and if you saw Him, then that means he was very pleased that you were here."

Elizabeth threw her arms around Father Clayton's neck. "Thank you, Father Clayton. I can't wait to hear the Bible stories. Daddy," Lizzy suddenly squealed. "There's Phoebe." She ran to Annette who had reached the bottom of the steps.

"Father, how is Walter, or John?" Tony asked the priest when they were alone.

"Oh, yes," he hesitated, remembering the embarrassing deception. "He's already on his way north and I understand he took your bottle of vitamins with him."

"That's great. I enjoyed your sermon," Tony said and shook the priest's hand. "Now, if I can pry my children away from Annette."

"Good luck with that," said Father Clayton. "I'm going to talk about forgiveness next Sunday; hope to see you and your family here."

"Hey man," Jared said when he recognized Nate leaping up the stairs.

"Sorry, I didn't make it back till this morning," Nate said and shook Jared's hand. "The Expo tied me up much longer than I thought. I worked past midnight and I have to be there at noon again today. How's everything here?"

"Great, I'll be ready to launch in the morning. I have ten articles and some stuff from YouTube and the blog is up. Sally wasn't as pissed as I thought she'd be about you launching the forum without her approval. Pretty ballsy move; don't do anything like that again. Check-in tomorrow if you're not busy. I may be crashed seven ways to Sunday by then."

"I'll make it up to you and contribute something about the Expo."

"Knock yourself out," Jared said. "I'm going down the street to get something to eat; can I get you something?"

"Your coffee is all I need." Nate sat down in front of Jared's laptop. *Now to see if Sally has anything interesting stored on Jared's computer.*

"Hey dude," Robby said when he found Scott waiting for him in his father's garage, "how come you weren't at church praying for my sister?"

"Sorry, man," Scott replied. "I've been texting back and forth with the head nurse in ICU; Marley's being moved to a room this afternoon."

"Yo, already," he gasped. "Sorry, I didn't mean to bite you like that. I saw your mom's car in the driveway earlier; I know you like to spend time with her when she's home."

"That's cool," Scott said. "She was called in about fifteen minutes ago. So, look at this." He played a video of Phoebe crossing the alley and slipping between two slats in the Harding's fence. "Just like she used to when Jim lived next door. You know what's weird?" Scott said and changed to a live feed of the street. "I've yet to record anyone coming or going at this house down the street. A Honda SUV pulled into the garage one day and nothing's stirred since."

"Seriously, dude?" Robby said. "You're spying on the neighbors now?

"It's just odd. I decrypted a complicated code *G* sent me," Scott said with pride. "It's the hardest one so far."

"What are you talking about?" Robby asked.

"I can usually crack his stuff in a matter of hours if that long. This one took me three days."

"Seriously, that's why you didn't come to the hospital; because you were doing something for that *G* pervert?"

"ICU only allows ten-minute visits," Scott replied, "and I didn't want to take time away from your family."

"I'm gonna let you off the hook this time," Robby said, "but you're coming with me this afternoon."

"Sure, Mom has no idea when she's coming home."

"Yo, so what was so complicated?" Robby quipped.

"It was an essay on solar power."

"And that took you three days?" Robby jabbed, "Woo-woo; what fun."

"Is writing music fun?" Scott countered. "Because I don't know if I'll ever truly understand what you call music."

Tony pulled up behind the Toyota 4-Runner in Annette's driveway. "Why would she let someone paint something like that on the sides of her car?"

"I think it's cool?" Nicky said from the front passenger seat.

"It's an offensive display of the American Flag."

Lizzy was in the back seat bouncing up and down in anticipation of seeing the ocean for the very first time. "Here they come!" she shouted when she saw Jeffrey and Justin and then Annette and Phoebe walking down the driveway.

Tony stepped out of the Olds. Annette's hair was pulled back in a ponytail, and she had on black sweatpants and a black New Orleans Saints hoodie sweater.

"You want to ride with us?" he yelled. "We've got room." Lizzy quickly slid over to make room. Annette unlocked her SUV and the boys walked around the back and lifted the rear door. "Look at all the junk in the back," he mumbled. He caught a glimpse of two skateboards and a boogie board before the boys slammed the door closed after throwing their towels inside. "Good idea, close it quick before something falls out," he muttered.

"Thanks," Annette answered. "But I'm takin the boys to their grandmother's later." She opened the driver's door and gave Tony a suspicious smile. "Follow me, if you can."

Tony nodded and backed the Olds out of the way. "I wonder what she meant by that?" he said while Annette backed the Toyota into the street in front of him. She hit the gas and sped toward the stop sign at the end of Jewel and turned onto Gold Coast without stopping. "Great!" he growled.

"Daddy, go!" Lizzy ordered from over his shoulder.

"I guess I'd better if we're going to find the beach. Lizzy put on your seat belt." He pressed the accelerator so hard that the tires squealed and Lizzy bounced against the back seat.

"Daddy, you left two black marks," Lizzy said after pulling herself up off the seat and looking out the back window.

Tony had no problem following Annette through Mesa or exiting onto I-5, but following her on the interstate was a different story. "She drives too fast," he complained. "She has children in the car," he said next; and then an afterthought, "I have children in the car." Then, "Oh God, I've lost her."

"I see her Daddy," Nicky said. "She's got her blinker on, merge right."

"What?" Tony huffed. "Okay, I see her now. Sea World Drive, Mission Bay Drive, remember that."

"Daddy, Sea World!" Lizzy shouted from the back seat. "I want to go to Sea World!"

"Okay, where the hell," Tony began when the next exit dumped him out into the middle of a six-lane road. "Another interstate?"

"Over there, over there," Nicky shouted. She pointed to the left. "She's getting into the exit lane; far left, far left."

"But that's two lanes over. How am I supposed to get all the way over there?" Tony slapped the turn signal down, yanked the steering wheel to the left, and crossed over the two lanes while horns blew around him. Somehow, he ended up behind her in the turning lane. "Whew!" he sighed and gave Nicky a half grin. He nodded to Lizzy in the back seat but she was staring at something else straight ahead.

"Look, Daddy! Look!" she squealed. "It's a roller coaster. It's like the one in Grant Park, remember Nicky?"

"Turn, turn," Nicky shouted. "The light is yellow; she turned already." More angry drivers blew their horns when Tony pressed the accelerator and slid onto Mission Blvd.

"Okay, I've lost her again."

"She's turning into a parking lot ahead on the right," Nicky yelled. "Get into the right lane!"

"Wow!" he heard Lizzy gasp. Tony turned his head to look for oncoming traffic. He caught a glimpse of Lizzy leaning against the side window. Her mouth was open and her eyes were trained on the amusement park. The girls swayed to one side and then forward when he turned into the parking lot and stopped.

"I don't see her," Nicky whispered.

"Me either," Lizzy said looking out the windows in the back seat.

Tony cruised the parking lot until he finally spotted the flags on the side of Annette's SUV. Jeffrey and Justin were already sitting on the curb, putting on their rollerblades and kneepads. Phoebe was sitting beside them in the grass. Annette was standing behind the truck smiling. "Don't say a word about keeping up," Tony growled. "You were driving entirely too fast, especially with a person trying to follow you."

"Daddy; you're embarrassing us!" Nicky whispered.

"You did that on purpose, didn't you?" Tony continued, "*Follow me if you can*." he mocked.

Annette's smile turned into a teasing frown. "That's the way I roll," she said and opened the back of the Toyota. "Right guys?" she said to Jeffrey and Justin, who were refreshing their rollerblade skills between parked cars.

"Absolutely," Jeffrey said.

"This is what you teach them," Tony said. Annette threw Justin their towels and then rummaged through the left side of the SUV and pulled out a rollerblade case, a football, and a Frisbee. "The back of your truck looks terrible, like a junk heap."

She looked up at him and smiled. "I never know what we might need; I'm certainly not going to drive all the way back to Mesa."

"It's just so mess…" he began.

"Unorganized?" Nicky interrupted, trying to stop her father from ruining the afternoon. "He's one of those *gotta have everything in its place* freaks, Nette."

"Yes, I am," he affirmed proudly; "except for the freak part."

"I straighten it up sometimes, but it always ends up like this again, so..." Annette closed the rear door, and they headed toward the boardwalk.

"Did your car come with that paint job?"

"Daddy," Nicky protested again.

"I'll introduce you to the airbrush artist," she replied smiling.

Nicky and Lizzy ran to the seawall that separated the sand from the boardwalk. They stared at the ocean and then laughed when a gust of ocean breeze blew their hair back and sprinkled sand against their faces. Tony joined his daughters at the four-foot wall and let his senses experience the Pacific Ocean for the first time.

"Lake Michigan," he whispered, "it smells like Lake Michigan."

"Yeah," Nicky replied with a similar sigh.

Did you go there often?" he asked, "did you and Lizzy go to Grant Park?"

"My friends and I used to take the Red Line uptown and hang out at the Navy Pier and Millennium Park. I took Lizzy to Grant once but the train ride scared her so much, I was afraid to risk it again."

"The wind is gusty today," Annette said when she caught up to them. "Hope it doesn't knock some of you off your blades."

Jeffrey and Justin whizzed past. "No problem here, but maybe for you, Nette," Justin jabbed as they both leaned and turned back toward the seawall.

"You guys want to rent some skates?" Nette asked and pointed to a store on the corner with a huge yellow sign on the roof with the word *Rental* in red letters, which apparently meant you could rent anything there. "Jose has regular skates if you're not sure about the blades."

"Can we Daddy, please?" Lizzy begged. "Then can we ride something over there?" She pointed to a whirling ride that was rising over the buildings.

"Well, uh." Tony stuttered, surprised that Lizzy would even ask. "Nicky?" he asked his oldest. "I'm willing to try blades if you are."

"Um," she said, not sure if she wanted to make a fool of herself in front of Jeffrey and Justin.

"Come on, Nicky," Jeffrey said. "I'll hold your hand."

"I'll hold her hand, thank you," Tony grumbled.

"Who'll hold my hand?" Lizzy whined.

"I will," Nette replied. "Phoebe and I will teach you how to skate." Lizzy clapped her hands.

"Have you ridden that?" Tony asked when they walked past *The Wave Machine*.

"That thing kicks my butt!" she said, laughing. Jeffrey and Justin laughed and admitted neither had lasted more than 10 seconds on their wave boards. Behind the Wave Machine were The Wave House Athletic Club and a wooden roller coaster called The Giant Dipper Annette explained was built in 1925 as part of the original Mission Beach Amusement Center, now called Belmont Park. "Yeah, they almost tore it down in the 80's because it became such an eye sore and was deemed too dangerous, but the citizens protested. I was told that Sally Samuels was involved in the "Save the Coaster" campaign back then and was instrumental in havin it designated a National Landmark. People say she was the reason this whole boardwalk was cleaned up. She pushed the city to build a homeless shelter on Broadway which motivated the panhandlers to stop congregating downtown." She pointed to three men huddled together by a trashcan next to the seawall. They each had on several layers of tattered clothing and carried dilapidated backpacks. One was standing next to a shopping cart filled with necessities such as blankets, pots, pillows, and cardboard. "They hang out in different parts of the city in the daytime but now they have a shelter to go to at night." She looked at Tony. "From what I hear, Sally's done some great things for the city even brought a lot of attention to the Mesa Village Retirement Community. No one understands why she wrote that article about her husband, but I think she must have had a good reason."

"I first met her when she bulled her way into Rick's office," Tony said. "And I've had a couple of run-ins with her that made me feel uncomfortable, like yesterday. She's someone I'd really like to steer clear of."

Annette led Tony to the walk-up window of the corner rental store while Jeffrey and Justin made figure-eights on the boardwalk. "Jose, mi buenos amigo y entrepreneur," Annette greeted the Latino at the counter.

"Ha, ha, ha; Nette, donde tengale estado?" Jose replied, "You been taking good care of my mural, still en buena forma? No dents, no scrapes? Aye, I appreciate you sending me clients. I need the business this time of year."

"Your beautiful work all over town is what sends clients to you, Jose. Everyone wants to know the identity of the anonymous *Jesus* tagger."

"I owe my talent to Jesus, and I give Him all the credit," Jose said.

"These are my new neighbors; can you fix em up with some blades?" Annette placed Phoebe on the counter.

"Absolutamente; Phoebe, are you ready for skates yet, nifia? You teach her to skate yet, Nette? It wouldn't surprise me." Jose had menacing tattoos that covered both of his bulging arms that swelled out of his sleeveless tee shirt. His chest and waist were thick, and his hands were rough and stained with paint. Elizabeth was captivated by the colorful murals that covered the walls of his store until he suddenly slammed a pair of skates on the counter in front of her. Only then did she notice how threatening he looked.

"Phoebe, stay here with Jose," Annette said, to which Phoebe replied with a yelp.

"No charge for you and your new neighbors," Jose whaled. "My welcoming gift to you," he said and dropped another pair on the counter with equal aggression for Tony and Nicky.

"Thank you, Jose," Tony said and reached over the counter and shook his hand. "Very nice place," he added. Every inch of the inside and outside walls was covered with painted landscapes of underwater life, desert plants, surfers on boards riding big curls, girls in bikinis sitting on towels on the sand, turtles, dolphins, and whales. Nicky insisted they skate north on the boardwalk to catch up with Jeffrey and Justin. Nette thought it best to keep Lizzy away from the rowdy boys. She held on tight at first, but after twenty minutes of skating around the boardwalk shops with no incidents, Lizzy began to loosen her grip. They took a break on a bench to watch the park rides in action.

"Nette," Lizzy said after a minute of watching screaming patrons ride the Big Dipper Roller Coaster and the Beach Blaster. "Have you ever seen God?"

"No, honey," she replied. "But there are stories in the Bible about people who heard God's voice, like Moses. God spoke to him in the form of a burning bush."

"Oh," Lizzy said, looking disappointed.

"What's the matter?" Annette asked.

"I saw a stream of light in the church today," she said. "It came from the angels in the windows above the altar. It shined on you, Nette, and there was a man standing behind you."

Annette's mouth went dry, making it difficult to speak. "Uh, what…behind me?" She looked over her shoulder toward Phoebe sitting on the counter at Jose's rental store. She had put Phoebe on the pew beside her, but at one point during the sermon, she had lost sight of her after she crawled over Charlie's lap. "Lizzy," Nette whispered. "I saw a light too, honey; it was the sun coming through the stained-glass windows. Maybe you imagined..."

"That's what Daddy always says," she sighed. "That I imagine things."

Annette patted the little girl on the knee. "Well, there's nothing wrong with having an imagination. I want you to draw what you saw for me tomorrow. And, you know what; your skating is no one's imagination." She took Lizzy by the hand and helped her to her feet. After a shaky start, they exited the park beside the last shop, where there was an elderly bearded vagrant wearing a sock hat, a dark green coat, and sunglasses leaning against the wall, holding his hand out. Annette tried to ignore the smelly unkempt man, but he brushed her wrist. She gently pushed Lizzy ahead of her and glared at him. "Stay away from us!" she scolded. Instead of asking for a handout, he pushed something into her palm. It was a small black object no bigger than a dime. Annette started to blast him for trying to pass her some type of contraband, but he spoke first.

"Give this to Sally," he said in a strained voice.

"What?" Nette grimaced.

"The reporter lady," he said, coughing. He took a deep breath and spoke again. "I overheard you talking about her. Tell her they're looking for me, so I have to lay low. It's important she gets this and soon. But…" He grabbed at her wrist, but she jerked it free. He lost his balance and almost fell, so Annette grabbed his arm while the old man steadied himself against the wall. "Don't let anyone see you, do you understand?" He groveled. "It would probably be a good idea if you pretended to give me something. They're watching." His head moved slightly to the left and right as if looking for *them.*

Annette pulled a dollar out of her sweatpants pocket and gave it to him. He limped away while bracing himself against the wall. He stumbled to his knees, and when he rose, the hood of his coat was over his head. "Don't let anyone see you," she heard him say again as he hobbled away.

Annette looked down at the small black object and slipped in into the same pocket she'd pulled the dollar from. *Why did I take this?* She turned to find Lizzy; she was drifting across the boardwalk.

"Nette," Lizzy yelled. "Look at me; I'm skating all by myself."

"Oh my God, Lizzy," Nette laughed. "Look at you! Let's go find your daddy." Annette bent down behind Lizzy and gave her a gentle push, and Lizzy shrieked with joy.

"Nette, do you think Daddy would let me paint my room like Jose's store?" Lizzy asked when they stopped at the rental store to pet Phoebe.

Jose leaned over the counter. "I'll give you some of my paint and help you get started." Then Jose whispered to Annette, "I saw you talking to Lee."

"You know that man?" she whispered. "He kinda scared me."

"Oh no, he's one of the good guys; you have my guarantee."

"Did you see me skating, Phoebe?" Lizzy asked; Phoebe yelped once. "Come on, Nette; let's show Daddy, he's right over there talking to that lady."

"Maybe we should wait just a minute," Annette warned. Tony was talking to a woman with a blonde ponytail, wearing white shorts and a yellow halter top. She was leaning against the seawall, and her body was doing some serious flirting.

When everyone was tired of skating, the beach caught their interest, and they chased the waves and played in the sand.

They threw the football and Frisbee until a dip in the temperature told them it was getting late.

Lizzy held Phoebe wrapped in a towel, and the teens walked ahead of Tony, who was keeping a parental eye on his daughter as they walked across the nearly vacant parking lot. "You've skated before," Annette said.

"Yeah, we had a rink in our neighborhood," Tony replied. "All us punks hung out there. My sister married the owner's son, and they turned it into a fitness center."

"Really," she said. "We had a small rink near the house back home. We were there every weekend until we got old enough to drive and date and all that stuff."

"Nette didn't even fall when that man grabbed her hand," Lizzy interrupted.

"What man?" Tony asked.

"A beggar stopped us and asked for money," she replied before Annette had a chance to speak.

"It's okay," Nette said quickly when Tony frowned. "Jose said he's harmless."

"Are you sure?"

"Shh!" she whispered. "Don't scare Lizzy by making a big deal of it; I handled it."

"Who was the lady with the ponytail, Daddy?" Lizzy asked.

"A woman from the cable company that knocked on the door a few days ago."

"What was she selling?" Annette asked and raised a suspicious eyebrow.

She opened the back door of the Toyota. A wave board and skateboard supported each side of the cargo area. A basketball and soccer gear were scattered around, along with towels, a shower bag, dirty socks, and wadded-up t-shirts. A bat, balls, and gloves were wrapped in a worn canvas bag. He saw various caps and jackets through the gaps in the clutter and a beach chair at the bottom of the pile. He picked up a neck brace and looked at Annette.

"Part of Justin's Halloween costume," she answered. "I gave the crutch away, and I used the hospital gown to clean something." Then she huffed, "You know I'm really tryin to keep from lettin you get on my last nerve, Dr. Harding."

They grinned at each other and then Tony thanked her for showing them the beach and for playing with Lizzy while he skated with Nicky. "I enjoyed throwing the football with the boys too. And, well, I guess I might be getting used to Jose's airbrush job."

"Okay, Doc," Annette said, grinning. "That's enough apologizing; be careful on the way home."

"Me?" he argued. "You be careful!"

"You might want to think about getting a Garmin."

Chapter 25

Ty opened a message from Colin that included a surveillance video of the boardwalk at Mission Beach.

Lee's well disguised, but we managed a sixty percent facial rec. He put something in this woman's hand. Gave us the slip at the train yard near Old Town. They influenced the yardmaster to search for him, but there was no trace.

He studied the images of friends having fun on the Mission Beach boardwalk. He froze the frame of Lee grabbing the wrist of the woman and another of him pressing something into her hand. *Any idea what he gave her?* Ty typed. *I don't think she knew him. She looks taken by surprise.*

Negative, appeared in the message block, and he went on to say that she works at Molly's Day Care, is the doctor's neighbor, and that Cams had them together a few other times since his move to Antrim Way.

"The doctor again," Ty sighed.

She coached Rick Samuels' grandson last summer where we can place Sally attending several times. Ops on Antrim are watching them.

Ty thought about the file he found hidden in a partition on Jared's hard drive as he stared at the stills; *The Nightcrawler Chronicles*, an outline of a story about a talented poodle and its master that coached t-ball. "Is this about you?" he asked the little dog, who seemed to be looking directly into the security camera mounted on a utility pole on a corner in front of a rental store.

It was 6:00 am when Annette tried the double doors at the main entrance to thc San Diego Daily Post. "You'd think they'd be open by now." She peered through the tinted glass while Phoebe sat patiently at her feet on a large blue mat imprinted with the newspaper logo. All she could see was dark silhouettes of office furniture. Phoebe whined, and Nette looked down at her. "What?" she asked. Phoebe looked up at a security camera in the upper right-hand corner of the blue canopy. "Great," she groaned. "I'm not supposed to let anyone see me. At least it's pointed the other way." To which Phoebe replied with a snort. A white Daily Post van passed them and turned into a driveway at the end of the building. "Well, Phoeb," she whispered. "Let's follow that van." Annette wrapped Phoebe inside her dark hoodie and followed the side of the building. She stayed within the shadows as she trotted behind of a row of tall hedges. She heard voices and banging noises at the rear of the building, where there was a loading dock. Two trucks pulled out and rushed past them; two more quickly backed into the empty spaces. Bundles of newspapers traveled down three conveyors where they were stacked onto plastic pallets and loaded into the trucks with forklifts. It was noisy and everyone was busy, too busy to notice Annette slip inside the building holding Phoebe tightly inside her sweater. She worked her way through rows of enormous rollers, sorters, and slicers until she came to a yellow door with a small square glass window that allowed her to see a man inside, sitting at a table with his back to the door, drinking a soda and reading a magazine. An open lunchbox and a half-eaten sandwich lay on the table in front of him. A directory next to another exit inside the room pointed the way to the main elevators. The man was wearing earplugs, so she took a chance and opened the door. She held her breath when he picked up the sandwich and took a bite and then laid it back down. She quickly tiptoed to the exit after seeing a security camera scanning the opposite direction. "My God, Phoeb, what am I doing?" They were in a long hallway with cameras on each end. Phoebe lifted her head from inside the sweater and looked up at them. Annette pulled the hood down over her forehead, hugged the wall and trotted toward the door marked *Stairs* while the red light on the cameras slowly rotated above her head. "The newsroom is supposed to be on the third floor, according to the legend on the wall," she whispered. "I'm never gonna get passed all these cameras." But when she reached the stairwell, the camera was pointed straight ahead instead of down the stairs. "Huh!" she grunted and scooted up the first set of stairs only to see another camera when she turned at the next flight; it too was pointed straight ahead which allowed her to make a run for it. Each time she turned to scale another set of stairs, the camera was pointed away from her, so she didn't stop until she reached the door stenciled with the number 3. She pulled on the door handle and found herself in front of an elevator bank. Two cameras were aimed at the elevator doors but both appeared jammed in position. Each wobbled and jerked as if trying to free itself from a bind. "What are the odds, Phoeb?" she whispered. "Phoeb?" she repeated and patted her sweater with both hands. "Where are you?" She spotted her trotting down a corridor past the elevator bank that had five doors on one side and a four-foot partition on the other that sectioned off a large newsroom. Her nose was pressed to the carpet. Annette saw three people with their eyes glued to their monitors in the newsroom, which was mostly cubbyholes of desks and computer terminals. TV monitors were attached to every wall broadcasting various news networks. Dark and empty offices bordered three sides of the great room. She crouched below the wall and followed Phoebe who had already nudged her way through the door of the second office with Sally's decorated name tile on the door. She heard an elevator door rumble, so she scrambled through the door and closed it. "Phoebe, where are you?" she whispered in the dark. A slim vertical window next to the door allowed her just enough light from the newsroom to see a knocked-over lamp, two air vents, and a smoke detector hanging from the wall. Everything that must have been on Sally's desk was on the floor. Phoebe crept from behind the desk and sat at her master's feet. "What happened in here?" Annette gasped and reached to pick her up. The door suddenly opened, and the light from the newsroom filled the office. Annette turned, but the door closed, and the room was dark again with a lone silhouette standing in front of the window.

"What are you doing in here?" an angry voice demanded.

"Uh, uh," Annette stuttered. The overhead light suddenly appeared, and she saw Sally closing the blinds. "Ms. Samuels, I-I know this looks weird but," she began. Sally gasped when saw Phoebe standing next to her desk and then looked at the lamp and the dangling covers and pieces of everything from her desk on the floor.

"Did you do this?"

"No, ma'am," Annette replied. "Well…" She looked at Phoebe. "It was like this when I walked in. I don't know…"

"Shut up, I'm calling Security." Sally pulled a cell phone from her bag.

"Are those cameras?" Annette whispered, and they both looked up at the exposed air vents.

"What's she doing?" Sally snarled. Phoebe was on her hind legs and pawing at one of the desk drawers.

"Phoebe, stop that!" Annette grabbed Phoebe away from the desk and held her close.

Sally took a key from her bag, unlocked the desk, and pulled open the drawer. "Where did this come from?" She picked up the small black rectangular object that the homeless man gave to Annette.

Annette reached into her sweater pocket, shifted Phoebe to the other arm, and checked the other pocket. The small object the old man gave her was gone and was now in Sally's hand. "That's, uh," Annette stuttered. "That's what-what I came here to give you."

Sally held the object between her fingers and frowned at Annette. She pulled on the ends, and it separated into two pieces. "It's a SIM card." They looked at each other in silence. "How did this get into my locked desk?"

"I-I don't know; I can't explain it," Annette whimpered. "It was in my pocket, but now," Annette looked at the card in Sally's hand and then at Sally again, "now it's not. A-a homeless man at the boardwalk told me to give it to you."

"He should have brought it to me himself," Sally groused. "This was foolish; it put you at risk."

"He said he has to lay low because someone is watchin him. He told me not to let anyone see me, and I don't think anyone did because..." She looked up at one of the opened vents, and the video camera turned on its side.
"Because…,"
Sally rubbed her forehead while Annette struggled for words.

"Stop trying to explain," Sally huffed and looked at Phoebe. "I've heard the stories."

"What stories?" Annette gasped.

"From the ballpark; never mind." Sally put her hand on the little dog's head, and Phoebe licked her hand. "Don't worry; no one really believes any of it."

"Thank God," Annette whispered.

"My nephew Daniel is certainly impressed with her," Sally said. Phoebe crawled out of Annette's arms and into Sally's. "Well, hello, Phoebe," she whispered. Phoebe put her nose to Sally's and licked her on the lips.

"I've tried to teach her not to do that," Annette apologized.

"It's all right," Sally cooed and scratched Phoebe on the head and then looked at Annette. "It's ridiculous trying to teach five-year-olds how to play ball."

"Not really," Annette argued, "the kids have fun. It's the parents that spoil it. They expect too much."

"They just expect to see a bigger return on their investment," Sally remarked. "That's why having a cute little dog around to entertain them is a good thing."

"They should play ball with their children in their backyards like my parents did my brother and me," Annette rebutted.

Sally released Phoebe back into Annette's arms. "Good point, but it costs those parents over two hundred dollars to register their child with the youth baseball leagues in San Diego County," she said. "That barely covers the cost of uniforms, use of the fields, umpires, and grounds personnel."

"I guess that's why Dr. Rick puts up the money for his team," Nette sighed. "Lord knows, Kevin would never…"

"Rick's spoiled brat son?" Sally laughed.

"Hmmm," Nette remarked, not really wanting to talk about Kevin Samuels.

"You were wise to give that nut case the brush off."

"I'm sorry if I did somethin wrong," Annette apologized.

"Just hope no one saw you." Sally looked around the room and then grabbed her shoulder bag and a long gray raincoat from a coat tree in the corner of the office. "Hide Phoebe in your sweater; I'm going to put this over you and walk you out of here. Where are you parked?"

"On a side street, a couple of blocks from here," Annette said.

Sally took her by the arm and pulled her through the walkway next to the news room and then guided her to a service elevator.

"Ms. Samuels," Annette said as the elevator descended, "did your husband do what you accused him of?" Sally didn't answer. She looked up at the camera in the right rear of the car and pulled the hood of the raincoat further down to better cover Annette's face. The elevator door opened into a parking garage. "I'm sorry I upset you, Mrs. Samuels," Annette whispered from under the hood.

"I know, but listen to me." Sally placed her hands on Annette's shoulders. "Don't come back here and don't try to contact me. What my friend gave you must remain our secret, like Phoebe." She looked at Phoebe, peeking through the opening in the coat.

"What exactly do you mean by that?" Annette gasped.

"Don't go to my condo, and if you see me somewhere, go the opposite way. Do you understand?" Annette nodded her head in silence. "There's something else," she sighed. "I saw the look on your face when you found me in Rick's office with Dr. Harding. You can't tell anyone that you saw me there," she added when Annette grimaced. "You'll put yourself in danger if you do. There's nothing going on between Dr. Harding and me."

"Why would I care if there was?"

"Now, I suggest you go to the coffee shop on the corner and ditch the coat." She pointed to the opposite side of the parking garage. "Go out the side entrance and follow the ally to the street, then circle around the next block and walk to your car from the opposite direction. There's more traffic now, so you might go unnoticed."

"You're kinda scarin me here."

"Good," she said and looked at Phoebe. "Keep your master safe." She watched them until they entered the coffee shop and took the small card from her pocket. She removed the battery cover from her cell and inserted the card into the SIM slot behind the battery.

A team of S3 Level techs from the Escondido facility relieved Ty and Colin from their duties at the Expo, leaving them free to concentrate on Sally again while Joseph Rodriguez and Willis Shepherd continued to demonstrate the enhancement capabilities to the Chinese guests. They selected one hundred random patrons, seeded them with specific instructions, and then ran them around the Expo like robots. The two senior agents shared a toast that evening in the Cabrillo room to celebrate their success. Early the next morning, Rodriguez's team alerted him of the surveillance malfunction in Sally's office building.

Tony was fifteen minutes early on his first official day as part of the Samuels Family Practice. An hour later, he was seeing his first patient and, thanks to his watch alarm, picked up Lizzy on time from Molly's. Nicky was home in time for dinner, and the threesome sat down together. "I looked in on Marley," Tony said, breaking the silence around the table. "She's going home in the morning."

"Wow," Lizzy gushed. "That's a miracle."

"That's good medicine, Lizzy," Tony corrected.

"Well, everybody else is calling it a miracle," Lizzy rebutted.

"That's because it involved brain surgery, and that scares people. She was lucky to have Dr. Samuels available to perform the surgery. What's going on with you, Nicky?" He asked, hoping for an equal amount of interest, or perhaps if he was lucky, she'd ask about his first day at work.

"Nothing," she replied and played with a piece of pork chop on her plate.

"How did your friends like your new cell phone?" he asked.

"No one really saw it. We have to keep them in our lockers; they get confiscated if we're caught using them."

"Oh," Tony replied. "Would you like to visit Marley after dinner?"

"I would! I would!" Lizzy yelled, bouncing up and down in her chair.

"I have homework," Nicky answered. "I'll call her on my new cell."

"Okay," Tony said. "Lizzy, you and I are going to clean up the kitchen so Nicky can do her homework."

"You need to take on some responsibility," he said to his youngest when she pooched out her lip. "It's not fair that Nicky does it all the time." He looked at Nicky and put his hand on her arm and gave it a gentle pat. "Right, honey?" He kept his hand there until she responded.

She pressed her lips together and mumbled, "Right."

After the visit and the girls were in bed, Tony walked outside to stand on the back porch. Something suddenly compelled him to walk across the alley to Annette's gate and knock. *That was stupid.* He turned to go home, but the gate opened.

"Doc," Annette sighed.

"I'm sorry," Tony said. "I didn't mean to disturb you."

"I sit out here all the time. I read or sometimes just sit and listen to Robby. How are the girls?" Her voice was soft, and her head was tilted lazily against the side of the gate. He couldn't stop the spontaneous smile that spread across his face. He felt all the frustration over Nicky's stubbornness, and Lizzy's daunting imagination melt away.

"They've gone to bed; I felt like talking to someone."

"Okay then; come on and sit down." She held the gate open wider and pointed to the wicker chairs on the porch. She led him across the broken stone path to the porch. "Would you like something to drink, a soda or decaf tea?"

"Where is Phoebe?

"Inside, I guess," she answered.

"Why are you frowning?" Tony asked.

"You cut your hair."

"Today was my first day at work."

"I kinda liked it the way it was," she said, smiling.

Tony hoped the shadows would hide his blushing.

"I like sittin out here at night." She sat back and pulled her legs up under her. "Robby's usually playin somethin' about now, but I suppose he's tired.

"I saw him at the hospital earlier."

"I hate hospitals; they make me nervous, and I'm sorry, but I don't have a lot of faith in doctors."

"Because of what you went through with your father," Tony sighed.

"So, how was your first day?" she asked.

"It felt great to be doing something familiar again. It's this single-father business that's frustrating. I bought Nicky the cell phone on our way home from the beach, and she acts like she could care less. I feel like I'm a big intrusion in her life, and we're never going to connect."

"You're doin great; she'll come around, be patient. In the meantime, y'all are creatin new memories together. A year from now, you'll look back and see how much better everything is, you'll see."

"Lizzy fell out of a chair in the backyard trying to reach for the stars. She almost fainted in church because she thought she saw God. I'm scared I'm going to lose her because she gets so caught up in the imaginary." Tony couldn't believe he had blurted that out. "I'm sorry, I didn't mean to…"

"It's okay," Annette interrupted. "We talked about the church thing a little bit when we were skatin. She wants to paint a mural on her bedroom wall like in Jose's shop. Jose volunteered to help her get started, with your permission. I think it would be good for her to paint the things she imagines. It puts it out there for the world to see and talk about. I think that would be important for her well-being."

"Mona showed me a picture she drew of our old apartment building," he said. "I recognized the brick casings around the windows, the curved front steps, and the double doors with the iron bars. She drew all these little details; I can't believe she even remembered all of it. She even told me the names of the neighbors that were standing in the windows, but she clammed up about the people on the roof."

"The roof," Annette sighed. "The night I stayed with her, she told me her mother used to take her to the roof and stand on the ledge," Annette paused, wondering if she should tell him the rest, "she talked about flying and wanted Lizzy to," she hesitated again, "go with her but she was too scared."

"Fly, as in jump?" Tony gasped. "Oh my God, what the hell was wrong with Carol?" he moaned. "No wonder Lizzy's so afraid of everything."

Annette put her hand on his shoulder. "Elizabeth's gonna be okay, Doc." She gently patted his shoulder as she watched him shake his head in disbelief. "She has you now."

"It was the drugs and the alcohol," he moaned.

"You know better than me what those things do to a person's brain," she whispered. "I've seen folks from back home do some pretty stupid things livin under the influence. You did the right thing movin away, as far as I'm concerned. You guys needed this."

Tony looked up at her. Tears stung his eyes.

Annette slid her hand from his shoulder to his back. "You're a good father."

"Carol might still be alive if I hadn't been so caught up in my own career."

"Doc, you have to put the past where it belongs; stop punishin yourself, or you'll never be able to move forward."

"Yeah," he sighed. "Like forward is so full of guarantees."

"Have a little faith. No one has ever told me that parenting is easy, even under the best circumstances. Coach Burns is letting Nicky sit out with JV on Friday. That's somethin to look forward to, isn't it?"

"Yeah, if she had told me about it," he replied. "I guess she doesn't want me there."

"But you're gonna go, aren't you?" Annette asked. "She wants you there, whether she's willin to admit it or not."

"No, she doesn't, she hates me," he muttered and hung his head. "She thinks I never went to her games, but I went every chance I could. I sat up high in the shadows so Carol wouldn't see me. She didn't want me anywhere near them."

Annette put her hand on Tony's shoulder again. "She'll be happy to see you there even if she doesn't show it. I remember being just like that when I was her age. My father and I fought all the time. It wasn't until I was older that I realized how much he loved me. Thank goodness I was able to tell him how much I appreciated…" She stopped when she felt a rush of emotions start to take over. "Just tell her you love her as often as you can. It may take a while, but she'll come around, I promise. By the way, did you tell Dr. Rick about finding Sally in his office?"

"I never got the chance," he replied. "It was strange; every time I looked for him, he was unavailable, according to Tonya. And I was pretty busy, being my first day and all."

"Maybe that's a good thing," she sighed; "maybe we should stay out of her drama."

Tony left Annette's backyard feeling like he might be on track after all. He had wanted to hug her, even kiss her before he left, but she kept her distance when they stood up and found themselves standing close together. He awkwardly thanked her and said goodnight. He headed straight to bed but noticed Lizzy's door partially open. He thought he heard the jingle of Phoebe's collar when he approached the door, so he opened it and stepped inside. Lizzy was asleep; he lifted the covers, but nothing was there. He looked down the hall; there was no shadowy figure. He went to bed, and he fell right to sleep for the first time since the move.

C: *You have surveillance from* The Post *waiting for you. Something screwy happened there this morning. Video in the whole place went down. Ops surveilled the woman with the dog driving there. Joseph is not pleased. What have you been doing all day?*

T: *Got bogged down at* The Voice. *Launch went better than expected. I'll get back to Sally ASAP.*

Chapter 26

"You up already?" Ty grunted into the cell phone, as Nate Roberts.

"Newspaper never sleeps, man," Jared replied. "And apparently, neither do bloggers."

"Can't make it today, dude. I put off some stuff yesterday to give you a hand."

"That's cool, plenty of volunteers showed up this morning wanting to be part of *The New Campus Voice*. I appreciate you sticking it out yesterday."

"No prob, check you later." Ty ended the call and turned on the COM unit in his ear. "Kemo, you got your ears on?" he said.

C: *Joseph wants you to follow up with the pharmacists at Vons.*

T: *Affirmative, but it's a waste of the precious time he's given us.*

C: *I've already loosened him up for you; shouldn't take long.*

T: *I should be looking for Lee, you know.*

C: *Sorry, direct order.*

The Chinese delegation spent the night at The Marriott downtown rather than the Escondido mansion after witnessing The Group's manipulative capabilities. The entourage returned by helicopter at 11:00 am. Joseph greeted them on the roof with the appropriate bow at the waist. "Follow me into the Cabrillo conference room." "Cabrillo," Delegate Chi Yong said as they boarded the elevator, "the famous explorer. I saw the monument to his honor atop one of your hills. He discovered the city of San Miguel?"

"Yes, in 1542," Rodriguez replied. "You will see an original portrait of him on the wall in the conference room. I carry his namesake, Juan Cabrillo Rodriguez."

"Yes," Mr. Yong replied, "and although you have Americanized your name, I see you have many mementos from the time period throughout your headquarters," he added as Rodriguez led him through the halls. They gathered in the conference room under the modest portrait. "Mr.

Rodriguez, we should get to business. We are not interested in whether randomly selected subjects will purchase 3DHD televisions or 10G tablets. Our economy might be struggling, but we have no problem manufacturing and marketing our goods worldwide. The stranglehold we have on your country is what you want relaxed, but thus far, you haven't demonstrated anything worth presenting to the Central Committee to barter such an agreement. You supposedly have the means to persuade people to buy certain products. We have marketing geniuses that create the same effect while providing us with enticing entertainment. I'm afraid that's all you've done here is entertain us."

"You said there was more," Delegate Hu Li added. "Perhaps we should see that today, right now, in fact. Otherwise, our helicopter is waiting to take us to your International Airport, where we shall board our private jet and return home."

"Yes, of course," Rodriguez said. He picked up a remote-control device, and a fluttering sound from the drapes on either side of the balcony slowly closing could be heard as the room darkened. "As I mentioned before, we run the entire Southwest Region of the United States from this complex." He went to the desk and slid a laptop closer. "And by that, I mean eighty percent of the population decides what they wear to work, whom they will hire or fire, what stocks they will trade, whether or not to fight with their spouses, what to serve for dinner, or whether to run their car off a cliff, all in accordance with what we influence them to do." The two members of the delegation sat down at the conference table when the large screen above them lit up. "We have the ability to turn an unfortunate event into something that is determined reasonable within twenty-four hours. We experienced such an event last weekend." A copy of Sally's oversized headline appeared across the screen. "This is an unfavorable article about one of our future political candidates. We have reduced the reaction to nothing more than sighs with our manipulation. We have people operating under our compliance within every level of government." Snapshots of faces materialized across the large screen. "Yes, even people that work in the White House. You may recognize many of them. And in a short time, our acquiescence will be complete. The Group has similar regional facilities throughout the U.S., but ours is the most proficient." A map of the U.S. divided into four sections appeared on the screen. "The Southwest Region is the most technologically advanced; therefore, that population is better saturated. He changed the screen to an array of surveillance cameras posted in various points of the State. "We allow much of the general public to run their own lives with the exception of those that display a potential to advance our causes." The array of live videos of recognizable locations changed every ten seconds, demonstrating the vastness of The Group's operation. "Every mission we initiate transpires peacefully and in accordance. We allow some controversy for appearance's sake, but in the end, we get what we want, and everyone is content."

"We've seen PowerPoint presentations before, Mr. Rodriguez," Yong said. "You still haven't demonstrated precisely what you're trying to sell us."

"There's a bill on the floor of the State Senate being voted on as we speak. Let's eavesdrop." Joseph Rodriguez began to type. Within seconds a view of the State Senate floor appeared on the big screen above them. "Ah, the off-shore drilling bill," he said, looking up from the keyboard. "The bill being debated on the floor is whether to allow the increase of oil drilling off the coast of California. I see they are about to call for a vote. What would you like the outcome, Mr. Yong, Mr. Li? Shall we flip a coin?"

"Oil drilling?" Yong sneered. "Your state environmentalists will never allow that. Your President has already passed laws that require all companies to look for alternative fuel sources."

"So that's a *no*?" Rodriguez asked.

"No!" Mr. Li grunted. "Make it *yes*, to make it interesting."

"*Yes*, it is, then." Rodriguez's fingers pattered across the keyboard, giving a command to the technicians in the North Quad to take control of the statesmen on the floor of the State Senate." He noticed one of the other Chinese council members pull out a cell phone and start texting. "Do you have a contact on the Senate floor?"

He looked up. "No, but ministers in our country have contacts in Sacramento."

"By all means, contact your Ministers," Rodriguez said. "We'll use them as verification." He turned to the monitor again. "It will take some time for the votes to be called. Is there something else I could demonstrate?"

The delegates looked at each other, and then Mr. Yong spoke. "Surprise us."

Joseph thought for a few seconds and then smiled.

"Annette, honey," Molly whined when she came out of her office. "Would you be a sweetheart and take the deposit to the bank for me?" Molly held a red canvas bank bag out to her. "Mona's been a little distracted today, and Lisa's interviewing a new parent."

"Sure, Molly," Nette replied and took the bag from her. "But I'm on my bike, you know. It'll take me a little longer."

"That's okay; just as long as you're back by three."

"I should be back long before that, and I'm taking Phoebe with me."

"Yes, but I wanted to…" she stuttered.

"I knew you were up to somethin," Nette laughed. "You were gonna dress her up again while I was gone, weren't you?"

"No, I just wanted her to play cards with me," she said, waddling behind Annette as she walked into the garage.

"Bye, Molly," Nette sang, teasing her. "See ya in a bit." She put Phoebe on the pillow in the basket and peddled away.

"Well, there's always Candy Crush," Molly sighed and went back into her office. She closed the door and pulled on the handles of one of the cabinets. Thirty brown stuffed poodles stared back at her.

"Play cards," Annette grumbled. "Doc worries about Lizzy. She's gonna grow out of her fantasies, but Molly seems to regress a little every day. It's just not fair," she said as they passed the church and turned onto Canyon Road. Phoebe replied with a whine.

C: *There's a demo going down at San Diego County Bank on the corner of Mesa and Canyon Rd. Joseph just gave the order.*

T: *I just finished with the pharmacist if you need me.*

C*: Sit tight; just giving you a heads-up because you're in the area.*

T: *10/4. The pharmacist filled a 90-day script for vitamins for John Smith.*

Said he heard Smith was headed up north-Canada.

Annette had to stand on the pedals to make it up Canyon Road's steep incline. A gas station/convenience store was on the corner at the top of the hill and across from the Mesa branch of the San Diego County Bank. The incline leveled off just before the store's driveway. Phoebe lifted her head and looked toward the bank. She barked twice and then leaped from the wire basket and scampered toward the convenience store. "Phoebe!" Nette yelled. A car turned in the parking lot and headed to the gas pumps, scarcely missing Phoebe. Annette dropped her bicycle in the driveway and ran behind the car. "Oh My God, oh My God!" she cried. The car stopped at a pump and she ran around the front looking on the ground. "Phoebe! Phoebe!" she cried. She looked in front of another car at the second pump.

"Annette?" she heard someone call out. When she turned, she saw a man standing next to a blue pickup truck on the other side of the service aisle. He was holding Phoebe and looking at her tag. "I thought this looked like Phoebe," he said and stepped over the isle. "I don't know how she recognized me, but she ran straight to me."

Annette put a hand on her forehead. "Tim," she gasped and rushed to him. "Oh God, Tim, she just jumped out of my basket; I thought for sure she'd been run over." She took Phoebe from him.

"What are you doing riding your bike on Canyon Road this time of day?"

"Oh no!" she gasped. "Molly's deposit; it's still in the basket." They both rushed over to where Annette dropped the bicycle. Tim lifted it upright by the handlebars and pushed it onto the sidewalk.

"Thank God, it's still under the pillow."

"But your bike is kind of messed up," Tim said. "Someone must have run over it." They both examined the bike and agreed it was unsafe to ride.

"I'm sorry about you and Mona," Nette sighed. "I wish there was somethin I could do to help, but she's so hard to get through to right now. Are you doin your part, you know, have you stopped the drinkin?"

"Nette," Tim said and shook his head. "Her leaving me has nothing to do with drinking. I stopped the minute she started using it as an excuse."

"Excuse?" she asked and pulled Phoebe close to her for comfort before hearing Tim's side of the story.

"She got tired of me drawing her attention away from her precious computer. Nothing else seems to matter to her except the degree. She shut everybody out; a little at first, which I didn't think too much about. I tried to tell the kids that their momma was just trying to better herself, but things just got worse. She became resentful of every little thing she had to do for us because it was taking her away from her assignments. I'm talking bitterly resentful; even with the kids. She said she couldn't take it anymore and left and went to her mother's. Now her mother is taking care of the kids while working on her college courses. She has put her degree over everything."

"You're not drinkin?" Annette asked.

"No!" He shook his head fervidly.

"I don't understand, Tim. Why would she make that up?"

"Her mother's worried too. She's been letting me see the kids behind Mona's back." They both quickly turned their heads when they heard popping noises. "What's that?" It sounded like it came from the bank.

"Oh, crap!" Annette gasped.

Tim grabbed the handlebars and turned the bike toward the convenience store. "Come on; let's get away from the street." They both hurried to the front of the store and turned around in time to see four black and white police cars pull up alongside and in front of the bank.

"Tim," Annette whispered. "That was gunfire." "I know," he replied. They heard two more shots, and then several more blacks and whites arrived. "Man, somebody must be robbing the bank. And it looks like it might be getting out of hand. Let's get out of here." Tim lifted her bicycle over the side of his truck and laid it down in the bed while Nette and Phoebe got in the passenger side. Tim pulled out of the parking lot onto Mesa Blvd and headed away from the bank.

T: *Kemo…a bank robbery?*
C: *How's the demonstration look from your angle?*
T: *Not too good for the guy inside. How's it supposed to end?*
C: *He's going to surrender.*
T: *I've got eyes on our woman and her dog. They're across the*
street at the convenience store, getting into a pickup truck.
C: *She was supposed to be inside the bank.*
T: *As part of the demo?*
C: *Affirmative; influenced daycare mgr. to send her there.*
Something must have been off. I'll review the video.
Lucky for Joseph, our visitors weren't aware of it.
T: *Two demos in one would have been cool.*

Annette didn't tell anyone that Tim drove her back to Molly's. And it was hard to avoid questions because her hands shook when she handed Molly the bank bag. She kept the incident to herself, only saying she hit a curb and fell and then tried to avoid Dr. Harding when he arrived to pick up Lizzy.

"I've been looking for you," he said when he found her in one of the bedrooms. "I want to show you Lizzy's impression of what she saw at church." He had a sheet of art paper in his hand. "You seem upset, is something wrong?"

She didn't want to talk about the bank or what might have happened if Phoebe hadn't jumped out of the basket. "Let me see it," she said. "Ohhh," she sighed when she looked at the drawing. She put her hand over her face and closed her eyes.

"Are you all right?" she heard him ask when her knees gave way. He grabbed her and quickly moved her to the bed and sat her down, then ran to the bathroom and returned with a wet washrag and a cup of water. The drawing was of a man standing behind a girl that resembled Annette sitting in a church pew. He was surrounded by the celestial sunrays and wearing a brown jacket like the one she bought her father for his birthday years ago.

"I had a wreck on my bike, I…"

"Let me look at you," he said.

"I'm fine, just a few scrapes; I just want to go home," she said and handed the drawing back to him. "Did you look at Mona's eyes?"

"Yes," he replied. "I told her to come in as soon as she can, but right now, I'm taking you home and making sure you're all right." Tony put the smashed bike in his trunk. "I'll take it home and see if I can fix it."

"Sure, thanks," she sighed.

Ty returned to his efficiency downtown to view the video of the bank robbery in Mesa. He watched the erratic behavior of the thief as he entered the bank and then slid a female teller a note. When she pushed an alarm under the counter, he pulled out a handgun and began waving it around. He fired two shots toward a security guard, missing him. Customers inside the bank scrambled to find an exit or somewhere to hide and hunkered down while the female teller gathered money from all the cash drawers and put it in a plastic shopping bag the man had pulled from his pocket. He fired two more shots at the front doors when he saw a policeman approach. He finally surrendered after forty-five minutes of telephone negotiations. Ty studied the video of the perimeter of the bank and the surveillance from the cameras outside the convenience store/gas station across the street. "Nightcrawler," He whispered after observing Annette drop her bicycle at the curb after her little dog jumped out of the handlebar basket and led her away from the danger that was about to present itself across the street. "It's as if you did that on purpose."

Annette sat in the wicker chair on her back porch, staring at the blue bicycle with the big white bow attached to the handlebars above Phoebe's basket. Doc presented it to her after giving up on straightening the frame of the old one. When she protested, he told her to consider it an early birthday present. Judging by the big smile on his face, she knew he was expecting more than the cool reaction she gave him. But she feared he would ask her for more details about what happened. "You're gonna have to stay home for a while," she told Phoebe after he left.

"Ruff, ruff," Phoebe yelped from the chair beside her.

"Because you did it again," Nette said, rebutting the two barks. "Accept this time it was me that you…" She squeezed her eyelids closed and took a deep breath when tears began to leak from under her eyelids, "that you saved," she choked out in a whisper. Phoebe sneezed and shook her head. She wiped the tears from her face with one hand. "It wasn't because you saw Tim."

Phoebe lowered her head between her front paws.

"You know, if people figure this out," she sobbed, "like Sally Samuels apparently has, our lives will be screwed. I can't explain you, Phoebe." She stood up and began to walk back and forth across the porch. "It's okay if you do things to help Lizzy," she said. Phoebe sat quietly and watched her master pace back and forth. "And I don't want to keep you away from Molly or the kids at the daycare, but stuff like today freaks me out." She stopped pacing and dropped to her knees in front of Phoebe and then rubbed the sides of her face with both hands. "I'm beggin you; you must keep a low profile. Stop doing things I can't explain."

Phoebe sat up. "Ruff," she whined and leaned forward and licked her master's wet cheeks.

Chapter 27

The Board at *The San Diego Daily Post* loosened its grip on Sally, allowing her major stories again, provided she worked from home and submitted her copy to David by email in light of the baffling incident in her office and their distorted security video footage. The blackout event at her condo justified her hiring a private security company to search her place and remove anything that resembled a camera or bugging device. Rodriguez assigned two additional tactical ops to her immediately after watching his surveillance screens go black and microphones silence. But when she left her building at noon, they lost her somewhere between G and Market Streets. Traffic cams on Broadway near the Courtyard Hotel picked her up two hours later. Ty smiled when he read the report as if proud of how skillful she was at giving the techs in Escondido and the added resources on the ground the slip. The Chinese Council Members remained in town for an additional day of demonstrations after witnessing the bank robbery in Mesa and receiving confirmation from their Ministers that the State Senate had passed the bill allowing expansion of oil drilling off the coast of California, which was remarkable considering the topical oil disasters in the Gulf of Mexico and China and the falling oil prices. They would be arriving at the mansion soon, and techs had already primed investors to initiate stock purchases and sales. Drivers were on standby to create an accident on the 805 that would back traffic up for two hours and simultaneously halt flight departures and arrivals from Lindbergh Field for six hours while Homeland Security Agents searched for the person who checked a suspicious suitcase containing several bottles of flammable liquid disguised as a mouth wash.

After submitting a report on his conversation with the pharmacist, Ty spent the rest of the night walking the downtown streets looking for Lee. He stayed close to West Harbor and the Gas Lamp District, observing the habits of street people. A light rail system carried pedestrians north and south. A person could ride from Tijuana to San Francisco if schooled in the transfer system between the bus, light rail, and the Coaster. He purchased a Metro Transit Card and rode around for hours. He traveled south to Chula Vista, east toward El Cajon, and west toward Mission Valley. He noticed three homeless men enter his coach at the Chula Vista station. They huddled close together at the farthest end of the car and only spoke to each other, and like many he observed that night, only allowed the tips of their khaki sleeves to show from under their layers of sweaters and coats. He followed the threesome when they exited at the Old Town station. They led him south along the rails and crushed rocks that were slick from the coastal humidity. They turned under an Interstate 5 overpass. It was dark under the tall concrete pilings, and the overhead traffic sounded like rolling thunder. It seemed a perfect place for the homeless to bed down at night. Ty carefully approached the edge of the first support piling. He expected to see many makeshift shelters, but the area was vacant. The traffic above made it impossible to hear anything like footsteps or voices that might guide him further, so he took a position in the shadows. Ten minutes later, two men turned the corner at the concrete pilings. They were carrying heavy backpacks that burdened their shoulders, separating their jackets and exposing their khaki shirts. They lumbered by him and vanished beyond the eight lanes that rumbled above. Ty followed them to the end of the wall just in time to see them enter a white wood-framed house across the frontage road through a garage door. He crouched in the shadows again when he heard a noise like someone dragging something over the rocks. When he looked up, he couldn't help but notice the streetlights casting a spotlight on part of the mountainous concrete walls. They were covered with colorful graffiti from top to bottom. The artist must have suspended himself with straps from the interstate guardrails in order to create clever animations from such a high level. There was blue ocean water and seagulls, swimmers and boats, houses and buildings, and people of various shapes, sizes, and colors doing everyday activities. Separating each scene was a stack of letters that read *J-e-s-u-s* from top to bottom. Aztec-style blocks and circles framed the colossal piece of art. Other tags marred the murals here and there, but they were faint scribbling against the massive canvas. A lone man pulling a wheeled suitcase was the cause of the disturbance.

"You need a warm place to sleep?" he whispered when he saw Ty.

"Yeah," Ty replied and walked into the light. He noticed a slip of khaki cuff protruding from under the man's coat. He hoped to be invited to the white house across the frontage road, but instead, the man grabbed his hand pushed his jacket sleeve up, and then quickly released him.

"There's a shelter on Broadway downtown," he said as if agitated. He pulled something from his coat pocket and handed it to him. It was an MTS card, just like the one he purchased to ride the transit system.

"Here," he whispered and put the card in his hand. "Take the light rail south and get off at the Broadway station; there's a shelter one block west." The man tugged on his arm and insisted he escort him to the boarding station until Ty convinced him he knew how to get there. He made his way back to the Old Town Station and embarked on the light rail that sped south to the Gas Lamp District station near his apartment. Many of the vagrants he'd observed tonight were indigent or alcoholics and unable to participate in society. Some were merely out of work, victims of the economy, but the men in the khaki shirts differed. Their association was more like a comradeship.

Ty's cell phone buzzed early the next morning. "Kemo," he answered.

"You should have checked in by now, bro," Colin reminded him.

"I was up late scouting the city; following homeless guys in khaki shirts. I'm sure they've formed some sort of solidarity, and they definitely exhibit signs of an agenda. I'm counting on them to lead me to Lee."

"You didn't file a report, and Joseph wants an update."

"Tell him what I just told you. How was the demo?"

"Our clients are fascinated but are pushing for more."

"I'm sure we can impress."

Annette recognized the sounds of an electric saw and hammering coming from inside Lewis's house next door as she walked up Charlie's front walk. She knocked and the elderly man's face erupted into a big smile when he opened the door. He called out to Lewis, who was sitting in the living room behind him.

"Lewis, look who's here? It's our little girl." But his expression quickly turned to that of concern when he read Annette's face.

"What's wrong, honey?" Charlie asked. He put an arm around her shoulder and escorted her into the living room. "Where's Phoebe?"

"I made her stay home."

"What'd she do this time?" Lewis chuckled. Lewis pointed the remote at the TV and turned it off. "Sit down," he said, using the remote to direct her to the sofa. "Tell us all about it."

"Okay, but promise me you won't tell anyone."

"You got it," Charlie said and sat down beside her. He and Lewis listened as she relayed how Phoebe diverted her from going to the bank just before it was robbed.

"People are startin to notice this stuff," she fretted. "Tim was even askin me a lot of questions when he gave us the ride back to Molly's."

"Phoebe's a smart little dog," Charlie said. "She can sense things that most humans can't." He gave her a reassuring pat on the hand. "But I'll tell you what, honey; how about Lewis and I spread the word around the village for everybody to keep a tight lip when it comes to Phoebe?" Charlie walked her to Molly's and felt that allowing her to talk about things might have lightened her burden; at least she was smiling. But he stewed over the situation on the way home and for the rest of the day.

Post assigned her to the Apple Store in Mission Valley, covering the line forming for the midnight unveiling of the new iPad. Colin's message reported the info through Ty's COM unit and he proceeded to the Apple Store in the Mission Valley Mall. He entered the store after tactical advised she had emailed her story, passing a Post photographer carrying his gear outside

"Crap," Sally grumbled under her breath when she saw him moving through the aisles. She hurried to the back of the store, but he caught up to her.

"It is you!" he said when they met face to face a few steps from a door that was marked for employees' use only. "I guess you're reporting on the new iPad launch. I met the manager at the Expo. He's going to sell me one ahead of the midnight sale. I couldn't mistake the red hair."

"It's auburn," she snapped back as if irritated. "Shouldn't you be at your post at the Expo?"

"Opening weekend is over," Nate said smiling, "so it's back to business."

"And what business is that Mr. Roberts?" she asked cynically.

"I thought I told you, I'm an IT consultant; I run my own business." He glanced around the store as if looking for the fictitious friend from the Expo. "Actually, if you think your readers might be interested, there's a Samsung Tablet coming out in six months with much broader apps."

"Well, that's nice," she said. "I was just leaving."

"Through the back door?" he asked.

"My camera guy is parked in the truck zone," she argued. "He's my ride."

"Allow me to be your ride and buy you lunch."

"You're kidding me, right?" she sneered.

"I have a car, although a bit more compact than your Mercedes and a little older; but it'll get us across the parking lot to the Italian restaurant on the corner."

"Italian, well, that is my favorite," she replied.

"Mine too, Ms. Samuels, Sally. It looks like we might at least have Italian in common and perhaps more."

All right, Mr. Roberts," she conceded. "Let's see where this goes." Nate turned his head and smiled at her several times as he drove across the mall parking lot to the restaurant. "Stop acting like an idiot Mr. Roberts," Sally complained; "how long has it been since you graduated from high school anyway?"

"Sorry for acting so childish; I'm just a little overwhelmed. I think I told you, I've read everything you've ever written."

"That's impossible," she argued. "I've been at The Post over twenty years."

"I know it's my parents; they've been collecting your stuff from as far back as when you were in college."

"And that's how you know so much about me because your parents were big fans of mine, and so now, you're my stalker?"

"God, Sally, no!" Nate found a space for the small car in a row close to the restaurant. He shut off the motor and turned to her. "I get you, Sally. I even understand why you haven't made the move to the national market."

Sally raised her chin as if to challenge his statement.

"This is your home," he said earnestly. "I remember my mother saying, 'Who will take care of San Diego if Sally leaves?'"

Sally frowned. How could he or his mother know anything about how she felt about anything?

"So, where is your mother?" she asked when they were seated inside.

"She lives in northern Cali and she's going to be very excited to hear I met you. My father died five years ago of a heart attack; he was just as big a fan, if not bigger."

"Well, I'm sorry," Sally whispered. She swapped water glasses with him as the waiter took their order and watched him dutifully after he took the first sip.

"I have to say," he continued, "Mother was sorely disappointed when you married Randy Samuels."

"Tell me something, Mr. Roberts," she asked suspiciously because something about him didn't make sense; "did you actually meet Jared by chance, or did you create the opportunity?"

"Well, both, I guess," he replied. "By chance at the Expo preopening, but to be honest, I knew you submitted stories to The Campus Voice, and I thought…" He shrugged his shoulders and sighed. "I was hoping for an opportunity to meet you. It sounds a little pathetic when I say it out loud."

"What sort of IT services do you specialize in?" she asked after their meals arrived.

"I build and maintain internet service, and I do system upgrades," he replied. "I have several clients, but the University sucks up most of my time." They both sat in silence for a while and picked at their food. "My mother's theory is, because your parents left you here in San Diego with the nuns for safekeeping, that deep down inside, you're still waiting for them, even though..."

His words touched a nerve that took away her ability to think of a good come-back. "Mr. Roberts," she choked out. "Your mother is wrong! I can't tell you how many years I agonized over their deaths and wondered why they left me in that awful place year after year. I finally concluded that they lived for their own amusement and that I was part of that entertainment for three months out of the year."

"Was living at the convent that bad?"

"I hated it there," she argued.

"Did you ever go to France to see where it happened?" Nate asked.

"Randy was going to take me, but our work never allowed us the time."

"Did you get details of the crash from the French police or the reporter that posted the original article?" he asked, but Sally only shook her head. "It couldn't have been that hard, given your connections."

"Maybe they would still be alive if they hadn't left me," she said, fighting back tears of both anger and pain.

Nate took her hand. "You need to know what happened; find out why they didn't come back. You'll never find closure until you do."

"What does it matter to you?" She quickly moved her hand away.

"Sally, I know it's been hard living alone," Nate whispered, "and Randy wasn't what you expected."

"Apparently, no one remembers the man he used to be," she countered. "I want that man back."

"Forget him," Nate said and leaned forward. He stared deep into her compelling green eyes and took hold of both her hands. She felt herself wanting to submit to his empathy, to confide in him. She missed having someone to unburden herself to the way she could with Randy. She pulled her hands away not wanting to fall for his *play on her weaknesses* game. "I'll help you, Sally," he whispered.

"You're being self-indulgent," she said.

Nate told her about a building on the San Diego City College grounds with vacant space enough for Jared to expand. It was wired with the high-speed Internet he needed for his digital publication, and the transfer would take only a day. It was a perfect location for interaction with other campuses.

"You should sell the idea to Jared yourself, Mr. Roberts, because I'm trying to distance myself from him."

"So, you never told him about the infamous story you were writing?"

"I would never put someone I cared about in jeopardy. If you really want to do something to help him, then remove my forum from the *Campus Voice;* help me disassociate myself from him completely."

"I'll do whatever you ask."

"Why should I trust you, Mr. Roberts?" Sally asked. "You've been selling yourself to me since the first night we met."

"Sally," Nate whispered; "please don't say anything or react to what you're about to see." She frowned at first, but then she nodded. Nate removed his contacts and pushed them deep into the leftover sauce on his plate.

"Your eyes," she gasped.

"Shh…don't," he whispered and covered her mouth with his hand.

She stared at him, stunned; his eyes were green, like hers. "That's not possible," she gasped. "Who are you?" she asked in a whisper so low that it seemed her lungs were out of air. She got up from her chair and stumbled away from the table. Nate quickly covered his eyes with his sunglasses and followed her outside. "Take me to Old Town," she said. Sally looked as if she had a special memory on every street they silently walked through in Old Town. When they came to Juan Street, she took a seat on the edge of a broken-down stone wall that bordered the block around a gift shop.

"This is obviously a special place for you," Nate said.

"There was a church here. I used to come here to hide from the nuns. My father said it was a safe place, but as you can see, it's been torn down and replaced by a gift shop. Its doors had the three crosses of Calvary embossed on them; the only things that were preserved. They're on the Calvary Catholic Church two blocks from here. There's a courtyard with a fountain in the back that's covered with weeds, and classrooms you can barely see anymore because of the overgrowth. It was all inside this wall that we're sitting on that used to be eight feet tall. It had its own history that, as you can see, no one seemed to care about. She looked at the street sign behind them. "I met a boy here named Juan who knew about its history. His family, several generations removed, went to school here."

"Juan, the same as the street," he remarked, looking at the sign.

"Crazy, isn't it? He could have made the name up on the spot; not very imaginative. He showed me a wine cellar under the church. I used to hide down there and write stories to show my parents. Sometimes I'd fall asleep and have to hustle to make it back to the convent in time for my first class. I wanted to be just like them, freelance, and travel the world. It all seemed so romantic, but it was really all bullshit."

"Do you still have the things you wrote from back then?" he asked.

"I left it all in the cellar. My parents were my voice; it died with them. I couldn't make myself come here for years, and when I finally did, the chapel was gone. I guess no one cared about this place. It wouldn't have been that hard to incorporate it into the Old Town museum." She looked up at the sign. "There was supposed to be a tunnel just off the wine cellar, according to Juan. I never got around to looking for it; he said it was unstable and warned me not to." She bowed her head. "I might have been able to save this place, like The Coaster at Belmont Park and...." she paused momentarily and sighed.

"You have to stop dwelling on the past, Sally," Nate whispered and put his arm around her. "You have so much to look forward to. There are a million readers out there that love you. I think my business partner, Colin, even thinks you walk on water. He wants to meet you, by the way; he's my best friend. You can trust him; I'd trust him with my life."

"How can you be so sure? Are you two…?" Sally asked frowning; "no, I would have picked up on the gay thing. I envy people that have best friends," she sighed. "I just never knew how to make that happen. People never stay; they come into my life, and then all of a sudden, they're gone. David and I had a thing for a while, you know; but he moved on. Then there was Randy… we were so perfect for each other. So perfect, but…."

"Yes?" Nate sighed and gently rubbed her shoulder.

"He got involved with…and they…" she stammered.

Nate listened carefully. Was she about to admit she knew what The Group had done to her husband? "He—became distracted, addicted…to power; it ruined him."

Nate sat quietly with her, hoping she would feel like confiding more of her feelings to him. "Nate, why do you hide your eyes? Why are they green, like mine?"

"I wish I could explain it to you. But they sometimes disturb people, clients," Nate sighed. "They're supposed to be a rarity; even run in families. They began to change color a few years ago. I wish it meant we are related?"

"Perhaps you were exposed to something," Sally interrupted.

"Exposed to something; what?"

"Something…I wish I could explain," she sighed.

"Sally, don't be so hard on yourself, or your parents. Maybe you should consider that Park and Aggie Stevens might have left you at the convent because they loved you."

"No, I don't think so," she rebutted bitterly. "It was a good place to dump me in good conscience."

Nate took something from his pants pocket and handed it to her. "Here, I found this on Jared's hard drive. Your story outline about a dog and its master is on this thumb drive."

"Jared's been trying to get me to write a book," she said and took the drive from him. "I told him to delete this. Everybody seems to want me to do something else with my life," she sighed, "other than what I want."

"Well, fiction has never exactly been your forte," Nate remarked.

"You're so right," she replied and stared at the tiny drive; "the truth is all there is. Nate, I'd like to be alone for a while, to think." She looked up at him and removed his sunglasses to look at his eyes once more. "I don't know how to have a best friend or a family. I guess it was just never meant to be."

Nate took the glasses from her and put them back on. "I'll get the car."

"No," she said. "I'll take the train."

"Sally, Jared will be safe at San Diego State," he assured her before they parted ways. "I'll make sure of it." He placed another one of his cell phones with the IT logo in her hand. "Please, call me if you need to talk; I promise this device is safe."

She took the phone and put it in her bag along with the drive. He followed her at a distance to the train boarding station. She took the light rail south which he also boarded three cars down and covertly disembarked with her at the Broadway station and followed her as she walked along the harbor.

"What ya doing with my picture of Leon?" Lewis asked Charlie when he walked into the living room holding a 5x7 framed picture in his hand. "I stopped at your place on the way home to check on the carpenters, and it caught my eye sitting on the hutch. It just got me thinking and wondering about whatever happened to him. I ain't heard from his son in a long time; I guess he gave up looking."

"What?" Lewis asked. The TV volume was up because of Lewis's slight hearing impairment, but Charlie didn't repeat himself. He shook his head and looked at the photo of clean-shaven Leon and Lewis and himself taken too many years ago to count before he and Lewis decided to grow mustaches and Leon's wife, Ellie, died suddenly of a burst aneurism.

"Lewis," he said. "Lewis…LEWIS…" Charlie repeated twice and then shouted. "Do you want to go to the senior center with me?"

"Oh," Lewis answered, "The senior center." He pointed the remote at the TV and turned it off. "Why didn't you say so? Scoot my walker over here."

"Come on." Charlie waved at him to hurry up. "I think the clinic is open today."

"You feelin sick," Lewis asked him as he opened the aluminum walker.

"No," Charlie gruffed, "I feel fine; but you should be pretty winded by the time we get there."

"Me?" Lewis contested. "I feel fine."

The two elder gentlemen sat in folding chairs outside the clinic office until Dr. Harding finished with the patient ahead of them.

"Afternoon, Doc," Charlie said sheepishly when he walked into the office and saw Tony examining the contents of an Automated External Defibrillator kit. "You have a minute?" Tony closed the box and reached out to grab Charlie's hand.

"Afternoon Doc," Lewis added, pushing his walker through the door behind Charlie

"Everything okay, guys?" Tony asked and looked back and forth at them standing in the small office; "Lewis, how about you?"

"We're fine, Doc," Charlie answered. "But you can look at Lewis if you want," he chuckled. "Actually, we came here to talk to you about something."

Tony frowned and smiled at the same time. “Okay, sit down; tell me what’s on your mind.” Tony grabbed an extra chair from outside, and Charlie closed the door and sat down.

“Doc,” Charlie said and leaned forward. “This has to be a confidential conversation; like between a doctor and patient kind of thing.”

“Well, of course, Charlie,” Tony replied. “If it’s about one of the residents, I have no problem making house calls.”

“No, no, not one of the residents; but there is someone we’d like you to keep an eye on for us. We can’t get around real fast like we used to and she lives right behind you over on Jewel. She could use someone, a friend, to talk to about things.”

“Yes, she’s worried about something right now,” Lewis interrupted. “She told us about it this morning.”

“Counseling’s not really my…” Tony began.

“She lost her father a few years ago,” Charlie continued. “And she lives by herself, and I think she’s a little more insecure than she’s willing to admit. I think if you’d kinda keep an eye on her, it might make her feel better.” He looked at Lewis, and they both nodded. “We’ve tried, but I think she needs someone closer to her own age; you know, someone she can relate to.”

“And don’t forget Phoebe,” Lewis broke in. Charlie quickly turned and glared at him and then shook his head.

“Charlie, are you talking about Annette?” Tony gasped.

“Well, yes...”

There was complete silence in the room for a few seconds while all three stared back and forth at each other. Then Tony took a deep breath and smiled. “That’s not very original, Charlie. You’re trying to fix me up with your friend, aren’t you? Nice try.” He shook a finger at both the old men. “Annette and I are already friends. We went to a barbeque at my boss’s house Saturday.” He smiled thinking about how mad she got at him for not keeping up with Kevin Samuels. “She’s a nice person, pretty and very independent. I don’t think she needs my help.”

Charlie didn’t reply with a smile or an apology. He lowered his head. “Something happened yesterday that sort of shook her up. I’m not sure how much longer we’ll be able to keep boosting her spirits.”

“Yes, I know; she had a wreck on her bicycle,” Tony said and recalled how strange she acted when he drove her home from

Molly's. "I tried to fix it, but a car had run over it, so I...did she tell you I bought her a new bicycle?"

"Yes, that's what gave me the idea that you might not mind keeping up with her for us." He got up from his chair.

"She made us promise not to tell anyone what really happened at the bank yesterday," Lewis added as he held onto the walker and pulled himself up. "You know, Phoebe saved my life last week when my bathroom caught fire."

"What happened at the bank?" Tony asked. "What are you talking about?"

"Phoebe called Gerry on the intercom so he could hear the smoke alarm and then made sure I stayed awake till he got there."

Charlie frowned at his friend. "You gotta big mouth, Lewis!" Then he turned to Tony. "It's best she tells you this stuff herself. Thanks for your time Doc." He shook Tony's hand. "Come on, Lewis," he growled.

Tony closed the clinic ten minutes after the two men left. He called Katie and told her not to cook dinner because he would make a pot of his world-famous spaghetti and meatballs, and her family should be at his house at six. He picked Lizzy up early and invited Annette to join them. She offered her picnic table and volunteered Robby and Scott to carry it across the alley to his back yard. They butted the table next to the glass-top table, and they all sat together and enjoyed the food and one another's company. Annette and Brad sat across from each other and talked as freely as they had before the infamous family intervention that had strained their relationship. Phoebe sat under the table and snacked on spaghetti and garlic bread that fell from the table, or that Lizzy slipped to her on the sly.

"You should know that Nette doesn't like it when people give Phoebe table food," Scott told her. She pulled on his shirt sleeve and beckoned him closer.

"Have you seen Molly's magic show?" she whispered in his ear.

"Yes, why?" he replied.

"Do you believe Phoebe is magic?" she asked.

"I believe that Phoebe is very intelligent, and for some people, it's hard to distinguish between the two," he replied.

"Does that mean yes?" she asked.

"I suppose," he replied, "but only because I haven't figured out how she does certain things."

At times, it seemed everyone was talking at once, which reminded Tony of how it used to be around his family table when he was a kid.

"Oh my God," Nette said after looking at her cell phone. "I just got a text from Jose; he's at my front door. I ran into him at University Mall, and he helped me pick out some paint and brushes for your mural, Lizzy. He volunteered to help you get started." She looked at Tony. "That is, if it's okay with you, Doc."

He smiled and waved his hand. "Go get Jose."

"There's my little magic puppy," Jose said when he sat at the table, and Phoebe jumped in his lap.

"Do you belong to Molly's Magic Club too, Jose?" Lizzy asked.

"Of course, I do; for a while now," he proclaimed.

Tony looked at Annette and wondered if there was a story behind Jose's statement. Annette sheepishly looked at Tony as if to say yes, there was. Tony examined Marley's eyes and assured Brad and Katie that he saw no evidence of pressure and that the redness would be gone soon.

Nicky confided to Robby that she saw Cass sitting in Jimmy's blue Pontiac smoking pot after basketball practice. "Cass asked me to hang out, but I told her I had to cut out."

"You know I had a thing for her last summer," Robby confessed. "I can't tell you who to hang out with, Nicky, but the dude with the Pontiac is a freak."

"Honestly, Robby," she said. "I don't think she cares about that dude. I think she just does stuff to piss off her dad. Besides, I'm an Aries, I don't follow the crowd."

"That's sic; no wonder I like you so much," Robby laughed and raised his voice so everyone could hear. "Yo, everybody, Nicky and Annette are both Aries. I'm a Cancer, the sensitive type."

"You're kidding me!" Tony gasped and glared at Annette. "You see what I mean?"

"I didn't, I swear," Annette said, laughing. "I put the books away."

"You guys are out of control," Tony said when everyone around the table took turns announcing their Zodiac signs.

"I put my faith in one thing," Jose added and pointed upward.

"As do I," Tony agreed. "So, that's enough of that garbage."

The conversations continued around the table. Brad announced he was having a swimming pool put in next month or whenever the rain stopped long enough. Tony said he was trying to figure out the best place to put the basketball goal he bought. Robby suggested over the garage door in the front of the house and volunteered to help; Annette gave him a thumbs-up sign.

"Scott, does your mother work around the clock?" Tony suddenly asked the ten-year-old. "I knocked on your door to invite her, but I guess she wasn't home. I don't even know what she looks like."

Scott appeared to be taken by surprise. "Ahem," he said, clearing his throat. "I thought I told you, Dr. Harding, she works at the airport, and they're extremely busy."

"I saw her," Lizzy said and bounced up and down in her seat. "I saw her the night of the fire standing by the curb in front of your house." She looked at Scott and smiled, pleased that she helped her friend and fellow believer.

"So, she does exist," Tony quipped.

"Security is shorthanded right now, Doc," Brad interjected, "and a slow screening process really jams up boarding. We all look out for him; that's what neighbors do for each other."

"Si," Jose said. "I know my little ones are safe when they are here with Nette."

"Let me know when she's home," Tony said. "I'd like to come over and introduce myself." Tony watched Annette over the course of the backyard gathering. He looked for the signs of the distress Charlie and Lewis spoke of. Outwardly, she seemed happy, and he wondered if he would have even noticed the occasional knitting of her brow or the melancholy in her eyes if they hadn't planted the idea in his mind. She caught him looking at her more than once and gave him a curious smile each time. The kids hung back after Brad and Katie left to play the Xbox at Nette's house, which she granted permission on the condition there would be no rowdiness because Marley was still healing. Jose gave Lizzy some ideas on how to get started on her mural.

"I should get one of those Xbox machines," Tony remarked later from across the picnic table. "Maybe Nicky would stay home more."

"That's why you bought the goal," Annette said.

"Yeah," he replied sheepishly, "and three more bicycles."

"What?" she gasped.

"I know," Tony moaned, "but I thought we could all ride together. I need to teach Lizzy; she did so well with the skates. Maybe I'll be caught up by Christmas. Their mother, well, she cleaned us out before she died."

"Oh," she sighed. "I didn't know; I should pay you back for the bicycle."

"No, no, I told you; it's your birthday present. I shouldn't have said anything." Tony rubbed his eyes. "Sometimes, thinking about how she stole the kid's college fund just sets me on fire. This evening was nice, wasn't it?"

She smiled at him. "I like the way you're handling things, Doc."

Tony smiled at her and then shook his head. "I don't know how you do it, but you always seem to make me feel better. You're a good cheerleader. I'm even getting used to being called Doc. It makes me think that everything really is different now."

Annette smiled at him again. "Well, Doc, it's about time for this cheerleader to go play referee."

"Wait," Tony said. "I've wanted to ask you; are you okay? I mean, after what happened yesterday."

"What do you mean?" she asked.

"You seemed upset when I brought the bike over. I was trying to cheer you up. Did I overstep our friendship? And I noticed this worrisome little frown on your face this afternoon." He touched her right eyebrow.

"I'm sorry about how I acted yesterday," she said softly.

"You're a very mysterious person; do you know that?" Tony said. "I'd like to know what makes you happy and do what I can to help you feel better about the things that worry you, like you do for me."

She squinted suspiciously. "Did Molly say something…or Charlie?"

"What? Uh-no, no," he stammered.

"Don't lie to me," she demanded. "If there's one thing I hate, it's a liar."

"No, I swear. Reading discomfort on people's faces is part of my training."

"Hum…" she groaned, considering his answer. "I'm sorry, I didn't mean to be so defensive; I'm kind of a private person. Besides, you wouldn't understand the things that worry me. You'd just think I was crazy, like my relatives that believe in horoscopes and card readin."

"I don't think you or your relatives are crazy," he said. "You should meet some of mine; I just overthink sometimes." They laughed and sighed at the same time. "That's why I like talking to you," Tony said with a serious look on his face. "You simplify things and then I know what I need to do. I want you to know that you can bounce anything that bothers you off me anytime if you think it'll help. I owe you big time for going with us to the barbeque, for taking us to the beach, and for listening to my whining."

There was a moment of silence, and Annette could hear her heart pounding in her ears. She found it difficult to swallow, as if the muscles in her throat were paralyzed. "Uh," she finally said. "I didn't know, I mean, you uh, gosh," she stammered. "That's a real sweet thing to say." She finally caught her breath. "I don't think you would feel that way if, I'm sure you wouldn't."

"Does it have something to do with Phoebe?" he asked.

"Why?" she asked suspiciously. "What have you heard?"

"Nothing," he replied quickly. "But I see what you mean about being defensive."

"I have to go." She swung her legs over the bench seat.

"I'm sorry, please. I was just trying to help." Tony climbed over the bench to follow her. "Just forget I said anything," he said and rushed around the end of the table. "You don't have to tell me anything you don't feel comfortable talking about."

"There's nothin to tell," she argued and marched to the gate.

"I'm sorry," he said, but she opened it and ran into the alley. "Wait," Tony yelled. "Your table…" When he heard Annette's gate slam closed, Tony's words were cut short. *Thanks a lot, Charlie.*

Chapter 28

"Your project is very interesting, Mr. Rodriguez," said Chi Yong, China's visiting Head of State Council Member, when the delegation arrived in Escondido the next morning. "It would be a tremendous enterprise for our country; therefore, it will be hard to negotiate tariff relief and complete forgiveness of debt without some kind of guaranteed results."

"Mr. Yong," Joseph replied, "our southeast operation has been responsible for increasing the neuronal connections in its subjects for generations, as well as passing the DNA markers on, making subsequent generations easier to control. Let me show you." Joseph touched a small square at the bottom of the large monitor. "We've been grooming this boy for three years." A school portrait of the oriental store owner/witness's son appeared on the monitor. "His family has been part of the enhancement program for fifteen years. When this young student is ready, we will have him enter the political field; a few years later he will announce his bid for President of the United States…and win."

"Someone of oriental decent President of your United States?" Yong exclaimed. "I cannot believe that! You must show me how this is done; the proof that the enhancement makes changes to the neuronal connections!"

"I will gladly give you the data from our thousands of experiments," Rodriguez replied, "tests we've conducted in the field and in our basement laboratory for the past thirty years. Share the information with the NPC, but our genetic enhancement therapy methods can only be revealed after a partnership has been agreed upon. Let me show you something else," he continued while Yong deliberated. "We currently have this woman primed for nomination." He walked to the screen and tapped another square. The face of a woman in a dark blue suit appeared beside the oriental boy's photo. He tapped another small square along the bottom of the screen and a younger woman's picture slid in. "Secretary of State Harris and her daughter," Joseph presented. "We've given Secretary Harris a strong voice in Washington. Our plan is to give her the nomination this summer at the DNC convention being held here in San Diego; her daughter will run the campaign and be instrumental in carrying the young votes. She will also be one of our options in eight years. The files we provide will show the thousands of people in authoritative positions who are currently under our influence in every branch of government. We are offering you an opportunity to partner with us. Your government's treatment of its citizens has given you a bad reputation in the world theater and rebellion has become more popular since the Hong Kong incident. Our offer will enable your new President to take over in 2016 the opportunity to manage his people without opposition and avoid the same consequences that other dictator countries are suffering. It is also our hope that you'll help us control your neighbors to the northeast."

"So, that's it, you want to use us to influence North Korea for you," Yong said.

"We will eventually infiltrate every country and control the world," Rodriguez said. "But time is running out. We need the added infrastructure because of the increasing worldwide nuclear threat. Our partnership would greatly speed up the process. We need the world to put pressure on North Korea, Iraq, Iran, Syria, and the other countries that are being run by radicals."

"Partners," Mr. Yong reflected. "Equal partners?"

"Equal, financially stable partners."

"I will take your proposal to our National Committee for consideration."

"Molly said you called in sick," Tony said as soon as he got to work and called Annette.

"Molly?" she replied from her cell phone as she drove north on Hwy. 15. Phoebe lay across her lap and looked up in response to the sound of the familiar name. "Did she call you or somethin?"

"Well," Tony sighed, "yes, she was concerned, you know Molly. She asked me to check on you."

"Yeah right; I just wish everyone would stop havin you check on me." Annette turned onto the scenic route 15. "I'm on my way to Escondido. In fact, I'm almost there. Jeffrey and Justin are movin up here today. I'm gonna help them unpack and I want to check the place out. I just don't trust Larry's judgment."

"Well, I'm glad you're okay. Will you be back later? I'm cooking steaks. Word is you don't do much cooking, so I thought you might like to join us."

"There are entirely too many words bein said about me."

"You can thank Robby for this one."

"I intend to. I'll have to let you know later…Oh!"

Tony heard Nette gasp. "Hello? Are you still there?"

"Yeah," she sighed. "I just passed the most magnificent Spanish home. It's built right into the side of the hill. That must have cost a few mills. Look, I appreciate the invitation, but I'll probably spend the night." Larry flagged the entrance to his driveway with a red shop rag tied to a fence post. He didn't tell her, however, that the driveway was a half-mile long. The house was two stories and had eggshell stucco. As she drove closer, she saw an attached three-car garage with a second-story loft and a pool area around the back with a hot tub and bathhouse. "And all you have to do is cut the grass and feed the livestock?" Annette asked Larry after he and the boys gave her a tour of the immediate grounds.

"Yep," Larry replied, "and keep this side of the mountain cleared ahead of the summer fires. What do you think?"

"It's kind of a weird arrangement but it sounds amazing, Larry," she sighed. "Look at you; your clothes are clean and wrinkle-free, your hair is combed, you even smell good."

"We've got a full fridge and a stocked pantry," Jeffrey added. "I put some steaks out to marinate for tonight."

"Steaks…" Nette whispered remembering Doc's invitation.

"Nette," Justin interrupted. "Come with me, I want to show you something." He led them to the barn and presented four new 4-wheelers and two dirt bikes. Her mouth dropped open. "Uh-uh, you didn't. Larry how…?"

"I swear Nette," Larry said. "Is this the greatest job ever, or what? I bought the kids new everything…Xbox One, Wii, Tablets, iPhones, games."

"And clothes," Jeffrey interrupted and held his arms out to display his new LeBron James crew shirt and matching basketball shorts.

"And I opened their savings accounts for college. Hey, that fourth off-road over there, the red one, is for you. Hop on and we'll show you the rest of the place."

Larry's property included a hill with spectacular views of two valleys. A dozen horses grazed in luscious stands of green grass on the south hillside that overlooked Lake Hodges. Kit Carson Park was on the north side beyond a small herd of cattle that lay lazily in the shade of a full eucalyptus tree. A steep mountain of brush, trees, and rocks bordered one end of the property. A ten-foot chain link fence with razor wire along the top barred entry and signs were affixed every twenty feet warning, *No Trespassing-Restricted Area* and *Danger-Falling Rock.*

"Larry," she asked, "what is that place?"

"The real estate lawyer said it was government-owned," he replied. "Who else would want a worthless pile of rock like that?"

"Reminds me of *Witch Mountain*," Jeffrey said laughing.

"There are cameras up there in the trees," Justin added. "I saw them with my binoculars."

"Maybe it's a secret nuclear bunker," Jeffrey jabbed. Larry put four steaks on the grill, which Jeffrey tended to, and Justin steamed corn and potatoes. They ate outside under the stars. Larry downed several beers during the process and fell asleep on the deck under a lounge chair next to the pool. "Daddy says he's gonna hire a housekeeper," Jeffrey said as they cleared the table outside and loaded the dishwasher.

"Why?" Nette sighed.

"He says we're gonna be too busy taking care of our land this summer."

"What about school?" Nette asked.

"We're gonna stay with Grandma the rest of this year," Justin replied, "then we're gonna enroll up here next fall."

"Oh," Nette whispered, thinking of how much she would miss them.

"We're gonna help Daddy cut grass and take care of the livestock," Jeffrey added.

"Nette, you can ride a horse, can't you?" Justin asked.

"Heck yeah, my brother in Colorado has horses; he taught me."

"You wanna go riding right now?" Justin asked.

"Uh, it's dark, dude," Nette replied.

"The moon's out, we can see fine, come on," Justin insisted. They raced each other to the barn. Phoebe followed as fast as her short legs would allow.

"This is the horse paddock," Jeffrey said as he caught his breath. "The cattle have one of their own. Daddy said we have to count the heard in the evening to make sure they all come in, or we have to go find them." He looked back toward the house and shrugged his shoulders. "I guess we should do that now," Jeffrey said. "Daddy probably won't be able to; he was snoring when we left." They saddled three horses and eased out of the paddock. Annette zipped Phoebe up inside her jacket and they slowly rode into the open moonlit landscape. The sky was clear and bountiful with stars. Lights from the distant houses glistened in the valleys.

"Is this the back side of that Spanish mansion I passed on the way here?" Nette asked.

"Yeah; you saw it?" Jeffrey asked.

"It took my breath away," Nette replied.

"I know how to get in there," Justin said. "I've seen a black SUV going in and out through a hidden driveway along the road." He took the binoculars from his jacket and handed them to her.

"I see the security cameras, Justin," she said as she scanned upward. "So, don't you dare do anything stupid to make your daddy lose this beautiful place."

"Chill, I'm just curious," he said and took the glasses from her. "Man, there's a helicopter." They all watched as the aircraft disappeared in the dark over the hill.

"If you ever see silos, bro, let me know cuz I'm calling Nette to come get us," Jeffrey said.

"If you see silos, I might just take your butts with me back to Louisiana!" Nette quipped. "Earthquakes are nerve-racking enough."

"Mr. Rodriguez," Chi Yong said, greeting the agent with a handshake after arriving by helicopter for an impromptu late-night meeting.

"You came alone," Rodriguez said as he led the sole delegate into the Cabrillo conference room.

"I have the authority to speak for us all. I have conferred with the National People's Congress by Skype."

Rodriguez led Mr. Yong to the balcony. "We can speak freely out here."

"The Congress has inquired about a timetable," Mr. Yong said after taking in the spectacular view.

"Six months. If you like, I can have a team of engineers fluent in Chinese return with you to Beijing with blueprints of the infrastructure we require. I will send technicians to train your people once the facility is built. It is expensive and the work is tedious because of certain risks, but I know how diligent your people are."

"The NPC is intrigued by the concept of gene enhancement therapy, Mr. Rodriguez, but you understand their restraint. They want to be certain your President is on board with this agreement."

"A select number of the most trusted Presidential advisors are aware of this project and our agreement. You will have a Presidential agreement in writing after the election and before the new facility is operational."

"We will meet again in a few weeks and discuss final terms," Mr. Yong said and the two men shook hands.

Willis Shepherd was waiting for Joseph in the conference room when he returned from escorting Mr. Yong to the helipad.

"This is working better than we anticipated, Shep," Rodriguez said and signaled him to join him on the balcony.

Shep chuckled and handed Joseph a glass of celebratory tequila. "It seems they now have a deeper understanding of how important this project is to them."

"Colin does excellent work, doesn't he?" Joseph remarked. "The stage is almost set. By this time next year, we'll be on our way to running the country and soon after, the world." They touched their glasses together. "What do you think about moving the nation's capital here to San Diego and changing its name back to San Miguel?" He turned to admire the Cabrillo portrait on the wall inside. "I've been dreaming for so long about giving the southwest back to its people, my people."

From the beginning of his employment with The Group, Ty Hemil had been listening to the conversations in Joseph's favorite meeting room. He had planted invisible devices throughout the walls of the entire mansion, including the balcony. He typed Colin a message using Phantom after removing his earpiece. *Kemo, it's time we had that beer.*

One hour, Colin replied. Ty began filling his backpack with bare essentials. He started putting on layers of clothes beginning with the khaki shirt he lifted from the Broadway Shelter. He corrupted all the equipment he didn't plan on taking with him and poured lighter fluid on the bed to start a fire. He pulled a hood over his head, left the efficiency, and was on board the light rail headed north before the assigned operative outside noticed the first streams of smoke seeping around the edges of the second-story windows.

Tony had just sent a late-night email to his sister Betty when he heard a ruckus in the alley. Frankie and Johnnie were barking angrily but by the time he rushed through the kitchen and opened the back door, their wailings were down to mournful yelps and were trotting back and forth against their enclosure when he opened the gate. "Good to know you two are on the job," he whispered. They both looked up at him wagging their tails.

Scott scrambled to the safety of his bedroom from his hiding place behind the hedgerow beside the Harding's. He was in a hurry to replay the video from the rooftop cameras. It produced a shadowy silhouette as it came into view in the alley. It stopped at Annette's gate and peered between the slats. The form walked further repeating the same motions at Dr. Harding's gate. Scott enlarged the dark silhouette, which revealed he was wearing goggles with protruded lenses. "Infrared," Scott gasped. He watched Dr. Harding step outside his gate just as the intruder exited onto Gold Coast. He suddenly realized that his sleuthing had turned into something more serious than the game-like comings and goings of the neighbors and the adventures of Nightcrawler. Scott was smarter than any kid in his grade level and confident in his ability to outwit adults. But at this moment, and for the first time he could remember, he was afraid and wished his mother was home instead of pulling another double shift. He called her cell but it went to voice mail. He texted Robby, *can u come over?* But he didn't reply. Annette was in Escondido and if he called Dr. Harding, he would overreact because he was home alone. There was one other option, to send the video file to Guardian. After seeing the *file sent* notice, he turned off the alien lava lamp and went to his window. He stared at the house down the block where there were no lights and no movement per usual. He closed the blind, crawled into bed, and stared at the laptop, hoping the intruder hadn't seen him hiding in the hedges. The rooftop motion sensors picked up something and began transmitting video of a San Diego Sheriff patrol car turning onto Antrim. Scott sat up. "He got it!" The camera over the garage followed the car to the end of the street until it turned left. The patrol car appeared again two minutes later at the rear of the house. The unit is parked on Gold Coast across from the entrance to the alley. "Thank you, G," Scott sighed, "you're a real Guardian." Scott lay down across his bed again but couldn't stop looking at the laptop screen and the patrol car. His cell phone buzzed; it was Robby.

"Sup dude," Robby asked, "had my Beats on."

"Nothing," Scott sighed. "Mom was called into work."

"You're soundin kinda weird, my man; you want me to come over?"

"Yes, please," Scott replied, relieved he wouldn't have to be alone.

Colin leaned against the railing on La Jolla's coastal boulevard and watched the waves surge below him and then brake against the arched rocks, propelling the seawater above his head. It was now forty-five minutes past the hour he had agreed to meet Ty in the bar across the street, their usual meeting place on their days off, where they often left notes for each other on a tiny pin drive behind a loose slat in the paneling near the floor in the men's room. He walked to the shoreline where thick jagged rocks and violent surf sprayed mist on his face after a report came over his COM that Ty's apartment had been gutted by fire. He tried to contact him once more even though the techs had reported the unit dead. There was nothing more to do but convince his superiors that his partner had gone under.

Sally looked over the city from her balcony holding the small cell phone that Nate gave her. She could see the tiny headlights moving across the Coronado Bridge, their reflections twinkling atop the ripples in the bay. Serious thoughts of leaving San Diego always made her stomach queasy, as if severing the connection would end the life source that beat inside her heart. Her parents' tragic demise wounded her deeply because they led such mysterious lives that she never understood. She thought about Randy, as she did every evening when she stood in this spot taking in the sea air. She had been convinced her loneliness was over when they married, but now she felt as isolated as when her parents died. She looked at the phone in her hand again, trying to decide if she should call Nate *to talk* as he suggested. Or, like before, allow the phone to drop from her hand and break into pieces on the street below. *Why are his eyes the same color as mine? The color is supposed to only run in families.* "It's not possible," she whispered and tightened her fingers around the phone. He had shushed her as if he thought someone was watching or listening, and there certainly could have been. But how would he know that unless he was one of them; they could have altered his eyes. She clinched the small phone tighter. "Something about him doesn't make sense."

Tony detoured through Jewel Street on his morning run. Annette's flagship was parked in her driveway. He was tempted to stop and knock on the door but he kept going and waited until he got out of the shower to call her; it went to voice mail. He never used to think about time when he was at St. Joe's, but today he found himself looking at his watch all day. When it alarmed at 5:30, he locked his office and hurried to the elevator. He laughed at himself when he started the Olds and revved the motor like a seventeen-year-old. He was in a hurry to pick up Lizzy but it was Annette that he wanted to see; they met up in Molly's kitchen.

"Glad you're back," he said and then sighed nervously thinking he'd sounded entirely too enthusiastic.

"Yeah," she replied. "I brought the boys home with me."

"I saw them with Todd this morning," he said and followed her to the living room where Lizzy was sitting on the floor in front of the TV with Claire.

"Actually, somethin's not right up at boy's new place," she said. "It's next to this government property that's fenced in like a prison."

"Come over for dinner tonight and we can talk about it."

"I'm kinda tired, maybe another time," she whispered.

"What's wrong with you?" Lisa said after Tony drove away with Lizzy. She had been in the kitchen eavesdropping. "It's obvious he's interested in you. Why don't you give him a chance?" she continued as Annette walked past the tall blonde and proceeded to the living room to pick up toys and put chairs and stools in their places. "Why do you always turn your back on guys who want to get to know you? How many times has this happened? How many times has Darren from the rec center asked you out?"

"I don't like Darren that way," Nette argued. "He's too young."

"It doesn't matter," Lisa argued. "You have to give somebody a chance; you have to give yourself a chance."

"I can't handle stupid men," she replied.

"Men need good women," she blurted out. "To keep them in balance; and believe it or not, we need them to balance us."

"Just drop it, Lisa, please!" Nette growled.

"Why, am I making too much sense?"

After Mrs. Carter picked up Claire, Annette looked for Molly in her office but it was empty. She reached to close a cabinet that was ajar; a stuffed poodle toppled out onto the floor. She opened the door to put it back and was astounded to see how many more animals were stored there. She found Molly lying down in one of the bedrooms. "Molly, are you feelin okay?" she asked, kneeling down beside her. She was holding the poodle that fell from the cabinet. "Why so many, Molly?" she asked, trying to hide her concern although her lips were trembling. "You never make them unless somebody's leavin."

"You girls do such a wonderful job of taking care of things around here; I just needed something to do. I enjoy making them."

"Okay then," Nette said and kissed her on the forehead and took Molly's hand. "I'm goin home now; please call me if you need anything."

"I will, dear; I'm fine; I'm just a little tired," Molly said. "See you tomorrow."

Robby was standing alongside Tony's driveway when he pulled into the garage with Lizzy. "Yo Doc, you ready to put up that goal?" he asked when Tony got out. He pointed to a space over the garage door with a spring-loaded tape measure and grinned, "Got my pop's tape measure." He held the yellow roll in his hand like it was a pistol then flipped it until the tape shot out four feet from its encasement; then he whipped it back inside with a flick of his wrist. "I've been practicing."

"I need to start dinner," Tony replied.

"Yo, just order pizza."

"Pizza, yay," Lizzy squealed after overhearing him and climbed out.

"Oh, what the hell," Tony replied. "Let me change clothes. Lizzy, go inside and watch TV."

Robby helped Tony put the screen door up first and then they mounted the backboard and goal over the garage. Tony noticed, all the while, that a few neighbors had ventured outside to watch them; some were sitting in lawn chairs. Robby moved the ladder to one side and they played a game of one-on-one that turned into a free throw game of *Around the World.*

"Do the neighbors always come out when your dad works outside?" Tony asked after beating Robby easily.

"They're just checkin you out, Doc," Robby teased. "I'm gonna order the pizza now and call Scott and Nette."

"I already asked Annette to eat with us, she was too tired."

"Oh, you did, huh?" Robby asked curiously and bumped him with his elbow."

"Mind your own business," Tony snarled. "And put my ladder away." Tony looked across the street again. The neighbors were folding their chairs; he waved to them, and they waved back. "Show's over," he whispered. "Robby's ordering the pizza, honey," Tony said on his way through the house but stopped when Lizzy didn't answer. "Did you hear me?" Her arms were above her head, and she was staring at the TV screen.

"Pizza, Robby's ordering the pizza; go look at the goal we put up." Tony gave up on getting her attention and hurried to the backyard to wipe the table off before the pizza arrived. When he returned, Lizzy was gone, and the TV was paused on a scene from Mary Poppins where the chimney sweep was dancing on the rooftop, balancing on one foot and with one leg in the air. His attention was quickly diverted from the eerie clown-like character to Robby and Scott's raised voices outside. When he reached the door, he saw Lizzy standing on the crown of the roof, just like the chimney sweep. "My God," Tony gasped and staggered from the house with his arms outstretched. "Lizzy, honey," he called carefully, not wanting to scare her, but she didn't hear him; she was looking straight ahead.

"Doc, I'm sorry," Robby cried. "I shoulda put the ladder up first."

Annette was standing next to the kitchen sink sipping bottled water when Phoebe burst through the doggy door barking. She turned toward the sink, trying to ignore her as she sprang up and down under her feet. "What is your problem?" Annette scolded and put the bottle down hard on the counter when the little dog started pouncing against her thigh. "Phoebe, I'm tired, I don't feel like playing." Phoebe kept jumping and whining. "Go see if Jeffrey and Justin want to play." Phoebe disappeared through the doggy door, and Annette watched her through the window over the sink. She ran to the gate and sat down, and then she stood up and sat down again as if anticipating her master's appearance through the back door. Seconds later, she bound through the plastic flap again, and this time, she growled and grabbed the hem of Annette's jeans. "I don't care; I'm tired."

"Ruff," Phoebe replied and pounced toward the door again.

"All right, what?" Annette followed Phoebe across the backyard, through the gate, and down the alley. "Slow down," she said, trying to keep up as the little dog turned down the trail between Doc and Brad's house. She passed the ladder leaning against the side of Doc's garage and noticed the basketball goal over the garage door. When she reached the front walk, she saw Robby, Scott, and Doc's eyes fixed upward. "Oh!" she gasped when she saw Lizzy standing on the roof, gazing into space.

"We can't even get her to look at us, Nette," Robby cried when he saw her.

Many more neighbors had gathered in their yards by now and Tony thought he heard someone suggest calling 911. "No, no," he shouted to them. "I've got this. Lizzy, Lizzy, honey!"

Scott looked at the cluster of neighbors and saw the living room curtain held back by someone in the house he'd been curious about. He took a picture and sent it to Guardian.

"How did you know?" Robby asked her and then looked down at Phoebe. "Oh, yeah. I'm gonna get my dad's rolled-up mattress from the garage."

"Good idea," she said and moved closer to Tony. "Why can't she hear you?"

"She scares me to death when she gets like this," Tony sighed.

"Mommy," Elizabeth's voice quivered, "I'm scared."

Charlie and Lewis had stopped to rest on a bench outside the gates of Mesa Village. "Hey, what's going on over there?" Lewis asked Charlie between gasps.

"That's Doc's house," Charlie reported.

"It certainly has brought out the neighbors," Lewis chuckled.

"Uh-oh," Charlie grunted. "His kid is on the roof." He stood up and walked to the edge of the sidewalk. "Hum, my eyesight ain't what it used to be, but ain't that Phoebe up there too?"

"How did she get up there?" Tony shouted when he saw the little dog standing next to his daughter.

"I guess the same way Lizzy did," Annette retorted.

"Certainly, not by the ladder," Tony grumbled.

"Phoebe!" Annette called out, ignoring Tony's contention. "Tell her to sit down."

"What?" Tony shouted.

"I meant to say, maybe she can get Elizabeth's attention." She looked up at the roof again. "Phoebe, talk to her!" Tony threw his hands up, losing his patience.

"Here's the mattress," Robby said and dropped the bedroll in front of them and removed the bungee cord. "Doc, you want me to climb the ladder and get her down?"

"Yes!" he blurted out.

"There's no time," Annette interrupted. "She's slippin. Phoebe, see if you can get her to slide down the edge on her butt, then Doc can catch her."

"No!" Tony shouted. Lizzy's feet slid off the crown a few inches.

"Okay, Mommy," Lizzy muttered. "I think I'm ready, I've been practicing." She spread her arms out beside her and tried to lift one foot. Phoebe began to bark, and Elizabeth's eyelids fluttered. "Phoebe, is that you?" She smiled when she saw her friend and suddenly realized where she was. Her eyes widened, and she gasped and then began to wave her arms as if grabbing for something to hold on to.

"She's panicking," Tony panted.

"Phoebe," Annette called out. "Do somethin!"

Phoebe barked once, and Elizabeth looked at her. "Are you sure?" she asked, and the little dog barked again.

"It's okay," Annette said. "Slide down to the edge; your daddy will catch you. Just like my daddy caught me, remember?"

Elizabeth looked at Annette. "When you were in the tree," she said. Annette nodded.

"No, are you crazy?" Tony scowled.

"What's the matter, you can catch her!" Annette retorted.

"Of course, that's not the point." Elizabeth's feet slid another foot, and she let out a gasp. "Now look at what you've done," Tony growled.

"What's your problem? She'll be fine," she replied. Suddenly Phoebe leaped from the roof and landed square in the middle of Annette's chest. "Oh!" she gasped when she felt the sudden blow. Elizabeth followed her lead and repelled off the roof, landing in her father's arms that he instinctively opened. He dropped to his knees on the mattress, clutching her tightly in his arms. Annette knelt down beside them.

"I told you he would catch you, sweetie," she whispered. "Just like my daddy." She gently slid her fingers through Lizzy's blond hair as she spoke.

"Get away from her," Tony shouted and pulled Elizabeth out of her reach. "I don't want you filling my daughter's head with any more of that horoscope, Voo Doo crap; do you hear me?" They both stood up at the same time facing each other. "Just stay away from her." Then he looked at Phoebe in Annette's arms. "And keep your dog away from her too."

"But Daddy," Elizabeth sniveled. Tears welled up in her eyes as she waved goodbye over his shoulder.

"Oh, my goodness," Charlie said to Lewis from their viewpoint on the bench across the street.

"He still doesn't get it," Lewis replied and shook his head.

"Yeah," Charlie sighed.

"He will," Lewis replied.

Charlie nodded. "Yes, he will, my friend."

Robby knocked on Dr. Harding's door ten minutes later, holding two pizza boxes; Scott was with him. "Yo, I'm sorry, Doc; seriously, I should have moved the ladder before ordering the pizza," Robby said. Tony turned away from them without speaking. They looked at each other and then stepped inside. "You got a little bent out of shape out there, didn't you, Doc?" Robby said, following him to the kitchen.

"You okay?" Scott asked Lizzy when he saw her lying on the sofa. The frozen rooftop scene was still on the TV screen; he picked up the remote and turned it off.

"Will you please talk to my daddy about Phoebe?" she whimpered.

"I'll see what I can do," he replied.

"You're not a father," Tony said, responding to Robby's remark. "And I'm tired of trying to understand what's going on in that crazy woman's head." He waved an arm in the direction of the alley.

Robby put the boxes down on the table. "So, Doc, no, I'm not a father. Honestly, I'm not sure I ever want to be, not unless...well, see, I was gonna run away with this little shorty I was crazy about last summer, but Nette and Phoebe stopped me. It would have been a mistake. She takes care of Jeffrey and Justin and any kid that needs her help. I can tell you sumpin fo-sho; I'm not getting married unless I find a chick just like Nette, because I know when I do, my life will be one awesome adventure." Tony growled something inaudible.

"Pizza, cool," Nicky said, interrupting them. She opened one of the boxes and picked up a slice and put the end of it to her mouth.

"You had practice?" Tony asked.

"Yeah; I heard about the big blowout in the front yard from the neighbors," Nicky replied, "Lizzy okay?"

"She's fine," Tony whispered. "Where are you going? He asked when Nicky carried her pizza to the screen door and pushed it open.

"Hey, you finally fixed the door," she remarked just before it slammed closed behind her.

"Fine, just go wherever you want," Tony sighed with frustration.

"What up, guys?" Nicky said when Jeffrey called out, inviting her inside. Justin was lying on Annette's sofa with his leg elevated and an ice pack wrapped around his knee. "Dude, what happened?"

"Skateboard," he said, reaching for the Velcro straps that held the pack around his knee. "Wanna see?"

"Oh, that's gross," Nicky cringed when she looked at the raw flesh.

"Yeah!" Justin said proudly. "Nette fixed me up with the ice pack."

"Keeps the swellin down," said Annette, who was sitting on the floor looking through Xbox games. "Remember that when you're jumpin ramps up at your dad's."

"You should have seen my knee when I hurt it playing football a few months ago," Jeffrey remarked, trying to one-up his brother.

"You guys see the big fight in my front yard?" Nicky asked. "I totally missed it."

"Naw, we missed it too," Justin said, pointing to his knee.

"What's the story, Nette; the whole block's buzzing about you and my dad."

"I'm not talkin about it," Nette snipped.

"I told you my dad's an a-hole," Nicky said. "I hope you cut him down to size."

Annette shook her head. "No comment."

"I'm just sayin that's all," Nicky said.

"She doesn't take sides between kids and parents," Justin explained.

Nicky's scrunched her mouth, making a face. "Yeah, well, it's cool.

Annette stood up and handed Justin a controller. "Your dad was scared; people panic and say stupid things when they're scared."

"So much for not taking sides," Nicky sneered.

"I'm not," she said. "Nicky, I understand why you're angry at your dad. He should have paid more attention and taken you guys out of South Chicago a long time ago. But you're gonna have to learn how to put the anger aside, or that's all you'll be is angry. You're a smart, talented girl; you can figure out how to do both."

"That's bullshit!" Nicky argued.

"You don't have to like what he did, and you may never have a normal father/daughter relationship, but you should respect him for what he's tryin to do now."

G: *So, Nightcrawler came to the rescue again. Hope the little girl's okay.*

Rec'd pic of the rental house; unfortunately, the window was too dark. Will be

sending another decoding exercise tonight.

S: *Kewl.*

Chapter 29

Sally tried to immerse herself in the work David assigned her, a school function in Chula Vista and a home invasion/robbery in National City, but she found herself looking for Nate to appear from out of the crowd everywhere she went. She found Lee true to his word when she looked for him along the harbor. She noticed a homeless woman moving oddly from bench to bench along the harbor walkway while she was feeding the hovering seagulls. The woman held her right fist out to each prospective donor, uncurled her fingers, and stared at them until they forked over a handout. Sally put a twenty in her threadbare gloved hand and asked if she knew Lee, but the woman only mumbled *thanks* and moved on. She received a text from Jared that read *The New Campus Voice* would be operating from San Diego City College the next day thanks to Nate. She didn't reply but checked the website when she got home; her forum was gone. She plugged her phone containing the new card into her laptop and logged onto the National Information System. Randy allowed her access to the site when they were together, and her security code was still good.

Joseph Rodriguez called Colin to the Cabrillo room and announced the deal with the Chinese appeared to be forthcoming.

"That's good news," Colin replied as he looked around the room he was rarely permitted to visit. He noticed more Spanish armament had been added to the décor since the last time he was above the sub-levels. "Our satellite link with their towers for the past ten years paid off." A map of the world lit up on the large flat screen on the wall above them, where the European and Asian continents glowed with a rhythmic pulse.

"Yes, it took time, given their structure, but we finally got the face time we needed. Having a facility there will enable us to lay our groundwork and penetrate the Asian continent and Europe. The remainder will fall in line as we continue positioning ourselves and the enhancement spreads." More countries became highlighted in their projected order of indoctrination.

"It's unimaginable that Syria, Pakistan, Afghanistan, or Iran could be softened," Colin sighed, "and North Korea."

"Libya, Syria, Israel, and Egypt," Rodriguez added. "There's urgency in these areas where fanatical factions have nuclear access. The world will never survive on negotiations alone."

"No sir, it won't," Colin sighed.

Rodriguez turned away from the map. "I called you up here to express my appreciation for the excellent work you did propagating China. As soon as we ink this deal, I'll be relocating you to Beijing to oversee the new headquarters. We need our undercover OP to surface because he's going with you. It would be catastrophic if he inadvertently did something to make our new partners nervous."

"The President and the joint chiefs are on board?" Colin asked.

"I'm not worried about the President or the joint chiefs. Debt forgiveness and tariff relief will override any concerns. Senator Harris will be nominated at the Convention this summer and history will be ours to make."

"What is our time frame in having Randal Samuels established politically?"

Rodriguez turned to the large screen again. "Actually, I've reconsidered using him at all. It may be the only way to get Ms. Samuels off our backs. Update Hemil when you hear from him."

"I should tell you; someone requested a background check on him at NSI," Colin added. "It came from an unspecified location and was highly encrypted. Ordinarily, the trace would be easy to decode, but its origin has been blocked with sophisticated routing. They accessed the profile we forged."

"Sally?" Rodriguez sighed.

"She was the reason we created it," Colin replied.

"Colin, tell me honestly, is there any reason to think Hemil has gone rogue?"

"No sir," Colin insisted. "I'm sure he's onto something that required the measure he took. He severed all connections to maintain credibility and work his way into the inner circle of the homeless man we've been looking for. Ty told me he was getting close."

"He advised you of no specific plan beforehand?" Rodriguez growled.

"No sir. He asked me to meet him in La Jolla but never showed up."

"La Jolla…oh yes; the bar with the rustic décor where you two hang out."

"Yes, sir," Colin replied, trying not to act surprised that Rodriguez knew about the place they met on their days off.

"I've ordered his extraction should tactically find him," the agent said. "I'd better like what I hear from him during debriefing, or you know what will happen."

"He'll make contact soon, sir." Colin tried to sound convincing because he knew his superior meant confinement in the basement.

"Would you like to guarantee that with your own well-being?" Rodriguez sneered.

"That would be foolish, sir," Colin replied. "Should I work on a reorientation for Randy?"

"Leave him and Sally to me."

"I'm keepin my distance until he apologizes," Annette huffed. "He's an idiot; just like the doctors that took care of Daddy." Phoebe watched her master pace the kitchen floor from under the table. "I was just beginnin to think we could be friends, but I guess he's no different than any other man. He's gonna have to work things out with his kids before tryin to understand us." Phoebe whined and then lay down with her head between her paws, thinking this could take a while, but all of a sudden, Annette left, slamming the door behind her. Phoebe emerged from under the table after hearing the gate slam closed. She sniffed around the edge of the plastic flap, pushed her nose through, and then jumped into the wicker chair and curled up next to her favorite fringed pillow.

Tony had argued himself to sleep and repeated the same discussion with himself for most of the morning's three-mile run. Had he been too harsh? No, she deserved everything he said to her. Should he apologize anyway? No, there's something strange about her and her dog; Lizzy should stay away from them. *But I like the way she makes me feel, and I miss talking to her*. Robby's words *awesome adventure* popped into his head. *Phoebe actually stabilizes Lizzy sometimes…no, no!* He slowed his pace when he saw Nette cross the street and headed to

Molly's. The argument continued through his shower and while he dressed for work. Then he was stunned when he saw the cologne with the wooden top sitting on his dresser again.

"We have a game Friday night," Nicky told him when he sat down to breakfast.

"That's great," Tony said, trying to act surprised.

"I doubt Coach Burns will put me in," Nicky sighed.

"Why wouldn't he; you're his star player, aren't you?"

"Daddy, get real. I'm the new kid, second string. Besides, his daughter's the real star."

"Did you hear that, Lizzy? Your sister has a game Friday night. We'll definitely be there, front and center. Lizzy, what's the matter?"

"Nothing," Lizzy sighed. Her eyes were cast down, and she hadn't touched her cereal.

"You can forget the silent treatment, young lady." He picked up the cereal box. "You're lucky I didn't put you on restriction because of that little stunt you pulled yesterday," he said as his cereal rattled in the bowl in front of him.

"That'll be the day when she's put on restriction," Nicky sneered. "Everybody's talking about your little tantrum, you know," she added sarcastically. "Have you apologized to Annette yet?"

"No!" he said sternly. "She should apologize to me for the crap she's put in Lizzy's head. She practically told Lizzy to jump off the roof."

"Scott said she was sliding down anyway," Nicky countered.

"Miss Nette didn't tell me to jump," Lizzy whined. "Phoebe said it would be okay. I don't expect you to understand because you're an adult."

"You, see?" Tony dropped his spoon, and it clunked in his bowl. "That's the crap I'm talking about."

"Annette was just trying to help," Nicky said defensively. "Believe me, she's not the reason Lizzy," she said and looked at her little sister. She stopped short of saying it was their mother that put the crap in Lizzy's head while he chose to be somewhere else. Thanks to him, they were forced to find their own way of coping with the bazaar life they lived. "You really don't get it, do you?" she blurted out.

"Okay, miss, smarty," Tony challenged. "Why did Lizzy climb up on the roof?"

"Why don't you ask her?" Nicky replied.

Tony bowed his head and lowered his voice to a whisper. "The TV was paused on the *Mary Poppins* movie," he whispered; "when she was on the roof, she thought she was talking to your mother…" He suddenly changed his tone. "Then Annette told her to jump! Lizzy imagined it was Phoebe." He pushed his chair away from the table. "You two hurry up and get ready. And Lizzy, I know you keep putting that cologne on my dresser."

"I thought I smelled that stuff again," Nicky sneered.

"I'm taking both of you to school," he announced.

"No, Todd's taking me like always," Nicky replied defiantly. "Why don't you just chill? It's over, and Lizzy's fine."

"I'm never going to be fine without Phoebe," Lizzy whined.

"I don't want to hear that name again. Do you two understand? Lizzy, you're riding with me, and I'm picking you up from school every day until I find another daycare." Tony stormed from the kitchen, and they heard his bedroom door slam.

"What am I gonna do, Nicky?" Lizzy cried. "I love Phoebe and who will play with Claire if I'm not there?"

"Oh, Lizzy, honey," Nicky said softly and moved her chair close to her sister. "Give him some time; it'll blow over, you'll see. Something more important will come up at work, and everything will be back like it was."

"I hope so," the little girl sobbed and leaned on her sister's shoulder.

Tony grabbed his wallet and keys from the dresser and headed for the door. "I almost forgot," he said and reached for the cologne bottle to throw it away, but it was gone.

Ty paid cash for a storage unit near Old Town. It came with a smelly coat and a musty mattress. He smudged his face with dirt to dupe the surveillance cameras and added a sock hat and darker sunglasses. He spent the next day following the local nomads who were riding the metro system, reaffirming his certainty of the kinship between those wearing the signature khaki shirts. They traveled from downtown to the Old Town station with regularity, trekked under the artful I-5 overpass and then disappeared into the garage attached to the white house across the frontage road. All the while, he kept watch over the single red dot on his GPS App that represented Sally's movements. He wished she would call; he could use another opportunity to work on their emotional bond.

Colin scrolled through hours of video of Ty's apartment and the La Jolla bar area not expecting to find him on any of it because he was a self-taught master of disguise and deception. He pulled what looked like a small sewing pin from under his shirt collar, put it in his COM unit, and listened to the recorded conversation between Rodriguez and Yong that Ty left for him in the bar restroom. It seemed Joseph was negotiating to satisfy his own personal agenda over and above the infiltration of China with the technology that would guide them to democracy. Colin dutifully destroyed the pin and wondered if it was time to bring his allegiance with The Group to an end. Something on the monitor that displayed surveillance of the north side of the mountain caught his attention. Security had pulled over a suspicious vehicle near the driveway of the leased property behind the mansion grounds. He grabbed a headset.

"This is operations, what do you have?" he ordered.

"Two males that claim to be friends of the new owner," a voice came back. "Found cocaine and two handguns."

"Escort them to the main highway and hold them there for state authorities," Colin commanded, and then he ordered a tech to handle the State Police dispatcher. He viewed recent footage of the property and recognized the tenant's sons from the boardwalk video and the woman with the dog. He designated a capable tech in the east quad to work out the details and have the boy's mother released from prison. If he didn't get out in front of this, Joseph certainly would.

Nette and Doris climbed the bleachers to the top row along with Jeffrey and Justin. They could hear Coach Burns all too clearly barking orders to each girl as they drilled, pointing out errors in form, release, whatever; it didn't matter because he always seemed to enjoy hearing his voice echo throughout the gym. "God, I hope this goes well for Nicky," Nette whispered to Doris.

"It'll be okay, Nette," Doris replied. "You told me she's a tough girl. And I'm here to hold you down; I mean to support you if things get out of hand."

"Ha, ha, Doris," Nette said.

"Oh look," Doris said, "there's Robby and Scott and, oh, Dr. Harding and Lizzy."

"I wasn't sure if he…" Nette began.

"Are you two speaking yet?" Doris asked sarcastically.

"Shut up, Doris."

Jeffrey and Justin let out a couple of whoops when the buzzer sounded in support of Mesa JV. Robby and Scott climbed the bleachers to join them. Lizzy turned and waved but remained sitting next to her daddy on the third row.

"Yo, look who's here, Nette," Robby said and nodded in Doc's direction.

"I don't care," she replied. "I'm here to support Nicky." Burns subbed her in the second quarter. She stayed with her opponent until they were twelve points down, then she snatched a pass away and threw a three-pointer. This produced cheers from the meager fans and an animation of criticism from Burns for not relaying the ball to the center. The ball was thrown back in, and Nicky stripped it mid-dribble when her intimidation caused a player to lose her timing; Nicky threw another three-pointer.

"Time," Burns yelled. "Sub," he bellowed and took Nicky out of the game. Annette got up from her seat, and Doris grabbed her by the shirt sleeve. Robby stood up and put his arms out to block her.

"Yo, Nette, look," he said, "Doc's got it." She looked down and saw Doc walking toward Coach Burns. He put out his hand, and they shook hands. They spoke briefly, and then he handed Burns a business card. They shook hands again, and Dr. Harding returned to his seat.

"What was that?" Nette scowled.

"I'll find out," Robby said and sprang down the bleachers before Annette could object. Scott texted Robby when he took too long.

"Doc told Burns that he looked flushed and offered him a free heart checkup," Scott reported, reading Robby's text.

"That was clever," Doris laughed. "He gave him something else to worry about besides bullying the girls."

"Humph!" Nette grunted.

Annette and her crew arrived at the senior center at the Mesa Village Retirement Community the next morning after passing through the drive-thru at McDonalds for breakfast. Robby was tinkering on the piano, and Scott played games on his iPhone. The older residents were mingling and catching up on each other's family news. Molly, Charlie, and Lewis were trying to win their pennies back from Lucy. Jeffrey had been trying to reach his dad all morning.

"I'm not drivin up there," Nette argued. "If he can't pick up his phone, then he's probably not in any shape to parent."

"What if something's wrong?" Justin asked while tugging on the straw of his drink. "What if he fell off one of the horses?"

Annette sighed. "I'm sorry, guys. I keep picturin him passed out in that lawn chair by the pool. We'll drive up later if he still doesn't answer. Right now, I'm gonna check on Molly." Jeffrey and Justin took their Mickey-D bags and sat at the table with Scott. Annette carried Phoebe to the poker table and sat between Molly and Lucy.

"Who's winnin?" she teased.

"Molly," Charlie complained and looked at Phoebe.

"Ruff," Phoebe growled.

"You two need to go over there with the kids and do your tricks so we can play a fair poker game."

"Charlie, hush!" Molly protested. "You're such a grouch today."

"He's down ten cents," Lewis interjected.

"Okay, come on, girl," Nette said. But Phoebe jumped in Molly's lap instead. "Come on, we're not welcome at this table."

"That's right, no cheating," Charlie teased.

"Go on," Molly said, giggling. Phoebe licked her on the cheek before jumping down but stopped and looked back at her before following her master. A short time later, the front door opened, and the Harding's walked in, accompanied by Charles Drake, his wife, and little Ray. Annette was sitting on the floor surrounded by kids and didn't see them until Lizzy slid down beside Phoebe, and then Doc's Nike's appeared in front of her. She looked up slowly.

"May we borrow the keys to the gym?" he asked.

"Sure; you can send Nicky over with it later." She looked away, pretending to reach for a dog treat. Tony looked at

Phoebe; she eased to the floor and put her head between her paws.

"Thanks," he said curtly. Charles Drake slapped him on the shoulder, reaffirming their plan to team up, making it awkward for Tony to reprimand Lizzy when she begged to stay and play with Phoebe. Jeffrey suddenly appeared next to Nicky, and the foursome left to shoot hoops. On their return from the gym, they met Lizzy running toward them from the rec room.

"Daddy!" she cried. "Nette said to get you!" She could barely get the rest out. "She said to hurry!"

The first thing Dr. Harding saw when he rushed through the doors was Annette on her knees on the floor and bent over Molly administering CPR compressions.

"How long has she been down?" Tony asked when he got to her.

"Three minutes, maybe," Annette answered, huffing as she pumped.

"Okay," he said. "I'll take over."

"No," she panted. "I'm trained in CPR."

"Nicky," Tony yelled and looked around until he found her standing between Robby and Jeffrey. He threw her his key ring. "Go get the AED kit off the wall in the clinic."

"Come on," Robby said when Nicky gasped. "I'll show you."

Tony felt for Molly's pulse while Annette pushed on her chest, and then he put his cheek close to her nose. Annette looked at him for reassurance, but he remained silent. Nicky and Robby returned with the AED. "Thanks, sweetheart," he said when he took it from her. "Okay, stop the compressions," he said to Annette, and she leaned back on her heels. "Undo her blouse for me so I can attach the EKG leads and the pads." Annette quickly got Molly ready. "No rhythm," he muttered after looking at the graph on the machine. He shocked her chest and checked the graph. "Nicky," he said and looked up at her. "There's a stethoscope in my drawer," he began, but she surprisingly handed it to him. He looked at her and smiled. "That's my girl."

"I found this too," she added and showed him a portable blood pressure machine.

"Great, honey," he said.

"Is there a heartbeat?" Annette said, panting.

"A weak one," he replied. "But there's another problem; she's not breathing. Her airway must be obstructed. Did someone call 911?"

"Yes, Charlie, the second she fell over," Annette whispered.

"I'll keep working on her until the ambulance arrives. If it doesn't arrive soon, I'll have to open an airway."

"Please, bring her back," Annette cried. "She's like a grandmother to me."

Tony applied the shock therapy again when the EKG suddenly reported no heartbeat. He listened to Molly's chest and looked at the graph again. "It's irregular," he said, "but it's something. Blood pressure is weak. Where's that ambulance? I'm going to need a few things," he said, looking at Annette. "There should be a first aid kit in here somewhere and I need something like a straw and a knife or a blade."

Charlie grabbed the straw from Justin's drink and sent him to the first aid kit in one of the cabinets. Lewis unfolded his pocket knife and handed it to Tony.

"I think we're set," he said. "Get the Betadine ready and open some of those alcohol packets and tear some strips of tape," he said to Annette and then looked at Lizzy. "Honey, you and little Ray go stand outside the door and watch for the ambulance; let me know the second you see it. Take Phoebe with you." Annette looked at Doc thinking he must have forgotten about forbidding them to be together. "Are you squeamish?" he asked after reading the graph once more. Annette shook her head and began to tear strips of tape and stick them to her arm. Tony wiped Lewis's pocket knife and Justin's straw with the alcohol pads and poured the Betadine on Molly's neck. "Her heartbeat should get stronger when she starts getting oxygen again."

"Do it, hurry," Annette whispered. Tony proceeded with the tracheotomy. There was bleeding, but Annette kept the area around the wound dry with cotton swabs from the first aid kit. She handed Tony the strips of tape when the straw was in place, and she anxiously waited for his sign of reassurance as the paper graph moved across the screen.

Father Clayton arrived and began a litany of prayers. Ten minutes later, Lizzy burst through the crowd with Phoebe in her arms, shouting to the top of her lungs that a helicopter had just landed in the street outside. Molly was breathing now. Her heartbeat was somewhat stronger, and her blood pressure was stable, but she still hadn't regained consciousness.

"It looks like a stroke," he told Mitch, the paramedic, and introduced himself. The ambulance had been delayed due to a multi-car pileup, so the hospital had dispatched the helicopter. "There's blood in her eyes, so there could be internal bleeding, and her right arm is drawn." Tony ran alongside Mitch and his partner as they rolled Molly to the helicopter. "Tell the ER to start TPA ASAP, and here's the EKG strip from the AED."

"Thanks, we've got TPA on board," Mitch shouted over the spinning blades above him. "Good thing you were here. Want to ride along?"

Tony looked back at Annette, who was standing in the doorway grasping Charlie's arm. "You want to go with Molly?" he shouted to her, but she shook her head. "We'll meet you there," he yelled to Mitch. "I work for Rick Samuels, and Molly's a good friend. Please take good care of her."

"You got it, Dr. Harding," Mitch replied and boarded the copter.

Tony hurried back to Annette, who was standing in front of a crowd that had moved outside to watch the helicopter take off with Molly on board. "They're giving her some meds to prevent stroke damage," he shouted over the engine's roar. Do you want me to take you to the hospital?" They both watched the plane lift in the air.

"No," she whispered. "I can't; she looked bad; I don't know if I can stand seeing her like this." She turned to Jeffrey and Justin. Nicky and Lizzy were standing beside her, along with Robby and Scott. "You guys can hang here if you want," she said. "I don't feel so good."

"You're shaking; let me drive you home," Tony whispered to her and then looked at Nicky, who nodded in approval. When they pulled into the driveway, he asked Nette if she had any wine or liquor in the house; she shook her head and reminded him she didn't drink. He escorted her inside, and they sat down on the sofa.

"Thank you so much for helpin Molly," she sobbed. "I know she's gettin older, and sometimes she acts a little off and…"

"Try not to worry," Tony interrupted. "They're very busy stabilizing her right now. I'll check on her in a little while after I know you're okay." Annette's crew, Jeffrey, Justin, Robby,

Scott, and Nicky, along with Lizzy carrying Phoebe, walked in the front door.

"Father Clayton's driving Charlie and some others to the hospital in his van," Jeffrey announced. "We thought we should keep you company, Nette."

Tony left her with the kids to check on Molly at the hospital. He called an hour later, saying Molly's blood pressure was still unstable, but her heart rate was good, and she was being closely monitored in the ICU. "No one's giving up on her, Nette; there's still a lot that can be done." Worried that she might never see Molly alive again, Annette mustered the courage to drive to the hospital. It started raining when she backed out of the driveway. She had told Phoebe to stay with Lizzy and the rest of the kids, but halfway down Canyon Rd. she jumped over the console from the back seat. It rained harder the closer she got to University Hospital. "I hope this isn't a bad omen," she whispered to her confidant. Nette waited in the SUV until it slacked up enough to make a run for the entrance. Phoebe watched her master through the streams of water running down the passenger side glass. Phoebe's face faded behind the abundant raindrops when the sliding doors opened and closed behind Annette.

Annette nervously made her way to the second floor. She recognized Charlotte, Molly's sister when she slipped past the ICU waiting room. Father Clayton was sitting beside her, along with a few neighbors. She leaned against the wall outside the ICU until the automatic doors opened when a nurse exited, enabling her to slip inside. Each room had glass walls with the curtains pulled back, allowing her to see each critical patient as she passed. A man was sitting next to and bent over a woman in one of the rooms. He was holding her hands and crying. Annette asked a nurse sitting outside the door what was wrong with the unresponsive woman.

"I'm afraid she's in renal failure," the nurse whispered. "She only has a few hours."

Annette pressed her hand against the glass; the woman looked as gaunt as her father had before he died. A room across from the nurse's station suddenly stirred with commotion. Two nurses jumped up from behind the counter and rushed across the hall. Annette approached the room and read Molly's name on the erasable board next to the door. The room was crowded with people in white coats, making it impossible to see what they were doing. The two nurses exited and returned to their post shaking their heads. One of them picked up a phone and asked for a doctor to be paged. Annette leaned against the wall and put her hands over her face. *This was a mistake; I never should have...I have to get out of here.* She hurried back toward the exit, looking back one last time. She saw Doc step out of Molly's room. Their eyes met and he gestured to her.

"Nette, it's okay, you can come in," he coaxed. She shook her head and kept going but he ran after her. "It's okay," he said when he caught up to her. "She's okay." Then she heard Molly's undisputable laugh. Tony put his arm around her. "She's going to be so happy to see you."

"How-how?" Annette stuttered. "There were so many people in her room."

"I was just about to call you." He guided her to Molly's room. "I don't know if it was good medicine or Father Clayton's prayers, but take a look."

Molly was sitting up in bed, and a nurse was shoving a wad of tubes into a red biohazard box and mumbling something like she wouldn't *need these anymore.*

"We took her off the breathing machine because all her vitals are normal."

"And quite suddenly," the nurse added. "I've never seen anything like it."

Molly held her arms out and Annette ran to her bedside and broke into tears as they hugged. "Honey, oh honey." Molly had to whisper because of the incision and bandage on her throat. "I'm still here." Then Molly pulled her closer and whispered in her ear. "And so was he."

"He, who?" Nette whispered.

"You know *him*; the one I always see when Phoebe does her magic."

Annette sat upright on the side of the bed and looked at Doc. "Are there side effects to these medicines?" she asked and then looked up at the three bags that were dripping drugs into her veins.

"Sometimes, but all her vitals are good." He pointed to one of the bags. "It takes the TPA a while to level the blood and oxygen," he said and looked at his watch. "She's been awake for fifteen minutes, so that means it took about four hours. That's better than average; sometimes it takes days."

"Fifteen?" Nette panted, realizing it had taken her at least twenty reluctant minutes to make her way to the ICU from the truck.

"Dr. Harding is taking good care of me, but you girls may have to run things at work for a few days."

"I'll leave you two alone so you can talk," Tony said. "We'll be watching the monitors out here."

"I knew you were here somewhere, dear," Molly said after Tony left the room. "How else would Phoebe have gotten here?"

"Molly, stop it. People are going to think you're talkin out of your head, and you'll never get out of here."

"Honey, there's no use trying to deny it; Phoebe is…"

"No, Phoebe is not; she's nothing!"

"Then how do you explain this and Lewis and everything else that happens? Where is she right now?"

"In the car!"

Molly touched Nette's damp hair. "There were raindrops on his coat, too."

Tony rushed around the nurse's station when Annette exited Molly's room. "Do you think her brain was damaged?" she asked him as they walked.

"Her cardiac doctor ordered an MRI, among other tests," he replied. They reached the window of the critically ill woman. The overhead lights were on, and the woman was sitting up in bed, sipping something from a cup. Her husband was talking to a doctor and smiling.

"I thought?" Annette gasped. The nurse from Molly's room rushed past her and entered the room.

"We just had our second miracle of the night." Annette looked again, and the woman put her feet over the edge of the bed, and the nurse helped her stand. Annette grabbed Doc's arm when she felt her knees buckling.

"Hey!" Tony gasped and caught her before she fell. "When was the last time you ate something?" He asked her after helping her to an empty room and handing her a cup of water. "Do you know the woman in that room?"

Annette shook her head and began crying. "I can't-I can't…I can't take this anymore," she sobbed.

"Let me take you home; the Olds is parked near the ER."

"No, Phoebe's waiting for me in the car."

"You mean Lizzy let her out of her sight?" he asked. "I'll drive the flagship, and we'll get my car tomorrow after church."

"Are you sure you won't be too embarrassed to drive it?"

"I'm kinda getting used to Jose's artwork. His influence has already covered a fourth of one of Lizzy's bedroom walls." On the way home, he told her how Scott had been texting the nurse's station to get updates and that Father Clayton had led Molly's sister and friends in prayer earlier in the waiting room. But it seemed like he was talking to himself because Annette didn't say a word, she just stared at Phoebe lying in her lap and picked at her damp hair. He drove the SUV into the garage and waited for her to look at him after he turned off the engine. "I'm sorry about going off on you the other day when Lizzy, well, you know. I shouldn't have blamed you or Phoebe because Lizzy is perfectly capable of doing that kind of thing on her own. I'm afraid I'm going to lose her someday to some freak accident, like Carol."

"Oh, Doc," Nette whispered. "I saw how scared you were, and I shouldn't have spouted off at you the way I did. I'm sorry too."

"I miss talking to you," he whispered and touched her on the arm.

Annette's living room was quiet and vacant of teenagers. "This place was full of kids when I left," she said. They pulled their cells out of their pockets and then looked at each other. "Oh," they both said at the same time and laughed after reading all the text messages they missed.

"Mine are at home, Scott is at Robby's, and yours are in the bedroom down the hall," Tony reported.

"Jeffrey heard from his dad," she read. "That's good." Phoebe pawed at Nette's foot; she picked her up and looked at Doc, wishing there was a rational way to explain her to him. They sat on the sofa, and Doc put his arm around her.

"Molly's in her sixties, Nette," he whispered. "She may have dodged a bullet this time, but you have to realize; you have to know, that at her age…"

"I know," she whispered and leaned her head against his shoulder. "I'm not ready to say goodbye to her yet. My father was only fifty-three."

"That's so young," he said and kissed her forehead. Phoebe jumped from the sofa and trotted into the kitchen as if on cue when Annette slipped her arms around Doc's waist and he put his arms around her as if both were trying to comfort one another from their losses. After a while, Annette looked up at him and kissed him on the lips, and before she realized it, they were lying on the sofa, on their way to making love. Annette sat up, and Tony began apologizing.

"Please stop saying you're sorry," she said. "It's my fault, I—"

"No, it's mine," Tony whispered. "You're emotionally vulnerable. Please don't hate me."

"No, I don't," she sighed. "But there is Nicky and Lizzy. And there's somethin I have to tell you, whenever I get the courage."

"You should know," he whispered, "that every time I'm with you, I feel my life change a little more for the better."

"Doc, please don't leave yet," Nette whispered. "Stay with me till I fall asleep." She led him to her bedroom, and they lay down together. Phoebe snuggled between them and put her cold nose against Tony's arm. He reached out to pet her, and she licked his hand. Then he smelled something familiar, the harsh fragrance of the cologne that kept showing up on his dresser.

"Do you smell that?" he whispered to Annette, but she was asleep. Phoebe walked with him to the gate. "Take care of my girl," he whispered; Phoebe gave him a snort that produced a nod. He expected to see Frankie and Johnnie's noses poke through the chain link fence when he passed, but they were asleep and didn't move.

"Daddy," Nicky whispered when she saw him pass her door. "You're back."

"Hey, honey; Miss Molly is doing much better," he said and sat down on the edge of her bed.

"How's Annette?" Nicky asked.

"Upset, of course," he replied. "But she finally went to sleep."

"Does this mean you're not mad anymore, and I can go to Molly's?" Lizzy whispered.

"Yes honey," Tony replied and hugged her as she scrambled to her knees and wrapped her arms around him. She asked her usual endless string of questions, so the threesome went to the kitchen, and Tony took the ice cream out of the freezer.

Frankie and Johnnie lay on their sides making high pitched pleas that could only be heard by the ears of other dogs; therefore, Dr. Harding had been insensible to their appeals when he passed. Phoebe looked at their stunned bodies through the fence as they struggled to make their legs move. A pair of warm hands suddenly reached down from out of nowhere and touched each of their heads at the same time, sending a regenerating sensation through their bodies. They quickly rose to their feet and ran around the yard with their tails between their legs, fearing the stranger that had sprayed them with strands of electricity might still be nearby. They ran into the shadows when they suddenly spotted him again standing at Annette's gate, reaching for the latch. The same hands that had brought the dogs back to life abruptly took hold of the accosters' wrist. His hand twisted backward, seemingly by itself, and pointed the shocking device at himself. Blue streaks of electricity shot out the end of the apparatus scorching the man's neck. His body jerked as the electricity seized his nervous system, knocking him to the ground. Frankie and Johnnie raised their heads from the shadows but ducked again when they heard footsteps.

Scott was lying across Robby's bed, waiting for the tune he picked out on the guitar to make sense, when he noticed the video icon on his laptop flash. He opened the quartered screen and observed activity in the alley on one of the cameras. "Dr. Harding brought Annette home," he reported to Robby. "He just crossed the alley, and there's Phoebe." Doc disappeared from view just as Robby grunted a response, but then he saw someone approach Annette's gate. Scott picked up his iPhone to text Guardian but stopped halfway through the message when the man's arms suddenly flew up over his head, and his body contorted and crumpled lifelessly to the ground. Scott began to revise his text when he saw two uniformed police officers appear and drag the man away. He forwarded the video to Guardian.

G: *He was brought in for questioning.*

S: *Is he one of the dudes from the rented house?*

G: *Can't say, but he's one of the reasons I guard your neighborhood.*

S: *Did Nightcrawler do that? Hello?*

Chapter 30

Rick Samuels greeted Tony with a hardy handshake Monday morning when they met behind the reception desk.

"Everybody's buzzing about how you saved Molly Ward, Dr. Harding," Tonya exhilarated so loudly that patients in the waiting room looked up from their magazines and phones. "How did you happen to be there at the right time?" Her excitement was unyielding.

Tony lowered his voice when he saw patients discretely pointing at him. "I was there with my daughters; please, I heard enough of this at church yesterday."

"Okay, Tonya, give him his caseload," Rick said, trying to redirect her attention, but Tonya couldn't help herself and winked at Tony when she handed him the patient files. "I've been called in to consult on Molly's case," Rick said as they walked toward their respective offices.

"Did something else present besides the obvious?" Tony asked. "You look concerned."

"Step in my office a minute." Rick led Tony to the conference room, closed the doors, and then used his key card to open the door to the new addition. It looked like a lab with rows of microscopes and test tubes, files, and monitors. One of the monitors had a slice of Molly's brain displayed.

"Evidence of bleeding," Tony said, pointing to a shaded area that traveled from the visual cortex to the outer edge near the skull. "This is where the vessel ruptured."

"Yes, and four hours later, it somehow cauterized itself," Rick stated. "Baffling, isn't it? The brain never ceases to amaze me."

"I guess that was our miracle. What caused this large area?" Tony pointed to an area surrounding the healed vessel.

"The reason why I've added her to my research."

"This is Marley Jones," Tony whispered when he noticed another monitor with a scan of Marley's brain on display.
Rick switched to another view of Molly's MRI. "I told you I've been studying cases with expanded gray matter throughout the cortices, and my theory is that they must have experienced a substantial increase in the volume of normal neuronal activity, thus stimulating the brain to accommodate the new pathways."

"Unfortunately, the skull doesn't have room enough for so much gray matter," Tony said. "Are you considering mutant genes or a virus; have you spoken to the State Board or The Surgeon General yet?"

"I sent them my findings once, some time ago, in fact, and they took it under advisement," Rick replied, shaking his head.

"Which means nothing will happen any time soon," Tony said. "That's how it went between the health department and St. Joe's. Unless a significant number of corpses piled up, something else was always more important."

Fortunately, Mrs. Ward is stable for now," Rick continued. "The medulla is where the artery bursts." He motioned to the brain stem. "It stopped communicating with the heart muscle and affected her breathing." Rick traced the vessels with his finger. "It's only because of the right sequence of events that she's alive. If it weren't for the AED and you're opening of the airway, allowing oxygen to feed her organs, we could be looking at a whole series of additional problems."

"It was lucky that Mitch had the TPA on board the air bus."

"As I said," Rick repeated, "the right sequence of events."

"I wanted you to see this since you were involved with both cases. I'm familiar with other neurosurgeons that have been able to successfully modify affected areas of their patient's brains as I did with Marley, but the procedure is always risky, and the results aren't always as good. Most patients have significant inflammation of the nerve cells around the optic nerve. I keep videos of their procedures and my research locked in this room where there are no cameras; I have more on DVDs at home."

"Your office?" Tony whispered.

"Yes, why?" Rick asked him.

"Oh, uh," Tony said, "I've been meaning to tell you something, but we kept missing each other. At your barbeque, I caught Sally in your office. She had several CD cases in her hand. I had every intention of telling you before now, but—"

"So, she wasn't just there looking for Randy," Rick sighed. "She has no business with those case files. She's going to be the death of my family."

"I don't understand," Tony said

"You can use my library too if you need to, but make sure this room remains locked."

Patients in the waiting room must have been passing the story of what happened at the senior center along to one another because it started every conversation all day. It was the same at church the day before, particularly because Father Clayton took a moment to pray for Molly and then gave thanks for placing a talented doctor in her midst when she fell ill. "After all," he prayed, "nothing happens without You're willing it, our Lord." He was anxious to see how Annette handled Molly's illness and was out the door one minute after five. When he entered the daycare, every child clutched a stuffed brown poodle.

"Molly makes one for each child when they leave us," Annette explained in a trembling voice. "She must have known it was her that was leavin because she made enough so every child could have one."

"Well, I have good news," Tony said. "Molly's been moved to the fifth floor." They made plans to visit after Nicky's practice. Later that night, they sat together on her back porch. "Rick shared something with me about Molly," Tony said. "Her MRI shows an enlarged area in her brain. It caused the aneurism and the stroke. Something similar happened to Marley but was caught in time before…" He paused and took a breath. "And, there have been other cases like theirs all over the southwest."

"I remember you said he'd seen it before," she sighed.

"Rick's been collecting information on these patients for some time."

"What else?" she asked, seeing the worried look on his face.

"I'm pretty sure Sally Samuels was taking some of those patient files from Rick's office when I walked in on her. Rick thinks she's going to use them for a story; he's probably right. But then he said something strange; I guess it wasn't so much what he said as the look on his face when he said it. He said Sally was going to be the death of his family."

"It was probably just an expression, but honestly, I think the Samuels family is perfectly capable of imploding on its own."

"And then I'll be looking for another job."

"So, who cares?" she said and took his hand. "You guys can move in with Phoebe and me."

"Always the simple solution with you," he said and kissed her hand. He smiled, thinking that he had never kissed a woman's hand before. "I'm almost afraid to say this, but I've seen a change in Nicky since she witnessed what happened to Molly. This morning, she asked me how old I was when I knew I wanted to be a doctor."

"What did you tell her?"

"The truth is that I used to get into so many street fights when I was a teenager and went to the ER so many times that it kinda started to feel like home. And I began to think, *I can do this*. Carol had a different vision of my career that looked more like Dr. Samuels' life with the big house and social life."

"Do you miss Chicago and St. Joe's?" she asked.

"No," he replied. "Well, that's not true, I do. But I was desperate to get us away from there. I couldn't see us making it as a family if we stayed."

"I get that," she whispered. "Maybe you and Nicky have turned a corner. Maybe she's lookin at you with different eyes now after seein what you actually do; I know I have."

Tony wanted to kiss her, but she appeared to be fighting their obvious connection.

Tom Burns was Tony's ten o'clock appointment the next morning. "Your secretary out there was trying to get money out of me," he grumbled while sitting on the exam table. "I told her you promised me this would be free."

"Tom, I'm a man of my word," Tony replied. "Your insurance will pay the Family Practice their part, and I'm going to waive the co-pay."

"As long as it's no money out of my pocket," he bellowed.

"I'm going to listen to your chest," Tony said taking a stethoscope from his pocket. "Then the nurse will take some blood, and we'll do an EKG. I'm going to give you a stress test too, but nothing strenuous. Tony walked to his car, thinking of nothing except seeing Annette in the next few minutes. Before he laid his head on his pillow tonight, he would have told her about Tom Burns' high blood pressure and pre-diabetes and everything else about his day. The ritual had become a soothing nightcap for him. He couldn't wait to be with the woman who was making him happier than he'd been in his life. When he reached the Olds, the euphoric cloud he was riding turned to frustration.

"You look disappointed, Dr. Harding," Sally said after seeing the look on his face. She was leaning against her red Mercedes that was parked next to his car. "I just wanted to ask you some questions about Molly Ward. The Post assigned me her story, and I understand you administered life support Saturday." She began to read from a notebook in her hand. "By using the AED on-site at the Mesa Village Retirement Community," she read, "and you may have performed some other life-sustaining procedure as well; is that correct?"

Tony groaned under his breath as he unlocked the car door. "The ER team saved her; that's all I have to say." He jerked the door open.

"Some people are saying that she suddenly sprang back to life in ICU and are calling it a miracle," she said, moving closer to the Olds. "Could you tell me about that?"

"No; ask the doctor of record." He got in, started the engine, and reached for the door handle, but she slid her body inside the door.

"Arthur Gallows saw something in you," she said and leaned in closer.

"Sally, put your hook away, I'm not biting."

"What happened to Molly Ward and Marley Jones?" she whispered.

Tony stared at Sally in silence; then she dropped her notepad on the ground below the door and stooped to pick it up. "They are both victims of an atrocity," she whispered, "like Andrew Barksdale and countless others."

"Write your story, Sally," Tony said, "but you won't get any quotes from me."

"I don't want the same thing to happen to Randy, Dr. Harding," she whimpered; "not to anyone else." She backed away from the door, allowing him to close it.

Ty sat in the grass under the concrete piling artistry that supported the I-5 overpass structure near the Old Town depot. It was after midnight, and a few non-members of Lee's elite army had bedded down around the corner from him beneath the two massive walls that presented the colorful images of San Diego and its multicultural citizenry. Ty's accommodations consisted of a sleeping bag and a cardboard box left behind by a former tenant. He assembled his bedroom, and after thirty minutes of waiting for the khaki-clad vagrants to trek by, he retrieved his smartphone and retraced the red dot that represented Sally's movements around the city. When he heard the sounds of footsteps upheaving the gray rocks, he flattened his residence and observed two men crossing the service road and heading toward the residential area across the frontage road. He followed them to the dubious backyard and watched them enter the garage by a side door. Ty knew it was never a good idea to enter an unfamiliar dark building alone. Colin would have told him to scope the place out in the daylight first. Colin would have been right because as soon as he closed the door behind him, the two men knocked his legs out from under him. He could smell their stench as they lay across his back during the struggle that followed. They pulled the backpack off him and rolled him over. He tried to tell them he was a friend looking for a place to sleep, but he felt a sting in his neck, and then everything went black. His hearing was the first of his senses to revive, but the distant sounds were too muffled to discern. Then he smelled something that reminded him of the lake in northern Cali where he used to go fishing as a kid. Concentrating seemed hard, and his thoughts kept drifting. He saw himself sitting on a dock and pushing a small boat down a ramp with his father. His eyelids were heavy as lead, but he managed to force his right eyelid up as far as a slit. He tried to observe as much as possible before giving in to the extreme effort. There were sheets of plywood nailed unevenly to thick square posts, and electrical cords were strung by hooks across the ceiling. Someone's hand suddenly forced his eyes closed. When he tried to reach for the hand, he discovered he was tied down. He heard shuffling around the room just before blacking out again. He woke a second time lying on his side on a somewhat softer mattress in a room with windows and rows of beds. This time he smelled cotton sheets and the aroma of food. It was dark outside, and someone nearby was snoring. He recalled the struggle in the garage and the brief revival. He felt a sharp sting when he laid his arm across his forehead to put pressure on his aching head; he pushed up his sleeve. "I was drugged," he moaned after ripping a band-aid off his arm that was covering a large puncture wound. His khaki shirt was gone as well.

"Hey, honey, are you okay?" a woman's voice asked. He could hear the sound of heavy footsteps approaching on the wood floor. "You've been sleeping a long time, but I saved you a plate if you feel like eating." The caring voice sounded familiar.

Ty recognized her from the broadcast of Old Walter's release from jail and as the woman he talked to at the Broadway St. Shelter the day he followed Sally.

"How long…what day is it?" he asked.

"It's Friday; you've been asleep for almost eighteen hours. Ordinarily, I call the cops when someone in your condition is brought to me, but you look like a kid that could use a break, and you weren't disturbing anybody, so I let you sleep it off."

"Sleep it off?" Ty sat up and held his aching head between his hands. "Oh," he moaned and pulled the hood of the sweater over his head so neither she nor anyone else could recognize him.

"Yeah, sleep off whatever you were on," the woman said. "In case you're wondering, you're at the Broadway Street Shelter."

He rubbed his eyes. "Where are my contacts?"

"Contacts?" she said, laughing. "You can afford contacts? Anyway, a railroad inspector found you in a stupor down at the yard; they said you might have been mugged and thought maybe you were one of my regulars."

"I think one of your regulars jumped me," he said and looked around. "Where's my backpack?"

"No backpack, no wallet, no ID," she said. "Is there someone I can call to come get you, honey?"

Ty rubbed his forehead. "I have a place near Old Town, but I guess I lost my metro card too," he said, patting down his pockets.

"I have a twenty-dollar card." She reached into her blouse pocket and handed him the small plastic card. "Here, take it. You don't seem the type to be living on the streets, so go home."

"Yes, ma'am," he sighed. "That plate, could I get it to go?"

Sally visited the harbor more often at night, hoping the sounds of the slapping water and seagull caws would help her relax. It was late, but a few restaurant and theater patrons were still meandering along the sidewalks. Several vagrants were out panhandling for whatever change they might collect off the last of the late-night crowd, including the old woman Maggie who she saw moving slowly through the multitude. Her begging method of uncurling her fingers and flattening her palm made her a recognizable figure to the regular Harbor Drive patrons. Sometimes she would impatiently pump her hand when the loiterers took too long. Maggie always took her time getting to Sally because she knew Sally was good for a twenty. Tonight, she shuffled to Sally before working the crowd leaving the pricey Captain's Catch.

"Hello Maggie," Sally said and quickly pulled a twenty from her coat pocket. "How are you tonight? I hope you're staying inside because it looks like rain again."

The woman never spoke; she only grunted, and when she rolled her fingers out in front of Sally, there was a wadded-up piece of paper in the palm of her frayed glove.

"From Lee," Maggie's raspy voice whispered.

"Lee, where is he?" Sally quickly asked. Maggie pumped her hand as if annoyed by Sally's question. Sally took the paper wad and replaced it with the twenty. Maggie curled her fingers up and moved onto the next bench as if nothing out of the ordinary had transpired. Sally palmed the paper wad and walked to the edge of the harbor where there was a street light and peeled it open. *Meet me at the warehouse...NOW!* Sally tore the paper into tiny pieces and threw it in the water below. She walked to her condo, entering through the parking garage. She took the stairs down to maintenance and followed the underground maze that took her across the street to the back of the warehouse. Inside, streetlights filtered through the frosted skylights and around the dock doors. All she could see were silhouettes of boxes filled with supplies for the local shelters. "Lee," she whispered and then heard a noise and followed the sound.

"In here." She recognized Lee's voice coming from behind a partially open steel door of an old walk-in safe. She slowly moved toward the light of his flashlight.

"Give me your phone," he ordered after she was inside and he had secured the door behind her. Lee handed her the flashlight in exchange for the cell phone. He put the phone on a countertop and pounded it with a hammer, destroying it. "Now give me the other one, the one he gave you."

"How did you know about this one?" she asked and took it from her bag.

"Caught this guy sneaking into my place." Lee displayed a photo on his cell phone.

"Nate," she gasped, "except he has a beard, and street clothes like yours. Why are his eyes closed; what did you do to him?"

"His real name is Ty Hemil, and I didn't hurt him; I drugged him, and he did a lot of talking. He's an operative working for The Group. You know that mega-corporation that has holdings everywhere in the state, including your newspaper, and, by the way, is your husband's financier."

"What? No! I checked him out with NSA," she bellowed as if upset but quickly restrained her feelings. "Thank God I listened to my instincts."

"You found what they wanted you to find. Why do you think your husband left your access open? Here's another phone. It's protected with a new encryption that will block anyone from cloning your phone. One of my guys extracted some interesting information from his phone and tablet that pretty much verified everything he told me after I gave him two doses of Sodium Pentothal. There's a name for what they did to my Ellie…brain enhancement. It's supposed to make people smarter, but what it really does is put them under their control."

"Did he explain how it works?" she gasped.

"Yeah, he did. The Group transmits an electromagnetic signal from their corporate mansion in Escondido that infects the brain through any electronic device. I have some friends camped at Lake Hodges near there; they're keeping an eye on the place for me until I get my equipment moved up there."

"You're leaving the tunnel I showed you?" she asked.

"It's not safe anymore."

"I'm told their place in Escondido is guarded like a fortress, but I believe I can take it."

"Lee," she whimpered, "Nate could be a victim of the enhancement. I'm working on something, another story. Please tell me what else he said; I could quote him as if from an anonymous source. Did any of your friends say anything about their eyes changing color?"

"No! Don't be taken in by these people, Sally. Think of the lives The Group has already altered with this enhancement; think of Randy. Isn't that why you came looking for me when you realized there was something wrong with him…that he was changing? You didn't think what I told you was possible, did you? You didn't believe me when I told you someone was taking people from the streets and using them as guinea pigs and then dumping them back where they found them confused and paralyzed by strokes. I think about what they did to my wife every day. People like your friend, Nate or Ty, whatever he calls himself, don't have the right to treat people like they're garbage."

"Lee, I know how you feel, but I don't think your wife would want you to do this. Whatever you're planning is insane, not justice."

"Okay, I'm insane," he snarled, "with grief and anger, and I'm going to get my revenge. The people on that hill are monsters. I should have packed that guy to Mexico through that tunnel."

"Why didn't you?" she whispered because he was staring at her strangely. He acted as if he had more to tell her, but he shook his head instead and snatched the flashlight from her. "Did you ask him about his eyes?"

"He works for The Group; you can't trust anything he says. They probably altered him so you'd make a fool of yourself; they do things like that. He claims he's trying to help you, and well, I guess in a way, he has by turning their attention elsewhere…to me."

"Lee," Sally sighed.

"I'll keep in touch if I can," he said, ignoring Sally's perplexed gaze. He opened the steel door, letting her know the meeting was over.

"Lee wait; there has to be another way. I have videos of surgeries that were performed to correct the effects of…the enhancement. They demonstrate how enlarged areas of the brain had to be surgically manipulated to prevent or stop hemorrhaging. I took them from Rick's home office. If I can get AP and enough papers to pick up my story, maybe the FBI or someone will launch an investigation. Maybe I could convince Rick to cooperate and testify in front of a Senate committee."

"That's too many ifs and maybes," he said. "They control too many people in high places. Listen, everyone appreciates what you did for Walter. It's clear they used him to cover up what they did to Barksdale. But it's time to cut off the snake's head and end this. I have to go now; I have work to do. I might not see you for a while. We tried it your way, Sally."

"I'll leave some money for you at the shelter."

"I don't need it," he contested. "You should keep your head down."

After the girls were in bed, Doc sat down with Annette on her back porch. He looked at Phoebe curled up in the chair next to them. "Why do Molly and Elizabeth talk about Phoebe as if..." Phoebe raised her head and looked at him.

"Yeah, well," Nette sighed nervously. Phoebe put her head down and turned her body away from them as if trying to hide. "Because Phoebe and Molly play cards and computer games and uh," she paused, "she swears she sees this guy in a brown jacket and floppy hat when Phoebe disappears during the magic act."

"Disappears?"

"Elizabeth saw her disappear at the magic show. That's why she's so in awe over Phoebe. Molly has this notion," she began but took a deep breath instead. "Never mind, it's crazy. It's just that she does things I can't explain sometimes, and it sort of wigs me out. She's inspired Lizzy's imagination, and I don't think that's such a bad thing." Annette bowed her head.

"What kind of things has she done?"

"Stuff you really don't want to hear."

"Please," he said and put his hand over hers.

"Well, remember the fire at Lewis'? Phoebe pressed the intercom button so Gerry could hear the smoke alarm." She paused for his reaction, but it seemed he was waiting to hear more. "She ran away from me on the way to the bank, making me chase after her. Gunshots went off a minute later; the bank was being robbed. It's as if she knew what was happenin and steered me away."

Tony nodded, remembering Charlie and Lewis' visit to the Mesa Village clinic. "What else?" he asked and squeezed her hand. She took a deep breath as if to muster more courage.

"The homeless man at the beach gave me somethin to give Sally Samuels so I went to The Daily Post the next mornin."

"What?" Doc gasped.

"Some really strange things happened while we were there. The security cameras kept turning in the opposite direction as I walked through the building, and somehow, the little card that he gave me got from my pocket to inside her locked desk."

"Why didn't you tell me you went there?" Tony asked. "That woman sneaked into Rick's house, remember, and stole from him?"

"I know, but the man said it was important that she get it right away, that someone was following him. Phoebe went in her office ahead of me and then I heard this racket. When I walked in, the room had been ransacked; the a/c vents were torn off the wall, exposing cameras. I think Phoebe did it."

"You shouldn't have gone there," he gasped.

"Sally unlocked her desk after she walked in on us; the card was in one of the drawers and had disappeared from my pocket. I don't know how that could have happened."

"Nette," Tony said and put both hands on her shoulders. "Sally is trying to stir up trouble; I don't want you involved. Promise me you won't do anything like that again."

"Okay, but you should also know about the woman and her daughter at the mall that Phoebe distracted long enough to keep them from being hit by a toolbox that fell through a skylight. And whether you want to admit it or not, Phoebe brought Lizzy to her senses and kept her from trying to fly off the roof." She closed her eyes. "And she does help Molly cheat at poker."

"Surely, you've considered these things to be coincidences," Tony whispered.

"Yes, over and over, a million times. But I can't explain how she disappears at the end of the magic act," she pleaded, "and then reappears on cue." Annette looked up at him. "I can tell by the look in your eyes that you don't believe any of this. But it's best you know this now before we, well, you know, get any closer."

"Look," he said and took both her hands. "I understand you believe Phoebe is special, and she is, without question. I've never seen a dog mimic human expression the way she does. And I know people have relationships with their pets and treat them like their own children. I'm trying," he said tenderly when Annette began to sob.

"She saved Molly and that other woman in ICU," she sobbed.

Tony put his arm around her as she cried hard on his shoulder. "I'm not going to dispute what you believe, Nette," he whispered, trying to console her. "Not anymore; not ever. We'll figure this out together. Your friendship is too important to me." Phoebe jumped down from the chair and climbed into Tony's lap. They each placed a hand on her. Phoebe looked up at Tony. The power of suggestion was a manipulative tool that he often used to get more participation out of lethargic patients than they were otherwise willing to give. And he was sure that's why he thought he saw something, a glint of mint green in Phoebe's eyes.

The next morning, Tony reversed his early morning route, hoping to catch Father Clayton. "You look like you have something on your mind, Doc," the priest said after they met up in front of the church and the idle chit-chat was over.

"I feel like I've found something here, Don," he said as they trotted along Gold Coast. "Something better than I could ever have hoped for when I left Chicago. I never expected to meet someone like Annette. It's because of her that I'm beginning to come to grips with the guilt I carry. I can actually see a future ahead for me and my girls. Something is bothering me, though."

"And that thing would be Phoebe," Father Clayton said immediately.

"W-well," Tony huffed, "how did you know?"

"Phoebe is hard to explain because of the things that have happened. Like Jim and Julia, for example, the couple that lived in your house."

"I heard Jim was blind and then regained partial sight."

"Jim and Julia, both swear it was Phoebe that cured him. Phoebe was in the garden with Jim when he suddenly saw a flash of light. Julia witnessed it happen from the back porch."

"She saw the flash?" Tony asked; Father Clayton nodded. "I know you're a man of the cloth, and you preach about miracles, but you realize there is a medical explanation for the flash of light he saw and that Julia most likely experienced it sympathetically?"

"His specialists had no real explanation for the sudden return of his sight. He and Julia are convinced to this day that it was Phoebe. I give God the credit for all such things. After all, the Bible states He uses both nature and His creatures to do His work. But there have been other incidents, and it's getting harder to keep Phoebe's magic under wraps."

"Magic!" Tony huffed. "Now you sound like Elizabeth. Surely you understand how the subconscious mind can turn a suggestion into reality."

"Of course; but that's what people have started to call it," the priest replied, "and that's why we must seek the truth through prayer. That's what I want you to do. Pray for Annette and maybe the truth will present itself to her and to you, to all of us.

I'm not sure she's completely come to terms with her father's death. She might see things differently if she could let go of him like you are trying to do with your guilt. Have the two of you, well, you know, made a physical commitment to each other yet?"

"No, no," Tony assured him. "I don't want to rush anything. To be honest, Don, the old Tony Harding wouldn't have waited. But something inside me has changed. I want to wait."

"Praise be to God," the priest replied as they turned toward Antrim.

"There is something else," Tony said just before they reached his house. "Why were you with Sally last week?"

"She asked me for my help, and I didn't turn her down," the priest replied. "Now our friend Walter is safe."

"What do you mean by safe?" Tony asked, but the priest only bowed his head. "Father, you can call on me for help anytime but please think twice when Sally's involved. She wants something from me…information...and I don't like being manipulated."

"Dr. Harding, we're being manipulated every minute of every day. Someone or something is always trying to influence our behavior, whether it's a salesman, a lifestyle, or something we see on television, it comes at us from all directions. What we have to do is take a step back and do what's best for ourselves, our family, and our community. Sally had to get Walter out of town before the judge changed his mind, and she believes her husband is having her followed. That's was the reason for the disguise."

They stopped momentarily in front of Tony's house. "I don't like her methods of getting things done," Tony said. "I caught her taking files from Rick's office. If she uses them to write an article, she could defile Rick's research. If there's anything you can do, maybe counsel her or persuade her to wait until Rick reaches something conclusive. I believe she has a vendetta against The Group because they're backing her husband's political career."

"Yes, I have heard her complain about The Group," Don said. "I'll pray about it, and if I receive direction, I'll surely do what I can." They shook hands and went their separate ways.

Chapter 31

Ty's stubble was nearly an inch long after two days of frequenting soup kitchens and eavesdropping on the conversations of fellow street dwellers. He heard rumors of a migration headed north, and it seemed to bear some truth because foot traffic through the overpass to the white frame house where he had been jumped was now nonexistent, so he returned and found it empty. A door in the kitchen stood open that led to a cellar. The memory of fishing materialized again when he descended the stairs, and he realized it was because of the distinct odor of mud. He recalled the plywood tacked to the thick beams that covered the dank walls of what he now realized was a tunnel, presumably one of many used by smugglers and illegals. But there were computer operators he remembered seeing on the opposite side of a burlap curtain that swayed back and forth during his brief awakening. He explored the north end with a flashlight, thinking perhaps it was the path to Sally's old chapel, but the interstate foundation blocked it. He plodded south about a quarter mile and found evidence of the occupancy he remembered. The excavation was larger and had empty shelves and tables along the plywood. Electrical outlets were strung on hooks, and he found six wooden beds crammed into an isolated area separated by the familiar-looking piece of burlap. "The thing about Sodium Pentothal," he whispered to the damp vacated hideout as he climbed back up the stairs to the kitchen, "it's only a truth serum for the weak-minded." Ty returned to the storage unit, packed his things into a newly acquired backpack, took the train north to Carlsbad, and found the local Salvation Army.

"Daddy look," Lizzy gasped as they approached Annette sitting on her front stoop, "Jeffrey and Justin are riding skateboards." Jeffrey came to a stop beside him and offered him the board.

"I don't think so," he said. "It's been too long."

"Well, I wouldn't want you to hurt yourself, man," Jeffrey quipped and slammed the board on the sidewalk.

Annette leaned her head to one side and grinned.

"Okay, I'll try it, once." Tony put a foot up on the board and pushed himself off. He was wobbly but somehow managed to stay upright. Later Annette egged him into riding Jeffrey's bike.

"Remember that picture in Nicky's album of you pullin a wheelie?" Nette teased. After working at it for a minute, he pulled the front wheel off the ground. They drank tea and sat on the porch while Lizzy ran Phoebe through her repertoire of tricks. Kids from the neighborhood came and went, if for no other reason than to tell Annette and Phoebe hello.

"Okay, now, I have a challenge for you," Tony taunted; "I'm going to teach you how to cook."

"Oh no," she protested. "I do just fine on McDonalds and frozen pizza." Then he bet her that he could teach her one of his mother's recipes every day. She balked vigorously at first, then finally agreed, only to moan and groan when she realized the first lesson would be that afternoon. Nicky walked in on them arguing in the kitchen. Her father was in the middle of tying the apron sash around her waist *the Harding way*. She intervened by volunteering to help. Tony and Annette laughed about it later that night when they sat on her back porch. Their goodnight kisses were becoming longer and more meaningful, making it more difficult for Tony to walk home alone across the alley. But he sensed a reluctance that somehow seemed to be connected to the way she talked about her father while running her fingers through Phoebe's soft coat. He was fully aware of how deep loss could stifle someone's life. He would give her all the time she needed.

The next day, the doorbell rang while Tony was heating leftovers from the first cooking lesson. He peered through the peephole and saw a woman dressed in a dark blue uniform and cradling a white flat box in her arms.

"Dr. Harding," she said when he opened the door. "I'm Brenda Bolton, Scott's mother. You wanted to meet me, *to see if I really exist*; I believe that is how you put it. I bought you an apple pie as a housewarming gift. Belated, I know, but I work such weird hours."

"So, I've heard; come in, Mrs. Bolton," Tony replied and held the door open. The woman was tall with long blonde hair that was pulled back in a twist. "I'm glad to finally meet you. Scott told me you work at the airport."

"Yes, Lindbergh; I'm pulling double shifts because of the Homeland Security upgrade, but honestly, I need the extra money."

"What is it that you do exactly?" he asked.

"Oh gosh, I work wherever they'll let me," she said, laughing. "Scott told me all about you, and by that, I mean you don't put up with any nonsense."

"I'm sorry, Brenda; I know we just met, but don't you think it's a little remiss of you to leave the responsibility of your son's welfare to your neighbors?"

"I appreciate your feelings, Dr. Harding. Scott's a brilliant little guy, something he inherited from his father, who…is out of the picture. I wouldn't do it if I thought he was in danger. Annette Rylan and Brad Jones have both been kind enough to look after him for me. I also have a security system and cameras set up around the perimeter of the house, and we text each other. I'm aware of everything that goes on. I'd be more worried if this weren't the great neighborhood it is."

"Do you know about the guy he talks to online, Guardian?"

"Of course; I had TSA check him out." He offered her coffee and a piece of pie just as she received an urgent text from the airport requesting her presence.

"Burns should be less hypertensive by now," Tony said to Annette in the car on the way to Nicky's game.

"What did you prescribe him?" Annette grinned cynically.

"Daddy," Lizzy interrupted, working her small frame between the front seats. She had a white envelope in her hand. "This was under your seat."

"I thought I gave this," Tony paused, recognizing the envelope with the USCSD logo that he caught Sally taking from his car, "to a patient." He quickly put it in the glove compartment. "Not important," he said, although he was curious as to how the envelope got under his seat and why it felt bulky.

"I haven't heard his big mouth all night," Annette commented at the half.

"He does seem less stressed, doesn't he?" Tony said, grinning.

"Yeah, that's what I said," Nette said. "The tall blonde Nicky is feeding the ball to is his daughter, Cass."

"He told me he had a daughter. I've seen her hanging out with a punk with a blue Trans Am in the mornings at school.

Yes, I follow them," he added when she gave him a questioning look.

"Jimmy's a street racer," she said. "Robby had a thing for Cass last summer. She wanted him to run away with her; she dumped him when he didn't go through with it." He read the compassion in her amazing blue eyes and didn't realize he had put his arm around her and was pulling her close to him. The third-quarter buzzer sounded, startling him back to his senses. She hadn't pulled away or even given him a warding-off sign. The crew went to Pizza Hut after the game, where they rearranged the tables so they could all sit together. The conversation started with how great Nicky played and the points she ran up and continued until the food arrived. Robby told a story about how Annette was twice banned from the gym for losing it when Burns went off on one of the players.

"You should have seen her swinging her fists, Doc," he said. Tony smiled at her when she blushed and remarked that he wouldn't expect anything less from the girl who would do anything to help a kid.

"I'm takin the boy's up to Larry's tonight," Nette said; "and I'm plannin on spendin the weekend. Larry's got plenty of room if y'all wanna come."

"How about it, Nicky," Tony said. "You guys want to spend the night up in Escondido?"

"Awesome!" Jeffrey exclaimed. "Nicky, I can't wait to show you our place. We have cattle and horses and 4-wheelers."

"Robby and Scott, how 'bout it," Nette asked, "You in?"

"Do you really have horses and cattle?" Lizzy squealed.

Joseph Rodriguez put his cell phone down hard on the conference table. Willis Shepherd was sitting at the opposite end of the table and looked up from his laptop.

"What's wrong?" his colleague asked.

"It's Sally," he growled and turned to the keyboard behind him. "Ops on the ground following her have confirmed she's planning another article."

"At least this time, we can get out in front of things by manipulating our people at the Post," Shepherd sighed.

"The order's been sent," the senior agent replied. A buzzing sound came from his breast pocket. He pulled out his cell phone and read the screen. "Colin just heard from Hemil." The screen behind him lit up, displaying Colin's station in Sub Level 3.

"The message was highly encrypted, sir," Colin said. "It took me a few minutes to transcribe." Willis moved closer to the monitor as Joseph magnified the image.

Found a tunnel under I-5 near Old Town where Lee's been squatting. He's organizing an attack on The Group HQ and has moved north; that's where I'm headed.

"You're certain it's from him?" Shepherd asked.

"He created the code that was used; it's as good as his signature."

"North; he wasn't more specific?" Rodriguez quizzed.

"He'll let me know when he finds him," Colin said. "Do you want me to send a team to search the tunnel?"

"Yes," Rodriguez growled.

"Do you think Hemil is on the right track, Joe?" Shepherd said. "This Lee fellow sounds like he's as dangerous as Sally."

"Sally the one that told him about the tunnel so they are definitely working together," Rodriguez grumbled.

Dinner at Larry's was under the stars and consisted of hamburgers, French fries, and brownies. Larry dug a pit down the hill away from the house and barns while everybody scavenged for wood to build a fire for roasting hot dogs and marshmallows.

"Annette taught me how to build a fire when we went camping out at Lake Jennings," Larry told Doc as he spread kindling in the bottom of the pit.

"You've known her a while?" Tony asked.

"Kids met her first, but it didn't take her long to start chewin my ass out to change my ways. I'm all they got, their mother's in prison. Annette got me thinking about how great my boys are and that I needed to straighten myself up, so here I am, up here in God's country." Later, they spread blankets on the grass, looked for falling stars, and then played cards and charades on the patio until after midnight. No one got up earlier than ten the next morning and only after hearing Tony beat on a pot with a metal spoon and yelling *breakfast*. Everyone came down the stairs complaining except for Lizzy, who pranced past everyone while following Phoebe out the back door. She was having the time of her life doing things she had never dreamed of.

Later, they rode horses and four-wheelers. Tony assembled two kites he retrieved from the trunk of his car that he intended to fly on their next trip to Mission Beach, but the strong Santa Ana winds quickly broke the strings and whisked them away. Justin saw the reflection of the blue and silver Mylar bird through his binoculars waving in a tree near the top of the posted hillside. Everyone took turns looking through the glasses and narrated the kite's futile escape attempts in spite of the whipping wind. There was no sign of the black and white Mylar shark. The cattle and horses strolled in that evening, and the kids helped Jeffrey and Justin feed them.

"This is what we'll be doing every day this summer," Justin bragged. "And clearing brush on the hillside. I'm going to explore that place one of these days." He looked at the dark rocky mountain that hovered in the distance.

"The government posts it," Nicky reminded him. "You'll be arrested."

"No, I won't," he argued. "I know exactly how to get in and out there."

Jeffrey shook his head. "You're not going to Witch Mountain without me."

"It's too risky, dude," Nicky contested.

"Nobody cares," Justin argued. "Anyway, I'm not gonna get caught."

"Man, I really dig this place," Robby sighed. "Let me know if you need some help this summer." Later they gathered around the pool. Larry marinated the steaks and started the grill. Tony took Annette by the hand and led her to the kitchen so they could prepare the salad, baked potatoes, and French bread, even though she argued against the idea all the way there. At one point, he just folded his arms, leaned against the stove, and grinned at her until she finished protesting. Lizzy and Phoebe were the after-dinner entertainment. The little dog went through her routines ending with Lizzy asking her to solve simple math problems, at which time she turned to Annette.

"Miss Nette," she whined, "would you please do the grand finale?"

"Oh no, I can't, honey, you know that," Nette replied softly.

"No one will tell," she begged.

"I don't have my magic scarf; it doesn't work unless…"

"I know where it is," Lizzy cried, jumped to her feet, and ran to Annette's Toyota.

"I forgot, it's hangin on the mirror," she moaned to Tony.

"I'll take care of this if you want," he offered.

"I don't have any music," Annette added.

"I have a guitar," Justin said and rushed into the house.

"I need a stage," Annette sighed, "and a tablecloth. Oh God, what am I doing?"

"Yeah! You gotta have the smoke and mirrors," Larry jeered. He must have downed more than the three beers he had at dinner because he snickered throughout Lizzy and Phoebe's act prompting Annette to kick his lounge chair several times. Justin returned with the guitar, which Robby took from him, and began to tune. Jeffrey and Nicky found a white sheet in the laundry room and covered the picnic table after Scott and Tony cleared it off. Lizzy retrieved the New Orleans Saints scarf and eagerly handed it to Nette.

Annette stood in front of the table. "All right, ladies and gentlemen; will the fabulous Phoebe please take her place on the stage?" Lizzy dashed to pick her up and gingerly placed her on the white cloth.

"You're gonna have to get another tablecloth," Larry slurred. "That one's paper thin; I can see right through it." He leaned over too far and fell out of his chair onto the stone patio and then laughed uncontrollably while he pulled himself back up. Robby plucked a simple tune while Annette held the Saints scarf above Phoebe.

"It's time," Tony overheard Annette whisper to Phoebe. Phoebe looked at her master and sat up on her hind legs. Robby vigorously strummed three chords just before Annette raised her voice.

"For the final performance of the evening…" She lowered the black and gold scarf and wrapped it around Phoebe. Annette's eyes scanned the small audience, and she smiled. "Abracadabra!" she yelled and pulled the scarf away. Phoebe was gone. Lizzy squealed and bounced on her knees.

Larry squeezed his eyes shut and then opened them again. He dropped from the chair and crawled on his hands and knees to the table. He grabbed the edge of the sheet and lifted it, accidentally pulling it off the table when he lost his balance. "I know she's under there," he garbled. He began fighting with the sheet and became entangled in it. "Where the hell did she go?" he whined when he finally freed himself, sat up, and looked around. Nicky looked to Jeffrey and then Justin for an explanation, but their faces were full of bitterness and embarrassment over their father's behavior. Tony's mouth was ajar when Lizzy grabbed him around the neck.

"Daddy, Daddy, now you have to believe," Lizzy squealed. All Tony could think to himself was Larry's barely coherent question. *Where the hell did she go?* Annette grabbed the sheet from the ground beside Larry, who was holding himself upright on one arm and massaging his forehead. Tony got up from his chair to help her but was suddenly startled by a shadowy figure of a man exiting their circle of light. Lizzy left her dismayed father to sit beside Scott, who had been recording the event on his phone. She squeezed his arm.

"Don't stop, there's more," she whispered.

"Oh where, oh where did my little dog go? Oh, where, oh where can she be?" Robby sang while strumming chords on the guitar. "With her ears cut long and her tail cut short, oh where, oh where can she be?" The wind seemed to assist Annette by lifting the sheet up and over the table and again by abruptly dying down, making it settle exactly into place. She took a deep breath.

"I hope this works after your disruption, Larry," she scolded. He staggered back to his chair that was lying on its side. She lifted the Saints scarf again by her fingertips, and Robby continued thrumming. "Ladies and gentlemen," she began, "may I present to you, Phoebe, the Magic Dog!" She jerked the scarf away, and to everyone's surprise, the little brown dog was in the same sitting-up position as before. Lizzy squealed and clapped and then turned to Scott to make sure he had recorded everything. Everyone else could only gasp and wonder how it was done. Annette looked at Tony; he was glaring at her, seemingly in shock. Then his eyes shifted over her shoulder. She turned, but there was nothing behind her but a stand of trees. When she turned back, he was standing beside her and staring into her eyes. He wrapped his arms around her before she could ask: "What is it?"

"I didn't think they'd ever go to bed," Justin said to his brother as they jogged across the field toward the horse barn.

"Did you ask Nicky if she wanted to come?"

"No, I didn't want to get her in trouble," Jeffrey replied as they opened one of the huge barn doors.

"Grab the bridles," Justin said. "We'll lead them down the hill behind the barn."

"And then where?" Jeffrey asked.

"To the hidden driveway, of course," Justin replied.

Scott could see the backyard and pool area from the upstairs bedroom he shared with Robby as he sent the recorded video to his friend Guardian. He glanced up just in time to see Jeffrey and Justin running across the yard.

Larry had too much to drink, he texted, *but Nette and Doc had everything under control.* He looked up again and saw Nicky following them. Robby leaned over Scott's shoulder to look out the window, startling him into dropping his cell phone. "You still up?"

"You scared me; you jerk." He picked his phone up from the floor. "It powered off; now I don't know if my video was sent."

"Yo, was that Nicky I just saw?" Robby asked.

"Yes," Scott replied. "She followed Jeffrey and Justin." They slipped out and met up with Nicky at the barn.

"What's goin down?" Robby whispered.

"They just took off," she said and pointed to the two open stalls. "They didn't even bother to saddle up. They're idiots."

"We better wake Nette and your dad." Robby turned to Scott. "I hope you're texting Nette."

"G will know what to do," he replied as he worked his thumbs up and down the keypad.

"Screw G, text Nette; never mind, I'm going to get her." Robby took off running back to the house.

Nicky walked out of the barn and looked up at the dark mountain. The Santa Ana wind eerily picked up its torrent and sent her long brown hair into motion. "They're gonna be so busted," she whispered. Scott almost lost his glasses in the wind surge while sending his message to Annette. "Who's G?" Nicky asked.

Tony didn't want to merely say goodnight to Annette and leave her standing at her bedroom door, but Lizzy was asleep in his arms, so he carried his daughter to the bedroom they were sharing. Phoebe trotted beside him and then jumped up on the bed and curled up beside her. He lay there thinking about what he witnessed and how hard it must have been for Annette to tell him about Phoebe. He remembered how she had trembled and fought back tears because she fully expected him to shake his head, walk away, and keep his distance from that point on. He wanted to be patient and let her decide for herself what was really happening. But there was no reasonable explanation for what he saw tonight. Where did Phoebe go when Annette pulled the scarf away? And who was the man he saw walking into the shadows? Annette had told him about Molly seeing a man in a coat and hat. He thought about the jingling noise he heard in Elizabeth's room just before seeing the shadowy figure in the hall. Was he a victim of mania? He eased out of bed, quietly stepped across the hall, and tapped on Annette's door.

"Doc," she whispered when she opened the door. "How's Lizzy?"

"She's fine," he said. "Did I wake you?"

"No."

"I couldn't sleep," he whispered.

"My mind won't shut off either," she said and held the door open inviting him inside. "Is everyone in bed?"

"The house is quiet except for Larry snoring downstairs." They moved closer to the bed, and Tony put his arms around her waist. "There's something I want to say to you before this night ends," he whispered.

"What?" she said softly and moved her hands up his arms toward his shoulders. They stared into each other's eyes, and time seemed to stand still as they inched closer together.

"I want to tell you something," he began, but Nette's cell phone alerted and shuffled around the top of the nightstand by the window. The mesmeric moment was broken, and Annette reached for it.

"Scott texted me somethin," she whispered. When she picked up the phone, she saw Jeffrey and Justin through the window riding bareback down the hill in front of the house, then she read Scott's text. "Oh God, they're goin over there." She ran out of the bedroom.

Robby met Annette on the staircase, gasping from running all the way from the barn. "Justin said he knew a way onto the property next door, Jeffrey went with him."

"I just saw them headin toward the road," she said. "I have to stop them before they get there."

"Where is she going?" Tony asked as he tore down the stairs behind her.

"She's going after the boys," Nicky said when she and Scott met him on his way through the kitchen.

"She was headed to the Toyota," Scott added.

"I thought you kids were in bed," Tony said, straining to keep from yelling and waking Lizzy. "Keep an eye on your sister so she doesn't freak out," he said and ran out the door. The 4-Runner was already moving, so he ran behind it, beating on the fender. Annette slowed just long enough for him to open the passenger door and jump inside, then she spun the tires as if trying to make up for the lost time, leaving a short strip of rubber behind on the long-sloping driveway. She stopped the truck when they reached the scenic 15.

"They were headed that way," she said, looking out her window. She suddenly lunged across his lap and opened the glove box. "There's a flashlight in here."

"I can't hear anything because of the wind in the trees," Tony said as he shined the flashlight on the ground. "Wait, I see a hoof print next to the road." They followed the occasional tracks to a blacktop driveway.

Phoebe raised her head and slid out from under Lizzy's arm. She brushed her nose against her cheek; Lizzy sighed and fell into a deeper sleep. Then she moved to the edge of the bed and jumped down.

The boys prompted their horses up the hill through the trees and brush until it was too thick to go further.

"Sounds like a freight train out here," Jeffrey said after sliding off the back of his horse. "The wind is making the horses nervous."

Justin slipped off his horse to survey the road. "We need to cross; there's another road over there behind those vines."

"We should go back, man," Jeffrey said. "Wait, did you see that flash?" he shouted. "Up there, on top of the building."

"Lightning?" Justin asked. "Man, there's another one; that can't be lightning. Uh-oh, I hear someone." They ducked in the bushes, but the horses were fretful and shuffling. "Pull off their bridles and let them go; they can be our decoy." They turned the horses loose on the blacktop road, and they galloped down the hill while Justin hid the bridles under a bush.

They heard a man's voice shouting over the gusts. "Everything is down on this side," he reported to someone over his phone. "Yes, cameras too. What did you say caused the power failure; a kite? No, it was just a couple of horses; I'll check further down the hill."

Jeffrey and Justin stared at one another for a minute before mustering the courage to peer over the bushes. "He's gone, let's get the hell out of here," Jeffrey whispered.

"No, I gotta know what's behind those vines," Justin replied. "He moved to the edge of the blacktop and then ran across the road.

"Crap!" Jeffrey whispered and followed his little brother.

Annette and Tony heard the clapping hooves approach just before the two horses galloped past them. "Watch out!" Tony yelled, instinctively pulling her out of the way.

"Oh God," she panted, watching the riderless horses prance down the drive. "Where are the boys?"

"I'll go look for them," Tony said. "Go back to the truck."

"No!" she argued.

"Please, I won't come back without them, I promise," he said.

"But you might need my help," she said and stepped ahead of him. He frowned, stepping in front of her, and then conceded, and they walked up the hidden drive together.

"Who's there?" a man's voice called out just as Annette discovered the bridals under the bushes. Tony shined the flashlight on the man and then on himself.

"We're looking for—uh, our horses," Tony yelled out. He shined the flashlight on the wad of bridles in Annette's hands.

"They should have just passed you," he said suspiciously and moved closer.

"Yes," Tony said. "But, there's one more. The wind spooked them, and they broke loose from their stalls."

"This property is posted as restricted." The man stopped about six feet from them. One of his hands was positioned at his waist and seemed to be propped on something that looked like the handle of a gun. "I must ask you to leave. We're on alert due to a power failure; the grounds are not safe. If we find your horse, we'll return it. Turn around; I'll escort you back to the road." Tony nodded and put a protecting arm around Annette. He looked up when the wind picked up again; small twigs and leaves pelted the ground around them. The man followed them to the end of the drive and remained there until they reached the 4-Runner and got inside.

"We have to go back," Annette whispered as Tony drove up Larry's driveway. "What's wrong?" she asked because of the perplexed look on his face.

"Nothing," he answered, but he was trying to make sense of what he just saw in the swaying treetops. "Nothing," he repeated, wondering what could have caused the fluorescent green streams of light in the canopies. "Does Larry have a pair of bolt cutters?"

"I do, in my toolbox in the back," she replied.

"There's a toolbox back there?"

"My daddy gave me a toolbox for my sixteenth birthday when he bought me my first car," she said as they traveled off-road toward the mountain. They pitched things over the back seat to reach the toolbox in a compartment under the floor. "I should take this bat just in case," Tony said and gave it a short practice swing.

"Oh!" Annette gasped and took it from him. "Someone must have used it as a fire poker," she said, examining the scorch marks on the end. "Wait till I find out who did this; my daddy gave me this too." The howling wind concealed the sound of their movements along the fence bordering the compound. They had stopped at the edge of the restricted property and parked under a tree with low-hanging branches. They scouted the fence line on foot hoping to find an easy way in. Annette grabbed Tony's arm. "I see something; it's them; I see Jeffrey's blonde hair; they're coming this way."

"Duck down," Tony warned, "just in case."

Jeffrey reached the fence first and clamped his fingers through the diamond-shaped links. "Stand on my shoulders," he ordered Justin. Tony and Annette burst from their hiding place. "Whoa!" Jeffrey yelled. "Doc, you scared the crap out of me."

"Shush! Quiet!" Annette scolded. Tony pushed the piercing wire apart with the bat after cutting enough links for Jeffrey and Justin to squeeze through.

"You're not gonna believe what we saw!" Jeffrey gushed as he looked back toward the compound.

"This way," Tony said and pointed the bat in the direction of the Toyota.

"I'm sorry, Nette," Justin said when they were safely inside the truck. "I didn't expect that place to be so, so scary, so creepy."

"What were you thinkin?" she scolded as Tony started the truck and pulled away.

"I don't know; I guess my curiosity got the best of me," Justin sighed.

"Oh Jesus," Tony said, looking in the rear-view mirror. "The wind blew the tree over that we were just parked under." He stopped and opened the door to look back because he also thought he saw the man with the hat again standing beside the uprooted tree. "What the hell?"

Robby, Nicky and Scott ran out to meet the 4-Runner when they saw it approach. Lizzy was still sleeping, and Larry had never stirred from the sofa.

"We told a guard that three horses got loose from the barn," Tony said when Nicky asked him what happened; "three…that's our story."

"Let's see what I got," Jeffrey said after they were safely inside the kitchen and crowded around his laptop. "This is going down in the elevator," he narrated. "It must have been stuck on automatic because it didn't stop when I pushed the buttons."

"It took us underground," Justin added. "The floors were marked with Sub numbers until we got to the one marked *Basement*."

"Oh, God, why did you do this?" Nette fretted.

"The doors to the place just opened when we walked up," Justin replied in their defense. "It was the same with the elevator."

"The basement made me think of American Horror Story," Jeffrey continued. "See this row of doors? The locks and handles are only on the outside, and the windows are skinny and reinforced with wire. The walls inside the rooms were padded. All these old guys in gray pj's were locked inside," he said as the video displayed three men lying in beds attached to the wall inside their rooms. "They look drugged or something." The shaky video showed one man curled up in a fetal position.

"That guy actually looks familiar," Tony sighed, "maybe from the hospital."

"We opened all the doors, but nobody moved, except for this one that took off running. There was another door marked *Do Not Enter*, in red letters, but we heard the elevator chime, and we ran to get back on."

"Yeah, it also read *Restricted Area*," Justin added.

"The doors opened on each floor all the way up," Jeffrey said as the video continued with brief shots of the area around the doors as they opened.

"Those people are wearing headsets and sitting in front of computers on the S2 and S1 floors," Tony muttered, "like a telemarketing center, maybe."

"The upper floors look like a normal residence," Annette remarked as the doors continued to open and close.

"It took us all the way to the roof," Jeffrey said. "We hid in the bell tower because people were running all over. We looked over the edge and saw the guy from the basement running into the woods and then a second or two later, two guys followed him."

"Hey, Doc," Justin said, "I overheard this one dude on the roof raving about a kite being tangled up in a transformer that caused some switches to explode."

"We snuck down the stairwell outside the bell tower," Jeffrey said, concluding the story.

"That place is 1000 times scarier than Witch Mountain," Justin sighed.

"May I copy this to my phone?" Scott asked.

"Don't do it," Robby said, "he'll send it to his internet buddy."

"No, I-I was-was just going to show it to my mother," Scott stuttered.

"Yeah, right," Robby said critically.

"No putting this on the internet," Tony warned. "We don't know what we're dealing with here."

"Why would they have people locked in the basement?" Nette asked. "What could be going on down there? Larry said that place has somethin to do with The Group, the company that owns Molly's. Thank God y'all got out of there without bein caught."

"The Group," Tony sighed.

"Maybe it's some kind of rehab," Nicky suggested.

"Maybe that's it, honey," Tony said, trying to agree with her rational answer, but not convinced of it in the least.

"They don't look like patients; they look like the people that live on the street," Nette sighed, thinking about the man on the boardwalk. "We should go home," she suddenly insisted. "Jeffrey, wake Larry up and tell him you're goin home with me. I don't want you guys up here…not ever again."

"But Nette," Justin said, "this is our home now."

"Just do it," Nette replied.

"I'll get Lizzy," Tony said. "Nicky, Robby, Scott; get your stuff." Tony slipped into the bedroom where Elizabeth lay sleeping with an arm around Phoebe. He felt something in Phoebe's hair when he moved Elizabeth's arm. "Leaves," he whispered, and Phoebe raised her head and looked at him. "And your feet are wet," he said after feeling her body all over. "Am I going nuts?" Phoebe's tag jingled when she shook her head.

Larry sat up and rubbed his face when Annette woke him to tell him they were leaving. "I'll see you next weekend?" he asked, yawning. Annette didn't answer, and then she made everyone promise not to say anything about what happened while they loaded their bags in the vehicles. Tony promised Elizabeth he would explain everything to her later.

"It's a secret," he said, "like Phoebe's magic."

"What do you mean one of them escaped?" Rodriguez yelled into the phone. "Find him! He could be one of Lee's allies; we barely got started on him." He turned to the keyboard; Colin's station appeared on the monitor. "Are we at full power?"

"Yes, sir," Colin replied. "Apparently a kite entangled itself in a transformer and tripped four safety switches that caused the power shut down. Our backup generators couldn't handle the sudden load, but we have fully recovered. Security found a small cut in the fence. They also found a small amount of blood on the roadside. The trail led to a steep drop off, and there are signs indicative of a fall."

"Damn!" Rodriguez growled.

Colin studied every frame of viable surveillance video taken at the time of the shutdown as the generators tried and failed to recoup the system. He assigned a team in the north quad to scrutinize the entire day's surveillance in and around the compound. In less than a minute, someone found footage of the wind simultaneously snapping two kites from their string and then whipping them up the forested mountain. Colin recognized Dr. Harding on the limp end of one of the strings and Annette Rylan standing near him. "Where are we on that early release?" he demanded from the tech in the east quad assigned to the project. "Put it in motion today." *God help you if this tactic doesn't keep you away from here.*

Chapter 32

Tony could have run ten miles and still not covered all the things flooding his mind. The weekend started out great, although overshadowed somewhat by Larry's drunkenness which was not so much an unfamiliar sight for him and his daughters considering where they came from, but one he hoped to never expose them to again. What troubled him the most was Phoebe's mysterious disappearing act that seemed to have produced a man who faded from the light surrounding the pool. And he was sure the shadowy figure standing by the fallen tree was one and the same. He thought about the menacing-looking guard that escorted him and Annette off the grounds when they were looking for the boys, the gusts of wind in the treetops that somehow illuminated the pitch dark above them, and more so, Jeffrey's account of what they saw inside the mansion that was verified by the images from his cell phone video. Thoughts of Marley and Molly suddenly appeared in the forefront of his mind, and he wondered if they somehow fit into the quandary. Maybe it was because the man who turned and looked directly into Jeffrey's cell phone before running out of the basement had the same acute bloodshot eyes as them before they fell ill. Then his memory served him Walter, the man he treated at Bonnie's, and a reenactment of Sally stuffing Rick's videos in her bag. He had resolved nothing by the time he reached his driveway.

Annette arrived early Monday to help Lisa in lieu of Molly's convalescence. They signaled shrugs to one another each time someone asked why Mona wasn't there yet. The phone rang after nine after the kids were fed and out to play. Annette answered in the kitchen and then fell to a squat on the floor after listening to the voice on the line. Lisa knelt down in front of her and grabbed the receiver; it was Tim. Mona's mother hadn't been able to wake her daughter and called an ambulance. She was in the ICU at UCSD in a coma and on life support; a CT scan showed evidence of a stroke and bleeding in the brain.

"Nette, call Doc and have him find out what's going on," Lisa said after hanging up with Tim. Annette shook her head and handed Lisa her cell.

"I can't," she sobbed. "Lisa, my knees are weak. I feel sick; I have—have to—to get some air." She crawled to her feet and stumbled out the back door.

Tonya placed two of Rick's patient files on top of Tony's. "Dr. Rick had an emergency this morning," she said. "He's wrapping things up now but said you could work a couple of his early appointments in with yours until he gets here." She lowered her voice. "He apparently doesn't trust the other doctors with his patients."

He took the files from her and, a short time later, heard Rick's voice in the hallway. He opened the elder's door after knocking and hearing a faint *come in.* Rick was sitting behind his desk, rubbing the sides of his head as if trying to soothe a headache; a DVD was lying on the desk in front of him.

"Another surgery," Tony guessed, seeing how weary Rick looked. "Not another abnormality?" Tony gasped, as he rushed past the father of medicine when Rick nodded and expelled a long sigh.

"I'm afraid so; one of the young ladies at Molly's, I'm afraid."

"Who?" Tony almost shouted. He picked up the disk; it had Mona's name written on it. "What's on here?"

"Aneurism; a pinched vessel; crowded gray matter," he moaned, "stroke. It was too advanced for a simple procedure to correct. I did what I could short of altering her mentality."

"You have to do something more than submit a report, Rick," Tony growled.

"I have tried and…"

"And what," Tony roared. "The Surgeon General didn't listen? Try again and keep trying."

Rick shook his head. "I'll handle it, son," Rick sighed. "I'll make another appeal, I promise. I'm exhausted right now. Please, go back to your patients; I need to go home and get some rest."

Tony's cell phone rang just as he stepped out of Rick's office; it was Lisa. "I just heard; I'm on my way to ICU now. Tell Annette I'll call her in a couple of hours." Tony slammed his patient files on the counter in front of Tonya. "I don't know when I'll be back. Divide these among Rick's not so trustworthy." Tonya was too shocked to reply and could only blink her eyes as she watched him leave by the rear hallway.

"Was that Dr. Anthony Harding?" Someone asked, startling her out of her dismay.

"Yes," Tonya replied as she turned around. She was taken aback when she saw the good-looking man standing on the other side of the counter. "Did you have an appointment with him?" she asked suggestively. "I'm afraid, I'm not sure..."

"I see he hasn't lost his passion," the man said with a smile. "I'm his friend Harry, from Chicago. I understand he practices here. Do you know where I might catch up with him?"

"I have no idea where he just rushed off to," Tonya said with her most flirtatious air. "I can give you his cell number; he said something about an emergency."

"Right," Harry nodded and copied the number to his cell phone. "I promise you sweetheart; every case is an emergency to Dr. Anthony Harding."

The automatic ICU doors flung open, and Tony stepped out into the hallway. He grabbed Harry's hand and arm. "Harry, you are a sight for sore eyes, my friend. What are you doing in San Diego?"

"I took a few days off to bring you something in person," Harry replied.

"You should have called."

"I wanted to surprise you, and to celebrate with my friend." Tony shook his head as if confused.

"There's a family consult room around the corner; we can talk there." He led him to a small cozy room that looked like a family living room.

"If you remember, my father had started building a case for you to take custody of the girls. Well, after Carol died, he went on to pursue some other things."

"What are you talking about, Harry?" Tony said, shrugging his shoulders.

"I know; that's why I wanted to tell you this in person. He started an investigation of her state-run insurance provider, the pharmacists, and the various doctors that enabled Carol to obtain the multiple scripts that kept her habit going. He's trying to prove they all share responsibility for what happened to her. He's ready to file suit on behalf of Nicky and Elizabeth. He even persuaded two representatives to propose legislation to refine the laws against such practices."

"I never gave any of that a thought," Tony said. "I presumed what happened to her was her own fault and possibly mine as well."

"It'll probably take years to resolve with so many defendants," Harry said. "But Dad is in litigation with the bank now over allowing Carol to make withdrawals from your personal savings account. He's hopeful to win a sizeable restitution on top of what they let her have."

"Restitution," Tony gasped. "Are you serious?"

"Yes," Harry replied. "I brought some papers with me that my dad wants you to sign." Tony grabbed Harry by the hand and pulled him in close.

"Harry, Harry, how can I ever thank you and your father?"

"Well, you know my father's a smart attorney," he said, grinning. "There will be money in it for the firm. Besides, Elizabeth is my God-daughter, and I take that responsibility seriously."

"Oh man," Tony sighed, overwhelmed by the news.

"Did you ever tell your family about Elizabeth?"

"No, I never could bring myself to; you're the only one that knows. I'm afraid if I tell someone, then I'll have to face the responsibility of finding her real father, and I'm not ready to do that. She's mine, and I don't want to share her with anyone, particularly if he's some deadbeat drug addict." He paused a few seconds to absorb Harry's news, then slapped him on the knee. "Come with me, I want to show you something interesting." Tony took Harry to Mona's room in the ICU. Tim was standing by her bed along with her mother.

"I should have known something was wrong," Tim cried in a whisper as if trying not to disturb Mona even though she was comatose. "She had turned into someone I didn't know anymore." He rubbed the tears from his face with his hands. "It was those damn computer courses. I know it sounds crazy, Dr. Harding, but that's when it started when she enrolled in that online college. She became obsessed, like an addict. Ask Annette; she was worried about her, too."

"Canbio' su cerebro," her mother added while incessantly staring at her daughter.

"She said her brain changed," Tim whispered. "She's right."

Tony and Harry looked at Mona's chart, and CT scans together on a monitor at the nurse's station. "This is unheard of," Harry commented, as slices of Mona's brain flicked by. "And you say there are others?"

"This makes the third one since I've been here. My boss, Dr. Rick Samuels, has records of others in his office."

"Do you think he'd mind if I looked at them?"

"He asked for my perspective and I have a keycard to his office." They left the ICU and headed to the fifth floor.

"So," Harry said when they were inside the elevator and the doors had closed, "tell me about Annette." His eyes widened when Tony suddenly smiled. "Ha! I knew it; I saw it on your face when Mona's husband said her name."

"She is special," Tony replied and rubbed his hand across his face while he blushed. "You'll meet her later, I promise because you're staying with us while you're here."

"Cool statue of Hypocrites," Harry remarked when they walked through Rick's office toward the conference room.

"Yeah, it gives me the creeps, too," Tony replied. Harry closed the conference room doors as if to give them privacy from the statue while Tony opened the door to Rick's new addition.

"Ricky, you're home early," Lorraine said when Rick surprised her in the kitchen. "Are you hungry?"

"No, I brought some work home," Rick replied and kissed her on the forehead. "There are too many interruptions at the hospital."

"You couldn't get any privacy in that new vault you just added? Oh well, I'm picking Daniel up in a couple of hours," Lorraine reminded. "Would you like me to take him to the park for a while so you can work?"

"I should be finished by then." He hesitated before leaving the kitchen. "Lorraine, Daniel's headaches and his eyes…they're okay, right?"

"Yes, dear," she insisted. "Limiting computer and TV time seems to have worked; he's fine."

"Good; and Kevin?"

"Yes, dear, he's better." Rick went to his office and locked the door behind him.

Lorraine hurried upstairs to her bedroom and closed the door. "Something's wrong," she hissed into her cell phone after punching in Kevin's number. "Your father just came home with a bizarre look on his face, saying he had some work to do. He asked me about Daniel's headaches and you. Did something happen? See if Uncle Randy knows something."

Ty sat on the ground under a tree in a park across the street from the Salvation Army in San Marcos, reading the latest issue of the San Diego Daily Post that he took from the local library. Contributing articles by Sally Samuels were his way of verifying she was okay since Lee had confiscated his computer. He laid the paper down when he noticed a light blue step-side pickup pull into the shelter parking lot. The driver jumped out, hustled around to the passenger door, and helped an ailing man get out. Ty casually walked over to the truck before entering the shelter and observed a khaki shirt in the bed of the truck with blood on it. He went to the bunk room, where a volunteer assessed the passenger's injured ankle. He put his pack on a nearby bed and sat down to eavesdrop.

"You got some bad scrapes on your arms, too," the volunteer said to the man whose face was smudged with dirt.

"Said he tripped and fell down a hill," the truck driver added. "I found him on the side of the road."

"Come on, I'll help you get cleaned up," the volunteer said and helped the man to his feet, supporting him with his shoulder.

"Said somebody was chasing him," the truck driver added. "Should I call an ambulance?" The limping man grumbled something indiscernible to the truck driver while he was being helped to the men's room. Thirty minutes later, the man hobbled back to the bunk with the support of a cane. He was shaven and wearing blue jeans and a black plaid flannel shirt. Ty had made himself at home in the bunk next to his.

"Hey man, what happened?" he asked.

"Nothing," the man said gruffly. "I fell; I'm fine." The truck driver left, and the volunteer returned to check on him.

"Are those clothes rednecks enough for you?" he jibed.

"I suppose," the injured man grumbled.

"You should stay out of the hills until you're well."

The man ambled out of the shelter at 3:00 am. Ty followed and watched him get into the same blue Chevy Stepside that seemed to be waiting for him on the far side of the park behind some bushes. Ty pulled the door handles of every vehicle along the street until he found an unlocked older model black F150 with technology conducive to easy hotwiring. It didn't take him long to catch up to the Chevy that was slowly negotiating the winding road out of town. He followed at a safe distance and soon began reading signs advertising Lake Hodges Campground. The driver ahead put his blinker on before the entrance, so Ty drove the black Ford into the woods. He searched the glove box and found a flashlight and a hunting knife, which he put in his backpack. A pair of jeans, a camouflage cap, and a jacket were behind the seat. He changed into the clothes and a pair of black work boots he found jammed between the cab and the truck bed. He grabbed his pack and trekked through the woods toward the campground. Twisting roads snaked around empty campsites at the perimeter. Most campers were clustered near the water where fishing boats were moored to logs or pulled up on the bank. The light blue truck passed him minus its passenger, which meant he had been dropped off somewhere in the campground. He came upon a smoking fire ring and a white aluminum pull camper whose door suddenly swung open. He recognized Lee when he stepped down the metal steps. He was wearing cowboy boots, jeans, and a brown sweatshirt; a different look for the homeless vagrant, yet similar to the man he followed. Lee grabbed a fishing pole lying against the tongue of the trailer and a small bait can and headed down an embankment. Ty found the shoreline and followed it until he saw Lee casting a line from the water's edge. The old man flung the rod like a pro making the hook and bait fly far out into the dark water; then he sat down on a weathered log to watch the floating bobber after it settled into place.

"I see you found us again." The old man spoke up without taking his eyes off the line. "Come on over here," he demanded. Ty eased closer and knelt on one knee beside him. "I never forget a man's stature or how he carries himself or his eyes." Lee turned his head to look at him. "I see you acquired another pair of contacts."

"I'm not here to harm you, Lee," Ty said bowing his head, acting embarrassed over what Lee knew about him. "Can we talk?"

"You work for The Group; I'm here to destroy them," Lee growled. "Is there anything else to discuss?"

"There are innocent people up there," Ty whispered. "Most of them don't realize what happened to them. My best friend Colin works there."

"So that's who you were communicating with? My guys haven't cracked your code yet, but they will."

"So, you still have my gear?"

"They killed my wife, Ellie," Lee groaned.

"I know your wife's case. The Group re-evaluated its transmission levels because of her. It was their only fatality until…"

"Barksdale?" Lee growled. "Ha! Bullshit!" Lee stood up, reeled in his line and cast it out again. "I dropped out of society after Ellie died," Lee said after settling back on the log. "Living on the street seemed to satisfy my need to be left alone. You see, most people treat us homeless like we're invisible. I started noticing things; people with symptoms just like Ellie had before she died…bloody eyes, headaches, talking to themselves about stuff they shouldn't know anything about. But you see, they got that way after they had disappeared for a week or two. None of them could remember where they'd been or what happened when they returned. I took some to the ER after they crashed. I even started writing their names down as they went missing and kept up with how long they were gone, which ones died, and which ones had to be institutionalized. Dozens are still unaccounted for." He stopped to take a breath as if overwhelmed with emotion. "Sally was reluctant at first, didn't believe me, but she began to take me seriously when her husband started showing the same symptoms."

"How can you be sure it wasn't something else? Street people are in poor health and often turn to alcohol and drugs."

"Being invisible let me overhear doctors discussing their conditions," Lee said, frowning deeply. "Something happened to their brains that caused vessels to become blocked; just like my Ellie and Anderson Barksdale." He shook his head and then looked back at the bobber and muttered under his breath.

"I don't know anything about your friends, Lee; I swear." Ty looked up in the direction of the mountain. "I know The Group is prepping Randy for an important role in politics."

"Sally has my notes," Lee continued, "and some videos of surgeries she stole from her brother-in-law. She wants to write an expose, but I have a swifter plan."

"Your plan will hurt and possibly kill innocent people."

"Putting an end to the things you told me about outweighs any harm that might come to the robots that work up there," Lee grunted.

"The Group is working toward the concept of creating a peaceful society; that's the reasoning behind the enhancement. They have the ability to proliferate dormant neuronal receptors in the brain with synthesized intelligence. It enters the brain through the senses, the key to our awareness and consciousness. The Group has the capability of creating false memories that spawn future actions. It's conveyed by electromagnetic energy. Computerization has made it faster and easier to target the key individuals they want to control. But sometimes the emotional response to the firing of the neurons causes skewed growth in brain cells."

"Because it's not natural," Lee groaned.

"True," Ty said, "evolution hasn't had time to catch up with what they're doing; the human brain won't be ready to tap into its full potential for another century. The government is trying to speed up the process."

"The government?" Lee gasped.

"It's a classified project; the ultimate goal is to create peace. Unfortunately, there are people in charge up there that are trying to satisfy their own agenda; and the project has become so costly that The Group is attempting to partner with the Chinese."

"Then I need to hurry," Lee groaned.

"If you're determined to do this, let me help you." Ty looked across the lake at the timbered mountain. "The man I followed here, the one that was hurt…were they after him?"

"He got caught scouting," Lee groaned, "they locked him up in an underground cell. He escaped before they got too far with their interrogation, but he's complaining of a headache, and his eyes have already turned red. He could get out when the power went out and two boys, teenagers, somehow came along and opened all the doors. There were others down there in too bad a shape to run."

"Teenagers?" Ty sighed. "The power failed? That place has backup-backup systems."

"My guy heard somebody say a kite blew something up on the roof; maybe it was those boys. He's lucky he didn't break his neck; it was a long fall."

"Are your men in these campsites?" Ty asked.

"I've told you too much already."

"Lee, if they are, you should disperse them to the shelters; tell them to scatter. They can use the truck I stashed up the trail, but they'll have to ditch it because I stole it. Believe me; people are looking for your guy right now."

The old man stared at him in silence while he considered the warning.

"I told Sally about you," he said. "That you work for The Group." Ty bowed his head as if in shame.

"So that's why she hasn't called me."

"Actually, I destroyed the phone you gave her." They both looked toward the water after hearing a loud plopping noise. The water was beginning to reflect the light of dawn, and they could see that Lee's cork had disappeared. He stood up, jerked the pole back, and turned the reel. They both chuckled and marveled over the ten-inch trout.

"Nice one; you gonna cook it?" Ty asked him.

"Naw," He had the fish off the hook by now and tossed it back in the lake.

"I have another question, Lee," Ty said after the trout hit the water. "You gave a woman with a little dog something on the boardwalk that she delivered to Sally. Is she part of Sally's agenda?" Lee tightened his lips and shook his head.

"I was being followed that day. I overheard her saying good things about Sally; I panicked."

"Everyone she's been in contact with, all her friends are under the microscope now. Colin is trying to deter any action they might decide to take. I need my tablet to get word to him and keep track of Sally."

"I feel like you're trying to reel me in like I did that trout." Lee picked up the bait can and secured the hook to the pole. "Come with me so I can search you. Which one of your names do you want to go by, Ty or Nate?"

"Sally knows me as Nate; let's go with that."

"Doc has told me very little about you, Harry, but it's nice to meet you," Nette said, as they stood in Tony's kitchen. Tony had dropped Harry at his house and waited with Annette at Molly's until Lizzy arrived, at which time they broke the news to her about Mona. "I wish I felt like bein more cordial, but the news about my friend has me pretty bummed."

"I understand," Harry sighed. "Would you like to go see her, you know, before, um..."

"She doesn't want to see Mona," Tony interrupted, "not like she is."

"Doc told you about Marley next door, and Molly?" Annette asked with a low, trembling voice.

"Yes," he replied and looked at Tony, not knowing if he had told her about the cases they reviewed earlier in Rick's office. Lizzy suddenly appeared in the kitchen carrying Phoebe in her arms.

"Daddy, Daddy, we have to take Phoebe to see Miss Mona right away!"

"Lizzy, honey, we can't take Phoebe to the hospital," Tony said and knelt down beside her. "Harry, this is Phoebe," he said, looking up at his friend. "She belongs to Annette; she and Lizzy have bonded, seriously bonded."

"I see that," Harry said, remembering the stories Tony told him about Elizabeth's profound imagination. "Elizabeth, do you remember me? I'm your godfather, Uncle Harry. You've grown at least three inches since I last saw you."

Lizzy hid behind her father and tightened her hold on Phoebe.

"Yeah, Lizzy gives Phoebe a real workout," Nette added and squatted down beside her. "I think Phoebe likes Lizzy more than me these days."

"But we have to," the little girl said, turning her appeal to Annette. "She made Miss Molly better. You can sneak her in."

"Annette doesn't feel like going to the hospital, sweetheart," Tony said to his daughter and ran his hand through her hair. "Hospitals upset her."

"You're going back to the hospital, aren't you?" Lizzy asked him.

"No, honey; Uncle Harry's here, and I don't do that anymore, remember." Elizabeth's eyes welled up, and she began to sob, and then she fell against her father. Tony put his arm around her, but she pushed him away.

"You saw her magic!" she yelled and ran to her room.

"I'm sorry, Harry," Tony apologized.

"I'll talk to her," Nette said and followed Lizzy.

"She's still very emotional," Harry said, avoiding any clinical term that would suggest a manic disorder.

"She's better actually," Tony said in her defense, "despite her obsessive relationship with Phoebe. Somehow it keeps her centered; that and the mural she's working on in her bedroom. Mona says…" he paused, remembering Mona's condition; "Mona said Lizzy has real talent."

"How bout we check on her later," Harry said. "I have to say this whole morphed architecture has sparked my curiosity. Come on, it'll be like old times, bouncing ideas around in the middle of the night."

"We used to thrive on fatigue," Tony said, smiling. We made some of our best diagnoses under the duress of exhaustion. But I made a promise to the kids and myself, Harry," he sighed. Tony grilled steaks, and they teamed up with Annette and the kids and played basketball in the driveway. Later Harry sat with Lizzy on her bed and admired his godchild's mural. It started in the left corner as a montage of her memories of Chicago and progressed to where her San Diego adventure began.

"Everyone is here," Harry whispered to Lizzy, "your new friends; and I can see that Phoebe is a big part of your life." Lizzy gave him a hug.

"She's a magic dog, Uncle Harry."

"Tell me about her magic?"

"I can't, Uncle Harry," she whispered. "It's a secret." Tony walked Annette home after the girls went to bed.

"Father Clayton emailed a prayer request to everyone in the parish," she whispered, "after giving Mona the last sacrament."

"I'm so sorry, Nette," Tony whispered. "My mother always said the more prayers said for a person, the more tranquil the transition is for everyone." Annette began to cry, and he pulled her close to him.

"What in God's name is happenin, Doc?" she cried. "Is this some kind of horrible virus? Molly spent so much time in her office on the computer, and Mona was obsessed with online college courses, just like Marley. This is all so crazy."

After spending a couple of hours sitting around the glass-top table in the backyard with Harry reminiscing over a couple of beers, Tony gave in to his friend's persistence and agreed to go to the hospital and check on Mona. They met Lizzy in the hallway next to the garage door. "Lizzy, honey, what are you doing up?"

"I-I was using the bathroom, and I heard voices," she said nervously.

"That was just me and Harry talking. Are you okay?" She bowed her head. "Where's Phoebe?" he asked. "I thought Annette left her with you tonight."

"She disappeared," Lizzy said in a low voice and then looked up at Harry. "I mean, I think she went home."

"Uncle Harry and I decided to check on Miss Mona; I was just coming to put you in bed with Nicky." Surprisingly, Elizabeth was delighted with the idea.

"I feel like I just got busted," Tony said as he drove down Gold Coast. "I'm not supposed to be doing this kind of thing anymore. Nicky's going to give me hell in the morning."

"I'll tell her I twisted your arm," Harry argued. Neither one noticed the small stowaway lying on the floorboard behind Harry's seat, even when Tony reached for the ID tag attached to his white coat lying across the back seat. Elizabeth had put Phoebe there and covered her with Tony's dark blue Nike sweater. Harry accidentally knocked the glove compartment door open with his knee when he got out, and the white envelope fell out.

"I forgot about that being in there," Tony said when Harry picked it up off the floor. "Lizzy found it under my seat, and unfortunately, there's only one person that could've put it there."

"It's from the hospital lab," Harry observed.

"Yes," Tony said, "Jane Doe returned this envelope to me."

"With something inside," Harry said after opening it.

"And a note with instructions to give this to her friend Jared Dawson at the *Campus Voice* should anything happen to her."

"Interesting; I can't wait to hear that story." Harry got out of the car and looked up at the large illuminated red sign with white letters in front of him. Then he looked at Tony from across the roof of the Olds. They both smiled at the same time. "I guess we never forget our roots," Harry said.

"I enter through these doors every chance I get," Tony said.

It took Rick more than the anticipated couple of hours to catch up on his work, and when Lorraine brought him a roast beef sandwich at lunchtime, she was taken aback by the stacks of files and CDs scattered across his desk and how quickly he ran to close his laptop after letting her in.

"I'll take Daniel to the park after school," she announced warily. "You look busy, dear."

"That would be great, Lorraine," he sighed as if relieved.

Lorraine left Kevin a voice message while she watched Daniel play on the monkey bars. "He's being very secretive about what he's working on. We need to talk after dinner." Randy Samuels arrived for dinner in response to his nephew's telephone invitation. The two brothers retreated to Rick's office for a cigar after their meal.

"What did Lorraine mean when she said you were locked up in here all day?" Randy asked, noticing Rick's clean desk.

"I had an emergency this morning, and it put me behind on some reports," Rick said as he reached inside the silver humidor on his desk and took out two cigars.

"Oh, anything serious?" Randy asked.

"Another brain abnormality that caused a hemorrhage, and sadly, it doesn't look like the young woman's going to make it." He took a deep breath. "Just like Anderson Barksdale."

"Barksdale, humph; what a disaster that trial turned out to be," he grumbled. "You want a Scotch?" Randy opened Rick's liquor cabinet.

"A real tragedy for sure," Rick sighed. "But other cases like his are mounting."

"Do you need my resources?" Randy asked and poured the whiskey into two glasses. Rick sighed and sat down behind his desk.

"No, this is beyond your scope, I'm afraid," he replied dolefully. "This is something I must take care of."

"Oh, how are you going to do that?" Randy quizzed. "I can't tell you how many of these humidors Sally looked at before deciding on this one," Randy continued when his brother didn't answer, and he helped himself to a cigar. "I would only admit this to you, Ricky," he sighed, staring at the humidor while moving the lid up and down, "but that house is too empty without her. Sometimes when I look at the ocean from the balcony, I…" he paused and smiled as if reminiscing. "I remember how much in love we were; I still love her dammit."

"Oh really?" Rick questioned in disbelief.

"I know," Randy said, exhaling loudly. "I can't help it; even after what she did." He went to the sofa and sat across it in a lounging position with his feet up. "I wish I'd never heard of Anderson Barksdale." He shook his head and took a drink and a long drag on the cigar. "So, what are you going to do about these cases?"

"There all have similarities to Barksdale," Rick reflected as he watched his brother suck on the cigar. "Arthur's been scouting the country looking for others, but the anomaly seems concentrated here in the southwest."

Randy expelled smoke as he spoke.

"Thousands of people die of hemorrhages every day."

"But these have significant changes to their brain's architecture," Rick replied. "Randy, when was the last time you had a complete physical?"

"What? Where did that come from?" Randy laughed and took sip of Scotch.

"I had one myself not long ago," Rick continued. "We're not getting any younger, you know. Come by the office before work in the morning. I'll reserve the machines. And don't forget to fast after midnight."

"You're serious? You better not make me late for court."

Lorraine leaned against the counter next to the sink with her arms folded and watched Kevin take dishes from the sink and stack them in the dishwasher. "Your father actually tried to hide what he was doing from me when I walked in. What do you think he was working on?"

"I heard there was another aneurism patient, and there have been others. He's putting together another paper for the Surgeon General and the State Medical Board."

"How do you know this?" she asked.

"I have my connections."

"Randy; The Group?" she asked and grabbed his arm. "So, was Sally right; that homeless man didn't kill Andy?" He jerked his arm away from her. "Oh, I wish you and Andy wouldn't have hacked into the county's computer system. Everything fell apart after that; Andy died, you lost your job, and Daniel had those headaches. Andy had headaches remember?" she gasped and stared at Kevin. "Kevin, did you and Andy do something more than hack into the county's computer system?" Kevin defiantly clanked the larger dishes together as he loaded them onto the bottom shelf; then, he slammed the door closed.

"What exactly are you asking, Mother?"

"I always suspected you and Andy did something more because of the way they reacted when he died. Is that why you and your uncle are still at odds? Please tell me that Daniel's headaches and eye strain weren't because of something you and Andy were doing. Tell me that he's not going to develop an aneurysm."

"Daniel is fine, Mother. And so am I, in case you're interested. I had headaches too for a while, remember?" Kevin grabbed a Heineken from the refrigerator and angrily popped the cap off. "I'm sure that my father will figure everything out with the help of his bright new protégé."

"Kevin," she panted in dismay as she watched him turn the bottle up and down nearly all the beer. "Of course, I'm glad you're okay, sweetheart. I'm just trying to understand."

"Father always insists on perfection," Kevin said mockingly and threw the bottle into the sink behind him. Lorraine gasped as she watched it bounce and splatter what was left of the beer all over the countertop and the floor. "Maya is his flawless little daughter," he grumbled. "His grandchildren are the smartest, and his staff is unsurpassed." Kevin's eyes squinted to narrow slits, his chest heaved, and his voice deepened. "I've heard it over and over all my life, and you know what? I'm sick of it!"

"Kevin, stop it!" Lorraine ordered. His face furrowed and turned red.

"Do you want to know why I hacked Uncle Randy's system? Well, I was trying to give myself an edge and make myself *perfect*. We stumbled onto a program The Group created. I'm not sure how, but it gave us clarity and intelligence; it changed us, Mother. How did we know Daniel was getting exposed?" Lorraine grabbed him by the shoulders with both hands and shook him.

"What did you do?" He grabbed her hands and shoved her away from him. She slipped on the wet tile and landed on the floor.

"Don't worry," he said, looking down at her, "The Group will take care of everything; they always do."

"My God, Kevin," Lorraine gasped and reached up to him. The sound of the heated conversation lured Rick into the kitchen.

"Kevin!" he shouted when he saw Lorraine struggling to get up and the scowl on his son's face while he held her down by her wrists. She mumbled a feeble excuse that she had only slipped as she crawled to her knees. "What did you do to your mother?" Rick growled. Kevin stared hypnotically at his father who was now bent over his mother, comforting her. He became fixated on the wooden block of knives on the counter next to him that held various carving utensils. He grabbed one of the large knives, cocked his arm back, and aimed it at the middle of his father's back. Randy entered the kitchen.

"What's all the fuss? Kevin!" he shouted when he saw the knife in his hand. He leaped at his nephew and tackled him to the floor.

"Get out!" Rick shouted as Kevin crawled to his feet and stormed out of the kitchen, yelling expletives at everyone. "Pack your bags and get out! Don't even think about taking Daniel with you."

"I'll take care of this," Randy said as he brushed himself off and ran after Kevin.

"You have a text message on your phone, Daddy," Nicky said when Tony and Harry sat at the breakfast table. "It's from Tonya. I fixed you some buttered toast, and there's jelly on the table."

"Thank you, sweetheart. I suppose she's wondering if I'm coming in today after the way I acted yesterday."

"I called a cab to take me to the airport while you were in the shower," Harry said after taking a bite of Nicky's toast. "I've disrupted things around here enough; sorry about making your dad go to the hospital last night, girls. You're not mad at me, are you Lizzy? You're awfully quiet." Lizzy shook her head and took a bite of her toast.

"Couldn't you stay just a little longer, Uncle Harry?" Nicky begged. "I'd like you to come to my game Friday."

"I wish I could, Nicky, but I cut out on a packed schedule. I suppose you're the star player like you were in South C? We did our best to make every game, didn't we?" he said, looking at Tony. "We had to hide from your mom, of course."

"What?" Nicky gasped, nearly choking on her coffee.

"Yeah," he replied. "She'd go nuts every time she saw your dad anywhere near you guys, so we hid in the shadows behind the support beams; you didn't tell her?" Tony and Nicky looked at one another in awkward silence. "Hey, when I come back, I'll make it a point to come check you out," he said, pointing to her with his butter knife. "You know the kid next door can't take his eyes off you?"

"Robby?" she said, laughing. "We're just friends. He's gaga over an ex-girlfriend."

"I suppose your dad has already put the fear of God into him," he snickered.

"Robby and I have come to an understanding," Tony chuckled.

"His sister is recovering nicely," Harry added with a serious nod.

"Thanks to Daddy," Elizabeth said. "He took her to the hospital."

"Thanks to Dr. Rick," Tony corrected.

"Come on, Doc," Harry said. "I like the new name, by the way; there's no telling what might have happened if you hadn't taken control of the situation. She might have—um—a; she might not be recovering as well as she is." Nicky looked at her father from the corner of her eyes and halfway smiled.

"Come on, man, you're embarrassing me," Tony sighed and got up from the table. "I've got something in my office for you to take back to Chicago." Harry's cab pulled up just as Todd drove off to school with the girls. He put the brown envelope with the legal documents containing Tony's signature in his carry-on bag before loading it into the back seat. "I had Scott make a copy of Jane Doe's memory card," Tony said. "I added the things we copied last night, plus an interesting video the boys made. It's in the envelope with the legal papers. Call me, and we can compare notes like we used to, except now it'll be over Skype or whatever Scott can hook me up with."

"Jane Doe obviously thinks she's in trouble," Harry said, "and is trusting you to help her."

"I wish we had more time to hash this out together," Tony replied.

"So do I," Harry agreed, "We were always a good team."

"I miss that, Harry," Tony said. The two men shook hands and bear-hugged before Harry slid into the seat. Tony's cell phone rang as the cab drove off.

"I'm on my way, Tonya," he answered after seeing her name on the screen. "No, you can tell me when I get there. Just have my patient files ready-what? She woke up? That's impossible!" Tony went directly to ICU. Mona's improvement wasn't as dynamic as Tonya had led him to believe on the phone, but her eyes were open, and she was answering simple yes and no questions with hand squeezes. Her mother prayed in Spanish, and Tim's eyes welled with tears when he saw him. His voice quaked as he relayed how the nurses suddenly started rushing in and out just before Mona opened her eyes.

"I thought she was dying, but actually, she was coming back to life." Rick was at the nurse's station paging through her chart and watching the monitor.

"When did this happen?" Tony asked.

"The nurse on duty noted a rise in her brain patterns around 2:00 am," he said, quoting from the chart. "Her readings are far from normal, and she's nowhere near out of the woods, but," he pointed to the monitor registering her current brain waves, "it's remarkable. The human body is miraculous."

"Was Phoebe with you last night?" Tony asked Annette when he called her from his office to tell her the encouraging news. "Harry and I ran into Elizabeth in the hallway last night; she said Phoebe had disappeared. I think she might have wrapped her in my sweater and put her in my car. I found the sweater on the floorboard behind my seat; I'm sure I left it in the dryer.

"I-I," she stammered and began to cry, "I don't know what time she came home. I don't know what to say."

"I know," Tony sighed, instead of saying how insane it sounded to think that Phoebe could have corrected Mona's condition. "Neither do I; we'll talk later."

He met Randy coming out of Rick's office, and the two men shook hands and exchanged *good mornings*. Tonya was her usual animated self, dressed in an orange mini skirt with matching imitation corn row braids decoratively pinned in her hair. She reported that Dr. Rick's brother had an *all-inclusive physical* before office hours, including an MRI of his brain, which made Tony pause and wonder why the extensive imaging tests. It never occurred to him that Randy might have been searching his brother's office for the Surgeon General report after being prompted to do so by his smartphone; or that Tonya would do the same after a compelling signal from her computer. Neither found what they were looking for.

"You're never gonna believe what happened," Annette said on the way home from Molly's that afternoon. "Out of the blue, Jeffrey and Justin's mother was released from prison due to over crowdin. She's on probation and stayin with her mother. No one had a clue this was gonna happen. I have my concerns, but at least it will keep them away from Larry's for a while."

Willis Shepherd sat in the conference room alongside Joseph Rodriguez, tediously reviewing video from Rick Samuel's home and office on the large overhead monitor.

"These are the images from the set of bookends we had his son rig," Rodriguez commented.

"No doubt he's compiled another report," Shepherd added.

"This is from the Family Practice parking lot this morning after the office search turned up nothing," Rodriguez continued. They watched a video on a split screen of a security guard parked his truck alongside Dr. Samuels' Cadillac. Rodriguez smiled as the guard gave into the impulse given him to use a flat pop-lock blade on the driver's door and then reach inside and grab a briefcase on the passenger seat. After prying it open, he took a stun gun and pressed it against the laptop inside until it produced smoke. Then he proceeded to melt the CDs in the same manner with the gun's electrical discharge.

"That should send him a clear message," Shepherd remarked.

Chapter 33

A yellow three-by-five invitation card decorated with daisies, bees, and butterflies, was pinned to the staff bulletin board announcing a party for Molly on Saturday at the Mesa Village Retirement Center.

"Bring a dish…hum," Nette sighed, wrinkling her nose.

"We've been waiting for Dr. Samuels' approval," Lisa said, peering over Nette's shoulder. "I think we could use a party." Annette agreed with a nod.

That afternoon, she sat at the kitchen table next to Tony while he paged through his mother's cookbook. "I've decided on the chicken and rice casserole," he said. "What are you going to bring?"

"Me?" she laughed. "I don't think…"

"Whatever you decide will be fine," he said, smiling in response to the baffled look on her face. "Do you think the boys will come?" he asked. "Have you met their mother?"

"Catrina," she said. "It's hard to tell what someone's like in ten minutes. She thanked me for bein their godmother and helpin her mother with the boys. She said the worst part of goin to prison was havin to leave them in Larry's custody. She doesn't act like an ex-con or near what Larry described, so I'm kinda confused." Tony closed the cookbook and put his hands over hers.

"They'll be back in your living room playing Xbox before you know it."

"Am I that obvious?" she said, laughing.

"Now, do you have any of your mother's recipes?"

"I have my grandmother's cookbook; it's in the bedroom.

"Why would you keep a cookbook in your bedroom?" he asked, climbing onto the wildflower-printed comforter and the bedside table to reach the top shelf. "I see you don't do much dusting up here. Wait a minute; what's this?" He held up the bottle of English Leather cologne by the wooden top.

"It was my father's," Annette said and crawled onto the bed. "The cookbook is there, leanin against the wall. Be careful…" The bottle suddenly slipped out of the decorative wooden top and fell on the bed next to Annette.

She picked it up and breathed in the quintessential fragrance from under the cap. "Oh my God, this is the mystery cologne, isn't it?" Tony stepped down off the nightstand with the cookbook under his arm and the wooden top in his hand, which Annette took from him. "The glue inside dried up a long time ago," she whispered as she put the top back on the cap. "Nothin else smells like it because it's so old," she whimpered. "This very smell was in your room."

"This is the bottle that keeps appearing on my dresser."

"I was afraid of that," Annette looked at him and then scrambled off the bed, but Tony grabbed her arm.

"Wait," he whispered and wrapped his arms around her. "I have to admit, I'm having trouble making sense of this," he said, taking the cologne from her. "But I'm trying."

"What am I gonna do, Doc? I'd give anything for things to just be normal."

"What's the fun in that?" he said, grinning at her. "Besides, I'm beginning to think that normal is learning how to deal with all the crazy things that are gonna happen whether we want them to or not."

Annette couldn't help but smile. Then she pulled him against her and closed her eyes. "Now I feel normal, and I haven't felt this way for a long time." She looked up at him; they kissed and then sank into the lush floral and kissed again.

People trickled into the senior center just before noon on Saturday. Annette made red beans and rice with sausage using a recipe from her grandmother's cookbook, which Doc gave an approving nod after a taste test. Robby strutted in with his guitar, wearing a SOA tee that showed part of a tattoo on his chest as well as the chain on his arm. He set up a keyboard adjacent to the hired DJ; Scott soon followed, carrying a laptop that he connected to Robby's keyboard. The guest of honor arrived fashionably late by one hour with her sister, Charlotte, dressed in her signature blue and white shapeless muumuu. She took her seat beside Charlie and Lewis at their usual poker table.

"Molly, I know this is who you really want to see," Annette said and placed Phoebe on her lap.

"Oh," Molly squealed. "How's my little girl?" she said, hugging Phoebe. "Oh, my sweet little darling, I miss our little talks." She kissed her on the nose, and in turn, Phoebe licked her on the lips. "I miss all of you so much; thank you, thank you." Nette sat on the floor next to her.

"Has Dr. Rick said when you can come back to work?"

"Oh, honey, I'm not coming back," she said and put her hand against Nette's cheek. "I'm going to stay with Charlotte. We are going to move into one of the houses in the new section. I recommended UCSD to allow Lisa to take over as manager. Something in my heart told me to spare you of that responsibility. Management is so stressful, just look at what it's done to me, and the children love you so much just as you are." She leaned closer and whispered. "This way, you can spend more time with Doc."

"Molly," Nette whined. "Will you never stop?" The DJ played soft music while people went through the reception line and filled their plates at the buffet table, and when the DJ took his break, Robby picked up his guitar and picked up the pace with some soft rock that Nicky refused to dance to because she was too embarrassed by her father and Nette's dance moves.

"Jose came by the house earlier to check on Lizzy's mural," Tony said as they swayed to a slow tune. "So, when are you going to tell me his story?"

"Oh, um," she said, bowing her head. She looked around to make sure no one was close enough to overhear. "I was drivin home from Chula Vista one night after takin some kid's home after ball practice. Just as I approached the Old Town exit on I-5, Phoebe started barkin and carryin on, jumpin from the front to the back. I thought I was goin to wreck. Then suddenly, she was gone;" she paused and took a breath, "you know what I mean. I took the Old Town exit," she continued when Tony nodded; "I stopped the car and started lookin for her. It's a bad part of town, but I had to find her. I looked up and saw this huge mural on the overpass wall with Jose's tag on it." She looked around again to make sure no one was listening. "Jose walked out of the shadows carryin Phoebe." She drew nearer to him in order to whisper in his ear. "He told me he was suspended over the edge of the overpass in a climbing harness painting when the strap broke. He saw someone lean over the side and put his hand out as he was falling. It didn't make sense to him how the guy thought he was gonna be able to reach the strap, but time seemed to slow down, and the man grabbed hold and then gently lowered him. Jose yelled out to him as he lay on the ground, but the man moved out of sight. When he sat up, Phoebe was sitting beside him." Annette put a hand on Tony's chest. "She put her paw on his chest like this. She does that to me sometimes; it's like she's tryin to comfort me."

"The man," Tony said. "Did he describe him?" Their rhythm had slowed to almost a standstill.

"It was too dark; he could make out the floppy hat and a jacket. Homeless people bed down on the ground under that overpass, but no one could do somethin like that."

"But we both know what happened," Tony whispered. Annette bowed her head. "It affected him so deeply that he changed the tag on all his artwork."

"From Jose' to *Jesus,*" Tony whispered, "the way he signed your truck and his work at the boardwalk."

"He doesn't like to talk about what happened; he just tells people that he gives all the glory for his talent to Jesus Christ, the son of God, who sent his son to save him." They were barely moving on the dance floor; they were dancing to a rhythm of their own. Annette couldn't help but wonder how many more of these uncanny tales Doc would be able to take. His eyes were endearing, and she wanted to kiss him right there in front of everyone, but his eyes shifted to the side door that led to the gym.

"Isn't that Cass?" he asked, moving closer to Nicky, who had braved a slow dance with Jeffrey. She immediately recognized her friend's stringy wind-blown bleach-blonde hair.

"I gave her one of those invitations." Jimmy appeared right behind her, tugging on her arm, trying to stop her. "She threw it back at me and said she had something better to do than to waste her time with our lame party."

"Where are you going?" Annette asked when Doc broke from them and headed to the door. Annette looked at Robby; he had already spotted Cass.

"Jimmy's trouble," Nicky whispered.

"Doc will take care of it," Nette sighed. When he returned ten minutes later, he confessed that he had to pin Jimmy against the wall when he became a smart ass. He told Cass she could stay, but she chose to leave with him.

"Robby shouldn't waste his time getting tattoos to compete with that punk," Tony told Nicky after taking her hand when the music started again. He gave her a crash course in rock-n-roll that lasted all of 15 seconds when she rushed back to the table thoroughly humiliated. When the music slowed, Tony grabbed Annette around the waist and pulled her in close.

"Where did you learn to dance anyway?" Nette laughed, staring into his chestnut eyes.

"I have two older sisters, remember?" he replied and then led her around a half circle. "I was their Guinea pig from the time I could stand. I learned a lot about girls from those two. Well, about most girls."

"You're full of surprises, Dr. Harding," she said.

"Yeah, you're right, so you'd better hold on," he whispered and spun her around.

"These are my favorite pictures from home," Annette told Tony later as they sat on her porch.

"This one, here," Tony said, stopping her on a page with a snapshot of a man standing beside a black pickup truck wearing a brown jacket and a floppy hat. "This looks like the guy I saw; although his face was never clear."

"I know how you feel about wacky beliefs, Doc," she said, closing the book. "I don't mean to be like the people who believe in aliens and UFOs or Voo Doo."

"It's been proven that when the mind doesn't understand what it's seeing," he said, "it fills in the blanks from memories of the things we know; but the problem is, I never met your father."

"Rick, we need to talk," Tony said when he met his boss in the hallway Monday morning. His elder looked tired and aged as he unlocked the door to his office.

"Is something wrong?" Tony asked, following Rick to his desk. "Is it Mona?"

"No, she's actually doing remarkably well," Rick sighed and then sat down. "After our talk last week, I went home and wrote another detailed report. I attached some videos and emailed them to the Surgeon General's office and the State Board."

"And?" Tony asked. "You received a rejection?" he asked when Rick bowed his head, looking dejected.

"It takes weeks to even get an acknowledgment," the elder said, not having the heart to tell him his email had failed and the hard copies destroyed.

"I looked over your case files," Tony said. "You're right about an outside stimulation. The damage to the optic nerve is definitely a clue."

Rick sat in silence, staring at his library of medical books. He suddenly got up, pulled a book from the shelf, and handed it to Tony.

"Neuro-ophthalmology," Tony said, reading the title. Rick pulled another book down.

"Lorraine and I have talked it over, son; I'm retiring right away…immediately. The practice is yours if you want it. If not, I'll start the search process. Tonya will be here to help you either way."

"Why would you leave a practice you just started?" Tony quizzed.

"Kevin and Lorraine had a horrible fight. I threw him out. Randy has him put up somewhere and is drawing up the necessary paperwork so we can have him committed. Lorraine is devastated."

"I'm sorry," Tony sighed. "But, you can still…"

"You're the only one that can run this place as I do," he said and handed him another book and then ran his fingers along the spines of the nearby reference books. "I can artificially strengthen weak arteries and repair bulges with injections and grafts, but I don't know how to slow neuronal communication. Marley and Mona, for example, their neurons were communicating so rapidly it reconstructed their intellectual cortex. The medication required to slow that process would cease normal brain function."

"Yes, I know," Tony said and took one last book from Rick entitled *Neuro Plasticity*.

"I had a case, it must have been twenty years ago," Rick continued; "when PET scans and MRI were at their threshold and before the Laser surgical techniques used today. A man brought his wife to the ER; she was suffering from severe headaches and blurred vision. Her eyes were bloodshot, like Marley's and Mona's, and there was pressure on the optic nerve. A scan showed a bulge in an artery, so I rushed her to surgery, but it burst during prep. Her husband was livid. He called me every day for months wanting to know why his wife died. He kept insisting it was the computer they bought. He rambled about how she was addicted to it, and her eyes got more bloodshot every time she used it. They would fight when he suggested she turn it off. It was a hard case to forget. Does any of that sound familiar?"

"That's why you can't quit," Tony said. "Let's figure this out together." Rick shook his head.

"No, I'm letting it go; I have to concentrate on keeping my family intact and well." The determination in his eyes told Tony that his boss had made up his mind.

Lorraine hurried down the stairs after seeing her husband standing in the family room staring out the French doors. "Sweetheart," she gasped when she reached him. "You're home early again." His abysmal stare frightened her when she touched him on the arm and he didn't look at her. "Ricky," she whispered. "What is it; did you hear from Randy? Did he find a hospital for Kevin?"

"He wasn't at work today, so I'm assuming that's what he's doing. Someone broke into my car," he whispered. "They destroyed my computer and my report. The file I emailed to the Surgeon General's office was intercepted; Randy's MRI was somehow deleted from the entire hospital system."

"How, why would someone…?" she gasped. He ignored the anxiety in her eyes when he finally turned and looked at her.

"Someone is doing everything they can to stop me from reporting my findings on a serious brain abnormality; an abnormality that I believe is affecting Kevin."

"And Andy?" her voice quivered. "Is-Kevin-going-to?" she stuttered. "He said something happened to them after they hacked into The Group system. He became violent when I pressed him about it; you saw him; oh my God, Daniel."

"Yes, it's been going on right under my nose. I've been trying to determine exactly how this anomaly is delivered. Somehow The Group knew about the report I was preparing." He slowly scanned the large family room. "Lorraine, I want you and Daniel to go to Myra's for a few days."

"Ricky," Lorraine moaned, "you're frightening me."

The Post lifted Sally's probation, leaving her free to cover high-profile stories again. It kept her busy during the day and her mind off Randy, Nate, Lee, The Group, and Jared. But at night, she drank too much wine and lamented over the story her conscience wouldn't let her forget. Her heart still yearned to present the story about the strange brain growth patterns that compressed arteries to the point of rupture, as demonstrated in Rick's small collection of video files. She could easily claim the facts were from an anonymous source. A statement from Lee was a tempting verification, but would readers believe a man who had been living on the streets for twenty years, even if he had specific names and dates of the fallen vagrants recorded in a journal? She was beginning to think perhaps Lee was right; maybe his plan was the best. She tried to call Randy's cell with the phone Lee gave her. There was a click, and his voice recited the outgoing message. "I miss you, Randy," she whispered into the phone. "I'm so sorry; I just needed to hear your voice."

The next morning, Tonya, dressed in black leggings and a long teal green velveteen shirt, approached Tony with two stacks of patient files. "Dr. Rick won't be in, Dr. Harding," she sighed, sounding overwhelmed. "He called to say you are in charge, and you should divvy up the patients."

"All right," Tony replied reluctantly and then looked across the patient waiting room. "I guess we're going to be backed up for a while; wait, what's she doing here?" He recognized a shapely young woman with a blonde ponytail and short skirt sitting in one of the chairs.

"That's your nine-thirty," Tonya whispered and winked at him, alleging his interest in the woman could be something more than a patient. "She specifically asked for you," she sighed sensually and twirled the black and green beads around her neck between her fingers. Tony flipped through the folders until he found the lovely Rebecca's file.

"Too bad we're so jammed up today; she's gonna have to take potluck." After seeing his last patient for the day, he let himself into Rick's office.

"Dr. Harding left Samuels' office carrying a file box," Shepherd conveyed to his partner after looking at the security video from Rick's office and parking lot.

"I sent the female operative to his office to distract him," Joseph growled.

"Sorry, your plan never came to fruition," Shepherd replied. "Our people on Antrim will find out what's in the box." Joseph pounded the keyboard in front of him.

"I'm going to have to devise something more serious to keep him out of our hair. It's time I made my point, as I did with Rick Samuels."

It took Father Clayton a few minutes to figure out where the late-night tapping was coming from since there was no vehicle parked in the driveway. He followed the sound to the back door and saw someone wearing a hooded sweater standing outside through the mini blinds. "Who's there?" he asked through the door.

"It's me, Father," a muffled voice replied.

"You'll have to do better than that," the priest insisted.

"Father, open the damn door!" It was a female voice. He opened the door and the mysterious visitor rushed inside. She asked if he was alone and then closed the blinds in the kitchen before pulling the hood back.

"I should have known, Sally," he sighed. "What happened this time? Good Lord your hands are shaking. Come into the prayer room. Would you like some tea or something stronger?" A few minutes later, she was sitting in the prayer room clutching a glass of wine and scrutinizing the images of Jesus, his mother, Mary, the Apostles, and various other saints and angels that adorned the humble chamber. A thick Bible lay open in front of the prayer stand. The kneeling cushion had two indents that surely were Father Clayton's impressions. "I was so sure I could shake things up enough to force Randy to come to his senses. But I didn't realize the extent of The Group's control over him, over everything; I feel so helpless and isolated."

"The Group," Father Clayton said while pulling a chair beside her. "I'm not sure what you mean, Sally, but there is always hope."

"I've put people in danger," she whispered. "Nothing short of an army can stop them." Father Clayton smiled at her.

"Then you must call on God's army." He looked at the kneeling stand. "Sometimes we have to leave it to Him. He will help if you ask." The priest lit the candle under the picture of Jesus gazing into the heavens hanging on the wall. "You can stay in the guest room if you like. I'll tell my housekeeper that I'm giving you a temporary refuge from an abusive situation. You should attend Mass this Sunday, Sally. The Word says when we gather in numbers to pray it is received with great profusion. And I've seen ample proof of it lately." He genuflected in front of the open Bible. "Would you like to walk over to the church with me?"

"No," she sighed, "I'd rather be alone." The worshipful images around the room seemed to be waiting in anticipation as she rose from her chair, stepped to the rail, and placed her knees inside the indentations. She clasped her fingers around her hands the way the nuns taught her as an unwilling child. She closed her eyes and began to pray while outside, an operative assigned to her sent her recorded conversation with Father Clayton to the Escondido mansion.

Tony enlisted Scott's help in sending a number of Rick's large case files to his friend Harry in an email. It took most of the night, and the ten-year-old wasn't used to sleeping on Dr. Harding's sofa; he was still awake when his iPhone vibrated. The text was from his mother at work, telling him she loved him. She hadn't expected him to see the message for a few more hours. It buzzed again. The second text was from Guardian, who fully expected him to be awake and to respond.

S: *Spending night with Dr. Harding; installed your firewall on his PC.*

Hope I didn't overstep. Was necessary in order to send large

confidential files to his friend in Chicago.

Scott's phone vibrated again when Guardian replied to his text, but a knock on the back door sidetracked him. Tony heard it, too, and they met in the doorway to the kitchen. Tony quickly opened the back door after looking through the blinds and seeing Annette standing on his porch, wiping tears from her cheeks.

"I don't understand, Doc," she sobbed. Phoebe eased through the door while Tony consoled her, cowering along the wall in the kitchen until she was safely under the table; Scott knelt down and beckoned her to come to him.

"My album was on the sofa," Annette sobbed. "I distinctly remember climbing on the bed and putting it back on the shelf. She put her paw on every person in each photo as I called their name; there were many she couldn't possibly have known."

When Scott left to go home, Annette was sitting at the table with a wet rag across her forehead, and Dr. Harding was sliding a cup of coffee in front of her. Scott looked down at his phone while he crossed the front yard. Guardian's text was still on the screen. He asked if there was any more news about Nightcrawler.

"*Affirmative*," he replied and relayed Annette's reason for being upset.

Tony placed his Nike sweater over Annette's shoulders and walked her home. "The girls will think I'm on my morning run."

"I'm sorry for freakin out like that," she sighed.

"You know you can freak out with me anytime you want," he said and pulled her closer to him.

The tires of the black Lincoln Navigator picked up gravel from the edge of the road and flung it over the side of the less barricaded area of scenic Hwy 15. There was no traffic to elude tonight, and it entered the discreet drive without concern. It was observed, however, by the two men crouched beneath the trees just below the road. Nate and Lee had been scouting the hillside around the fortified Spanish mansion, looking for a viable assault route. "The only entrance beside the main gate is the drive that Navigator just turned into. It forks and leads to an underground parking lot and a breezeway entrance that's controlled by a technician on Sub Level 1. There are stairs to the bell tower and the roof with a well-guarded helicopter pad."

"How far down is the parking lot?" Lee asked.

"One level," Nate replied, "and fortified with security cameras. Colin will help us, but we'll have to make a significant distraction. You know if they get their hands on you, they'll give you something much stronger than what you gave me; and then after you spill your guts, they'll dump your body out in the ocean."

"Why did you tell me all that stuff if you weren't under?" Lee asked.

"I was trying to scare you out of doing something like this."

"I'll take them down first before they can get their hands on me."

"I'm not going in there without an escape plan," Nate whispered.

"I don't care if I escape," Lee sighed.

"I want my friend to get out of there alive. Colin and I got into this because we believed in the enhancement project. We were convinced it made people intelligent and creative and gave them the ability to live more fulfilled lives."

"So that's what you do up there," Lee said, "make people smarter and fulfilled? What about the ones you killed?"

"I swear, Lee; I was never told about that. Colin and I deal with high-priority matters that require fine-tuning. Theoretically, The Group is trying to create and maintain a harmonious society."

"You knew about the Ellie…and Barksdale. Why are you here with me?"

"Because," Nate paused, "I realized you can't have a perfect society when the people running things are imperfect, vindictive, and greedy," he said. "Our superiors want to take the project in a direction of their own."

The Navigator stopped at the door within the vine-covered stone breezeway. Four operatives quickly exited and pulled two lifeless forms from the back of the vehicle and carried them inside the complex, and then the SUV sped away.

Chapter 34

The top two rows of one section of the bleachers were noticeably made up of Nicky Harding fans because with every score she made, some sort of cheer, whistle, or dog howl erupted from there, and it didn't take long for the rest of the scanty crowd to be drawn in. Coach Burns put Nicky and Cass on the bench at the half after they had run the score up by 70 points.

"My father is such an ass," Cass grumbled.

"It's cool," Nicky replied. "You should come with us to get pizza after the game. It'll give you and Robby a chance to, you know, make up."

"Who says I want to hook up with that loser again?" Cass huffed.

"Just come with us anyway," Nicky laughed. "It'll be fun." As it turned out, Cass came along, but so did her father after Dr. Harding unwittingly added him to Nicky's invitation. It put a damper on Cass's mood. She and Robby barely spoke to each other, but there was a lot of glancing and looking away.

Tony was now spending his nights reading the books Rick gave him until his watch alarm sounded at 11:00, at which time he would trek across the alley to say goodnight to Annette. He considered skipping tonight's study because it was late when they got home from pizza, but once he opened Rick's book on neuroplasticity, he became engrossed and forgot to turn the alarm on. When he heard a knock on the door, he immediately realized his mistake and headed to the back door, thinking it was Annette. But when he reached the living room, he realized the knock was coming from the front door, and without looking through the peephole, opened it.

Annette was lying in her bed wondering why she hadn't heard from Doc. "If somethin's wrong, he'd call, wouldn't he?" she asked Phoebe, who was lying beside her. "He's probably readin those books again. I guess the girls are right about him forgettin about time. Is this somethin I should be worried about? Maybe if I put on one of those skinny dresses Marley gave me and sneak over there, I can make him forget about the books."

Scott was distracted from his tablet when he saw a car pull up in front of the Harding house. A woman wearing a gray raincoat and shiny red high heels stepped out and walked to the front door. Scott shook Robby, who was sprawled across his bed sleeping, and motioned for him to come to the window.

"Yo, what's she doing here so late?" Robby gasped when he recognized the strikingly attractive Rebecca. Scott pulled up the four views from the roof-mounted cameras.

"I'll get her license number and have, uh-oh," he panted when he saw activity on another camera. "Annette's crossing the alley! Look at the dress she's wearing!" Scott had seen her in dresses at church before, but never anything as seductive as the scanty blue dress and heels she had on.

"Crap!" Robby shouted and ran from the room. Scott followed him to the alley holding the tablet, but Annette was already at Doc's back door, looking through the window and turning the doorknob. Annette slipped off the heels and quietly moved through the kitchen to not wake the girls. She saw Tony standing inside the front door with a woman when she reached the living room. Her coat was on the floor, and she had nothing but a pair of red stilettos and a tiny red thong. Her arms were wrapped around his neck, and he had his hands on her waist. The blue heels slipped out of Annette's hand when the woman hooked her leg around his calf.

"You bastard," she yelled and ran out the kitchen door, slamming it behind her.

"We should do something," Scott whispered from their hiding place at the corner of the fence. "I have no idea how to intervene in a situation like this."

"We need to duck cuz shit's fixin to hit the fan," Robby sighed. Twenty seconds went by that seemed more like twenty minutes. The gate suddenly flew open. They watched Annette slam it closed behind her and march across the alley and then pull her gate open and slam it closed with the exact same vigor.

"I've never seen her like that," Scott gasped. They heard a car door slam behind them, so they scrambled to the front yard just in time to see Rebecca speeding away. Frankie and Johnnie were yelping by now, so they hurried back to the alley. Doc was standing outside his gate holding Annette's blue heels.

"Did you guys see Nette?" he huffed.

"Yeah," Robby panted. "What happened to make her so mad, Doc?"

"Damn," he replied and rubbed the back of his neck. "She saw something she shouldn't have." Frankie and Johnnie put their wet noses through the fence links as if sympathizing.

"Yeah, man," Robby said, "we saw who was at your front door."

"Wait!" Tony rebutted, "I didn't invite her over. I had no idea it was her at the door." Phoebe trotted up and pawed at Tony's pant leg. Then they heard a door slam and a motor start. Tony picked up Phoebe and they all rushed to Annette's front yard just in time to see the 4-runner back out of the driveway and then leave rubber on the pavement as it sped away. "I guess she's pretty mad," Tony sighed. Phoebe snorted, seemingly in agreement.

"Here," Scott said and held the tablet up so Doc could see the quartered screen. He replayed Annette standing at Tony's back door seconds after Rebecca was let in the front.

"What did she see, Doc?" Robby quizzed.

"This is a horrible misunderstanding," Tony sighed. "That woman just showed up on my doorstep, forced her way in, and then laughed at me when I shoved her out the door."

"What are you gonna do?" Scott sighed.

"I'm going to find her and explain," Tony declared to which Phoebe yelped once. "Here," Tony said and handed Phoebe to Robby. "And watch the girls. Don't wake them up, and no funny business," he added, pointing a finger at the teenager. "You, keep an eye on him," he said, pointing to Scott.

"Yes, sir," Scott replied.

Annette had turned right onto Gold Coast, so Tony headed in the same direction, slowing as he went by the rectory, thinking she might have stopped and unburdened herself to Father Clayton. He stared at the stop sign when he reached Canyon Road, realizing he had no idea which way to turn. Then he saw a pair of black tire marks on the road heading north toward Mesa Blvd. He rode up and down Mesa Blvd. twice and cruised through the mall parking lot but didn't see the tagged Toyota anywhere. He was about to give up when he caught a glimpse of the flagship parked in front of a sports bar on a side street. *She must really be pissed; this is the last place I would expect to find her.* She was sitting at the bar talking to Darren from the rec center when he went inside. The music was loud and she was laughing about something he said to her. She looked beautiful, from her light brown hair reflecting the colors of the lights over the mirrored shelves of liquor bottles to the clingy short blue dress she had on that exposed all her curves. Her tanned, slim legs even made the flip-flops she was wearing look sexy. The bartender put drinks in front of her and Darren, and they moved from the bar to sit at a table. Darren saw him first when he turned to sit down; then Annette, when she looked to see who Darren was looking at.

"Hey, Doc," Darren said and walked toward him. "What are you doing here? Hey, Nette, look who's here?"

"Shut up, Darren!" Annette growled as she stormed past them and headed to the door. Tony grabbed her by the arm.

"I thought you didn't drink?" he gruffed, looking at the drink in her hand. "And what are you doing here with Darren?" He regretted his words as soon as they came out of his mouth. She jerked her arm away from him.

"Well, I guess you were wrong, Dr. Harding," she snarled back at him. "And I guess I was wrong too; sooner or later, old habits re-surface." She walked out the door.

"Annette, wait," he said, following her outside. "It wasn't what it looked like." She stopped and turned around, and then threw her drink in his face and ran to her truck. Tony expected to taste the bitter sting of alcohol on his lips but realized it was only water and wiped his face with his hand. Darren appeared behind him.

"You're gonna have to give that sweet thing a little time to cool off, Doc," he said, chuckling.

"Shut up, Darren!" Tony growled and left him standing alone in front of the sports bar. He went home but told the boys he couldn't find her. Darren was probably right; she needed time to cool off. But he stared at the ceiling all night, thinking and worrying, wondering if she would ever believe him. He never told her about Rebecca. They talked about everything else, his apprehensions with parenting, Rick's cases, Sally's badgering. Why didn't he tell her he had a stalker? *Why did I try and turn things around on her with Darren? God, how am I going to fix this?* He sneaked a peek at Lizzy, who was sleeping soundly while he made coffee the next morning. Nicky's door was closed. He could put off telling them about the fight a little while longer. Two cups of Folgers weren't much help as he sat alone at the kitchen table. He was worn out from lack of sleep and worry. He used to thrive on exhaustion, but this was a different kind of burden. Robby and Scott startled him when they burst in through the back door. And to his surprise, Nicky was with them.

"She's gone, Doc," Robby blurted out. "Her truck's in the driveway, but she's gone. We found this on her computer." He handed Tony two sheets of paper.

"Nicky, what are you doing with these guys?" he began but saw the angst in her eyes. "How did you get into her house?"

"Yo, all us kids know she keeps a key under the mat on the back porch," Robby answered as if surprised that he didn't.

"This is the last site she visited," Scott reported. "It's a Delta flight itinerary. And this is an email to her mother in Louisiana," he added, pointing to the second sheet.

"She must have taken a cab to the airport," Robby added, "and took Phoebe with her because we can't find her either."

"Her flight leaves in forty-five minutes," Tony said, looking at his watch. He jumped to his feet and headed to the garage. He could feel the adrenaline pumping as he wove through traffic on southbound I-5. He kept telling himself all the way there that if he could just keep her from getting on the plane, then everything would be okay. He would apologize for being such a jerk the night before, and he would explain that Rebecca was the one making the advances, that the seduction seemed to be a setup. He would beg her to understand. It took him thirty minutes to get to the airport and another ten to find a parking space. He ran into the terminal with the flight confirmation in his hand, but he was stopped at the bottom of the escalator because he didn't have a boarding pass. He tried to convince the security agent that it was an emergency, but he was referred to the Emergency Services desk. He turned to look for it, knowing it would take too long.

"Doctor Harding?" a woman's voice called out. "Is that you?"

"Brenda?" he gasped when he turned around. Scott's mother walked toward him, dressed in an airport security uniform with Phoebe in her arms.

"I was hoping someone would show up for her. Annette didn't consider getting her a ticket, so I agreed to take her home."

"Has her plane left?" Tony asked and took Phoebe from her. "I-I have to..."

"Scott texted me," she said; "he said you two had a fight." Tony closed his eyes and opened his mouth to speak, but nothing came out. "Her plane has boarded already," she said and looked at her watch; "come with me." She led him to a courtesy cart and drove him through the concourse with the lights flashing and the horn beeping until they reached the gate that boarded to Houston, the first leg of Annette's trip. All the chairs were empty, the boarding doors were closed, and the attendant was gone. Brenda exited the cart and rushed to the desk. Tony followed her with Phoebe in his arms. She picked up a radio from its dock on the counter and called for the plane's captain. "I'm sorry, Dr. Harding," she sighed when the captain replied with a loud "Negative". They walked to the observation window and watched the Boeing 747 turn toward its assigned runway and then, five minutes later, take off. Brenda looked at him sympathetically. "I'm sorry; we were just too late. Is there anything else I can do? Perhaps I could have the tower radio the captain and get a message to her."

"No," Tony sighed and bowed his head. "I don't think that would help. Thank you for trying." Each time Tony looked at Phoebe in the passenger seat next to him on the way home, she was staring at him. Her expression made him think she felt as dejected as he was. "Why didn't she buy you a ticket?" he finally asked her. Phoebe replied with a mournful sound. "She takes you everywhere. She would have bought you a ticket." Phoebe stared at him in silence. "She left you behind; you followed her." Phoebe let out a single bark in response. "So, what do we do now?" Phoebe groaned and eased down in the seat and put her head between her front paws. "We'll give her a few days to cool off. She'll be back."

"That was close," Willis Shepherd said as he observed the concourse activity recorded by the security cameras at Lindbergh. "He almost made it in time. At least we were able to slow him down by controlling the traffic lights; the ones he didn't run, that is."

"It's only a matter of time before the doctor gets discouraged and goes back to Chicago," Rodriguez responded. "Now, when Hemil brings us the vagrant, we'll have this situation wrapped up. Then we can get on with the business at hand with the Chinese."

"What are your plans for Sally?" Joseph replaced the airport boarding scene on the monitor with a black-and-white view from a security camera in the basement. Willis watched as the image changed and displayed the inside of one of the locked rooms where Sally lay unconscious on a narrow bed attached to a padded concrete wall and dressed in a smock and pants like the men in Jeffrey's video. The screen split to display the inside of a room two doors down where Randy was shown in the same institutional-type clothing and then expanded to include the room next to his where his nephew Kevin was displayed in the same dire condition.

"They must never leave here alive," Willis warned.

"She ruined our investment," Joseph sneered. "For what? Love is a destructive emotion."

Charlie, Lewis, and Molly, along with her sisters Charlotte and Lucy Jones, sat in their usual places at the poker table in the Mesa Village Senior Center, trying to concentrate on the cards in their hands. Charlie repeatedly lifted the stack of pennies in front of him and annoyingly dropped them one by one. Word had reached them of Annette and Doc's argument and her flight home.

"I can't believe it," Molly whined. "And she left Phoebe; that's not like her."

"Lucy; did Brad or Katie say what the fight was about?" Charlie asked from across the table.

"Robby only had sketchy details." Lucy's voice quivered as she tried to keep from crying. "It happened in the middle of the night, is all he said. What are we going to do around here without her to cheer us up?"

"Did he say how Doc's taking it?" Molly asked. "Poor Phoebe," she sighed. "I just can't believe she didn't take her."

"We should get her mother's address and send Annette a card," Lewis suggested. "We can have everybody write her a note and sign it. Maybe if she sees how much we miss her, she'll come back."

"Actually, that's not a bad idea, Lewis," Charlie said as he continued to plunk the pennies. "Molly, can you and Charlotte take care of that?"

"Yes, of course," Molly said, "but we'll have to send more than one card if everybody's gonna write something. Do any of you have her mother's address?"

"I'll get it," Charlie said and snatched his pennies.

"Where ya going?" Lewis asked.

"To get that address," Charlie growled loud enough for Lewis to hear, "and the story from the horse's mouth."

Tony opened the door when he recognized Charlie through the peephole.

"Please come in, Charlie," he sighed. "People have been calling me all morning, so I'm not surprised to see you."

"So, it's true," Charlie asked, "you two had a fight, and she went back to Louisiana?"

"Yes," Tony replied. He grabbed two beers, and they went to the back porch.

"That didn't help; given her trust issues," Charlie said after Tony explained what happened. "She's more forgiving with kids because of their innocence and with folks my age because we've seen it all and don't care about some things anymore. But she doesn't have much patience with people of her own generation who do stupid things."

"And that's just what I did, Charlie," Tony said. "Instead of explaining everything to her, like I did to you, I got mad; I even made it sound like she had done something wrong."

"People usually do that when they're feeling guilty about something," Charlie remarked.

"You're right," Tony sighed. "I never told her about the woman who was stalking me. I kept her to myself; maybe deep down inside, I wanted something to happen. And I've been feeling myself slip back into that obsessive person I was before Carol died. I've been spending too much time studying neuro-ophthalmology and neglecting the people I love."

"Neuro-what?" Charlie snarled.

"Rick gave me some books from his library on the subject and some patient files. He wanted my opinion, to see if the optic nerve system could be used as a potential gateway source for changes he's been finding in the intellectual cortex."

"Sounds important," Charlie said.

"It doesn't seem so significant right now."

"What does the intellectual cortex do?"

"It's where new information is stored. There's no consequence when neurons pass information normally, but it can be detrimental when it receives too much at once and begins to activate latent neurons and create new cells that grow out of proportion. People have died as a result of it. Rick believes that Anderson Barksdale was a victim of the disorder. He managed to get a brain scan before he was taken to the M.E. for autopsy. He left me a copy. Barksdale died as a result of a ruptured artery that was compressed because of the change in his brain's architecture. Sally Samuels has been trying to get her hands on all this information."

"For another story," Charlie pondered. "Well, we all figured there'd be another one."

"Rick wrote a report on the abnormality but then suddenly decided to retire," Tony sighed. "He asked me to take over the practice, but I can't neglect my family like I did before."

"Don't be so hard on yourself for reacting like any man would when it comes to a pretty woman's flirtations," Charlie said resolutely. "And what happened in the past with your wife wasn't completely your fault, you know. She should have had your back when it came to your work. Nicky's attitude is a result of your wife's excuses for her own weakness, and Nicky's gonna figure that out someday. What you need to do is get yourself on a plane and bring Annette back here and go on with your life as a doctor, a father, and maybe even a husband again."

"The two of you seem to share the same simplistic logic," Tony said. "No wonder you're friends."

"This architecture disorder," Charlie said, "is that what happened to Molly and Marley and Mona?"

"I'm certain of it," Tony sighed. "I may even know who's responsible. But I have to put that aside for now."

"This sounds like something that certainly deserves someone's attention." Charlie stood up and stepped down off the porch. "Now come and help me look for her mother's address. Is the key still under the mat?

It was late afternoon; Nate and Lee had four trout on a string in their box. "I remember how excited my father used to get when they put new bait out at the hardware store," Nate said as he shuffled through Lee's small tackle box.

"Where do you and your father fish?" Lee asked.

"A river up in the mountains," Nate replied, "but, my father's not around anymore."

"Dead?" Lee asked, but Nate didn't reply.

"Hey, you're in the weeds," Nate said.

"Damn!" Lee grunted. "The trollin motor is hung up."

"Lee!" Nate whispered. "Turn off the motor, look."

"It's a boat," Lee growled, "moving along the bank at the base of the hill. Think they're looking for us?"

"It disappeared in the brush," Nate whispered. "There's an inlet behind the tall grass; let's take a look."

"Her name is Stella Mae," Charlie said, looking over Scott's shoulder. "I met her not long after Annette moved here. Nice woman, but not quite ready to make new friends so soon after her husband passed."

"Really, Charlie?" Tony asked and gave the old man a suspicious squint while Scott searched Annette's contacts.

"She was here to scrutinize her daughter's new house and neighbors," Charlie said defensively. "I think I-we made a good impression."

"Here's her email address," Scott said. "And telephone number, and there's a link to Google Maps."

"Annette told me they lived on a river." Charlie leaned closer to observe the aerial view of the home sight.

"Too many trees," Tony remarked, "can't see the house."

"The street view isn't much better," Scott reported; "just the beginning of what appears to be a long gravel driveway."

"Her father built the house," Charlie added. "Zoom out again so Doc can see what highway he'll have to take from the airport. What, you can do this," Charlie said when Tony looked at him and frowned. "This way, she can't hang up on you or send your call to voice mail." A few seconds later, Robby appeared with Nicky, along with Lizzy carrying Phoebe. A minute later, Jeffrey and Justin knocked on the front door with their mother, announcing that they'd heard the news. A mixed account came from everyone at once when they asked what happened, and when the voices quieted, everyone was looking at Doc.

"I know you all think the next move is mine," Tony whined. "But she chose to leave without giving us a chance to talk this out."

"But Daddy," Lizzy whined and drew Phoebe closer to her. "She won't talk to you, so you have to talk to her in person."

"Stella might talk some sense into her," Charlie groaned in appeasement. "I'm gonna take this address to Molly."

"All right, everybody out," Tony said. "Power down her computer," he said to Scott, who was feverishly texting on his cell phone.

"Are you texting Nette?" Lizzy asked. He smiled and shook his head.

"A friend."

Stella opened the front door, holding Coco on one arm. Annette put her single suitcase to rest against a column and gave her mother a generous hug.

"Where's Phoebe?" Stella asked after their long embrace.

"I left her with a neighbor," Annette sighed. "Sorry, Coco," she said and massaged her on the top of the head.

"Your email was a little vague," Stella said, frowning as her daughter rolled her suitcase inside. "Is everything okay?" Annette made a face and shook her head.

"I knew this would happen; I should have known better than to trust him."

"But," Stella started to argue, "Oh come on, sit down, baby girl." She put an arm around her daughter and drew her close. "It'll be all right. But you just brought the one suitcase? I guess that means you ain't plannin on stayin long."

"I was in a hurry," Nette answered as they entered the family room. "You still have my stuff in my closet, don't you?"

"Well…" Stella said.

"Mom," Nette panted. "What did you do?"

"I-I donated your old stuff to the church for a benefit garage sale. Just your clothes," she explained further when she saw the alarm in her daughter's eyes. "Your room is just like you left it."

"Thank God!" Annette gasped. Stella beckoned her to sit down on the sofa.

"Now tell me what happened."

"Why are men such jerks?"

"Oh, I see," Stella said, "you're in love with the doctor.

"No, I certainly am not!" Annette insisted.

"I have eyes," Stella argued.

"What's that supposed to mean?" Nette asked.

"Your friend Robby's been sendin me pictures for the past four hours; I see how the two of you look at each other."

"There's nothin to see now," Annette said scornfully.

"I know love when I see it." Annette bowed her head. "So, you found out he wasn't perfect, and it's over?"

"You never take my side," Annette snapped.

"There are no sides. Everybody makes mistakes; isn't that what you tell the children you mentor?"

"The key word there is children, mother!" Annette argued.

"And who's actin like a child right now?"

"One thing's for sure; I certainly regressed by lettin myself fall for that liar," Annette groaned.

"He must be really special to get you mad enough to run home to your mama and was able to talk you into cookin."

"I wish I'd never told you that."

"I'll fix you some lunch, and then you can rest. A good night's sleep in your old bed might help clear your mind."

"You're probably right," Annette sighed. "I brought you a couple of pretty neat shells I found for your terrarium."

"It's still on the shelf," she said, pointing to a set of shelves next to the fireplace.

"What's this?" Annette asked and reached into the wide-mouthed glass bowl of sand and remnants from the sea. I don't remember this turquoise stone."

"Oh, that belonged to your father," Stella replied from the kitchen. "His father's great-great-great grandfather was Cherokee. Have you never heard the story about the Indian brave who tied his pony to the tent of his woman for 13 days? I've been waiting for the right time to give it to you."

"But you should give this to Keith," she said while rubbing the stone with her fingers and thinking how much it resembled the one the little boy at the cave dwellings tried to give her on her trip across the country. "It's obviously been passed down to the men in the family."

"But you two were so close. I thought…you know."

"It's Keith's, Mom; I don't think I need it."

Nate sat in silence at the table in the camper while Lee fried trout filets on the small three-burner stove.

"You're thinking about that boat," Lee said, observing the frown on Nate's face. "That inlet is likely full of cameras, like everywhere else." Nate didn't respond. "I could jam them, but that would ruin my element of surprise." Lee dished the trout into two paper plates and set them on the table along with several packages of restaurant catsup.

"I thought I knew everything about that place," Nate groaned.

"Humph," Lee grunted. "You don't even know what goes on in the basement."

"Lee, where's my laptop? I need to contact Colin."

"Stored under your seat," Lee mumbled, "Along with some of my ammo."

Chapter 35

"Well, this is it," Tony said to Scott, who was sitting beside him in front of his computer, "a presentation of two hundred patient cases with abnormal brain architecture, as complete as I can get it. I couldn't have done this without you, kid." Scott grinned when Doc patted him affectionately on the arm. "I'm going to send this to the Surgeon General and every medical journal I can think of until someone pays attention," he added, holding a small thumb drive between his fingers; "as soon as I get back, that is. Convincing Annette to come home is first on my agenda."

"It could merit you a Nobel prize consideration, Dr. Harding," Scott remarked.

"Not when a crime is being committed. I need a safe place to hide this and Rick's reference material," he said, pointing to the box on the floor.

"Annette has a place," he said eagerly. They trekked across the alley to Annette's house and retrieved the key from under the mat. Scott led Doc to her bedroom closet. "Pull up the corner of the carpet under the shoe boxes." Tony peeled the carpet back and found a zip lock bag containing money and Jeffrey's thumb drive. "We can surround the file box with her shoe boxes." Unfortunately, and unbeknownst to Tony, an operative from the rental house was crouched in the shrubs outside the bedroom wall with an ultrasound recording device pressed against the stucco.

"Brad and Katie are going to keep an eye on the house while we're gone," Tony told Nicky after breakfast while he helped her clear the dishes. "Have you and Lizzy started packing? I booked a flight for tomorrow morning. It's four hours with an hour's layover in Houston, so bring your music and games. I bought Phoebe a ticket; I'm picking up a pet carrier today."

"We're not going, Daddy," Nicky interrupted. "Next week is Spring Break; we'll be fine right here. Phoebe will keep Lizzy company; we're used to staying by ourselves, remember?"

"Honey," Tony began, and then grabbed her and wrapped his arms around her. "I'm so sorry about your mother; please forgive me; she was sick, and I should have never left you alone with her. I was such an idiot; I should have fought harder for you. I want you to know how proud I am of you for being so brave."

"You're right, Daddy," she sighed, "you should have stepped up. Just bring Annette back with you; please."

"I love you, sweetheart," Tony said, trying to fight back the tears, but they streamed down his face anyway. Nicky wrapped her arms around his waist.

"Bring her back, Daddy."

Sunday morning Father Clayton asked the congregation to pray for a traveling parishioner. Robby played soft hymnal music from the choir loft that turned into the tune "Blue Bayou," and then the choir began to hum along to the unrehearsed song.

Tony handed his ticket to Brenda, who was standing behind the same boarding desk they had rushed to in the courtesy cart a week earlier. She smiled and wished him good luck and a safe flight. He responded with a nod and said he hoped the kids would be safe while he was gone.

"They will be," she whispered. "Our neighbors will see to it. Besides, I heard Charlie packed a bag and will be staying at your house."

"Did you read the latest in *The Post* regarding Sally?" Willis Shepherd asked his cohort after reading the hourly reports from the Cabrillo room. "They're reporting she's taking a sabbatical."

"Really," Joseph said, nodding his head in approval. "And there's a press release from the D.A. office," Joseph announced in return. "Randal Samuels is in Sacramento for a month shadowing the Governor." Joseph began to chuckle. "I can't wait to see the look on Sally's face when she realizes what she's done."

"There's news from Mesa," Willis said when an alert appeared. "The doctor is on his way to Louisiana; time to initiate the next phase."

Tony rented a car at Alexandria International Airport and set the navigation system to the address Scott found for Stella Mae Rylan. The fifty-minute drive to Natchitoches brought him to the gravel driveway they had found on *Google Street.* A black mailbox was posted next to the culvert with the name *Rylan* hand-painted in white letters. He followed the drive through a stand of trees that opened up to the front lawn and a two-story house. Plants hung along the porch between the columns that surrounded the ground floor. Flourishing white and pink dogwoods, crepe myrtles, and large oak trees abounded, along with willows and huge fuchsia azaleas and bridal wreaths. The air was sweet with springtime blossoms. The birds seemed to sing louder when he approached the steps…as if to greet him. He had never heard so many varieties singing all at once. He tapped the metal knocker against the hardwood door, and his heart picked up several paces while he waited for someone to answer. He had rehearsed several speeches during the five-hour junket but had never decided which one to use. He walked along the porch when there was no response, looking through windows and a screened porch along the side until he reached the concrete steps at the rear of the house. The backyard was grassy and shady and ended at the river, where there was a boat dock. A party barge was drifting gradually down the middle of the river. The captain waved to him and turned the boat toward the dock.

"You lookin for Stella?" the man at the wheel hollered out just before his boat bumped the dock.

"Yes," Tony yelled back, "and her daughter, Annette." The man laughed and waved his arm, beckoning him to jump on board.

"Stella's at the riverfront park," he said. "I'll take you there." Tony sat on a cushioned seat against the railing, and the man eased away from the dock. "You must be the doctor fella Nette's all mad at," he said.

"What?" Tony said. "Oh, yes, I'm Dr. Tony Harding. How did you…"

"Oh yeah, we know all about you. I'm Stella's brother, Nicholas. I give rides back and forth along the river when there are festivities downtown. Our week-long spring fling is just gettin started. I saw Annette a couple of hours ago with a bunch of kids slidin down the bank on flattened cardboard."

"Sounds like my girl, all right," Tony said, smiling. Nicholas let Tony off at the Front Street levee. He climbed the grassy hill to the historic section of town where music was playing, and vendors were selling crafts, souvenirs, clothes, and food. He asked one of the vendors if he knew Stella and was directed to a woman with strawberry blonde hair pulled back in a ponytail sitting on a wrought iron bench up the hill with a dog in her lap.

"Yes?" Stella said, looking up at Tony through her sunglasses as he approached. "Ah, you must be Doc; I recognize you from the dozens of pictures I've been gettin all week." Stella patted the bench seat with her hand, signaling him to sit beside her.

"Excuse me for staring," Tony said, "but your dog looks just like…"

"This is Coco, Phoebe's mother."

"How is she, Ms. Rylan?" Tony asked as he held his hand out for Coco to smell. "Do you think she's ready to talk to me?"

"You can call me Stella," she said, taking off her sunglasses to see him more clearly. "She's been pretty busy visitin people she ain't seen since she left. We haven't really talked about your little spat. I figured we'd end up spendin too much of our time arguing about it, so I just left it alone." Stella stopped a boy passing by who was eating a corn dog. "This is my nephew, Jacob. Where did Nette go after y'all got through hidin eggs, honey?"

"She went down to the cemetery with some flowers," Jacob replied while licking mustard from his lips.

"Take Dr. Hardin down there, will you please?"

"Sure, come on," Jacob said and took another bite of his dog, "follow me."

"Thank you, Ms. Stella," Tony said. "I hope to see you and Coco later."

"Me too," she said, grinning. Tony gave Coco a farewell pat on the head and followed Jacob. Stella put her sunglasses back on and cuddled Coco closer. She watched them wind through the crowds gathered around the entrances of the many antique stores on Front Street until she lost sight of them when they turned to cross the Cane River Bridge. Jacob pointed his cleaned corn dog stick at a large Live Oak tree after leading Tony through the cemetery gate. He didn't see her at first because of the breadth of the tree, but he saw her sitting on the ground leaning against it when he got closer. She was twirling a yellow daisy by its stem between her fingers and staring at the tombstone in front of her. He dreaded how she might react; perhaps she would stomp off while telling him to go to hell. A small dried limb crackled under his foot, making her look up. She jumped to her feet immediately. But she ran to him and wrapped her arms around him; they held each other for a long time. No words were necessary, all was forgiven. She took his hand and led him to her father's plot.

"Daddy," she said, addressing the headstone. "This is the man I was tellin you about." She looked at Tony, "before I told him goodbye. I don't think I ever really did that…tell him goodbye…until today." They walked to the river and hitched a ride with Nicholas. "I had made up my mind, Doc," she said as the barge slowly moved down the river. "I was coming back." Nicholas dropped them off at the Rylan boat dock, and they went upstairs to her bedroom and consummated their love for each other. Then they talked for hours; Doc heard about the wonderful southern culture and how much fun growing up in the rural countryside was.

"I hope I can measure up to what your daddy would have wanted for you," Tony said. "I grew up in the projects; they produce criminals. The only respect I got from my father was when I came home bloody and bruised from fighting." He went on to explain the sequence of events with Rebecca and about the drive, and the box of files he hid in Annette's bedroom closet, Rick's peculiar behavior, and his abrupt retirement. "I'm not sure what the reaction will be when I submit my report to the AMA. It could cause a terrible turmoil. I think it may have played a part in Rick's decision. But I don't want to take over his practice. I don't care if I lose my job; some things are more important."

"He couldn't have left just because of the report," Annette replied. "There had to be another reason. Don't worry, everything will work itself out." Nicholas took them back to the Front Street area. The night's festivities began with a spectacular fireworks display over the river that ended with the lighting of thousands of lights along its banks. They ate the southern cuisine, played carnival games, danced to the live bands, and had a good time with Annette's family, neighbors, and the thousands of festival goers. When they arrived back at the Rylan house, Tony asked Annette to marry him. "What about the girls?" Annette asked after accepting the proposal with a long embrace and passionate kiss. "Do you think they're ready?"

"We'll have time to rehearse something on the flight home." But Stella woke them in the middle of the night. She was holding Coco in one arm as she vigorously shook Tony's shoulder. "Hurry, hurry, y'all need to get up and come see," she gasped. Tony sat up immediately and saw his cell phone on the nightstand lit up with a dozen missed calls from Nicky. He grabbed it and jumped out of bed; Annette followed. Stella led them to a laptop on the nightstand in her bedroom. A video was streaming of a house engulfed in flames. Robby's face appeared on the screen for a split second before he turned Scott's tablet to show the fire trucks and flashing red and blue lights. Water was fruitlessly dousing a house from four directions, and then the view shifted back to the burning building.

"It's your house, Nette!" he cried.

"They said it's too hot," Scott's voice said from somewhere off-camera." Robby's face appeared again. "Nette," he gasped. "We can't find Phoebe. Man, I hope she's just hiding somewhere. Yo, what do we do?"

"Is this live?" Tony asked Stella, and she nodded anxiously. "Find the Fire Marshal," he shouted. "Tell him we'll be back tomorrow afternoon, and we're expecting a full investigation." Annette sat down on the bed and stared at the screen.

"I-I can't believe it," she gasped. "My house, it's destroyed; and Phoebe…"

Stella disconnected the call and sat down beside her.

"I'm sure she's fine, honey." She gave her daughter a reassuring hug, and Coco crawled in her lap and made a sympathetic whining noise. Tony called Nicky to make sure they were safe. She had taken Lizzy to Robby's soundproofed bedroom to shield her from the commotion. She confirmed that the house looked like a total loss and that Phoebe was nowhere to be found. He could hear Lizzy crying, so he asked Nicky to put her on.

"You know Phoebe can take care of herself, sweetheart," he said to her. "You know what she can do."

"You really believe that Daddy?" she whined.

"Yes, sweetheart, I do."

Their flight arrived the next afternoon. Annette was unbuckling her seatbelt before Tony turned onto Jewel. She spread both hands across the dash of the Toyota to brace herself for the hard stop in front of what was left of her house. Charlie was standing next to the yellow tape and metal barricades that were around the perimeter. A police unit was parked in the driveway. Tony had told Stella about his marriage proposal before they left, while Annette was showering.

"What did she say?" Stella had asked as if there was some doubt that her unpredictable daughter would accept. Then she took off the wedding ring set that Sonny Rylan gave her forty-five years ago, folded his hand around it and said she was very happy and proud. But Annette and Tony didn't talk about wedding plans or how they would break the news to the girls as they sat next to each other on the plane. Tony kept the rings safely tucked away in his pocket. They briefly discussed living arrangements and what Annette would need but not much else. Tony kept a reassuring arm around her because she appeared to be in shock and couldn't talk about any particular subject for very long.

"Oh my God, Charlie!" she sobbed into his shoulder when she reached him.

"I know, honey," he whispered, "I know; I'm just glad you weren't home; it went out of control so fast." He nodded hello to Tony as he consoled her. "You know that we haven't found Phoebe yet? We're not allowed past the barricades because it's still so hot. The heat scorched the sides of your neighbors' houses. It was all they could do to keep them from catching fire. Hell, half the block was evacuated until they got it under control. The Fire Marshal said an accelerant must have been used, maybe jet fuel."

"It gets hotter than gasoline," Tony said, "and almost impossible to put out. I remember my father saying it's used to make sure buildings burn quickly, for insurance scams, or sometimes to cover up a theft or a murder." He saw Scott and Brenda standing in the alley across the smoldering rubble. The fire department had knocked down the wooden fence to fight the fire from the rear. "I should check on the kids," he said and drove Annette to his house and away from the dreadful scene.

"That should keep them occupied for a while," Joseph Rodriguez said to Willis Shepherd. "Colin has already taken care of the Fire Marshall and has instructed our team to keep matters going sideways."

"Did you read the report that the head of the Chinese National Party has requested a meeting with the President?" Shepherd asked.

"Yes," Rodriguez replied, "but there will be no audience with the President. Secretary Harris has been instructed to explain that it's too risky for the President to go on record about the enhancement project or acknowledge it in any way."

"Another alert," Shepherd reported; "Colin's getting something from Hemil; a weather report?"

"It's a *Phantom* program." Nate turned the laptop so that Lee could read the text on the screen. "Colin and I use it to communicate. It's like a 3D illusion print." Lee looked at the screen and then at Nate and squinted suspiciously. "We've been using it since we were in college," Nate continued. "I turned it into an encrypted stereogram program that only the two can see."

"What is this garbage I'm reading about a storm?" Lee said, frowning at the screen.

"It's a legitimate weather forecast for the southwestern United States that I used as the cover; there's a hidden message in the script. I just asked Colin about the inlet and if it's possible to use it to enter the bunker. I also told him to be on standby to shut down the security system when the time comes. We're gonna need his help to pull this off, Lee. And before you ask, yes, I trust him."

"I've been thinking," Lee said. "If you take out the generators on the roof, like what happened with the kite, then no one should notice me entering the inlet. How long will it take him to answer?"

"Not long, but we might have another problem," Nate said, looking up from his tablet. "Look at the U.S. Geological Survey site. The USGS has issued a warning about this weather event. There's a jet stream moving a tropical storm across the extreme South Pacific. It's carrying a huge amount of water and an atmospheric river has developed extending toward the west coast. It will likely stall when it reaches the mountains." He pointed to a weather chart on the screen. A huge red mass was stretched across the South Pacific. "This is a satellite view of the storm and the AR." There was a long green finger-shaped graphic jutting out from the storm and headed in a northeasterly direction. "Some call it an ARkstorm; a combination of the atmospheric river term and the Noah's Ark story. It's projected to reach us in less than a week and stall in the Sierra Nevada."

"We'll have a flood of biblical proportions," Lee gasped. "We can use it to our advantage."

"There will be mudslides; the lake will rise; the inlet may close before..."

"Then I'll need to go in before the water gets too high," Lee said.

"This can't be right," Nate groaned after switching to *The Post* website; "Sally's taken a sabbatical. Did she say anything to you about taking time off?"

"No, I broke off contact with her before I moved up here."

"Oh, no," Nate muttered. "There was a house fire on Jewel near The Mesa Retirement Village; Annette Rylan's house; fortunately, she was out of town. This was *them*; you know." He switched to his tracking program. "I encoded a signal to a thumb drive I gave Sally. Oh God, Lee," he groaned; "she's here; they've got her."

"Shh, what's that noise?" Lee whispered after a few minutes of woeful silence. "Do you hear a scratching noise?"

"Yeah," Nate replied. Lee pulled back a curtain behind his seat.

"I don't see anything."

"It's the door," Nate said and got up from the table to open it.

"Why it's a mutt!" Lee exclaimed when Phoebe jumped inside the trailer. "There's a collar and tag. Who do you belong to; someone in the campground?"

Phoebe leaped into Lee's lap and licked him on the face.

"Lee, don't you recognize this dog?" Nate said. "It's her dog. The Group sent a team to torch her house; they must have taken her."

"She got away," Lee added. Phoebe looked up at Lee and barked once. "Here's a phone number," he said after looking at the tag. "Google it."

"It's hers, all right," Nate said after reading the search results. But how did she find us?" Phoebe looked at Nate and cocked her head. Lee found a bowl and gave the little dog some water.

"Look at her lap it up," he chuckled. "I think I have some leftover bacon and some canned chicken." Nate's tablet lit up with a reply from Colin.

"It's the weather report," Lee reported to his new friend when he saw the icon on the screen.

"He can help us with the security, but he's not aware of the inlet. He confirmed the fire and said the University is buying out Dr. Samuels' practice; he's retiring."

"They got to him too," Lee sighed. "They're going after everyone," he said to his new four-legged friend.

Annette finally fell asleep in Elizabeth's bed at 4:00 am. After walking the living room floor for a while, Tony noticed Scott's light on when he looked outside. He walked over and tapped on the window.

"Dr. Harding," Scott said after raising the window. "I couldn't sleep either. I'm really sorry about your report and the files."

"Yeah," Tony sighed. "Please tell me you had your security cameras on."

"Well, I," Scott began, but he was interrupted by his mother when she suddenly entered the bedroom.

"I'm sorry, Dr. Harding," she said and shuffled Scott away from the window. "I was home, and I had turned them off."

"Hi, Brenda. I hoped they caught something that would give us an idea of how the fire started."

"I'm really sorry about this," she said. "Please tell Annette to let me know if there's anything I can do. Good night."

"Good night," he sighed when she abruptly closed the window. He called Rick on his cell while he walked across his front yard. "Rick, Annette's house…" Tony began when Rick answered.

"Yes, I heard; I'm sorry, son," Rick moaned through the phone. "I hope no one was hurt."

"Do you know why this happened?" Tony asked. "Is this why you left the practice; because you were threatened? You left Andrew Barksdale's MRI and your research for me to find; you knew what I'd do."

"Yes," he replied. "I'm sorry; I wish I could help you, son, but…"

"Is my family in danger?" Tony interrupted.

"I don't think so," he whispered, "not anymore…good night."

Father Clayton stopped by the next morning to offer Annette his support. Nicky and Marley donated some of their clothes and Lizzy was excited that she would be sharing her room with Phoebe when she came home. "I heard Phoebe is missing." He held her hands as he spoke. "I'm praying she'll come home. The church has a fund set up for parishioners in crises; just let me know what you need." Tony motioned him into the kitchen. There were many things he wanted to confide, but he didn't know how or where to begin, or if he should at all.

"I know this is going to sound strange, but I need to get in touch with Sally."

"*The Post* reported she's on sabbatical," he replied. "She usually goes on retreat at St. Jude's in Old Town. She's gone there before to decompress; it's where she grew up. I'll contact the Monsignor. Oh, look." Father Clayton pointed to a book lying on the counter next to the sink. "Isn't that Nette's family cookbook? Not everything was lost, praise the Lord," he said as Tony rushed to pick it up.

"Nette," Tony called out. "We must have left your grandmother's cookbook here," he began, but Lizzy interrupted.

"Nette," Elizabeth yelled, appearing from the hallway. "Look! Phoebe must still be here. I found this in Daddy's bedroom." She was holding the vintage bottle of English Leather in her hands. Annette looked at the bottle and then ran past Tony who was holding the cookbook out to her. She exited the back door, ran across the yard, and opened the gate. Tony followed her, as did Lizzy, Father Clayton, and Nicky, who had just emerged from her room with Annette's white photo album in her arms.

"You can't go in there!" Tony hollered when he saw her turn into her backyard. "It's not safe!" She stopped at the concrete steps and looked at the pile of ash where the wicker chairs used to be. The bicycle Doc bought her was a melted mound of spaghetti-like metal. Only two feet of the stucco wall was left standing, and clumps of embers and remnants of what used to be cabinets, appliances, and furniture.

"Where is she?" she whimpered, feeling Tony's hands on her shoulders. Father Clayton, Lizzy, and Nicky stopped in the middle of the backyard.

"Wow, there's really nothing left," Nicky whispered. "But there's this," she added and held up the white album.

"She tried to save this stuff for me," Annette sobbed. She looked at what was left of her bedroom. "And it may have killed her."

"No," Tony whispered, trying to console her; "she'll come home; she'll find a way."

The insurance adjuster arrived two days later and completed his inspection while Annette sat waiting in a plastic lawn chair in the backyard.

"The Fire Marshall's report states an electrical short in the kitchen caused it," Annette said as if disputing the information on the form the adjustor handed her.

"Yes, my company will accept that," he replied. "It'll move the demolition and rebuilding process along quicker."

"But it's not true. Someone set my house on fire!" She stood up, knocking the chair backward.

"Well, we can't really prove that," the adjuster said. "Look, I know you probably had some sentimental items that can never be replaced, but you'll be generously compensated. I know you didn't have anything to do with it, and no one was hurt."

"My dog is missin," Annette groaned.

"The Fire Marshall found no remains," the adjuster remarked. "I suggest you get another dog. What address would you like us to mail the check to?"

Tony inspected the house as well, hoping against hope that he would find the drives or something left of the box of reference materials, but when he brushed the debris away from where the closet used to be, there was nothing but ash.

Annette bought a Nintendo, and Doc's house became the new hangout. They cooked in the evenings and listened to Robby's tunes. Rick's name was removed from the name tiles at work, and the practice was now *USCSD Family Practice.* Lisa hired Catrina in Mona's absence. Nicky's basketball team worked its way to the top of the JV bracket, and Lizzy added more strokes to her mural. Tony tried to reach Harry, but according to an email from Betty, a supervisor at the hospital said he had taken vacation time. Annette and Doc sat on his back porch every night to discuss their day.

"After experiencing the serenity of your mother's porch, I understand your ritual," he said one night. "The only things missing are the cooing doves and the crickets; and the frogs just before a rain." Tony had taken the wedding set Stella gave him to the jewelers and had the rings resized and cleaned. "I want to do this again," he said and got down on one knee. He took the engagement ring out of his pocket and put it on her finger. “Marry me.” She said yes, and they woke Nicky and Elizabeth. They all celebrated over ice cream on the back porch. Annette was coming around to the idea that there was a whole new life ahead of her, but she would never forget the faithful companion that got her to this point. She might have never left home if it hadn’t been for Phoebe being by her side.

Chapter 36

Sally awoke lying on her side on a hard mattress, opened her eyes, and found she barely had the strength to push herself onto her back. Her mouth was dry, so it was difficult to even utter a wince when her right arm fell hard against the cold vinyl wall, and her left gave way and flopped lifelessly over the edge of the bed, overextending her elbow, causing a shooting pain up her arm. "What's wrong with me?" She whispered as she drifted in and out of sleep.

"She's coming out of it," Joseph said to Willis when the report of her stirring reached him. "I should go down and welcome her."

"To her temporary home," Willis said as if giving him a reminder.

Sally opened her eyes again. *Why is everything gray? No, there's a light.* Then she saw a figure come into view, someone was standing over her. "What happened?" she whispered to the man in the dark suit as she struggled to sit up.

"Have some water," the man said and sat down beside her and helped her to an upright position. "Your favorite brand, I believe," he whispered and put a bottle of Evian to her lips. "Don't worry, Sally, I plan to take very good care of you."

"Who are you, what happened, how long have I been here?" she asked as she looked at her plain lavender scrubs and the man with a hint of a Spanish accent with dark hair and tinted glasses. He took the empty bottle from her and left the room without saying another word. She heard a lock turn after he closed the door. "Wait! Where am I?" she said, stumbling to the door. She looked out the slender window in the door but could only see a wall of concrete cinder blocks through the reinforced wire. *The last thing I remember is being in Father Clayton's prayer room.* She was brought a food tray by a man in a charcoal gray uniform an hour later. She thought, as she looked at the bacon and eggs on her plate, that she would need her strength when it came time to make a run for it. She might not get far, but she might see something that would tell her where she was.

"Here are your patient files, Dr. Harding," Tonya said while handing Tony a small stack of folders per the morning ritual they had assumed since his return from Louisiana.

"Thank you, Tonya," he replied. "Did someone change the security code on Rick's door? I tried to return some books to his library; my card didn't work."

"Yes," she replied. "The Group had me change it for security reasons. Give me your keycard, I'll update it. Congrats on your engagement, Dr. Harding. I knew it wouldn't be long before you were off the market." Tony walked across the hall to Rick's office during a break between patients. The green light blinked when he inserted the card, and the door opened. As he replaced the books, he couldn't shake the eerie feeling the ominous pale granite statue of Hippocrates was giving him. "That's better," he whispered after turning the statue around to face the library wall. He slipped his card into the slot to open the door to the addition, but the box didn't light up. He moved the handle, and the door opened; the room was empty. *Nothing is left; all our proof is gone.* He heard Tonya calling his name from Rick's office.

"There you are," Tonya said when Tony appeared through the conference room door.

"It's so strange in here without Rick," he said, watching her turn the statue back around. "Can't you just leave that thing the way I put it?" Tonya quickly left the office after telling him his next patient had arrived. He reached to turn the statue again, but the head came off in his hand, exposing the inside cavity. There was a camera lens set inside each of the eyes. He dropped it, and it broke it into pieces on the floor, revealing an array of circuit boards. He looked around, wondering if there were more hidden cameras in the office. "Tonya!" he yelled. He found her sitting at the reception desk with her back to him, but for some reason, she couldn't hear him calling out to her. "Tonya!" he repeated, but her attention was fixed on her PC monitor.

"Yes, Dr. Harding?" she sighed and turned around; she looked dazed.

"Tonya, there's a camera in the head of the Hypocrites statue," he huffed.

"Yes," she said and blinked her eyes as if confused, "I know, they're everywhere. The Group installed those ages ago." Tony remembered Annette's story about the cameras in Sally's office.

"In my office?" he asked, but her eyes rolled up as if she was fainting. "Tonya?" Her eyelids closed. "Tonya!" He grabbed her by the shoulders when she fell forward and then eased her to the floor. After finding no pulse in her neck, he raised her eyelids with his fingers; they were bloodshot. Blood began to ooze from her ears and the corners of her eyes. By the time the EMT arrived with the crash cart, it was too late, in spite of Tony's wholehearted CPR efforts.

Sally quickly sat up on the side of the bed when she heard the lock turn. Judging by the number of meals she'd been served and the yellow-tinged bruise on her arm, this was possibly her third day of captivity, and she was certain The Group was responsible. She was sure they had tried to poison her, had bugged her office, and planted some sort of tracking device under her skin…the night I met Nate Roberts at Jared's…he must be the reason I'm here. *Lee tried to warn me about him.* Why else would she be locked in a soundproof, padded room with two cameras pointed at her? The uniformed guard walked in with another tray. When he bent over to put it on the bed, she bolted into the hallway. A row of doors was on her left and an elevator to the right; she headed for the elevator. But when she got there and pushed the button, it didn't light up. She ran back and met the guard running out of her room. She pushed him back inside and slammed the door closed. She looked inside the room next to hers through the slender window in the door. She began yelling and beating on the door when she recognized Walter lying on the bunk. The door was locked, and the room soundproofed, but she thought she saw one of his bare feet move. The guard caught up to her by the time she reached the second door and grabbed her around the neck, but not before she had time to recognize Randy. He was motionless, his face gaunt and his skin pale. "No!" she screamed and desperately tried to free herself by kicking the guard and scratching his face. "Randy!" she screamed while the guard dragged her back to her room and threw her onto the floor. The guard exited quickly, locking the door behind him. Sally scrambled to her feet and ran to the window. "Randy!" she sobbed. The guard returned five minutes later with a shackle and four feet of chain and secured her ankle to the bunk bed.

"Senator Harris negotiated a handshake agreement," Willis said to his partner. "We'll have our deal with the Chinese in a few days." Rodriguez was standing in front of the portrait of his famous ancestor.

"We are one step closer to world peace," he said as if speaking to the horseman, "and to the reclamation of San Miguel."

"Don't you think it's time to take care of our guests in the basement?"

"Yes, I think everyone's accounted for now. Hemil has informed Colin he will have Lee here in a couple of days; the doctor and the woman with the dog have diverted their interests to restoring their lives since her house was destroyed. We will have all these little annoyances wrapped up very shortly."

"It's unfortunate that Randal wavered so badly," Willis sighed. "His love for Sally ended up making him useless to us."

"Yes," Joseph said. "We'll influence *The Post* to release a cover story stating that he and Sally are reconciling and starting over…in Italy."

"Joe," Willis sighed, "it's obvious you hold some sort of affection for this woman. It's not going to interfere with what must be done?"

"Not to worry Willis; but first, I want her to understand a few things."

"Don't take too long, the Governor has issued a state of emergency because of the severe weather outside. Flooding and mudslide warnings are in effect. We may have to take some measures ourselves."

"I'm aware," Joseph replied. "I'm having my artifact collection moved down to the bunker."

"You know, I'm as proud of my heritage as anyone, Joe," Willis said. "But I let go of my hostility a long time ago; I embrace my equality. Why is it you aren't able to do the same?"

"Because unlike you, Willis, my people have no public voice," Rodriguez replied. "Too many still live in disparity and work for practically nothing. We are still spat upon, sneered at, and denied the benefit of citizenship because the Americans look at us as low-class degenerates. When we take over, I'll declare the southwest from Texas to the Pacific for the new, *New Mexico*. North America will be divided, but all attempts at governing themselves will fail, and it will gladly allow our prosperous country to take it over."

"How will our new partners fit into this?" Willis asked.

"Once we are established in China, we will use the enhancement to take control of them and their finances. In time, the new, *New Mexico* will be the richest and most powerful country in the world."

Tony ran through the rain to his car, not noticing the elderly Hispanic man in the black raincoat standing next to the Olds. He was holding a large black umbrella imprinted with three silver crosses which he quickly shared with Tony. The man gave him a small piece of paper and then tipped his black derby exposing his long gray streaked hair. Without saying a word, he left Tony holding the umbrella and quickly got into a black Ford Escape; the tires spewed water in the flooding parking lot as it sped away.

"We're in for another week of this, according to Channel 4," Annette said later that evening while handing Tony a cup of hot chocolate as he sat watching the rain from the back porch.

"The streets are getting more dangerous," Tony said. "Don't try to drive anywhere too far; just call me if you need to go any further than Molly's."

"Sure," Annette replied. "You know it's weird. I had my doubts about Catrina when Lisa hired her, but she's actually pretty amazing with kids. How could Larry have been so wrong about her?"

"I don't know; I just hope she's not," he sighed, "another victim. I'm sorry, I didn't mean to…"

"Doc, I'm so sorry about Tonya," Annette whimpered. "Is the practice going to be okay?"

"Everything will be fine..." he began but shook his head as if arguing with himself. "What happened to Tonya might as well be my fault. It goes against everything I believe in to stand by and do nothing, but if I continue pursuing this abnormality, I'm sure I'll be putting you and the girls in danger." He put his cup down and took the crumpled note from his shirt pocket. "A man gave me this in the parking lot today. I told Don a few weeks ago that I wanted to talk to Sally. He thought she was on a retreat, staying at a church in Old Town, but according to this note from the Monsignor, she's not there. She's been working on a story that connects The Group to brain disorders, and now no one can tell me where she is. I'm sure Rick left the practice because he felt threatened when something happened to the second report he tried to send the AMA. I haven't been able to reach Harry. My sister even went to the hospital to look for him, but they told her he was on vacation. He would never take so much time off. What worries me is that I sent him copies of everything," he said sorrowfully while crumpling the note in his hand. "I hid Rick's files and the original report in your closet; I'm sure that's why your house was destroyed and Phoebe is missing. My back is against the wall here." He was almost sobbing. "I don't know what I'll do if anything happens to you and the girls."

"Well," she finally said after thinking for a minute. "You know, my daddy always said, when you've done all you can, it's time to turn it over to the Lord."

"Always the simple solution," Doc whispered and took her hand.

"This is too big for us to fix," she said. "Sometimes we don't have any choice but to leave it to Him."

"Took advantage of the break in the weather," Lee yelled to Nate as he trudged up the slick muddy hill to the campsite. "Look at the string of fish we caught?" Lee was holding his rod and a string of six trout. "You know *night crawlers* are what they call worms used as bait in the South. A befitting name you gave her; she pointed out exactly where I should cast my line."

"Sure, Lee," Nate replied from his lawn chair beside the camper door. "You shouldn't get too attached; it's time to make our move."

"Watch this, I taught her a few tricks." Lee threw a small stick out beyond the awning. Phoebe ran to fetch it and brought it back to him. "Now, sit up, girl." Phoebe brought her front paws up and sat up. "Good girl. You deserve a treat." Lee opened a bag of dog food he bought at the bait stand.

"You know somebody already taught her those tricks," Nate said, recalling Sally's outline that included a list of feats that Nightcrawler could perform.

"Yeah, yeah," Lee groaned; "the number on the tag."

"Don't let this temporary break in the weather fool you, it's stalled in the mountains and is turning back around. We need to do this before the water in the inlet gets any higher."

"Someone will find you," Lee said, looking down at Phoebe, "and call the number; then you'll be back with your master again." Lee leaned over and stroked Phoebe on the head as she ate the dog food from his hand. "I've had a lot of fun with you," he sighed, "And I ain't had much to smile about in a long time. Guess I'll get started loading the boat."

"Loading the boat; with what?"

"With the rest of the ammo I have stockpiled under my bed. Don't worry; I'll share it with you. I acquired some uniforms and gas masks too. My guy who escaped from up there got a good look at what the guards were wearing; he found some uniforms at the Thrift Store that were close enough. See if your friend found me a way inside from the inlet. I'd like to set my charges as close to the base of the structure as possible. I might be able to activate them remotely if this weather doesn't short out my wiring," he groaned. Phoebe followed behind Lee as he trudged back down the hill. "Come on, Nightcrawler; let's go clean out the boat."

"Lee, you know you're never gonna make it out of there," Nate said, but Lee kept walking.

Tony made the clinic at the village available even though it was doubtful anyone would challenge the weather, so he was surprised when he heard a door slam in the rec room. He stepped outside his office and saw Father Clayton walking toward him with a troubled look on his face. "Don, what are you doing out in this mess; is someone sick?"

"Dr. Harding!" He huffed. "I'm worried." He looked at the coat rack outside the clinic office and saw the umbrella with the three crosses hanging next to Tony's raincoat. "I see the Monsignor at St. Jude's contacted you."

"Have you heard from Sally?" Tony asked.

"No, she came to the rectory one night a few weeks ago very upset. I left her alone in my prayer room while I went to the church; when I returned, she was gone. She left a note that she was going on a sabbatical at St. Jude's, but no one there has seen or heard from her."

"Don, do you think something's happened to her because of a story she's working on?"

"You know I'm sworn to silence," he whispered and bowed his head. "But Sally believes the people who are funding Randy's political career are angry with her over the article she wrote and have been spying on her."

"I guess by people, she means The Group?" Tony sighed. "Tonya said they had cameras everywhere in the hospital just before she died, or maybe she just meant *everywhere*."

"The Group is partnered with thousands of corporations." Tony squeezed his eyes closed,

"Including San Diego Cable Technology, I suppose."

"Yes," Father Clayton replied. "All of the media, USCSD, and practically all businesses in Southern California."

"That's how it's delivered," Tony whispered. "No wonder that woman kept showing up," he sighed. "She was trying to seduce me into taking the SDCT enhancement service. It's the cable service, Don," he said, seeing the puzzled look on the priest's face. "SDCT has augmented the cable signal. It must be extremely potent, considering what it does to the optic nerve. They replaced the cable on our street after Marley fell ill; something must have gone wrong."

"Doc, what are you…?" the priest gasped.

"Don," Tony interrupted, "do you know what makes humans unique? It's our ability to take in information from all our senses at once and then make conscious, intelligent decisions. They're using the sense of sight to infiltrate the minds of their victims. Our brains naturally produce light energy that turns on neurons. SDCT must be producing some sort of electromagnetic signal that enlightens neurons, only sometimes too many at once, forcing the creation of new matter cells in order to facilitate the mass activity, consequently, crimping vessels in the process. That's what happened to Anderson Barksdale and what nearly happened to Marley, Molly, and Mona. And most likely Tonya, but I'll never know because her family had her remains cremated."

"You'd think they'd want an explanation for their daughter's sudden death," Father Clayton remarked.

"There's exceptional work being done in optogenetics labs where information is inserted into the brain artificially. Under controlled conditions, certain neurons can be turned on with light. Scientists have also found that specific colors control precise behavior; they can even generate false memories."

"Unbelievable," the priest moaned.

"I've been reading about successful trials with patients suffering from psychosis or serious brain disorder, both naturally occurring or due to injury; but only under controlled conditions and with the use of external hardware."

"But why aren't you and I affected, and Sally and Dr. Samuels; why some and not others?"

"I keep thinking about something Sally said to me when we first met; something about Rick hiring me because of my work ethic. Maybe people with deep conviction, like Rick, Sally, and you, Don; maybe our neurons have developed a structure that wards off the influence. The stronger the commitment, the better neurons are able to discount the unscrupulous." A noise came from the rec room that struck fear into Father Clayton while he tried to comprehend the possibility that The Group was actually practicing mind control.

"Someone else is here!" he gasped. They both hurried outside to the large room. "Thank God, it's only your daughter and Robby."

"Yo, Doc, we've been trying to call you man," Robby blurted out. "I guess the weather has the cell towers messed up."

"Larry checked Jeffrey and Justin out of school," Nicky said. "Annette is driving Catrina up to Escondido to bring them back."

"No! We agreed to never go back there," Tony gasped.

"The Group headquarters is up there," Father Clayton said.

"And I told her not to go anywhere in this weather."

"She tried calling you Doc," Robby pleaded. Robby and Nicky followed him to the door. Father Clayton retrieved the raincoat and umbrella from the coat rack and ran after them.

"Where's Lizzy?" Tony asked Nicky as he put on the raincoat.

"At my house, with Marley and Scott," Robby replied.

"Nicky, watch your sister until I get back."

"Daddy, I want to go," Nicky begged.

"No, the roads are too dangerous."

"Please let me go with you," Nicky pleaded and threw her arms around him.

Overcome with emotion over his daughter's display of affection, Tony opened the umbrella, put an arm around her, and guided her to the passenger side of the Olds.

"Sally, I won't let you leave this room unless I'm sure you're going to behave," Joseph Rodriguez said from inside the doorway of her cell-like room. "I'd like to forgo the sedatives because I really want you alert for this little outing." Sally backed away from the man whose face was rough and aged and yet somehow familiar.

"Come with me," he said and unlocked the chain from around the leg of the bed. He rolled it up in his hand, and she followed him out the door at a safe distance. "Don't worry about them," he said when she turned to look at the row of doors behind her. She also saw a door with a keypad box on the wall next to it and a uniformed guard sitting in front of a desk two feet away. Rodriguez pushed the elevator button and then pressed his hand to a black glass panel. He began to grumble when the doors failed to open. "That damn storm has everything screwed up." He pressed four numbers on the keypad above the glass, which Sally memorized while pretending to nervously look around. The floor numbers lit up inside the elevator car as it rose. They got off on L2 after passing S2, S1, and Ll. They passed people in an entryway who were rushing around, carrying pieces of ornamented furniture and pushing dollies stacked with boxes of china. A man was disassembling a set of armor and another removing a shield and a pair of swords from a wall. "I had hoped to present my entire collection to you, but everything is being moved because of the storm." He led her to the Cabrillo conference room, politely offered her a seat in an elaborately designed chair, and laid the chain on the floor. She could see the rain coming down hard outside through the closed balcony doors as she looked around for an escape route. "Sally, I could have blindfolded you," Joseph said, realizing her cognizance. "But I've wanted to show you my residence for a long time. These magnificent chandeliers and paintings, the rugs, flooring, window dressings, furniture, and the chair you're sitting in are all of authentic Spanish design. I regret the precautions we've been forced to take at this time. I've worked hard on my collection and I was hoping to impress you."

"Do I know you?" she asked.

"I suppose we both look a little different than we did as children. But who could ever mistake those beautiful green eyes and auburn hair?"

"St. Jude's?" She stood and followed him to the portrait of Juan Cabrillo Rodriguez, dragging the chain behind her.

"He's so stately in his armor, standing beside his white steed in full battle gear. This is my grandfather, several generations past, of course." Sally read the name under the portrait.

"Juan!" she gasped. "So, I didn't just make you up. I took my parents' death very hard; I never went back to the chapel."

"I know," he whispered. "I went there for months hoping to console you."

"What happened," she asked, "how did you end up here, working for this God-awful company?"

"I'm in charge of the entire Southwest region. You might say, partly because of you. You taught me the basics I needed to keep up in school; I was able to further my education and go to college. You always had your dreams, your stories. You didn't let the heartbreak of losing your parents stop you. We are alike in that way. Neither one of us gave up our dreams, even in the face of adversity. My dream is to raise my people out of poverty. I'm going to give them back the opportunities the Americans took away."

"Juan," Sally sighed and moved closer to him. "I thought I was doing something really good by helping you."

"I saved the things you left in the wine cellar," he said. "They're in a storage box. I always hoped I would be able to give them to you in person someday, to let you know how grateful I was for your kindness and to tell you how much I care for you."

"Juan," Sally said, softly, "how many people are locked up below with Randy and Walter? Are you experimenting on people?"

"Sally, always the reporter," he whispered. "I'm afraid your friend Walter didn't make it; pneumonia," he sighed. "Only Randy and his nephew are left."

"Oh God! Walter," she whimpered and closed her eyes despairingly.

"The Group has been working toward creating a gifted society for 30 years. We've been hugely successful here in the southwest. Soon I'll be the leader..." He stopped himself short and looked around the room that he knew contained substantial surveillance. "The Group's enhancement project has provided us control over enough people in Washington to facilitate a partnership with the Chinese. In time, we will gain control of their assets, and eventually, they will be working for us. Ultimately citizens in every country like Russia and Iran will be living peacefully under our scrutiny." He smiled at her eerily. "Sally, I'd love to do all this with you by my side; I have great plans." He leaned in close and whispered in her ear. "Soon, the Southwest will secede and join with Mexico to form a new country. I'll be its president; let me reward you for the kindness you showed me." He placed his hand gently on her cheek. "You can be the first lady," he sighed. "Together, we will raise my people out of poverty." Sally wanted to tell him he was crazy.

"What about Randy?" she asked daringly. "Will Randy be safe, and his nephew?"

"Hum, I'm not sure," he replied and backed away. "Alright, I suppose I could make them comfortable; but that will depend on you." She put her hands over her mouth, trying to be brave and not cry out.

"Did you take control of Randy because of me, or did I happen along and interfere with your plans for him?"

"Your relationship with Randy worked well for my purposes for a while."

"So, it was me," Sally sighed, "Juan, this idea, plan, whatever, is barbaric and will never stand up. What do you think will happen after you're gone; someone else will take over and dictate an agenda of their own liking. Do you think anyone else will have the same passion for your people? That's the way it is; that's the way it's been throughout history. Leave the God-fearing citizens of our country out of it and allow them to live their lives by following their own hearts and beliefs. Your ancestors were Christians, Juan, remember? This plan is pure evil."

"Your case has worth, Sally." Juan smiled at her lovingly. "We could be a great team," he chuckled. "Like you and Randy used to be. I can see where your compassion could actually help me maintain balance." He put his hand to her cheek again but Sally angrily spat in his face. "My darling Sally," he said while wiping the phlegm away with his handkerchief; "you can't maintain the good without the evil. That's one of the keys to the enhancement's success; by allowing a certain amount of evil to prevail." He tapped the keys on his cell phone and then stepped closer. "Actually, I just wanted to see you one last time, for old time's sake," he said, putting his hand around her throat; "and for you to see me." He snickered and squeezed tighter, then he let go and pushed her away. "One of the guards will take you back to the basement. I'll have the box delivered to you, but should go through it quickly."

The guard led Sally to the elevator by the chain; he used the same four numbers as Juan to open the doors. They rode down in silence, and when they reached the door to her room, she jerked on the chain, throwing him off balance. A kick to the groin put him on his knees. She pulled a fire extinguisher off the wall next to the elevator and hit him on the head twice, knocking him out. She looked up and saw a camera in one corner of the ceiling. She threw the canister at it and knocked it askew. There was another one above the door at the end of the hall, so she aimed the nozzle at it and covered it with foam. Then she snatched the keys from the guard's belt and freed herself from the ankle shackle. She somberly peeked through the window of the empty room next to hers where Walter had been kept and then moved to Randy's door, wiping tears from her eyes while nervously fumbling through the key ring until she found the one that unlocked his door. She shook him and called out to him, but he didn't move. The guard lying on the floor began to stir, so she ran for the door at the end of the hallway. The four numbers released the lock, and the door opened. She trudged up five flights of stairs to the bell tower through a steady stream of water. At the top, she found another set of stairs leading to the ground. She raced down them and ran for her life through a driving rain into the woods.

The guard from the basement staggered into the Cabrillo conference room with one hand pressed against the top of his head. Blood seeped from between his fingers, and his clothes were soaking wet. "Sir, I'm sorry, she got away from me! She knew the security code and opened the door to the roof. Now the basement is flooding with water from the stairwell. What do you want me to do with the others?" Rodriguez pressed the keyboard, but it failed to respond to his request to display the security cameras.

"What about the safe room?"

"The door is intact, sir," the guard replied.

"Let them drown; go to the east quadrant and organize a team. Find her!" Shepherd walked in just as the guard rushed out. He was waving his cell phone.

"We're being summoned to the situation room in the north quad." All monitors on one wall in the large room displayed a different version of a weather map. Rodriguez and Willis didn't recognize the man with the high-level Red ID tag that was gesturing at them.

"We've started the evacuation process," the man said. "All hard drives are being pulled; what we can't retrieve, we will wipe clean. There's a helicopter on the roof waiting to transport the data to a secure location. I need to go to the basement and make sure our work there is secure; if not, we'll take it with us."

"Who are you?" Joseph demanded. "Who sent you here?"

"D.C.," the man said and reached in his pocket for his ID. "I was originally dispatched here to investigate why one of your senior operatives is communicating with one of your tactical using an unapproved encryption."

"Get Colin Sadler in here and see what he has to say," Rodriguez growled.

"So, you know who I'm talking about," the agent said. "I'm keeping him in place for now in case your man, Ty Hemil, attempts to contact him again. His last coded message to Sadler said he was within five miles of here. He's planning an assault and is with someone named Lee."

"That's a cover story," Rodriguez growled. "He's bringing Lee in."

"Well, let's sort this out, shall we," the agent from DC said. He took out his cell phone pressed several buttons on the keypad, and held it up. The recorded conversation between Rodriguez and Shepherd, the same recording that Ty sent to Colin, began to play. "My superiors are concerned about certain statements in this conversation. You see, they're not aware of a plan to move the nation's capital to San Diego or turn the Southwest into a country of its own. Because this conversation suggests treason, I'm also here to take you and Mr. Shepherd into custody along with Mr. Samuels, who I believe is locked in your basement."

Rodriguez looked at Willis Shepherd.

"Did you do this?" he snarled.

"Mr. Rodriguez," the agent groaned, "your partner has remained loyal to your cause. It was you who underestimated our scrutiny and the coalition we already share with the NPC."

"But our efforts convinced them to consider debt forgiveness in exchange for the enhancement program," Rodriguez argued. "That should count for something."

"As of this moment, it counts for nothing," the DC agent replied.

Chapter 37

The rain pounded against Lee's raincoat as he trolled along the bank after crossing Lake Hodges in his aluminum fishing boat. Water had already covered the top of his feet, endangering his payload of weapons, ammo, hand grenades, and bomb-making materials that he had been stealing from military box cars for years. Twenty feet from the inlet opening, for better or worse, he would soon be inside and able to set charges that would bring down the beast that altered minds and killed his wife and hundreds of others. He silenced the murmuring trolling motor after hearing a noise that sounded like a dog barking but decided it was only his conscience reprimanding him for leaving Nightcrawler behind in the camper. He continued, using his paddle to move the boat closer to the shoreline and the mouth of the inlet. He turned his head when he heard the noise again; this time, he saw her standing at the water's edge. "How in the hell?" he muttered, remembering how awful he felt when he closed the door on her. Nate had sent a coded message to his friend Colin instructing him to shut down the security system in exactly twenty minutes, the time he estimated it would take Lee to reach the inlet and for him to reach the roof of the complex and initiate an assault. Lee would set off his load of C4 and homemade bombs, and Nate would take out the generators with the pipe bombs that Lee had constructed. Nate was relieved to hear that an evacuation plan had been executed because of the storm. Colin had found no schematic identifying a route to the inlet, so he would shut down the nearby hallways and the electrified fences and gates. His evacuation was on hold because of the arrival of a high-ranking agent from DC.

"You're gonna have to stop that barking," Lee strained to whisper. Nightcrawler ran up the hill, stopped, and started barking again. "Shush!" Lee hissed. He used the paddle to pole the boat to the bank, tied it to a bush, and trudged up the hill. He was out of breath by the time he caught up to her and sat down to rest but then heard something that sounded like one of the freight trains going through the Old Town switchyard. He looked to his right and saw a slurry of water and mud crashing down the hill. He let out a long distressful moan as he watched it bury his boat when it reached the water's edge. A wave of solid mud followed that was cutting a much wider path so he scooped up Nightcrawler and clumsily plodded up the hill to get out of its way. He stopped to rest again just below the road. "I've got to keep going," he said, looking at his watch. "It's just about time. I guess I'll just have to use what I've got left." He opened the backpack he was carrying to let her see the pipe bombs and grenades inside. Phoebe whined and shook her head. "And there's always this, providing my payload is sealed tight enough." He raised a flap on his outside coat pocket and let her sniff the remote detonating device inside. He stumbled up onto the silt-filled road; Phoebe trotted behind him. He crossed and stopped in front of the iron gates. He looked at his watch again. "Thirty seconds," he panted. "You need to get out of here now; find someplace safe, maybe that house up the road where those kids live; Nate says you know them." Phoebe looked up at him, tilted her head, then turned and ran up the mud-sheeted road. It was time. Lee slowly raised his hands, spread his fingers, and grabbed the bars. "Whew," he said, relieved that the gates were no longer electrified. He made his way up a brick walkway to the front doors. He heard a rumble and looked up past the stained windows and clay canopies and saw a cloud of smoke rolling off the roof. That meant Nate was in place and using the tear gas and pipe bomb he gave him to shut down the generators. The lights on either side of the doors flickered and went dark. He grabbed two tear gas canisters and a gas mask from his pack, shoved the bronze door handles down and rushed inside.

Tony drove slowly through the deluge along the winding scenic Hwy. 15. Nicky helped him navigate the fallen rocks along the dark shoulder and in the middle of the road that, at times, forced him to drive dangerously close to the edge of the mountain, further causing the edge to give way due to the disturbance of his wheels. Water streamed against the wheels and he was relieved when they finally reached Larry's driveway, which put them on higher ground for the moment. He and Nicky ran inside under the shelter of the umbrella after parking behind Annette's 4-Runner. Annette and Catrina were coming down the stairs when they entered through the kitchen.

"Doc, Nicky, what are you doin here?" Nette asked.

"Look, I understand why you came up here," Tony told her. "But we all need to get off this mountain now. Where are Jeffrey and Justin?" he asked, realizing the house was dark, "and Larry?"

"We don't know," she said. "Catrina and I have been lookin everywhere; there's no power."

"Did you check the barn?" Nicky said.

"No, good idea; I'll go look," Nette said.

"We'll all go," Tony said. They got in Annette's 4-Runner and headed to the barn. The horses and cattle were locked in their barns with food in their troughs and hay spread all around. "They apparently took care of business before they left, which is what we need to do." When they drove back to the house, Larry and the boys were waiting on the porch.

"What are you guys doing here?" Jeffrey shouted over the sound of the driving rain. "Mom?" Catrina jumped out of the 4-Runner, ran to her boys, and hugged them.

"We drove north to I-15," Larry shouted, "but the traffic is bottlenecked at the intersection."

"The State Troopers are up there searching cars," Justin added.

"Doc, we met your Olds coming up the drive," Larry said. Tony hadn't even noticed his car was gone.

"We didn't know what to think; it turned into the road that goes to Witch Mountain," Jeffrey said, looking toward the mansion. "The woman driving it looked like Sally Samuels."

"Who?" Tony said.

"What's she doing up here?" Annette added.

"This must be where she's been all this time?" Tony muttered. His first thought was to try and go after her, but he shook his head, dismissing the idea. "We'll have to take the flagship and your truck, Larry."

"We're riding with Nette," Justin said.

"Larry, you'll have to be careful. Water is crossing the road south of here, and I had to dodge rocks."

"Catrina," Larry said, looking at his ex-wife, "ride with me, please." She sighed and then nodded. "Looks like you and Nicky are riding with us, Doc," Larry said. "Nette's already down the driveway." They could barely see her tail lights through the heavy rain.

"Let's not waste time either," Tony said after he closed the umbrella inside Larry's truck.

"I never felt thunder like that," Larry said when they reached the road.

"Me either," Tony whispered. "I'm not sure that was thunder."

"I found her, sir; driving an Oldsmobile and bogged down in the mud near the bell tower," a security guard announced, interrupting Rodriguez and Shepherd, who were still trying to explain the recording, as well as a newly transcribed communication between Colin and Ty about a plan to alter the power and security systems. Sally was vigorously resisting the guard's tight grip around her arm while he pulled her further into the room. She had made her way down the mountain after escaping from the basement by following the private road and stumbling onto Larry's ranch. She was surprised but grateful to find Dr. Harding's Oldsmobile parked in the driveway. She called out, but when no one answered and after finding the keys in the ignition, she jumped inside and went back for Randy and Kevin.

"What is this woman doing here?" The DC agent growled.

"So, you came back," Rodriquez touted arrogantly, "for Randy."

"What should I do with her?" the guard asked.

"This is entirely your fault, Sally," Joseph growled. "If you weren't such a meddlesome bitch, none of this would be happening. You and your high and mighty ideas…just like when we were children." Shepherd frowned at Rodriguez through his dark glasses after hearing the telltale quiver of emotion in his partner's voice.

"Get some help," the DC agent bellowed to the guard. He took a gun out from under his coat and ordered Sally to sit down in a nearby chair. The cell phone in his pocket vibrated. “All right, check it out,” he told the caller. He turned to Shepherd and Rodriguez. “Sadler just received another message from Hemil stating they abandoned their plan because of the storm and are now on their way to the Salvation Army twenty miles away.” Sally recalled Lee telling her Nate’s real name, Ty Hemil. *Do ‘they’ mean that Lee is with him?*

“Let’s move this situation to the basement,” the DC agent ordered when an additional four guards arrived. “We’ll pick up Sadler on the way; this woman can perish alongside her husband and the two of you,” he said, directing his gun at Rodriguez and Shepherd. Shepherd reacted by rushing at the agent. One of the guards grabbed him and after a struggle between the two mammoth forces, they fell to the floor and wrestled while exchanging blows to the face and jabs to the ribs. When it looked as if the guard was the weaker of the two and unable to subdue Shepherd, the other two stepped up and struck Shepherd in the head with the butt of their rifles.

“You can’t do this,” Rodriguez growled. “It’s against policy.”

“I was sent here to clean up your mess,” the agent bellowed back at him. “And it would appear that most of it is right here in this room.” Everyone in the room tensed up when they heard a loud explosion coming from somewhere above their heads. Battery-powered spotlights came on after the lights flickered.

“What the hell was that?” Rodriguez growled.

“Let’s go ask Sadler,” the agent ordered. The guards followed their superiors to the elevator, pushing their prisoners ahead of them.

“Another failure up top, sir,” Colin reported when he saw the DC agent marching toward his station. “We should leave…” he paused when he saw Sally being escorted by a guard and blood running down the side of Shepherd’s face. “I can’t guarantee how long the backup systems will work under these conditions,” he continued slowly, realizing something must be going terribly wrong. “Most of the technicians have evacuated.” Colin frowned as he spoke after seeing that Rodriguez looked roughed up as well.

“You’re coming with us, Sadler,” the agent ordered.

"Of course," Colin said and hesitantly joined the marshaled group. Sally stood next to Joseph in front of the elevator that was to take them to the basement.

"You see, Juan," she said and looked around at their captors, "it seems that someone with a different agenda has already altered your plans to uplift your people."

"Your parents dumped you in that place so they could go off and play," Joseph groaned. "What did they teach you; to save an amusement park, to renovate the downtown area and a retirement community?"

"To give the homeless decent shelters for one thing," a muffled, graveled voice behind them broke in. They heard something like metal hit the floor and roll toward them. The entire area in front of the elevator suddenly filled with irritating smoke. The agent ordered everyone inside the elevator except for two guards that he directed to seize the man in the gas mask who was now running back toward the north quadrant. Another loud boom shook the elevator as it descended. The guards shoved their captives into the basement that was now three feet deep with water. Once in the basement, the DC agent opened the door marked *restricted.* The room looked like a morgue with stainless steel beds and overhead operating room lamps. He exited less than a minute later, carrying a silver briefcase and shouting orders to the guards to get on the elevator to the roof.

"Sir, why am I not going with you?" Colin asked.

"Kill this one now, we'll throw him out in route," the agent ordered. One of the guards lifted his rifle and pulled the trigger. Everyone crouched down when three loud shots rang out. "You got him, there's blood spatter on the wall," he growled when their target disappeared under the water. "Find him!" The guards searched but came up empty. "There's no time; let his body wash down the mountain." The elevator doors closed, and Colin rose from the water, holding his shoulder in the doorway of one of the cells; blood was pumping through his shirt. "Sir," he addressed his mentor, "why are we being left behind?"

"Because you and that smart-ass have been sending unapproved coded messages to each other discussing a plan to destroy this place," Rodriguez groaned. "Now, find us a way out of here!" Colin made a pressure bandage out of his shirtsleeve while he checked the door that led to the roof and bell tower. "It's locked; try your palm on the glass." Joseph and Willis both tried the plate and the four-digit code over and over to no avail. When pounding his body against the steel door produced nothing, Shepherd found an ax and began to strike the lock and the door.

Lee threw a grenade and a pipe bomb at the guards chasing him; debris and blood blew in all directions when the canisters exploded. He proceeded to climb the stairs to the roof to join Nate, which was an arduous task for the older man. He could barely hear the shouting over his own gasps from inside the facemask when he opened the door.

"Face down on the ground!" the voices were yelling through the haze of smoke and rain. He stumbled forward until several figures dressed in black and gray fatigues and wearing helmets appeared through his fogged mask. They were pointing their rifles at Nate lying face down on the flat roof. One of the soldier's jackets was open, revealing DHS in yellow letters across his protective vest. Lee took off the face mask and began to shout. "Hey! Hey! Over here!" They immediately pointed their rifles at him and repeated the order. "Are you Navy?" Lee panted when he saw the word Miramar stitched in red letters over their pockets. One of the DHS agents lifted his rifle barrel and protective headgear while the rest kept their rifles trained on him.

"Homeland Security; identify yourself!" the woman's voice demanded.

"We don't have time, ma'am," Lee said. "Sally Samuels and some others are being taken to the basement." Suddenly the Washington agent, along with the three remaining security guards, appeared through the cloud of smoke. They headed toward what they thought was their awaiting helicopter. "That's the guys that were holding guns on everybody; you need to stop them, ma'am."

"Excuse me, sirs," she shouted. "Your helicopter has been seized and taken to a US Department of Homeland Security facility. Step over here and tell me who you are and what your purpose is here." Nate took the opportunity to jump to his feet and run to the stairs.

"Someone's pounding on the door down there," he shouted through the thrashing rain, "but the stairwell is flooded."

"See if the elevator will take us down," Lee yelled to the woman the soldiers were addressing as their commander, "if that's okay with you, ma'am."

The DHS commander spouted instructions to her squad to take the DC agent and his men into custody.

"You two lead the way," she ordered, "and don't try anything, because these men have my permission to shoot you."

"Someone, help me," Sally cried from inside Randy's room, where she had raised him to a sitting position in his bunk. The water was four feet deep now and was almost to their waist.

"I'll help you stand him up on the bed," Colin said, wading inside. "I'm afraid the water is seeping in through the door pretty fast."

"You're bleeding," Sally whimpered.

"I'm fine," Colin replied.

"Randy's nephew, he's in the next room," she pleaded.

"We're going to get out of here," Colin tried to assure her. "My friend is coming for us." Sally worked her shoulder under Randy's arm after Colin stood him against the wall.

"Thank you," she asked. "What's your name?"

"Colin Sadler, Ms. Samuels. That noise we heard was from my friend Ty. You know him as Nate Roberts. He'll be here soon."

"You're Nate's business partner," she said, recalling the conversation at the restaurant, "and best friend," she added, looking at him closely for some sort of clue as to what else that relationship might truly consist of.

"Yes, we've known each other for a long time."

"I don't understand; your friend has done a good job of keeping me confused. Do you work for The Group or not?"

"We did," he replied, looking around at the dire situation they were in. "There's not enough time to explain that right now. I should go check on Kevin." Blood continued to stream from the gaping wound on the back of Shepherd's head. He was now pounding on the elevator door with the axe after realizing his efforts were only letting more water in from the stairwell.

"I hear the elevator," he shouted. Water gushed into the shaft as the soldiers inside the elevator pried the damaged door open about three feet. They pushed both Rodriguez and Shepherd against the wall after they tried to rush through the tight opening before everyone else.

"Hey Kemo; what the hell?" Ty said to his friend when he got off the elevator and met up with Colin carrying Kevin over one shoulder. "Is that blood?"

"Looks like you ended up saving my ass instead of the other way around," Colin gibed.

"Where's Sally?" Colin led him to the room where they found her straining to hold up Randy's large frame.

"Nate," she cried, "we have to get Randy and Kevin out of here, those people did something to them." Nate, Colin, and the soldiers helped Sally through the water and carried Randy and Kevin to the elevator. "Lee," Sally gasped when she recognized him standing inside the door. "I was sure you…"

"Would blow myself up?" he snarled. "I would have if it wasn't for…well, it wasn't cuz I didn't try." He thought better of admitting that Nightcrawler had misdirected him and that her estranged friend had helped him plan the assault. The water escaped through the door which never quite closed completely as the elevator lifted the crowded car. They listened to its motor struggle and then shut down. The soldiers pried the door open again to find they'd only moved up two levels to S1; water rushed over their feet as they disembarked.

"Looks like all four quadrants are flooded," Colin shouted over the buckling sounds around them. "We should hurry."

"How much further?" Sally asked.

"It's just one flight to ground level; we can take the stairs," Colin yelled. Rodriguez and Shepherd remained inside the elevator pushing buttons, thinking it might start moving again with the load lightened; it did.

"Commander said to let them go," shouted one of the soldiers when Lee lunged toward the elevator. "They'll get 'em up top."

"I'll take care of them now," Lee growled and reached inside his pack.

"No," Nate shouted. "The explosion could trap us all down here."

"They're the ones responsible for killing my Ellie," Lee blurted out.

"You have to save yourself, Lee," Sally cried.

"No," he said, shaking his head. "This is it; I have nothing else to live for."

"Lee," Nate begged; "Remember how that little dog Nightcrawler made you feel?" he said, glancing at Sally. "You said you felt something you hadn't felt in a long time…happiness; you're going to be happy again when this is over."

"Please come with us, Lee," Sally pleaded over the moaning walls. Nate and another soldier struggled to carry Kevin and Randy up the next flight of stairs through the thick mud that was oozing down the stairs after Lee surrendered to their pleas. The door to the ground level was blocked with muck and concrete debris and wouldn't budge, so they continued climbing. The walls they were bracing themselves against suddenly shook violently, and the stairwell behind them fell away. They watched as the water below besieged and carried the stairs away. A soldier in the rear of the group fell when the step under his feet crumbled, but his well-trained comrade quickly grabbed him by his Kevlar. Nate used his jacket as a rope to assist when the vest's Velcro tabs began to pull apart. With their man rescued, they noticed sections of the upper levels collapsing with the disintegrating mountain. They hurried to the door-marked roof, but no matter how hard the uniformed soldiers rammed and pried, the frame was badly twisted and completely jammed. Their rifle bullets had no effect, and then Lee produced two small square packages of C4 with fuses from his pack and set them over the door hinges. They hovered away from the door on the only part of the stairs left standing as he lit the ordnance, praying the blast wouldn't send them into the abyss below. A portion of the steel door blew away that was just big enough to squeeze through one at a time.

"We're interrogating everyone at EMR-ISAC at Miramar," the commander shouted as the rescued group huddled together. "Anyone requiring medical treatment will be attended to there," she dictated, observing Randy and Kevin's limp bodies being maneuvered through the breached door and Colin's bloody shoulder. Rodriguez and Shepherd had never made it to the roof. "You two ride with me," she said, nodding to Nate and Lee. "I have some questions."

"We should hurry," Nate shouted. "The building is coming down."

"We're not going to be much safer in the sky," the DHS commander added.

"You got a spotlight on this rig?" Lee asked the senior officer as their plane lifted. "Shine it through those trees; I think I just saw the two that got away down there." Lee reached into his pack and, one by one, pulled the pins from three grenades and tossed them out the door. The saturated ground exploded, creating an avalanche of trees and mud. "Ha-ha! That should slow them down."

"I'll take that pack, sir," the commander ordered. "Slide it over here."

"Did you get the evidence you needed?" Nate asked, noticing the silver briefcase beside her on the floor, but she didn't reply. He and Colin's stint with The Group was over, and he wondered what was next: perhaps endless hours of interrogation from DHS, the FBI, and possibly the CIA, and maybe prison. He looked over the edge of the open door and amazingly saw a reflection. "Look," he yelled; "I see three crosses."

"Just like the ones on the doors of the cathedral in Old Town," Lee noted when he looked down.

"Put a spot on the road," the commander yelled out.

"Two people are standing under an umbrella," Nate shouted over the sound of the helicopter motor as he leaned over the edge.

"Put us down," she shouted to the pilot. "Carefully; but be prepared to take off again if it gives way."

"I saw her turn south," Larry said as he drove slowly around the bend in the road that would take them in front of the Spanish mansion. "But I've lost her taillights; I can't even see the road."

"Larry, stop!" Tony yelled from the front passenger seat. Catrina and Nicky were sitting behind them in the extended cab. "It's a mudslide." Larry put the truck in reverse and backed up ten feet after his headlights revealed a five-foot-thick avalanche of mud surging across the road in front of them. The two men opened their doors and carefully stepped outside. Larry watched in bewilderment as the flow relentlessly carried boulders and asphalt over the edge of the disintegrated road and twisted guardrail. Tony carefully stepped to the side of the road and balanced himself against a tree. He thought he saw something that looked like the end of a skateboard sticking out of the steadily moving mud and then a sheared boogie board. "Larry?" Tony yelled out, paying little attention to the rain hitting his face. "Is that—" Then he saw something else: *stars…stripes.* No!" he gasped, realizing it was the side of Annette's SUV pushed against a tree, thirty feet below. "God, no!" he shouted while he hurried down the hill as fast as he dared. Larry started to follow him but stopped and yelled down to Tony.

"Doc, wait, I've got some rope and a winch." He rushed to his truck and quickly told Catrina that Jeffrey and Justin were trapped below with Annette. "Catrina, I don't have time to be scared," he said when she screamed out. "You and Nicky need to get bâck up the road." He handed her an umbrella. "Somewhere higher, safer. I'm going to brace the truck against one of those concrete road posts and shine the lights down the hill. I'll run the cable down to Doc as far as I can and then use the rope. We'll get them out." By the time Tony reached the 4-Runner, Jeffrey and Justin were climbing out the passenger side door.

"Annette's hurt, Doc," Jeffrey cried. "I can't get her to wake up. I found the neck brace, but I couldn't get it on her. There's blood, Doc," he said, trying to be brave and control the quiver in his voice.

"Okay, you did great," Tony said. "That's your dad's rope coming down; you two follow it up to the road. Your mother and Nicky are up there waiting for you; I'll get her out." The boys met their father on his way down with the rope; they heard a noise and looked back. The oozing mud had caught the rear bumper, turned the SUV, and bent it around the side of the tree. "Larry, hurry, we need to secure the truck," Tony yelled. The boys kept climbing, and Larry helped Tony tie the rope to the frame. Tony crawled into the front seat while Larry scrambled up the slick hill to tighten the winch. He called out to Annette; she let out a moan as if responding. Jeffrey had deflated the airbags and unlocked her seatbelt. Tony quickly put his arms around her and pulled her to the passenger side. The left side of her head was bleeding badly, and her left arm appeared to be broken. He spotted the neck brace on the floor and secured it around her neck and then yanked the Saints bandana from the rear-view mirror and tied it around her head. Everything from the back of the truck was scattered everywhere. While he looked around for something to make a splint or stretcher out of, he suddenly felt a jolt. He held on as the truck slid another five feet and slammed against a large rock. He looked behind him; the rope was stretched tight and appeared to be unraveling. The side of the truck started to cave in under the pressure of the mud, causing the windshield to shatter. He instinctively bent over Annette, shielding her from the glass. He heard another sound; like a voice in his head. *I can't hold this much longer*, the voice warned. He looked over the dash and saw a man bracing his hands against the front fender holding the truck in place. The lights from Larry's truck had illuminated the raindrops, casting light and shadows in all directions and making it impossible to see him clearly, except for the water bouncing off his floppy hat. "Who…" Tony began, but the voice in his head interrupted. *Hurry!* He slipped his arms underneath Annette and lifted her out of the seat. He desperately trudged through the mud to reach the rope tied to Larry's winch. But the muck sucked both Nikes off his feet and then pushed him down and dragged him six feet until it pressed him against a tree. He tightened his grip around Annette as the lava-like mud flowed across his legs, pinning him down. He heard a snap and a whip and saw the rope fly through the air. He looked back; the SUV was gone, and there was no sign of anyone, only the debris rushing by. Tony struggled to move his legs, but they were trapped under the weight of the mud. It seemed the sludge was getting deeper and more forceful with every thrash he made to free himself. The twisted body of a man wearing a security guard jacket drifted by; his neck was broken, and his arms were dislocated at each joint. He felt like a spectator, watching pieces of furniture and chunks of concrete and rubbish pass. The mud pushed another body passed them, jerking and turning, and then another, and another. A woman with her hair and face covered with dark mud churned violently by, and he wondered if it might be Sally. A surge of thick mud abruptly pushed and shoved them sideways. In a few seconds, they, too, would be swept down the hill and end up twisted within the mire. The force snatched him away from the tree, but instead of suffocating under the muck, he seemed to be caught on something. Then he lost his grip on Annette; he flailed his arms, grabbing for her, but he was grabbing at air. He screamed out her name, but he couldn't even hear his own voice. He suddenly felt like he was suspended, free. Had he already passed into the next world? Does it happen this fast? No, he could feel something under his arms, a limb or a branch.

"We've got you, sir." Was it another voice in his head? Before Tony had time to comprehend what was happening, he felt something cinch around his waist. Someone in black and gray fatigues was pushing him forward, and at the same time, he was being pulled up the hill with some type of hoist.

"Nette," he cried out and tried to look behind him.

"The lady's in the basket, sir," the voice yelled. "You'll both be topside in a sec. My commander has called for a Medevac." Nicky ran to her mud-sodden father as soon as she saw him on the edge of the road.

"Daddy, you're okay; I was so scared," she cried and wrapped her arms around him.

"Honey," he said, after they hugged for a long time. "You should know; Nette has a bad head injury. We won't know how serious it is until we get her to the hospital," he said when he saw the alarm in her eyes.

"Dr. Harding!" Tony heard a woman's voice shout out to him.

“Daddy, you’re never gonna believe who’s here,” Nicky whispered as they walked toward the uniformed woman.

“Commander,” one of the uniformed men shouted from somewhere within the veil of rain. “Medevac is here.”

“Dr. Harding, you should hurry if you’re going to get on board with Annette.”

“Brenda?” Tony gasped. Scott’s mother was the last person he expected to see. “DHS, Homeland Security?” he asked when he read the yellow letters across her vest.

“Yes,” she answered. “We don’t have time to talk…go!”

“Does Scott know…?” She interrupted him with a nod. “Please,” Tony begged. “Get Rick Samuels to UCSD; even if you have to handcuff and drag him there.” Brenda keyed her radio and ordered a unit to locate Rick Samuels as she ran back to a waiting helicopter. She signaled Nate and Lee, who were standing outside the door, to get inside as she spoke. Nate stepped inside and reached out to give Lee a hand up but he was bent down as if retrieving something he’d dropped.

“Come on,” the old man said, grinning as he stood up with Nightcrawler in his arms. “I’m glad you’re okay!” he said to her. When he got in, he saw the DHS commander staring at him peculiarly. “I found her, or she found me at our camp at the lake.” She recognized Phoebe immediately, of course. But she would keep that to herself until after his debriefing. Judging from the smile on his face, Phoebe’s presence could be helpful with that. Phoebe sniffed his right coat pocket as if looking for a treat. Lee nodded and reached inside. “Is everyone off the ground?” Lee asked Brenda as the helicopter lifted.

“Affirmative,” she said. “Why?” The helicopter suddenly vibrated and jerked sideways. The pilot quickly compensated for the gust that was knocking them around in the air. A fireball shot past the open door, and they could hear debris hitting the underside of the copter.

“What did you do?” Nate asked his friend.

“Ha, it worked!” Lee laughed as if surprised and stroked Phoebe. The pilot turned the helicopter and everyone on board observed the fireball below and the remainder of the mansion cascade down the mountain.

"You realize that you probably just destroyed crucial evidence?" Brenda shouted. Nate touched Lee's shoulder, letting him know he understood.

"Daddy," Nicky sobbed while he wrapped a blanket around her. "They should put ice on her arm to reduce the swelling." Larry, Catrina, Jeffrey, and Justin huddled together in blankets on one side of the Medevac while a medic rigged an IV. "That's what she does when one of us gets hurt. Maybe he could pack some over her head too."

"Hey, you have ice packs on board, don't you?" he addressed the medic. Jeffrey and Justin twisted the instant ice packs to initiate the cooling as the medic pulled them from a slide-out storage bin. They passed them to Nicky, and she carefully placed them around Annette's arm and against the side of the pressure bandage the medic had wrapped around her head.

"Look," Nicky gasped. "She's moving her arms and hands. That's a good sign, right?"

"Honey, honestly," Tony whispered. "It's involuntary movement; it means her brain is swelling. She needs to get into surgery as soon as we get to the hospital to relieve the pressure." He scrambled to the front of the helicopter and sat next to the pilot.

"Hey, Doc," the pilot said before Tony had a chance to say a word. "I should have known it was you down there saving somebody."

"Mitch," Tony exclaimed when he recognized the man behind the control stick as the pilot that rushed Molly to the ER when she fell ill at the rec center.

"Yeah," he replied. "It's been all hands on deck this week."

"Well, right now, we need to get Annette to the hospital ASAP and hope that Brenda means DHS can get Dr. Samuels there in time. She has a serious head injury."

"Annette," Mitch asked, "the lady with the little dog?" Tony nodded. Mitch pushed his radio communication button and began to speak directly to the ER at UCSD. "Inbound carrying accident victim with a serious head injury. Dr. Rick Samuels is en route to perform surgery; have the patient ready for his arrival." He turned and smiled at Tony. "That'll make the attendings scramble."

“Thanks, man,” Tony sighed. The vibration from Lee’s exploding boat reached them, shaking the Medevac.

“It’s okay,” Mitch said; “I’m starting to get used to flying in this weather.”

Chapter 38

Mitch found Tony and Nicky clean scrubs from the hospital supply room when they reached the hospital. "And I found these in the lost and found," he said, putting a pair of white socks to his nose, "they smell clean, and a pair of Crocs."

"Thanks again, Mitch," Tony said. "I really need to get up to trauma," he said, looking down at his mud-caked clothes. Before stepping into the shower, he called Brad to ask him to have Father Clayton take care of notifications and not say anything to Elizabeth just yet. Tony and Nicky hugged once more before they went in to check on Annette. "Sweetheart, you're too young to have gone through all the things you have. You took care of your mother when she wasn't capable and then lost her to the accident. And you took care of Lizzy, even though…" He took her hands and looked into her tear-filled eyes. "Even though..."

"I got my education in South C, remember Daddy?" Nicky interrupted. "You weren't around when Mom got pregnant."

"She takes up so much of my time," he said; "I really miss what you and I had. I wish with all my heart that I would have been a better father and I could have that back." They hugged and cried together. "I wish I could tell you Annette's going to be okay. We have to rely on Rick, and time and prayer." Five minutes later, Dr. Rick Samuels arrived with a four-man military escort.

"Where's the patient?" he demanded when everyone in the ER turned around and looked at him and the entourage dressed in military fatigues.

"She's in trauma-eval, Dr. Samuels," one of the male attendants answered. Rick headed to the elevator, but suddenly stopped and turned around.

"You don't have to follow me," he impatiently told his escort.

"We're just following orders, sir," one of the soldiers said in a disciplined regimental tone. "We are to deliver you to the patient."

"I don't understand why all this is necessary. I would have come knowing it was Dr. Harding who requested it. You scared my wife half to death when you landed on our front lawn." He got no response from the chaperons. "Let's go then." Thirty minutes later, Dr. Samuels and Tony were staring at three digitized MRI images in a dark room next to the OR, where a team was busy preparing Annette for surgery. "You know what has to be done," he said.

"Yeah," Tony sighed. "There was involuntary motion on the way in."

"Well, I don't know if it was your idea to use the ice packs but it helped slow the bleeding and swelling; it may have given us some time. You see how large the skull fracture is and the fissures; I'll have to replace it with a plate later if she..." he said and looked at Tony. "At least the opening will relieve the pressure from the swelling and hopefully prevent permanent damage. We'll take care of the upper left arm in a few days if she makes it through the next 48 hours. You can assist if you like.

Three hours later, Tony left the OR to check on Nicky in the waiting room after watching Rick remove a four-inch rectangle of skull bone. Rick remarked, while suctioning as much blood as possible from within the folds of her brain, that her small frame must have missed the side airbags altogether. He used medication to clot the bleeding, but there was bruising and swelling that could take weeks or months to heal. There was a crowd of at least thirty people in the hall outside the surgery waiting room when Tony turned the corner after exiting the double doors of the OR. Jose was the first to reach out his hand. He said something to him, but he either didn't understand him because he was speaking Spanish or because he was overwhelmed by the crowd he saw inside the waiting room through the glass. Charlie and Lewis, Molly, and her sister Charlotte were there, along with many other Mesa Village residents. Robby was sitting next to Nicky on a sofa, along with Todd and Marley; Jeffrey and Justin, still in their muddy pants and shoes, were in a row of chairs across from them. Larry and Catrina stood beside them with their arms around each other. He recognized parents from the daycare,

Mrs. Magnoli, and her daughter, Crystal. Her father shook his hand using the once badly broken arm. Doris and Jim stood in the hall with their two boys, Tom Burns and Cass, and many others he didn't recognize. Father Don appeared from within the crowd in the waiting room and rushed over.

"Dr. Harding," he said. "Can you believe how many lives Annette has touched?"

"All-all these people?" he stammered.

"Amazing, isn't it? I just spoke with Julia. Do you remember Julia and Jim, the couple that used to live in your house? They will be here tomorrow. Oh, and Annette's mother, Stella, is flying in tonight. Doc, please tell me, how was the surgery; how is she? Dr. Harding?"

"I wish I had something positive for you, Don," he finally said after watching another group of people stop outside the waiting room door. "But it's just too soon. There was bleeding and bruising in her brain, and a lot of swelling. Rick did the best he could; the next 48 hours should tell us what direction this will go. Uh-uh, I-I don't know what I'm going to say to Annette's mother. She must be out of her mind." He looked at Nicky through the glass windows. "I'm gonna need Nicky to help me with Lizzy."

"I'll send her out and forward your report to everyone," the priest said. "We're all praying, you know." He put his hand on Tony's shoulder. "We're rotating the prayers around the room so they're constant." Todd volunteered to drive Doc and Nicky home. Cass took Nicky's place next to Robby on the sofa.

"It'll be daylight soon, somewhere behind those rainclouds," Tony whispered to Nicky and Todd as they stood outside Brad and Katie's front door.

"I just heard the radio announce the ARkstorm is lifting," Todd added before the door slowly opened.

"Dr. Harding," Scott whispered. "I've been researching brain injuries; the statistics are all over the place." Tony walked the worried 10-year-old to the sofa and sat him down.

"Her brain has been severely traumatized," Tony said, noticing Scott's tablet on the coffee table displaying a diagram of the brain. "Dr. Rick removed some skull…"

"To prevent damage from swelling," Scott interrupted; "unless the blow concussed it so badly that..." He paused… "It could take months to heal or for her to wake up."

"Yes," Tony replied. Scott had certainly done his research. "I'm trying to be hopeful. Her strong spirit will help her make it through this. This is the hardest part, the waiting."

"Time is not necessarily a bad thing," Scott said, bowing his head. "Dr. Harding, I'm sorry." He took off his glasses and began to wipe his eyes, but the tears fell faster than he could keep up. Tony put his arms around him so he could cry on his chest.

"It's okay, kid; it's gonna be okay. Have you heard from your mother?"

"She'll be home in a couple of hours," he sniffled.

"I could use you and Nicky's help telling Lizzy what happened," Tony said, thinking how much the kid really needed his mother right now. "She listens to you."

"Sure," Scott said. "I can do that." Tony borrowed Brad's truck to drive back to the hospital after two short hours of sleep. Lizzy's summation had been simple, "…if only Phoebe were here." He avoided the waiting room and accessed the ICU through the doctor's entrance at the rear of the ward. He found Rick standing next to Annette's bed, watching a screen that displayed five horizontal lines representing her brain waves. "Minimal activity in Delta," Tony observed.

"As are the others; but it's early," Rick sighed. "The brain is still traumatized."

"Yes," Tony replied solemnly, looking at the secured ventilator tube, the IV needles flowing to both arms and the crown of sensors that led to the clicking machines reporting her brain waves and other vitals.

"You're probably not aware, but my brother was brought in by ambulance just as I was finishing up with Annette."

"Randy? No, what happened?"

"He presented with a stroke; Sally was with him."

"Sally?" Tony gasped, remembering Jeffrey and Justin's account of seeing her drive the Olds onto The Group's property.

"Apparently, they've been trying to reconcile. He told me recently that he still loved her. His condition has been complicated, however, by the brain abnormality; I'm afraid he's critical. I'm sending him to Johns Hopkins in Baltimore."

"But, his MRI; surely it must have..."

"His MRI never saw the light of day," Rick interrupted. "It was deleted from the hospital system."

"The Group; those sun-of-a-bitches," Tony grumbled. Rick stared at him in silence. "What? They're not watching anymore. Their headquarters has been destroyed; I was there; we were there," he said, looking at Annette's life-supported body.

"Sally's with Randy in room three," Rick finally said after a long silence and then left the room. Tony held Annette's hand and listened to the breathing machine as it assisted her lungs. Exhausted after hours of staring at the nearly flat brain waves trail across the small screen and trying to will them to rise and grow closer together, he walked across the ward to room three. Sally was dressed in pajamas and a bathrobe, sitting in a chair, and bent over Randy.

"Thank God!" she cried when she realized he was standing in the doorway. "Thank God, you're okay. How's Annette? Rick said she was seriously hurt."

"We won't know for some time," Tony sighed.

"They had me and Randy and Kevin locked in the basement of that evil place," she said looking back at her husband. "I saw your car; I took it. I'm sorry, but I had to try and get them out."

"Rick didn't tell me about Kevin, but I'm glad you made it out of there," he said, remembering the woman he saw being carried down the hill by the mud. "So, Rick doesn't know where you were?"

"DHS gave me a narrative. The truth is, The Group kidnapped us. We were locked up in their basement. Walter was there." She began to cry. "But they killed him; after all we did to try and save him. I don't know what their narrative is to explain Kevin, but I know he's in very bad shape. He put his arms around her to console her, but all he could think about was the devastation The Group had caused.

"At least it's over."

The ICU waiting room was much smaller. Robby and Marley were propped up against each other on a loveseat. Nicky and Elizabeth sat with their arms around each other. Molly and her sister were gone, but Charlie and Lewis, Father Clayton, and some others sat in a row of chairs, taking turns praying. Tony reported there was no change in Annette's condition and tried to convince everyone it was still early, according to his prior experience with trauma patients at St. Joe's. When Brenda Bolton and Scott stepped off the elevator, he hurried to meet them in the hall. "How are you, kid?" Tony greeted Scott with a handshake. "Brenda, thank you so much for..."

"Thank me for what, Dr. Harding?" she quickly interrupted.

"Of course," Tony scowled. "That's right; you just work at the airport."

"Mom, I'm going to talk to Robby," Scott said while handing her his tablet.

"That's fine, honey," she replied and turned to Tony. "Is there someplace where we can talk privately?" He led her to the patient consult room. "One moment," she said before they sat down. She took a small device from her purse and walked around the small room with it held out in front of her. "It's okay to talk in here."

"Seriously?" Tony growled. They sat down and Brenda powered on Scott's tablet. "Does Scott know what you do?" he quizzed.

"To a limited degree," she replied and put the tablet in Tony's lap after pressing two icons. "We have a pact to never talk about it openly. This is from inside the facility above where we found you; it was the southwest headquarters of The Group. DHS ordered our team to search for it after this went viral on YouTube yesterday. The Director's office was being overrun with inquiries about subversion and a possible terrorism link." Tony frowned as he studied the video.

"This is Jeffrey's recording of the night he and Justin snuck onto the property. Wait this—this is my report and possibly the files Sally stole from Rick. But everything was lost in the fire," he said and then turned to her. "Scott promised he wouldn't copy it."

"He didn't," Brenda said. "He told me about helping you only after this went viral. DHS traced its origin to an online college newspaper at SDSU."

"Jared Dawson," Tony whispered; "Sally's friend."

"We've been watching The Group for a number of years. Scott has helped us break their codes, unknowingly, of course. I can't elaborate on the full scope of their activities, but our hand was forced when this spread throughout the internet. A federal judge issued a search warrant, and as it turned out, none too soon. They were in the midst of evacuating and taking crucial evidence with them. We were able to confiscate a cache of evidence; it details their methods of...well..."

"Controlling people's behavior," he groaned.

"Yes," she replied slowly. "Everything we find there shall be classified and will be used to prevent this from happening again." She touched the screen, and a photo gallery appeared. "These are photos of people whose remains we found at the bottom of Lake Hodges and in the debris in and around the complex."

"I know this woman," Tony sighed when he saw a photo of Rebecca in the photo array. "I'm sure they had her stalking me." She switched to a video of bulldozers pushing through mud and people wearing white hazmat suits loading plastic body bags into the backs of ambulances.

"A statement has been released that an anonymous student from SDSU submitted the videos to the web publication. Subscribers began sharing it, and soon it exploded into a hot topic, creating all kinds of conspiracy theories."

"Anonymous student? You have a narrative for everything," he whispered. "So, this is what you do; investigate atrocities and then lie to the public? And what are you going to do with the stuff you found there?"

"Doc," she whispered. "We want our citizens to live in peace; not in fear of people like The Group. I'm not privy to what was done with what we found."

"Then we're still in danger of someone else using this enhancement. Wouldn't it be nice if something as organic as discipline, values, and convictions could fend off what The Group was trying to do?"

"If only people weren't so complicated," she sighed. "DHS owes you and Dr. Samuels, and Sally and her friends a debt of thanks for your steadfast work. You managed to put all the pieces together. I'm curious, though; I know why Dr. Samuels stopped trying after two of his attempts to expose the enhancement failed. But why didn't you try to do something with the information you had before you went to Louisiana; before Annette's house burned?"

"Because getting her back was the most important thing in the world to me; more than putting my family in danger, and certainly more than your accolades. Let me ask you something; why do you involve your son in government conspiracies? He might be a genius, but he's a ten-year-old in his heart. He needs his mother around to have fun with and to get a hug from when he needs it. Not that any of us minds taking care of him, but he should know it's you he can depend on, not us or someone named Guardian. Who the hell is Guardian?"

"You're right, of course, Doc," Brenda sighed. "I created Guardian."

"You?" Tony sneered. "Why does that not surprise me?"

"Me or one of my staff when I'm not unavailable. I would never leave my son completely unsupervised. He's the reason I took this assignment with DHS. I'm going to trust you with something that you can't tell anyone, not even Annette. His father was gifted, or so we thought; he died before Scott was born…from an aneurysm. His autopsy revealed an unusual amount of gray matter and altered neurons, like the others. Scott inherited his father's DNA; and the mutant cells. I agreed to help DHS with their investigation in exchange for new identities and relocation to Mesa and their promise to protect Scott. Honestly, I don't know what the FBI was waiting on, but the video forced their hand. I'm good at what I do, Doc; just like you. And I love my son just as much as you love your daughters. Our households will always be different because of our commitment and vigilance. Our children are going to grow up and be better adults because of the examples we give them."

"I learned the hard way what happens when you're an absent parent. I'd give anything if I could have the time back that I lost with my kids. I'm never going to put anything ahead of them again. That's the example I want to give them; that nothing is more important than they are."

Brenda looked at her cell phone. "Someone is on their way up; we should meet them." Three minutes later, they were standing in front of the elevator. When the door opened, Brenda directed the first man who stepped out, wearing sunglasses and carrying an overnight bag, to the ICU. The next person to step out was his friend Harry.

"It was you!" Tony gasped after giving him a bear hug. "You sent the videos to Jared."

"I found out who Jared Dawson was," he explained, "and his relationship to Jane Doe. I called him after reading she took time off, and The Post kept giving me the runaround."

"Yeah, Betty got the same crap from St. Joe's about you. I was afraid—well, never mind about that; I'm glad you're safe." The last man to step out of the elevator was older, wearing a dark plaid shirt, jeans, and work boots, and was carrying something wrapped in a towel. Lizzy leaped from her seat in the waiting room when she saw Phoebe wriggle her head out from under the towel. The old man gingerly put the little dog in her arms when he saw the look on her face when she ran up to him.

"Where did you find her?" Lizzy exclaimed. "She's been missing for weeks. Oh Phoebe, Phoebe, I missed you so much!" She cuddled her closely while Phoebe licked her face.

"She's been keeping me company," Lee said, "I was told her family was here at the hospital and anxious to get her back."

"Anthony Harding," Tony said, holding out his hand. "I can't tell you how much this means to us—to Elizabeth. Have we met? You look familiar."

"My name is Lee," the old man said. "I found her, or she found me up at Lake Hodges. DHS picked me and my friend off the mountain, like they did you. We crossed paths up there in the chaos."

"Phoebe was on the mountain?" Tony gasped, remembering the voice in his head and the illusionary figure holding Annette's truck in place.

Charlie slowly rose from his chair in the waiting room after looking long and hard at the man talking to Dr. Harding.

"Leon, is that you?" he said hesitantly when he reached the group standing in front of the elevator.

"Charlie?" Lee said. "Charlie, look at you; you done got old," he added as the two old friends hugged each other.

"Where have you been all these years?" Charlie asked. "Your family hired a PI to look for you, you know; we thought you were dead. Lewis," he bellowed and took Lee by the arm and pulled him into the waiting room, "look who this is?"

"Daddy," Lizzy said anxiously, "you have to take Phoebe to Nette."

"They're not going to allow her in ICU, honey," Tony said, bending down and hugging his daughter and petting Phoebe on the head. "Look at the mud on her."

"But you have to," she begged. "She can make her well. Put her in a bag and sneak her in."

"Let's wait until Rick moves her to a floor where there'll be less scrutiny," Tony tried to reason. "They like to keep things sterile in the ICU."

"But Daddy; I thought you believed," Elizabeth whimpered. "But Daddy," she kept repeating as he ushered her to where Nicky was sitting in the waiting room. She gave in when Annette's friends suddenly gathered around to welcome Phoebe back home. When the excitement died, she carried the little dog to a bench in a secluded corner. "You know what to do," she whispered.

Something made Sally raise her head in spite of the hypnotic flutter of Randy's breathing machine that had made it impossible to keep her eyes open. A tall man wearing sunglasses and toting a suitcase was standing inside the door. "Nate," she sighed. "I never expected to see you again, except for maybe in a prison cell. Is your friend, okay?"

"Colin is fine, and you're right, but at least we're free to walk around with one of these on." He raised his right pant leg and showed her the blackstrap with the electronic disk around his ankle. "I brought you some clothes." He put the suitcase down just inside the door.

"He's in bad shape," Sally said and touched Randy's face. "Your people did a good job of swiping him of everything. Rick's sending him to Johns Hopkins."

Nate took off the sunglasses and put his hand on her shoulder. "I'm sorry, Sally; I never expected them to do this to their golden boy," he said as he looked at Randy's comatose face. "Whoa!" he huffed and staggered backward.

"What's wrong?" Sally gasped.

"I saw someone or something—uh, right there," he said, pointing at the monitor displaying Randy's vitals.

"What do you mean?"

"Nothing," he said, repeatedly squeezing his eyes open and shut. "My contacts must have scarred my eyes, but I have no doubt who that is." Sally followed his eyes and looked through the glass window; Jared stared back at them.

"Jared, you shouldn't be here," she said after rushing out of the room to meet him.

"I had to make sure you're okay," he sighed. "Why is *he* here?" Jared glared at Nate through the glass. "Doesn't he work for *them*?"

"He's cooperating with DHS," she replied.

"How can you be so sure? Maybe you should stick with the first impression you had of him."

"Lizzy," Tony whispered to his daughter, who was asleep on a bench in the waiting room. "Time to go home."

"Did Annette wake up?" she said when she saw Phoebe lying beside her on the cushioned seat.

"No, honey, not yet," he answered. "But we have to go; you guys have school tomorrow."

"I don't understand," Lizzy whined and looked at Phoebe. "Why didn't she wake up?"

Tony tried to explain to her again at breakfast that Annette's brain was bruised and swollen and that no one could say for sure how long it would take to heal. "Dr. Rick's going to take her off the meds that are making her sleep tomorrow," he said to his frowning daughter, who was holding Phoebe in her lap after being freshly bathed and blow-dried. "After that, we'll have to wait and see what happens."

"Man, I hope this goes well," Harry said sympathetically as they watched the girls leave for school with Robby and Todd. "Sounds like Elizabeth was expecting her to wake up by now. It's hard for someone her age to understand how these things work."

"Elizabeth believes, I, we, uh," Tony stammered and shook his head. How could he explain Phoebe without sounding certifiably insane, even to his best friend who had been with him through all his emotional highs and lows with Carol?

"Well, I guess that's just Elizabeth," Harry said, "right?"

"Yeah," Tony sighed. "Harry, I don't know what I'm going to do if Annette…I asked her to marry me, you know."

"That's great, man," Harry said, smiling. "Look, why don't we take Phoebe to the hospital? I've read that coma patients sometimes respond to familiar things, especially when there's an emotional connection." They entered ICU with Phoebe under Tony's white coat through the doctor's entrance and immediately noticed a bustling of activity in Randy's room. Tony handed Phoebe to Harry and instructed him to take her to Annette's room when he saw two orderlies push Randy's bed through the door and down the hallway.

"Is Randy on his way to Johns Hopkins already?" he asked when he caught up with Sally, who was right behind the orderlies, along with the man wearing sunglasses who got off the elevator at the same time as Harry.

"They're transporting him upstairs first," she replied. "Rick wants to make sure he's stable before traveling. Dr. Harding," she said, grabbing his arm as they turned the corner and headed toward the exit doors, "he woke up during the night, and he recognized me."

"That's impossible, I mean, unbelievable. I don't understand, but that's excellent news." Tony met up with Harry outside Annette's door.

"What's all that about?" Harry asked as they watched the entourage around the bed, moving down the hallway of glass windows. "And who's the guy with the sunglasses?"

"Randy regained consciousness," Tony replied. "That dude's been hovering over Sally since he got here."

"He looks a little seedy to me," Harry remarked. Harry had placed Phoebe beside Annette's good arm. She lifted her head and looked at Tony through the glass with her bright brown eyes. Tony opened his mouth and almost spoke to her out loud. *Why…why not Annette; why not both Annette and Randy?* She put her head down and Tony turned away and steadied his body against the window as he felt himself giving way to the same anguish he felt so many times over Carol's behavior. "Someone else is here," Harry whispered.

"Stella!" Tony panted when he recognized the woman sitting in a chair next to Annette's bed, whom he had assumed was a nurse. "Why didn't you call me," he said after rushing inside, "I would have picked you up."

"Your Father Clayton took care of us," she replied. She was stroking Coco in her lap and desperately trying to remain calm, but her voice was trembling as she looked at her daughter, who was lying so lifeless and dependent on machines. "He was kind enough to arrange for us to stay in the hospitality wing." She looked at her daughter again. "I don't know if I can do this again, Doc." Tears were rolling down her face. "This feels so much like Sonny's last days. Coco was lying beside him, just like Phoebe was next to her now. Every once in a while, he would touch her to make sure she was still there, and she'd lick his hand." She laid her hand on Phoebe's head. "But she doesn't even know Phoebe's here; she doesn't know I'm here; she doesn't know anything."

"Rick is changing her meds; she could wake up soon," Tony sighed and put his hand on Phoebe's back. "She's going to wake up, right Phoebe?"

Chapter 39

Sally woke up to a woodsy panorama outside the passenger window of Nate's Jeep Cherokee rental. She had dozed off shortly after the pit stop they made at a small gas station/convenience store where she had purchased an off-brand bottled water and a nutrition bar. "I didn't mean to fall asleep on you," she sighed, turning her head back to look at him. "We were talking, and I just…"

"It's okay," Nate said, grinning from behind his sunglasses. "It's a long boring ride to where we're going; you didn't miss anything." She looked at the half-empty bottle in the cup holder. She remembered thinking when she broke the seal that there was no reason to think her drinks would be tampered with anymore. The nutrition bar tasted nasty, but that was to be expected, so why did she feel groggy? Was she just being paranoid?

"How did you get permission to leave town with the ankle bracelet?" she asked, as she straightened from her slumped position; "and what is it that I must see before leaving for Baltimore?" Nate checked the rear-view mirror before answering.

"You'll see, shortly. They tried to convince me that wearing the bracelet was for my protection, but I have a problem trusting the government with my safety."

"Do you know if they ever found Juan?"

"Lee and I saw Joseph and Willis running through the woods from the helicopter. He threw three grenades out the door that exploded on the ground; maybe he got them. There were a lot of dead and injured pulled from the debris, but no one's ever going to tell me if they were among them."

"I hope Annette Rylan recovers from her injuries," she sighed. "I never intended for her to get caught up in this."

"She's the reason you had me delete the Nightcrawler outline, isn't she? It was really weird how that little dog found me and Lee. There is certainly something special about her."

"Yes," Sally replied, "and peculiar how Randy suddenly got better. The Nightcrawler story can never be told."

"You're not saying she had something to do with that? I assumed the stories in your outline were fictitious." Sally turned her head away and looked out the passenger window again as if avoiding his question. "Sally, remember the night I brought the suitcase to the hospital, and I thought I saw something, someone."

"You saw Jared, right?"

"I saw a man standing next to Randy's bed," he said, shaking his head, "but when I blinked, he was gone; Randy woke up a few hours later. Lee brought Nightcrawler to the hospital to return her to Annette; she is in bed next to her across the ward from Randy. There were similar accounts in your outline."

"I can't talk about it," she sighed, "because there is no explanation, so there's no proper ending. Please, are we in the Calaveras?" she asked, trying to change the subject.

"Yes, I grew up in a little town a few miles ahead. Sally, I have things that I can't explain either, not with words. Things you must see for yourself in order to believe."

"Your friend Colin said as much, but I don't know why you have to be so mysterious. Remember, I have a flight out of LAX tomorrow afternoon." The road took them through the middle of a little town where Nate pointed out a small school he attended with his brother and many places along the way that seemed to bring back good memories judging by the smile on his face. It took them about a minute to travel from one end to the other; then, their journey continued up the mountain for another five miles. Nate turned onto an even narrower road composed of asphalt and gravel mix.

"It's been a while since I've been up here. The road looks a little washed; I hope the house survived the storm. Dad used to keep everything a lot more ship-shape than this."

"So that's where you're taking me?" Nate didn't answer because they had come upon a modest stone-and-mortar home, typical of one built to withstand the mountain winter weather. It was surrounded by nearly three acres of partially cleared land with patches of yellow-flowered weeds that were swaying in the light breeze that also produced an eerie whooshing sound through the tops of the pines. There was a faded green wooden barn behind the house.

"Everything looks good," Nate said. He took his time surveying the grounds as he drove toward the barn. "I should put the Jeep inside."

"Why can't we just drive up to the house?" Sally asked while observing a small trickle of smoke coming from a chimney, an array of solar panels attached to a pole behind the house, and two small satellite dishes attached to the roof. A feeling of dread came over her when Nate drove into the dark barn. It got worse when he turned off the motor and got out in what seemed like a big hurry to close the two large doors. The memory of the basement and the cell she was confined in rushed to the forefront of her mind. The barn suddenly became dismal and menacing, and she realized she didn't really know for sure where he had taken her. There were no road signs, and she had only guessed they were in the Calaveras Mountains. Why had she been so fuzzy-headed when she woke up? Why didn't she think to check the GPS on her cell? She checked her coat pocket for her phone and then the seat; it was gone. Her bag wasn't on the floor next to her feet where she put it. Panic began to build as she thought perhaps, she was made to fall asleep, and as far as anyone knew, she was on her way to Baltimore. She heard Lee's voice in her head through the dead silence of the barn, warning her that Nate worked for The Group and remembered Jared telling her she should have gone with her first impression of Nate. She began to ask herself other questions, such as what was his real reason for removing the ankle bracelet and why he had stuck so close to her at the hospital. Was this where Juan Cabrillo Rodriguez was hiding, waiting for her? Was Juan's obsession with her the reason she was brought here? After all, it had been his reason for indoctrinating Randy.

"Looking for this?" Nate asked after opening the passenger door and allowing her to watch him take her phone from his inside coat pocket and see that the battery had been removed. Sally got out and backed away from the car.

"Nate, what's going on here?"

"I couldn't take the chance that someone would follow us," he replied and moved toward her. "I have a commitment that I plan to keep."

"No!" she yelled and ran to the doors and pushed them apart. A man wearing a gray hoodie over a black baseball cap was approaching quickly. He was clearly holding something in his right pocket; perhaps a gun. "Oh, my God," she gasped.

Nate caught up to her and grabbed her.

"Kemo!" he yelled.

"Hi-yo," the man answered. "Get back inside!" They each grabbed an arm, pulled her back inside the barn, and closed the doors.

"Mother okay?" Nate asked after forcing Sally down on a hay bale.

"She sent me out here to make sure you weren't followed." The man said. Sally gasped when he removed the hood and she recognized Colin. "And she said to stop using the nicknames," Colin added.

"What did you do with your ankle bracelet, bro?" Nate asked.

"Well," Colin said and lifted his pants leg, "my cat has plenty of food, litter, and a new collar." Sally leaped from her seat on the hay bale and scrambled for the doors. Nate clutched her arm and pulled her backward. She jerked loose and ran around the Jeep, and grabbed the driver's door. Colin pulled her hand away from the door handle and shoved her against the door. Nate was there in an instant to help pin her against the truck.

"You work for The Group," Sally cried. "Is *mother* some sort of code word?"

"Please, Sally," Nate huffed. "Stop fighting. We're brothers; this is our home; that's why we brought you here." Sally stopped struggling, and they loosened their hold. "Give her your sweater, Kemo-uh-Kerry," Nate said.

"I'm glad to hear your husband is doing better, Sally," Colin said, smiling as if proud to be able to say something comforting and then slipped his sweater around her. He removed a device from the pocket that she thought held a gun. It looked like one of Nate's calling card cell phones.

"Destroy any of these you have left; Mother says the encryption is compromised."

"What is this place?" Sally demanded. Neither one answered, but it was clear they were keeping something to themselves.

"I suppose it's time," Nate said, looking back and forth between them.

"I'll watch things from out here for a while," Colin said. Nate put an arm around Sally's shoulder and led her outside and across the property towards the house. "It's best we walk slowly and normally, just in case."

"Why?" she asked. As they moved across the grassy yard and got closer to the house, Nate's silence made her all the more anxious. "I'm not going in the house until you tell me why you brought me here," she said when they reached the front porch.

"Sally," Nate said, "None of us was sure how you'd react to what you're going to see inside." He put his hand on her shoulders. "I want you to know that this was always the plan…the real mission. I'll take you to L.A. immediately if you like, but you have to go in the house first." He guided her across the porch and pushed the door open. The house was warm from the wood stove that was standing on a hearth and smelled of sweet apples and cinnamon. A woman was standing at the sink drying her hands with a checkered hand towel; she turned around when she heard the door creek.

"Michael, honey, what took you so long?" she asked recognizing his tall stature. "Kerry's been here for three days-Kerry; is that you, Kerry?"

"No," Sally said. "It's not." She pulled back the hood. The gray-haired woman, who looked to be in her late sixties, grabbed the edge of the sink with one hand to steady herself. She moved forward, helping herself along by propping herself against the dining table and the door. "Michael, you and Kerry did it!" she gasped. "I can't believe it!" Sally moved closer and immediately noticed the woman's green eyes-her mother's eyes. "Who," she began, "no, this isn't possible. This is some sort of trick." Sally shook her head in disbelief, turned around and headed to the door.

"Sally, please," the woman begged. Nate blocked her path by holding his arms out.

"Get out of my way," Sally growled, "Nate or Michael; whoever you are."

"Your father and I had to start over as different people with new identities," the woman cried out. "I never wanted to leave you, but it was the only way out and make sure you would be safe."

"Out?" Sally demanded and turned to face the woman again. "Safe from what?"

"The CIA," her mother whimpered. "We worked for the CIA; we were emissaries posing as freelance writers. We planned to resign by the time you graduated from high school." She pulled one of the chairs out from the table and sat down; she appeared to be overcome with exhaustion. "We naively thought they would let us," she sobbed. "The trestle collapse was no accident, but we were late; we missed the train by five minutes. A trusted friend helped us out of the country and back into the U.S. and arranged our new identities. We moved as close to you as we dared."

"And you just started a whole new life without me?" Sally huffed and looked at Nate. "You could have gotten word to me; I would have kept your secret." Sally's eyes began to sting from the tears she was trying to suppress. "Maybe I wouldn't have felt so alone."

"We were afraid to try and contact you," her mother replied. "You were a headstrong child and you grew up to be just as impetuous and determined; we knew you wouldn't stop until you found us. Too many people knew you were our daughter. You would have led whoever tried to kill us right to our door, and they would have spared no one. When Kerry and Michael were old enough, we told them about you; as if they didn't already know you were someone special because of the things we collected about you over the years."

"Kerry and I applied to The Group's headquarters after we were told you were investigating the behavioral changes," Michael added.

"We're still somewhat in the loop," her mother interrupted. "It's a small loop that's getting smaller every year, I'm afraid. But our good friend who helped us exit

France still moves within certain circles in Washington. We still communicate, secretly, of course. He warned us we would suffer horrible consequences if we got too close. And then you married one of their political prospects. You were in danger and given your spirit, we felt we had to intervene. Your father and I promised one another we would never get involved with such projects again, but you were putting yourself in danger." Sally suddenly felt overwhelmed and sat down in a leather recliner beside a table that bore a stack of San Diego Daily Post newspapers along with a pair of black-rimmed reading glasses.

"I missed you and Daddy so much." Sally began to cry and wiped her eyes with her hands. Nate handed her a napkin and knelt down beside her. "And Daddy is gone?" she sighed, remembering that he told her his father had died of a heart attack. A man's voice rang out from the doorway.

"Not yet," he said and leaned his fishing rod against the wall and then threw his string of fish on the floor outside the door. "Sally, my God!" he hollered and rushed to her. Sally barely had time to stand before he had scooped her up in his arms. "My baby girl," he cried. "Oh, my baby girl," Park Stevens repeated over and over.

"Daddy," Sally moaned and wrapped her arms around him.

A week passed without any significant change in Annette's condition, so Dr. Samuels moved her to the fifth floor. The telltale monitors that displayed minimal brain activity were now recording the info within the confines of the nurse's station. Tony checked on her four times a day and Elizabeth brought Phoebe to visit every day after school. Phoebe would lick her master's face, but there was no retort; no grumbling, no shooing, no complaining. Robby downloaded her favorite tunes to his MP3 in hopes the familiar sounds coming from the ear buds would spark a reaction. Stella stayed by her side and was considering Dr. Samuels' suggestion that she allow him to remove the ventilator.

"This is too much," Stella said to Tony one afternoon through her tears. "I can't stand watchin her deteriorate little by little each day."

"She's very much alive, Stella," Tony replied trying to encourage both himself and the sobbing mother. "We just need to give her brain more time. I've thought about it; I can bring her home and turn my office into a hospital room. Annette's house will be finished soon; you can move in there."

"I lost count of the people who have come to see her. I can't believe how many friends she made in the two years she's been here."

"She touched a lot of lives."

"That's why my decision has been so hard to make."

"Decision?" Tony asked.

"I know you love her, Doc," Stella said, "but I'm her legal guardian. So, if she manages to breathe on her own after Dr. Samuels removes the ventilator, I'm gonna take her back to Louisiana where she can be surrounded by the things she grew up with." She stroked Coco, who was always somewhere within her reach. "Coco's due to have a litter in a couple of weeks; I'd like for that to happen at home."

Tony visited the hospital chapel every morning before work; Father Clayton dedicated prayers to her recovery at each Mass. But when another week went by without any change, the ventilator was removed. To everyone's relief, Annette continued to breathe on her own. Stella began consulting doctors about the travel arrangements with the small miracle behind her. Tony made tacos and burritos and refried beans the following Friday. He invited the neighbors for dinner and broke the news to them about Stella's decision. Everyone went home with sad faces after passing on dessert. Saturday morning, he went to the Mesa Village rec room, where he found Charlie, Lewis, and Molly.

"You should go to the hospital before Stella takes her back to Louisiana," he told them. "It might be the last time you see her for a while." Charlie put an arm around Molly while she cried. Tony called Doris and then Jose. "I don't know the names of everyone that came to the hospital," he said to each of them. "Please see that they know her mother will be moving her in the next few days." Then he walked down the street to the rectory.

"I can't tell you how sorry I am, Doc," the priest whispered as they sat in the reverently lit prayer room. "I've been praying every minute of every day for her recovery. I have to admit, I've asked God a thousand times why this had to happen to her." He looked around at all the pious faces on the shelves and walls. "I'm not supposed to question God's work; this is His world after all. He put us here, but it's understood that He's going to come for us someday because He loves us and wants us for Himself. But my heart is in pain and it keeps telling me that none of you deserves this. I wish I had something better to offer you, but right now I'm feeling a little too human."

"Thank you for that, Don," Tony whispered. "Stella's determined to take Annette back to Louisiana. The truth is, maybe I do deserve this for the way I neglected Carol and my girls. Maybe this is God's way of punishing me." He rested his head in his cupped hands. "Elizabeth was so convinced that Phoebe would make Annette well. I think I even fooled myself into believing it."

"You must learn to forgive yourself, Doc," the priest whispered and put a reassuring hand on his shoulder. "God forgave you the minute you asked Him to. You and Carol were too young to know what marriage would be like; you both made mistakes. And we can't entirely discount how that little dog has affected the hearts of so many. You know the Bible says that God put the animals on earth for mankind to use for food and clothing, to pull our plows and carry our gear, even to open our hearts with their unwavering loyalty and companionship."

"So, the *magic* we all witnessed was just something we opened ourselves up to, something we wanted, needed to see? Or maybe, it was something we were set up to believe by an artificial entity," he sighed.

"Are you talking about SDCT again, Doc?" Father Clayton asked. "Is it really possible that they did something to us? I don't know about all that, but it's been proven that pets have a way of softening the hardest of hearts, opening people up to receive love; even believing in something greater. I'd call that magic, wouldn't you?"

"Where are the prayers going, Don?" Tony wept. "Why isn't she getting better?"

"There certainly is a lot of spiritual energy being spent right now, isn't there? Believe me, it's being received and its power will be manifested in some way. Often, we only recognize it in retrospect."

"Energy, power, magic?" He quizzed, shaking his head. "I thought it was a sin to entertain such ideas. Sometimes I feel like I fell off the edge of the earth when I moved here," he sighed, thinking about The Group and the hundreds of thousands of people that its enhancement project must have mentally altered. "I'm not sure what's real anymore."

"Love is real; it was given to us by God. But unfortunately, in order for us to be able to experience love, He also had to give us free will. Let me give you something." The priest reached behind him and took a brown leather bible from a small bookshelf. "This is the Word of God; it holds the answers to all your questions."

"Will it tell me how to make Stella change her mind?"

"Try it," Don said and handed the book to him. "And be ready to be amazed."

Tony invited Stella for a walk while the nurses bathed Annette the next morning. She carried Coco on one arm as he led her to the courtyard below where Rick once occupied his fifth-floor office. The plants in the small beds had multiplied threefold since that first day when he looked down on them. They sat on one of the iron benches and listened to the fountain's peaceful trickling.

"Stella, the girls and I want to go with you when you take Annette home. I'd like to make sure she has everything she needs, the equipment at your house is running properly, and, more importantly, the people around her know what to do on a daily basis and in case of an emergency. I think the room next to the screened-in porch downstairs would be perfect. She can see the river from there."

"I think that's a wonderful idea, Doc." Stella laid a hand over his. "You and the girls can stay as long as you like; you know I have plenty of room." Tony visited the hospital chapel later that day. He fell to his knees in front of the wooden cross on the wall in the room full of empty pews. "God, please forgive me for my past transgressions," he sobbed. "I know it was You who put Annette in my life;

please, don't take her away." He heard a sound, an abrupt deafening sound, like speakers that had been turned up too loud. It was a blaring voice that left him incapacitated and incapable of forming another thought. It echoed inside his skull as it repeated the words *take care of my daughter* over and over as if on a loop until it was indiscernible. He pressed his hands against the sides of his head to try and relieve the pain but could only slump into a fetal position on the floor. It stopped just as suddenly as it started. He rose to his elbows and looked around the empty chapel, trying to figure out what happened. He tried to stand, but his knees buckled, forcing him to sit back on the floor. He closed his eyes, thinking he had truly lost his mind. If this meant he was a victim of The Group, he would need an MRI, treatment, and therapy. When he opened his eyes, he saw Phoebe sitting on the floor in front of him. She jumped up on the pew behind him and grabbed hold of his coat collar with her mouth. Tony frowned when she pulled on it; he wanted her to leave him alone. "How did you get down here?" Phoebe whined and then pulled at his shoulder. "Phoebe, please," he yelled and brushed her away; then he turned around and spoke to her directly: "Please stop it." Phoebe obeyed and sat down. "Just go-" he began, but she disappeared before his eyes. Tony stood up and called out her name but all he saw was the chapel door arbitrarily swing open and close on its own. He rushed out of the chapel and didn't bother to wait on the elevator; he took the stairs two at a time all the way up to the fifth floor. Stella was standing beside the bed when he burst into Annette's room; Phoebe was lying in the bed as if she had never moved from her master's side.

"Doc," Stella cried; "she moved her hand and turned her head." Tony rushed to the nurse's station to look at her graphs, which showed brainwaves that were now pronounced and closer together, but she was still unresponsive. "Doc, what do you think; is she gonna wake up now?" Stella asked after calling out to her daughter numerous times.

"I don't know," he replied. He pulled a chair up beside the bed and sat down. He stared at her for thirty minutes before drifting off to sleep, resting his head on her hand.

Stella and Coco lay on the sofa that was expanded to make a bed. She awoke fifteen minutes later to a room filled with fog. She could feel its dampness on her skin and taste its moisture on her tongue. The fog was eerily tinted green; the same as that dreadful morning when her husband lay dying in his hospital bed. Over time she concluded that the cloud hovering over his bed was her husband's spirit leaving his body. And just like that early morning, she felt something touch her on the cheek just before the room suddenly cleared as if someone had turned on a vacuum. She jumped to her feet and rushed to her daughter's bedside. Tony felt something move his hair and tickle his forehead. He opened his eyes expecting to find Phoebe sniffing his face, but she was asleep with her head across Annette's stomach. He felt his hair move again, and he swatted at the annoyance. When he lifted his head, he saw Annette looking at him and smiling. "Thank God," he gushed.

"Doc, you look terrible," she said with a scratchy voice. "You have dark circles under your eyes. Mom, what are you doing here?" she asked when she saw her mother standing at the foot of the bed holding Coco. "Why are you crying?" Phoebe whined but didn't move. "Hey, girl," Nette whispered and then reached for her faithful friend. "When did she come home?" she asked Tony. "What happened; how long have I been here? Why is my arm in a cast?"

"Slow down; one question at a time," Tony whispered, amazed and relieved that her memory was intact. "You were in a bad accident," he whispered and scooted Phoebe closer so she could put her arm around her.

"What, no kisses?" she asked after rubbing her cheek against Phoebe's nose. "Aren't you happy to see me? Why is she acting so weird? Did something happen to her?"

"Because he's gone," Stella whispered. "He was here, and now he's gone!"

"What did you say, Mom?"

"Your father," Stella sobbed and quickly left the room. Tony followed her out into the hall.

"Stella, wait," he called out, catching up to her before she escaped into the ladies' room.

"I thought she had died," she sobbed, looking back toward Annette's room. "I thought I saw her spirit leave her body, but it was Sonny; he's been here all along, and now he's gone for good."

"Stella, I told you she would wake up," Tony sighed and wrapped his arms around her while she clutched Coco close to her chest. "There were so many prayers. She's going to be okay now; she's going to need our help, but she's going to be okay."

"He let her go," she whispered. "He let her go because she has you now."

Chapter 40

"Ok, how many, Lewis?" Charlie asked his friend from across the poker table in the Mesa Village Retirement Community rec room.

"What?" Lewis replied.

"I said, how many cards?" Charlie bellowed louder.

"Here," Lewis said and threw down all five of his cards.

"Leon?" Charlie asked while tolerantly dealing Lewis five cards. His old friend, now a resident of the Village, carefully scrutinized the cards in his hand.

"One," he finally said.

"One?" Charlie asked suspiciously. "Hum," he grunted under his breath and dealt him a single card. "Okay, anyone else; Molly, Lucy? Don't let this guy worry you," he said, glancing at Leon. "As I recall, he always did more bluffing than winning."

"That's what the game is all about, ladies," Leon returned sarcastically. "Feels good playing poker with you again, Charlie; you were always such a good sport when it came to losing."

"Charlie quit being a grouch and give me two cards," Molly said and then let out a sigh. "You've been in a sour mood since Annette and Doc decided to spend the summer in Louisiana."

"And I suppose you're okay with Phoebe not being around to help you cheat?" Charlie grumbled.

"Ha! You mean Nightcrawler," Leon said, "she sure could point out the good fishing hot spots."

"Shush!" Lucy whispered, when she glanced over Charlie's shoulder and saw Father Clayton in his casual street clothes enter the room. "Father, we were just talking about how much we miss Annette and Doc and Phoebe. Their wedding ceremony was so beautiful."

"I think it will go down as one of my all-time favorites for some time to come," Father Clayton agreed. "You mind if I join your game?"

"Pull up a chair," Charlie replied.

"Nette looked so brave walking down the aisle holding on to her brother's arm… and the cane," Lucy said as the priest sat between her and Molly. "I just couldn't stop crying." She held her cards close to her heart as she spoke. "I wish Doc wouldn't have left The Family Practice; we need him around here."

"And Lisa could really use Nette's help at the daycare," Molly added. "They're coming back, aren't they, Father?"

"Molly, you know as well as I that she has many months of therapy ahead of her," Father Clayton replied. "And, you remember Doc's best man, Harry?"

"Yeah," Charlie replied. "His father is some kind of big wig lawyer in Chicago. I heard he was able to get Doc a lot of money from the doctors that prescribed his wife all those pills she was hooked on, and from the bank that let her take all his money. Oh, well, I see where you're going with this; who knows if they'll come back?"

"Brad finally gave in and let Robby go for a visit," Lucy said. "Nicky had been texting him and making the place sound like a fun park; swimming, fishing, jet-skiing, 4-wheeler riding at something they call Mud-Fest.

"Jeffrey and Justin have been hounding Catrina, too," Molly said. "Father, did you notice how much Nette's brother looks like their father? It's uncanny."

"How do you know what her father looked like?" Charlie countered with an impatient croon.

"Because I saw him," Molly replied. "I mean, I saw a picture of him," she quickly corrected herself when Charlie frowned at her suspiciously.

"Leon, whatever happened to that guy Nate you stayed with at Lake Hodges?" Father Clayton asked.

"Said he was going home, but he made sure not to tell me where that is," Leon replied. "I heard from Sally though, after she and Randy returned from Baltimore. They're looking at property in the Calaveras Mountains."

"That's hard to believe," the priest said. "She's lived in the city all her life."

"Did you guys know Charlie and Stella are Facebook friends now?" Lewis interrupted.

"Lewis, have I ever told you, you've gotta big mouth!" Charlie groaned.

"Do you have some inside information you're not telling us, Charlie?" Molly insisted.

“Lucy,” Charlie said loudly, making her jump in her seat. “How many cards do you want?”

“I don’t want any,” she returned anxiously.

“Charlie!” Molly fussed. “Stop being so cantankerous.”

“Then stop making a big deal out of my friendship with Stella. I just wanted to thank her for giving me and Lewis one of Coco’s puppies. Now, is anybody going to ante up?”

“Just give me five off the top,” Father Clayton said. “I’ll bet they’ll be back in time for school to start.”

“We’re going to make millions with this program,” Michael said to his brother Kerry from the back room of the hardware store they now owned in the small town near their mountain home. “I think we’ve covered all random probabilities.”

“So, just how interested is Microsoft in this program?” Kerry asked and picked up the yellow tablet with columns of code symbols. “Wait, I just heard the bell over the door,” he said, dropping the tablet.

“Darn customers,” Michael complained. “They keep interrupting.”

“I much prefer running the store to what we were doing before,” Kerry said.

“If it just wasn’t so boring,” Michael said and followed Kerry to the doorway.

“It’s not my fault you’re ADD,” Kerry jabbed.

“Wait,” Michael whispered and grabbed Kerry’s arm. “It’s him.”

“The guy Mother and Dad always keep out of hearing range when he comes around,” Kerry whispered. “He’s wearing a fishing hat and sunglasses; as if we wouldn’t recognize him.”

“Yeah, he normally has a priest’s collar on,” Michael said.

“I’ve heard Mother call him Monsignor before,” Kerry whispered.

“You go talk to him,” Michael said. “I’ll record it.”

“Good morning,” Kerry said to the elderly gentleman browsing the shelves. He placed behind the register and laid his cell phone on the counter. A flat-screen TV above his head was tuned to a muted news channel.

"The kid at the gas station told me about this place when I asked about antiques," the elderly Hispanic man said. "Hardware stores in small towns are usually good sources of interesting finds."

"I keep the basic electrical, plumbing stuff, and paint supplies so folks don't have to go all the way down the mountain," Kerry said and glanced at the door to the back room where Michael was hiding in the shadows. "There are some old tools in those boxes on the back table that were here when I bought the place." Kerry's cell phone buzzed; he chuckled when he read the text. "This is Al from the gas station telling me he sent you here. Cell phone service is a little slow here in the mountains. He says you bought a fishing hat and a Vitamin Water." After ten minutes of browsing, the old man walked to the register with a rusty wood planer.

"I see Fox News is still running the story about The Group," the man said. "Those news channels sure know how to run things in the ground."

"Yeah, I suppose," Kerry said, and turned to look up at the flat screen displaying footage of the hollowed-out mansion and the crumbled mountain. "I've heard all I care to about that secret government operation. One of many, I'm sure," he chuckled.

"They better hope Sally Samuels never gets wind of them," the man countered.

"I'm sorry?" Kerry asked, pretending to be confused. "What did she have to do with that? I must have missed that report; but as you see, I keep the TV muted most of the time. Actually, wasn't it a YouTube video that exposed that place?" Kerry told the man there was no charge for the planner as it was of no cost to him when he laid his wallet on the counter. He couldn't help but notice the three silver embossed crosses.

"You have a blessed day, young man," the man said after putting his wallet away and lifting his fishing hat, exposing his gray-streaked hair.

"I saw the wallet," Michael said when he joined Kerry behind the front display window.

"As was intended, I'm sure," Kerry whispered. "The question is, do the crosses mean we're safe, or is it a warning? I've heard Mother say they always mean one or the other."

"A clear reminder for sure, that we should remain vigilant," Michael said as they watched the man get in his truck and drive away.

Scott looked up from his tablet and quickly covered the device with his arms to protect it from the cascading water from Robby's cannonball landing after dropping from the rope into the otherwise calm Cane River. Nicky dropped into the water after him and then Lizzy. Robby yelled and waved to Scott to grab the rope and jump in. Lizzy plodded up the bank to give him the message in person with Phoebe following, water dripping from her hair, along with Daisy, one of Coco's puppies and the newest member of Lizzy's animal entourage. "In a minute," he shouted, hovering more closely over his tablet as the two poodles stopped near him to shake water from their coats. Phoebe ran up the hill to the porch swing in Stella's back yard where Annette and Doc sat wrapped in towels; Daisy pranced behind Lizzy when she turned and headed down to the boat dock.

G: *We haven't talked about Nightcrawler or the magic show for a while.*

S: *Annette doesn't do the magic any more since the accident.*

Anyway, magic is an illusion, sleight of hand, skilled deception.

G: *So, is this your conclusion regarding NC?*

S: *There is no scientific explanation; therefore, I have no resolution.*

G: *Made sure you and Robby mind your manners.*

S: *Affirmative.*

G: *Taking late flight Friday; should be there early Saturday. Jeffrey and*

Justin will be with me. So glad to be working behind the counter at

Lindbergh again. Love you.

S: *Love you too, Mom.*

Scott moved the tablet to higher ground, took off his glasses, and gingerly tip-toed down the bank. He stepped up to the knotted rope, took hold with both hands and then looked up the hill behind him at Nette and Doc. Nette looked up from drying Phoebe with her towel; Doc raised his hand and gave him a thumbs-up sign.

"I still have to pinch myself sometimes," Doc said after Scott launched himself off the bank, arms and legs flailing, and then landed in the water awkwardly on his stomach.

"What do you mean?" Annette asked, looking up from her toweling.

"I can't believe how much my life has changed this past year," he said. "It's as if something or someone pointed me in the right direction…to you," he added, putting an arm around her, "and now, here I am, sitting on this swing on Cane River and listening to what must be every songbird in the South and watching butterflies and squirrels. And who would've thought I'd have the relationship I do with my daughters…and ever pick up a Bible?" He placed a hand on Phoebe's back. Annette placed her hand over his.

"I know; it's amazin how we all found each other."

"Oh, my phone is vibrating," Doc said and reached into his pocket. "Ha!" Look who's coaching your T-Ball team?"

"Doctor Rick!" she said after looking at the photo on the screen. "Daniel is getting so tall." She scrolled to the next picture, which included the assistant coach. "Huh!" she grunted. "Kevin."

"Lorraine admitted him to a mental hospital in Orange County. They've developed a therapy using external hardware based on Rick's research, for the neuronal impairment that consists of a series of exercises that, as you can see, have been proven effective. That's huge in light of what happened to Andrew Barksdale and many others. Sometimes I wonder if we all might have been affected to a degree."

"You're referring to Phoebe?" she asked.

"Okay, I guess I'm still trying to make sense of it," he replied.

"Those things did happen, just not anymore," she said and gently rubbed Phoebe's ears. "Maybe someone should tell her story…now that it's over."

"Someone like Sally? It's not exactly her type of reporting. But what was going on in that mountain," he whispered as if someone might be listening; "now that's her kind of story."

"Maybe she could tell both. She's the only one who would tell it right."

"The things Phoebe used to do, Don would call a mystery," Doc said. "Not Lizzy, of course." Phoebe watched them share a long kiss on the lips before Tony stood up and took her by the hand. "Come on," he said. "Let's go back in."

Annette looked at the cane leaning against the porch railing. "Sure."

"Hold on, I've got you," he said, handing her the support she was now accustomed to relying on. She held on tight to his waist as he helped her stand. "Training dormant brain cells to perform new tasks is difficult, but it can only be accomplished by repetition," he said.

"Great!" she laughed; "just what I need, another therapeutic anecdote from Dr. Rick's library." Phoebe stayed behind on the swing and rolled herself up in the towel. She wriggled her head out to watch Doc help her master slowly maneuver down the embankment toward the river. Annette suddenly stopped and squeezed Doc's arm when she felt a warm sensation, like an electrical charge, surge down in her back;, then her hips and legs began to tingle. Elizabeth looked up from feeding cracker crumbs to the tiny bream swimming under the dock when she heard Nette's aluminum cane bouncing on the ground. Nette was staring at Phoebe in the swing. Stella saw her daughter throw the cane down from a window in the dining room and quickly walked outside onto the porch with Coco in her arms. Her daughter was smiling broadly at Doc. It was the same look she teased her brother with when they were kids.

"What are you doing?" Doc asked, bewildered.

"Racin you to the rope, silly," she laughed. "Last one in's a rotten egg!" She broke into a run down the bank without any difficulty and grabbed hold of the rope. She swung out wide over the water and let go. Doc ignored the swaying rope and dove in behind her after stumbling down the hill and yelling at her to slow down.

"You're right," she laughed when Doc came up out of the water beside her. "Swimming is good therapy."

"Yes, it is," he replied and looked back for Phoebe. Stella was sitting in the swing now with both dogs in her lap. *No, she didn't do this*, he thought to himself. Suddenly Nicky caught his attention when she let out a yell just before jumping off Robby's shoulders. He was reminded again of how wonderfully things had changed in spite of all the tragedy when he saw Scott treading water nearby and Elizabeth on the dock playing with Daisy. When he turned back, Annette splashed him in the face with a hand paddle of water. "Awe," he growled, "it's on now." The kids heard the threat and they all swam closer in order to take part in the water fight. Elizabeth looked up the embankment as well, wondering if Phoebe was responsible for Annette's surprising recovery, but the two dogs' attention was totally on Stella, who was feeding them treats.

"It had to be her," Elizabeth whispered to Daisy, but when she looked across the boat dock, her newest friend was nowhere to be found. She swung her body around to look for her. "There you are." The little black and white puppy jumped across her legs, barked twice, and then shook her head. "Are you saying it wasn't her; then who?" Elizabeth sighed. She looked into Daisy's eyes and gasped. "You?" she panted after seeing a glint of mint green emitting deep within her irises. "Of course, your mama must still…" she began while looking at Phoebe and Coco, now both curled up on Stella's lap. "Okay, but this will be *our* secret forever." Elizabeth giggled because she suddenly felt a shower of water pelting her on the back; the water fight had migrated to the dock.

THE END

Made in the USA
Columbia, SC
20 February 2025